0 250 500 750 Kilometers
0 250 500 Miles
Norwegian Sea
ICELAND
Reykjavík
SWEDEN
NORWAY
Oslo
North Sea
Copenhagen
DENMARK
NETHERLANDS
Amsterdam
Berlin
Dublin
IRELAND
UNITED KINGDOM
London
BELGIUM
Brussels
GERMANY
Rhine R.
Paris
LUXEMBOURG
Seine R.
LIECHTENSTEIN
Vienna
Atlantic Ocean
FRANCE
Bern
SWITZERLAND
Ljubljana
SLOVENIA
Po R.
ITALY
Rome
Ebro R.
Corsica
PORTUGAL
Madrid
Sardinia
SPAIN
Lisbon
Balearic Isl.
Sicily
Tunis
Algiers
Rabat
TUNISIA
Tripoli
MOROCCO
ALGERIA
WESTERN SAHARA

ctic Ocean
FINLAND
elsinki
Tallinn
ESTONIA
Riga
LATVIA
THUANIA
Vilnius
Minsk
BELARUS
Warsaw
ND
Kiev
RUSSIA
Moscow
Don R.
Dnieper R.
UKRAINE
VAKIA
islava
Budapest
GARY
MOLDOVA
Chisinau
ROMANIA
Belgrade
Bucharest
KAZAKHSTAN
Volga R.
Caspian Sea
Black Sea
LAVIA
Sofia
BULGARIA
kopje
MACEDONIA
BANIA
GEORGIA
Tbilisi
ARMENIA
Yerevan
Baku
AZERBAIJAN
Ankara
TURKEY
GREECE
Athens
Crete
Tigris R.
Euphrates
Tehran
CYPRUS
SYRIA
LEBANON
Beirut
Damascus
Baghdad
IRAN
ranean Sea
ISRAEL
Jerusalem
Amman
JORDAN
IRAQ
R.
Cairo
Kuwait
KUWAIT
Nile R.
SAUDI
ARABIA
BYA
EGYPT
QATAR

SECOND EDITION

Western Civilization

A Brief History

Volume II: Since 1500

Jackson J. Spielvogel
The Pennsylvania State University

WADSWORTH
THOMSON LEARNING

Australia • Canada • Mexico • Singapore • Spain
United Kingdom • United States

WADSWORTH
THOMSON LEARNING™

History Publisher: *Clark Baxter*
Senior Development Editor: *Sue Gleason*
Assistant Editor: *Jennifer Ellis*
Senior Marketing Manager: *Diane McOscar*
Senior Print Buyer: *Mary Beth Hennebury*
Senior Production Editor: *Michael Burggren*
Permissions Editor: *Bob Kauser*
Interior Designer: *Norman Baugher*
Cover Designer: *Carole Lawson*
Copy Editor: *Bruce Emmer*
Production Service: *Jon Peck, Dovetail Publishing Services*

Maps: *MapQuest.com, Inc.*
Photo Researcher: *Sarah Evertson, Image Quest*
Compositor: *New England Typographic Service*
Printer/Binder: *Quebecor World Taunton*
Cover Printer: *Phoenix Color Corp.*

Cover Image: Green, Charles (1840–1898). *Christmas comes but once a year!* Private collecion. © Photographic Library, London/Art Resources, NY

Photo Credits begin on page 645 which constitutes a continuation of the copyright page

Printed in the United States of America
1 2 3 4 5 6 7 05 04 03 02 01

For permission to use material from this text, contact us:
Web: www.thomsonrights.com
Fax: 1-800-730-2215
Phone: 1-800-730-2214

Wadsworth/Thomson Learning
10 Davis Drive
Belmont, CA 94002-3098
USA

For more information about our products, contact us:
Thomson Learning Academic Resource Center
1-800-423-0563
http://www.wadsworth.com

International Headquarters
Thomson Learning
International Division
290 Harbor Drive, 2nd Floor
Stamford, CT 06902-7477
USA

UK/Europe/Middle East/South Africa
Thomson Learning
Berkshire House
168-173 High Holborn
London WC1V 7AA
United Kingdom

Asia
Thomson Learning
60 Albert Street, #15-01
Albert Complex
Singapore 189969

Canada
Nelson Thomson Learning
1120 Birchmount Road
Toronto, Ontario M1K 5G4
Canada

Library of Congress Cataloging-in-Publication Data

Spielvogel, Jackson J.
Western civilization : a brief history / Jackson J. Spielvogel.—2nd ed.
p. cm.
Includes bibliographical references and index.
ISBN 0-534-58707-0 (comprehensive vol. : alk. paper)
ISBN 0-534-58708-9 (vol I. : alk. paper)
ISBN 0-534-58709-7 (vol II. : alk. paper)
ISBN 0-534-58710-0 (instructor's edition : alk. paper)
1. Civilization, Western—History. I. Title.
CB245.S63 2001
909'.09821—dc21 2001026221

This book is printed on acid-free recycled paper.

About the Author

JACKSON J. SPIELVOGEL is associate professor emeritus of history at The Pennsylvania State University. He received his Ph.D. from The Ohio State University, where he specialized in Reformation history under Harold J. Grimm. His articles and reviews have appeared in such journals as Moreana, Journal of General Education, Catholic Historical Review, Archiv für Reformationsgeschichte, *and* American Historical Review. *He has also contributed chapters or articles to* The Social History of Reformation, The Holy Roman Empire: A Dictionary Handbook, Simon Wiesenthal Center Annual of Holocaust Studies, *and* Utopian Studies. *His work has been supported by fellowships from the Fulbright Foundation and the Foundation for Reformation Research. At Penn State, he helped inaugurate the Western civilization courses as well as a popular course on Nazi Germany. His book* Hitler and Nazi Germany *was published in 1987 (fourth edition, 2001). He is the co-author (with William Duiker) of* World History, *published in January 1994 (third edition, 2001). Professor Spielvogel has won five major university-wide teaching awards. During the year 1988–1989, he held the Penn State Teaching Fellowship, the university's most prestigious teaching award. In 1996, he won the Dean Arthur Ray Warnock Award for Outstanding Faculty Member, and in 1997, he became the first recipient of the Schreyer Institute's Student Choice Award for innovative and inspiring teaching.*

To Diane,
whose love and support
made it all possible

Brief Contents

Detailed Contents

CHAPTER 17

The Eighteenth Century: An Age of Enlightenment 343

CHAPTER 18

The Eighteenth Century: European States, International Wars, and Social Change 362

CHAPTER 19

A Revolution in Politics: The Era of the French Revolution and Napoleon 383

CHAPTER 20

The Industrial Revolution and Its Impact on European Society 405

CHAPTER 28
Cold War and a New Western World, 1945–1970 578

CHAPTER 29
The Contemporary Western World (Since 1970) 603

Maps

Chronologies

Preface

We are often reminded how important it is to understand today's world if we are to deal with our growing number of challenges. And yet that understanding will be incomplete if we in the Western world do not comprehend the meaning of Western civilization and the role Western civilization has played in the world. For all of our modern progress, we still greatly reflect our religious traditions, our political systems and theories, our economic and social structures, and our cultural heritage. I have written this brief history of Western civilization to assist a new generation of students in learning more about the past that has helped create them and the world in which they live.

I began this project with two primary goals. First, I wanted to write a well-balanced work in which the political, economic, social, religious, intellectual, cultural, and military aspects of Western civilization would be integrated into a chronologically ordered synthesis. Second, I wanted to avoid the approach that is quite common in other brief histories of Western civilization—an approach that makes them collections of facts with little continuity from section to section. Instead, I sought to keep the story in history. Narrative history effectively transmits the knowledge of the past and is the form that best enables students to remember and understand the past. At the same time, I have not overlooked the need for the kind of historical analysis that makes students aware that historians often disagree in their interpretations of the past.

To enliven the past and let readers see for themselves the materials that historians use to create their pictures of the past, I have included in each chapter primary sources (boxed documents) that are keyed to the discussion in the text. The documents include examples of the religious, artistic, intellectual, social, economic, and political aspects of Western life. Such varied sources as a Roman banquet menu, advice from a Carolingian mother to her son, marriage negotiations in Renaissance Italy, the diary of a German soldier at Stalingrad, and a debate in the Reformation era all reveal in a vivid fashion what Western civilization meant to the individual men and women who shaped it by their activities.

Each chapter has a lengthy introduction and conclusion to help maintain the continuity of the narrative and to provide a synthesis of important themes. Anecdotes in the chapter introductions convey more dramatically the major theme or themes of each chapter. Detailed chronologies reinforce the events discussed in the text while timelines at the end of each chapter enable students to see at a glance the major developments of an era. An annotated bibliography at the end of each chapter reviews the most recent literature on each period and also gives references to some of the older, "classic" works in each field. Extensive maps and illustrations serve to deepen the reader's understanding of the text. To facilitate understanding of cultural movements, illustrations of artistic works discussed in the text are placed next to the discussions. New to the second edition are focus questions and chapter outlines at the beginning of each chapter, which should help students to gain a quick overview and guide them to the main subjects of each chapter. A glossary of important terms and a pronunciation guide have also been added to the second edition.

As preparation for the revision of *Western Civilization: A Brief History*, I reexamined the entire book and analyzed the comments and reviews of colleagues who have found the book to be a useful instrument for introducing their students to the history of Western civilization. In making revisions for the second edition, I sought to build upon the strengths of the first edition and, above all, to maintain the balance, synthesis, and narrative qualities that characterized that edition. To keep up with the ever-growing body of historical scholarship, new or revised material has been added throughout the book on many topics, including, for example, civilization in Mesopotamia and Egypt; ancient Israel; Homer; Sparta; Aristotle's views of women; women in the Hellenistic world; Roman values and attitudes; literature in the late Roman Republic; late Roman Empire; women in early Christianity and the new Germanic kingdoms; the rise and spread of Islam; the Vikings; the Black Death; Catherine of Siena; Christine de Pizan; marriage and childbirth in Renaissance Italy; European discovery and expansion in the sixteenth and seventeenth centuries; Artemisia Gentileschi; Judith Leyster and Dutch realism; Louis XIV; limits of absolutism; nobility in the eighteenth century; female utopian socialists; the economy of Latin America; revolution of 1848 in Italy; Napoleon II; women and work in the nineteenth century; women and the Paris commune; Impressionism; Marie Curie; women reformers and the "new woman" in the nineteenth century; Asian response to imperialism; the history of

Canada; social repercussions of the Great Depression; movies in the 1920s and 1930s; new attitudes toward sexuality in the 1920s; history of the United States and Canada since 1945; decolonization; the women's liberation movement; and the war in Kosovo. Throughout the revising process, I also worked to craft a book that I hope students will continue to find very readable. New subheadings were added in many chapters in the second edition in order to facilitate the reader's comprehension of the content of the chapters.

To provide a more logical arrangement of the material, I have also made organizational changes in Chapters 1, 6, 14, 28, and 29. Chapters 9, 10, and 11 on the High Middle Ages were reorganized and condensed to form two new chapters entitled "The Recovery and Growth of European Society in the High Middle Ages" and "A New World of Cities and Kingdoms." Moreover, all "Suggestions for Further Reading" at the end of each chapter were thoroughly updated, and new illustrations were added to almost every chapter.

The enthusiastic response to the primary sources (boxed documents) led me to evaluate the content of each document carefully and add new documents throughout the text, including "The Twelve Tables," "West Meets East: An Exchange of Royal Letters," "British Victory in India," "Declaration of the Rights of Man and the Citizen," "A Leader of the Paris Commune," "Hesse and the Unconscious," and "Margaret Thatcher: Entering a Man's World." For the second edition, the maps have been revised where needed and, as in previous editions, are carefully keyed to all text references. New maps have also been added, including "The Columbian Exchange" and "The Holocaust."

Because courses in Western civilization at American and Canadian colleges and universities follow different chronological divisions, a one-volume edition and a two-volume edition of this text are being made available to fit the needs of instructors. Teaching and learning ancillaries include the following:

For the Instructor

Instructor's Manual with Test Bank Prepared by Kevin Robbins, Indiana University Purdue University Indianapolis. This new Instructor's Manual contains chapter outlines, suggested lecture topics, and discussion questions for the maps and artwork as well as the primary source documents located in the text. World Wide Web sites and resources, video collections, suggested student activities, and secondary sources for lecture preparation are also included. Exam questions include essays, identifications, and multiple-choice questions. Available in two volumes.

ExamView Instructors can create, deliver, and customize tests and study guides (both print and online) in minutes with this easy-to-use assessment and tutorial system. ExamView offers both a Quick Test Wizard and an Online Test Wizard that guide the user step by step through the process of creating tests, while its unique "WYSIWYG" capability allows users to see the test they are creating on the screen exactly as it will print or display online. Tests of up to 250 questions using up to 12 question types can be built. Using ExamView's complete word processing capabilities, instructors can enter an unlimited number of new questions or edit existing questions. Available for Windows and Macintosh.

Full Color Map Acetate Package This package includes maps from the text and from other sources. More than 100 four-color images are provided in a handy three-ring binder. Map commentary is provided by James Harrison, Siena College.

Map Slides 100 full-color map slides.

Lecture Enrichment Slides Prepared by Dale Hoak and George Strong, College of William and Mary. These 100 slides contain images of famous paintings, statues, architectural achievements, and interesting photos. The authors supply commentary for each slide.

History Video Library A completely new selection of videos to go with the second edition. Over 50 titles to choose from, with coverage spanning from "Egypt: A Gift to Civilization" to "Children of the Holocaust."
CNN Today Videos For *Western Civilization*, the perfect lecture launchers contain video clips ranging from one to five minutes long.

Sights and Sounds of History Video Uses focused video clips, photos, artwork, animations, music, and dramatic readings to bring history to life. The video segments average four minutes long and are available on VHS. These make excellent lecture launchers.

HistoryLink An advanced PowerPoint presentation tool containing text-specific lecture outlines, figures, and images that allows instructors to quickly deliver dynamic lectures. In addition, it provides the flexibility to customize each presentation by editing what we have provided or by adding one's own collection of slides, videos and animations. All of the map acetates and selected photos have also been incorporated into each of the lectures. In addition, the extensive Map Commentaries for each map slide are available through the "Comments" feature of PowerPoint.

For the Student

Study Guide Prepared by James Baker, Western Kentucky University. Includes chapter outlines, chapter summaries, and seven different types of questions for each chapter. Available in two volumes.

Exploring the European Past: Text and Images A completely customizable reader that brings to life the events, people, and movements that helped define Western civilization. Each reading begins with an introduction that sets the time and tone, followed by primary source and then secondary source documents, each with a series of critical thinking questions. Every reading is brought to life

Internet Guide for History, 3/e Prepared by John Soares. This newly revised and up-to-date internet provides exercises by topic. It can be found on the web at http://history.wadsworth.com.

Western Civilization, Canadian Supplement Prepared by Maryann Farkus, Dawson College. Discusses Canadian history and culture in the context of Western

Introduction to Students of Western Civilization

Civilization, as historians define it, first emerged between five thousand and six thousand years ago when people began to live in organized communities with distinct political, military, economic, and social structures. Religious, intellectual, and artistic activities also assumed important roles in these early societies. The focus of this book is on Western civilization, a civilization that for most of its history has been identified with the continent of Europe. Its origins, however, go back to the Mediterranean basin, including lands in North Africa and the Middle East, as well as Europe itself. Moreover, the spread of Europeans abroad led to the development of offshoots of Western civilization in other parts of the world.

Because civilized life includes all the deeds and experiences of people organized in communities, the history of a civilization must embrace a series of studies. An examination of Western civilization therefore requires us to study the political, economic, social, military, cultural, intellectual, and religious aspects that make up the life of that civilization and show how they are interrelated. In so doing, we need also at times to focus on some of the unique features of Western civilization. Certainly, science played a crucial role in the development of modern Western civilization. Although such societies as those of the Greeks, the Romans, and medieval Europeans were based largely on a belief in the existence of a spiritual order, Western civilization experienced a dramatic departure toward a natural or material view of the universe in the seventeenth-century Scientific Revolution. Science and technology have been important in the growth of modern and largely secular Western civilization, although antecedents to scientific development also existed in Greek, Islamic, and medieval thought and practice.

Many historians have also viewed the concept of political liberty, the fundamental value of every individual, and the creation of a rational outlook, based on a system of logical, analytical thought, as unique aspects of Western civilization. Of course, Western civilization has also witnessed the frightening negation of liberty, individualism, and reason. Racism, violence, world wars, totalitarianism—these too must form part of the story. Finally, regardless of our concentration on Western civilization and its characteristics, we need to take into account that other civilizations have influenced Western civilization and it, in turn, has affected the development of other civilizations.

In our examination of Western civilization, we need also to be aware of the dating of time. In recording the past, historians try to determine the exact time when events occurred. World War II in Europe, for example, began on September 1, 1939, when Hitler sent German troops into Poland and ended on May 7, 1945, when Germany surrendered. By using dates, historians can place events in order and in relation to one another and try to determine the development of patterns over periods of time.

If someone asked you when you were born, you would reply with a number, such as 1982. In the United States, we would all accept that number without question because it is part of the dating system followed in the Western world (Europe and the Western Hemisphere). In this system, events are dated by counting backward or forward from the birth of Jesus Christ (assumed to be the year 1). An event that took place four hundred years before the birth of Jesus would be dated 400 B.C. ("before Christ"). Dates after the birth of Jesus are labeled A.D. These letters stand for the Latin words *anno Domini*, which mean "in the year of the Lord." Thus an event that took place 250 years after the birth of Jesus is written A.D. 250, meaning "in the year of the Lord 250." It can also be written as 250, just as you would not give your birth year as A.D. 1982, but simply as 1982.

Historians also make use of other terms to refer to time. A decade is ten years, a century is one hundred years, and a millennium is one thousand years. The expression "fourth century B.C." refers to the fourth period of one hundred years counting backward from 1, the assumed date of the birth of Jesus. Since the first century B.C. would be the years 100 B.C. to 1 B.C., the fourth century B.C. would be the years 400 B.C. to 301 B.C. We could say, then, that an event in 350 B.C. took place in the fourth century B.C.

The phrase "fourth century A.D." refers to the fourth period of one hundred years after the birth of Jesus. Since the first period of one hundred years would be the years 1 to 100, the fourth period of one hundred years, or fourth century, would be the years 301 to 400. We could say, then, for example, that an event in 350 took place in the fourth century. In similar manner, the first millennium B.C. refers to the years 1000 B.C. to 1 B.C.; the second millennium A.D. refers to the years 1001 to 2000.

Some historians now prefer to use the abbreviations B.C.E. (for "before the Common Era") and C.E. (for "Common Era") instead of B.C. and A.D. This is especially true of world historians, who prefer to use terminology that is not so Western or Christian oriented. The dates remain the same, of course: 1950 B.C.E. and 1950 B.C. would be the same year. In keeping with current usage by many historians of Western civilization, this book will use the terms B.C. and A.D.

The dating of events can also vary from people to people. Most people in the Western world use the Western calendar, also known as the Gregorian calendar after Pope Gregory XIII, who refined it in 1582. The Hebrew calendar, by contrast, uses a different system in which the year 1 is the equivalent of the Western year 3760 B.C., considered by Jews to be the date of the creation of the world. The Western year 2000 is thus the year 5760 on the Jewish calendar. The Islamic calendar begins year 1 on the day Muhammad fled Mecca, which is the year 622 on the Western calendar. Thus the Western year 2000 is the year 1348 on the Islamic calendar.

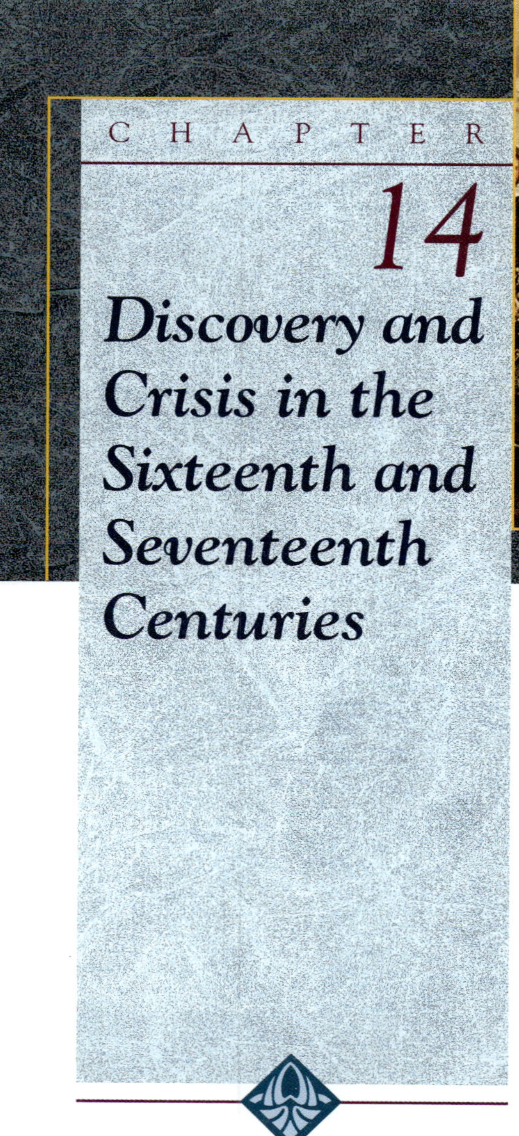

CHAPTER

14

Discovery and Crisis in the Sixteenth and Seventeenth Centuries

CHAPTER OUTLINE

FOCUS QUESTIONS

- Why did Europeans begin to amass overseas empires during the sixteenth century, and what effects did this experience have on both the Europeans and conquered peoples?
- What role did religion play in the European wars of the sixteenth century and the Thirty Years' War of the seventeenth century?
- How did the religious policy, the foreign policy, and the governments of Philip II of Spain and Elizabeth I of England differ?
- What economic and social crises did Europe experience between 1560 and 1650?
- How did the turmoil in Europe between 1560 and 1650 contribute to the witchcraft craze and to the artistic and intellectual developments of the period?

BY THE MIDDLE of the sixteenth century, it was apparent that the religious passions of the Reformation era had brought an end to the religious unity of medieval Europe. The rift between Catholics and Protestants was instrumental in fueling a series of wars that dominated much of European history between 1560 and 1650. The struggles fought in Germany at the beginning of the seventeenth century (known as the Thirty Years' War) were especially brutal and devastating. When the Catholic general Johann Tilly captured Neubrandenburg, his forces massacred the city's three thousand defenders. A month later, the army of the

Protestant leader Gustavus Adolphus retaliated by slaughtering the entire garrison of two thousand men at Frankfurt-an-der-Oder. Noncombatants suffered as well, as is evident from the contemporary description by Otto von Guericke of the sack of Magdeburg. Once the city had been captured, Tilly's forces were let loose: "Then there was nothing but beating and burning, plundering, torture, and murder." All the buildings were looted of anything valuable, and then the city was "given over to the flames, and thousands of innocent men, women, and children, in the midst of a horrible noise of heartrending shrieks and cries, were tortured and put to death in so cruel and shameful a manner that no words would suffice to describe." Thus "in a single day this noble and famous city, the pride of the whole country, went up in fire and smoke, and the remnant of its citizens, with their wives and children, were taken prisoners and driven away by the enemy."

The wars worsened the economic and social crises that were besetting the continent. The fact that Europe unrelentingly suffered wars, rebellions, constitutional crises, economic depression, social disintegration, a witchcraft craze, and demographic perturbations between 1560 and 1650 has led some historians to speak of those ninety years as an age of crisis in European life.

Crisis, however, often creates opportunities, and nowhere is that more apparent than in the geographical discoveries that made this an era of European expansion into new worlds. Although the discovery of new territories began before the sixteenth century, it was not until the sixteenth and seventeenth centuries that Europeans began to comprehend the significance of their discoveries and to exploit them for material gain.

◆ An Age of Discovery and Expansion

Never has the dynamic and even ruthless energy of Western civilization been more apparent than in its expansion into the rest of the world. By the sixteenth century, the Atlantic seaboard had become the center of a commercial activity that raised Portugal and Spain and later the Dutch Republic, England, and France to prominence. The age of expansion was a crucial factor in the European transition from the agrarian economy of the Middle Ages to a commercial and industrial capitalistic system. Expansion also led Europeans into new and lasting contacts with non-European peoples that inaugurated a new age of world history.

The Motives

Europeans had long been attracted to lands outside of Europe. Indeed, a large body of fantasy literature about "other worlds" blossomed in the Middle Ages. In *The Travels of John Mandeville* in the fourteenth century, the author spoke of lands (which he had never seen) filled with precious stones and gold. Other lands were more frightening, "where the folk be great giants of twenty-eight foot long, or thirty foot long. . . . And they eat more gladly man's flesh than any other flesh," as well as lands farther north full of "cruel and evil women. And they have precious stones in their eyes. And they be of that kind that if they behold any man with wrath they slay him at once with the beholding."[1] Other writers spoke of mysterious Christian kingdoms: the magical kingdom of Prester John in Africa and a Christian community in southern India that was supposedly founded by Thomas, the apostle of Jesus.

Although Muslim control of Central Asia cut Europe off from the countries farther east, the Mongol conquests in the thirteenth century had reopened the doors. The most famous medieval travelers to the East were the Polos of Venice. Niccolò and Maffeo, merchants from Venice, accompanied by Niccolò's son Marco, undertook the lengthy journey to the court of the great Mongol ruler Kublai Khan (1259–1294) in 1271. An account of Marco's experiences, the *Travels*, proved to be the most informative of all the descriptions of Asia by medieval European travelers. Others followed the Polos, but in the fourteenth century, the conquests of the Ottoman Turks and then the breakup of the Mongol Empire reduced Western traffic to the East. With the closing of the overland routes, a number of people in Europe became interested in the possibility of reaching Asia by sea to gain access to the spices and other precious items of the region. Christopher Columbus had a copy of Marco Polo's *Travels* in his possession when he began to envision his epoch-making voyage across the Atlantic Ocean.

An economic motive thus loomed large in Renaissance European expansion. Merchants, adventurers, and government officials had high hopes of finding precious metals and new areas of trade. Many European explorers and conquerors did not hesitate to express their desire for material gain. One Spanish

the Atlantic on August 3, 1492. On October 12, he

comes.

conquistador explained that he and his kind went to the New World to "serve God and His Majesty, to give light to those who were in darkness, and to grow rich,

the Arabian Sea and reached the port of Calicut on the southwestern coast of India, on May 18, 1498. On arriving in Calicut, da Gama announced to his

some wives accompanied their husbands abroad, many ordinary European women found new opportunities for marriage in the New World because of the lack of white women. Indeed, as one commentator bluntly put it, even "a whore, if handsome, can make a wife for some rich planter."[5] In the violence-prone world of early Spanish America, a number of women also found themselves rich after their husbands were killed unexpectedly. In one area of Central America, women owned about 25 percent of the landed estates by 1700.

European expansion also affected the conquerors in the economic arena. Wherever they went in the New World, Europeans sought to find sources of gold and silver. One Aztec commented that the Spanish conquerors "longed and lusted for gold. Their bodies swelled with greed, and their hunger was ravenous; they hungered like pigs for that gold."[6] Rich silver deposits were found and exploited in Mexico and southern Peru (modern Bolivia). When the mines at Potosí in Peru were opened in 1545, the value of precious metals imported into Europe quadrupled. It has been estimated that between 1503 and 1650, some 16 million kilograms (over 35 million pounds) of silver and 185,000 kilograms (400,000 pounds) of gold entered the port of Seville, triggering a price revolution that reverberated throughout the Spanish economy.

But gold and silver were only two of the products that became part of the exchange between the New World and the Old. Europeans brought their horses and sheep and also took up the cultivation of wheat. Into Seville flowed sugar, dyes, cotton, vanilla, and hides from livestock raised on the grass-covered plains of South America. New agricultural products such as potatoes, coffee, corn, and tobacco were also imported. Because of its trading posts in Asia, Portugal soon challenged the Italian states as the chief entry point of the eastern trade in spices, jewels, silks, carpets, ivory, leather, and perfumes, although the Venetians clung tenaciously to the spice trade until they lost out to the Dutch in the seventeenth century. Economic historians believe that the increase in the volume and area of European trade as well as the rise in liquid capital due to this expansion were crucial factors in producing a new era of commercial capitalism that represented the first step toward the global economy we know today.

European expansion, which was in part a product of European rivalries, also deepened those rivalries and increased the tensions among European states. Bitter conflicts arose over the cargoes coming from the New World and Asia. Although the Spanish and Portuguese entered the competition first, the Dutch, French, and English soon became involved on a large scale and by the seventeenth century were challenging the Portuguese and Spanish monopolies.

Politics and the Wars of Religion in the Sixteenth Century

By the middle of the sixteenth century, Calvinism and Catholicism had become militant religions dedicated to spreading the word of God as they interpreted it. Although this religious struggle for the minds and hearts of Europeans is at the heart of the religious wars of the sixteenth century, economic, social, and political forces also played important roles in these conflicts. Of the sixteenth-century religious wars, none were more momentous or shattering than the French civil wars known as the French Wars of Religion.

The French Wars of Religion (1562–1598)

Religion was at the heart of the French civil wars of the sixteenth century. The growth of Calvinism led to persecution by the French kings but did little to stop the spread of Calvinism. Huguenots (as the French Calvinists were called) came from all layers of society: artisans and shopkeepers hurt by rising prices and a rigid guild system, merchants and lawyers in provincial towns whose local privileges were tenuous, and members of the nobility. Possibly 40 to 50 percent of the French nobility became Huguenots, including the house of Bourbon, which stood next to the Valois dynasty in the royal line of succession and ruled the southern French kingdom of Navarre. The conversion of so many nobles made the Huguenots a potentially dangerous political threat to monarchical power. Though the Calvinists constituted only about 7 percent of the population, they were a strong-willed and well-organized minority.

The Catholic majority greatly outnumbered the Calvinist minority. The Valois monarchy was staunchly Catholic, and its control of the Catholic church gave it little incentive to look favorably on Protestantism. At the same time, an extreme Catholic party—known as the ultra-Catholics—favored strict opposition to the Huguenots and were led by the Guise family. Possessing the loyalty of Paris and large sections of northern and northwestern France, they could recruit and pay for large armies and received support abroad from the papacy and Jesuits who favored their noncompromising Catholic position.

The religious issue was not the only factor that contributed to the French civil wars. Towns and provinces, which had long resisted the growing power of monarchical centralization, were only too willing to join a revolt against the monarchy. This was also true of the nobility, and the fact that so many of them were Calvinists created an important base of opposition to the crown. The French Wars of Religion, then, based a major constitutional crisis for France and temporarily halted the development of the French centralized territorial state. The claim of the ruling dynasty of the state to a person's loyalties was temporarily superseded by loyalty to one's religious belief. For thirty years, battles raged in France between Catholic and Calvinist parties, who obviously considered the unity of France less important than religious truth. But there also emerged in France a group known as the *politiques* who placed politics before religion and believed that no religious truth was worth the ravages of civil war. The *politiques* ultimately prevailed, but not until both sides had become exhausted by bloodshed.

Finally, in 1589, Henry of Navarre, the political leader of the Huguenots and a member of the Bourbon dynasty, succeeded to the throne as Henry IV (1589–1610). Realizing, however, that he would never be accepted by Catholic France, Henry took the logical way out and converted to Catholicism. With his coronation in 1594, the Wars of Religion finally came to an end. The Edict of Nantes in 1598 solved the religious problem by acknowledging Catholicism as the official religion of France while guaranteeing the Huguenots the right to worship and to enjoy all political privileges, including the holding of public offices.

Philip II and the Cause of Militant Catholicism

The greatest advocate of militant Catholicism in the second half of the sixteenth century was King Philip II of Spain (1556–1598), the son and heir of Charles V. Philip's reign ushered in an age of Spanish greatness, both politically and culturally. Philip's first major goal was to consolidate and secure the lands he had inherited from his father. These included Spain, the Netherlands, and possessions in Italy and the New World. For Philip, this meant strict conformity to Catholicism, enforced by aggressive use of the Spanish Inquisition, and the establishment of strong monarchical authority. Establishing this authority was not an easy task because Philip had inherited a governmental structure in which each of the various states and territories of his empire stood in an individual relationship to the king. Philip did manage, however, to expand royal power by making the monarchy less dependent on the traditional landed aristocracy.

Crucial to an understanding of Philip II is the importance of Catholicism to the Spanish people and their ruler. Driven by a heritage of crusading fervor, the Spanish had little difficulty seeing themselves as a nation of people divinely chosen to save Catholic Christianity from the Protestant heretics. Philip II, the "Most Catholic King," became the champion of Catholicism throughout Europe, a role that led him to spectacular victories and equally spectacular defeats. Spain's leadership of a "holy league" against Turkish encroachments in the Mediterranean resulted in a stunning victory over the Turkish fleet in the Battle of Lepanto in 1571. But Philip's attempt to crush the revolt in the Netherlands and his tortured policy with England's Queen Elizabeth led to his greatest misfortunes.

The Revolt of the Netherlands

As one of the richest parts of Philip's empire, the Spanish Netherlands was of great importance to the "Most Catholic King." Philip's attempt to strengthen his control in the Netherlands, which consisted of seventeen provinces (modern Netherlands, Belgium, and Luxembourg), soon led to a revolt. The nobles, who stood to lose the most politically if their jealously guarded privileges and freedoms were weakened, strongly opposed Philip's efforts. Resentment against Philip was also aroused by the collection of taxes when the residents of the Netherlands realized that these revenues were being used for Spanish interests. Finally, religion became a major catalyst for rebellion when Philip attempted to crush Calvinism. Violence erupted in 1566, when Calvinists—especially nobles—began to destroy statues and stained-glass windows in Catholic churches. Philip responded by sending the duke of Alva with ten thousand veteran Spanish and Italian troops to crush the rebellion.

But the revolt became organized, especially in the seven northern provinces where the Dutch, under the leadership of William of Nassau, the prince of

CHRONOLOGY

The Wars of Religion in the Sixteenth Century

The French Wars of Religion	1562–1598
Coronation of Henry IV	1594
Edict of Nantes	1598
Outbreak of revolt in the Netherlands	1566
Battle of Lepanto	1571
Spanish Armada	1588
Twelve-year truce (Spain and the Netherlands)	1609
Independence of the United Provinces	1648

Orange, offered growing resistance. The struggle dragged on for decades until 1609, when a twelve-year truce ended the war, virtually recognizing the independence of the northern provinces. These seven northern provinces, which began to call themselves the United Provinces of the Netherlands in 1581, soon emerged as the Dutch Republic, although the Spanish did not formally recognize them as independent until 1648. The ten southern provinces remained a Spanish possession (see Map 14.2).

The England of Elizabeth

After the death of Queen Mary in 1558, her half-sister Elizabeth, the daughter of Henry VIII and Anne Boleyn, ascended the throne of England. During Elizabeth's reign, England rose to prominence as the relatively small island kingdom became the leader of the Protestant nations of Europe, laid the foundations for a world empire, and experienced a cultural renaissance.

Intelligent, cautious, and self-confident, Elizabeth moved quickly to solve the difficult religious problem she inherited from her half-sister. Elizabeth's religious policy was based on moderation and compromise. The Catholic laws of Mary's reign were repealed, and a new Act of Supremacy designated Elizabeth as "the only supreme governor" of both church and state. The church service used during the reign of Edward VI was revised to make it more acceptable to Catholics. The Church of England under Elizabeth was basically Protestant, but of a moderate sort that kept most people satisfied in the second half of the sixteenth century.

Caution, moderation, and expediency also dictated Elizabeth's foreign policy. Fearful of other countries' motives, Elizabeth realized that war could be

MAP 14.2 The Height of Spanish Power Under Philip II.

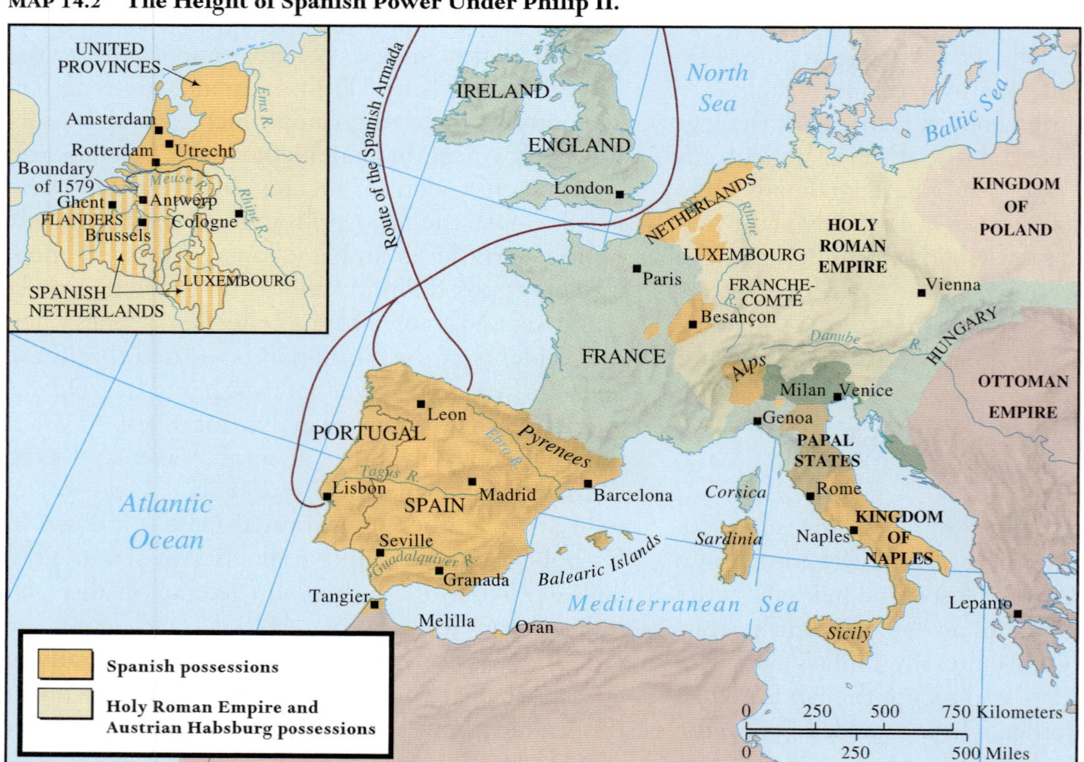

PROCESSION OF QUEEN ELIZABETH I. **Intelligent and learned, Elizabeth was familiar with Latin and Greek and spoke several European languages. Served by able administrators, she ruled for nearly forty-five years and generally avoided open military action against any major power. Her participation in the revolt of the Netherlands, however, brought England into conflict with Spain. This picture, painted near the end of her reign, shows the queen on a ceremonial procession.**

disastrous for her island kingdom and her own rule. While encouraging English piracy and providing clandestine aid to French Huguenots and Dutch Calvinists to weaken France and Spain, Elizabeth pretended complete aloofness and avoided alliances that would force her into war with any major power. Gradually, however, Elizabeth was drawn into conflict with Spain. After years of resisting the idea of invading England as too impractical, Philip II of Spain was finally persuaded to do so by advisers who assured him that the people of England would rise against their queen when the Spaniards arrived. Moreover, Philip was easily convinced that the revolt in the Netherlands would never be crushed as long as England provided support for it. In any case, a successful invasion of England would mean the overthrow of heresy and the return of England to Catholicism, surely an act in accordance with the will of God. Philip therefore ordered preparations for an armada (fleet of warships) to spearhead the invasion of England in 1588.

The armada proved a disaster. The Spanish fleet that finally set sail had neither the ships nor the troops that Philip had planned to send. A conversation between a papal emissary and an officer of the Spanish fleet before the armada departed reveals the fundamental flaw:

> "And if you meet the English armada in the Channel, do you expect to win the battle?"
>
> "Of course," replied the Spaniard.
>
> "How can you be so sure?" [asked the emissary]
>
> "It's very simple. It is well known that we fight in God's cause. So, when we meet the English, God will surely arrange matters so that we can grapple and board them, either by sending some strange streak of weather, or, more likely, just by depriving the English of their wits. If we can come to close quarters, Spanish valor and Spanish steel (and the great masses of soldiers we shall have on board) will make our victory certain. But unless God helps us by a miracle the English, who have faster and handier ships than ours, and many more long-range guns, and who know their advantage just as well as we do, will never close with us at all, but stand aloof and knock us to pieces with their culverins, without our being able to do them any serious hurt. So," concluded the captain, and one fancies a grim smile, "we are sailing against England in the confident hope of a miracle."[7]

The hoped-for miracle never materialized. The Spanish fleet, battered by a number of encounters with the English, sailed back to Spain by a northward route around Scotland and Ireland where it was further battered by storms. Although the English and Spanish would continue their war for another sixteen years, the defeat of the Spanish Armada guaranteed for the time being that England would remain a Protestant country. Although Spain made up for its losses within a year and a half, the defeat was a psychological blow to the Spaniards.

◆ Economic and Social Crises

The period of European history from 1560 to 1650 witnessed severe economic and social crises as well as political upheaval. The inflation-fueled prosperity of the sixteenth century showed signs of slackening by the beginning of the seventeenth century. Economic contraction began to be evident in some parts of Europe by the 1620s. In the 1630s and 1640s, as imports of silver from the Americas declined, economic recession intensified, especially in the Mediterranean area. The industrial and financial center of Europe in the Renaissance, Italy was now becoming an economic backwater. Spain's economy was also seriously failing by the 1640s.

Population trends of the sixteenth and seventeenth centuries also reveal Europe's worsening conditions. The sixteenth century was a period of expanding population, possibly related to a warmer climate and increased food supplies. It has been estimated that the population of Europe increased from 60 million in 1500 to 85 million by 1600, the first major recovery of European population since the devastation of the Black Death in the mid-fourteenth century. However, records also indicate a leveling off of the population by 1620 and even a decline by 1650, especially in central and southern Europe. Europe's longtime adversaries—war, famine, and plague—continued to affect population levels. Another "little ice age" after the middle of the sixteenth century, when average temperatures fell, affected harvests and gave rise to famines. These economic problems created social tensions that were also evident in the witchcraft craze.

The Witchcraft Craze

Hysteria over witchcraft affected the lives of many Europeans in the sixteenth and seventeenth centuries. Witchcraft trials were prevalent in England, Scotland, Switzerland, Germany, some parts of France and the Low Countries, and even New England in America.

Witchcraft was not a new phenomenon in the sixteenth and seventeenth centuries. Its practice had been part of traditional village culture for centuries, but it came to be viewed as both sinister and dangerous when the medieval church began to connect witches to the activities of the devil, thereby transforming witchcraft into a heresy that had to be extirpated. After creation of the Inquisition in the thirteenth century, people were accused of a variety of witchcraft practices and, following the biblical injunction, "Thou shalt not suffer a witch to live," were turned over to secular authorities for burning at the stake or, in England, hanging.

What distinguished witchcraft in the sixteenth and seventeenth centuries from these previous developments was the increased number of trials and executions of presumed witches. Perhaps more than a hundred thousand people were prosecuted throughout Europe on charges of witchcraft. As more and more people were brought to trial, the fear of witches as well as the fear of being accused of witchcraft escalated to frightening proportions. Although larger cities were affected first, the trials spread to smaller towns and rural areas as the hysteria persisted well into the seventeenth century (see the box on p. 293).

The accused witches usually confessed to a number of practices, most often after intense torture. But even when people confessed voluntarily, certain practices stand out. Many said that they had sworn allegiance to the devil and attended sabbats, nocturnal gatherings where they feasted, danced, and even copulated with the devil in sexual orgies. More common, however, were admissions of using evil incantations and special ointments and powders to wreak havoc on neighbors by killing their livestock, injuring their children, or raising storms to destroy their crops.

A number of contributing factors have been suggested to explain why the witchcraft craze became so widespread in the sixteenth and seventeenth centuries. Religious uncertainties clearly played some part. Many witchcraft trials occurred in areas where Protestantism had been recently victorious or in regions, such as southwestern Germany, where Protestant-Catholic controversies still raged. As religious passions became inflamed, accusations of being in league with the devil became common on both sides. Recently, however, historians have emphasized the importance of social conditions, especially the problems of a society in turmoil, in explaining the witchcraft hysteria. At a time when the old communal values that stressed working together for the good of the community were disintegrating, property owners became more fearful of the growing numbers of poor among them and transformed them psychologically into agents of the devil. Old women were particularly susceptible to suspicion. Many of them, no longer the recipients of the local charity found in traditional society, may even have tried to survive by selling herbs, potions, or secret remedies for healing. When problems arose—and there were many in this crisis-laden period—these same people were the most likely scapegoats.

That women should be the chief victims of witchcraft trials was hardly accidental. Nicholas Rémy, a witchcraft judge in France in the 1590s, found it "not unreasonable that this scum of humanity, i.e., witches, should be drawn chiefly from the feminine sex."[8] To another judge, it came as no surprise that witches would confess to sexual experiences with Satan: "The

A Witchcraft Trial in France

Persecutions for witchcraft reached their high point in the sixteenth and seventeenth centuries when tens of thousands of people were brought to trial. In this excerpt from the minutes of a trial in France in 1652, we can see why the accused witch stood little chance of exonerating herself.

The Trial of Suzanne Gaudry

28 May, 1652. . . . Interrogation of Suzanne Gaudry, prisoner at the court of Rieux. . . . [During interrogations on May 28 and May 29, the prisoner confessed to a number of activities involving the devil.]

Deliberation of the Court—June 3, 1652

The undersigned advocates of the Court have seen these interrogations and answers. They say that the aforementioned Suzanne Gaudry confesses that she is a witch, that she had given herself to the devil, that she had renounced God, Lent, and baptism, that she has been marked on the shoulder, that she has cohabited with the devil and that she has been to the dances, confessing only to have cast a spell upon and caused to die a beast of Philippe Cornié. . . .

Third Interrogation—June 27

The prisoner being led into the chamber, she was examined to know if things were not as she had said and confessed at the beginning of her imprisonment.

—Answers no, and that what she has said was done so by force.

Pressed to say the truth, that otherwise she would be subjected to torture, having pointed out to her that her aunt was burned for this same subject.

—Answers that she is not a witch. . . .

She was placed in the hands of the officer in charge of torture, throwing herself on her knees, struggling to cry, uttering several exclamations, without being able, nevertheless to shed a tear. Saying at every moment that she is not a witch.

The Torture

On this same day, being at the place of torture.

This prisoner, before being strapped down, was admonished to maintain herself in her first confessions and to renounce her lover.

—Says that she denies everything she has said, and that she has no lover. Feeling herself being strapped down, says that she is not a witch, while struggling to cry . . . and upon being asked why she confessed to being one, said that she was forced to say it.

Told that she was not forced, that on the contrary she declared herself to be a witch without any threat.

—Says that she confessed it and that she is not a witch, and being a little stretched [on the rack] screams ceaselessly that she is not a witch. . . .

Asked if she did not confess that she had been a witch for twenty-six years.

—Says that she said it, that she retracts it, crying that she is not a witch.

Asked if she did not make Philippe Cornié's horse die, as she confessed.

—Answers no, crying Jesus-Maria, that she is not a witch.

The mark having been probed by the officer, in the presence of Doctor Bouchain, it was adjudged by the aforesaid doctor and officer truly to be the mark of the devil.

Being more tightly stretched upon the torture-rack, urged to maintain her confessions.

—Said that it was true that she is a witch and that she would maintain what she had said.

Asked how long she has been in subjugation to the devil.

—Answers that it was twenty years ago that the devil appeared to her, being in her lodgings in the form of a man dressed in a little cow-hide and black breeches. . . .

Verdict

July 9, 1652. In the light of the interrogations, answers and investigations made into the charge against Suzanne Gaudry, . . . seeing by her own confessions that she is said to have made a pact with the devil, received the mark from him, . . . and that following this, she had renounced God, Lent, and baptism and had let herself be known carnally by him, in which she received satisfaction. Also, seeing that she is said to have been a part of nocturnal carols and dances.

For expiation of which the advice of the undersigned is that the office of Rieux can legitimately condemn the aforesaid Suzanne Gaudry to death, tying her to a gallows, and strangling her to death, then burning her body and burying it here in the environs of the woods.

The Face of War in the Seventeenth Century

The Thirty Years' War was the most devastating war Europeans had experienced. Destruction was especially severe in Germany. We have a firsthand account of the face of war in Germany from a picaresque novel called Simplicius Simplicissimus, *written by Jakob von Grimmelshausen. The author's experiences as a soldier in the Thirty Years' War gave his descriptions of the effect of the war on ordinary people a certain vividness and reality. This selection describes the fate of a peasant farm, an experience all too familiar to thousands of German peasants between 1618 and 1648.*

Jakob von Grimmelshausen, Simplicius Simplicissimus

The first thing these horsemen did in the nice back rooms of the house was to put in their horses. Then everyone took up a special job, one having to do with death and destruction. Although some began butchering, heating water, and rendering lard, as if to prepare for a banquet, others raced through the house, ransacking upstairs and down; not even the privy chamber was safe, as if the golden fleece of Jason might be hidden there. Still others bundled up big packs of cloth, household goods, and clothes, as if they wanted to hold a rummage sale somewhere. What they did not intend to take along they broke and spoiled. Some ran their swords into the hay and straw, as if there hadn't been hogs enough to stick. Some shook the feathers out of beds and put bacon slabs, hams, and other stuff in the ticking, as if they might sleep better on these. Others knocked down the hearth and broke the windows, as if announcing an everlasting summer. They flattened out copper and pewter dishes and baled the ruined goods. They burned up bedsteads, tables, chairs, and benches, though there were yards and yards of dry firewood outside the kitchen. Jars and crocks, pots and casseroles all were broken, either because they preferred their meat broiled or because they thought they'd eat only one meal with us. In the barn, the hired girl was handled so roughly that she was unable to walk away, I am ashamed to report. They stretched the hired man out flat on the ground, stuck a wooden wedge in his mouth to keep it open, and emptied a milk bucket full of stinking manure drippings down his throat; they called it a Swedish cocktail. He didn't relish it and made a very wry face. By this means they forced him to take a raiding party to some other place where they carried off men and cattle and brought them to our farm. Among these were my father, mother, and [sister] Ursula.

Then they used thumbscrews, which they cleverly made out of their pistols, to torture the peasants, as if they wanted to burn witches. Though he had confessed to nothing as yet, they put one of the captured hayseeds in the bake-oven and lighted a fire in it. They put a rope around someone else's head and tightened it like a tourniquet until blood came out of his mouth, nose, and ears. In short, every soldier had his favorite method of making life miserable for peasants, and every peasant had his own misery. My father was, as I thought, particularly lucky because he confessed with a laugh what others were forced to say in pain and martyrdom. No doubt because he was the head of the household, he was shown special consideration; they put him close to a fire, tied him by his hands and legs, and rubbed damp salt on the bottoms of his feet. Our old nanny goat had to lick it off and this so tickled my [father] that he could have burst laughing. This seemed so clever and entertaining to me—I had never seen or heard my [father] laugh so long—that I joined him in laughter, to keep him company or perhaps to cover up my ignorance. In the midst of such glee he told them the whereabouts of hidden treasure much richer in gold, pearls, and jewelry than might have been expected on a farm.

I can't say much about the captured wives, hired girls, and daughters because the soldiers didn't let me watch their doings. But I do remember hearing pitiful screams from various dark corners and I guess that my mother and our Ursula had it no better than the rest.

Art: Mannerism and the Baroque

The artistic Renaissance came to an end when a new movement called Mannerism emerged in Italy in the 1520s and 1530s. The age of the Reformation had brought a revival of religious values accompanied by much political turmoil. Especially in Italy, the worldly enthusiasm of the Renaissance gave way to anxiety, uncertainty, suffering, and a yearning for spiritual experience. Mannerism reflected this environment in its deliberate attempt to break down the High Renaissance principles of balance, harmony, and moderation. Italian Mannerist painters deliberately distorted the rules of proportion by portraying elongated figures that conveyed a sense of suffering and a strong emotional atmosphere filled with anxiety and confusion.

Mannerism spread from Italy to other parts of Europe and perhaps reached its apogee in the work of El Greco (1541–1614). Doménikos Theotocópoulos (called "the Greek"—El Greco) was from Crete, but after studying in Venice and Rome, he moved in the 1570s to Spain, where he became a church painter in Toledo. El Greco's elongated figures, portrayed in unusual shades of yellow and green against an eerie background of turbulent grays, reflect well the artist's desire to create a world of intense emotions.

EL GRECO, *LAOCOÖN*. Mannerism reached high expression in the work of El Greco. Born in Crete, trained in Venice and Rome, and settling finally in Spain, El Greco worked as a church painter in Toledo. Pictured here is his version of the *Laocoön*, a famous piece of Hellenistic sculpture that had been discovered in Rome in 1506. The elongated, contorted bodies project a world of suffering, while the somber background scene of the city of Toledo adds a sense of terror and doom.

Mannerism was eventually replaced by a new movement—the Baroque—that dominated the artistic world for another century and a half. The Baroque began in Italy in the last quarter of the sixteenth century and spread to the rest of Europe. Baroque artists sought to harmonize the classical traditions of Renaissance art with the intense religious feelings fostered by the revival of religion in the Reformation. Although Protestants were also affected, the Baroque was most wholeheartedly embraced by the Catholic reform movement, as is evident at the Catholic courts, especially those of the Habsburgs in Madrid, Prague, Vienna, and Brussels. Eventually the Baroque style spread to all of Europe and Latin America.

In large part, Baroque art and architecture reflected the search for power that was characteristic of much of the seventeenth century. Baroque churches and palaces featured richly ornamented facades, sweeping staircases, and an overall splendor that were meant to impress people. Kings and princes wanted other kings and princes as well as their subjects to be in awe of their power. The Catholic church, which commissioned many new churches, wanted people to see the triumphant power of the Catholic faith.

Baroque painting was known for its use of dramatic effects to heighten emotional intensity. This style was especially evident in the works of the Flemish painter Peter Paul Rubens (1577–1640), a prolific artist and an important figure in the spread of the Baroque from Italy to other parts of Europe. In his artistic masterpieces, bodies in violent motion, heavily fleshed nudes, a dramatic use of light and shadow, and rich sensuous pigments converge to show intense emotions. The restless forms and constant movement blend together into a dynamic unity.

Perhaps the greatest figure of the Baroque was the Italian architect and sculptor Gian Lorenzo Bernini (1598–1680), who completed Saint Peter's basilica and designed the vast colonnade enclosing the piazza in front of it. Action, exuberance, profusion, and dramatic effects mark his work in the interior of Saint Peter's, where Bernini's *Throne of St. Peter* hovers in midair, held by the hands of the four great doctors of the Catholic church. Above the chair, rays of golden light drive a mass of clouds and angels toward the spectator.

PETER PAUL RUBENS, *THE LANDING OF MARIE DE' MEDICI AT MARSEILLES.* **The Fleming Peter Paul Rubens played a key role in spreading the Baroque style from Italy to other parts of Europe. In *The Landing of Marie de' Medici at Marseilles,* Rubens made a dramatic use of light and color, bodies in motion, and luxurious nudes to heighten the emotional intensity of the scene. This was one of a cycle of twenty-one paintings dedicated to the queen mother of France.**

ARTEMISIA GENTILESCHI, *JUDITH BEHEADING HOLOFERNES.* **Artemisia Gentileschi painted a series of pictures portraying scenes from the lives of courageous Old Testament women. In this painting, a determined Judith, armed with her victim's sword, struggles to saw off the head of Holofernes. Gentileschi realistically and dramatically shows the bloody nature of Judith's act.**

Less well known than the male artists who dominated the seventeenth-century art world in Italy but prominent in her own right was Artemisia Gentileschi (1593–1653). Born in Rome, she studied painting under her father's direction. In 1616, she moved to Florence and began a successful career as a painter. At the age of twenty-three, she became the first woman to be elected to the Florentine Academy of Design. Although she was known internationally in her day as a portrait painter, her fame now rests on a series of pictures of heroines from the Old Testament, including Judith, Esther, and Bathsheba. Most famous is her *Judith Beheading Holofernes*, a dramatic rendering of the biblical scene in which Judith slays the Assyrian general Holofernes in order to save her besieged town from the Assyrian army.

A Golden Age of Literature: England and Spain

Periods of crisis often produce great writing, and so it was of this age, which was characterized by a golden age of theater. In both England and Spain, writing for the stage reached new heights between 1580 and 1640. The golden age of English literature is often called the Elizabethan era because much of the English cultural flowering of the late sixteenth and early seventeenth centuries occurred during the reign of Queen Elizabeth. Elizabethan literature exhibits the exuberance and pride associated with English exploits at the time (see the box on p. 300). Of all the forms of Elizabethan literature, none expressed the energy and intellectual versatility of the era better than drama. Of all the dramatists, none is more famous than William Shakespeare (1564–1614).

Shakespeare was the son of a prosperous glovemaker from Stratford-upon-Avon. When he appeared in London in 1592, Elizabethans were already addicted to the stage. By 1576, two professional theaters run by actors' companies were in existence. Elizabethan theater became a tremendously successful business. In or near London, four to six theaters were open six afternoons a week. London theaters ranged from the Globe, which was a circular unroofed structure holding three thousand spectators, to the Blackfriars, which was roofed and held only five hundred. In the former, the admission charge of only a penny or two enabled even the lower classes to attend, while the higher prices charged in the latter attracted the well-to-do. Elizabethan audiences varied greatly, consisting as they did of nobles, lawyers, merchants, and even vagabonds—putting pressure on playwrights to write works that pleased all.

William Shakespeare: In Praise of England

William Shakespeare is one of the most famous playwrights of the Western world. He was a universal genius, outclassing all others in his psychological insights, depth of characterization, imaginative skills, and versatility. His historical plays reflected the patriotic enthusiasm of the English in the Elizabethan era, as this excerpt from Richard II *illustrates.*

❋ *William Shakespeare,* Richard II

This royal throne of kings, this sceptered isle,
This earth of majesty, this seat of Mars,
This other Eden, demi-Paradise,
This fortress built by Nature for herself
Against infection and the hand of war,
This happy breed of men, this little world,
This precious stone set in the silver sea,
Which serves it in the office of a wall
Or as a moat defensive to a house
Against the envy of less happier lands—
This blessed plot, this earth, this realm, this England,
This nurse, this teeming womb of royal kings,
Feared by their breed and famous by their birth,
Renowned for their deeds as far from home,
For Christian service and true chivalry,
As is the sepulcher in stubborn Jewry [the Holy Sepulcher in Jerusalem]
Of the world's ransom, blessed Mary's Son—
This land of such dear souls, this dear dear land,
Dear for her reputation through the world,
Is now leased out, I die pronouncing it,
Like a tenement or pelting farm.
England, bound in with the triumphant sea,
Whose rocky shore beats back the envious siege
Of watery Neptune, is now bound in with shame,
With inky blots and rotten parchment bonds.
That England, what was wont to conquer others,
Hath made a shameful conquest of itself.
Ah, would the scandal vanish with my life,
How happy then were my ensuing death!

Shakespeare was a "complete man of the theater." Although best known for writing plays, he was also an actor and a shareholder in the chief performing company of the time, the Lord Chamberlains' Company, which played in theaters as diverse as the Globe and the Blackfriars. Shakespeare has long been recognized as a universal genius. He was a master of the English language, but this technical proficiency was matched by an incredible insight into human psychology. Whether in his tragedies or comedies, Shakespeare exhibited a remarkable understanding of the human condition.

The theater was one of the most creative forms of expression during Spain's golden century. The first professional theaters created in Seville and Madrid in the 1570s were run by actors' companies as in England. Soon a public playhouse could be found in every large town, including Mexico City in the New World. Touring companies brought the latest Spanish plays to all parts of the Spanish empire.

Beginning in the 1580s, the agenda for playwrights was set by Lope de Vega (1562–1635). Like Shakespeare, he was from a middle-class background. He was an incredibly prolific writer; almost one-third of his fifteen hundred plays survive. They have been characterized as witty, charming, action-packed, and realistic. Lope de Vega made no apologies for the fact that he wrote his plays to please his audiences. In a treatise on drama written in 1609, he stated that the foremost duty of the playwright was to satisfy public demand. He remarked that if anyone thought he had written his plays for fame, "undeceive him and tell him that I wrote them for money."

One of the crowning achievements of the golden age of Spanish literature was the work of Miguel de Cervantes (1547–1616), whose *Don Quixote* has been acclaimed as one of the great literary works of all time. Each of the two main figures of this work personifies a side of the Spanish character. The knight Don Quixote from La Mancha is the visionary who is so involved in his lofty ideals that he is oblivious to the hard realities around him. To him, for example, windmills appear as four-armed giants. In contrast, the knight's fat and earthy squire, Sancho Panza, is the rationalist who cannot get his master to see the realities in front of him. But after adventures that take them to all parts of Spain, each comes to see the value of the other's perspective. We are left with Cervantes' conviction that idealism and realism, visionary dreams and the hard work of reality, are both necessary to the human condition.

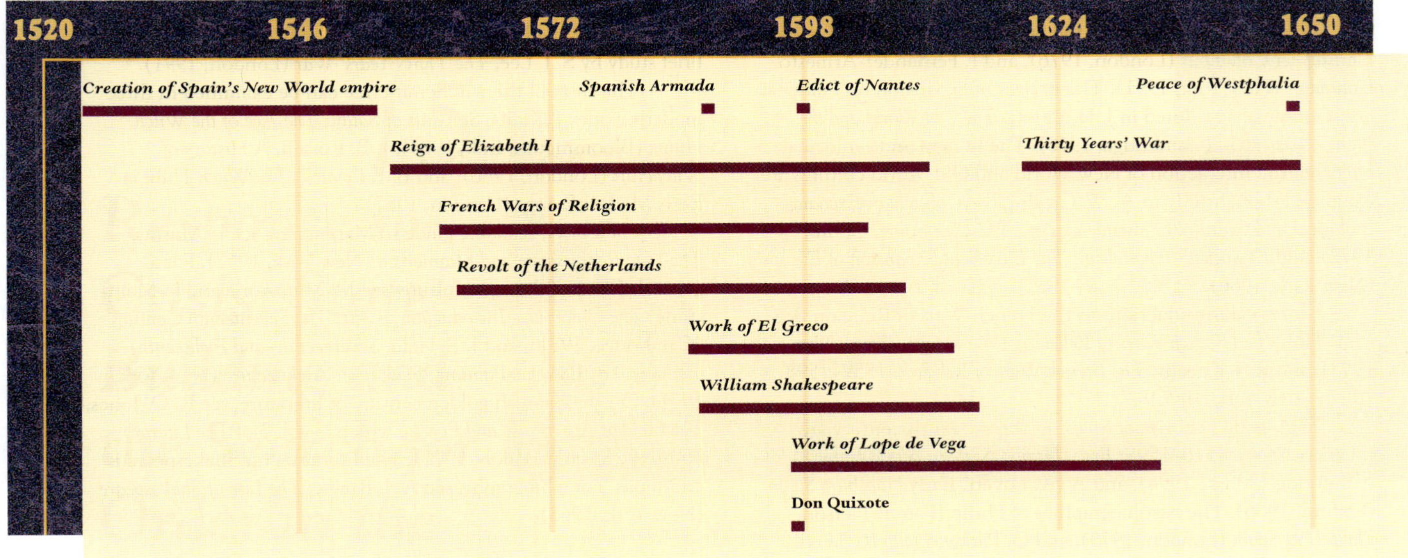

Conclusion

Between 1560 and 1650, Europe attempted to adjust to a whole range of change-laden forces. Populations contracted as economic expansion gave way to economic recession. The discovery of new trade routes to the East and the "accidental" discovery of the Americas led Europeans to venture outside the medieval world in which they had been enclosed for virtually a thousand years. The conquest of the Americas brought out the worst and some of the best of European civilization. The greedy plundering of resources and the brutal enslavement and virtual annihilation of millions of New World inhabitants were hardly balanced by attempts to create new institutions, convert the natives to Christianity, and foster the rights of the indigenous peoples.

In the sixteenth century, the discoveries made little impact on Europeans preoccupied with the problems of dynastic expansion and, above all, religious division. It took one hundred years of religious warfare complicated by serious political, economic, and social issues—the worst series of wars and civil wars since the collapse of the Roman Empire in the west—before Europeans finally admitted that they would have to tolerate different ways of worshiping God. That men who were disciples of the Apostle of Peace would kill each other—often in brutal and painful fashion—aroused skepticism about Christianity itself. As one German writer put it in 1650: "Lutheran, popish, and Calvinistic, we've got all these beliefs here; but there is some doubt about where Christianity has got to." It is surely no accident that the search for a stable, secular order of politics and for order in the universe through natural laws played such important roles in the seventeenth century. The religious wars of the sixteenth and seventeenth centuries opened the door to the secular perspectives that have characterized modern Western civilization.

Notes

1. Quoted in J. R. Hale, *Renaissance Exploration* (New York, 1968), p. 32.
2. Quoted in J. H. Parry, *The Age of Reconnaissance: Discovery, Exploration, and Settlement, 1450 to 1640* (New York, 1963), p. 33.
3. Quoted in Richard B. Reed, "The Expansion of Europe," in Richard De Molen, ed., *The Meaning of the Renaissance and Reformation* (Boston, 1974), p. 308.
4. Quoted in Mary B. Campbell, *The Witness and the Other World: Exotic European Travel Writing, 400–1600* (Ithaca, N.Y., 1991), p. 197.
5. Quoted in G. V. Scammell, *The First Imperial Age: European Overseas Expansion, c. 1400–1715* (London, 1989), p. 62.
6. Miguel Leon-Portilla, ed., *The Broken Spears: The Aztec Account of the Conquest of Mexico* (Boston, 1969), p. 51.
7. Quoted in Garrett Mattingly, *The Armada* (Boston, 1959), pp. 216–217.
8. Quoted in Joseph Klaits, *Servants of Satan: The Age of the Witch Hunts* (Bloomington, Ind., 1985), p. 68.
9. Ibid.

Suggestions for Further Reading

General works on the period from 1560 to 1650 include C. Wilson, *The Transformation of Europe, 1558–1648* (Berkeley, Calif., 1976), and R. Bonney, *The European Dynastic States, 1494–1660* (Oxford, 1991).

The best general accounts of European discovery and expansion are G. V. Scammell, *The First Imperial Age: European Overseas Expansion, c. 1400–1715* (London, 1989); J. H. Parry, *The Age of Reconnaissance: Discovery, Exploration, and Settlement, 1450 to 1650* (New York, 1963); and B. Penrose, *Travel and Discovery in the Renaissance, 1420–1620* (New York, 1962). On the medieval background to European expansion, see J. R. S. Phillips, *The Medieval Expansion of Europe* (New York, 1988). On European perceptions of the world outside Europe, see M. B. Campbell, *The Witness and the*

wars that more and more Europeans came to think of politics in secular terms.

One of the responses to the crises of the seventeenth century was a search for order. As the internal social and political rebellions and revolts died down, it became apparent that the privileged classes of society—the aristocrats—remained in control, although the various states exhibited important differences in political forms. The most general trend saw an extension of monarchical power as a stabilizing force. This development, which historians have called absolutism or absolute monarchy, was most evident in France during the flamboyant reign of Louis XIV, regarded by some as the perfect embodiment of an absolute monarch. In his memoirs, the duc de Saint-Simon, who had firsthand experience of French court life, said that Louis was "the very figure of a hero, so imbued with a natural but most imposing majesty that it appeared even in his most insignificant gestures and movements." The king's natural grace gave him a special charm as well: "He was as dignified and majestic in his dressing gown as when dressed in robes of state, or on horseback at the head of his troops." His life was orderly: "Nothing could be regulated with greater exactitude than were his days and hours." His self-control was impeccable: "He did not lose control of himself ten times in his whole life, and then only with inferior persons." But even absolute monarchs had imperfections, and Saint-Simon had the courage to point them out: "Louis XIV's vanity was without limit or restraint," which led to his "distaste for all merit, intelligence, education, and, most of all, for all independence of character and sentiment in others," as well as his "mistakes of judgment in matters of importance."

But absolutism was not the only response to crisis in the seventeenth century. Other states, such as England, reacted differently to domestic crisis, and another very different system emerged where monarchs were limited by the power of their representative assemblies. Absolute and limited monarchy were the two poles of seventeenth-century state building.

◆ The Practice of Absolutism: Western Europe

Absolute monarchy or absolutism meant that the sovereign power or ultimate authority in the state rested in the hands of a king who claimed to rule by divine right—that kings received their power from God and were responsible to no one (including parliaments) except God. But what did sovereignty mean? The late-sixteenth-century political theorist Jean Bodin believed that sovereign power consisted of the authority to make laws, tax, administer justice, control the state's administrative system, and determine foreign policy. These powers made a ruler sovereign.

France and Absolute Monarchy

France during the reign of Louis XIV (1643–1715) has traditionally been regarded as the best example of the practice of absolute monarchy in the seventeenth century. French culture, language, and manners reached into all levels of European society. French diplomacy and wars shaped the political affairs of western and central Europe. The court of Louis XIV seemed to be imitated everywhere in Europe. Of course, the stability of Louis' reign was magnified by the instability that had preceded it.

The fifty years of French history before Louis XIV came to power were a time in which royal and ministerial governments struggled to avoid the breakdown of the state. The line between order and anarchy was often a thin one. The situation was especially complicated by the fact that in 1610 and 1643, when Louis XIII and Louis XIV, respectively, succeeded to the throne, they were only boys, leaving the government dependent on royal ministers. Two especially competent ministers played crucial roles in maintaining monarchical authority.

Cardinal Richelieu, Louis XIII's chief minister from 1624 to 1642, initiated policies that eventually strengthened the power of the monarchy. By eliminating the political and military rights of the Huguenots while preserving their religious ones, Richelieu transformed the Huguenots into more reliable subjects. Richelieu acted more cautiously in "humbling the pride of the great men," the important French nobility. He understood the influential role played by the nobles in the French state. The dangerous ones were those who asserted their territorial independence when they were excluded from participating in the central government. Proceeding slowly but determinedly, Richelieu developed an efficient network of spies to uncover noble plots and then crushed the conspiracies and executed the conspirators, thereby eliminating a major threat to royal authority.

When Louis XIV succeeded to the throne in 1643 at the age of four, Cardinal Mazarin, the trained successor of Cardinal Richelieu, dominated the government. An Italian who had come to France as a papal legate and then became naturalized, Mazarin attempted to carry on Richelieu's policies until his death in 1661. The most important event during Mazarin's rule was the Fronde, a revolt led primarily by nobles who wished to curb the centralized administrative power being built up at the expense of the provincial nobility. The Fronde was crushed by 1652, and with its end, a vast number of French people concluded that the best hope for stability in France lay in the crown. When Mazarin died in 1661, the greatest of the seventeenth-century monarchs, Louis XIV, took over supreme power.

LOUIS XIV. Louis XIV was determined to be the sole ruler of France. He eliminated the threat of the high nobility by removing them from the royal council and replacing them with relatively new aristocrats whom he could dominate. This portrait by Hyacinth Rigaud captures the king's sense of royal dignity and grandeur.

THE REIGN OF LOUIS XIV (1643–1715)

The day after Cardinal Mazarin's death, Louis XIV, at the age of twenty-three, expressed his determination to be a real king and the sole ruler of France:

> Up to this moment I have been pleased to entrust the government of my affairs to the late Cardinal. It is now time that I govern them myself. You [secretaries and ministers of state] will assist me with your counsels when I ask for them. I request and order you to seal no orders except by my command. . . . I order you not to sign anything, not even a passport . . . without my command; to render account to me personally each day and to favor no one.[1]

His mother, who was well aware of Louis' proclivity for fun and games and getting into the beds of the maids in the royal palace, laughed aloud at these words. But Louis was quite serious.

Louis proved willing to pay the price of being a strong ruler (see the box on p. 306). He established a conscientious routine from which he seldom deviated, but he did not look on his duties as drudgery because he judged his royal profession to be "grand, noble, and delightful." Eager for glory (in the French sense of achieving what was expected of one in an important position), Louis created a grand and majestic spectacle at the court of Versailles. Consequently, Louis and his court came to set the standard for monarchies and aristocracies all over Europe. The great French writer Voltaire dubbed the period from 1661 to 1715 the "Age of Louis XIV," and historians have tended to call it that ever since.

Although Louis may have believed in the theory of absolute monarchy and consciously fostered the myth of himself as the Sun King, the source of light for all of his people, historians are quick to point out that the realities fell far short of the aspirations. Despite the centralizing efforts of Cardinals Richelieu and Mazarin, France still possessed a bewildering system of overlapping authorities in the seventeenth century. Provinces had their own regional courts, their own local Estates, their own sets of laws. Members of the high nobility with their huge estates and clients among the lesser nobility still exercised much authority. Both towns and provinces possessed privileges and powers seemingly from time immemorial that they would not easily relinquish.

One of the keys to Louis' power was that he was able to restructure the central policy-making machinery of government because it was part of his own court

Louis XIV: Kingly Advice

Throughout his reign, Louis XIV was always on stage, acting the role of the wise "Grand Monarch." In 1661, after he became a father, Louis began his Memoirs for the Dauphin, *a frank collection of precepts for the education of his oldest son and heir to the throne. He continued to add to the* Memoirs *over the next twenty years.*

Louis XIV, Memoirs for the Dauphin

Kings are often obliged to do things which go against their inclinations and offend their natural goodness. They should love to give pleasure and yet they must often punish and destroy persons on whom by nature they wish to confer benefits. The interest of the state must come first. One must constrain one's inclinations and not put oneself in the position of berating oneself because one could have done better in some important affair but did not because of some private interest, because one was distracted from the attention one should have for the greatness, the good and the power of the state. Often there are troublesome places where it is difficult to make out what one should do. One's ideas are confused. As long as this lasts, one can refrain from making a decision. But as soon as one has fixed one's mind upon something which seems best to do, it must be acted upon. This is what enabled me to succeed so often in what I have done. The mistakes which I made, and which gave me infinite trouble, were the result of the desire to please or of allowing myself to accept too carelessly the opinions of others. Nothing is more dangerous than weakness of any kind whatsoever. In order to command others, one must raise oneself above them and once one has heard the reports from every side one must come to a decision upon the basis of one's own judgment, without anxiety but always with the concern not to command anything which is of itself unworthy either of one's place in the world or of the greatness of the state. Princes with good intentions and some knowledge of their affairs, either from experience or from study and great diligence in making themselves capable, find numerous cases which instruct them that they must give special care and total application to everything. One must be on guard against oneself, resist one's own tendencies, and always be on guard against one's own natural bent. The craft of a king is great, noble and delightful when one feels worthy of doing well whatever one promises to do. But it is not exempt from troubles, weariness and worries. Sometimes uncertainty causes despair, and when one has spent a reasonable time in examining an affair, one must make a decision and take the step which one believes to be best. When one has the state in view, one works for one's self. The good of the one constitutes the glory of the other. When the former is fortunate, eminent and powerful, he who is the cause thereof becomes glorious and consequently should find more enjoyment than his subjects in all the pleasant things of life for himself and for them. When one has made a mistake, it must be corrected as soon as possible, and no other consideration must stand in the way, not even kindness.

and household. The royal court located at Versailles was an elaborate structure that served three purposes simultaneously: it was the personal household of the king, the location of central governmental machinery, and the place where powerful subjects came to find favors and offices for themselves and their clients, as well as the main arena where rival aristocratic factions jostled for power. The greatest danger to Louis' personal rule came from the very high nobles and princes of the blood (the royal princes) who considered it their natural function to assert the policy-making role of royal ministers. Louis eliminated this threat by removing them from the royal council, the chief administrative body of the king and overseer of the central machinery of government, and enticing them to his court where he could keep them preoccupied with court life and out of politics. Instead of the high nobility and royal princes, Louis relied for his ministers on nobles who came from relatively new aristocratic families. His ministers were expected to be subservient; said Louis, "I had no intention of sharing my authority with them."

Louis' domination of his ministers and secretaries gave him control of the central policy-making machinery of government and thus authority over the traditional areas of monarchical power: the formulation of foreign policy, the making of war and peace, the assertion of the secular power of crown against any religious authority, and the ability to levy taxes to fulfill these functions. However, Louis had considerably less success with the internal administration of the kingdom. The traditional groups and institutions of French society—the nobles, officials, town councils, guilds, and representative Estates in some provinces—were simply too powerful for the king to have direct control over the lives of his subjects. As a result, the control of the central government over the provinces and the people was carried out largely by careful bribery of the important people to see that the king's policies were executed.

The maintenance of religious harmony had long been considered an area of monarchical power. The desire to keep it led Louis to pursue an anti-Protestant policy, aimed at converting the Huguenots to Catholicism. In October 1685, Louis issued the Edict of Fontainebleau. In addition to revoking the Edict of Nantes, the new edict provided for the destruction of Huguenot churches and the closing of their schools. Although forbidden to leave France, it is estimated that 200,000 Huguenots left for shelter in England, the United Provinces, and the German states.

PALACE OF VERSAILLES. Louis XIV spent untold sums of money on the construction of a new royal residence at Versailles. The enormous palace also housed the members of the king's government and served as home for thousands of French nobles. As the largest royal residence in Europe, Versailles impressed foreigners and became a source of envy for other rulers.

The cost of building palaces, maintaining his court, and pursuing his wars made finances a crucial issue for Louis XIV. He was most fortunate in having the services of Jean-Baptiste Colbert (1619–1683) as controller-general of finances. Colbert sought to increase the wealth and power of France through mercantilism, a set of principles that dominated economic thought in the seventeenth century. According to the mercantilists, the prosperity of a nation depended on a plentiful supply of bullion or gold and silver. For this reason, it was desirable to achieve a favorable balance of trade in which goods exported were of greater value than those imported, promoting an influx of gold and silver payments that would increase the quantity of bullion. To encourage exports, governments should stimulate and protect export industries and trade by granting trade monopolies, encouraging investment in new industries through subsidies, and improving transportation systems by building roads, bridges, and canals. By placing high tariffs on foreign goods, they could be kept out of the country and prevented from competing with domestic industries. Colonies were also deemed valuable sources of raw materials and markets for finished goods. As a system of economic principles, mercantilism focused on the role of the state, believing that state intervention in some aspects of the economy was desirable for the sake of the national good.

Colbert was an avid practitioner of mercantilism. To decrease the need for imports and increase exports, he founded new luxury industries and granted special privileges, including tax exemptions, loans, and subsidies to individuals who established new industries. To improve communications and the transportation of goods internally, he built roads and canals. To decrease imports directly, Colbert raised tariffs on foreign manufactured goods and created a merchant marine to carry French goods.

Both the increase in royal power that Louis pursued and his desire for military glory led the king to develop a professional army numbering 100,000 men in peacetime and 400,000 in time of war. Louis made war an almost incessant activity of his reign. To achieve the prestige and military glory befitting the Sun King as well as to ensure the domination of his Bourbon dynasty over European affairs, Louis waged

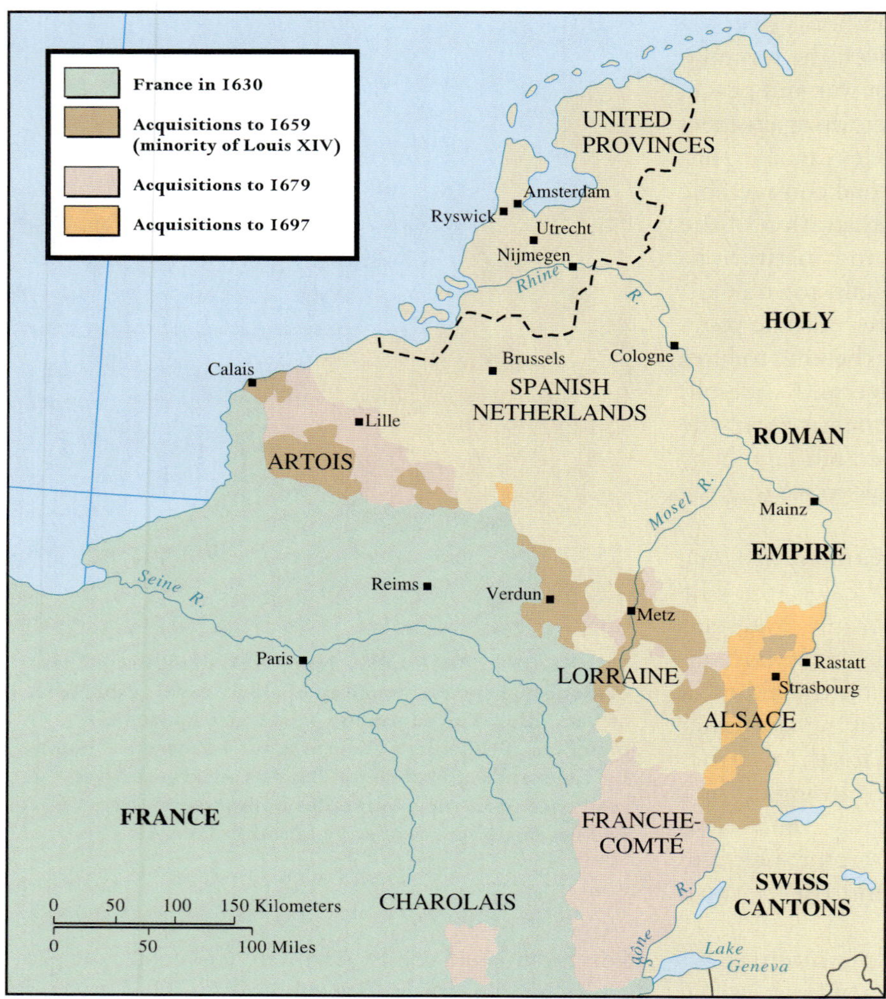

MAP 15.1 Territories Won in the Wars of Louis XIV.

four wars between 1667 and 1713 (see Map 15.1). His ambitions roused much of Europe to form coalitions to prevent destruction of the European balance of power Bourbon hegemony would cause. Although Louis added some territory to France's northeastern frontier and established a member of his own Bourbon dynasty on the throne of Spain, he also left France impoverished and surrounded by enemies.

The Decline of Spain

At the beginning of the seventeenth century, Spain possessed the most populous empire in the world, controlling almost all of South America and a number of settlements in Asia and Africa. To most Europeans, Spain still seemed the greatest power of the age, but the reality was quite different. The treasury was empty; Philip II went bankrupt in 1596 from excessive expenditures on war, and his successor did the same in 1607 by spending a fortune on his court. The armed forces were obsolescent, the government was inefficient, and the commercial class was weak in the midst of a suppressed peasantry, a luxury-loving class of nobles, and an oversupply of priests and monks. Spain continued to play the role of a great power, but appearances were deceiving.

During the reign of Philip III (1598–1621), many of Spain's weaknesses became all too apparent. Interested only in court luxury or miracle-working relics, Philip III allowed his first minister, the greedy duke of Lerma, to run the country. The aristocratic Lerma's primary interest was accumulating power and wealth for himself and his family. As important offices were filled with his relatives, crucial problems went unsolved.

At first, the reign of Philip IV (1621–1665) seemed to offer hope for a revival of Spain's energies, especially in the capable hands of his chief minister, Gaspar de Guzman, the count of Olivares. This clever, hardworking, and power-hungry statesman dominated the king's every move and worked to revive the interests of the monarchy. A flurry of domestic reform decrees, aimed at curtailing the power of the church and the landed aristocracy, was soon followed by a political reform program whose purpose was to further centralize the government of all Spain and its possessions in monarchical hands. All of these efforts met with little real success, however, because both the number (estimated at one-fifth of the population) and power of the Spanish aristocrats made them too strong to curtail in any significant fashion.

At the same time, most of the efforts of Olivares and Philip were undermined by their desire to pursue Spain's imperial glory and by a series of internal revolts. Spain's involvement in the Thirty Years' War led to a series of frightfully expensive military campaigns that led to internal revolts and years of civil war. Unfortunately for Spain, the campaigns also failed to produce victory. As Olivares wrote to King Philip IV, "God wants us to make peace; for He is depriving us visibly and absolutely of all the means of war."[2] The defeats in Europe and the internal revolts of the 1640s ended any illusions about Spain's greatness. The actual extent of its economic difficulties is still debated, but there is no question about its foreign losses. Dutch independence was formally recognized by the Peace of Westphalia in 1648, and the Peace of the Pyrenees with France in 1659 meant the surrender of certain border regions, such as the Catalonian province of Roussillon, to France.

Absolutism in Central and Eastern Europe

During the seventeenth century, a development of great importance for the modern Western world took place in central and eastern Europe, the appearance of three new powers: Prussia, Austria, and Russia.

The German States

The Peace of Westphalia, which officially ended the Thirty Years' War in 1648, left each of the more than three hundred German states comprising the Holy Roman Empire virtually autonomous and sovereign. Of these states, two emerged in the seventeenth and eighteenth centuries as great European powers.

THE RISE OF BRANDENBURG-PRUSSIA

The development of Brandenburg as a state was largely the story of the Hohenzollern dynasty. By the seventeenth century, the dominions of the house of Hohenzollern, now called Brandenburg-Prussia, consisted of three disconnected masses in western, central, and eastern Germany (see Map 15.2).

MAP 15.2 The Growth of Brandenburg-Prussia.

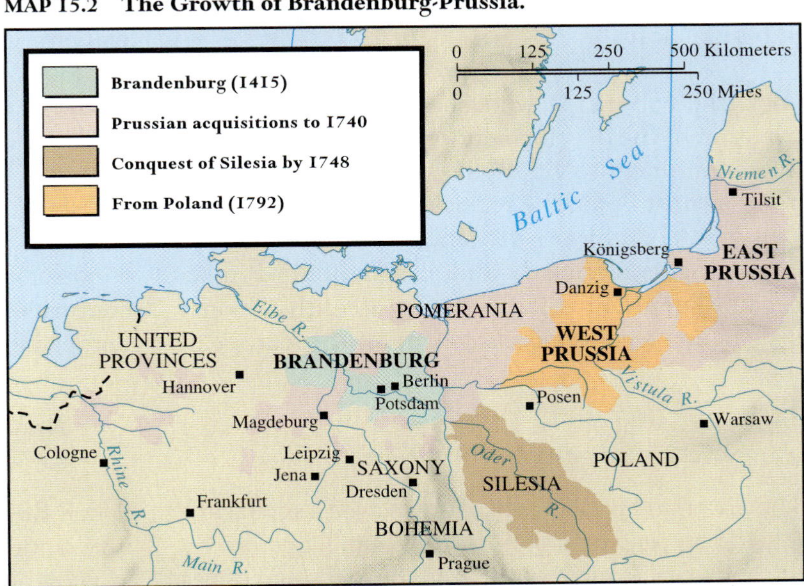

CHRONOLOGY

Absolutism in Western Europe

France	
Louis XIII	1610–1643
Cardinal Richelieu as chief minister	1624–1642
Ministry of Cardinal Mazarin	1642–1661
Fronde	1648–1652
Louis XIV	1643–1715
Edict of Fontainebleau	1685
Spain	
Philip III	1598–1621
Philip IV	1621–1665

The foundation for the Prussian state was laid by Frederick William the Great Elector (1640–1688). Realizing that Brandenburg-Prussia was a small, open territory with no natural frontiers for defense, Frederick William built a competent and efficient standing army. By 1678, he possessed a force of forty thousand men that absorbed more than 50 percent of the state's revenues. To sustain the army and his own power, Frederick William established the General War Commissariat to levy taxes for the army and oversee its growth and training. The Commissariat soon evolved into an agency for civil government as well. Directly responsible to the elector, the new bureaucractic machine became his chief instrument to govern the state. Many of its officials were members of the Prussian landed aristocracy, the Junkers, who also served as officers in the all-important army.

Frederick William was succeeded by his son Frederick III (1688–1713), who made one significant contribution to the development of Prussia. In return for his commitment to aid the Holy Roman Emperor in a war against Spain, he received the title of king in Prussia in 1701. Elector Frederick III was transformed into King Frederick I, and Brandenburg-Prussia became simply Prussia. In the eighteenth century, Prussia emerged as a great power on the European stage.

The Emergence of Austria

The Austrian Habsburgs had long played a significant role in European politics as Holy Roman Emperors. By the end of the Thirty Years' War, the Habsburg hopes of creating an empire in Germany had been dashed. In the seventeenth century, the house of Austria made a difficult transition; the German Empire was lost, but a new empire was created in eastern and southeastern Europe.

The nucleus of the new Austrian Empire remained the traditional Austrian hereditary possessions: Carinthia, Carniola, Styria, and Tyrol (see Map 15.3). To these had been added the kingdom of Bohemia and parts of northwestern Hungary in the sixteenth century. In the seventeenth century, Leopold I (1658–1705) encouraged the eastward movement of the Austrian Empire, but he was sorely challenged by the revival of Turkish power. Having moved into Transylvania, the Turks eventually pushed westward and laid siege to Vienna in 1683. A European army, led by the Austrians, counterattacked and decisively defeated the Turks in 1687. Austria took control of Hungary, Transylvania, Croatia, and Slovenia, thus establishing an Austrian Empire in southeastern Europe. At the end of the War of Spanish Succession (1702–1713), Austria gained possession of the Spanish Netherlands and received formal recognition of its occupation of the Spanish possessions in Italy (Milan, Mantua, Sardinia, and Naples), thus making Austria the dominant power in divided Italy. By the beginning of the eighteenth century, the house of Austria had acquired a new empire of considerable size.

The Austrian monarchy, however, never became a highly centralized, absolutist state, primarily because it contained so many different national groups. The Austrian Empire remained a collection of territories held together by a personal union. The Habsburg emperor was archduke of Austria, king of Bohemia, and king of Hungary. Each of these areas, however, had its own laws, Estates-General, and political life. The landed aristocrats throughout the empire were connected by a common bond of service to the house of Habsburg, as military officers or government bureaucrats, but there was no common sentiment to tie the regions together. By the beginning of the eighteenth century, Austria was a populous empire in central Europe of great potential military strength.

Russia: From Fledgling Principality to Major Power

A new Russian state had emerged in the fifteenth century under the leadership of the principality of Moscow and its grand dukes. In the sixteenth century,

CHRONOLOGY

Absolutism in Central and Eastern Europe

Brandenburg-Prussia	
Frederick William the Great Elector	1640–1688
Elector Frederick III (King Frederick I)	1688–1713
Austrian Empire	
Leopold I	1658–1705
Turkish siege of Vienna	1683
Russia	
Ivan IV the Terrible	1533–1584
Time of Troubles	1598–1613
Michael Romanov	1613–1645
Peter the Great	1689–1725
First trip to the West	1697–1698
Great Northern War	1701–1721
Founding of St. Petersburg	1703
Battle of Poltava	1709
Holy Synod	1721

Ivan IV the Terrible (1533–1584), who was the first ruler to take the title of tsar (Russian word "Caesar"), expanded the territories of Russia eastward, after finding westward expansion blocked by the powerful Swedish and Polish states. Ivan also extended the autocracy of the tsar by crushing the power of the Russian nobility, known as the boyars. Ivan's dynasty came to an end in 1598 and was followed by a resurgence of aristocratic power in a period of anarchy known as the Time of Troubles. It did not end until the Zemsky Sobor, or national assembly, chose Michael Romanov in 1613 as the new tsar, beginning a dynasty that lasted until 1917.

In the seventeenth century, Muscovite society was highly stratified. At the top was the tsar, who claimed to be a divinely ordained autocratic ruler. Russian society was dominated by an upper class of landed aristocrats who, in the course of the seventeenth century, managed to bind their peasants to the land. An abundance of land and a shortage of peasants made serfdom desirable to the landowners, who sustained a highly oppressive system. Townspeople were also controlled. Many merchants were not allowed to move from their cities without government permission or to sell their businesses to anyone outside their class. In the seventeenth century, merchant and peasant revolts as well as a schism in the Russian Orthodox church created very unsettled conditions. In the midst of these political and religious upheavals, Russia was experiencing more frequent contacts with the West and Western ideas were beginning to penetrate a few Russian circles. At the end of the seventeenth century,

MAP 15.3 The Growth of the Austrian Empire.

Peter the Great noticeably accelerated this westernizing process.

THE REIGN OF PETER THE GREAT (1689–1725)

Peter the Great was an unusual character. A strong man, towering 6 feet 9 inches tall, Peter was coarse in his tastes and rude in his behavior. He enjoyed a low kind of humor—belching contests and crude jokes—and vicious punishments—flogging, impalings, and roastings (see the box on p. 313). Peter received a firsthand view of the West when he made a trip there in 1697–1698 and returned to Russia with a firm determination to westernize or Europeanize Russia. Perhaps too much has been made of Peter's desire to westernize a "backward country." Peter's policy of Europeanization was largely technical. He admired European technology and gadgets and desired to transplant these to Russia. Only this kind of modernization could give him the army and navy he needed to make Russia a great power.

PETER THE GREAT. Peter the Great wished to westernize Russia, especially in the realm of technical skills. His foremost goal was the creation of a strong army and navy in order to make Russia a great power. A Dutch painter created this portrait of the armored tsar during his visit to the West in 1697.

As could be expected, one of his first priorities was the reorganization of the army and the creation of a navy. Employing both Russians and Europeans as officers, he conscripted peasants for twenty-five-year stints of service to build a standing army of 210,000 men. Peter has also been given credit for forming the first Russian navy.

Peter reorganized the central government, partly along Western lines. In 1711, he created a senate to supervise the administrative machinery of state while he was away on military campaigns. In time, the Senate became something like a ruling council, but its ineffectiveness caused Peter to borrow the Western institution of "colleges," or boards of administrators entrusted with specific functions, such as foreign affairs, war, and justice. To impose the rule of the central government more effectively throughout the land, Peter divided Russia into eight provinces and later, in 1719, into fifty. Although he hoped to create a "police state," by which he meant a well-ordered community governed in accordance with law, few of his bureaucrats shared his concept of honest service and duty to the state. Peter hoped for a sense of civic duty, but his own forceful personality created an atmosphere of fear that prevented it.

To satisfy his insatiable need of money for an army and navy that absorbed as much as four-fifths of the state revenue, Peter adopted Western mercantilistic policies to stimulate economic growth. He tried to increase exports and develop new industries while exploiting domestic resources like the iron mines in the Urals. But his military needs were endless, and he came to rely on the old expedient of simply raising taxes, imposing additional burdens on the hapless peasants who were becoming ever more oppressed in Peter's Russia.

Peter also sought to gain state control of the Russian Orthodox church. In 1721, he abolished the position of patriarch and created a body called the Holy Synod to make decisions for the church. At its head stood a procurator, a layman who represented the interests of the tsar and assured Peter of effective domination of the church.

Immediately upon returning from his first trip to the West in 1698, Peter began to introduce Western customs, practices, and manners into Russia. He ordered the preparation of the first Russian book of etiquette to teach Western manners. Among other things, it pointed out that it was not polite to spit on the floor or scratch oneself at dinner. Because Westerners did not wear beards or the traditional long-skirted coat, Russian beards had to be shaved

Peter the Great Deals with a Rebellion

During his first visit to the West in 1697–1698, Peter received word that the Streltsy, an elite military unit stationed in Moscow, had revolted against his authority. Peter hurried home and crushed the revolt in a very savage fashion. This selection is taken from an Austrian account of how Peter dealt with the rebels.

Peter and the Streltsy

How sharp was the pain, how great the indignation, to which the tsar's Majesty was mightily moved, when he knew of the rebellion of the Streltsy, betraying openly a mind panting for vengeance! He was still tarrying at Vienna, quite full of the desire of setting out for Italy; but, fervid as was his curiosity of rambling abroad, it was, nevertheless, speedily extinguished on the announcement of the troubles that had broken out in the bowels of his realm. Going immediately to Lefort . . . , he thus indignantly broke out: "Tell me, Francis, how I can reach Moscow by the shortest way, in a brief space, so that I may wreak vengeance on this great perfidy of my people, with punishments worthy of their abominable crime. Not one of them shall escape with impunity. Around my royal city, which, with their impious efforts, they planned to destroy, I will have gibbets and gallows set upon the walls and ramparts, and each and every one of them will I put to a direful death." Nor did he long delay the plan for his justly excited wrath; he took the quick post, as his ambassador suggested, and in four weeks' time he had got over about three hundred miles without accident, and arrived the 4th of September, 1698,—a monarch for the well deposed, but an avenger for the wicked.

His first anxiety after his arrival was about the rebellion—in what it consisted, what the insurgents meant, who dared to instigate such a crime. And as nobody could answer accurately upon all points, and some pleaded their own ignorance, others the obstinacy of the Streltsy, he began to have suspicions of everybody's loyalty. . . . No day, holy or profane, were the inquisitors idle; every day was deemed fit and lawful for torturing. There was as many scourges as there were accused, and every inquisitor was a butcher. . . . The whole month of October was spent on lacerating the backs of culprits with the knout and with flames; no day were those that were left alive exempt from scourging or scorching; or else they were broken upon the wheel, or driven to the gibbet, or slain with the ax. . . .

To prove to all people how holy and inviolable are those walls of the city which the Streltsy rashly meditated scaling in a sudden assault, beams were run out from all the embrasures in the walls near the gates, in each of which two rebels were hanged. This day beheld about two hundred and fifty die that death. There are few cities fortified with as many palisades as Moscow has given gibbets to her guardian Streltsy.

and coats shortened, a reform Peter personally enforced at court by shaving off his nobles' beards and cutting their coats at the knees with his own hands. Outside the court, the edicts were enforced by barbers and tailors planted at town gates with orders to cut the beards and cloaks of all who entered or left. Anyone who failed to conform was to be "beaten without mercy."

One group of Russians benefited greatly from Peter's cultural reforms—women. Having watched women mixing freely with men in Western courts, Peter shattered the seclusion of upper-class Russian women and demanded that they remove the traditional veils that covered their faces. Peter also decreed that social gatherings be held three times a week in the large houses of St. Petersburg where men and women could mix for conversation, card games, and dancing, which Peter had learned in the West. The tsar also now insisted that women could marry of their own free will.

The object of Peter's domestic reforms was to make Russia into a great state and military power. His primary goal was to "open a window to the west," meaning an ice-free port easily accessible to Europe. This could only be achieved on the Baltic, but at that time the Baltic coast was controlled by Sweden, the most important power in northern Europe. Desirous of these lands, Peter, with the support of Poland and Denmark, attacked Sweden in the summer of 1700, believing that the young king of Sweden, Charles XII, could easily be defeated. Charles, however, proved to be a brilliant general. He smashed the Danes, flattened the Poles, and, with a well-disciplined force of only eight thousand men, routed the Russian army of forty thousand at the Battle of Narva (1700). The Great Northern War (1701–1721) soon ensued.

But Peter fought back. He reorganized his army along Western lines and at the Battle of Poltava in July 1709 decisively defeated Charles's army. Although the war dragged on for another twelve years, the Peace of Nystadt in 1721 gave formal recognition to what Peter had already achieved: the acquisition of Estonia, Livonia, and Karelia (see Map 15.4). Sweden became a second-rate power while Russia was now the great European state Peter had wanted. Already in 1703, in these northern lands on the Baltic, Peter had begun the construction of a new city, St. Petersburg, his window to the west and a symbol that Russia was looking westward to Europe. The lives of thousands of peasants were lost during its construction. Finished during Peter's lifetime, St. Petersburg remained the Russian capital until 1917.

Peter modernized and westernized Russia to the extent that it became a great military power and, by his death in 1725, an important member of the European state system. But his policies were also detrimental to Russia. Westernization was a bit of a sham, because Western culture reached only the upper classes while the real object of the reforms, the creation of a strong military, only added more burdens to the masses of the Russian people. The forceful way in which Peter the Great brought westernization led his people to distrust Europe and Western civilization.

The Limits of Absolutism

In recent decades, historical studies of local institutions have challenged the traditional picture of absolute monarchs. It is misleading to think that these rulers actually controlled the lives of their subjects. In 1700, government for most people still meant the local institutions that affected their lives: local courts, local tax collectors, and local organizers of armed forces. Kings and ministers might determine policies and issue guidelines, but they still had to function through local agents and had no guarantee whatever that their wishes would be carried out. A mass of urban and provincial privileges, liberties, and exemptions (including from taxation) and a whole host of corporate bodies and interest groups—provincial and national Estates, clerical officials, officeholders who had bought or inherited their positions, and provincial nobles—limited what monarchs could achieve. The most successful rulers were not those who tried to destroy the old system but rather those like Louis XIV who knew how to use the old system to their advantage. Above all other considerations stood the

MAP 15.4 The Expansion of Russia.

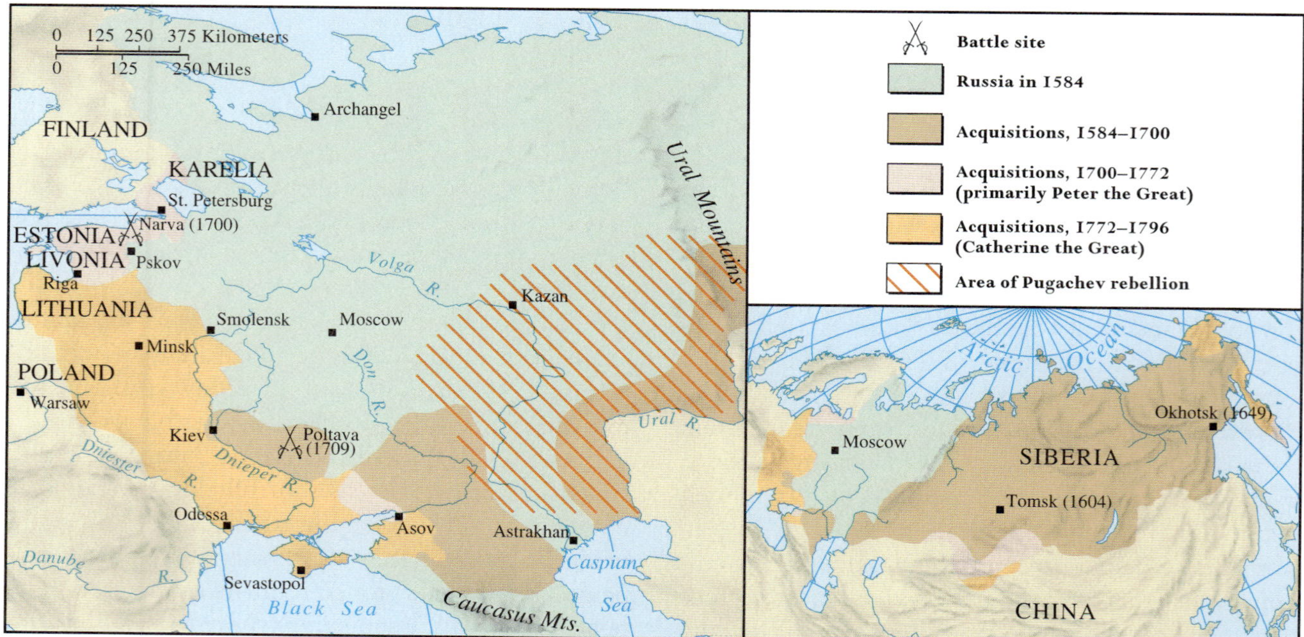

landholding nobility. Everywhere in the seventeenth century, the landed aristocracy played an important role in the European monarchical system. As military officers, judges, officeholders, and landowners in control of vast, untaxed estates, their power remained immense. In some places, their strength even put severe limits on how effectively monarchs could rule.

Limited Monarchy: The Dutch Republic and England

Almost everywhere in Europe in the seventeenth century, kings and their ministers were in control of central governments. But not all European states followed the pattern of absolute monarchy. In western Europe, two great states—the Dutch Republic and England—successfully resisted the power of hereditary monarchs.

The Golden Age of the Dutch Republic

The seventeenth century has often been called the golden age of the Dutch Republic as the United Provinces held center stage as one of Europe's great powers. Like France and England, the United Provinces was an Atlantic power, underlining the importance of that shift of political and economic power in the seventeenth century from the Mediterranean Sea to the countries on the Atlantic seaboard. As a result of the sixteenth-century revolt of the Netherlands, the seven northern provinces, which began to call themselves the United Provinces of the Netherlands in 1581, became the core of the modern Dutch state. The new state was officially recognized by the Peace of Westphalia in 1648.

With independence came internal dissension. There were two chief centers of political power in the new state. Each province had an official known as a stadholder who was responsible for leading the army and maintaining order. Beginning with William of Orange and his heirs, the house of Orange occupied the stadholderate in most of the seven provinces and favored the development of a centralized government with themselves as hereditary monarchs. The States General, an assembly of representatives from every province, opposed the Orangist ambitions and advocated a decentralized or republican form of government. For much of the seventeenth century, the republican forces were in control. But in 1672, burdened with war against both France and England, the United Provinces allowed William III (1672–1702) of the house of Orange to establish a monarchical regime. However, his death in 1702 without direct heirs enabled the republican forces to gain control once more. The Dutch Republic would not be seriously threatened again by the monarchical forces.

Underlying Dutch prominence in the seventeenth century was its economic prosperity, fueled by the role of the Dutch as carriers of Europe trade. But war proved disastrous to the Dutch Republic. Wars with France and England placed heavy burdens on Dutch finances and manpower. English shipping began to challenge what had been Dutch commercial supremacy, and by 1715, the Dutch were experiencing a serious economic decline.

England and the Emergence of Constitutional Monarchy

One of the most prominent examples of resistance to absolute monarchy came in seventeenth-century England where king and Parliament struggled to determine the role each should play in governing the nation. But the struggle over this political issue was complicated by a deep and profound religious controversy. Along with the victory of Parliament came the foundation for constitutional monarchy by the end of the seventeenth century.

REVOLUTION AND CIVIL WAR

With the death of Queen Elizabeth in 1603, the Tudor dynasty became extinct, and the Stuart line of rulers was inaugurated with the accession to the throne of Elizabeth's cousin, King James VI of Scotland, who became James I (1603–1625) of England. Although used to royal power as king of Scotland, James understood little about the laws, institutions, and customs of the English. He espoused the divine right of kings—the belief that kings receive their power directly from God and are responsible to no one except God. This viewpoint alienated Parliament, which had grown accustomed under the Tudors to act on the premise that monarch and Parliament together ruled England as a "balanced polity." Parliament expressed its displeasure with James's claims by refusing his requests for additional monies needed by the king to meet the increased cost of government. Parliament's power of the purse proved to be its trump card in its relationship with the king.

CHRONOLOGY

Limited Monarchy and Republics

United Provinces of the Netherlands	
Official recognition	1648
House of Orange	
William III	1672–1702
England	
James I	1603–1625
Charles I	1625–1649
Petition of Right	1628
Civil Wars	1642–1648
Commonwealth	1649–1653
Death of Cromwell	1658
Restoration of monarchy	1660
Charles II	1660–1685
Declaration of Indulgence	1672
Test Act	1673
James II	1685–1688
Declaration of Indulgence	1687
Glorious Revolution	1688
Bill of Rights	1689

Some members of Parliament were also alienated by James's religious policy. The Puritans—Protestants within the Anglican church inspired by Calvinist theology—wanted James to eliminate the episcopal system of church organization used in the Church of England (in which the bishop or *episcopos* played the major administrative role) in favor of a Presbyterian model (used in Scotland and patterned after Calvin's church organization in Geneva, where ministers and elders—also called presbyters—played an important governing role). James refused because he realized that the Anglican church, with its bishops appointed by the crown, was a major support of monarchical authority. But the Puritans were not easily cowed and added to the rising chorus of opposition to the king. Many of England's gentry, mostly well-to-do landowners below the level of the nobility, had become Puritans, and these Puritan gentry not only formed an important and substantial part of the House of Commons, the lower house of Parliament, but also held important positions locally as justices of the peace and sheriffs. It was not wise to alienate them.

The conflict that began during the reign of James came to a head during the reign of his son Charles I (1625–1649). In 1628, Parliament passed a petition of right that the king was supposed to accept before being granted any taxes. This petition prohibited taxes without Parliament's consent, arbitrary imprisonment, the quartering of soldiers in private houses, and the declaration of martial law in peacetime. Although he initially accepted it, Charles later reneged on the agreement because of its limitations on royal power. In 1629, Charles decided that because he could not work with Parliament, he would not summon it to meet. From 1629 to 1640, Charles pursued a course of "personal rule," which forced him to find ways to collect taxes without Parliament's cooperation. These expedients aroused opposition from middle-class merchants and landed gentry who believed the king was attempting to tax without Parliament's consent.

The king's religious policy also proved disastrous. The attempt of Charles to impose more ritual on the Anglican church struck the Puritans as a return to Catholic popery. Charles's efforts to force them to conform to his religious policies infuriated the Puritans, thousands of whom abandoned England for the "howling wildernesses" of America.

Grievances mounted until England finally slipped into a civil war (1642–1648) that was won by the parliamentary forces. Most important to Parliament's success was the creation of the New Model Army by Oliver Cromwell, the only real military genius of the war. The New Model Army was composed primarily of more extreme Puritans known as the Independents, who, in typical Calvinist fashion, believed they were doing battle for the Lord. It is striking to read in Cromwell's military reports such statements as "Sir, this is none other but the hand of God; and to Him alone belongs the glory."

Between 1648 and 1660, England faced a trying situation. After the execution of Charles I on January 30, 1649, Parliament abolished the monarchy and the House of Lords and proclaimed England a republic or commonwealth. But Cromwell and his army, unable to work effectively with Parliament, dispersed it by force. As the members of Parliament departed in April 1653, Cromwell shouted after them: "It's you that have forced me to do this, for I have sought the Lord night and day that He would slay me rather than put upon me the doing of this work." With the certainty of one who is convinced he is right, Cromwell had destroyed both king and Parliament.

Finally, Cromwell dissolved Parliament and divided the country into eleven regions, each ruled by a major general who served virtually as a military governor. Unable to establish a constitutional basis for a

OLIVER CROMWELL. Oliver Cromwell was a dedicated Puritan who formed the New Model Army and defeated the forces supporting King Charles I. Unable to work with Parliament, he came to rely on military force to rule England. Cromwell is pictured here in 1649, on the eve of his military campaign in Ireland.

working government, Cromwell had resorted to military force to maintain the rule of the Independents, ironically using even more arbitrary policies than those of Charles I.

Oliver Cromwell died in 1658. After floundering for eighteen months, the military establishment decided that arbitrary rule by the army was no longer feasible and reestablished the monarchy in the person of Charles II (1660–1685), the son of Charles I. The restoration of the Stuart monarchy ended England's time of troubles, but it was not long before England experienced yet another constitutional crisis.

Restoration and a Glorious Revolution

The restoration of the monarchy and the House of Lords did not mean that the work of the English Revolution was undone. Parliament kept much of the power it had won, arbitrary courts were still abolished, Parliament's role in government was acknowledged, and the necessity for its consent to taxation was accepted. Yet Charles continued to push his own ideas, some of which were clearly out of step with many of his subjects.

Charles was sympathetic to and perhaps even inclined to Catholicism. Moreover, Charles's brother James, heir to the throne, did not hide the fact that he was a Catholic. Parliament's suspicions were therefore aroused in 1672 when Charles took the audacious step of issuing a declaration of indulgence that suspended the laws that Parliament had passed against Catholics and Puritans after the restoration of the Anglican church as the official church of England. Parliament would have none of it and induced the king to suspend the declaration. Propelled by strong anti-Catholic sentiment, Parliament then passed the Test Act of 1673, specifying that only Anglicans could hold military and civil offices.

The accession of James II (1685–1688) to the crown virtually guaranteed a new constitutional crisis for England. An open and devout Catholic, his attempt to further Catholic interests made religion once more a primary cause of conflict between king and Parliament. In 1687, James issued a declaration of indulgence that suspended all laws that excluded Catholics and Puritans from office. Parliamentary outcries against James's policies stopped short of rebellion because members knew that he was an old man and his successors were his Protestant daughters Mary and Anne, born to his first wife. But on June 10, 1688, a son was born to James II's second wife, also a Catholic. Suddenly the specter of a Catholic hereditary monarchy loomed large. A group of prominent English noblemen invited the Dutch chief executive, William of Orange, husband of James's daughter Mary, to invade England. William and Mary raised an army and invaded England while James, his wife, and their infant son fled to France. With almost no bloodshed, England had undergone its "Glorious Revolution," not over the issue of whether there would be monarchy but rather over who would be monarch.

The events of late 1688 constituted only the initial stage of the Glorious Revolution. In January 1689, Parliament offered the throne to William and Mary, who accepted it along with the provisions of a bill of rights (see the box on p. 318). The Bill of Rights affirmed Parliament's right to make laws and levy taxes and made it impossible for kings to oppose or do without Parliament by stipulating that standing armies could be raised only with the consent of Parliament.

The Bill of Rights

In 1688, the English experienced yet another revolution, a bloodless one in which the Stuart king James II was replaced by Mary, James's daughter, and her husband, William of Orange. After William and Mary had assumed power, Parliament passed a bill of rights that specified the rights of Parliament and laid the foundation for a constitutional monarchy.

The Bill of Rights

Whereas the said late King James II having abdicated the government, and the throne being thereby vacant, his Highness the prince of Orange (whom it has pleased Almighty God to make the glorious instrument of delivering this kingdom from popery and arbitrary power) did (by the device of the lords spiritual and temporal, and diverse principal persons of the Commons) cause letters to be written to the lords spiritual and temporal, being Protestants, and other letters to the several counties, cities, universities, boroughs, and Cinque Ports, for the choosing of such persons to represent them, as were of right to be sent to parliament, to meet and sit at Westminster upon the two and twentieth day of January, in this year 1689, in order to such an establishment as that their religion, laws, and liberties might not again be in danger of being subverted; upon which letters elections have been accordingly made.

And thereupon the said lords spiritual and temporal and Commons, pursuant to their respective letters and elections, being now assembled in a full and free representation of this nation, taking into their most serious consideration the best means for attaining the ends aforesaid, do in the first place (as their ancestors in like case have usually done), for the vindication and assertion of their ancient rights and liberties, declare:

1. That the pretended power of suspending laws, or the execution of laws, by regal authority, without consent of parliament is illegal.
2. That the pretended power of dispensing with the laws, or the execution of law by regal authority, as it has been assumed and exercised of late, is illegal.
3. That the commission for erecting the late court of commissioners for ecclesiastical causes, and all other commissions and courts of like nature, are illegal and pernicious.
4. That levying money for or to the use of the crown by pretense of prerogative, without grant of parliament, for longer time or in other manner than the same is or shall be granted, is illegal.
5. That it is the right of the subjects to petition the king, and all commitments and prosecutions for such petitioning are illegal.
6. That the raising or keeping a standing army within the kingdom in time of peace, unless it be with consent of parliament, is against law.
7. That the subjects which are Protestants may have arms for their defense suitable to their conditions, and as allowed by law.
8. That election of members of parliament ought to be free.
9. That the freedom of speech, and debates or proceedings in parliament, ought not to be impeached or questioned in any court or place out of parliament.
10. That excessive bail ought not to be required, nor excessive fines imposed, nor cruel and unusual punishments inflicted.
11. That jurors ought to be duly impaneled and returned, and jurors which pass upon men in trials for high treason ought to be freeholders.
12. That all grants and promises of fines and forfeitures of particular persons before conviction are illegal and void.
13. And that for redress of all grievances, and for the amending, strengthening, and preserving of the laws, parliament ought to be held frequently.

The rights of citizens to petition the sovereign, keep arms, have a jury trial, and not be subject to excessive bail were also confirmed. The Bill of Rights helped fashion a system of government based on the rule of law and a freely elected Parliament, thus laying the foundation for a constitutional monarchy.

The Bill of Rights did not settle the religious questions that had played such a large role in England's troubles in the seventeenth century. The Toleration Act of 1689 granted Puritan Dissenters the right of free public worship (Catholics were still excluded). Although the Toleration Act did not mean complete religious freedom and equality, it marked a departure in English history because few people would ever again be persecuted for religious reasons.

Many historians have viewed the Glorious Revolution as the end of the seventeenth-century struggle between king and Parliament. By deposing one king and establishing another, Parliament had destroyed the divine-right theory of kingship (William was, after all, king by grace of Parliament, not God) and confirmed its right to participate in the government. Parliament did not have complete control of the government, but it now had an unquestioned right to participate in affairs of state. During the next century, it would gradually prove to be the real authority in the English system of constitutional monarchy.

Responses to Revolution

The English revolutions of the seventeenth century prompted very different responses from two English political thinkers, Thomas Hobbes and John Locke. Thomas Hobbes (1588–1679), who lived during the English Civil War, was alarmed by the revolutionary upheavals in his contemporary England. His name has since been associated with the state's claim to absolute authority over its subjects, which he elaborated in his major treatise on political thought known as the *Leviathan,* published in 1651.

Hobbes claimed that in the state of nature, before society was organized, human life was "solitary, poor, nasty, brutish, and short." Humans were guided not by reason and moral ideals but by animalistic instincts and a ruthless struggle for self-preservation. To save themselves from destroying each other (the "war of every man against every man"), people contracted to form a commonwealth, which Hobbes called "that great Leviathan (or rather, to speak more reverently, that mortal god) to which we owe our peace and defense." This commonwealth placed its collective power in the hands of a sovereign authority, preferably a single ruler, who served as executor, legislator, and judge. This absolute ruler possessed unlimited power. In Hobbes's view, subjects may not rebel; if they do, they must be suppressed.

John Locke (1632–1704), author of a political work called *Two Treatises of Government,* viewed the exercise of political power quite differently from Hobbes and argued against the absolute rule of one man. Like Hobbes, Locke began with the state of nature before human existence became organized socially. But unlike Hobbes, Locke believed that humans lived then in a state of equality and freedom rather than a state of war. In this state of nature, humans had certain inalienable natural rights—to life, liberty, and property. Like Hobbes, Locke did not believe that all was well in the state of nature. Since there was no impartial judge in nature, people found it difficult to protect these natural rights. So they mutually agreed to establish a government to ensure the protection of their rights. This agreement established mutual obligations: government would protect the rights of people, and the people would act reasonably toward their government. But if a government broke this agreement—if a king, for example, failed to live up to his obligation to protect the natural rights or claimed absolute authority and made laws without the consent of the community—the people might form a new government. For Locke, however, the community of people was primarily the landholding aristocracy who were represented in Parliament, not the landless masses. Locke was hardly an advocate of political democracy, but his ideas proved important to both the Americans and the French in the eighteenth century and were used to support demands for constitutional government, the rule of law, and the protection of rights.

Economic Trends in the Seventeenth Century

The seventeenth century was marked by economic contraction, although conditions varied by country or region. Trade, industry, and agriculture all felt the pinch of a depression, which some historians believe bottomed out between 1640 and 1680. Translated into everyday life, for many people the economic contraction of the seventeenth century meant scarce food, uncertain employment, and high rates of taxation.

Population was also affected. Based on the birthrate of the seventeenth century, demographers would expect the European population to have doubled every twenty-five years. In reality, the population either declined or increased only intermittently as a result of a variety of factors. Infant mortality rates were high, 30 percent in the first year of life and 50 percent before the age of ten. Epidemics and famines were again common experiences in European life. The last great epidemic of bubonic plague spread across Europe in the middle and late years of the seventeenth century. The Mediterranean region suffered from 1646 to 1657, when the plague killed off 130,000 persons in

Naples alone. In 1665, it struck England and devastated London, killing 20 percent of its population.

Overseas Trade and Colonies

As we saw in our discussion of Colbert's policies in France, one of the principles of mercantilism was a high regard for colonies as sources of raw materials and markets for finished goods. Mercantilist theory on the role of colonies was matched in practice by Europe's overseas expansion. With the development of colonies and trading posts in the Americas and the East, Europeans entered an age of international commerce in the seventeenth century. We should remember, however, that local, regional, and intra-European trade still dominated. About one-tenth of English and Dutch exports were shipped across the Atlantic; slightly more went to the East. What made the transoceanic trade rewarding, however, was not the volume but the value of its goods. Dutch, English, and French merchants were bringing back products that were still consumed largely by the wealthy but were beginning to make their way into the lives of artisans and merchants. Pepper and spices from the Indies, West Indian and Brazilian sugar, and Asian coffee and tea were becoming more readily available to European consumers. The first coffee and tea houses opened in London in the 1650s and spread rapidly to other parts of Europe.

In 1600, much overseas trade was still carried by the Spanish and Portuguese, who alone possessed colonies of any significant size. But war and steady pressure from their Dutch and English rivals eroded Portuguese trade in both the West and the East. The Spanish also maintained an enormous South American empire, but Spain's importance as a commercial power declined rapidly in the seventeenth century.

The Dutch became a major economic power in the seventeenth century. The Dutch East India Company, formed in 1602 to exploit the riches of the East, gradually took control of most of the Portuguese bases in the East and opened trade with China and Japan. Its profits were spectacular in the first ten years. The Dutch West India Company, created in 1621, was less successful. One of its projects was the North American colony of New Netherlands, which stretched from the mouth of the Hudson River as far north as Albany. In 1664, the English seized New Netherlands and renamed it New York, and the Dutch West India Company soon went bankrupt.

The Dutch overseas trade and commercial empire faced two major rivals in the seventeenth century—the English and the French. The English had founded their own East India Company in 1601 and proceeded to create a colonial empire in the New World along the Atlantic seaboard of North America. French commercial companies in the East experienced much difficulty. Though due in part to a late start, the problems of the French also demonstrated the weakness of a commerce dependent on political rather than economic impetus (see the box on p. 321). The East India Companies set up by Henry IV and Richelieu all failed. The French had greater success in North America, where in 1663 Canada was made the property of the crown and administered like a French province. But the French failed to provide adequate men or money, allowing their continental wars to take precedence over the conquest of the North American continent. Already in 1713, by the Treaty of Utrecht, the French began to cede some of their American possessions to their English rival.

The World of European Culture

The seventeenth century witnessed remarkable talent. In addition to the intellectuals responsible for the Scientific Revolution (see Chapter 16), the era was blessed with a number of prominent thinkers, artists, and writers.

Art: French Classicism and Dutch Realism

In the second half of the seventeenth century, France replaced Italy as the cultural leader of Europe. Rejecting the Baroque style as overly showy and passionate, the French remained committed to the classical values of the High Renaissance. French late classicism, with its emphasis on clarity, simplicity, balance, and harmony of design, was, however, a rather austere version of the High Renaissance style. Its triumph reflected the shift in seventeenth-century French society from chaos to order. While rejecting the emotionalism and high drama of the Baroque, French classicism continued the Baroque's conception of grandeur in the portrayal of noble subjects, especially those from classical antiquity.

The supremacy of Dutch commerce in the seventeenth century was paralleled by a brilliant flowering of Dutch painting. Wealthy patricians and

West Meets East: An Exchange of Royal Letters

Economic gain was not the only motivation of Western rulers who wished to establish a European presence in the East. In 1681, King Louis XIV of France wrote a letter to the king of Tonkin asking permission for Christian missionaries to proselytize in Vietnam. The king of Tonkin politely declined the request.

A Letter to the King of Tonkin

Most high, most excellent, most mighty and most magnanimous Prince, our very dear and good friend, may it please God to increase your greatness with a happy end!

We hear from our subjects who were in your Realm what protection you accorded them. We appreciate this all the more since we have for you all the esteem that one can have for a prince as illustrious through his military valor as he is commendable for the justice which he exercises in his Realm. . . . Since the war which we have had for several years, in which all of Europe had banded together against us, prevented our vessels from going to the Indies, at the present time, when we are at peace after having gained many victories and expanded our Realm through the conquest of several important places, we have immediately given orders to the Royal Company to establish itself in your kingdom as soon as possible. . . . We have given orders to have brought to you some presents which we believe might be agreeable to you. But the one thing in the world which we desire most, both for you and for your Realm, would be to obtain for your subjects who have already embraced the law of the only true God of heaven and earth, the freedom to profess it, since this law is the highest, the noblest, the most sacred and especially the most suitable to have kings reign absolutely over the people.

We are even quite convinced that, if you knew the truths and the maxims which it teaches, you would give first of all to your subjects the glorious example of embracing it. We wish you this incomparable blessing together with a long and happy reign, and we pray God that it may please Him to augment your greatness with the happiest of endings.

Your very dear and good friend,
Louis

Answers from the King of Tonkin to Louis XIV

The King of Tonkin sends to the King of France a letter to express to him his best sentiments. . . . Your communication, which comes from a country which is a thousand leagues away, and which proceeds from the heart as a testimony of your sincerity, merits repeated consideration and infinite praise. Politeness toward strangers is nothing unusual in our country. There is not a stranger who is not well received by us. How then could we refuse a man from France, which is the most celebrated among the kingdoms of the world and which for love of us wishes to frequent us and bring us merchandise? These feelings of fidelity and justice are truly worthy to be applauded. As regards your wish that we should cooperate in propagating your religion, we do not dare to permit it, for there is an ancient custom, introduced by edicts, which formally forbids it. Now, edicts are promulgated only to be carried out faithfully; without fidelity nothing is stable. How could we disdain a well-established custom to satisfy a private friendship? . . . This then is my letter. We send you herewith a modest gift which we offer you with a glad heart.

This letter was written at the beginning of winter and on a beautiful day.

burghers of Dutch urban society commissioned works of art for their guild halls, town halls, and private dwellings. Following the wishes of these patrons, Dutch painters became primarily interested in the realistic portrayal of secular, everyday life. This interest in painting scenes of everyday life is evident in the work of Judith Leyster (c. 1609–1660), who established her own independent painting career, a remarkable occurrence in seventeenth-century Europe. Leyster became the first woman member of the painting guild of St. Luke in Haarlem, which enabled her to set up her own workshop and take on three male pupils. Musicians playing their instruments, women sewing, children laughing while playing games, and actors performing

JUDITH LEYSTER, *SELF-PORTRAIT.* Although Judith Leyster was a well-known artist to her Dutch contemporaries, her fame diminished soon after her death. In the late nineteenth century, however, a Dutch art historian rediscovered her work. In her *Self-Portrait,* painted in 1635, she is seen pausing in her work in front of one of the scenes of daily life that made her such a popular artist in her own day.

are the subjects of Leyster's portraits. But she was also capable of introspection, as is evident in her *Self-Portrait*.

The finest example of the golden age of Dutch painting was Rembrandt van Rijn (1606–1669). Although Rembrandt shared the Dutch predilection for realistic portraits, he became more introspective as he grew older. He refused to follow his contemporaries, whose pictures were largely secular in subject matter; half of his paintings focused on scenes from biblical tales. Since the Protestant tradition of hostility to religious pictures had discouraged artistic expression, Rembrandt stands out as the one great Protestant painter of the seventeenth century.

The Theater: The Triumph of French Neoclassicism

As the great age of theater in England and Spain was drawing to a close around 1630, a new dramatic era began to dawn in France that lasted into the 1680s. Unlike Shakespeare in England and Lope de Vega in Spain, French playwrights wrote more for an elite

REMBRANDT VAN RIJN, *SYNDICS OF THE CLOTH GUILD.* The Dutch experienced a golden age of painting during the seventeenth century. The burghers and patricians of Dutch urban society commissioned works of art, and these quite naturally reflected the burghers' interests, as this painting by Rembrandt illustrates.

audience and were forced to depend on royal patronage. Louis XIV used theater as he did art and architecture—to attract attention to his monarchy. French dramatists cultivated a classical style that emphasized the clever, polished, and correct over the emotional and imaginative. Many of the French works of this period derived their themes and plots from Greek and Roman sources.

Jean-Baptiste Molière (1622–1673) enjoyed the favor of the French court and benefited from the patronage of the Sun King. He wrote, produced, and acted in a series of comedies that often satirized the religious and social world of his time. In *The Misanthrope*, he mocked the corruption of court society, while in *Tartuffe*, he ridiculed religious hypocrisy. Molière's satires, however, sometimes got him into trouble. The Paris clergy did not find *Tartuffe* funny and had it banned for five years. Only the protection of Louis XIV saved Molière from more severe harassment.

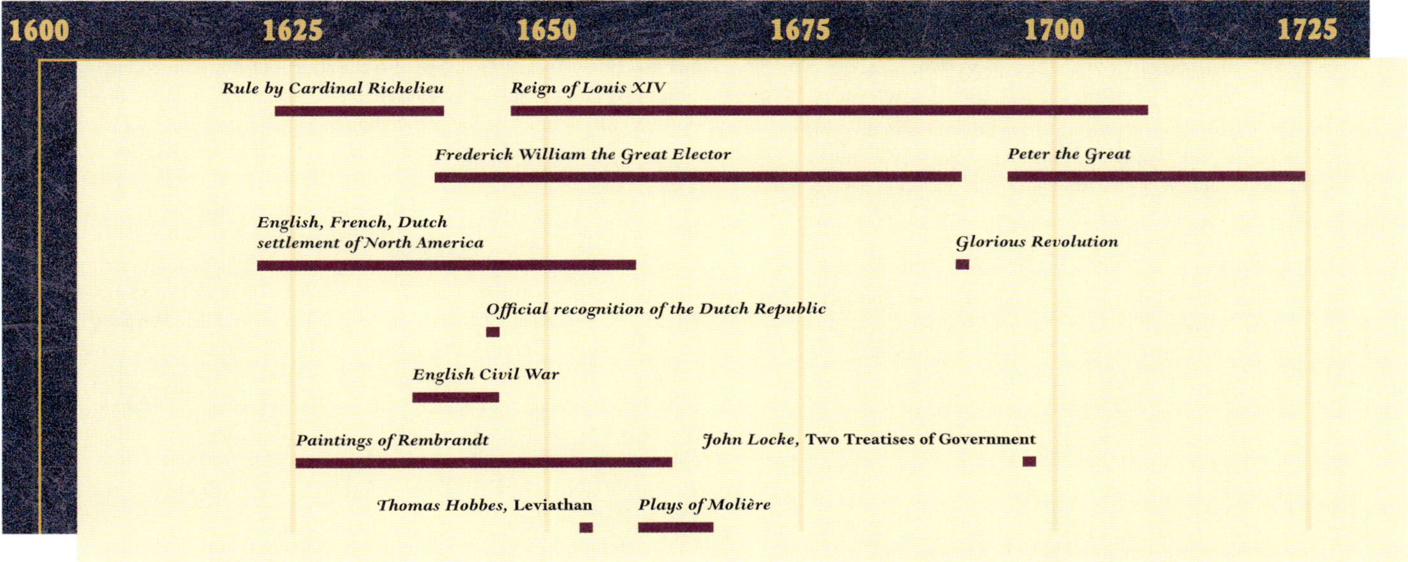

Conclusion

To many historians, the seventeenth century has assumed extraordinary proportions. The divisive effects of the Reformation had been assimilated and the concept of a united Christendom, held as an ideal since the Middle Ages, had been irrevocably destroyed by the religious wars, making possible the emergence of a system of nation-states in which power politics took on increasing significance. The growth of political thought focusing on the secular origins of state power reflected the changes that were going on in seventeenth-century society.

Within those states, there slowly emerged some of the machinery that made possible a growing centralization of power. In those states called absolutist, strong monarchs, with the assistance of their aristocracies, provided the leadership for greater centralization. But in England, where the landed aristocracy gained power at the expense of the monarchs, the foundations were laid for a constitutional government in which Parliament provided the focus for the institutions of centralized power. In all the major European states, a growing concern for power and dynastic expansion led to larger armies and greater conflict. War remained an endemic feature of Western civilization.

But the search for order and harmony continued, evident in art and literature. At the same time, although it would be misleading to state that Europe had become a secular world, it is fair to say that religious preoccupations and values were losing ground to secular considerations. The seventeenth century was a transitional period to a more secular spirit that has characterized modern Western civilization until the present. No stronger foundation for this spirit could be found than in the new view of the universe that was created by the Scientific Revolution of the seventeenth century, and it is to that story that we now turn.

Notes

1. Quoted in John B. Wolf, *Louis XIV* (New York, 1968), p. 134.
2. Quoted in J. H. Elliott, *Imperial Spain, 1469–1716* (New York, 1963), p. 338.

Suggestions for Further Reading 

In addition to the general works listed in Chapter 14, see also D. H. Pennington, *Europe in the Seventeenth Century*, 2d ed. (New York, 1989); T. Munck, *Seventeenth Century Europe, 1598–1700* (London, 1990); and R. S. Dunn, *The Age of Religious Wars, 1559–1715*, 2d ed. (New York, 1979).

For brief accounts of seventeenth-century French history, see R. Briggs, *Early Modern France, 1560–1715* (Oxford, 1977), and J. B. Collins, *The State in Early Modern France* (Cambridge, 1995). A solid and very readable biography of Louis XIV is J. B. Wolf, *Louis XIV* (New York, 1968). For a brief study, see P. R. Campbell, *Louis XIV, 1661–1715* (London, 1993). Also of value are the works by O. Bernier, *Louis XIV* (New York, 1988), and P. Goubert, *Louis XIV and Twenty Million Frenchmen*, trans. A. Carter (New York, 1970). A now classic work on life in Louis XIV's France is W. H. Lewis, *The Splendid Century* (Garden City, N.Y., 1953). Well-presented summaries of revisionist views on Louis's monarchical power are R. Mettam, *Power and Faction in Louis XIV's France* (Oxford, 1988), and W. Beik, *Absolutism and Society in Seventeenth Century France* (Cambridge, 1985). C. W. Cole, *Colbert and a Century of French Mercantilism*, 2 vols. (London, 1939), is still the fundamental study.

Good general works on seventeenth-century Spanish history include J. Lynch, *Spain Under the Habsburgs*, 2d ed. (New York, 1981), and the relevant sections of J. H. Elliott, *Imperial Spain, 1469–1716* (New York, 1963; rev. ed. 1977). The important minister Olivares is examined in J. H. Elliott, *The Count-Duke of Olivares: The Statesman in an Age of Decline* (London, 1986).

An older but still valuable survey of the German states in the seventeenth century can be found in H. Holborn, *A History of Modern Germany, 1648–1840* (London, 1965). An important recent work is M. Hughes, *Early Modern Germany, 1477–1806* (Philadelphia, 1992). On the creation of an Austrian state, see R. J. W. Evans, *The Making of the Habsburg Monarchy, 1550–1700* (Oxford, 1979), and C. Ingrao, *The Habsburg Monarchy, 1618–1815* (Cambridge, 1994). The older work by F. L. Carsten, *The Origins of Prussia* (Oxford, 1954), remains an outstanding study of early Prussian history.

On Russian history before Peter the Great, see the classic work by V. O. Klyuchevsky, *A Course in Russian History: The Seventeenth Century* (Chicago, 1968). Works on Peter the Great include L. Hughes, *Russia in the Age of Peter the Great* (New Haven, Conn., 1998); M. S. Anderson, *Peter the Great*, 2d ed. (New York, 1995); and the massive popular biography by R. K. Massie, *Peter the Great* (New York, 1980).

Good general works on the period of the English Revolution include M. A. Kishlansky, *A Monarchy Transformed* (London, 1996); G. E. Aylmer, *Rebellion or Revolution? England, 1640–1660* (New York, 1986); and A. Hughes, *The Causes of the English Civil War* (New York, 1991). On the war itself, see R. Ashton, *The English Civil War: Conservatism and Revolution, 1604–1649* (London, 1976). On Oliver Cromwell, see R. Howell Jr., *Cromwell* (Boston, 1977), and P. Gaunt, *Oliver Cromwell* (Cambridge, Mass., 1996). For a general survey of the post-Cromwellian era, see J. R. Jones, *Country and Court: England, 1658–1714* (London, 1978). A more specialized study is W. A. Speck, *The Revolution of 1688* (Oxford, 1988). On Charles II, see the scholarly biography by R. Hutton, *Charles II* (Oxford, 1989). Locke's political ideas are examined in J. H. Franklin, *John Locke and the Theory of Sovereignty* (London, 1978). On Thomas Hobbes, see D. D. Raphael, *Hobbes* (London, 1977).

On the United Provinces, there is a valuable but very lengthy study by J. Israel, *The Dutch Republic: Its Rise, Greatness, and Fall* (New York, 1995). See also the short but sound introduction by K. H. D. Haley, *The Dutch in the Seventeenth Century* (London, 1972). Of much value is S. Schama, *The Embarrassment of Riches: An Interpretation of Dutch Culture in the Golden Age* (New York, 1987).

On the economic side of the seventeenth century, there are the three volumes by F. Braudel, *Civilization and Capitalism in the 15th to 18th Century*, which obviously cover much more than just the seventeenth century: *The Structures of Everyday Life* (London, 1981), *The Wheels of Commerce* (London, 1982), and *The Perspective of the World* (London, 1984). Two single-volume comprehensive surveys are J. de Vries, *The Economy of Europe in an Age of Crisis* (Cambridge, 1976), and R. S. Duplessis, *Transitions to Capitalism in Early Modern Europe* (Cambridge, 1997). On overseas trade and colonial empires, see C. R. Boxer, *The Dutch Seaborne Empire, 1600–1800* (New York, 1965), and R. Davis, *English Overseas Trade, 1500–1700* (London, 1973).

French theater and literature are examined in A. Adam, *Grandeur and Illusion: French Literature and Society, 1600–1715*, trans. J. Tint (New York, 1972). For an examination of French and Dutch art, see A. Merot, *French Painting in the Seventeenth Century* (New Haven, Conn., 1995), and S. Slive, *Dutch Painting, 1600–1800* (New Haven, Conn., 1993).

For additional reading, go to InfoTrac College Edition, your online research library at http://web1.infotrac-college.com

Enter the search terms *Louis XIV* using Key Terms.

Enter the search terms *Peter the Great* using Key Terms.

Enter the search terms *Oliver Cromwell* using Key Terms.

Enter the search term *mercantilism* using the Subject Guide.

CHAPTER

16

Toward a New Heaven and a New Earth: The Scientific Revolution and the Emergence of Modern Science

CHAPTER OUTLINE

- Background to the Scientific Revolution
- Toward a New Heaven: A Revolution in Astronomy
- Advances in Medicine
- Women in the Origins of Modern Science
- Toward a New Earth: Descartes, Rationalism, and a New View of Humankind
- Science and Religion in the Seventeenth Century
- The Spread of Scientific Knowledge
- Conclusion

FOCUS QUESTIONS

- What developments during the Middle Ages and Renaissance contributed to the Scientific Revolution of the seventeenth century?
- What did Copernicus, Kepler, Galileo, and Newton contribute to a new vision of the universe, and how did it differ from the Ptolemaic conception of the universe?
- What role did women play in the Scientific Revolution?
- What problems did the Scientific Revolution present for organized religion, and how did both the church and the emerging scientists attempt to solve these problems?
- How were the ideas of the Scientific Revolution disseminated, and what impact did they have on society?

I*N ADDITION TO POLITICAL, economic, social, and intellectual crises, the seventeenth century witnessed an intellectual one. The Scientific Revolution questioned and ultimately challenged conceptions and beliefs about the nature of the external world and reality that had crystallized into a rather strict orthodoxy by the Late Middle Ages. Derived from the works of ancient Greeks and Romans and grounded in Christian thought, the medieval worldview had become almost overpowering. But the breakdown of Christian unity during the Reformation and the subsequent religious wars had created an environment in which Europeans became more* *comfortable with challenging both the ecclesiastical and political realms. Should it surprise us that a challenge to intellectual authority soon followed?*

The Scientific Revolution taught Europeans to view the universe and their place in it in a new way. The shift from an earth-centered to a sun-centered cosmos had an emotional as well as intellectual effect on those who understood it. Thus the Scientific Revolution, popularized in the eighteenth-century Enlightenment, stands as the major force in the transition to the largely secular, rational, and materialistic perspective that has defined the modern Western mentality since its full acceptance in the nineteenth and twentieth centuries.

The transition to a new worldview, however, was far from easy. In the seventeenth century, the Italian scientist Galileo, an outspoken advocate of the new worldview, found that his ideas were strongly opposed by the authorities of the Catholic church. Galileo's position was clear: "I hold the sun to be situated motionless in the center of the revolution of the celestial bodies, while the earth rotates on its axis and revolves about the sun." Moreover, "nothing physical that sense-experience sets before our eyes . . . ought to be called in question (much less condemned) upon the testimony of biblical passages." But the church had a different view, and in 1633, Galileo, now sixty-eight and in ill health, was called before the dreaded Inquisition in Rome. He was kept waiting for two months before he was tried and found guilty of heresy and disobedience. Completely shattered by the experience, he denounced his errors: "With a sincere heart and unfeigned faith I curse and detest the said errors and heresies contrary to the Holy Church." Legend holds that when he left the trial rooms, Galileo muttered to himself: "And yet it does move!" In any case, Galileo had been silenced, but his writings remained, and they began to spread through Europe. The actions of the Inquisition had failed to stop the spread of the new ideas of the Scientific Revolution.

In one sense, the Scientific Revolution was not a revolution. It was not characterized by the explosive change and rapid overthrow of traditional authority that we normally associate with the word revolution. *The Scientific Revolution did overturn centuries of authority, but only in a gradual and piecemeal fashion. Nevertheless, its results were truly revolutionary. The Scientific Revolution was a key factor in setting Western civilization on its modern secular and material path.*

◆ Background to the Scientific Revolution

To say that the Scientific Revolution brought about a dissolution of the medieval worldview is not to say that the Middles Ages was a period of scientific ignorance. Many educated Europeans took an intense interest in the world around them since it was, after all, "God's handiwork" and therefore an appropriate subject for study. Late medieval scholastic philosophers had advanced mathematical and physical thinking in many ways, but the subjection of these thinkers to a strict theological framework and their unquestioning reliance on a few ancient authorities, especially Aristotle and Galen, limited where they could go. Many "natural philosophers," as medieval scientists were known, preferred refined logical analysis to systematic observations of the natural world. A number of changes and advances in the fifteenth and sixteenth centuries may have played a major role in helping "natural philosophers" abandon their old views and develop new ones.

The Renaissance humanists mastered both Greek and Latin and made available new works of Ptolemy and Archimedes as well as Plato. These writings made it apparent that even the unquestioned authorities of the Middle Ages, Aristotle and Galen, had been contradicted by other thinkers. The desire to discover which school of thought was correct stimulated new scientific work that sometimes led to a complete rejection of the classical authorities.

Renaissance artists have also been credited with making an impact on scientific study. Their desire to imitate nature led them to rely on a close observation of nature. Their accurate renderings of rocks, plants, animals, and human anatomy established new standards for the study of natural phenomena. At the same time, the "scientific" study of the problems of perspective and correct anatomical proportions led to new insights. "No painter," one Renaissance artist declared, "can paint well without a thorough knowledge of geometry."[1]

Technical problems, such as calculating the tonnage of ships accurately, also served to stimulate scientific activity because they required careful observation and accurate measurements. Then, too, the invention of new instruments and machines, such as the telescope and microscope, often made new scientific discoveries possible. Above all, the printing press had an indirect but crucial role in spreading innovative ideas quickly and easily.

Mathematics, so fundamental to the scientific achievements of the sixteenth and seventeenth centuries, was promoted in the Renaissance by the rediscovery of the works of ancient mathematicians and the influence of Plato, who had emphasized the importance of mathematics in explaining the universe. Applauded as the key to navigation, military science, and geography, mathematics was also regarded as the key to understanding the nature of things. According to Leonardo da Vinci, since God eternally geometrizes, nature is inherently mathematical: "Proportion is not only found in numbers and measurements but also in sounds, weights, times, positions, and in whatsoever power there may."[2] Copernicus, Kepler, Galileo, and Newton were all great mathematicians who believed that the secrets of nature were written in the language of mathematics.

Another factor in the origins of the Scientific Revolution may have been magic. Renaissance magic was the preserve of an intellectual elite from all of Europe. By the end of the sixteenth century, Hermetic magic had become fused with alchemical thought into a single intellectual framework. This tradition believed that the world was a living embodiment of divinity. Humans, who it was believed also had that spark of divinity within, could use magic, especially mathematical magic, to understand and dominate the world of nature or employ the powers of nature for beneficial purposes. Was it Hermeticism, then, that inaugurated the shift in consciousness that made the Scientific Revolution possible, since the desire to control and dominate the natural world was a crucial motivating force in the Scientific Revolution? Scholars debate the issue, but histories of the Scientific Revolution frequently overlook the fact that the great names we associate with the revolution in cosmology—Copernicus, Kepler, Galileo, and Newton—all had a serious interest in Hermetic ideas and the fields of astrology and alchemy. The mention of these names also reminds us of one final consideration in the origins of the Scientific Revolution: it resulted largely from the work of a handful of great intellectuals.

◆ Toward a New Heaven: A Revolution in Astronomy

The greatest achievements in the Scientific Revolution of the sixteenth and seventeenth centuries came in the fields most dominated by the ideas of the Greeks—astronomy, mechanics, and medicine. The cosmological views of the Late Middle Ages had been built on a synthesis of the ideas of Aristotle, Claudius Ptolemy (the greatest astronomer of antiquity who lived in the second century A.D.), and Christian theology. In the resulting Ptolemaic or geocentric conception, the universe was seen as a series of concentric spheres with a fixed or motionless earth as its center. Composed of material substance, the earth was imperfect and constantly changing. The spheres that surrounded the earth were made of a crystalline, transparent substance and moved in circular orbits around the earth. Circular movement, according to Aristotle, was the most "perfect" kind of motion and hence appropriate for the "perfect" heavenly bodies thought to consist of a nonmaterial, incorruptible "quintessence." These heavenly bodies, pure orbs of light, were embedded in the moving, concentric spheres, and in 1500 the number of known spheres was ten. Working outward from the earth, eight spheres contained the moon, Mercury, Venus, the sun, Mars, Jupiter, Saturn, and the fixed stars. The ninth sphere imparted to the eighth sphere of the fixed stars its motion, while the tenth sphere was frequently described as the prime mover that moved itself and imparted motion to the other spheres. Beyond the tenth sphere was the Empyrean Heaven—the location of God and all the saved souls. This Christianized Ptolemaic universe, then, was finite. It had a fixed outer boundary in harmony with Christian thought and expectations. God and the saved souls were at one end of the universe, while humans were at the center. They had been given power over the earth, but their real purpose was to achieve salvation.

Copernicus

In May 1543, shortly before his death, Nicolaus Copernicus (1473–1543), who had studied mathematics and astronomy first at Krakow in his native Poland and later at the Italian universities of Bologna and Padua, published his famous book *On the Revolutions of the Heavenly Spheres*. Copernicus was not an accomplished observational astronomer and relied for his data on the records of his predecessors. But he was a mathematician who felt that Ptolemy's geocentric system was too complicated and failed to accord with the observed motions of the heavenly bodies (see the box on p. 330). Copernicus hoped that his heliocentric (sun-centered) conception would offer a more accurate explanation.

Copernicus argued that the universe consisted of eight spheres with the sun motionless at the center and the sphere of the fixed stars at rest in the eighth sphere. The planets revolved around the sun in the order of Mercury, Venus, the earth, Mars, Jupiter, and Saturn. The moon, however, revolved around the earth. Moreover, according to Copernicus, what appeared to be the movement of the sun and the fixed stars around the earth was really explained by the daily rotation of the earth on its axis and the journey of the earth around the sun each year.

The heliocentric theory had little immediate impact; most people were not yet ready to accept Copernicus' thinking. But doubts about the Ptolemaic system were growing. The next step in destroying the geocentric conception and supporting the Copernican system was taken by the German scientist Johannes Kepler.

Kepler

The work of Johannes Kepler (1571–1630) illustrates well the narrow line that often separated magic and science in the early Scientific Revolution. An avid astrologer, Kepler possessed a keen interest in Hermetic thought and mathematical magic. In a book written in 1596, he elaborated on his theory that the universe was constructed on the basis of geometric figures, such as the pyramid and the cube. Believing that the harmony of the human soul (a divine attribute) was mirrored in the numerical relationships existing between the planets, he focused much of his attention on discovering the "music of the spheres." Kepler was also a brilliant mathematician and astronomer who took a post as imperial mathematician to Emperor Rudolf II. Using the detailed astronomical data of his predecessor, Kepler derived laws of planetary motion that confirmed the heliocentric theory. In his first law, he contradicted Copernicus by showing that the orbits of the planets around the sun were not circular but elliptical, with the sun at one focus of the ellipse rather than at the center.

Kepler's work effectively eliminated the idea of uniform circular motion as well as the idea of crystalline spheres revolving in circular orbits. The basic structure of the traditional Ptolemaic system had been destroyed, and people had been freed to think in new ways of the paths of planets revolving around the sun. By the end of Kepler's life, the Ptolemaic system was rapidly losing ground to the new ideas. Important questions remained unanswered, however. What were the planets made of? And how does one explain

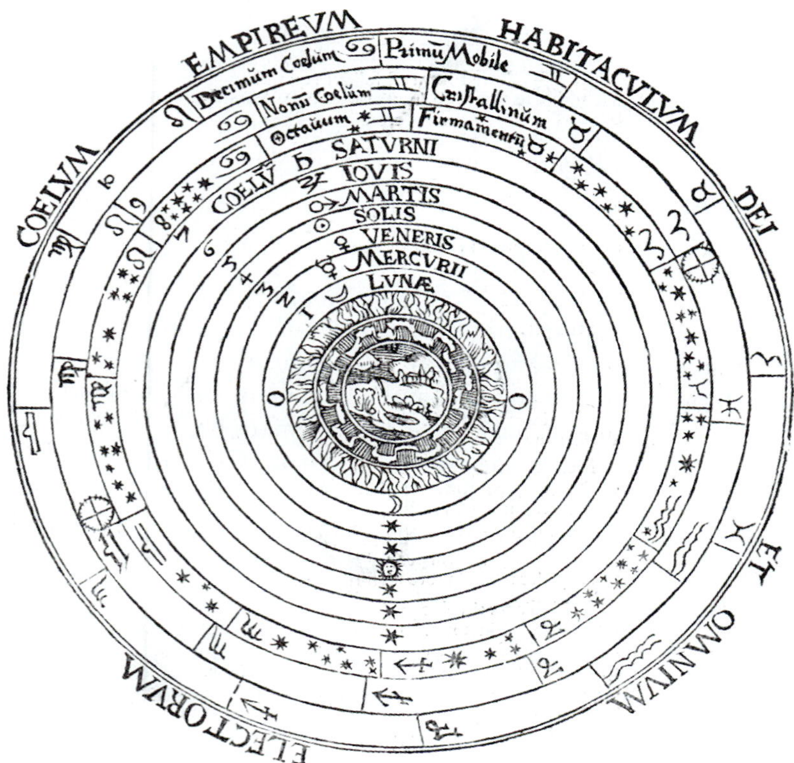

MEDIEVAL CONCEPTION OF THE UNIVERSE. **As this sixteenth-century illustration shows, the medieval cosmological view placed the earth at the center of the universe, surrounded by a series of concentric spheres. The earth was imperfect and constantly changing, whereas the heavenly bodies that surrounded it were perfect and incorruptible. Beyond the tenth and final sphere was heaven, where God and all the saved souls were located.**

motion in the universe? It was an Italian scientist who achieved the next important breakthrough to a new cosmology by answering the first question.

Galileo

Galileo Galilei (1564–1642) taught mathematics, first at Pisa and later at Padua, one of the most prestigious universities in Europe. Galileo was the first European to make systematic observations of the heavens by means of a telescope, thereby inaugurating a new age in astronomy. He had heard of a Flemish lens grinder who had created a "spyglass" that magnified objects seen at a distance and soon constructed his own. Instead of peering at terrestrial objects, Galileo turned his telescope to the skies and made a remarkable series of discoveries: mountains on the moon, four moons revolving around Jupiter, the phases of Venus, and sunspots. Galileo's observations seemed to destroy yet another aspect of the traditional cosmology in that the universe seemed to be composed of a material substance similar to that of earth rather than an ethereal or perfect and unchanging substance.

Galileo's revelations, published in the *The Starry Messenger* in 1610, stunned his contemporaries and probably did more to make Europeans aware of the new picture of the universe than the mathematical theories of Copernicus and Kepler (see the box on p. 331). But even in the midst of his newfound acclaim, Galileo found himself increasingly suspect by the authorities of the Catholic church. The Roman Inquisition (or Holy Office) of the Catholic church condemned Copernicanism and ordered Galileo to abandon the Copernican thesis. The report of the Inquisition ran: "The doctrine that the sun was the center of the world and immovable was false and absurd, formally heretical and contrary to Scripture, whereas the doctrine that the earth was not the center of the world but moved, and has further a daily motion, was philosophically false and absurd and theologically at least erroneous."[3] It is apparent from the Inquisition's response that the church attacked the Copernican system because it threatened not only Scripture but also the entire prevailing conception of the universe. The heavens were no longer a spiritual world but a world of matter. Humans were no longer at the center, and God was no longer in a specific place. The new system raised such uncertainties that it seemed prudent simply to condemn it. In 1633, Galileo was found guilty of teaching the condemned Copernician system and was forced to recant his errors.

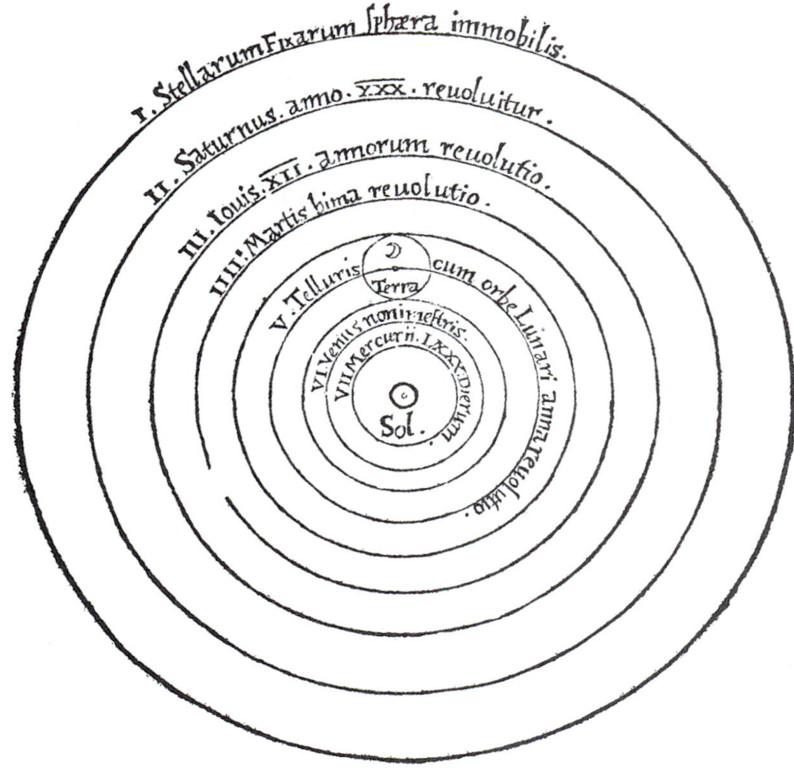

THE COPERNICAN SYSTEM. **The Copernican system was presented in *On the Revolutions of the Heavenly Spheres,* published shortly before Copernicus' death. As shown in this illustration from the first edition of the book, Copernicus maintained that the sun was the center of the universe and that the planets, including the earth, revolved around it. Moreover, the earth rotated daily on its axis.**

On the Revolutions of the Heavenly Spheres

Nicolaus Copernicus began a revolution in astronomy when he argued that the sun and not the earth was at the center of the universe. Expecting controversy and scorn, Copernicus hesitated to publish the work in which he put forth his heliocentric theory. He finally relented, however, and managed to see a copy of it just before he died.

Nicolaus Copernicus, On the Revolutions of the Heavenly Spheres

For a long time, then, I reflected on this confusion in the astronomical traditions concerning the derivation of the motions of the universe's spheres. I began to be annoyed that the movements of the world machine, created for our sake by the best and most systematic Artisan of all, were not understood with greater certainty by the philosophers, who otherwise examined so precisely the most insignificant trifles of this world. For this reason I undertook the task of rereading the works of all the philosophers which I could obtain to learn whether anyone had ever proposed other motions of the universe's spheres than those expounded by the teachers of astronomy in the schools. And in fact first I found in Cicero that Hicetas supposed the earth to move. Later I also discovered in Plutarch that certain others were of this opinion. I have decided to set his words down here, so that they may be available to everybody:

> Some think that the earth remains at rest. But Philolaus the Pythagorean believes that, like the sun and moon, it revolves around the fire in an oblique circle. Heraclides of Pontus and Ecphantus the Pythagorean make the earth move, not in a progressive motion, but like a wheel in a rotation from the west to east about its own center.

Therefore, having obtained the opportunity from these sources, I too began to consider the mobility of the earth. And even though the idea seemed absurd, nevertheless I know that others before me had been granted the freedom to imagine any circles whatever for the purpose of explaining the heavenly phenomena. Hence I thought that I too would be readily permitted to ascertain whether explanations sounder than those of my predecessors could be found for the revolution of the celestial spheres on the assumption of some motion of the earth.

Having thus assumed the motions which I ascribe to the earth later on in the volume, by long and intense study I finally found that if the motions of the other planets are correlated with the orbiting of the earth, and are computed for the revolution of each planet, not only do their phenomena follow therefrom but also the order and size of all the planets and spheres, and heaven itself is so linked together that in no portion of it can anything be shifted without disrupting the remaining parts and the universe as a whole. . . .

Hence I feel no shame in asserting that this whole region engirdled by the moon, and the center of the earth, traverse this grand circle amid the rest of the planets in an annual revolution around the sun. Near the sun is the center of the universe. Moreover, since the sun remains stationary, whatever appears as a motion of the sun is really due rather to the motion of the earth.

The condemnation of Galileo by the Inquisition seriously hampered further scientific work in Italy, which had been at the forefront of scientific innovation. Leadership in science now passed to the northern countries, especially England, France, and the Dutch Netherlands. By the 1630s and 1640s, no reasonable astronomer could overlook that Galileo's discoveries combined with Kepler's mathematical laws had made nonsense of the Ptolemaic-Aristotelian world system and clearly established the reasonableness of the Copernican model. Nevertheless, the problem of explaining motion in the universe and tying together the ideas of Copernicus, Galileo, and Kepler had not yet been solved. This would be the work of an Englishman who has long been considered the greatest genius of the Scientific Revolution.

Newton

Born in the English village of Woolsthorpe, Isaac Newton (1642–1727) showed little promise until he attended Cambridge University. In 1669, he accepted a chair of mathematics at the university. During an intense period of creativity from 1684 to 1686, he wrote

The Starry Messenger

The Italian Galileo Galilei was the first European to use a telescope to make systematic observations of the heavens. His observations, as reported in The Starry Messenger *in 1610, stunned European intellectuals by revealing that the celestial bodies were not perfect and immutable, as had been believed, but were apparently composed of material substance similar to the earth. In this selection, Galileo describes how he devised a telescope and what he saw with it.*

Galileo Galilei, The Starry Messenger

About ten months ago a report reached my ears that a certain Fleming had constructed a spyglass by means of which visible objects, though very distant from the eye of the observer, were distinctly seen as if nearby. Of this truly remarkable effect several experiences were related, to which some persons gave credence while others denied them. A few days later the report was confirmed to me in a letter from a noble Frenchman at Paris, Jacques Badovere, which caused me to apply myself whole-heartedly to inquire into the means by which I might arrive at the invention of a similar instrument. This I did shortly afterwards, my basis being the theory of refraction. First I prepared a tube of lead, at the ends of which I fitted two glass lenses, both plane on one side while on the other side one was spherically convex and the other concave. Then placing my eye near the concave lens I perceived objects satisfactorily large and near, for they appeared three times closer and nine times larger than when seen with the naked eye alone. Next I constructed another one, more accurate, which represented objects as enlarged more than sixty times. Finally, sparing neither labor nor expense, I succeeded in constructing for myself so excellent an instrument that objects seen by means of it appeared nearly one thousand times larger and over thirty times closer than when regarded without natural vision.

It would be superfluous to enumerate the number and importance of the advantages of such an instrument at sea as well as on land. But forsaking terrestrial observations, I turned to celestial ones, and first I saw the moon from as near at hand as if it were scarcely two terrestrial radii. After that I observed often with wondering delight both the planets and the fixed stars, and since I saw these latter to be very crowded, I began to seek (and eventually found) a method by which I might measure their distances apart. . . .

Now let us review the observations made during the past two months, once more inviting the attention of all who are eager for true philosophy to the first steps of such important contemplations. Let us speak first of that surface of the moon which faces us. For greater clarity I distinguish two parts of this surface, a lighter and a darker; the lighter part seems to surround and to pervade the whole hemisphere, while the darker part discolors the moon's surface like a kind of cloud, and makes it appear covered with spots. . . . From observation of these spots repeated many times I have been led to the opinion and conviction that the surface of the moon is not smooth, uniform, and precisely spherical as a great number of philosophers believe it (and the other heavenly bodies) to be, but is uneven, rough, and full of cavities and prominences, being not unlike the face of the earth, relieved by chains of mountains and deep valleys.

his major work, *Mathematical Principles of Natural Philosophy,* known simply as the *Principia* by the first word of its Latin title. In this work, Newton spelled out the mathematical proofs demonstrating his universal law of gravitation. Newton's work was the culmination of the theories of Copernicus, Kepler, and Galileo. While each had undermined some part of the Ptolemaic-Aristotelian cosmology, no one until Newton had pieced together a coherent synthesis for a new cosmology.

In the first book of the *Principia*, Newton defined the basic concepts of mechanics by elaborating the three laws of motion: every object continues in a state of rest or uniform motion in a straight line unless deflected by a force, the rate of change of motion of an object is proportional to the force acting on it, and to every action there is always an equal and opposite reaction. In Book Three, Newton applied his theories of mechanics to the problems of astronomy by demonstrating that these three laws of motion govern the planetary bodies as well as terrestrial objects. Integral to his whole argument was the universal law of gravitation to explain why the planetary bodies did not go off in straight lines but continued in elliptical orbits about the sun. In mathematical terms, Newton explained that every object in the universe was attracted to every other object with a force (gravity) that is directly proportional to the product of their masses and inversely proportional to the square of the distances between them.

The implications of Newton's universal law of gravitation were enormous, even if it took another century before they were widely recognized. Newton had demonstrated that one universal law, mathematically proved, could explain all motion in the universe. The secrets of the natural world could be known by human investigations. At the same time, the Newtonian synthesis created a new cosmology in which the world was seen largely in mechanistic terms. The universe was one huge, regulated, and uniform machine that operated according to natural laws in absolute time, space, and motion. Although Newton believed that God was "everywhere present" and acted as the force that moved all bodies on the basis of the laws he had discovered, later generations dropped his spiritual assumptions. Newton's world-machine, conceived as operating absolutely in space, time, and motion, dominated the modern worldview until the twentieth century, when the Einsteinian revolution based on a concept of relativity superseded the Newtonian mechanistic concept.

Newton's ideas were soon accepted in England but were resisted on the Continent, and it took much of the eighteenth century before they were generally accepted everywhere in Europe. They were also reinforced by developments in other fields, especially medicine.

ISAAC NEWTON. Pictured here is a portrait of Isaac Newton by Godfrey Kneller. With a single law of universal gravitation, Newton was able to explain all motion in the universe. His great synthesis of the work of his predecessors created a new picture of the universe, one in which the universe was viewed as a great machine operating according to natural laws.

Advances in Medicine

Although the Scientific Revolution of the sixteenth and seventeenth centuries is associated primarily with the dramatic changes in astronomy and mechanics that precipitated a new perception of the universe, a third field that had been dominated by Greek thought in the Late Middle Ages, medicine, also experienced a transformation. Late medieval medicine was dominated by the teachings of the Greek physician Galen, who had lived in the second century A.D.

Galen's influence on the medieval medical world was pervasive in anatomy, physiology, and disease. Galen had relied on animal, rather than human, dissection to arrive at a picture of human anatomy that was quite inaccurate in many instances. Even when Europeans began to practice human dissection in the Late Middle Ages, instruction in anatomy still relied on Galen. While a professor read a text of Galen, an assistant dissected a cadaver for illustrative purposes. Physiology, or the functioning of the body, was also dominated by Galenic hypotheses, including the belief that there were two separate blood systems, one controlling muscular activities and containing bright red blood moving upward and downward through the arteries, the other governing the digestive functions and containing dark red blood that ebbed and flowed in the veins.

Two major figures are associated with the changes in medicine in the sixteenth and seventeenth centuries: Andreas Vesalius and William Harvey. The new anatomy of the sixteenth century was the work of the Belgian Andreas Vesalius (1514–1564). His study of medicine at Paris involved him in the works of Galen, the great ancient authority. Especially important to him was a recently discovered text of Galen, *On Anatomical Procedures,* that led Vesalius to emphasize practical research as the principal avenue for understanding human anatomy.

After receiving a doctorate in medicine at the University of Padua in 1536, he accepted a position there as professor of surgery. In 1543, he published his masterpiece, *On the Fabric of the Human Body.* This book was based on his Paduan lectures, in which he deviated from traditional practice by personally dissecting a body to illustrate what he was discussing. Vesalius's anatomical treatise presented a careful examination of the individual organs and general structure of the human body. The book would not have been feasible without the artistic advances of the Renaissance and the technical developments in the art of printing. Together, these advances made possible the creation of illustrations superior to any hitherto produced.

Vesalius' hands-on approach to teaching anatomy enabled him to overthrow some of Galen's most glaring errors. He did not hesitate, for example, to correct Galen's assertion that the great blood vessels originated from the liver since his own observations made it clear that they came from the heart. Nevertheless, Vesalius still clung to a number of Galen's erroneous assertions, including the Greek physician's ideas on the ebb and flow of two kinds of blood in the veins and arteries. It was not until William Harvey's work on the circulation of the blood that this Galenic misperception was corrected.

Englishman William Harvey (1578–1657) attended Cambridge University and later Padua, where he earned a doctorate of medicine in 1602. His reputation rests on his book *On the Motion of the Heart and Blood,* published in 1628. Although questions had been raised in the sixteenth century about Galen's physiological principles, no major challenge to his system had emerged. Harvey's work, based on meticulous observations and experiments, led him to reject the ancient Greek's contentions. Harvey demonstrated that the heart was the beginning point of the circulation of blood in the body, that the same blood flows in both veins and arteries, and that the blood makes a complete circuit as it passes through the body. Although Harvey's work dealt a severe blow to Galen's theories, his ideas did not begin to achieve general recognition until the 1660s, when the capillaries, which explained how the blood passed from the arteries to the veins, were discovered. Harvey's theory of the circulation of the blood laid the foundation for modern physiology.

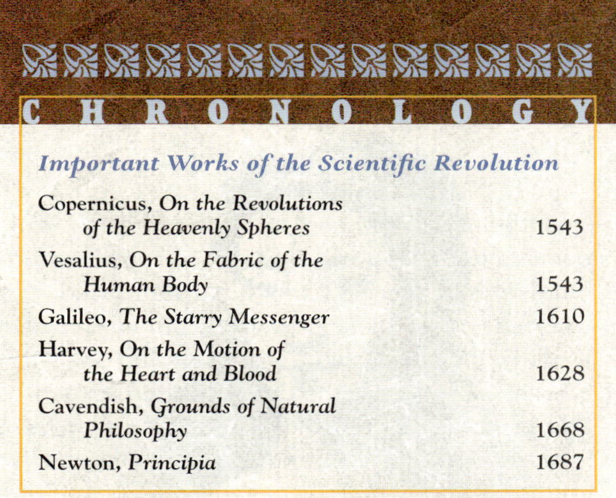
CHRONOLOGY

Important Works of the Scientific Revolution

Copernicus, *On the Revolutions of the Heavenly Spheres*	1543
Vesalius, *On the Fabric of the Human Body*	1543
Galileo, *The Starry Messenger*	1610
Harvey, *On the Motion of the Heart and Blood*	1628
Cavendish, *Grounds of Natural Philosophy*	1668
Newton, *Principia*	1687

Women in the Origins of Modern Science

During the Middle Ages, except for members of religious orders, women who sought a life of learning were severely hampered by the traditional attitude that a woman's proper role was as a daughter, wife, and mother. But in the late fourteenth and early fifteenth centuries, new opportunities for elite women emerged as enthusiasm for the new secular learning called humanism encouraged Europe's privileged and learned men to encourage women to read and study classical and Christian texts. The ideal of a humanist education for some of the daughters of Europe's elite persisted into the seventeenth century.

Much as they were drawn to humanism, women were also attracted to the Scientific Revolution. Unlike females educated formally in humanist schools, women attracted to science had to obtain a largely informal education. European nobles had the leisure and resources that gave them easy access to the world of learning. This door was also open to noblewomen who could participate in the informal scientific networks of their fathers and brothers. One of the most prominent female scientists of the seventeenth century, Margaret Cavendish (1623–1673), came from an aristocratic background. Cavendish was not a popularizer of science for women but a participant in the crucial scientific debates of her time. Despite her achievement, however, she was excluded from membership in the Royal Society (see "The Spread of Scientific Knowledge" later in the chapter), although she was once allowed to attend a meeting. She wrote a number of works on scientific matters, including *Observations upon Experimental Philosophy* and

"which one shows to the curious, but which has no use at all, any more than a carousel horse."[6]

◆ Toward a New Earth: Descartes, Rationalism, and a New View of Humankind

The fundamentally new conception of the universe contained in the cosmological revolution of the sixteenth and seventeenth centuries inevitably had an impact on the Western view of humankind. Nowhere is this more evident than in the work of the Frenchman René Descartes (1596–1650), an extremely important figure in Western history. Descartes began by reflecting the doubt and uncertainty that seemed pervasive in the confusion of the seventeenth century and ended with a philosophy that dominated Western thought until the twentieth century.

The starting point for Descartes' new system was doubt, as he explained at the beginning of his most famous work, *Discourse on Method,* written in 1637:

> From my childhood I have been familiar with letters; and as I was given to believe that by their means a clear and assured knowledge can be acquired of all that is useful in life, I was extremely eager for instruction in them. As soon, however, as I had completed the course of study, at the close of which it is customary to be admitted into the order of the learned, I entirely changed my opinion. For I found myself entangled in so many doubts and errors that, as it seemed to me, the endeavor to instruct myself had served only to disclose to me more and more of my ignorance.[7]

Descartes decided to set aside all that he had learned and begin again. One fact seemed beyond doubt—his own existence:

> But I immediately became aware that while I was thus disposed to think that all was false, it was absolutely necessary that I who thus thought should be something; and noting that this truth *I think, therefore I am,* was so steadfast and so assured that the suppositions of the skeptics, to whatever extreme they might all be carried, could not avail to shake it, I concluded that I might without scruple accept it as being the first principle of the philosophy I was seeking.[8]

With this emphasis on the mind, Descartes asserted that he would accept only things that his reason said were true.

From his first postulate, Descartes deduced an additional principle, the separation of mind and matter. Descartes argued that since "the mind cannot be doubted but the body and material world can, the two must be radically different." From this came an absolute dualism between mind and matter, or what has also been called Cartesian dualism. Using mind or human reason, the path to certain knowledge, and its best instrument, mathematics, humans can understand the material world because it is pure mechanism, a machine that is governed by its own physical laws because it was created by God—the great geometrician.

Descartes' conclusions about the nature of the universe and human beings had important implications. His separation of mind and matter allowed scientists to view matter as dead or inert, as something that was totally separate from themselves and could be investigated independently by reason. The split between mind and body led Westerners to equate their identity with mind and reason rather than with the whole organism. Descartes has rightly been called the father of modern rationalism. His books were placed on the papal Index of Forbidden Books and condemned by many Protestant theologians. The radical Cartesian split between mind and matter, and

DESCARTES WITH QUEEN CHRISTINA OF SWEDEN. René Descartes was one of the primary figures in the Scientific Revolution. Claiming to use reason as his sole guide to truth, Descartes posited a sharp distinction between mind and matter. He is shown here, standing to the right of Queen Christina of Sweden. The queen had a deep interest in philosophy and invited Descartes to her court.

between mind and body, had devastating implications not only for traditional religious views of the universe but also for how Westerners viewed themselves.

Science and Religion in the Seventeenth Century

In Galileo's struggle with the Holy Office of the Catholic church, we see the beginning of the conflict between science and religion that has marked the history of modern Western civilization. Since time immemorial, theology had seemed to be the queen of the sciences. It was natural that the churches would continue to believe that religion was the final measure of everything. To the emerging scientists, however, it often seemed that theologians knew not of what they spoke. These "natural philosophers" then tried to draw lines between the knowledge of religion and the knowledge of "natural philosophy" or nature. Galileo had clearly felt that it was unnecessary to pit science against religion when he wrote that

> in discussions of physical problems we ought to begin not from the authority of scriptural passages, but from sense-experiences and necessary demonstrations; for the holy Bible and the phenomena of nature proceed alike from the divine word, the former as the dictate of the Holy Ghost and the latter as the observant executrix of God's commands. It is necessary for the Bible, in order to be accommodated to the understanding of every man, to speak many things which appear to differ from the absolute truth so far as the bare meaning of the words is concerned. But Nature, on the other hand, is inexorable and immutable; she never transgresses the laws imposed upon her, or cares a whit whether her abstruse reasons and methods of operation are understandable to men.[9]

To Galileo, it made little sense for the church to determine the nature of physical reality on the basis of biblical texts that were subject to radically divergent interpretations. The church, however, decided otherwise in Galileo's case and lent its great authority to one scientific theory, the Ptolemaic-Aristotelian cosmology, no doubt because it fit so well with its own philosophical views of reality. But the church's decision had tremendous consequences. For educated individuals, it established a dichotomy between scientific investigations and religious beliefs. As the scientific beliefs triumphed, it became almost inevitable that religious beliefs would suffer, leading to a growing secularization in European intellectual life—precisely what the church had hoped to combat by opposing Copernicanism. Many seventeenth-century intellectuals were both religious and scientific and believed that the implications of this split would be tragic. Some believed that the split was largely unnecessary, while others felt the need to combine God, humans, and a mechanistic universe into a new philosophical synthesis. One individual, Pascal, illustrates how one European intellectual responded to the implications of the cosmological revolution of the seventeenth century.

Blaise Pascal (1623–1662) was a French scientist who sought to keep science and religion united. Pascal had a brief but checkered career. He was an accomplished scientist and a brilliant mathematician who excelled at both the practical (he invented a calculating machine) and the abstract (he devised a theory of probability and did work on conic sections). After a profound mystical vision on the night of November 23, 1654, which assured him that God cared for the human soul, he devoted the rest of his life to religious matters. He planned to write an "apology for the Christian religion" but died before he could do so. He did leave a set of notes for the larger work, however, which in published form became known as *Pensées* or *Thoughts*.

In the *Pensées*, Pascal tried to convert rationalists to Christianity by appealing to both their reason and their emotions. Humans were, he argued, frail creatures, often deceived by their senses, misled by reason, and battered by their emotions. And yet they were beings whose very nature involved thinking: "Man is but a reed, the weakest in nature; but he is a thinking reed."[10]

Pascal was determined to show that the Christian religion was not contrary to reason: "If we violate the principles of reason, our religion will be absurd, and it will be laughed at."[11] Christianity, he felt, was the only religion that recognized people's true state of being as both vulnerable and great. To a Christian, a human being was both fallen and at the same time God's special creation. But it was not necessary to emphasize one at the expense of the other—to view humans as only rational or only hopeless. Pascal even had an answer for skeptics in his famous wager: God is a reasonable bet; it is worthwhile to assume that God exists. If he does, we win all; if he does not, we lose nothing.

Despite his own background as a scientist and mathematician, Pascal refused to rely on the scientist's world of order and rationality to attract people to God: "If we submit everything to reason, there will be no mystery and no supernatural element in our religion." In the new cosmology of the seventeenth century, "finite man," Pascal believed, was lost in the new infinite world, a realization that frightened him: "The

Pascal: "What Is a Man in the Infinite?"

Perhaps no intellectual in the seventeenth century gave greater expression to the uncertainties generated by the cosmological revolution than Blaise Pascal. Himself a scientist, Pascal's mystical vision of God's presence caused him to pursue religious truths with a passion. His work, the Pensées, *consisted of notes for a larger, unfinished work justifying the Christian religion. In this selection, Pascal presents his musings on the human place in an infinite world.*

❋ *Blaise Pascal,* Pensées

Let man then contemplate the whole of nature in her full and exalted majesty. Let him turn his eyes from the lowly objects which surround him. Let him gaze on that brilliant light set like an eternal lamp to illumine the Universe; let the earth seem to him a dot compared with the vast orbit described by the sun, and let him wonder at the fact that this vast orbit itself is no more than a very small dot compared with that described by the stars in their revolutions around the firmament. But if our vision stops here, let the imagination pass on; it will exhaust its powers of thinking long before nature ceases to supply it with material for thought. All this visible world is no more than an imperceptible speck in nature's ample bosom. No idea approaches it. We may extend our conceptions beyond all imaginable space; yet produce only atoms in comparison with the reality of things. It is an infinite sphere, the center of which is everywhere, the circumference nowhere. In short, it is the greatest perceptible mark of God's almighty power that our imagination should lose itself in that thought.

Returning to himself, let man consider what he is compared with all existence; let him think of himself as lost in his remote corner of nature; and from this little dungeon in which he finds himself lodged—I mean the Universe—let him learn to set a true value on the earth, its kingdoms, and cities, and upon himself. What is a man in the infinite? . . .

For, after all, what is a man in nature? A nothing in comparison with the infinite, an absolute in comparison with nothing, a central point between nothing and all. Infinitely far from understanding these extremes, the end of things and their beginning are hopelessly hidden from him in an impenetrable secret. He is equally incapable of seeing the nothingness from which he came, and the infinite in which he is engulfed. What else then will he perceive but some appearance of the middle of things, in an eternal despair of knowing either their principle or their purpose? All things emerge from nothing and are borne onward to infinity. Who can follow this marvelous process? The Author of these wonders understands them. None but He can.

eternal silence of those infinite spaces strikes me with terror" (see the box above). The world of nature, then, could never reveal God: "Because they have failed to contemplate these infinites, men have rashly plunged into the examination of nature, as though they bore some proportion to her. . . . Their assumption is as infinite as their object." A Christian could only rely on a God who through Jesus cared for human beings. In the final analysis, after providing reasonable arguments for Christianity, Pascal came to rest on faith. Reason, he believed, could take people only so far: "The heart has its reasons of which the reason knows nothing." As a Christian, faith was the final step: "The heart feels God, not the reason. This is what constitutes faith: God experienced by the heart, not by the reason."[12]

In retrospect, it is obvious that Pascal failed to achieve his goal. Increasingly, the gap between science and traditional religion grew wider as Europe continued along its path of secularization. Of course, traditional religions were not eliminated, nor is there any evidence that churches had yet lost their numbers. That would happen later. Nevertheless, more and more of the intellectual, social, and political elites began to act on the basis of secular rather than religious assumptions.

◆ The Spread of Scientific Knowledge

During the seventeenth century, scientific learning and investigation began to increase dramatically. Major universities in Europe established new chairs of science, especially in medicine. Royal and princely patronage of individual scientists became an international phenomenon. Of great importance to the work of science, however, was the creation of a scientific method and new learned societies that enabled the new scientists to communicate their ideas to each other and to disseminate them to a wider, literate public.

The Scientific Method

In the course of the Scientific Revolution, attention was paid to the problem of establishing the proper means to examine and understand the physical realm. This creation of a scientific method was crucial to the evolution of science in the modern world. Curiously enough, it was an Englishman with few scientific credentials who attempted to put forth a new method of acquiring knowledge that made an impact on English scientists in the seventeenth century and other European scientists in the eighteenth century. Francis Bacon (1561–1626), a lawyer and lord chancellor, rejected Copernicus and Kepler and misunderstood Galileo. And yet in his unfinished work *The Great Instauration* (*The Great Restoration*), he called for his contemporaries "to commence a total reconstruction of sciences, arts, and all human knowledge, raised upon the proper foundations." Bacon did not doubt humans' ability to know the natural world, but he believed that they had proceeded incorrectly: "The entire fabric of human reason which we employ in the inquisition of nature is badly put together and built up, and like some magnificent structure without foundation."[13]

Bacon's new foundation—a correct scientific method—was to be built on inductive principles. Rather than beginning with assumed first principles from which logical conclusions could be deduced, he urged scientists to proceed from the particular to the general. From carefully organized experiments and systematic, thorough observations, correct generalizations could be developed. Bacon was clear about what he believed his method could accomplish. His concern was more for practical than for pure science. He stated that "the true and lawful goal of the sciences is none other than this: that human life be endowed with new discoveries and power." He wanted science to contribute to the "mechanical arts" by creating devices that would benefit industry, agriculture, and trade. Bacon was prophetic when he said that "I am laboring to lay the foundation, not of any sect or doctrine, but of human utility and power." And how would this "human power" be used? To "conquer nature in action."[14] The control and domination of nature became a central proposition of modern science and the technology that accompanied it. Only in the twentieth century did some scientists ask whether this assumption might not be at the heart of the modern ecological crisis.

Descartes proposed a different approach to scientific methodology by emphasizing deduction and mathematical logic. Descartes believed that one could start with self-evident truths, comparable to geometrical axioms, and deduce more complex conclusions. His emphasis on deduction and mathematical order complemented Bacon's stress on experiment and induction. It was Newton who synthesized them into a single scientific methodology by uniting Bacon's empiricism with Descartes's rationalism. This scientific method began with systematic observations and experiments, which were used to arrive at general concepts. New deductions derived from these general concepts could then be tested and verified by precise experiments.

The Scientific Societies

The first of the scientific societies appeared in Italy, but those of England and France were ultimately of more significance. The English Royal Society evolved out of informal gatherings of scientists at London and Oxford in the 1640s, although it did not receive a formal charter from King Charles II until 1662. The French Royal Academy of Sciences also arose out of informal scientific meetings in Paris during the 1650s. In 1666, Louis XIV bestowed on the group a formal recognition. The French Academy received abundant state support and remained under government control; its members were appointed and paid salaries by the state. In contrast, the Royal Society of England received little government encouragement, and its fellows simply co-opted new members.

Early on, both the English and French scientific societies formally emphasized the practical value of scientific research. The Royal Society created a committee to investigate technological improvements for industry; the French Academy collected tools and machines. This concern with the practical benefits of science proved short lived, however, as both societies came to focus their primary interest on theoretical work in mechanics and astronomy. The construction of observatories at Paris in 1667 and at Greenwich, England, in 1675 greatly facilitated research in astronomy by both groups. While both the English and French societies made useful contributions to scientific knowledge in the second half of the seventeenth century, their true significance arose from their example that science should proceed along the lines of a cooperative venture.

LOUIS XIV AND COLBERT VISIT THE ACADEMY OF SCIENCES. **In the seventeenth century, individual scientists received royal and princely patronage, and a number of learned societies were established. In France, Louis XIV, urged on by his minister Colbert, gave formal recognition to the French Academy in 1666. In this painting by Henri Testelin, Louis XIV is shown seated, surrounded by Colbert and members of the French Royal Academy of Sciences.**

Science and Society

The importance of science in the history of modern Western civilization is usually taken for granted. But how did science become such an integral part of Western culture in the seventeenth and early eighteenth centuries? Recent research has stressed that one cannot simply assert that people perceived that science was a rationally superior system. An important social factor, however, might help explain the relatively rapid acceptance of the new science.

It has been argued that the literate mercantile and propertied elites of Europe were attracted to new science because it offered new ways to exploit resources for profit. Some of the early scientists made it easier for these groups to accept the new ideas by demonstrating how the ideas could be applied directly to specific industrial and technological needs. Galileo, for example, consciously sought an alliance between science and the material interests of the educated elite when he assured his listeners that the science of mechanics would be quite useful "when it becomes necessary to build bridges or other structures over water, something occurring mainly in affairs of great importance." At the same time, Galileo stressed that science was fit for the "minds of the wise" and not for "the shallow minds of the common people." This made science part of the high culture of Europe's wealthy elites at a time when that culture was being increasingly separated from the popular culture of the lower classes.

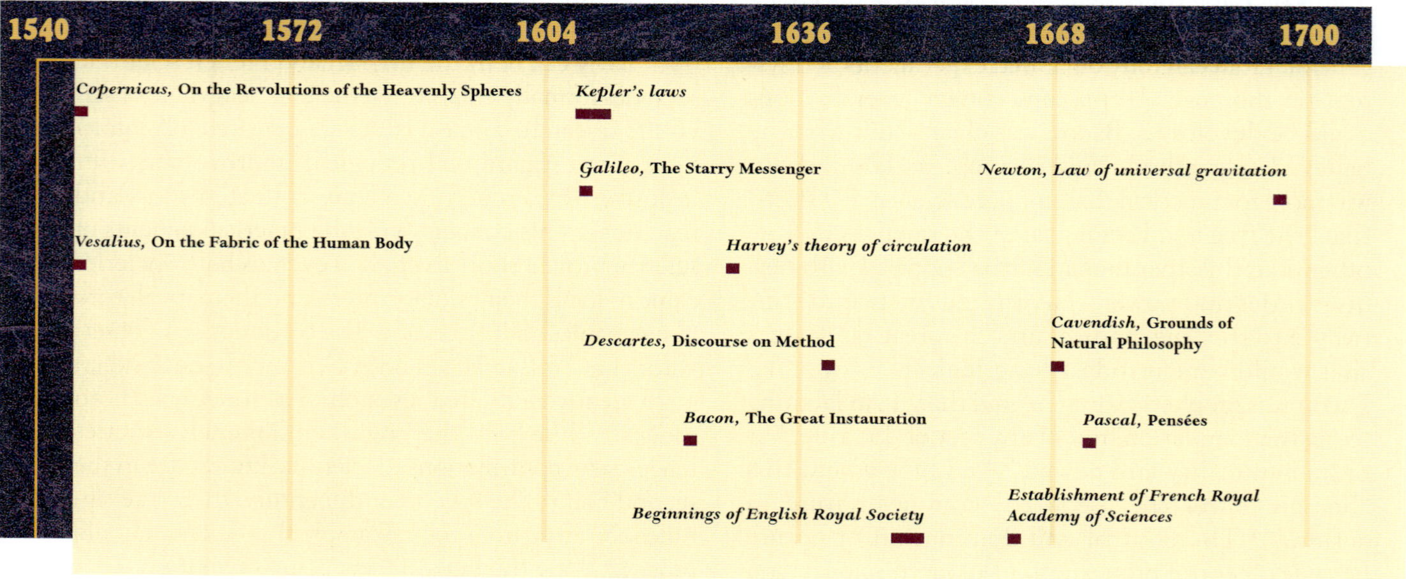

Conclusion

The Scientific Revolution represents a major turning point in modern Western civilization. In the Scientific Revolution, the Western world overthrew the medieval, Ptolemaic-Aristotelian worldview and arrived at a new conception of the universe: the sun at the center, the planets as material bodies revolving around the sun in elliptical orbits, and an infinite rather than finite world. With the changes in the conception of heaven came changes in the conception of earth. The work of Bacon and Descartes left Europeans with the separation of mind and matter and the belief that by using only reason, they could in fact understand and dominate the world of nature. The development of a scientific method furthered the work of scientists, and the creation of scientific societies and learned journals spread its results. Although traditional churches stubbornly resisted the new ideas and a few intellectuals pointed to some inherent flaws, nothing was able to halt the replacement of the traditional ways of thinking by new ways that created a more fundamental break with the past than that represented by the breakup of Christian unity in the Reformation.

The Scientific Revolution forced Europeans to change their conception of themselves. At first, some were appalled and even frightened by its implications. Formerly, humans on earth had been at the center of the universe. Now the earth was only a tiny planet revolving around a sun that was itself only a speck in a boundless universe. Most people remained optimistic despite the apparent blow to human dignity. After all, had Newton not demonstrated that the universe was a great machine governed by natural laws? Newton had found one—the universal law of gravitation. Could others not find other laws? Were there not natural laws governing every aspect of human endeavor that could be found by the new scientific method? Thus the Scientific Revolution leads us logically to the age of the Enlightenment of the eighteenth century.

Notes

1. Quoted in Alan G. R. Smith, *Science and Society in the Sixteenth and Seventeenth Centuries* (London, 1972), p. 59.
2. Edward MacCurdy, *The Notebooks of Leonardo da Vinci* (London, 1948), vol. 1, p. 634.
3. Quoted in John H. Randall, *The Making of the Modern Mind* (Boston, 1926), p. 234.
4. Quoted in Londa Schiebinger, *The Mind Has No Sex? Women in the Origins of Modern Science* (Cambridge, Mass., 1989), pp. 52–53.
5. Ibid., p. 85.
6. Quoted in Phyllis Stock, *Better than Rubies: A History of Women's Education* (New York, 1978), p. 16.
7. René Descartes, *Philosophical Writings*, ed. and trans. Norman K. Smith (New York, 1958), p. 95.
8. Ibid., pp. 118–119.
9. Stillman Drake, ed. and trans., *Discoveries and Opinions of Galileo* (New York, 1957), p. 182.
10. Pascal, *Pensées*, trans. J. M. Cohen (Harmondsworth, England, 1961), p. 100.
11. Ibid., p. 31.
12. Ibid., pp. 52–53, 164, 165.
13. Francis Bacon, *The Great Instauration*, trans. Jerry Weinberger (Arlington Heights, Ill., 1989), pp. 2, 8.
14. Ibid., pp. 2, 16, 21.

Suggestions for Further Reading 

Four general surveys of the entire Scientific Revolution are A. G. R. Smith, *Science and Society in the Sixteenth and Seventeenth Centuries* (London, 1972); J. R. Jacob,*The Scientific Revolution: Aspirations and Achievements, 1500–1700* (Atlantic Highlands, N.J., 1998); S. Shapin, *The Scientific Revolution* (Chicago, 1996); and J. Henry, *The Scientific Revolution and the Origins of Modern Science* (New York, 1997). Also of much value is A. G. Debus, *Man and Nature in the Renaissance* (Cambridge, 1978), which covers the period from the mid-fifteenth through the mid-seventeenth centuries. On the relationship of magic to the beginnings of the Scientific Revolution, see the pioneering works by F. Yates, *Giordano Bruno and the Hermetic Tradition* (New York, 1964) and *The Rosicrucian Enlightenment* (London, 1975).

A good introduction to the transformation from the late medieval to the early modern worldview is A. Koyré, *From the Closed World to the Infinite Universe* (New York, 1958). Also still of value is A. Koestler, *The Sleepwalkers: A History of Man's Changing Vision of the Universe* (New York, 1959). On the important figures of the revolution in astronomy, see E. Rosen, *Copernicus and the Scientific Revolution* (New York, 1984); M. Sharratt, *Galileo: Decisive Innovator* (Oxford, 1994); S. Drake, *Galileo, Pioneer Scientist* (Toronto, 1990); M. Casper, *Johannes Kepler,* trans. C. D. Hellman (London, 1959), the standard biography; and R. S. Westfall, *The Life of Isaac Newton* (New York, 1993). On Newton's relationship to alchemy, see M. White, *Isaac Newton: The Last Sorcerer* (Reading, Mass., 1997).

The standard biography of Vesalius is C. D. O'Malley, *Andreas Vesalius of Brussels, 1514–1564* (Berkeley, Calif., 1964). The work of Harvey is discussed in G. Whitteridge, *William Harvey and the Circulation of the Blood* (London, 1971). A good general account of the development of medicine can be found in W. P. D. Wightman, *The Emergence of Scientific Medicine* (Edinburgh, 1971).

The importance of Francis Bacon in the early development of science is underscored in P. Zagorin, *Francis Bacon* (Princeton, N.J., 1998). A good introduction to the work of Descartes can be found in G. Radis-Lewis, *Descartes: A Biography* (Ithaca, N.Y., 1998).

For histories of the scientific academies, see R. Hahn, *The Anatomy of a Scientific Institution: The Paris Academy of Sciences, 1666–1803* (Berkeley, Calif., 1971), and M. Purver, *The Royal Society, Concept and Creation* (London, 1967).

On the subject of women and early modern science, see the comprehensive and highly informative work by L. Schiebinger,

The Mind Has No Sex? Women in the Origins of Modern Science (Cambridge, Mass., 1989). See also C. Merchant, *The Death of Nature: Women, Ecology, and the Scientific Revolution* (San Francisco, 1980). The social and political context for the triumph of science in the seventeenth and eighteenth centuries is examined in M. Jacobs, *The Cultural Meaning of the Scientific Revolution* (New York, 1988) and *The Newtonians and the English Revolution, 1689–1720* (Ithaca, N.Y., 1976).

For additional reading, go to InfoTrac College Edition, your online research library at http://web1.infotrac-college.com

Enter the search term *Copernicus* using Key Terms.

Enter the search terms *Galileo not Jupiter* using Key Terms.

Enter the search terms *Isaac Newton* using Key Terms.

Enter the search terms *Rene Descartes* using Key Terms.

CHAPTER

17

The Eighteenth Century: An Age of Enlightenment

CHAPTER OUTLINE

- The Enlightenment
- Culture and Society in an Age of Enlightenment
- Religion and the Churches
- Conclusion

FOCUS QUESTIONS

- What intellectual developments led to the emergence of the Enlightenment?
- Who were the leading figures of the Enlightenment, and what were their main contributions?
- In what type of social environment did the philosophes thrive, and what role did women play in that environment?
- What innovations in art, music, and literature occurred in the eighteenth century?
- How did popular culture and popular religion differ from high culture and institutional religion in the eighteenth century?

THE EARTH-SHATTERING WORK of the "natural philosophers" in the Scientific Revolution had affected only a relatively small number of Europe's educated elite. In the eighteenth century, this changed dramatically as a group of intellectuals known as the philosophes popularized the ideas of the Scientific Revolution and used them to undertake a dramatic examination of all aspects of life. In Paris, the cultural capital of Europe, women took the lead in bringing together groups of men and women to discuss the new ideas of the philosophes. At her fashionable home in the Rue St. Honoré, Marie-Thérèse de Geoffrin, wife of a wealthy merchant, held sway over gatherings that became the talk of France and even Europe. Distinguished foreigners, including a future king of Sweden and a future king of Poland, competed to receive invitations.

When Madame Geoffrin made a visit to Vienna, she was so well received that she exclaimed, "I am better known here than a couple of yards from my own house." Madame Geoffrin was an amiable but firm hostess who allowed wide-ranging discussions as long as they remained in good taste. When she found that artists and philosophers did not mix particularly well (the artists were high-strung and the philosophers talked too much), she set up separate meetings. Artists were invited only on Mondays; philosophers, on Wednesdays. These gatherings were but one of many avenues for the spread of the ideas of the philosophes. And those ideas had such a widespread impact on their society that historians ever since have called the eighteenth century the Age of Enlightenment.

For most of the philosophes, "enlightenment" included the rejection of traditional Christianity. The religious wars and intolerance of the sixteenth and seventeenth centuries had left intellectuals so disgusted with religious fanaticism that they were open to the new ideas of the Scientific Revolution. Whereas the great scientists of the seventeenth century believed that their work exalted God, the intellectuals of the eighteenth century read the same conclusions a different way and increasingly turned their backs on Christian orthodoxy. Consequently, European intellectual life in the eighteenth century was marked by the emergence of the secularization that has characterized the modern Western mentality ever since. While some historians have argued that this secularism first arose in the Renaissance, it never developed then to the same extent that it did in the eighteenth century. Ironically, at the same time that reason and materialism were beginning to replace faith and worship, a great outburst of religious sensibility manifested itself in music and art. Clearly, the growing secularization of the eighteenth century had not yet captured the hearts and minds of all Europeans.

◆ The Enlightenment

In 1784, the German philosopher Immanuel Kant defined the Enlightenment as "man's leaving his self-caused immaturity." Whereas earlier periods had been handicapped by the inability to "use one's intelligence without the guidance of another," Kant proclaimed as the motto of the Enlightenment: "Dare to Know! Have the courage to use your own intelligence!" The eighteenth-century Enlightenment was a movement of intellectuals who dared to know. They were greatly impressed with the accomplishments of the Scientific Revolution, and when they used the word *reason*—one of their favorite words—they were advocating the application of the scientific method to an understanding of all life. All institutions and all systems of thought were subject to the rational, scientific way of thinking if people would only free themselves from the shackles of past, worthless traditions, especially religious ones. If Isaac Newton could discover the natural laws regulating the world of nature, they too by using reason could find the laws that governed human society. This belief in turn led them to hope that they could make progress toward a better society than the one they had inherited. *Reason, natural law, hope, progress*—these were common words in the heady atmosphere of the eighteenth century.

The Paths to Enlightenment

Although the intellectuals of the eighteenth century were much influenced by the scientific ideas of the seventeenth century, they did not always acquire this knowledge directly from the original sources. After all, Newton's *Principia* was not an easy book to read or comprehend. Scientific ideas were spread to ever-widening circles of educated Europeans not so much by scientists themselves as by popularizers. Especially important as the direct link between the Scientific Revolution of the seventeenth century and the intellectuals of the eighteenth was Bernard de Fontenelle (1657–1757). In his *Plurality of Worlds*, he used the form of an intimate conversation between a lady aristocrat and her lover to present a detailed account of the new mechanistic universe. Scores of the educated elite of Europe learned the new cosmology in this lighthearted fashion.

Although the Reformation had attempted to restore religion as the central focus of people's lives, it was perhaps inevitable that the dogmatic controversies, religious intolerance, and religious warfare engendered by it would open the door to the questioning of religious truths and values. The overthrow of medieval cosmology and the advent of scientific ideas and rational explanations in the seventeenth century likewise affected the belief of educated men and women in the traditional teachings of Christianity. Skepticism about religion and a growing secularization of thought were important factors in the emergence of the Enlightenment.

THE POPULARIZATION OF SCIENCE: FONTENELLE AND THE *PLURALITY OF WORLDS*. **The most important popularizer of the ideas of the Scientific Revolution was Bernard de Fontenelle who, though not a scientist himself, had much knowledge of scientific matters. In this frontispiece illustration to his *Plurality of Worlds*, an aristocratic lady listens while her astronomer-friend explains the details of the new cosmology.**

Skepticism about Christianity as well as European culture itself was nourished by travel reports. In the course of the seventeenth century, traders, missionaries, medical men, and navigators began to publish an increasing number of travel books that gave accounts of many different cultures. By the end of the seventeenth century, this travel literature began to have an impact on the minds of educated Europeans. The realization that there were highly developed civilizations with different customs in other parts of the world forced Europeans to evaluate their own civilization relative to others. Practices that had once seemed grounded in reason now appeared to be matters of custom.

A final source of inspiration for the Enlightenment came primarily from two Englishmen, Isaac Newton and John Locke. Newton was frequently singled out for praise as the "greatest and rarest genius that ever rose for the ornament and instruction of the species." One English poet declared: "Nature and Nature's Laws lay hid in Night; God said, 'Let Newton be,' and all was Light." Enchanted by the grand design of the Newtonian world-machine, the intellectuals of the Enlightenment were convinced that by following Newton's rules of reasoning, they could discover the natural laws that governed politics, economics, justice, religion, and the arts. The world and everything in it were like a giant machine.

John Locke's theory of knowledge had a great impact on eighteenth-century intellectuals. In his *Essay Concerning Human Understanding*, written in 1690, Locke denied Descartes's belief in innate ideas. Instead, argued Locke, every person was born with a *tabula rasa*, a blank mind:

> Let us then suppose the mind to be, as we say, white paper, void of all characters, without any ideas. How comes it to be furnished? Whence comes it by that vast store which the busy and boundless fancy of man has painted on it with an almost endless variety? Whence has it all the materials of reason and knowledge? To this I answer, in one word, from experience. . . . Our observation, employed either about external sensible objects or about the internal operations of our minds perceived and reflected on by ourselves, is that which supplies our understanding with all the materials of thinking.[1]

Our knowledge, then, is derived from our environment, not from heredity; from reason, not from faith. Locke's philosophy implied that people were molded by their environment, by the experiences that they received through their senses from their surrounding world. By changing the environment and subjecting people to proper influences, they could be changed and a new society created. And how should the environment be changed? Newton had already paved the way by showing how reason enabled enlightened people to discover the natural laws to which all institutions should conform. No wonder the philosophes were enamored of Newton and Locke. Taken together, their ideas seemed to offer the hope of a "brave new world" built on reason.

The Philosophes and Their Ideas

The intellectuals of the Enlightenment were known by the French term *philosophes*, although not all of them were French and few were philosophers in the strict sense of the term. They were literary people, professors, journalists, statesmen, economists, political scientists and, above all, social reformers. They came from both the nobility and the middle class, and a few even stemmed from lower-middle-class origins. Although it was a truly international and cosmopolitan movement, the Enlightenment also enhanced the dominant role already being played by French culture; Paris was its recognized capital. Most of the leaders of the Enlightenment were French. The French philosophes in turn affected intellectuals elsewhere and created a movement that enveloped the entire Western world, including the British and Spanish colonies in America (see Map 17.1).

Although the philosophes faced different political circumstances depending on the country in which they lived, they shared common bonds as part of a truly international movement. Although they were called philosophers, what did philosophy mean to

MAP 17.1 The Enlightenment in Europe.

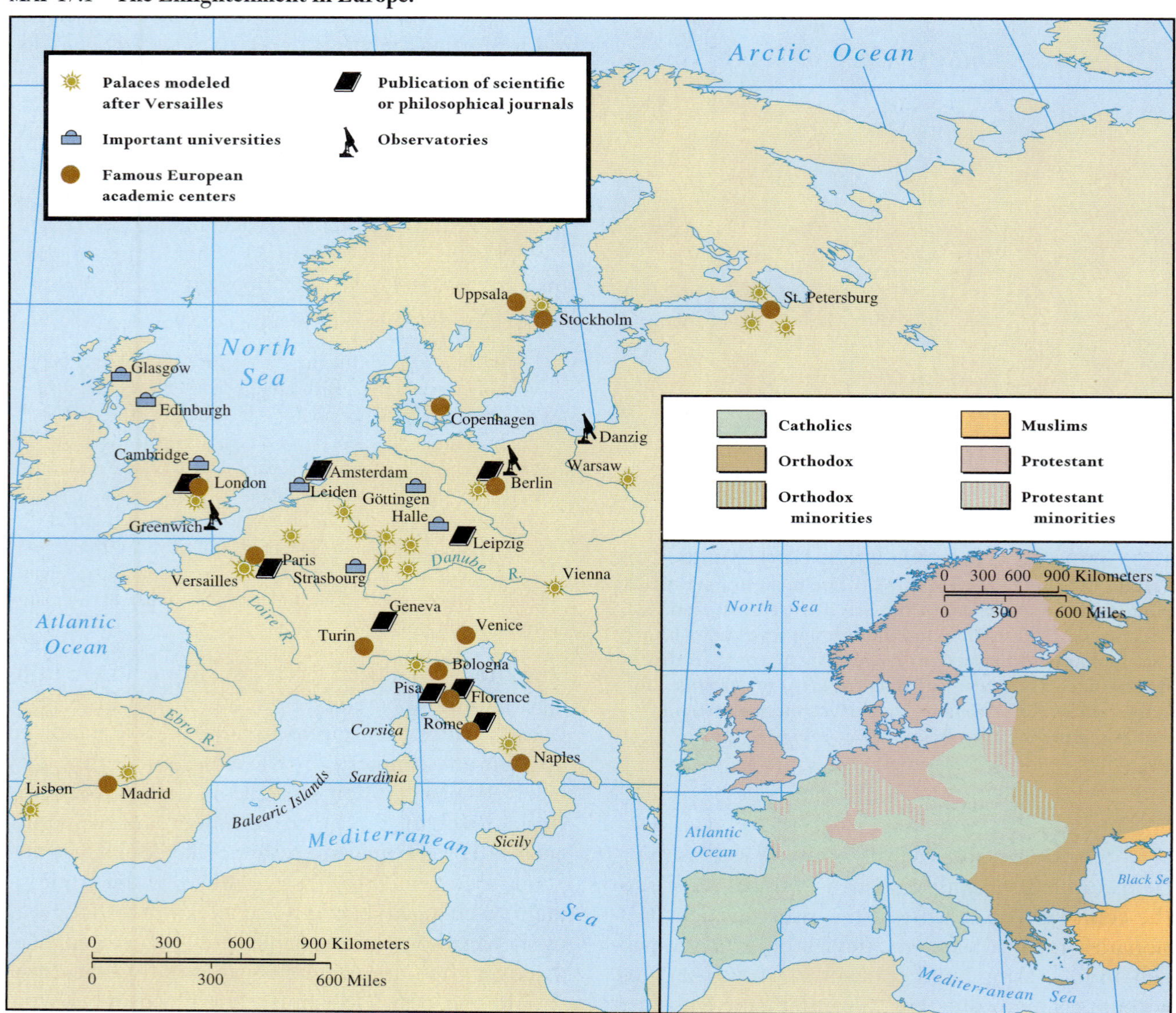

them? The role of philosophy was to change the world, not just to discuss it. As one writer said, the philosophe is one who "applies himself to the study of society with the purpose of making his kind better and happier." To the philosophes, rationalism did not mean the creation of a grandiose system of thought to explain all things. Reason was scientific method, and it meant an appeal to facts and experience. A spirit of rational criticism was to be applied to everything, including religion and politics.

Although the philosophes constituted a kind of "family circle" bound together by common intellectual bonds, they often disagreed. Spanning almost an entire century, the Enlightenment evolved over time, with each succeeding generation becoming more radical as it built on the contributions of the previous one. A few people, however, dominated the landscape completely, and we might best begin our survey of the ideas of the philosophes by looking at the three French giants—Montesquieu, Voltaire, and Diderot.

MONTESQUIEU AND POLITICAL THOUGHT

Charles de Secondat, baron de Montesquieu (1689–1755), came from the French nobility. He received a classical education and then studied law. In his first work published in 1721, the *Persian Letters*, he used the format of two Persians supposedly traveling in western Europe and sending their impressions back home to enable him to criticize French institutions, especially the Catholic church and the French monarchy. Much of the program of the French Enlightenment is contained in this work: the attack on traditional religion, the advocacy of religious toleration, the denunciation of slavery, and the use of reason to liberate human beings from their prejudices.

His most famous work, *The Spirit of the Laws*, was published in 1748. This treatise was a comparative study of governments in which Montesquieu attempted to apply the scientific method to the social and political arena to ascertain the "natural laws" governing the social relationships of human beings. Montesquieu distinguished three basic kinds of governments: republics, suitable for small states and based on citizen involvement; monarchy, appropriate for middle-sized states and grounded in the ruling class's adherence to law; and despotism, apt for large empires and dependent on fear to inspire obedience. Montesquieu used England as an example of the second category, and it was his praise and analysis of England's constitution that led to his most far-reaching and lasting contribution to political thought—the importance of checks and balances created by means of a separation of powers. He believed that England's system, with its separate executive, legislative, and judicial powers that served to limit and control each other, provided the greatest freedom and security for a state. The translation of his work into English two years after publication ensured its being read by American philosophes who incorporated its principles into the American constitution (see Chapter 19).

VOLTAIRE AND THE ENLIGHTENMENT

The greatest figure of the Enlightenment was François-Marie Arouet, known simply as Voltaire (1694–1778). Son of a prosperous middle-class family from Paris, Voltaire received a classical education typical of Jesuit schools. Although he studied law, he wished to be a writer and achieved his first success as a playwright. Voltaire was a prolific author and wrote an almost

VOLTAIRE. François-Marie Arouet, better known as Voltaire, achieved his first success as a playwright. A philosophe, Voltaire was well known for his criticism of traditional religion and his support of religious toleration.

The Attack on Religious Intolerance

Although Voltaire's attacks on religion were in no way original, his lucid prose, biting satire, and clever wit caused his works to be widely read and all the more influential. These two selections present different sides of Voltaire's attack on religious intolerance. The first is from his straightforward treatise The Ignorant Philosopher, *and the second is from his only real literary masterpiece, the novel* Candide, *where he uses humor to make the same fundamental point about religious intolerance.*

Voltaire, The Ignorant Philosopher

The contagion of fanaticism then still subsists. . . . The author of the *Treatise upon Toleration* has not mentioned the shocking executions wherein so many unhappy victims perished in the valleys of Piedmont. He has passed over in silence the massacre of six hundred inhabitants of Valtelina, men, women, and children, who were murdered by the Catholics in the month of September, 1620. I will not say it was with the consent and assistance of the archbishop of Milan, Charles Borome, who was made a saint. Some passionate writers have averred this fact, which I am very far from believing; but I say, there is scarce any city or borough in Europe, where blood has not been spilt for religious quarrels; I say, that the human species has been perceptibly diminished, because women and girls were massacred as well as men; I say, that Europe would have had a third larger population, if there had been no theological disputes. In fine, I say, that so far from forgetting these abominable times, we should frequently take a view of them, to inspire an eternal horror for them; and that it is for our age to make reparation by toleration, for this long collection of crimes, which has taken place through the want of toleration, during sixteen barbarous centuries.

Let it not then be said, that there are no traces left of that shocking fanaticism, of the want of toleration; they are still everywhere to be met with, even in those countries that are esteemed the most humane. The Lutheran and Calvinist preachers, were they masters, would, perhaps, be as little inclined to pity, as obdurate, as insolent as they upbraid their antagonists with being.

Voltaire, Candide

At last [Candide] approached a man who had just been addressing a big audience for a whole hour on the subject of charity. The orator peered at him and said:

"What is your business here? Do you support the Good Old Cause?"

"There is no effect without a cause," replied Candide modestly. "All things are necessarily connected and arranged for the best. It was my fate to be driven from Lady Cunégone's presence and made to run the gauntlet, and now I have to beg my bread until I can earn it. Things should not have happened otherwise."

"Do you believe that the Pope is Antichrist, my friend?" said the minister.

"I have never heard anyone say so," replied Candide; "but whether he is or he isn't, I want some food."

"You don't deserve to eat," said the other. "Be off with you, you villain, you wretch! Don't come near me again or you'll suffer for it."

The minister's wife looked out of the window at that moment, and seeing a man who was not sure that the Pope was Antichrist, emptied over his head a chamber pot, which shows to what lengths ladies are driven by religious zeal.

endless stream of pamphlets, novels, plays, letters, philosophical essays, and histories. His writings brought him both fame and wealth.

Although he touched on all of the themes of importance to the philosophes, Voltaire was especially well known for his criticism of traditional religion and his strong attachment to the ideal of religious toleration (see the box above). He lent his prestige and skills as a polemicist to fight cases of intolerance in France. In 1763, he penned his *Treatise on Toleration*, in which he argued that religious toleration had created no problems for England and Holland and reminded governments that "all men are brothers under God." As he grew older, Voltaire became ever more strident in his denunciations. "Crush the infamous thing," he thundered repeatedly—the infamous thing being religious fanaticism, intolerance, and superstition.

Throughout his life, Voltaire championed not only religious tolerance but also deism, a religious outlook shared by most other philosophes. Deism was built on the Newtonian world-machine, which implied the existence of a mechanic (God) who had created the universe. To Voltaire and most other philosophes, God had no direct involvement in the world he had created; God simply allowed it to run according to its own natural laws. Jesus might be a "good fellow," as Voltaire called him, but he was not divine as Christianity claimed.

DIDEROT AND THE *ENCYCLOPEDIA*

Denis Diderot (1713–1784) was the son of a skilled craftsman from eastern France who became a freelance writer so that he could be free to study and read in many subjects and languages. One of his favorite topics was Christianity, which he condemned as fanatical and unreasonable. As he grew older, his literary attacks on Christianity grew more vicious. Of all religions, Christianity, he maintained, was the worst, "the most absurd and the most atrocious in its dogma." This progression reflected his own movement from deism to atheism, ending with a basic materialistic conception of life: "This world is only a mass of molecules."

Diderot's most famous contribution to the Enlightenment was the twenty-eight-volume *Encyclopedia, or Classified Dictionary of the Sciences, Arts, and Trades*, that he edited and referred to as the "great work of his life." Its purpose, according to Diderot, was to "change the general way of thinking." It did precisely that in becoming a major weapon of the philosophes' crusade against the old French society. The contributors included many philosophes who expressed their major concerns. They attacked religious superstition and advocated toleration as well as a program for social, legal, and political improvements that would lead to a society that was more cosmopolitan, more tolerant, more humane, and more reasonable. In later editions, the price of the *Encyclopedia* was drastically reduced, dramatically increasing its sales and making it available to doctors, clergymen, teachers, lawyers, and even military officers. The ideas of the Enlightenment were spread even further as a result.

TOWARD A NEW "SCIENCE OF MAN"

The Enlightenment belief that Newton's scientific methods could be used to discover the natural laws underlying all areas of human life led to the emergence in the eighteenth century of what the philosophes called a "science of man" or what we would call the social sciences. In a number of areas, philosophes arrived at natural laws that they believed governed human actions. If these "natural laws" seem less than universal to us, it reminds us how much the philosophes were people of their times reacting to the conditions they faced. Nevertheless, their efforts did at least lay the foundations for the modern social sciences.

The Physiocrats and Adam Smith have been viewed as founders of the modern discipline of economics. The leader of the Physiocrats was François Quesnay (1694–1774), a highly successful French court physician. Quesnay and the Physiocrats claimed they would discover the natural economic laws that governed human society. Their major "natural law" of economics represented a repudiation of mercantilism, specifically its emphasis on a controlled economy for the benefit of the state. Instead the Physiocrats stressed that the existence of the natural economic forces of supply and demand made it imperative that individuals should be left free to pursue their own economic self-interest. In doing so, all of society would ultimately benefit. Consequently, they argued that the state should in no way interrupt the free play of natural economic forces by government regulation of the economy but rather just leave it alone, a doctrine that subsequently became known by the French term *laissez-faire* ("let it alone").

The best statement of *laissez-faire* was made in 1776 by a Scottish philosopher, Adam Smith (1723–1790), when he published his famous work *Inquiry into the Nature and Causes of the Wealth of Nations*, known simply as *The Wealth of Nations*. Like the Physiocrats, Smith believed that the state should not interfere in economic matters; indeed, he gave to government only three basic functions: it should protect society from invasion (army); it should defend individuals from injustice and oppression (police); and it should keep up public works, such as roads and canals, that private individuals could not afford. Thus in Smith's view, the state should be a kind of "passive policeman" that remains out of the lives of individuals. In emphasizing the economic liberty of the individual, the Physiocrats and Adam Smith laid the

A Social Contract

Although Jean-Jacques Rousseau was one of the French philosophes, he has also been called "the father of Romanticism." His political ideas have proved extremely controversial. While some political theorists have hailed him as the prophet of democracy, others have labeled him an apologist for totalitarianism. This selection is taken from one of his most famous books, The Social Contract.

❋ *Jean-Jacques Rousseau,* **The Social Contract**

Book 1, Chapter 6: The Social Pact

"How to find a form of association which will defend the person and goods of each member with the collective force of all, and under which each individual, while uniting himself with the others, obeys no one but himself, and remains as free as before." This is the fundamental problem to which the social contract holds the solution. . . .

Chapter 7: The Sovereign

Despite their common interest, subjects will not be bound by their commitment unless means are found to guarantee their fidelity.

For every individual as a man may have a private will contrary to, or different from, the general will that he has as a citizen. His private interest may he speak with a very different voice from that of the public interest; his absolute and naturally independent existence may make him regard what he owes to the common cause as a gratuitous contribution, the loss of which would be less painful for others than the payment is onerous for him; and fancying that the artificial person which constitutes the state is a mere rational entity, he might seek to enjoy the rights of a citizen without doing the duties of a subject. The growth of this kind of injustice would bring about the ruin of the body politic.

Hence, in order that the social pact shall not be an empty formula, it is tacitly implied in that commitment—which alone can give force to all others—that whoever refused to obey the general will shall be constrained to do so by the whole body, which means nothing other than that he shall be forced to be free; for this is the condition which, by giving each citizen to the nation, secures him against all personal dependence, it is the condition which shapes both the design and the working of the political machine, and which alone bestows justice on civil contracts—without it, such contracts would be absurd, tyrannical and liable to the grossest abuse.

foundation for what became known in the nineteenth century as economic liberalism.

THE LATER ENLIGHTENMENT

By the late 1760s, a new generation of philosophes who had grown up with the worldview of the Enlightenment began to move beyond their predecessors' beliefs. Most famous was Jean-Jacques Rousseau (1712–1778). Almost entirely self-educated, he spent a wandering existence as a youth holding various jobs in France and Italy. Eventually he made his way to Paris, where he was introduced into the circles of the philosophes. He never really liked the social life of the cities, however, and frequently withdrew into long periods of solitude.

Rousseau's political beliefs were presented in two major works. In his *Discourse on the Origins of the Inequality of Mankind,* Rousseau argued that people had adopted laws and governors in order to preserve their private property. In the process, they had become enslaved by government. In his celebrated treatise *The Social Contract,* published in 1762, Rousseau tried to harmonize individual liberty with governmental authority (see the box above). The social contract was basically an agreement on the part of an entire society to be governed by its general will. If any individual wished to follow his own self-interest, he should be forced to abide by the general will. "This means nothing less than that he will be forced to be free," Rousseau said, because the general will represented a community's highest aspirations, what was best for the entire community. Thus liberty was achieved through being forced to follow what was best for all people because, he believed, what was best for all was best for each individual. To Rousseau, because everybody was responsible for framing the general will, the creation of laws could never be delegated to a parliamentary body:

> Thus the people's deputies are not and could not be its representatives; they are merely its agents; and they cannot decide anything finally. Any law which the people has not ratified in person is void; it is not law at all. The English people believes itself to be free; it is gravely mistaken; it is free only during the election of Members of Parliament; as soon as the Members are elected, the people is enslaved; it is nothing.[2]

This is an extreme, idealistic statement, but it is the ultimate statement of participatory democracy.

Another influential treatise by Rousseau also appeared in 1762. Titled *Émile*, it is one of the Enlightenment's most important works on education. Written in the form of a novel, the work was really a general treatise "on the education of the natural man." His fundamental concern was that education should encourage rather than restrict children's natural instincts. Life's experiences had shown Rousseau the importance of the promptings of the heart, and what he sought was a balance between heart and mind, between sentiment and reason. This emphasis on heart and sentiment made him a precursor of the intellectual movement called Romanticism that dominated Europe at the beginning of the nineteenth century.

But Rousseau did not necessarily practice what he preached. His own children were sent to foundling homes, where many children died young. Rousseau also viewed women as "naturally" different from men: "to fulfill [a woman's] functions, an appropriate physical constitution is necessary to her. . . . She needs a soft sedentary life to suckle her babies. How much care and tenderness does she need to hold her family together?" In Rousseau's *Émile*, Sophie, who was Émile's intended wife, was educated for her role as wife and mother by learning obedience and the nurturing skills that would enable her to provide loving care for her husband and children. Not everyone in the eighteenth century, however, agreed with Rousseau, making ideas of gender an important issue in the Enlightenment.

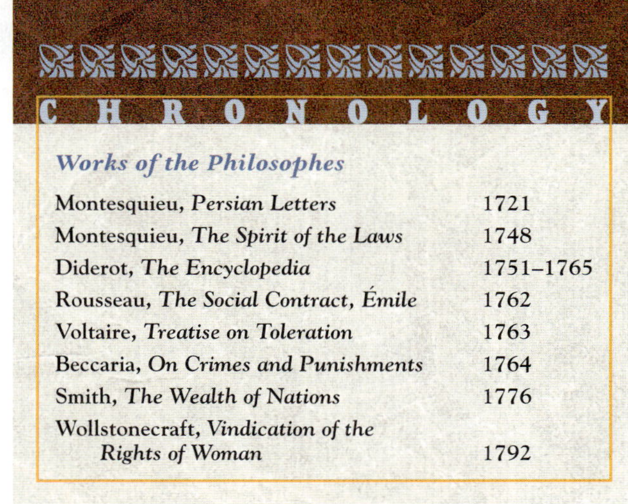

CHRONOLOGY

Works of the Philosophes

Montesquieu, *Persian Letters*	1721
Montesquieu, *The Spirit of the Laws*	1748
Diderot, *The Encyclopedia*	1751–1765
Rousseau, *The Social Contract, Émile*	1762
Voltaire, *Treatise on Toleration*	1763
Beccaria, *On Crimes and Punishments*	1764
Smith, *The Wealth of Nations*	1776
Wollstonecraft, *Vindication of the Rights of Woman*	1792

THE "WOMAN QUESTION" IN THE ENLIGHTENMENT

For centuries, men had dominated the debate about the nature and value of women. In general, many male intellectuals had argued that the base nature of women made them inferior to men and made male domination of women necessary (see Chapter 16). In the seventeenth and eighteenth centuries, many male thinkers reinforced this view by arguing that it was based on "natural" biological differences between men and women. Like Rousseau, they argued that the female constitution made women mothers. Male writers, in particular, were critical of the attempts of some women in the Enlightenment to write on intellectual issues, arguing that women by nature were intellectually inferior to men. Nevertheless, there were some Enlightenment thinkers who offered more positive views of women. Diderot, for example, maintained that men and women were not all that different, and Voltaire asserted that "women are capable of all that men are" with regard to intellectual activity.

It was women thinkers, however, who added new perspectives to the "woman question" by making specific suggestions for improving the conditions of women. Mary Astell (1666–1731), daughter of a wealthy English coal merchant, argued in 1697 in *A Serious Proposal to the Ladies* that women needed to become better educated. Men, she believed, would resent her proposal, "but they must excuse me, if I be as partial to my own sex as they are to theirs, and think women as capable of learning as men are, and that it becomes them as well."[3]

The strongest statement for the rights of women in the eighteenth century was advanced by the English writer Mary Wollstonecraft (1759–1797), viewed by many as the founder of modern European feminism. In *Vindication of the Rights of Woman*, written in 1792, Wollstonecraft pointed out two contradictions in the views of women held by such Enlightenment thinkers as Rousseau. To argue that women must obey men, she said, was contrary to the beliefs of the same individuals

The Rights of Women

Mary Wollstonecraft responded to an unhappy childhood in a large family by seeking to lead an independent life. Few occupations were available for middle-class women in her day, but she survived by working as a teacher, chaperone, and governess to aristocratic children. All the while, she wrote and developed her ideas on the rights of women. This excerpt is taken from her Vindication of the Rights of Woman, *written in 1792. This work led to her reputation as the foremost British feminist thinker of the eighteenth century.*

Mary Wollstonecraft, Vindication of the Rights of Woman

It is a melancholy truth—yet such is the blessed effect of civilization—the most respectable women are the most oppressed; and, unless they have understandings far superior to the common run of understandings, taking in both sexes, they must, from being treated like contemptible beings, become contemptible. How many women thus waste life away the prey of discontent, who might have practiced as physicians, regulated a farm, managed a shop, and stood erect, supported by their own industry, instead of hanging their heads surcharged with the dew of sensibility, that consumes the beauty to which it at first gave luster. . . .

Proud of their weakness, however, [women] must always be protected, guarded from care, and all the rough toils that dignify the mind. If this be the fiat of fate, if they will make themselves insignificant and contemptible, sweetly to waste "life away," let them not expect to be valued when their beauty fades, for it is the fate of the fairest flowers to be admired and pulled to pieces by the careless hand that plucked them. In how many ways do I wish, from the purest benevolence, to impress this truth on my sex; yet I fear that they will not listen to a truth that dear-bought experience has brought home to many an agitated bosom, nor willingly resign the privileges of rank and sex for the privileges of humanity, to which those have no claim who do not discharge its duties. . . .

Would men but generously snap our chains, and be content with rational fellowship instead of slavish obedience, they would find us more observant daughters, more affectionate sisters, more faithful wives, and more reasonable mothers—in a word, better citizens. We should then love them with true affection, because we should learn to respect ourselves; and the peace of mind of a worthy man would not be interrupted by the idle vanity of his wife. . . .

that a system based on the arbitrary power of monarchs over their subjects or slave owners over their slaves was wrong. The subjection of women to men was equally wrong. In addition, she argued that the Enlightenment was based on an ideal of reason innate in all human beings. If women have reason, then they too are entitled to the same rights that men have. Women, Wollstonecraft declared, should have equal rights with men in education and in economic and political life as well (see the box above).

The Social Environment of the Philosophes

The social backgrounds of the philosophes varied considerably, from the aristocratic Montesquieu to the lower-middle-class Diderot and Rousseau. The Enlightenment was not the preserve of any one class, although obviously its greatest appeal was to the aristocracy and upper middle classes of the major cities. The common people, especially the peasants, were little affected by the Enlightenment.

Of great importance to the Enlightenment was the spread of its ideas to the literate elite of European society. Although the publication and sale of books and treatises were crucial to this process, the salon was also a factor. Salons came into being in the seventeenth century but rose to new heights in the eighteenth. The salons were the elegant drawing rooms in the urban houses of the wealthy where invited philosophes and guests gathered to engage in witty, sparkling conversations often centered on the new ideas of the philosophes. In France's rigid hierarchical society, the salons were important in bringing together writers and artists with aristocrats, government officials, and wealthy bourgeoisie.

As hostesses of the salons, women found themselves in a position to affect the decisions of kings, sway political opinion, and influence literary and artistic taste. Salons provided havens for people and views unwelcome in the royal court. When Diderot's *Encyclopedia* was suppressed by the French authorities, Marie-Thérèse de Geoffrin (1699–1777), a wealthy bourgeois widow whose father had been a valet, welcomed the encyclopedists to her salon and offered financial assistance to complete the work in secret. Madame Geoffrin was not without rivals, however. The marquise du Deffand (1697–1780) had abandoned her husband in the provinces and established herself in Paris, where her ornate drawing room attracted many of the Enlightenment's great figures, including Montesquieu and Voltaire.

Although the salons were run by women, the reputation of a salon depended on the stature of the males a hostess was able to attract. Despite this male domination, however, both French and foreign observers complained that females exerted undue influence in French political affairs. While exaggerated, this perception led to the decline of salons during the French Revolution toward the end of the century.

The salon served an important role in making possible conversation and sociability between upper-class men and women as well as spreading the ideas of the Enlightenment. But other means of spreading Enlightenment ideas were also available. Coffeehouses, cafés, reading clubs, and public lending libraries established by the state were gathering places to exchange ideas. Secret societies also developed. The most famous was the Freemasons, established in London in 1717, France and Italy in 1726, and Prussia in 1744. It was no secret that the Freemasons were sympathetic to the ideas of the philosophes.

◆ Culture and Society in an Age of Enlightenment

The intellectual adventure fostered by the philosophes was accompanied by both traditional practices and important changes in the eighteenth-century world of culture and society.

Innovations in Art, Music, and Literature

Although the Baroque and neoclassical styles that had dominated the seventeenth century continued into the eighteenth century, by the 1730s a new style known as Rococo began to affect decoration and architecture all over Europe. Unlike the Baroque, which stressed majesty, power, and movement, Rococo emphasized grace and gentle action. Rococo rejected strict geometrical patterns and had a fondness for curves; it liked to follow the wandering lines of natural objects, such as seashells and flowers. It made much use of interlaced designs colored in gold with delicate

THE SALON OF MADAME GEOFFRIN. An important factor in the development of the Enlightenment was the spread of new ideas to the literate elites of European society. Salons were an important part of this process. Madame Geoffrin, who presided over one of the best-known Parisian salons, is shown here, the third figure from the right in the front row.

ANTOINE WATTEAU, *THE PILGRIMAGE TO CYTHERA*. Antoine Watteau was one of the most gifted painters in eighteenth-century France. His portrayal of aristocratic life reveals a world of elegance, wealth, and pleasure. In this painting, Watteau depicts a group of aristocratic pilgrims about to depart the island of Cythera, where they have paid homage to Venus, the goddess of love.

VIERZEHNHEILIGEN, INTERIOR VIEW. Pictured here is the interior of the Vierzehnheiligen, the pilgrimage church designed by Balthasar Neumann. As this illustration shows, the Baroque-Rococo style of architecture produced lavish buildings in which secular and spiritual elements became easily interchangeable. Elaborate detail, blazing light, rich colors, and opulent decoration were blended together to create a work of stunning beauty.

contours and graceful curves. Highly secular, its lightness and charm spoke of the pursuit of pleasure, happiness, and love.

Some of Rococo's appeal is evident in the work of Antoine Watteau (1684–1721), whose lyrical views of aristocratic life—refined, sensual, civilized, with gentlemen and ladies in elegant dress—revealed a world of upper-class pleasure and joy. Underneath that exterior, however, was an element of sadness as the artist revealed the fragility and transitory nature of pleasure, love, and life.

Another aspect of Rococo was that its decorative work could easily be used with Baroque architecture. The palace of Versailles had an enormous impact on Europe. "Keeping up with the Bourbons" became important as the Austrian emperor, the Swedish king, German princes, Italian princes, and even a Russian tsar built grandiose palaces. While imitating Versailles's size, they were modeled less after the French classical style of Versailles than after the seventeenth-century Italian Baroque, as modified by a series of brilliant German and Austrian sculptor-architects. This Baroque-Rococo architectural style of the eighteenth century was used in both palaces and churches, and often the same architects did both. This is evident in the work of one of the greatest architects of the eighteenth century, Balthasar Neumann (1687–1753).

Neumann's two masterpieces are the pilgrimage church of the Vierzehnheiligen (Fourteen Saints) in southern Germany and the Bishop's Palace known as the Residenz, the residential palace of the Schönborn prince-bishop of Würzburg. Secular and spiritual become easily interchangeable as lavish and fanciful ornament, light, bright colors, and elaborate and rich detail greet us in both buildings.

The eighteenth century was one of the greatest in the history of European music. In the first half of the century, two composers—Handel and Bach—stand out as musical geniuses. Johann Sebastian Bach (1685–1750) came from a family of musicians. Bach held the post of organist and music director at a number of small German courts before becoming director of liturgical music at the church of St. Thomas in Leipzig in 1723. There Bach composed his Mass in B Minor, his St. Matthew's Passion, and the cantatas and motets that have established his reputation as one of the greatest composers of all time. Above all for Bach, music was a means to worship God; in his own words, his task in life was to make "well-ordered music in the honor of God."

The other great musical giant of the early eighteenth century, George Frederick Handel (1685–1759), was, like Bach, born in Saxony in Germany and in the same year. Unlike Bach, however, he was profoundly secular in temperament. After studying in Italy, where he began his career writing operas in the Italian manner, in 1712 he moved to England, where he spent most of his adult life trying to run an operatic company. Although patronized by the English royal court, Handel wrote music for large public audiences and was not adverse to writing ambitious, unusual-sounding pieces. The band for his Fireworks Music, for example, was supposed to be accompanied by 101 cannon. Although he wrote much secular music, ironically, the worldly Handel is probably best known for his religious creations. His *Messiah* has been called "one of those rare works that appeal immediately to everyone, and yet is indisputably a masterpiece of the highest order."[4]

Bach and Handel perfected the Baroque musical style, with its monumental and elaborate musical structures. Two geniuses of the second half of the eighteenth century—Haydn and Mozart—were innovators who wrote music called classical rather than Baroque. Their renown caused the musical center of Europe to shift from Italy to the Austrian Empire.

Franz Joseph Haydn (1732–1809) spent most of his adult life as musical director for the wealthy Hungarian princes, the Esterhazy brothers. Haydn was incredibly prolific, composing 104 symphonies in addition to string quartets, concerti, songs, oratorios, and Masses. His visits to England in 1790 and 1794 introduced him to a world where musicians wrote for public concerts rather than princely patrons. This "liberty," as he called it, induced him to write his two great oratorios, *The Creation* and *The Seasons*, both of which were dedicated to the common people.

Wolfgang Amadeus Mozart (1756–1791) was a child prodigy who gave his first harpsichord concert at six and wrote his first opera at twelve. He, too, sought a patron, but his discontent with the overly demanding archbishop of Salzburg forced him to move to Vienna, where his failure to find a permanent patron made his life miserable. Nevertheless, he wrote music prolifically and passionately—string quartets, sonatas, symphonies, concerti, and operas—until he died at thirty-five, a debt-ridden pauper. *The Marriage of Figaro*, *The Magic Flute*, and *Don Giovanni* are three of the world's greatest operas. Mozart composed with an ease of melody and a blend of grace and precision that arguably no one has ever surpassed.

The eighteenth century was also decisive in the development of the novel. The modern novel grew out of the medieval romances and the picaresque stories of the sixteenth century. The English are credited with establishing the "modern novel as the chief vehicle" for fiction writing. With no established rules, the novel was open to much experimentation. It also proved especially attractive to women readers and women writers.

The High Culture of the Eighteenth Century

Historians and cultural anthropologists have grown accustomed to distinguishing between a civilization's high culture and its popular culture. High culture usually means the literary and artistic world of the educated and wealthy ruling classes; popular culture refers to the written and unwritten lore of the masses, most of which is passed down orally. By the eighteenth century, European high culture consisted of a learned world of theologians, scientists, philosophers, intellectuals, poets, and dramatists, for whom Latin remained a living and truly international language. Their work was supported by a wealthy and literate lay group, the most important of whom were the landed aristocracy and the wealthier upper classes in the cities.

Especially noticeable in the eighteenth century was an expansion of both the reading public and publishing. One study of French publishing, for example, reveals that French publishers were issuing about sixteen hundred titles yearly in the 1780s, up from three hundred titles in 1750. Though many of these titles were still aimed at small groups of the educated elite, some were also directed to the new reading public of the middle classes, which included women and urban artisans. The growth of publishing houses made it possible for authors to make money from their works and be less dependent on wealthy patrons.

An important aspect of the growth of publishing and reading in the eighteenth century was the development of magazines for the general public. Great Britain, an important center for the new magazines, saw 25 periodicals published in 1700, 103 in 1760, and 158 in 1780. Along with magazines came daily newspapers. The first was printed in London in 1702, but by 1780, thirty-seven other English towns had their own newspapers. Filled with news and special features, they were relatively cheap and were available free of charge in coffeehouses.

Popular Culture

Popular culture refers to the written and unwritten literature and the social activities and pursuits that are fundamental to the lives of most people in a society. The distinguishing characteristic of popular culture is its collective and public nature. Group activity was especially evident in the festival, a broad name used to cover a variety of celebrations: community festivals in Catholic Europe that celebrated the feast day of the local patron saint; annual festivals, such as Christmas and Easter, that go back to medieval Christianity; and Carnival, which was celebrated in the Mediterranean world of Spain, Italy, and France as well as in Germany and Austria. All of these festivals were special occasions on which people ate, drank, and celebrated to excess. In traditional societies, festival was a time for relaxation and enjoyment because much of the rest of the year was taken up with unrelieved work. As the poet Thomas Gray in 1739 said of Carnival in Turin: "This Carnival lasts only from Christmas to Lent; one half of the remaining part of the year is passed in remembering the last, the other in expecting the future Carnival."[5]

Carnival began around the start of the year and lasted until the first day of Lent, the forty-day period of fasting and purification leading up to Easter. Because people were expected to abstain from meat, sex, and most recreations during Lent, Carnival was a time of great indulgence. Hearty consumption of food, especially meat and other delicacies, and heavy drinking were the norm. Carnival was a time of intense sexual activity as well. Songs with double meanings could be sung publicly at this time of year, whereas at other times they would be considered offensive. A float of Florentine key makers, for example, sang this ditty to the ladies: "Our tools are fine, new and useful / We always carry them with us / They are good for anything / If you want to touch them, you can." Finally, Carnival was a time of aggression, a time to release pent-up feelings. Most often this took the form of verbal aggression, since people were allowed to openly insult other people and even to criticize their social superiors and authorities. Certain acts of physical violence

A LONDON COFFEEHOUSE. Coffeehouses first appeared in Venice and Constantinople but quickly spread throughout Europe by the beginning of the eighteenth century. In addition to drinking coffee, patrons of coffeehouses could read magazines and newspapers, exchange ideas, play chess, smoke, and engage in business transactions. In this scene from a London coffeehouse of 1705, well-attired gentlemen make bids on commodities. Bidding went on until pins, which had been stuck in the sides of lit candles, fell to the table. Bidding stopped when patrons could "hear a pin drop."

were also permitted. People pelted each other with apples, eggs, flour, and pig's bladders filled with water.

The same sense of community evident in festival was also present in the chief gathering places of the common people, the local taverns or cabarets. Taverns functioned as a regular gathering place for neighborhood men to talk, play games, conduct small business matters, and of course drink. In some countries, the favorite drinks of poor people, such as gin in England and vodka in Russia, proved devastating as poor people regularly drank themselves into oblivion. Gin was cheap; the classic sign in English taverns, "Drunk for a penny, dead drunk for two pence," was literally true. In England, the consumption of gin rose from two to five million gallons between 1714 and 1733 and declined only when complaints finally led to strict laws to restrict sales in the 1750s.

In the eighteenth century, the separation between elite and poor grew ever wider. In 1500, popular culture was for everyone; a second culture for the elite, it was the only culture for the rest of society. But between 1500 and 1800, the nobility, clergy, and bourgeoisie abandoned popular culture to the lower classes. This was, of course, a gradual process, and in abandoning the popular festivals, the upper classes were also abandoning the popular worldview as well. The new scientific outlook had brought a new mental world for the upper classes, and they now viewed such things as witchcraft, faith healing, fortune telling, and prophecy as the beliefs of "such as are of the weakest judgment and reason, as women, children, and ignorant and superstitious persons."

Crime and Punishment

By the eighteenth century, most European states had developed a hierarchy of courts to deal with crimes. Except in England, judicial torture remained an important means of obtaining evidence before a trial. Courts used the rack, thumbscrews, and other instruments to obtain confessions in criminal cases. Punishments for crimes were often cruel and even spectacular. Public executions were a basic part of traditional punishment and were regarded as a necessary means of deterring potential offenders in an age when a state's police arm was too weak to ensure the capture of criminals. Although nobles were excuted by simple beheading, lower-class criminals condemned to death were tortured, broken on the wheel, or drawn (eviscerated) and quartered. The death penalty was still commonly used in property as well as criminal cases. By 1800, more than two hundred crimes were subject to the death penalty in England. In addition to executions, European states resorted to forced labor in mines, forts, and navies. England also sent criminals as indentured servants to colonies in the New World and, after the American Revolution, to Australia.

Appalled by the unjust laws and brutal punishments of their times, some philosophes had sought to create a new approach to justice. The most notable effort was made by the Italian philosophe Cesare Beccaria (1738–1794). In his essay *On Crimes and Punishments*, written in 1764, Beccaria argued that punishments should serve only as deterrents, not as exercises in brutality: "Such punishments . . . ought to be chosen as will make the strongest and most lasting impressions on the minds of others, with the least torment to the body of the criminal."[6] Beccaria was also opposed to the use of capital punishment. It was spectacular but failed to stop others from committing crimes. Imprisonment, the deprivation of freedom, made a far more lasting impression. Moreover, capital punishment was harmful to society because it set an example of barbarism: "Is it not absurd, that the laws, which detest and punish homicide, should, in order to prevent murder, publicly commit murder themselves?"[7]

By the end of the eighteenth century, a growing sentiment against executions and torture led to a decline in both corporal and capital punishment. A new type of prison, in which criminals were placed in cells and subjected to discipline and regular work to rehabilitate them, began to replace the public spectacle of barbarous punishments.

◆ Religion and the Churches

The music of Bach and the pilgrimage and monastic churches of southern Germany and Austria make us aware of a curious fact. While much of the great art and music of the time was religious, the thought of the time was antireligious as life became increasingly secularized and men of reason attacked the established churches. And yet most Europeans were still Christians. Even many of those most critical of the churches accepted that society could not function without religious faith.

In the eighteenth century, the established Catholic and Protestant churches were basically conservative institutions that upheld society's hierarchical structure, privileged classes, and traditions. Although churches experienced change because of new state policies, they did not sustain any dramatic internal changes. In both Catholic and Protestant countries, the parish church run by priest or pastor remained the center of religious practice. In addition to providing religious services, the parish church kept records of births, deaths, and marriages, provided charity for the poor, supervised whatever primary education there was, and cared for orphans.

Toleration and Religious Minorities

One of the chief battle cries of the philosophes had been a call for religious toleration. Out of political necessity, a certain level of tolerance of different creeds had occurred in the seventeenth century, but many rulers still found it difficult to accept. Louis XIV had turned back the clock in France at the end of the seventeenth century, insisting on religious uniformity and suppressing the rights of the Huguenots. Even devout rulers continued to believe that there was only one path to salvation; it was the true duty of a ruler not to allow subjects to be condemned to hell by being heretics. Persecution of heretics continued; the last burning of a heretic took place in 1781.

The Jews remained the despised religious minority of Europe. The largest number of Jews (known as the Ashkenazic Jews) lived in eastern Europe. Except in relatively tolerant Poland, Jews were restricted in their movements, forbidden to own land or hold many jobs, forced to pay burdensome special taxes, and also subject to periodic outbursts of popular wrath. The resulting pogroms, in which Jewish communities were looted and massacred, made Jewish existence precarious and dependent on the favor of their territorial rulers.

Another major group was the Sephardic Jews who had been expelled from Spain in the fifteenth century. Although many had migrated to Turkish lands, some of them had settled in cities, such as Amsterdam, Venice, London, and Frankfurt, where they were relatively free to participate in the banking and commercial activities that Jews had practiced since the Middle Ages. The highly successful ones came to provide valuable services to rulers, especially in central Europe. But even these Jews were insecure because their religion set them apart from the Christian majority and served as a catalyst to social resentment.

Some Enlightenment thinkers in the eighteenth century favored a new acceptance of Jews. They argued that Jews and Muslims were human and deserved the full rights of citizenship despite their religion. Many philosophes denounced persecution of the Jews but made no attempt to hide their hostility and ridiculed Jewish customs. Diderot, for example, said that the Jews had "all the defects peculiar to an ignorant and superstitious nation." Many Europeans favored the assimilation of the Jews into the mainstream of society, but only by the conversion of Jews to Christianity as the basic solution to the "Jewish problem." This, of course, was not acceptable to most Jews.

The Austrian emperor Joseph II (1780–1790) attempted to adopt a new policy toward the Jews, although it too was limited. It freed Jews from nuisance taxes and allowed them more freedom of movement and job opportunities, but they were still restricted from owning land and worshiping in public. At the same time, Joseph encouraged Jews to learn German and work toward greater assimilation into Austrian society.

Popular Religion in the Eighteenth Century

Despite the rise of skepticism and the intellectuals' belief in deism and natural religion, religious devotion remained active in the eighteenth century. It is difficult to assess precisely the religiosity of Europe's Catholics. The Catholic parish church remained a center of life for the entire community. How many people went to church regularly cannot be known exactly, but it has been established that 90 to 95 percent of Catholic populations did go to Mass on Easter Sunday, one of the church's most important celebrations.

After the initial century of religious fervor that gave rise to Protestantism in the sixteenth century, Protestant churches in the seventeenth century had settled down into well-established patterns controlled by state authorities and served by a well-educated clergy. Protestant churches became bureaucratized and bereft of religious enthusiasm. In Germany and England, where rationalism and deism had become influential and moved some theologians to a more "rational" Christianity, the desire of ordinary Protestant churchgoers for greater depths of religious experience led to new and dynamic religious movements.

One of the most famous movements—Methodism—was the work of John Wesley (1703–1791). An ordained Anglican minister, Wesley underwent a mystical experience in which "the gift of God's grace" assured him of salvation and led him to become a missionary to the English people, bringing the "glad tidings" of salvation to all people, despite opposition from the Anglican church, which criticized this emotional mysticism or religious enthusiasm as superstitious nonsense. To Wesley, all could be saved by experiencing God and opening the doors to his grace.

The Conversion Experience in Wesley's Methodism

After his own conversion experience, John Wesley traveled extensively to bring the "glad tidings" to other people. It has been estimated that he preached over forty thousand sermons, some of them to audiences numbering twenty thousand listeners. Wesley gave his message wherever people gathered—in the streets, hospitals, private houses, and even pubs. In this selection from his journal, Wesley describes how emotional and even violent conversion experiences could be.

The Works of the Reverend John Wesley

Sunday, May 20 [1759], being with Mr. B—11 at Everton, I was much fatigued, and did not rise: but Mr. B. did, and observed several fainting and crying out, while Mr. Berridge was preaching: afterwards at Church, I heard many cry out, especially children, whose agonies were amazing: one of the eldest, a girl of ten or twelve years old, was full in my view, in violent contortions of body, and weeping aloud, I think incessantly, during the whole service. . . . The Church was equally crowded in the afternoon, the windows being filled within and without, and even the outside of the pulpit to the very top; so that Mr. B. seemed almost stifled by their breath; yet feeble and sickly as he is, he was continually strengthened, and his voice, for the most part, distinguishable; in the midst of all the outcries. I believe there were present three times more men than women, a great part of whom came from far; thirty of them having set out at two in the morning, from a place thirteen miles off. The text was, *Having a form of godliness, but denying the power thereof.* When the power of religion began to be spoken of, the presence of God really filled the place: and while poor sinners felt the sentence of death in their souls, what sounds of distress did I hear! The greatest number of them who cried or fell, were men: but some women, and several children, felt the power of the same almighty Spirit, and seemed just sinking into hell. This occasioned a mixture of several sounds; some shrieking, some roaring aloud. The most general was a loud breathing, like that of people half strangled and gasping for life: and indeed almost all the cries were like those of human creatures, dying in bitter anguish. Great numbers wept without any noise: others fell down as death: some sinking in silence; some with extreme noise and violent agitation. I stood on the pew-seat, as did a young man in the opposite pew, an able-bodied, fresh, healthy countryman: but in a moment, while he seemed to think of nothing less, down he dropped with a violence inconceivable. The adjoining pews seemed to shake with his fall: I heard afterwards the stamping of his feet; ready to break the boards, as he lay in strong convulsions, at the bottom of the pew. Among several that were struck down in the next pew, was a girl, who was as violently seized as he. . . . Among the children who felt the arrows of the Almighty, I saw a sturdy boy, about eight years old, who roared above his fellows, and seemed in his agony to struggle with the strength of a grown man. His face was as red as scarlet: and almost all on whom God laid his hand, turned either very red or almost black. . . .

The violent struggling of many in the above-mentioned churches, has broken several pews and benches. Yet it is common for people to remain unaffected there, and afterwards to drop down on their way home. Some have been found lying as dead on the road: others, in Mr. B.'s garden; not being able to walk from the Church to his house, though it is not two hundred yards. . . .

In taking the Gospel to the people, Wesley preached to the masses in open fields, appealing especially to the lower classes neglected by the socially elitist Anglican church. He tried, he said, "to lower religion to the level of the lowest people's capacities." Wesley's charismatic preaching often provoked highly charged and even violent conversion experiences (see the box above). Afterward, converts were organized into so-called Methodist societies or chapels in which they could aid each other in doing the good works that Wesley considered a component of salvation. Although Wesley sought to keep Methodism within the Anglican church, after his death it became a separate and independent sect. Methodism represents an important revival of Christianity and proved that the need for spiritual experience had not been expunged by the eighteenth-century search for reason.

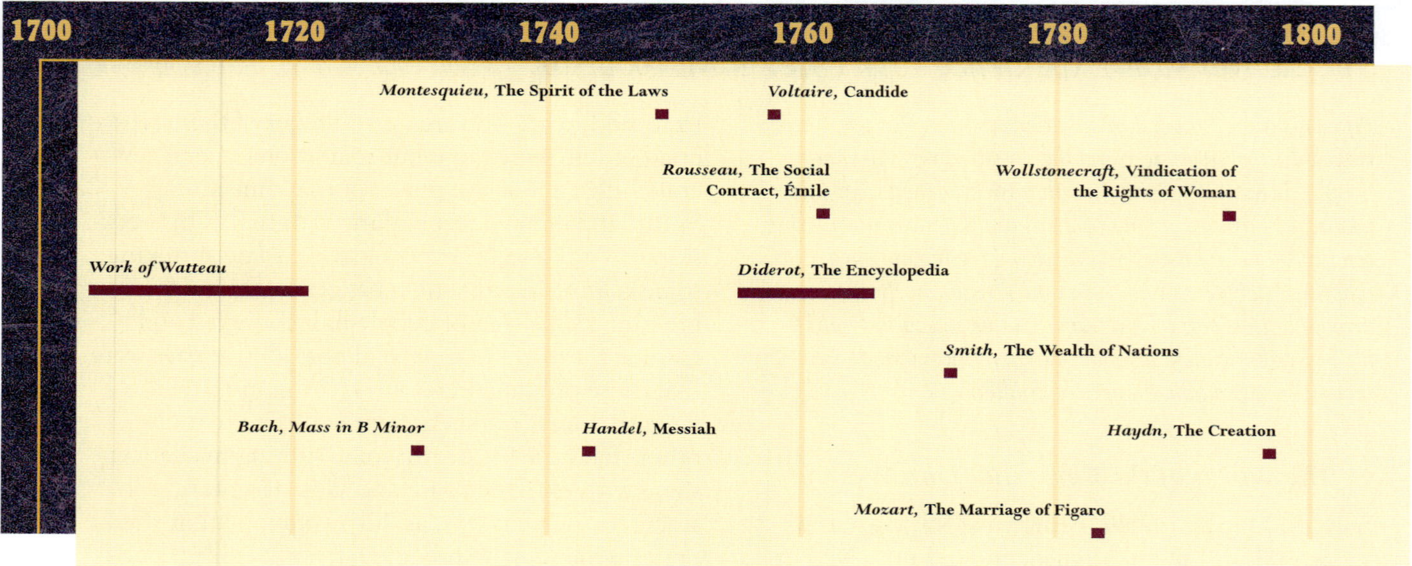

Conclusion

One prominent historian of the eighteenth century has appropriately characterized it as a century of change and tradition. Highly influenced by the new worldview ushered in by the Scientific Revolution and especially the ideas of Locke and Newton, the philosophes hoped that they could create a new society by using reason to discover the natural laws that governed it. Like the Christian humanists of the fifteenth and sixteenth centuries, they believed that education could produce better human beings and a better human society. By attacking traditional religion as the enemy and creating the new "sciences of man" in economics, politics, and justice, the philosophes laid the foundation for a modern worldview based on rationalism and secularism.

But it was also an age of tradition. While secular thought and rational ideas began to pervade the mental world of the ruling elites, most people in eighteenth-century Europe still lived by seemingly eternal verities and practices—God, religious worship, and farming. The most brilliant architecture and music of the age were religious. And yet the forces of secularization were too strong to stop. In the midst of intellectual change, economic, political, and social transformations of great purport were taking shape that by the end of the eighteenth century were to lead to both political and industrial revolutions. It is time now to examine the political, economic, and social traditions and changes of the century.

Notes

1. John Locke, *An Essay Concerning Human Understanding* (New York, 1964), pp. 89–90.
2. Jean-Jacques Rousseau, *The Social Contract*, trans. Maurice Cranston (Harmondsworth, England, 1968), p. 141.
3. Mary Astell, *A Serious Proposal to the Ladies*, in Moira Ferguson, ed., *First Feminists: British Women Writers, 1578–1799* (Bloomington, Ind., 1985), p. 190.
4. Kenneth Clark, *Civilization* (New York, 1969), p. 231.
5. Quoted in Peter Burke, *Popular Culture in Early Modern Europe* (New York, 1978), p. 179.
6. Cesare Beccaria, *An Essay on Crimes and Punishments*, trans. E. D. Ingraham (Philadelphia, 1819), pp. 59–60.
7. Ibid., p. 60.

Suggestions for Further Reading

Two sound, comprehensive surveys of eighteenth-century Europe are I. Woloch, *Eighteenth-Century Europe* (New York, 1982), and M. S. Anderson, *Europe in the Eighteenth Century* (London, 1987). See also R. Birn, *Crisis, Absolutism, Revolution: Europe, 1648–1789*, 2d ed. (Fort Worth, Tex., 1992).

Good introductions to the Enlightenment can be found in N. Hampson, *A Cultural History of the Enlightenment* (New York, 1968); U. Im Hof, *The Enlightenment* (Oxford, 1994); D. Goodman, *The Republic of Letters: A Cultural History of the French Enlightenment* (Ithaca, N.Y., 1994); and D. Outram, *The Enlightenment* (Cambridge, 1995). A more detailed synthesis can be found in P. Gay, *The Enlightenment: An Interpretation*, 2 vols. (New York, 1966–1969). For a short, popular survey on the French philosophes, see F. Artz, *The Enlightenment in France* (Kent, Ohio, 1968). Also of value are E. J. Wilson and P. H. Reill, *Encyclopedia of the Enlightenment* (New York, 1996), and J. W. Yolton, ed., *The Blackwell Companion to the Enlightenment* (Cambridge, Mass., 1995). Studies of the major Enlightenment intellectuals include J. Sklar, *Montesquieu* (Oxford, 1987); H. T. Mason, *Voltaire: A Biography* (Baltimore, 1981); P. N. Furbank, *Diderot: A Critical Biography* (New York, 1992); and M. Cranston, *The Noble Savage: Jean-Jacques Rousseau* (New York, 1991). On women in the eighteenth century, see N. Z. Davis and A. Farge, eds., *A History of Women: Renaissance and Enlightenment Paradoxes* (Cambridge, Mass., 1993); C. Lougee, *Le Paradis des Femmes: Women, Salons, and Social Stratification* (Princeton, N.J., 1976); O. Hufton, *The Prospect Before Her: A History of*

Women in Western Europe, 1500–1800 (New York, 1998); and B. S. Anderson and J. P. Zinsser, *A History of Their Own*, vol. 2 (New York, 1988).

Two readable general surveys on the arts and literature are M. Levy, *Rococo to Revolution* (London, 1966), and H. Honour, *Neo-Classicism* (Harmondsworth, England, 1968). On the eighteenth-century novel, see G. J. Barker-Benfield, *The Culture of Sensibility: Sex and Society in the Eighteenth-Century English Novel* (Chicago, 1992). On the growth of literacy, see R. A. Houston, *Literacy in Early Modern Europe: Culture and Education, 1500–1800* (New York, 1988). Different facets of crime and punishment are examined in the important works by M. Foucault, *Discipline and Punish: The Birth of the Prison* (New York, 1977), and J. Langbein, *Torture and the Law of Proof* (Chicago, 1977).

Important studies on popular culture include P. Burke, *Popular Culture in Early Modern Europe* (New York, 1978), and R. Darnton, *The Great Cat Massacre and Other Episodes in French Cultural History* (New York, 1984).

A good introduction to the religious history of the eighteenth century can be found in G. R. Cragg, *The Church and the Age of Reason, 1648–1789* (London, 1966). The problem of religious toleration is examined in J. I. Israel, *European Jewry in the Age of Mercantilism, 1550–1750*, 2d ed. (New York, 1989). On John Wesley, see H. Rack, *Reasonable Enthusiast: John Wesley and the Rise of Methodism* (New York, 1989).

For additional reading, go to InfoTrac College Edition, your online research library at http://web1.infotrac-college.com

Enter the search term *Enlightenment* using the Subject Guide.

Enter the search term *Voltaire* using Key Terms.

Enter the search term *Diderot* using Key Terms.

Enter the search term *Rousseau* using Key Terms.

CHAPTER

18

The Eighteenth Century: European States, International Wars, and Social Change

CHAPTER OUTLINE

- The European States
- Wars and Diplomacy
- Economic Expansion and Social Change
- The Social Order of the Eighteenth Century
- Conclusion

FOCUS QUESTIONS

- What do historians mean by the term enlightened absolutism, and to what degree did eighteenth-century Prussia, Austria, and Russia exhibit its characteristics?
- What were the causes and results of the Seven Years' War?
- What changes occurred in agriculture, finance, industry, and trade during the eighteenth century?
- Who were the main groups making up the European social order in the eighteenth century, and how did the conditions in which they lived differ both between groups and between different parts of Europe?

HISTORIANS HAVE OFTEN DEFINED the eighteenth century chronologically as spanning the years from 1715 to 1789. Politically, this makes sense because 1715 marks the end of the age of Louis XIV and 1789 was the year in which the French Revolution erupted. This period has often been portrayed as the final phase of Europe's old order, swept away by the violent upheaval and reordering of society associated with the French Revolution. Europe's old order, still largely agrarian, dominated by kings and landed aristocrats, and grounded in privileges for nobles, clergy, towns, and provinces, seemed to continue a basic pattern that had prevailed in Europe since medieval times. But new ideas and new practices were also beginning to emerge. Just as a new intellectual order based on rationalism and secularism was emerging in Europe from the intellectual reorientation of the Scientific Revolution and the Enlightenment, demographic, economic, and social patterns were beginning to change in ways that heralded the emergence of a modern new order.

The ideas of the Enlightenment seemed to proclaim a new political age as well. Catherine the Great, who ruled Russia from 1762 to 1796, wrote to Voltaire: "Since 1746 I have been under the greatest obligations to you. Before that period I read nothing but romances, but by chance your works fell into my hands, and ever since then I have never ceased to read them, and have no desire for books less well written than yours, or less instructive." The empress also invited Diderot to Russia and, when he arrived, urged him to speak frankly "as man to man." Diderot did, offering her advice for a far-ranging program of political and financial reform. But Catherine's apparent eagerness to make enlightened reforms was tempered by skepticism. She said of Diderot: "If I had believed him everything would have been turned upside down in my kingdom; legislation, administration, finance—all would have been turned topsy-turvy to make room for impractical theories." For Catherine, enlightened reform remained more a dream than a reality, and in the end, the waging of wars to gain more power was more important.

In the eighteenth century, the process of centralization that had characterized the growth of states since the Middle Ages continued as most European states enlarged their bureaucratic machinery and consolidated their governments in order to collect the revenues and build the armies they needed to compete militarily with the other European states. International competition continued to be the favorite pastime of eighteenth-century rulers. Within the European state system, the nations that would dominate Europe until World War I—Britain, France, Austria, Prussia, and Russia—emerged as the five great powers of Europe. Their rivalries led to major wars. In the midst of this state building and war making, dramatic demographic, economic, and social changes gave rise to a radical transformation in the way Europeans would raise food and produce goods.

The European States

Most European states in the eighteenth century were ruled by monarchs. Although the seventeenth-century justification for strong monarchy on the basis of divine right continued into the succeeding century, as the eighteenth century became increasingly secularized, divine-right assumptions were gradually superseded by influential utilitarian arguments. The Prussian king Frederick II expressed these well when he attempted to explain the services a monarch must provide for his people:

> These services consisted in the maintenance of the laws; a strict execution of justice; an employment of his whole powers to prevent any corruption of manners; and defending the state against its enemies. It is the duty of this magistrate to pay attention to agriculture; it should be his care that provisions for the nation should be in abundance, and that commerce and industry should be encouraged. He is a perpetual sentinel, who must watch the acts and the conduct of the enemies of the state. . . . If he be the first general, the first minister of the realm, it is not that he should remain the shadow of authority, but that he should fulfill the duties of such titles. He is only the first servant of the state.[1]

This utilitarian argument was reinforced by the praises of the philosophes.

Enlightened Absolutism?

There is no doubt that Enlightenment thought had some impact on the political development of European states in the eighteenth century. Closely related to the Enlightenment idea of natural laws was the belief in natural rights, which were thought to be inalienable privileges that ought not to be withheld from any person. These natural rights included equality before the law, freedom of religious worship, freedom of speech and the press, and the right to assemble, hold property, and pursue happiness. The United States' Declaration of Independence summarized the Enlightenment concept of natural rights in its opening paragraph: "We hold these truths to be self-evident, that all men are created equal; that they are endowed by their creator with certain unalienable rights; that among these are life, liberty and pursuit of happiness."

But how were these natural rights to be established and preserved? In the opinion of most philosophes, most people needed the direction provided by an enlightened ruler. What, however, made rulers enlightened? They must allow religious toleration, freedom of speech and the press, and the rights of private property. They must foster the arts, sciences, and education. Above all, they must not be arbitrary in their rule; they must obey the laws and enforce them fairly for all subjects. Only strong monarchs seemed capable of overcoming vested interests and effecting the reforms society needed. Reforms then should come from above—from the rulers rather than from the people. Distrustful of the masses, the philosophes believed that absolute rulers, swayed by enlightened principles, were the best hope of reforming their societies.

The extent to which rulers actually did so is frequently discussed in the political history of Europe in the eighteenth century. Many historians once assumed that a new type of monarchy emerged in the later eighteenth century, which they called "enlightened despotism" or "enlightened absolutism." Monarchs such as Frederick II of Prussia, Catherine the Great of Russia, and Joseph II of Austria supposedly followed the advice of the philosophes and ruled by enlightened principles, establishing a path to modern nationhood. Recent scholarship, however, has questioned the usefulness of the concept of enlightened absolutism. We can best determine the extent to which it can be applied by surveying the development of the European states and then making a judgment about the enlightened absolutism of the later eighteenth century.

The Atlantic Seaboard States

As a result of overseas voyages in the sixteenth century, the European economic axis began to shift from the Mediterranean to the Atlantic seaboard. In the seventeenth century, English and Dutch influence expanded as Spain's and Portugal's declined. By the eighteenth century, Dutch power had waned, and it fell to the English and French to build the commercial empires that ultimately fostered a true global economy.

FRANCE: THE LONG RULE OF LOUIS XV

In the eighteenth century, France experienced an economic revival as the Enlightenment gained strength. The French monarchy, however, was not overly influenced by the philosophes and resisted reforms as the French aristocracy grew stronger.

Louis XIV had left France with enlarged territories, an enormous debt, an unhappy populace, and a five-year-old great-grandson as his successor. Louis XV (1715–1774) did not begin to rule in his own right until 1743. But Louis was both lazy and weak, and ministers and mistresses soon began to influence the king, control the affairs of state, and undermine the prestige of the monarchy. The loss of an empire in the Seven Years' War, accompanied by burdensome taxes, an ever-mounting public debt, more hungry people, and a frivolous court life at Versailles forced even Louis to realize the growing disgust with his monarchy.

The next king, Louis's twenty-year-old grandson, who became Louis XVI (1774–1792), knew little about the operations of the French government and lacked the energy to deal decisively with state affairs. His wife, Marie Antoinette, was a spoiled Austrian princess who devoted much of her time to court intrigues. As France's financial crises worsened, neither Louis nor his queen seemed able to fathom the depths of despair and discontent that soon led to violent revolution.

GREAT BRITAIN: KING AND PARLIAMENT

The success of the Glorious Revolution in England had prevented absolutism without clearly inaugurating constitutional monarchy. The eighteenth-century British political system was characterized by a sharing of power between king and Parliament, with Parliament gradually gaining the upper hand. (The United Kingdom of Great Britain came into existence in 1707 when the governments of England and Scotland were united; the term *British* came to refer to both English and Scots.) The king chose ministers responsible to himself who set policy and guided Parliament; Parliament had the power to make laws, levy taxes, pass the budget, and indirectly influence the king's ministers. The eighteenth-century British Parliament was dominated by a landed aristocracy that historians usually divide into two groups: the peers, who sat for life in the House of Lords, and the landed gentry, who sat in the House of Commons and served as justices of the peace. The two groups had much in common: both were made up of landowners with similar economic interests, and they frequently intermarried.

The deputies to the House of Commons were chosen from the boroughs and counties but not by popular voting. Who was eligible to vote in the boroughs varied widely, enabling wealthy landed aristocrats to gain support by patronage and bribery; the result was a number of "pocket boroughs" controlled by a single person (hence "in his pocket"). The duke of Newcastle, for example, controlled the representatives from seven boroughs. It has been estimated that out of 405 borough deputies, 293 were chosen by fewer than 500 voters. This aristocratic control also extended to the county delegates, two from each of

England's forty counties. Although all holders of property worth at least 40 shillings a year could vote, members of the leading landed gentry families were elected over and over again.

In 1714, a new dynasty—the Hanoverians—was established when the last Stuart ruler, Queen Anne (1702–1714), died without an heir. The crown was offered to the Protestant rulers of the German state of Hanover. Because the first Hanoverian king, George I (1714–1727), did not speak English and neither he nor George II (1727–1760) had much familiarity with the British system, their chief ministers were allowed to handle Parliament. Many historians believe that this exercise of ministerial power was an important step in the development of the modern cabinet system in British government.

Robert Walpole served as prime minister from 1721 to 1742 and pursued a peaceful foreign policy to avoid new land taxes. But new forces were emerging in eighteenth-century England as growing trade and industry led an ever-increasing middle class to favor expansion of trade and world empire. The exponents of empire found a spokesperson in William Pitt the Elder, who became prime minister in 1757 and furthered imperial ambitions by acquiring Canada and India in the Seven Years' War (see "The Seven Years' War" later in this chapter).

Despite his successes, however, Pitt the Elder was dismissed by the new king, George III (1760–1820), in 1761 and replaced by the king's favorite, Lord Bute. However, discontent over the electoral system and the loss of the American colonies (see Chapter 19) brought public criticism of the king. In 1780, the House of Commons affirmed that "the influence of the crown has increased, is increasing, and ought to be diminished." King George III managed to avoid drastic change by appointing William Pitt the Younger (1759–1806), son of William Pitt the Elder, as prime minister in 1783. Supported by the merchants, industrial classes, and the king, Pitt managed to stay in power. George III, however, remained an uncertain

CHRONOLOGY

France and Britain in the Eighteenth Century

France	
Louis XV	1715–1774
Louis XVI	1774–1792
Great Britain	
The Stuarts	
Queen Anne	1702–1714
The Hanoverians	
George I	1714–1727
George II	1727–1760
Robert Walpole	1721–1742
William Pitt the Elder	1757–1761
George III	1760–1820
William Pitt the Younger	1783–1801

THE BRITISH HOUSE OF COMMONS. **A sharing of power between king and Parliament characterized the British political system in the eighteenth century. Parliament was divided into the House of Lords and the House of Commons. This painting shows the House of Commons in session in 1793 during a debate over the possibility of war with France. William Pitt the Younger is addressing the chamber.**

supporter because of periodic bouts of insanity (he once mistook a tree in Windsor Park for the king of Prussia). Thanks to Pitt's successes, however, serious reform of the corrupt parliamentary system was avoided for another generation.

Absolutism in Central and Eastern Europe

Of the five major European powers, three were located in central and eastern Europe and came to play an increasingly important role in European international politics (see Map 18.1).

PRUSSIA: THE ARMY AND THE BUREAUCRACY

Two able Prussian kings in the eighteenth century, Frederick William I and Frederick II the Great, further developed the two major institutions—the army and the bureaucracy—that were the backbone of Prussia. Frederick William I (1713–1740) promoted the evolution of Prussia's highly efficient civil bureaucracy by establishing the General Directory. It served as the chief administrative agent of the central government, supervising military, police, economic, and financial affairs. Frederick William strove to maintain a highly efficient bureaucracy of civil service workers. It had its own code in which the supreme values were obedience, honor, and service to the king as the highest duty. As Frederick William asserted: "One must serve the king with life and limb, with goods and chattels, with honor and conscience, and surrender everything except salvation. The latter is reserved for God. But everything else must be mine."[2] Close, personal supervision of the bureaucracy became a hallmark of the eighteenth-century Prussian rulers.

Frederick William's other major concern was the army. By the end of his reign, it had grown from 45,000 to 83,000 men. Though the tenth-largest nation in physical size and thirteenth in population in Europe, Prussia had the fourth-largest army, after France, Russia, and Austria. The nobility or landed aristocracy known as Junkers, who owned large estates with many

MAP 18.1 Europe in 1763.

serfs, were the officers in the Prussian army. They too had a strong sense of service to the king or state. Prussian nobles believed in duty, obedience, and sacrifice. At the same time, because of its size and its reputation as one of the best armies in Europe, the Prussian army was the most important institution in the state.

Frederick the Great (1740–1786) was one of the best-educated and most cultured monarchs in the eighteenth century. He was well versed in Enlightenment thought and even invited Voltaire to live at his court for several years. His intellectual interests were despised by his father, who forced his intelligent son to prepare for a career in rulership (see the box on p. 368). A believer in the king as the "first servant of the state," Frederick became a conscientious ruler who made few innovations in administration. His diligence in overseeing its operation, however, made the Prussian bureaucracy well known for both efficiency and honesty.

For a time, Frederick seemed quite willing to follow the philosophes' suggestions for reform. He established a single code of laws for his territories that eliminated the use of torture except in treason and murder cases. He also granted a limited freedom of speech and the press as well as complete religious toleration—no difficult task since he had no strong religious convictions anyway. Although Frederick was well aware of the philosophes' condemnation of serfdom, he was too dependent on the Prussian nobility to interfere with it or with the hierarchical structure of Prussian society. In fact, Frederick was a social conservative who made Prussian society even more aristocratic than it had been before. Frederick reversed his father's policy of allowing commoners to have power in the civil service and reserved the higher positions in the bureaucracy for members of the nobility. The upper ranks of the bureaucracy came close to constituting a hereditary caste.

Like his predecessors, Frederick the Great took a great interest in military affairs and enlarged the Prussian army (to 200,000 men). Unlike his predecessors, he had no objection to using it. Frederick did not hesitate to take advantage of a succession crisis in the Habsburg monarchy to seize the Austrian province of Silesia for Prussia. This act aroused Austria's bitter hostility to Prussia and embroiled Frederick in two major wars, the War of the Austrian Succession and the Seven Years' War. Although the latter war left his country exhausted, Frederick succeeded in keeping Silesia. After the wars, the first partition of Poland with Austria and Russia in 1772 gave him the Polish territory between Prussia and Brandenburg and created greater unity for the scattered lands of Prussia. By the end of his reign, Prussia was recognized as a great European power.

FREDERICK II AT SANS-SOUCI. Frederick II, known as Frederick the Great, was one of the most cultured and best-educated European monarchs. In this painting, he is shown visiting the building site of his residential retreat, Sans-Souci, at Potsdam.

THE AUSTRIAN EMPIRE OF THE HABSBURGS

The Austrian Empire had become one of the great European states by the beginning of the eighteenth century. The city of Vienna, center of the Habsburg monarchy, was filled with magnificent palaces and churches built in the Baroque style and became the music capital of Europe. And yet Austria, a sprawling assemblage of many different nationalities, languages, religions, and cultures, found it difficult to provide common laws and administrative centralization for its people. Although Empress Maria Theresa (1740–1780) managed to make administrative reforms that helped centralize the Austrian Empire, these reforms were done for practical reasons—to strengthen the power of the Habsburg state—and were accompanied by an enlargement and modernization of the armed forces. Maria Theresa remained staunchly

Frederick the Great and His Father

As a young man, the future Frederick the Great was quite different from his strict and austere father, Frederick William I. Possessing a high regard for French culture, poetry, and flute playing, Frederick resisted his father's wishes that he immerse himself in governmental and military affairs. Eventually, Frederick capitulated to his father's will and accepted the need to master affairs of state. These letters, written when Frederick was sixteen, illustrate the difficulties in their relationship.

Frederick to His Father, Frederick William I (September 11, 1728)

I have not ventured for a long time to present myself before my dear papa, partly because I was advised against it, but chiefly because I anticipated an even worse reception than usual and feared to vex my dear papa still further by the favor I have now to ask; so I have preferred to put it in writing.

I beg my dear papa that he will be kindly disposed toward me. I do assure him that after long examination of my conscience I do not find the slightest thing with which to reproach myself; but if, against my wish and will, I have vexed my dear papa, I hereby beg most humbly for forgiveness, and hope that my dear papa will give over the fearful hate which has appeared so plainly in his whole behavior and to which I cannot accustom myself. I have always thought hitherto that I had a kind father, but now I see the contrary. However, I will take courage and hope that my dear papa will think this all over and take me again into his favor. Meantime I assure him that I will never, my life long, willingly fail him, and in spite of his disfavor I am still, with most dutiful and childlike respect, my dear papa's

Most obedient and faithful servant and son,
Frederick

Frederick William to His Son Frederick

A bad, obstinate boy, who does not love his father; for when one does one's best, and especially when one loves one's father, one does what he wishes not only when he is standing by but when he is not there to see. Moreover you know very well that I cannot stand an effeminate fellow who has no manly tastes, who cannot ride or shoot (to his shame be it said!), is untidy about his person, and wears his hair curled like a fool instead of cutting it; and that I have condemned all these things a thousand times, and yet there is no sign of improvement. For the rest, haughty, offish as a country lout, conversing with none but a favored few instead of being affable and popular, grimacing like a fool, and never following my wishes out of love for me but only when forced into it, caring for nothing but to have his own way, and thinking nothing else is of any importance.

This is my answer.

Frederick William

Catholic and conservative and was not open to the wider reform calls of the philosophes. But her successor was.

Joseph II (1780–1790) was determined to make changes; at the same time, he carried on his mother's chief goal of enhancing Habsburg power within the monarchy and Europe. Joseph was an earnest man who believed in the need to sweep away anything standing in the path of reason. As he expressed it: "I have made Philosophy the lawmaker of my empire; her logical applications are going to transform Austria."

Joseph's reform program was far-reaching. He abolished serfdom and tried to give the peasants hereditary rights to their holdings. A new penal code was instituted that abrogated the death penalty and established the principle of equality of all before the law. Joseph introduced drastic religious reforms as well, including complete religious toleration and restrictions on the Catholic church. Altogether, Joseph II issued six thousand decrees and eleven thousand laws in his effort to transform his empire.

Joseph's reform program proved overwhelming for Austria, however. He alienated the nobility by freeing the serfs and alienated the church by his attacks on the monastic establishment. Even the serfs were unhappy, unable to comprehend the drastic changes inherent in Joseph's policies. His attempt to rationalize the administration of the empire by imposing German as the official bureaucratic language alienated the non-German nationalities. As Joseph complained, there were not enough people for the kind of bureaucracy he needed. His deep sense of failure is revealed in the epitaph he wrote for his gravestone: "Here lies Joseph II who was unfortunate in everything that he undertook." His successors undid many of his reform efforts.

RUSSIA UNDER CATHERINE THE GREAT

Peter the Great was followed by a series of six successors who were made and unmade by the palace guard. After the last of these six, Peter III, was murdered by a faction of nobles, his German wife emerged as autocrat of all the Russians. Catherine II (1762–1796) was an intelligent woman who was familiar with the works of the philosophes. She claimed that she wished to reform Russia along the lines of Enlightenment ideas, but she was always shrewd enough to realize that her success depended on the support of the palace guard and the gentry class from which it stemmed. She could not afford to alienate the Russian nobility.

Initially, Catherine seemed eager to pursue reform. She called for the election of an assembly in 1767 to debate the details of a new law code. In her *Instruction*, written as a guide to the deliberations, Catherine questioned the institution of serfdom, torture, and capital punishment and even advocated the principle of the equality of all people in the eyes of the law. But a year and a half of negotiation produced little real change.

CATHERINE THE GREAT. Autocrat of Russia, Catherine was an intelligent ruler who favored reform. She found it expedient, however, to retain much of the old system in order to keep the support of the landed nobility. In this portrait by Dmitry Levitsky, she is shown in legislative regalia in the Temple of Justice in 1783.

In fact, Catherine's subsequent policies had the effect of strengthening the landholding class at the expense of all others, especially the Russian serfs. To reorganize local government, Catherine divided Russia into fifty provinces, each of which was in turn subdivided into districts ruled by officials chosen by the nobles. In this way, the local nobility became responsible for the day-to-day governing of Russia. Moreover, the gentry were now formed into corporate groups with special legal privileges, including the right to trial by peers and exemption from personal taxation and corporal punishment. The Charter of the Nobility formalized these rights in 1785.

Catherine's policy of favoring the landed nobility led to even worse conditions for the Russian peasants and provoked a rebellion. Led by an illiterate Cossack, Emelyan Pugachev, the rebellion spread across southern Russia. But the insurrection soon faltered, and Pugachev was captured, tortured, and executed. Catherine responded to the failed revolt with even harsher measures against the peasantry. All rural reform was halted, and serfdom was expanded into newer parts of the empire.

Catherine proved a worthy successor to Peter the Great by expanding Russia's territory westward into Poland and southward to the Black Sea. Russia gained land to the south by defeating the Turks. In the Treaty of Kuchuk-Kainarji in 1774, the Russians also gained the privilege of protecting Greek Orthodox Christians in the Ottoman Empire. Russian expansion westward came at the expense of neighboring Poland. In the three partitions of Poland in 1772, 1793, and 1795, Russia gained about 50 percent of Polish territory; Austria and Prussia took the rest.

Enlightened Absolutism Revisited

Of the three major rulers most closely associated traditionally with enlightened absolutism—Joseph II, Frederick II, and Catherine the Great—only Joseph II sought truly radical changes based on Enlightenment

CHRONOLOGY

Central and Eastern Europe in the Eighteenth Century

Prussia	
Frederick William I	1713–1740
Frederick II the Great	1740–1786
Austrian Empire	
Maria Theresa	1740–1780
Joseph II	1780–1790
Russia	
Peter III	1762
Catherine II the Great	1762–1796
Pugachev's rebellion	1773–1775
Charter of the Nobility	1785
Poland	
First partition	1772
Second partition	1793
Third partition	1795

ideas. Both Frederick and Catherine liked to be cast as disciples of the Enlightenment, expressed interest in enlightened reforms, and even attempted some. But the policies of neither seemed seriously affected by Enlightenment thought. Necessities of state and maintenance of the existing system took precedence over reform. Indeed, many historians maintain that Joseph, Frederick, and Catherine were all guided primarily by a concern for the power and well-being of their states and that their policies were not all that different from those of their predecessors. In the final analysis, heightened state power was used to build armies and wage wars to gain more power. Nevertheless, in their desire to forge stronger state systems, these rulers did pursue such enlightened ideas as legal reform, religious toleration, and the extension of education, since these served to create more satisfied subjects and strengthened the state in significant ways.

It would be foolish, however, to overlook the fact that political and social realities limited the ability of enlightened rulers to make reforms. Everywhere in Europe, the hereditary aristocracy was still the most powerful class in society. Enlightened reforms were often limited to changes in the administrative and judicial systems that did not seriously undermine the powerful interests of the European nobility. Although aristocrats might join the populace in opposing monarchical extension of centralizing power, as the chief beneficiaries of a system based on traditional rights and privileges for their class, they were certainly not willing to support a political ideology that trumpeted the principle of equal rights for all.

◆ Wars and Diplomacy

The philosophes condemned war as a foolish waste of life and resources in stupid quarrels of no value to humankind. Despite their words, the rivalry among states that led to costly struggles remained unchanged in the European world of the eighteenth century. Europe consisted of a number of self-governing states guided by the self-interest of the ruler. And as Frederick the Great of Prussia said, "The fundamental rule of governments is the principle of extending their territories."

International rivalry and the continuing centralization of the European states were closely related. The need for taxes to support large armies and navies created its own imperative for more efficient and effective control of power in the hands of bureaucrats who could collect taxes and organize states for the task of winning wars. At the same time, the development of large standing armies ensured that political disputes would periodically be resolved by armed conflict rather than diplomacy. Between 1715 and 1740, it had seemed that Europe preferred peace. But in 1740, a major conflict erupted over the succession to the Austrian throne.

After the death of the Habsburg emperor Charles VI (1711–1740), King Frederick II of Prussia took advantage of the succession of a woman, Maria Theresa, to the throne of Austria by invading Austrian Silesia. The vulnerability of Maria Theresa encouraged France to enter the war against its traditional enemy, Austria; in turn, Maria Theresa made an alliance with Great Britain, which feared French hegemony over Continental affairs. All too quickly, the Austrian succession had set off a worldwide conflagration. The War of the Austrian Succession (1740–1748) was fought not only in Europe, where Prussia seized Silesia and France occupied the Austrian Netherlands, but also in the East, where France took Madras in India from the British, and in North America, where the British captured the French fortress of Louisbourg at the entrance to the St. Lawrence River. By 1748, all parties were exhausted and agreed to a peace that guaranteed the return of all occupied territories except for Silesia to their original owners. Prussia's refusal to return Silesia guaranteed another war, at least between the two hostile central European powers of Prussia and Austria.

The Seven Years' War (1756–1763)

Maria Theresa refused to accept the loss of Silesia and prepared for its return by rebuilding her army while working diplomatically to separate Prussia from its chief ally, France. In 1756, Austria achieved what was soon labeled a diplomatic revolution. French-Austrian rivalry had been a fact of European diplomacy since the late sixteenth century. But two new rivalries made this old one seem superfluous: Britain and France over colonial empires, and Austria and Prussia over Silesia. France abandoned Prussia and allied with Austria. Russia, which saw Prussia as a major hindrance to Russian goals in central Europe, joined the new alliance. In turn, Great Britain allied with Prussia. This diplomatic revolution of 1756 now led to another worldwide war.

There were three major areas of conflict: Europe, India, and North America (see Map 18.2). Europe witnessed the clash of the two major alliances: the British and Prussians against the Austrians, Russians, and French. With his superb army and military prowess, Frederick the Great of Prussia was able for some time to defeat the Austrian, French, and Russian armies. Eventually, however, Frederick's forces were gradually worn down and faced defeat until a new Russian tsar, Peter III, withdrew Russia's troops from the conflict. His withdrawal guaranteed a stalemate and resuscitated the desire for peace. The European conflict was ended by the Peace of Hubertusburg in 1763. All occupied territories were returned, with the exception that Austria officially recognized Prussia's permanent control of Silesia.

The Anglo-French struggle in the rest of the world had more decisive results. Known as the Great War for Empire, it was fought in India and North America. The French had returned Madras to Britain after the War of the Austrian Succession, but jockeying for power continued as the French and British supported opposing native Indian princes. The British under Robert Clive (1725–1774) ultimately won out,

MAP 18.2 The Seven Years' War.

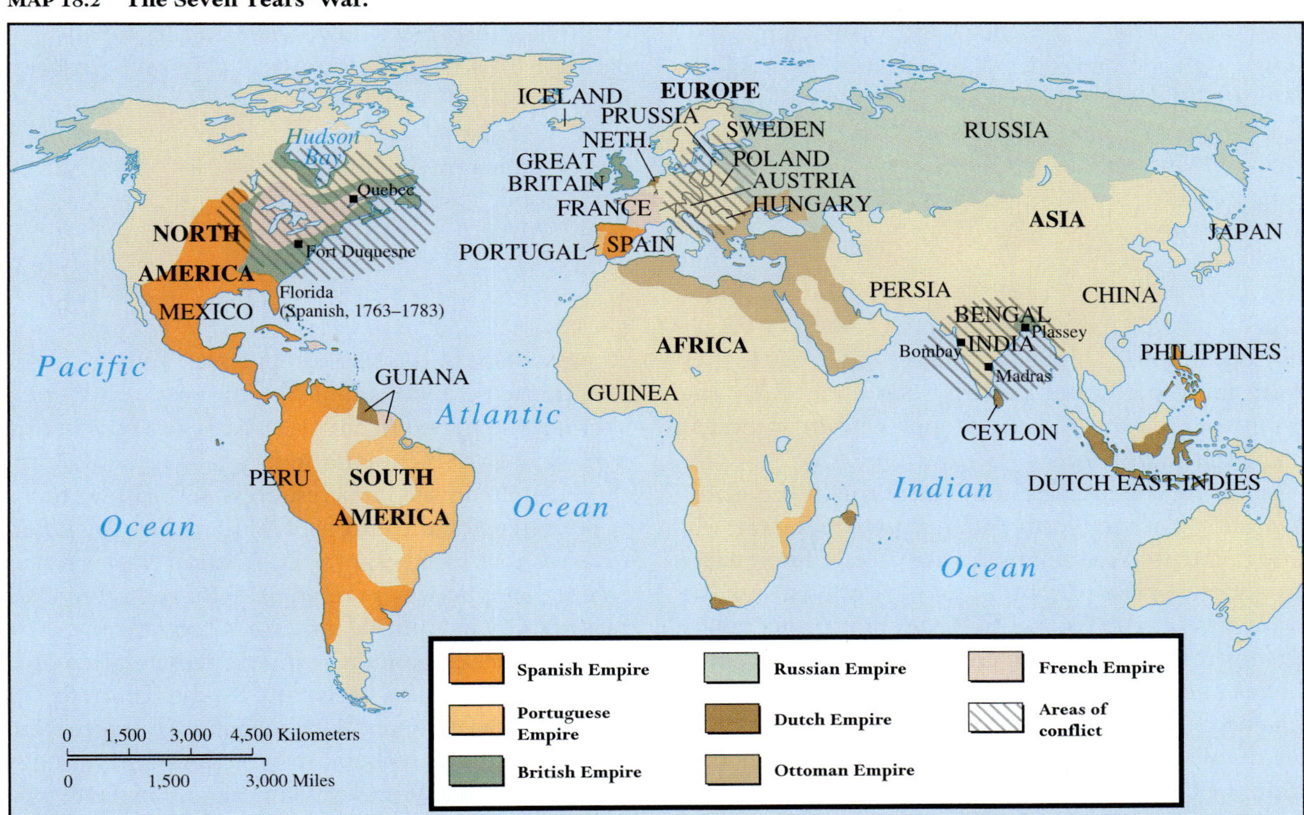

British Victory in India

After the war of the Austrian Succession, the French and British continued to maneuver for advantage in India. The success of the British in defeating the French was due to Robert Clive, who, in this excerpt from one of his letters, describes his famous victory at Plassey, north of Calcutta (June 23, 1757). This battle demonstrated the inability of native Indian soldiers to compete with Europeans and signified the beginning of British control in Bengal. Clive claimed to have a thousand Europeans, two thousand sepoys (local soldiers), and eight pieces of cannon available for this battle.

Robert Clive's Account of His Victory at Plassey

At daybreak we discovered the [governor's] army moving toward us, consisting, as we since found, of about fifteen thousand horse and thirty-five thousand foot, with upwards of forty pieces of cannon. They approached apace, and by six began to attack with a number of heavy cannon, supported by the whole army, and continued to play on us very briskly for several hours, during which our situation was of the utmost service to us, being lodged in a large grove with good mud banks. To succeed in an attempt on their cannon was next to impossible, as they were planted in a manner round us and at considerable distances from each other. We therefore remained quiet in our post, in expectation of a successful attack upon their camp at night. About noon the enemy drew off their artillery and retired to their camp. . . .

On finding them make no great effort to dislodge us, we proceeded to take possession of one or two more eminences lying very near an angle of their camp, from whence, and an adjacent eminence in their possession, they kept a smart fire of musketry upon us. They made several attempts to bring out their cannon, but our advanced fieldpieces played so warmly and so well upon them that they were always driven back. Their horse exposing themselves a good deal on this occasion, many of them were killed, and among the rest four or five officers of the first distinction; by which the whole army being visibly dispirited and thrown into some confusion, we were encouraged to storm both the eminence and the angle of their camp, which were carried at the same instant, with little or no loss; though the latter was defended (exclusively of blacks) by forty French and two pieces of cannon; and the former by a large body of blacks, both horse and foot. On this a general rout ensued, and we pursued the enemy six miles, passing upwards of forty pieces of cannon they had abandoned, with an infinite number of carts and carriages filled with baggage of all kinds. . . . It is computed there are killed of the enemy about five hundred. Our loss amounted to only twenty-two killed and fifty wounded, and those chiefly blacks.

not because they had better forces but because they were more persistent (see the box above). By the Treaty of Paris in 1763, the French withdrew and left India to the British.

By far the greatest conflicts of the Seven Years' War took place in North America (where the war was known as the French and Indian War). There were two primary areas of contention. One consisted of the waterways of the Gulf of St. Lawrence, protected by the fortress of Louisbourg and by forts near the Great Lakes and Lake Champlain that protected French Quebec and French traders. The other was the unsettled Ohio River valley. As the French moved south from the Great Lakes and north from their forts on the Mississippi, they began to establish forts from the Appalachians to the Mississippi River. To British settlers in the thirteen colonies to the east, this French activity threatened to cut off a vast area of the continent from British exploitation.

Despite initial French successes, British fortunes were revived by the efforts of William Pitt the Elder, who was convinced that the destruction of the French colonial empire was a prerequisite for the survival of Britain's own colonial empire. Accordingly, Pitt decided to make a minimal effort in Europe while concentrating resources, especially the British navy, on the war in the colonies. Although French troops were greater in number, the ability of the French to use them in the New World was contingent on naval support. The defeat of French fleets in major naval bat-

THE DEATH OF GENERAL WOLFE. The great powers of Europe fought the Seven Years' War in Europe, India, and North America. Despite initial French successes in North America, the British went on to win the war. This painting by Benjamin West presents a heroic rendering of the death of General James Wolfe, the British commander who defeated the French forces at the Battle of Quebec.

tles in 1759 gave the British an advantage because the French could no longer easily reinforce their garrisons. A series of British victories soon followed. On the night of September 13, 1759, British forces led by General James Wolfe scaled the heights outside Quebec and defeated the French under General Louis-Joseph Montcalm on the Plains of Abraham. Both generals died in the battle. The British went on to seize Montreal, the Great Lakes area, and the Ohio valley. The French were forced to make peace. By the Treaty of Paris, they ceded Canada and the lands east of the Mississippi to England. Their ally Spain transferred Spanish Florida to British control; in return, the French gave their Louisiana territory to the Spanish. By 1763, Great Britain had become the world's greatest colonial power.

Economic Expansion and Social Change

The eighteenth century witnessed the beginning of economic changes in Europe that ultimately had a strong impact on the rest of the world. Rapid population growth, an agricultural revolution, industrialization, and an increase in worldwide trade characterized the economic patterns of the eighteenth century.

Population and Food

Despite regional variations, Europe's population began to grow around 1750 and continued a slow upward movement. It has been estimated that the total European population was around 120 million in 1700, expanded to 140 million by 1750, and then grew to 190 million by 1790; thus the growth rate in the second half of the century was double that of the first half. These increases occurred during the same time that several million Europeans were going abroad as colonists. A falling death rate was perhaps the most important cause of population growth. What accounted for the decline in the death rate? More plentiful food and better transportation of available food supplies led to some improvement in diet and relief from devastating famines. Also of great significance in lowering death rates was the disappearance of bubonic plague.

More food was in part a result of improvements in agricultural practices and methods in the eighteenth century, especially in Britain, parts of France, and the Low Countries. Eighteenth-century agriculture was characterized by increases in food production that can be attributed to four interrelated factors: more farmland, healthier and more abundant livestock, increased yields per acre, and an improved climate.

Climatologists believe that the "little ice age" of the seventeenth century declined in the eighteenth, especially evident in the moderate summers that provided more ideal growing conditions. The amount of land under cultivation was increased by abandoning the old open-field system in which part of the land was left to lie fallow to renew it. New crops, such as alfalfa and clover, which stored nitrogen in their roots, restored the soil's fertility and also provided winter fodder for livestock, enabling landlords to maintain an ever-larger number of animals. The more numerous livestock made available more animal manure, which was used to fertilize fields and produce better yields per acre. Also important to the increased yields was the spread of new vegetables, including two important American crops, the potato and maize (Indian corn). Although they were not grown in quantity until after 1700, they had been brought to Europe from America in the sixteenth century and were part of what some historians have called the Columbian exchange—a reciprocal exchange of plants and animals between Europe and America (see Map 18.3). The potato became a staple in Germany, the Low Countries, and especially Ireland, where repression by British landlords forced large numbers of poor peasants to survive on small pieces of marginal land. The potato took relatively little effort to produce in large quantities. High in carbohydrates and calories, rich in vitamins A and C, it could be easily stored for winter use.

In the eighteenth century, the English were the leaders in adopting the new techniques that have been characterized as an agricultural revolution. This early modernization of English agriculture with its noticeable increase in productivity made possible the feeding of an expanding population about to enter a new world of industrialization and urbanization.

New Methods of Finance and Industry

A decline in the supply of gold and silver in the seventeenth century had created a chronic shortage of money that undermined the efforts of governments

MAP 18.3 The Columbian Exchange.

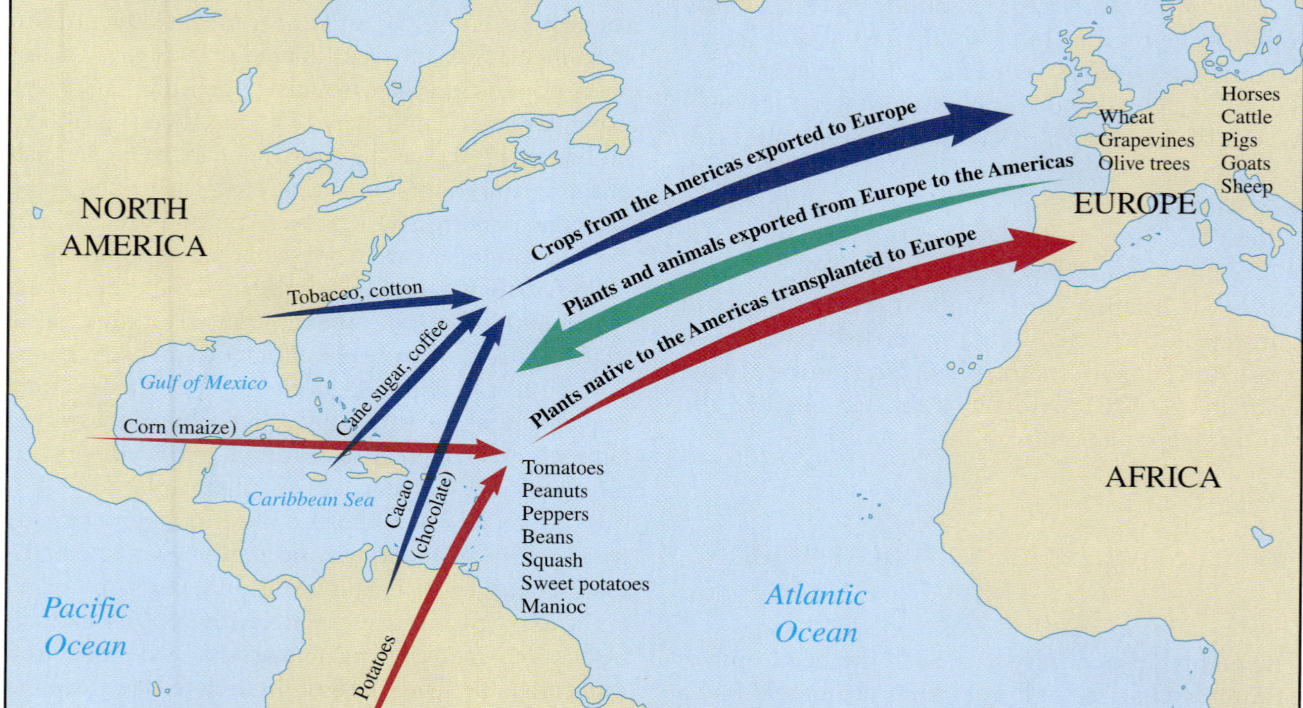

to meet their needs. The establishment of new public and private banks and the acceptance of paper notes made possible an expansion of credit in the eighteenth century.

Perhaps the best example of this process can be observed in England, where the Bank of England was founded in 1694. Unlike other banks accustomed to receiving deposits and exchanging foreign currencies, the Bank of England also made loans. In return for lending money to the government, the bank was allowed to issue paper "banknotes" backed by its credit. These soon became negotiable and provided a paper substitute for gold and silver currency.

The most important product of European industry in the eighteenth century was textiles, most of which were still produced by traditional methods. In cities that were textile centers, master artisans used timeworn methods to turn out finished goods in their guild workshops. But textile production was shifting to the countryside in parts of Europe by the eighteenth century. Industrial production in the countryside was done by the so-called putting-out or domestic system in which a merchant-capitalist entrepreneur bought the raw materials, mostly wool and flax, and "put them out" to rural workers who spun the raw material into yarn and then wove it into cloth on simple looms. Capitalist entrepreneurs sold the finished product, made a profit, and used the profit to manufacture more. This system became known as the cottage industry because spinners and weavers did their work on spinning wheels and looms in their own cottages. The cottage industry was truly a family enterprise since women and children could spin while men wove on the looms, enabling rural people to earn incomes that supplemented their pitiful wages as agricultural laborers. The cottage system used traditional methods of manufacturing and spread to many areas of rural Europe in the eighteenth century. But in the second half of the century, significant changes began to occur that would soon revolutionize industrial production (see Chapter 20).

Toward a Global Economy: Mercantile Empires and Worldwide Trade

Although bankers and industrialists would come to dominate the economic life of the nineteenth century, in the eighteenth century merchants and traders still reigned supreme. Intra-European trade accounted for most of the activity as wheat, timber, and naval stores from the Baltic, wines from France, wool and fruit from Spain, and silk from Italy were exchanged along with a host of other products. But the eighteenth century witnessed only a slight increase in this trade while overseas trade boomed. From 1716 to 1789, total French exports quadrupled, whereas intra-European trade, which constituted 75 percent of these exports in 1716, constituted only 50 percent of the total in 1789. This increase in overseas trade has led some historians to speak of the emergence of a global economy in the eighteenth century. By the beginning of the century, Spain, Portugal, and the Dutch Republic, which had earlier monopolized overseas trade, found themselves increasingly overshadowed by France and Britain. The rivalry between these two great western European powers was especially evident in the Americas and the East.

COLONIAL EMPIRES

Both the French and British colonial empires in the New World included large parts of the West Indies and the North American continent. In the former, the British held Barbados, Jamaica, and Bermuda while the French possessed Martinique, Saint Domingue, and Guadeloupe. On these tropical islands, both the British and the French had developed plantation economies, worked by African slaves, which produced tobacco, cotton, coffee, and sugar, all products increasingly in demand in Europe.

The French and British colonies on the North American continent were structured in different ways. French North America (Canada and Louisiana) was run autocratically as a vast trading area, where valuable furs, leather, fish, and timber were acquired. However, the inability of the French state to get its people to emigrate to these North American possessions left them thinly populated.

British North America had come to consist of thirteen colonies on the eastern coast of the present United States. They were thickly populated, containing about 1.5 million people by 1750, and were also prosperous. Supposedly run by the British Board of Trade, the Royal Council, and Parliament, these thirteen colonies had legislatures that tended to act independently. Merchants in such port cities as Boston, Philadelphia, New York, and Charleston resented and resisted regulation from the British government.

Both the North American and West Indian colonies of Britain and France were assigned roles in keeping with mercantilist theory. They provided raw materials for the mother country while buying the latter's manufactured goods. Navigation acts regulated what could be taken from and sold to the colonies. Theoretically, the system was supposed to provide a balance of trade favorable to the mother country.

British and French rivalry was also evident in the Spanish and Portuguese colonial empires in Latin America. The decline of Spain and Portugal had led these two states to depend even more on resources from their colonies, and they imposed strict mercantilist rules to keep others out. Spain, for example, tried to limit all trade with its colonies to Spanish ships. But the British and French were too powerful to be excluded. The British cajoled the Portuguese into allowing them into the lucrative Brazilian trade. The French, however, were the first to break into the Spanish Latin American market when the French Bourbons became kings of Spain. Britain's entry into Spanish American markets first came in 1713, when the British were granted the privilege, known as the *asiento*, of transporting 4,500 slaves a year into Spanish Latin America.

THE SALE OF SLAVES. The slave trade was one of the most profitable commercial enterprises of the eighteenth century. This painting shows a Western slave merchant negotiating with a local African leader over slaves at Gorée, Senegal, in West Africa in the late eighteenth century.

The rivalry also extended to the East, where Britain and France competed for the tea, spices, cotton, hardwoods, and luxury goods of India and the East Indies. The rivalry between the two countries was played out by their state-backed national trading companies. In the course of the eighteenth century, the British defeated the French and by the mid-nineteenth century had assumed control to the entire Indian subcontinent.

GLOBAL TRADE

To justify references to a global economy, historians have usually pointed to the patterns of trade that interlocked Europe, Africa, the East, and the American continents. One such pattern involved the influx of gold and silver into Spain from its colonial American empire. Much of this gold and silver made its way to Britain, France, and the Netherlands in return for manufactured goods. British, Dutch, and French merchants in turn used their profits to buy tea, spices, silk, and cotton goods from China and India to sell in Europe. Another important source of trading activity came from the plantations of the Western Hemisphere. Plantations, extending from the southern colonies of North America through the West Indies and into Brazil, were worked by African slaves and produced tobacco, cotton, coffee, and sugar to meet European demand. A third pattern of trade involved British merchant ships, which carried British manufactured goods to Africa, where they were traded for a cargo of slaves, which were then shipped to Virginia and paid for with tobacco, which was in turn shipped back to Britain, where it was processed and then sold in Germany for cash.

Of all the goods traded in the eighteenth century, perhaps the most profitable and certainly the most infamous were African slaves. The need for slaves on the plantations in the Americas made the eighteenth century the high point of the Atlantic slave trade. It has been estimated that of the total 9.3 million slaves transported from Africa, almost two-thirds were taken in the eighteenth century.

Slaving ships sailed from a European port to the African coast, where Europeans had established bases. There merchants could trade manufactured goods, rum, and brandy for blacks captured by African middlemen. The captives were closely packed into cargo ships, 300 to 450 per ship, and chained in holds without sanitary facilities or enough space to stand up; there they remained during the voyage to America, which took at least one hundred days (see the box

The Atlantic Slave Trade

One of the most odious practices of early modern Western society was the Atlantic slave trade, which reached its height in the eighteenth century. Blacks were transported in densely packed cargo ships from the western coast of Africa to the Americas to work as slaves in the plantation economy. Not until late in the eighteenth century did a rising chorus of voices raise serious objections to this trade in human beings. This excerpt presents a criticism of the slave trade from an anonymous French writer.

Diary of a Citizen

As soon as the ships have lowered their anchors off the coast of Guinea, the price at which the captains have decided to buy the captives is announced to the Negroes who buy prisoners from various princes and sell them to Europeans. Presents are sent to the sovereign who rules over that particular part of the coast, and permission to trade is given. Immediately the slaves are brought by inhuman brokers like so many victims dragged to a sacrifice. White men who covet that portion of the human race receive them in a little house they have erected on the shore, where they have entrenched themselves with two pieces of cannon and twenty guards. As soon as the bargain is concluded, the Negro is put in chains and led aboard the vessel, where he meets his fellow sufferers. Here sinister reflections come to his mind; everything shocks and frightens him and his uncertain destiny gives rise to the greatest anxiety. . . .

The vessel sets sail for the Antilles, and the Negroes are chained in a hold of the ship, a kind of lugubrious prison where the light of day does not penetrate, but into which the air is introduced by means of a pump. Twice a day some disgusting food is distributed to them. Their consuming sorrow and the sad state to which they are reduced would make them commit suicide if they were not deprived of all the means for an attempt upon their lives. Without any kind of clothing it would be difficult to conceal from the watchful eyes of the sailors in charge any instrument apt to alleviate their despair. The fear of a revolt, such as sometimes happens on the voyage from Guinea, is the basis of a common concern and produces as many guards as there are men in the crew. The slightest noise or a secret conversation among two Negroes is punished with utmost severity. All in all, the voyage is made in a continuous state of alarm on the part of the white men, who fear a revolt, and in a cruel state of uncertainty on the part of the Negroes, who do not know the fate awaiting them.

When the vessel arrives at a port in the Antilles, they are taken to a warehouse where they are displayed, like any merchandise, to the eyes of buyers. The plantation owner pays according to the age, strength, and health of the Negro he is buying. He has him taken to his plantation, and there he is delivered to an overseer who then and there becomes his tormentor. In order to domesticate him, the Negro is granted a few days of rest in his new place, but soon he is given a hoe and a sickle and made to join a work gang. Then he ceases to wonder about his fate; he understands that only labor is demanded of him. But he does not know yet how excessive this labor will be. As a matter of fact, his work begins at dawn and does not end before nightfall; it is interrupted for only two hours at dinnertime. The food a full-grown Negro is given each week consists of two pounds of salt beef or cod and two pots of tapioca meal. . . . A Negro of twelve or thirteen years or under is given only one pot of meal and one pound of beef or cod. In place of food some planters give their Negroes the liberty of working for themselves every Saturday; others are even less generous and grant them this liberty only on Sundays and holidays.

above). As soon as the human cargo arrived in the New World, the slaves entered the plantation economy. Here the "sugar factories," as the sugar plantations in the Caribbean were called, played an especially prominent role. The French colony of Saint Domingue (later Haiti) had half a million slaves working on three thousand plantations by the last two decades of the eighteenth century. This colony produced 100,000 tons of sugar a year, but at the expense of a high death rate from the brutal treatment of the slaves. It was not until the 1790s that the French abolished slavery. The British followed suit in 1808.

The Social Order of the Eighteenth Century

The pattern of Europe's social organization, first established in the Middle Ages, continued well into the eighteenth century. Social status was still largely determined not by wealth and economic standing but by the division into the traditional "orders" or "estates" determined by heredity. This divinely sanctioned division of society into traditional orders was supported by Christian teaching, which emphasized the need to fulfill the responsibilities of one's estate. Although Enlightenment intellectuals attacked these traditional distinctions, they did not die easily. In the Prussian law code of 1794, marriage between noble males and middle-class females was forbidden without a government dispensation. Even without government regulation, however, different social groups remained easily distinguished everywhere in Europe by the distinctive, traditional clothes they wore.

Nevertheless, some forces of change were at work in this traditional society. The ideas of the Enlightenment made headway as reformers argued that the idea of an unchanging social order based on privilege was hostile to the progress of society. However, not until the revolutionary upheavals at the end of the eighteenth century did the old order finally begin to disintegrate.

The Peasants

Because society was still mostly rural in the eighteenth century, the peasantry constituted the largest social group, making up as much as 85 percent of Europe's population. There were rather wide differences, however, between peasants from area to area. The most important distinction—at least legally—was between the free peasant and the serf. Peasants in Britain, northern Italy, the Low Countries, Spain, most of France, and some areas of western Germany shared freedom despite numerous regional and local differences. Legally free peasants, however, were not exempt from burdens. Some free peasants in Andalusia in Spain, southern Italy, Sicily, and Portugal lived in a poverty more desperate than that of many serfs in Russia and eastern Germany. In France, 40 percent of free peasants owned little or no land whatever by 1789.

Small peasant proprietors or tenant farmers in western Europe were also not free from compulsory services. Most owed tithes, often one-third of their crops. Although tithes were intended for parish priests, in France only 10 percent of the priests received them. Instead they wound up in the hands of towns and aristocratic landowners. Moreover, in addition to giving up their crops, some peasants also owed a variety of dues and fees. Local aristocrats claimed hunting rights on peasant land and had monopolies over the flour mills, community ovens, and wine and oil presses needed by the peasants. Hunting rights, dues, fees, and tithes were all deeply resented.

The local villages in which they dwelt remained the centers of peasants' social lives. Villages, especially in western Europe, maintained public order; provided poor relief, a village church, and sometimes a schoolmaster; collected taxes for the central government; maintained roads and bridges; and established common procedures for sowing, plowing, and harvesting crops. But villages were often dominated by richer peasants and proved highly resistant to innovations, such as new agricultural practices.

The Nobility

The nobles, who constituted about 2 or 3 percent of the European population, played a dominating role in society. Being born a noble automatically guaranteed a place at the top of the social order, with all of the attendant special privileges and rights. The legal privileges of the nobility included judgment by their peers, immunity from severe punishment, and exemption from many forms of taxation. Especially in central and eastern Europe, the rights of landlords over their serfs were overwhelming.

Nobles also played important roles in military and government affairs. Since medieval times, landed aristocrats had functioned as military officers. While monarchs found it impossible to exclude commoners from the ranks of officers, the tradition remained that nobles made the most natural and hence the best officers. The eighteenth-century nobility also played a significant role in the administrative machinery of state. In some countries, such as Prussia, the entire bureaucracy reflected aristocratic values. Moreover, in most of Europe, the landholding nobles controlled much of the life of their local districts.

Although the nobles clung to their privileged status and struggled to keep others out, almost everywhere the possession of money made it possible to enter the ranks of the nobility. Rights of nobility were frequently attached to certain lands, so purchasing the lands made one a noble; the acquisition of government offices also often conferred noble status.

THE ARISTOCRATIC WAY OF LIFE. The eighteenth-century country house in Britain fulfilled the desire of aristocrats for both elegance and privacy. The painting above by Richard Wilson shows a typical English country house of the eighteenth century surrounded by a simple and serene landscape. Thomas Gainsborough's *Conversation in the Park,* shown at left, captures the relaxed life of two aristocrats in the park of their country estate.

 *The Inhabitants of Towns and Cities*

Townspeople were still a distinct minority of the total population except in the Dutch Republic, Britain, and parts of Italy. At the end of the eighteenth century, about one-sixth of the French population lived in towns of two thousand inhabitants or more. The biggest city in Europe was London, with one million inhabitants; Paris numbered between 550,000 and 600,000. Altogether, Europe had at least twenty cities in twelve countries with populations over 100,000, including Naples, Lisbon, Moscow, St. Petersburg, Vienna, Amsterdam, Berlin, Rome, and Madrid.

Although urban dwellers were vastly outnumbered by rural inhabitants, towns played an important role in Western culture. The contrasts between a large city with its education, culture, and material consumption and the surrounding, often poverty-stricken countryside were striking, as evidenced by this British traveler's account of Russia's St. Petersburg in 1741:

> The country about Petersbourg has full as wild and desert a look as any in the Indies; you need not go above 200 paces out of the town to find yourself in a wild wood of firs, and such a low, marshy, boggy country that you would think God when he created the rest of the world for the use of mankind had created this for an inaccessible retreat for all sorts of wild beasts.[3]

Peasants often resented the prosperity of towns and their exploitation of the countryside to serve urban interests. Palermo in Sicily used one-third of the island's food production while paying only one-tenth of the taxes. Towns lived off the countryside not by buying their goods and crops but by using tithes, rents, and feudal dues to acquire peasant produce.

Many cities in western and even central Europe had a long tradition of patrician oligarchies that continued to control their communities by dominating town and city councils. Despite their domination, patricians constituted only a small minority of the urban population. Just below the patricians stood an upper crust of the middle classes: nonnoble officeholders, financiers and bankers, merchants, wealthy rentiers who lived off their investments, and important professionals, including lawyers. Another large urban group was the petty bourgeoisie or lower middle class made up of master artisans, shopkeepers, and small traders. Below them were the laborers or working classes. Much urban industry was still done in small guild workshops by masters, journeymen, and apprentices. Urban communities

Poverty in France

Unlike the British, who had a system of public-supported poor relief, the French responded to poverty with ad hoc policies when conditions became acute. This selection is taken from an intendant's report to the controller-general at Paris describing his suggestions for a program to relieve the grain shortages expected for the winter months.

M. de la Bourdonnaye, Intendant of Bordeaux, to the Controller-General, September 30, 1708

Having searched for the means of helping the people of Agen in this cruel situation and having conferred with His Eminence, the Bishop, it seems to us that three things are absolutely necessary if the people are not to starve during the winter.

Most of the inhabitants do not have seed to plant their fields. However, we decided that we would be going too far if we furnished it, because those who have seed would also apply [for more]. Moreover, we are persuaded that all the inhabitants will make strenuous efforts to find some seed, since they have every reason to expect prices to remain high next year. . . .

But this project will come to nothing if the collectors of the taille continue to be as strict in the exercise of their functions as they have been of late and continue to employ troops [to force collection]. Those inhabitants who have seed grain would sell it to be freed from an oppressive garrison, while those who must buy seed, since they have none left from their harvest and have scraped together a little money for this purchase, would prefer to give up that money [for taxes] when put under police constraint. To avoid this, I feel it is absolutely necessary that you order the receivers-general to reduce their operations during this winter, at least with respect to the poor. . . .

We are planning to import wheat for this region from Languedoc and Quercy, and we are confident that there will be enough. But there are two things to be feared: one is the greed of the merchants. When they see that general misery has put them in control of prices, they will raise them to the point where the calamity is almost as great as if there were no provisions at all. The other fear is that the artisans and the lowest classes, when they find themselves at the mercy of the merchants, will cause disorders and riots. As a protective measure, it would seem wise to establish two small storehouses. . . . Ten thousand ecus [30,000 livres] would be sufficient for each. . . .

A third point demanding our attention is the support of beggars among the poor, as well as of those who have no other resources than their wages. Since there will be very little work, these people will soon be reduced to starvation. We should establish public workshops to provide work as was done in 1693 and 1694. I should choose the most useful kind of work, located where there are the greatest number of poor. In this manner, we should rid ourselves of those who do not want to work and assure the others a moderate subsistence. For these workshops, we would need about 40,000 livres, or altogether 100,000 livres. The receiver-general of the taille of Agen could advance this sum. The 60,000 livres for the storehouses he would get back very soon. I shall await your orders on all of the above.

Marginal Comments by the Controller-General

Operations for the collection of the taille are to be suspended. The two storehouses are to be established; great care must be taken to put them to good use. The interest on the advances will be paid by the king. His Majesty has agreed to the establishment of the public workshops for the able-bodied poor and is willing to spend up to 40,000 livres on them this winter.

also had a large group of unskilled workers who served as servants, maids, and cooks at pitifully low wages.

Despite an end to the ravages of plague, eighteenth-century cities still experienced high death rates, especially among children, because of unsanitary living conditions, polluted water, and a lack of sewage facilities. One observer compared the stench of Hamburg to an open sewer that could be smelled for miles around. Overcrowding also exacerbated urban problems as cities continued to absorb rural immigrants. But cities proved no paradise for them, for unskilled workers found few employment opportunities. The result was a serious problem of poverty in the eighteenth century (see the box above).

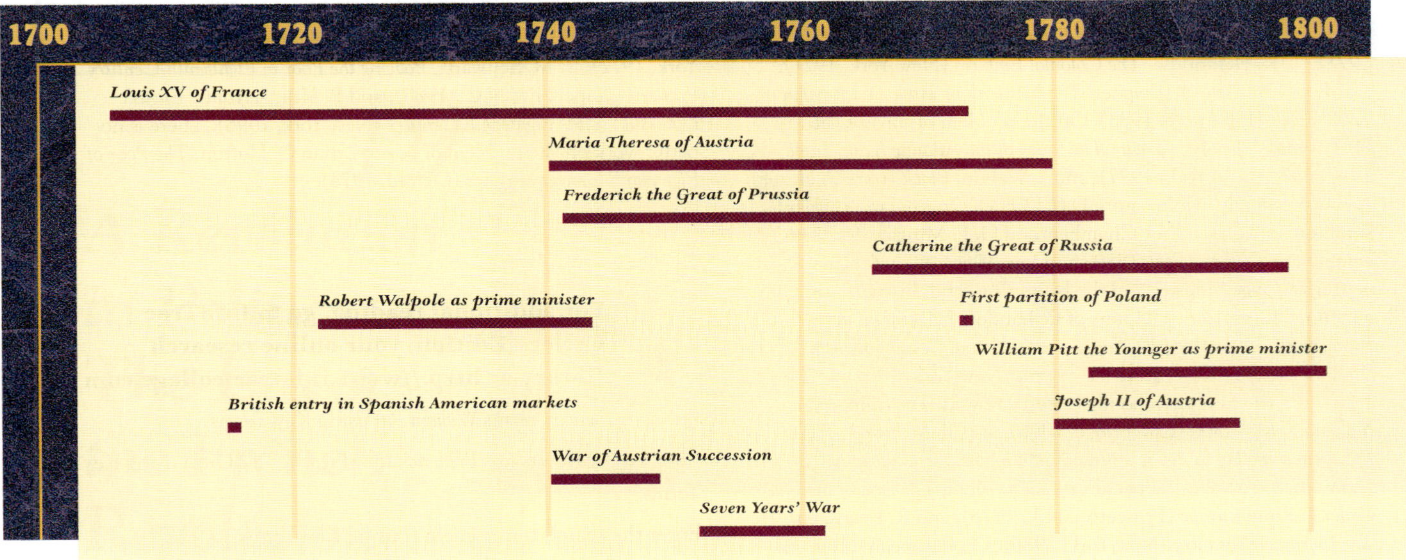

Conclusion

Everywhere in Europe at the beginning of the eighteenth century, the old order remained strong. Nobles, clerics, towns, and provinces all had privileges, some medieval in origin, others the result of the attempt of monarchies in the sixteenth and seventeenth centuries to gain financial support from their subjects. Everywhere in the eighteenth century, monarchs sought to enlarge their bureaucracies to raise taxes to support the new large standing armies that had originated in the seventeenth century. The existence of these armies made wars more likely. The existence of five great powers, two of them (France and Britain) in conflict in the East and the New World, initiated a new scale of strife; the Seven Years' War could legitimately be viewed as the first world war. The wars altered some boundaries on the European continent but were perhaps more significant for the victories that marked the emergence of Great Britain as the world's greatest naval and colonial power. Everywhere in Europe, increased demands for taxes to support these conflicts led to attacks on the privileged orders and a desire for change not met by the ruling monarchs.

At the same time, sustained population growth, dramatic changes in finance, trade, and industry, and the growth of poverty created tensions that undermined the traditional foundations of the old order. The inability of that old order to deal meaningfully with these changes led to a revolutionary outburst at the end of the eighteenth century that marked the beginning of the end for that old order.

Notes

1. Frederick II, *Forms of Government,* in Eugen Weber, *The Western Tradition* (Lexington, Mass., 1972), pp. 538, 544.
2. Quoted in Reinhold A. Dorwart, *The Administrative Reforms of Frederick William I of Prussia* (Cambridge, Mass., 1953), p. 36.
3. Igor Vinogradoff, "Russian Missions to London, 1711–1789: Further Extracts from the Cottrell Papers," *Oxford Slavonic Papers,* New Series (1982), 15:76.

Suggestions for Further Reading

For a good introduction to the political history of the eighteenth century, see the relevant chapters in the general works by Woloch, Anderson, and Birn listed in Chapter 17. See also G. Treasure, *The Making of Modern Europe, 1648–1780* (London, 1985); W. Doyle, *The Old European Order, 1660–1800* (Oxford, 1978); and O. Hufton, *Europe: Privilege and Protest, 1730–1789* (London, 1980). On enlightened absolutism, see H. M. Scott, ed., *Enlightened Absolutism: Reform and Reformers in Later Eighteenth-Century Europe* (Ann Arbor, Mich., 1990). Good studies of individual states include J. B. Owen, *The Eighteenth Century, 1714–1815* (London, 1975), on England; P. R. Campbell, *The Ancien Régime in France* (Oxford, 1988); E. Wangermann, *The Austrian Achievement, 1700–1800* (London, 1973); R. Vierhaus, *Germany in the Age of Absolutism* (Cambridge, 1988); J. Gagliardo, *Germany Under the Old Regime* (London, 1991); J. Lynch, *Bourbon Spain, 1700–1808* (Oxford, 1989); H. W. Koch, *A History of Prussia* (London, 1978); and P. Dukes, *The Making of Russian Absolutism, 1613–1801,* 2d ed. (London, 1990). Good biographies of some of Europe's monarchs include R. Asprey, *Frederick the Great: The Magnificent Enigma* (New York, 1986); I. De Madariaga, *Catherine the Great: A Short History* (New Haven, Conn., 1990); D. Deales, *Joseph II,* vol. 1 (Cambridge, 1987); and T. C. W. Blanning, *Joseph II* (New York, 1994). For a study of one of the wars of this age, see R. S. Browning, *The War of Austrian Succession* (London, 1995).

A good introduction to European population can be found in M. W. Flinn, *The European Demographic System, 1500–1820* (Brighton, England, 1981). An interesting perspective on economic history can be found in F. Braudel, *Capitalism and Material Life, 1400–1800* (New York, 1973). The subject of mercantile empires

of the fall of the Bastille by the Duc de La Rochefoucauld-Liancourt, he exclaimed, "Why, this is a revolt." "No, Sire," replied the duke, "it is a revolution."

Historians have long held that the modern history of Europe began with two significant transformations—the French Revolution and the Industrial Revolution (on the latter, see Chapter 20). Accordingly, the French Revolution has been portrayed as the major turning point in European political and social history when the institutions of the "old regime" were destroyed and a new order was created based on individual rights, representative institutions, and a concept of loyalty to the nation rather than the monarch. This perspective has certain limitations, however.

France was only one of a number of places in the Western world where the assumptions of the old order were challenged. Although some historians have used the phrase "democratic revolution" to refer to the upheavals of the late eighteenth and nineteenth centuries, it is probably more appropriate to speak not of a democratic movement but of a liberal movement to extend political rights and power to the bourgeoisie "possessing capital," people not of the aristocracy who were literate and had become wealthy through capitalist enterprises in trade, industry, and finance. The years preceding and accompanying the French Revolution included attempts at reform and revolt in the North American colonies, Britain, the Dutch Republic, some Swiss cities, and the Austrian Netherlands. The success of the American and French Revolutions makes them the center of attention for this chapter.

Not all of the decadent privileges that characterized the old European regime were destroyed in 1789, however. The revolutionary upheaval of the era, especially in France, did create new liberal and national political ideals, summarized in the French revolutionary slogan, "Liberty, Equality, Fraternity," that transformed France and were then spread to other European countries through the conquests of Napoleon.

◆ The Beginnings of the Revolutionary Era: The American Revolution

At the end of the Seven Years' War in 1763, Great Britain had become the world's greatest colonial power. In North America, Britain controlled Canada and the lands east of the Mississippi (see Map 19.1). After the Seven Years' War, British policy makers sought to obtain new revenues from the thirteen American colonies to pay for British army expenses in defending the colonists. An attempt to levy new taxes by the Stamp Act in 1765 led to riots and the law's quick repeal.

The Americans and the British had different conceptions of empire. The British envisioned a single empire with Parliament as the supreme authority throughout. Only Parliament could make laws for all the people in the empire, including the American colonists. The Americans, in contrast, had their own representative assemblies. They believed that neither the king nor Parliament had any right to interfere in their internal affairs and that no tax could be levied without the consent of an assembly whose members actually represented the people.

Crisis followed crisis in the 1770s until 1776, when the colonists decided to declare their independence from the British Empire. On July 4, 1776, the Second Continental Congress announced a declaration of independence written by Thomas Jefferson. A stirring political document, the Declaration of Independence affirmed the Enlightenment's natural rights of "life, liberty, and the pursuit of happiness" and declared the colonies to be "free and independent states absolved from all allegiance to the British crown." The war for American independence had formally begun.

Of great importance to the colonies' cause was the assistance provided by foreign countries that were eager to gain revenge for earlier defeats at the hands of the British. The French supplied arms and money to the rebels from the beginning of the war, and French officers and soldiers also served in the American Continental Army under George Washington as commander in chief. When the British army of General Cornwallis was forced to surrender to a combined American and French army and French fleet under Washington at Yorktown in 1781, the British government decided to call it quits. The Treaty of Paris, signed in 1783, recognized the independence of the American colonies and granted the Americans control of the territory from the Appalachians to the Mississippi River.

Toward a New Nation

The thirteen American colonies had gained their independence as the United States of America, but a fear of concentrated power and concern for their

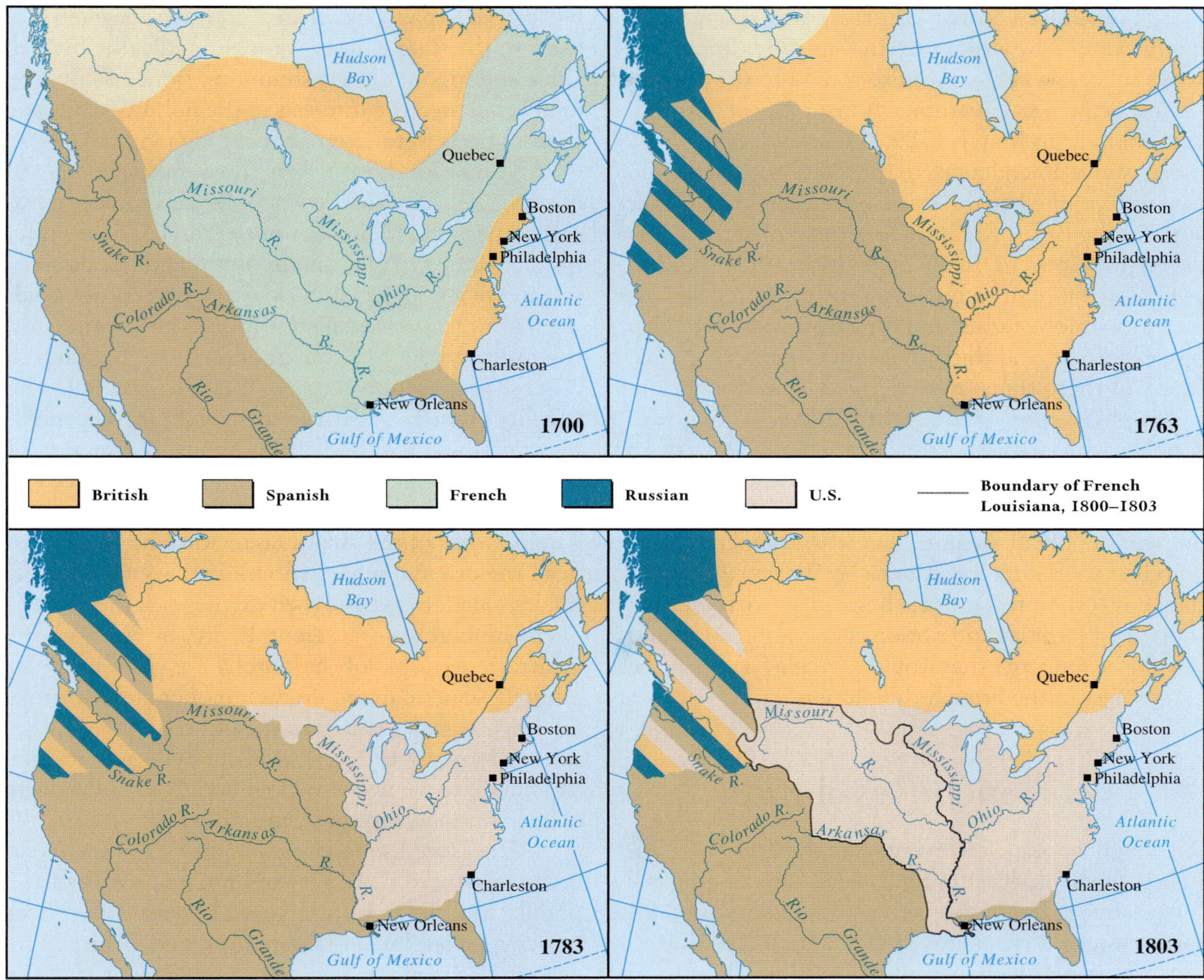

MAP 19.1 North America, 1700–1803.

own interests caused them to have little enthusiasm for establishing a united nation with a strong central government. The Articles of Confederation, ratified in 1781, did little to provide for a strong central government. A movement for a different form of national government soon arose. In the summer of 1787, fifty-five delegates attended a convention in Philadelphia to revise the Articles of Confederation. The convention's delegates—wealthy, politically experienced, and well educated—rejected revision and decided to devise a new constitution.

The proposed constitution created a central government distinct from and superior to the governments of the individual states. The national government was given the power to levy taxes, raise a national army, regulate domestic and foreign trade, and create a national currency. The central or federal government was divided into three branches, each with some power to check the functioning of the others. A president would serve as the chief executive with the power to execute laws, veto the legislature's acts, supervise foreign affairs, and direct military forces. Legislative power was vested in the second branch of government, a bicameral legislature composed of the Senate, elected by the state legislatures, and the House of Representatives, elected directly by the people. The Supreme Court and other courts "as deemed necessary" by Congress served as the third branch of government. They would enforce the Constitution as the "supreme law of the land."

The United States Constitution was approved by the states—by a slim margin—in 1788. Important to its success was the promise to add to it a "bill of rights" as the new government's first piece of business. Accordingly, in March 1789, the new Congress proposed twelve amendments to the Constitution; the ten that were ratified by the states have been known ever since as the Bill of Rights. These guaranteed freedom of religion, speech, the press, petition, and assembly, as well as the right to bear arms, be protected against unreasonable searches and arrests, trial by jury, due process of law, and the protection of property rights. Many of these rights were derived from the natural rights philosophy of the eighteenth-century philosophes, which was popular among the American colonists. Many European intellectuals saw the American Revolution as the embodiment of the Enlightenment's political dreams. And when French officers who had fought in the American War for Independence returned to France, they did so with ideas of individual liberties and notions of republicanism and popular sovereignty that would soon play a role in the early stages of the French Revolution.

The French Revolution

Although we associate events like the French Revolution with sudden changes, such events involve long-range problems as well as immediate precipitating forces. The causes of the French Revolution must be sought in a multifaceted examination of French society and its problems in the late eighteenth century.

Background to the French Revolution

The long-range or indirect causes of the French Revolution must first be sought in the condition of French society. Before the Revolution, French society was grounded in the idea of privilege or an inequality of rights. The population of 27 million was divided, as it had been since the Middle Ages, into legal categories known as the three orders or estates.

THE THREE ESTATES

The First Estate consisted of the clergy and numbered about 130,000 people. The church owned approximately 10 percent of the land. Clergy were exempt from the *taille*, France's chief tax, although the church had agreed to pay a "voluntary" contribution every five years to the state. Clergy were also radically divided, since the higher clergy, stemming from aristocratic families, shared the interests of the nobility while the parish priests were often poor commoners.

The Second Estate was the nobility, composed of no more than 350,000 people who nevertheless owned perhaps 30 percent of the land. The nobility had continued to play an important and even crucial role in French society in the eighteenth century, holding many of the leading positions in the government, the military, the law courts, and the higher church offices. The French nobility was also divided. The nobility of the robe derived its status from officeholding, a pathway that had often enabled commoners to attain noble rank. These nobles now dominated the royal law courts and important administrative offices. The nobility of the sword claimed to be descended from the original medieval nobility. As a group, the nobles sought to expand their privileges at the expense of the monarchy—to defend liberty by resisting the arbitrary actions of monarchy, as some nobles asserted—and to maintain their monopolistic control over positions in the military, church, and government. Moreover, the possession of privileges remained a hallmark of the nobility. Common to all nobles were tax exemptions, especially from the *taille*.

The Third Estate, the commoners of French society, constituted the overwhelming majority of the population. They were divided by vast differences in occupation, level of education, and wealth. The peasants, who alone made up 75 to 80 percent of the total population, were by far the largest segment of the third estate. They owned about 35 to 40 percent of the land, although these holdings varied from area to area and more than half the peasants had little or no land on which to support themselves. Serfdom no longer existed on any large scale in France, but French peasants still had obligations to their local landlords that they deeply resented. These "relics of feudalism," survivals from an earlier age, included the payment of fees for the use of village facilities, such as the flour mill, community oven, and winepress, as well as tithes to the clergy.

Another part of the Third Estate consisted of skilled artisans, shopkeepers, and other wage earners in the cities. Although the eighteenth century had been a period of rapid urban growth, 90 percent of French towns had fewer than ten thousand inhabitants, and only nine cities had more than fifty thousand. In the eighteenth century, consumer prices rose faster than wages, with the result that these urban groups experienced a noticeable decline in purchasing power. In Paris, for example, income lagged behind food prices and well behind a 140 percent rise in rents for working people in skilled and unskilled trades. The economic discontent of this segment of the third estate—and often simply the struggle for survival—led the common people to play an important role in the French Revolution, especially in the city of Paris.

About 8 percent, or 2.3 million people, constituted the bourgeoisie or middle class who owned about 20 to 25 percent of the land. This group included merchants, bankers, and industrialists who controlled the resources of trade, finance, and manufacturing and benefited from the economic prosperity after 1730. The bourgeoisie also included professional people—lawyers, holders of public offices, doctors, and writers. Many members of the bourgeoisie sought security and status through the purchase of land. They had their own set of grievances because they were often excluded from the social and political privileges monopolized by nobles. At the same time, remarkable similarities existed at the upper levels of society between the wealthier bourgeoisie and the nobility. It was still possible for wealthy middle-class individuals to enter the ranks of the nobility by obtaining public offices and entering the nobility of the robe. During this century, 6,500 new noble families were created in this way. Moreover, the new and critical ideas of the Enlightenment proved attractive to both aristocrats and bourgeoisie. Members of both groups shared a common world of liberal political thought. Both aristocratic and bourgeois elites, long accustomed to a new socioeconomic reality based on wealth and economic achievement, were increasingly frustrated by a monarchical system resting on privileges and on an old and rigid social order based on the concept of estates. The opposition of these elites to the old order ultimately led them to take drastic action against the monarchical regime, although they soon split over the problem of how far to proceed in eliminating traditional privileges. In a real sense, the Revolution had its origins in political grievances.

OTHER PROBLEMS FACING THE FRENCH MONARCHY

The inability of the French monarchy to deal with new social realities was exacerbated by specific problems in the 1780s. Although France had enjoyed fifty years of growth overall, periodic economic crises still occurred. Bad harvests in 1787 and 1788 and an incipient manufacturing depression resulted in food shortages, rising prices for food and other necessities, and unemployment in the cities. The number of poor, estimated by some analysts at almost one-third of the population, reached crisis proportions on the eve of the Revolution.

The immediate cause of the French Revolution was the near collapse of government finances. French governmental expenditures continued to grow due to costly wars and royal extravagance. On the verge of a complete financial collapse, the government of Louis XVI was finally forced to call a meeting of the Estates-General, the French parliamentary body that had not met since 1614.

The Estates-General consisted of representatives from the three orders of French society. In the elections for the Estates-General, the government had ruled that the Third Estate should get double representation (it did, after all, constitute 97 percent of the population). Consequently, while both the First Estate (the clergy) and the Second Estate (the nobility) had about three hundred delegates each, the commoners had almost six hundred representatives. Two-thirds of the latter were people with legal training, and three-fourths were from towns with over two thousand inhabitants, giving the Third Estate a particularly strong legal and urban representation. Most members of the Third Estate advocated a regular constitutional government that would abolish the fiscal privileges of the church and nobility as the major way to regenerate France.

FROM ESTATES-GENERAL TO NATIONAL ASSEMBLY

The Estates-General opened at Versailles on May 5, 1789. It was divided from the start over the question of whether voting should be by order or by head (each delegate having one vote). Traditionally, each order would vote separately; each would have veto power over the other two, thus guaranteeing aristocratic control over reforms. But the Third Estate was opposed to this approach and pushed its demands for voting by head. Since it had double representation, with the assistance of liberal nobles and clerics, it could turn the three estates into a single-chamber legislature that would reform France in its own way. Most delegates still desired to make changes within a framework of respect for the authority of the king;

THE TENNIS COURT OATH. **Finding themselves locked out of their regular meeting place on June 20, 1789, the deputies of the Third Estate met instead in the nearby tennis courts of the Jeu de Paume and committed themselves to continue to meet until they established a new constitution for France. In this painting, the neoclassicist Jacques-Louis David presents a dramatic rendering of the Tennis Court Oath.**

revival or reform did not mean the overthrow of traditional institutions. But when the First Estate declared in favor of voting by order, the Third Estate felt compelled to respond in a significant fashion. On June 17, 1789, the Third Estate voted to constitute itself a "national assembly" and decided to draw up a constitution. Three days later, on June 20, the deputies of the Third Estate arrived at their meeting place only to find the door locked; thereupon they moved to a nearby indoor tennis court and swore (in what became known as the Tennis Court Oath) that they would continue to meet until they had produced a French constitution. These actions of June 17 and June 20 constitute the first step in the French Revolution since the Third Estate had no legal right to act as the National Assembly. This bold move, largely the work of the lawyers of the Third Estate, was soon in jeopardy, however, as the king sided with the First Estate and threatened to dissolve the Estates-General. Louis XVI now prepared to use force.

The intervention of the common people, however, in a series of urban and rural uprisings in July and August 1789, saved the Third Estate from the king's attempt to stop the revolution. The most famous of the urban risings was the fall of the Bastille (see the box on p. 390). Parisians organized a popular force and on July 14 attacked the Bastille, a royal armory. But the Bastille had also been a state prison, and though it now contained only seven prisoners (five forgers and two insane people), its fall quickly became a popular symbol of triumph over despotism. Paris was abandoned to the insurgents, and Louis XVI was soon informed that the royal troops were unreliable. Louis's acceptance of that reality signaled the collapse of royal authority; the king could no longer enforce his will. The fall of the Bastille had saved the National Assembly.

At the same time, independent of what was going on in Paris, popular revolts broke out in numerous cities. The collapse of royal authority in the cities was paralleled by peasant insurrections in the countryside. A growing resentment of the entire landholding system, with its fees and obligations, created the conditions for a popular uprising. The fall of the Bastille and the king's apparent capitulation to the demands of the Third Estate now encouraged peasants to take matters into their own hands. From July 19 to August 3, peasant rebellions occurred throughout France. The agrarian revolts served as a backdrop to the Great Fear, a vast panic that spread like wildfire through France between July 20 and August 6. Fear of invasion by foreign troops, aided by a supposed aristocratic plot, encouraged the formation of more citizens' militias and permanent committees. The greatest impact of the agrarian revolts

STORMING OF THE BASTILLE. Louis XVI planned to use force to dissolve the Estates-General, but a number of rural and urban uprisings by the common people prevented this action. The fall of the Bastille, depicted here by an unidentified painter, is perhaps the most famous of the urban risings.

and Great Fear was on the National Assembly meeting in Versailles.

The Destruction of the Old Regime

One of the first acts of the National Assembly was to destroy the relics of feudalism or aristocratic privileges. On the night of August 4, 1789, the National Assembly in an astonishing session voted to abolish seigneurial rights as well as the fiscal privileges of nobles, clergy, towns, and provinces. On August 26, the assembly provided the ideological foundation for its actions and an educational device for the nation by adopting the Declaration of the Rights of Man and the Citizen (see the box on p. 391). This charter of basic liberties began with a ringing affirmation of "the natural and imprescriptible rights of man" to "liberty, property, security and resistance to oppression." It went on to affirm the destruction of aristocratic privileges by proclaiming an end to exemptions from taxation, freedom and equal rights for all men, and access to public office based on talent. The monarchy was restricted, and all citizens were to have the right to take part in the legislative process. Freedom of speech and the press were coupled with the outlawing of arbitrary arrests.

The Declaration also raised another important issue. Did the proclamation's ideal of equal rights for all men also include women? Many deputies insisted that it did, at least in terms of civil liberties, provided

The Fall of the Bastille

On July 14, 1789, Parisian crowds in search of weapons attacked and captured the royal armory known as the Bastille. It had also been a state prison, and its fall marked the triumph of "liberty" over despotism. This intervention of the Parisian populace saved the Third Estate from Louis XVI's attempted counterrevolution.

A Parisian Newspaper Account of the Fall of the Bastille

First, the people tried to enter this fortress by the Rue St.-Antoine, this fortress, which no one has ever penetrated against the wishes of this frightful despotism and where the monster still resided. The treacherous governor had put out a flag of peace. So a confident advance was made; a detachment of French Guards, with perhaps five to six thousand armed bourgeois, penetrated the Bastille's outer courtyards, but as soon as some six hundred persons had passed over the first drawbridge, the bridge was raised and artillery fire mowed down several French Guards and some soldiers; the cannon fired on the town, and the people took fright; a large number of individuals were killed or wounded; but then they rallied and took shelter from the fire. . . . Meanwhile, they tried to locate some cannon; they attacked from the water's edge through the gardens of the arsenal, and from there made an orderly siege; they advanced from various directions, beneath a ceaseless round of fire. It was a terrible scene. . . . The fighting grew steadily more intense; the citizens had become hardened to the fire; from all directions they clambered onto the roofs or broke into the rooms; as soon as an enemy appeared among the turrets on the tower, he was fixed in the sights of a hundred guns and mown down in an instant; meanwhile cannon fire was hurriedly directed against the second drawbridge, which it pierced, breaking the chains; in vain did the cannon on the tower reply, for most people were sheltered from it; the fury was at its height; people bravely faced death and every danger; women, in their eagerness, helped us to the utmost; even the children, after the discharge of fire from the fortress, ran here and there picking up the bullets and shot; [and so the Bastille fell and the governor, De Launey, was captured]. . . . Serene and blessed liberty, for the first time, has at last been introduced into this abode of horrors, this frightful refuge of monstrous despotism and its crimes.

Meanwhile, they get ready to march; they leave amidst an enormous crowd; the applause, the outbursts of joy, the insults, the oaths hurled at the treacherous prisoners of war; everything is confused; cries of vengeance and of pleasure issue from every heart; the conquerors, glorious and covered in honor, carry their arms and the spoils of the conquered, the flags of victory, the militia mingling with the soldiers of the fatherland, the victory laurels offered them from every side, all this created a frightening and splendid spectacle. On arriving at the square, the people, anxious to avenge themselves, allowed neither De Launey nor the other officers to reach the place of trial; they seized them from the hands of their conquerors, and trampled them underfoot one after the other. De Launey was struck by a thousand blows, his head was cut off and hoisted on the end of a pike with blood streaming down all sides. . . . This glorious day must amaze our enemies, and finally usher in for us the triumph of justice and liberty. In the evening, there were celebrations.

that, as one said, "women do not aspire to exercise political rights and functions." Olympe de Gouges, a playwright and pamphleteer, refused to accept this exclusion of women from political rights. Echoing the words of the official declaration, she penned a Declaration of the Rights of Woman and the Female Citizen, in which she insisted that women should have all the same rights as men. The National Assembly ignored her demands.

In the meantime, Louis XVI had remained inactive at Versailles. He did refuse, however, to promulgate the decrees on the abolition of feudalism and the Declaration of Rights, but an unexpected turn of events soon forced the king to change his mind. On October 5, thousands of Parisian women, described by one eyewitness as "detachments of women coming up from every direction, armed with broomsticks, lances, pitchforks, swords, pistols and muskets," marched to

Declaration of the Rights of Man and the Citizen

One of the important documents of the French Revolution, the Declaration of the Rights of Man and the Citizen, was adopted in August 1789 by the National Assembly. The declaration affirmed that "men are born and remain free and equal in rights," that governments must protect these natural rights, and that political power is derived from the people.

Declaration of the Rights of Man and the Citizen

The representatives of the French people, organized as a national assembly, considering that ignorance, neglect, and scorn of the rights of man are the sole causes of public misfortunes and of corruption of governments, have resolved to display in a solemn declaration the natural, inalienable, and sacred rights of man, so that this declaration, constantly in the presence of all members of society, will continually remind them of their rights and their duties. . . . Consequently, the National Assembly recognizes and declares, in the presence and under the auspices of the Supreme Being, the following rights of man and citizen:

1. Men are born and remain free and equal in rights; social distinctions can be established only for the common benefit.
2. The aim of every political association is the conservation of the natural and imprescriptible rights of man; these rights are liberty, property, security, and resistance to oppression.
3. The source of all sovereignty is located in essence in the nation; no body, no individual can exercise authority which does not emanate from it expressly.
4. Liberty consists in being able to do anything that does not harm another person. . . .
6. The law is the expression of the general will; all citizens have the right to concur personally or through their representatives in its formation; it must be the same for all, whether it protects or punishes. All citizens being equal in its eyes are equally admissible to all honors, positions, and public employments, according to their capabilities and without other distinctions than those of their virtues and talents.
7. No man can be accused, arrested, or detained except in cases determined by the law, and according to the forms which it has prescribed. . . .
10. No one may be disturbed because of his opinions, even religious, provided that their public demonstration does not disturb the public order established by law.
11. The free communication of thoughts and opinions is one of the most precious rights of man: every citizen can therefore freely speak, write, and print. . . .
12. The guaranteeing of the rights of man and citizen necessitates a public force; this force is therefore instituted for the advantage of all, and not for the private use of those to whom it is entrusted. . . .
14. Citizens have the right to determine for themselves or through their representatives the need for taxation of the public, to consent to it freely, to investigate its use, and to determine its rate, basis, collection, and duration.
15. Society has the right to demand an accounting of his administration from every public agent.
16. Any society in which guarantees of rights are not assured nor the separation of powers determined has no constitution.
17. Property being an inviolable and sacred right, no one may be deprived of it unless public necessity, legally determined, clearly requires such action, and then only on condition of a just and prior indemnity.

Versailles, 12 miles away, and insisted that the royal family return to Paris. On October 6, the king complied. As a goodwill gesture, he brought along wagonloads of flour from the palace stores. All were escorted by women armed with pikes (some of which held the severed heads of the king's guards), singing, "We are bringing back the baker, the baker's wife, and the baker's boy" (the king, queen, and their son). The king now accepted the National Assembly's decrees and was virtually a prisoner in Paris.

Because the Catholic church was viewed as an important pillar of the old order, it soon felt the impact of reform. Most of the lands of the church were confiscated, and the church was also secularized. In July 1790, the Civil Constitution of the Clergy was put into effect. Both bishops and priests of the Catholic church were to be elected by the people and paid by the state. All clergy were also required to swear an oath of allegiance to the Civil Constitution. Only 54 percent of the French parish clergy took the oath, and the majority of bishops refused. The Catholic church, still an important institution in the life of the French people, now became an enemy of the Revolution.

A NEW CONSTITUTION

By 1791, the National Assembly had completed a new constitution that established a limited, constitutional monarchy. There was still a monarch (now called "king of the French"), but he enjoyed few powers not subject to review by the new Legislative Assembly. The Legislative Assembly, in which sovereign power was vested, was to sit for two years and consist of 745 representatives chosen by an indirect system of election that preserved power in the hands of the more affluent members of society. Only active citizens (men over the age of twenty-five paying taxes equivalent in value to three days' unskilled labor) could vote for electors (men paying taxes equal in value to ten days' labor). This relatively small group of fifty thousand electors then chose the deputies. To qualify as a deputy, one had to pay taxes equal in value to fifty-four days' labor.

By 1791, a revolutionary consensus that was largely the work of the wealthier bourgeoisie had moved France into a drastic reordering of the old regime. By mid-1791, however, this consensus faced growing opposition from clerics angered by the Civil Constitution of the Clergy, lower classes hurt by a rise in the cost of living, peasants angry that dues had still not been abandoned, and political clubs like the Jacobins who offered more radical solutions to France's problems. In addition, by mid-1791, the government was still facing severe financial difficulties due to massive tax evasion. Despite all of their problems, however, the bourgeois politicians in charge remained relatively unified on the basis of their trust in the king. But Louis XVI disastrously undercut them. Upset with the whole turn of revolutionary events, he attempted to flee France in June 1791 and almost succeeded before being recognized, captured, and brought back to Paris. In this unsettled situation, with a discredited and seemingly disloyal monarch, the new Legislative Assembly held its first session in October 1791. France's relations with the rest of Europe soon led to Louis' downfall.

Over a period of time, some Europeans had become concerned about the French example and feared that revolution would spread to their countries. On August 27, 1791, Emperor Leopold II of Austria and King Frederick William II of Prussia invited other European monarchs to use force to reestablish monarchical authority in France. Insulted by this threat, the Legislative Assembly declared war on Austria on April 20, 1792.

The French fared badly in the initial fighting, and loud recriminations were soon heard in Paris. A frantic search for scapegoats began; as one observer noted, "Everywhere you hear the cry that the king is betraying us, the generals are betraying us, that nobody is to be trusted; . . . that Paris will be taken in six weeks by the Austrians. . . . We are on a volcano ready to spout flames."[1] Defeats in war coupled with economic shortages in the spring reinvigorated popular groups that had been dormant since the previous summer and led to renewed political demonstrations, especially against the king. Radical Parisian political groups, declaring themselves an insurrectionary "commune," organized a mob attack on the royal palace and Legislative Assembly in August 1792, took the king captive, and forced the assembly to suspend the monarchy and call for a national convention, chosen on the basis of universal male suffrage, to decide on the future form of government. The French Revolution was about to enter a more radical stage as power passed from the assembly to the new Paris Commune, composed of many who proudly called themselves the *sans-culottes*, ordinary patriots without fine clothes. Although it has become customary to equate the more radical sans-culottes with working people or the poor, many were merchants and better-off artisans who were often the elite of their neighborhoods.

The Radical Revolution

In September 1792, the newly elected National Convention began its sessions. Although it was called to draft a new constitution, it also acted as the sovereign ruling body of France. Socially, the composition of the National Convention was similar to its predecessors. Dominated by lawyers, professionals, and property owners, two-thirds of its deputies were under forty-five, and almost all had had political experience as a result of the Revolution. Almost all were also intensely distrustful of the king and his activities. It was therefore no surprise that the Convention's first major step on September 21 was to abolish the monarchy and establish a republic. At the beginning of 1793, the Convention passed a decree condemning Louis XVI to death. With his execution on January 21, 1793, the destruction of the old regime was complete. There could be no turning back. But the dispatch of the king produced new challenges by creating new enemies for the Revolution both at home and abroad while strengthening groups that were already opposed to it.

In Paris, the local government, the Commune, led by the newly appointed minister of justice, Georges Danton, favored radical change and put constant pressure on the Convention, pushing it to ever more radical positions. Moreover, the National Convention still did not rule all of France. Peasants in the west as well as inhabitants of France's major provincial cities refused to accept the authority of the Convention. Domestic turmoil was paralleled by a foreign crisis. By the time the king was executed, most of Europe—an informal coalition of Austria, Prussia, Spain, Portugal, Britain, the Dutch Republic, and Russia—had aligned against France, and by late spring some members of the coalition were poised to invade France in an effort to destroy the revolutionaries and reestablish the old regime.

To meet these crises, the Convention gave broad powers to an executive committee of twelve known as the Committee of Public Safety, which came to be dominated by Maximilien Robespierre, the leader of the Jacobins. For a twelve-month period, this committee gave the country the leadership it needed to weather the domestic and foreign crises of 1793.

A NATION IN ARMS

To meet the foreign crisis and save the republic from its foreign enemies, the Committee of Public Safety decreed a universal mobilization of the nation on August 23, 1793:

> Young men will fight, young men are called to conquer. Married men will forge arms, transport military baggage and guns and prepare food supplies. Women, who at long last are to take their rightful place in the revolution and follow their true destiny, will forget their futile tasks: their delicate hands will work at making clothes for soldiers; they will make tents and they will extend their tender care to shelters where the defenders of the [nation] will receive the help that their wounds require. Children will make lint of old cloth. It is for them that we are fighting: children, those beings destined to gather all the fruits of the revolution, will raise their pure hands toward the skies. And old men, performing their missions again, as of yore, will be guided to the public squares of the cities where they will kindle the courage of young warriors and preach the doctrines of hate for kings and the unity of the Republic.[2]

EXECUTION OF THE KING. At the beginning of 1793, the National Convention sentenced the king to death, and on January 21 of that year, Louis XVI was executed. As seen in this engraving by Carnavalet, the execution of the king was accomplished using a new revolutionary device, the guillotine.

In less than a year, the French revolutionary government had raised an army of 650,000; by September 1794, it numbered 1,169,000. The Republic's army was the largest ever seen in European history. It pushed the allies back across the Rhine and even conquered the Austrian Netherlands to the north (see Map 19.2).

Historians have focused on the importance of the French revolutionary army as an important step in the creation of modern nationalism. Previously, wars had been fought between governments or ruling dynasties by relatively small armies of professional

MAP 19.2 French Conquests in the Revolutionary Wars.

soldiers. The new French army, however, was the creation of a "people's" government; its wars were now "people's" wars. The entire nation was to be involved in the war. But when dynastic wars became people's wars, warfare increased in ferocity and lack of restraint. Although innocent civilians had suffered in the earlier struggles, now the carnage became appalling at times. The wars of the French revolutionary era opened the door to the total war of the modern world.

THE COMMITTEE OF PUBLIC SAFETY AND THE REIGN OF TERROR

To meet the domestic crisis, the National Convention and the Committee of Public Safety established the Reign of Terror. Revolutionary courts were organized to protect the revolutionary Republic from its internal enemies (see the box on p. 397). In the course of nine months, sixteen thousand people were officially killed under the blade of the guillotine, a revolutionary device for the quick and efficient separation of heads from bodies. But the true number of the Terror's victims was probably closer to fifty thousand. The bulk of the Terror's executions took place in places that had been in open rebellion against the authority of the National Convention. The Terror demonstrated no class prejudice. Estimates are that the nobles constituted 8 percent of its victims; the middle classes, 25; the clergy, 6; and the peasant and laboring classes, 60. To the Committee of Public Safety, this bloodletting was only a temporary expedient. After the wars and domestic emergencies were

CITIZENS ENLISTING IN THE NEW FRENCH ARMY. To save the Republic from its foreign enemies, the National Convention created a new revolutionary army of unprecedented size. In this painting, citizens joyfully hasten to sign up at recruitment tables set up in the streets. Officials are distributing coins to those who have enrolled.

over, there would arise a "republic of virtue" in which the Declaration of Rights of the Man and Citizen would be fully established.

Military force in the form of revolutionary armies was used to bring recalcitrant cities and districts back under the control of the National Convention. Because Lyons was France's second city after Paris and had defied the National Convention during a time when the Republic was in peril, the Committee of Public Safety decided to make an example of it. By April 1794, a total of 1,880 citizens of Lyons had been executed. When guillotining proved too slow, cannon fire and grapeshot were used to blow condemned men into open graves. A German observed:

> Whole ranges of houses, always the most handsome, burnt. The churches, convents, and all the dwellings of the former patricians were in ruins. When I came to the guillotine, the blood of those who had been executed a few hours beforehand was still running in the street. . . . I said to a group of sans-culottes that it would be decent to clear away all this human blood. Why should it be cleared? one of them said to me. It's the blood of aristocrats and rebels. The dogs should lick it up.[3]

In western France, revolutionary armies were also brutal in defeating the rebel armies. The commander of the revolutionary army ordered that no quarter be given: "The road to Laval is strewn with corpses. Women, priests, monks, children, all have been put to death. I have spared nobody." Perhaps the most notorious act of violence occurred in Nantes, where victims were executed by sinking them in barges in the Loire River.

 THE "REPUBLIC OF VIRTUE"

Along with the Terror, the Committee of Public Safety took other steps both to control France and to create a new republican order and new republican citizens. By spring 1793, it was sending "representatives on mission" as agents of the central government to all parts of France to implement the laws dealing with the wartime emergency. The committee also attempted to provide some economic controls by establishing price limits on goods declared of first necessity, ranging from food and drink to fuel and clothing. The controls failed to work very well since the government lacked the machinery to enforce it.

In its attempts to create a new order, the National Convention also pursued a policy of dechristianization. A new calendar was instituted in which years would no longer be numbered from the birth of Jesus but from September 22, 1792, the first day of the French Republic. The new calendar also eliminated Sundays and church holidays. The word *saint* was removed from street names, churches were pillaged and closed by revolutionary armies, and priests were encouraged to marry. In Paris, the cathedral of Notre

Dame was designated a "temple of reason"; in November 1793, a public ceremony dedicated to the worship of reason was held in the former cathedral in which patriotic maidens adorned in white dresses paraded where the high altar had once stood.

By the summer of 1794, the French had been successful on the battlefield against their foreign foes. The military successes meant that the Terror no longer served much purpose. But the Terror continued because Robespierre, now its dominant figure, had become obsessed with purifying the body politic of all the corrupt. Many deputies in the National Convention feared, however, that they were not safe while Robespierre was free to act. An anti-Robespierre coalition in the National Convention gathered enough votes to condemn him. Robespierre was guillotined on July 28, 1794.

Reaction and the Directory

After the death of Robespierre, revolutionary fervor began to give way to the Thermidorean Reaction, named after the month of Thermidor on the new French calendar. The Terror began to abate. The National Convention curtailed the power of the Committee of Public Safety, shut down the Jacobin club, and attempted to provide better protection for its deputies against the Parisian mobs. Churches were allowed to reopen for public worship. Economic regulation was dropped in favor of laissez-faire policies, another clear

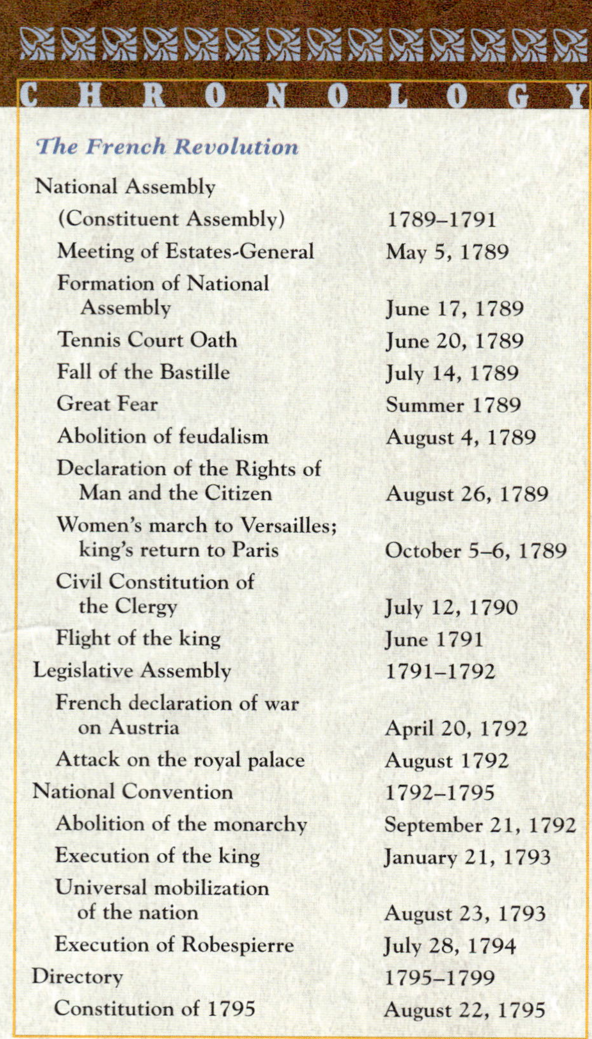

CHRONOLOGY

The French Revolution

Event	Date
National Assembly (Constituent Assembly)	1789–1791
Meeting of Estates-General	May 5, 1789
Formation of National Assembly	June 17, 1789
Tennis Court Oath	June 20, 1789
Fall of the Bastille	July 14, 1789
Great Fear	Summer 1789
Abolition of feudalism	August 4, 1789
Declaration of the Rights of Man and the Citizen	August 26, 1789
Women's march to Versailles; king's return to Paris	October 5–6, 1789
Civil Constitution of the Clergy	July 12, 1790
Flight of the king	June 1791
Legislative Assembly	1791–1792
French declaration of war on Austria	April 20, 1792
Attack on the royal palace	August 1792
National Convention	1792–1795
Abolition of the monarchy	September 21, 1792
Execution of the king	January 21, 1793
Universal mobilization of the nation	August 23, 1793
Execution of Robespierre	July 28, 1794
Directory	1795–1799
Constitution of 1795	August 22, 1795

WOMEN PATRIOTS. **Women played a variety of roles in the events of the French Revolution. This picture shows a women's patriotic club discussing the decrees of the National Convention, an indication that some women had become highly politicized by the upheavals of the Revolution.**

A Victim of the Reign of Terror

The Reign of Terror created a repressive environment in which even innocent people could be accused of crimes against the Republic. As seen in this letter by Anne-Félicité Guinée, wife of a wigmaker, merely insulting an official could lead to arrest and imprisonment.

Letter of Anne-Félicité Guinée

Citizen Anne-Félicité Guinée, twenty-four years old . . ., informs you that she was arrested at the Place des Droits de l'Homme, where I had gone to get butter. I point out to you that for a long time I have had to feed the members in my household on bread and cheese and that, tired of complaints from my husband and my boys, I was compelled to go wait in line to get something to eat. For three days I had been going to the same market without being able to get anything, despite the fact that I had waited from 7 or 8 A.M. until 5 or 6 P.M. After the distribution of butter on the twenty-second, . . . a citizen came over to me and said that I was in very delicate condition. To that I answered, "You can't be delicate and be on your legs for so long. I wouldn't have come if there were any other food." He replied that I needed to drink milk. I answered that I had men in my house who worked and that I couldn't nourish them with milk, that I was convinced that if he, the speaker, was sensitive to the difficulty of obtaining food, he would not vex me so, and that he was an imbecile and wanted to play despot, and no one had that right. Here, on the spot, I was arrested and brought to the guard house. I wanted to explain myself. I was silenced and dragged off to prison. . . . About 7 P.M., I was led to the Revolutionary Committee [of the section], where I was called a counterrevolutionary and was told I was asking for the guillotine because I told them I preferred death to being treated ignominiously the way he was treating me. . . . I was asked if I knew whom I had called a despot. I answered, "I didn't know him," and I was told that he was the commander of the post. I said that he was more [a commander] beneath his own roof than anyone, given that he was there to maintain order and not to provoke bad feelings. . . . I was told that I had done three times more than was needed to get the guillotine and that I would be explaining myself before the Revolutionary Tribunal. The next day, I was taken to the Revolutionary Committee, which, without waiting to hear me, had me taken to the Mairie, where I stayed for nine days without a bed or a chair with vermin and with women addicted to all sorts of crimes. . . .

On the ninth day I was transferred to the prison of La Force. . . . In the end I can give you only the very slightest idea of all the horrors that are committed in these terrible prisons. . . . I was thrown together not with women but with monsters who gloried in all their crimes and who gave themselves over to all the most horrible excesses. One day, two of them fought each other with knives. Day and night I lived in mortal fear. The food that was sent in to me was grabbed away immediately. That was my cruel situation for seventeen days. My whole body was swollen from . . . the poor treatment I had endured. . . .

[Anne-Félicité Guinée was discharged provisionally after the authorities realized that she was pregnant.]

indication that moderate forces were again gaining control of the Revolution. In addition, a new constitution was adopted in August 1795 that reflected this more conservative republicanism and a desire for a stability that did not sacrifice the ideals of 1789.

To avoid the dangers of another single legislative assembly, the Constitution of 1795 established a national legislative assembly consisting of two chambers: a lower house, known as the Council of 500, which initiated legislation, and an upper house, the Council of Elders, which accepted or rejected the proposed laws. The 750 members of the two legislative bodies were chosen by electors who had to be owners or renters of property worth between 100 and 200 days' labor, a requirement that limited their number to thirty thousand. The Council of Elders elected five directors from a list presented by the Council of 500 to act as the executive committee or Directory.

The period of the Directory was an era of stagnation, corruption, and graft, a materialistic reaction to the suffering and sacrifices that had been demanded in the Reign of Terror and the Republic of Virtue.

Napoleon and Psychological Warfare

In 1796, at the age of twenty-seven, Napoleon Bonaparte was given command of the French army in Italy, where he won a series of stunning victories. His use of speed, deception, and surprise to overwhelm his opponents is well known. In this selection from a proclamation to his troops in Italy, Napoleon also appears as a master of psychological warfare.

Napoleon Bonaparte, Proclamation to the French Troops in Italy (April 26, 1796)

Soldiers:

In a fortnight you have won six victories, taken twenty-one standards, fifty-five pieces of artillery, several strong positions, and conquered the richest part of Piedmont [in northern Italy]; you have captured 15,000 prisoners and killed or wounded more than 10,000 men. . . . You have won battles without cannon, crossed rivers without bridges, made forced marches without shoes, camped without brandy and often without bread. Soldiers of liberty, only republican troops could have endured what you have endured. Soldiers, you have our thanks! The grateful Patrie [nation] will owe its prosperity to you. . . .

The two armies which but recently attacked you with audacity are fleeing before you in terror; the wicked men who laughed at your misery and rejoiced at the thought of the triumphs of your enemies are confounded and trembling.

But, soldiers, as yet you have done nothing compared with what remains to be done. . . . Undoubtedly the greatest obstacles have been overcome; but you still have battles to fight, cities to capture, rivers to cross. Is there one among you whose courage is abating? No. . . . All of you are consumed with a desire to extend the glory of the French people; all of you long to humiliate those arrogant kings who dare to contemplate placing us in fetters; all of you desire to dictate a glorious peace, one which will indemnify the Patrie for the immense sacrifices it has made; all of you wish to be able to say with pride as you return to your villages, "I was with the victorious army of Italy!"

Speculators made fortunes in property by taking advantage of the Republic's severe monetary problems. At the same time, the government of the Directory faced political enemies from both the left and the right of the political spectrum. On the right, royalists who dreamed of restoring the monarchy continued their agitation. On the left, Jacobin hopes of power were revived by continuing economic problems. Battered by the left and right, unable to find a definitive solution to the country's economic problems, and still carrying on the wars left from the Committee of Public Safety, the Directory increasingly relied on the military to maintain its power. This led to a coup d'état in 1799 in which the successful and popular military general Napoleon Bonaparte was able to seize power.

The Age of Napoleon

Napoleon dominated both French and European history from 1799 to 1815. In a sense, Napoleon brought the Revolution to an end in 1799, but he was also a child of the Revolution; indeed, he even called himself the son of the Revolution. The French Revolution had made possible his rise first in the military and then to supreme power in France. Even beyond this, Napoleon had once said, "I am the Revolution," and he never ceased to remind the French that they owed to him the preservation of all that was beneficial in the revolutionary program.

The Rise of Napoleon

Napoleon was born in 1769 in Corsica, only a few months after France had annexed the island. The son of a lawyer whose family stemmed from the Florentine nobility, the young Napoleon obtained a royal scholarship to study at a military school in France. When the Revolution broke out in 1789, Napoleon was a lieutenant, but the Revolution and the European war that followed broadened his sights and presented him with new opportunities.

Napoleon rose quickly through the ranks. In 1794, when he was only twenty-five, the Committee of Public Safety promoted him to the rank of brigadier general. Two years later, he was made commander of the French armies in Italy (see the box on p. 398), where he won a series of stunning victories and dictated peace to the Austrians in 1797. Throughout his Italian campaigns, Napoleon won the confidence of his men by his energy, charm, and ability to comprehend complex issues quickly and make decisions rapidly. These qualities, combined with his keen intelligence, ease with words, and supreme confidence in himself, enabled him throughout the rest of his life to influence people and win their firm support. He returned to France as a conquering hero. After a disastrous expedition to Egypt in 1799, Napoleon returned to Paris, where he participated in the coup d'état that ultimately led to his virtual dictatorship of France. He was only thirty years old at the time.

With the coup of 1799, a new form of the Republic was proclaimed in which, as first consul, Napoleon directly controlled the entire executive authority of government. He had overwhelming influence over the legislature, appointed members of the administrative bureaucracy, controlled the army, and conducted foreign affairs. In 1802, Napoleon was made consul for life and in 1804 returned France to monarchy when he crowned himself Emperor Napoleon I. The revolutionary era that had begun with an attempt to limit arbitrary government had ended with a government far more autocratic than the monarchy of the old regime.

The Domestic Policies of Emperor Napoleon

Napoleon once claimed that he had preserved the gains of the Revolution for the French people. The ideal of republican liberty had, of course, been destroyed by Napoleon's thinly disguised autocracy. But were revolutionary ideals maintained in other ways? An examination of his domestic policies will enable us to judge the truth or falsehood of Napoleon's assertion.

In 1801, Napoleon established peace with the oldest and most implacable enemy of the Revolution, the Catholic church. Both sides gained from the Concordat that Napoleon arranged with the pope. Napoleon agreed to recognize Catholicism as the religion of a majority of the French people. Although the Catholic church was permitted to hold processions again and reopen the seminaries, the pope agreed not to raise the question of the church lands confiscated in the Revolution. As a result of the Concordat, the Catholic church was no longer an enemy of the French government. At the same time, the agreement reassured those who had acquired church lands during the Revolution that they would not be stripped of them, an assurance that obviously made them supporters of the Napoleonic regime.

Napoleon's most famous domestic achievement was his codification of the laws. Before the Revolution,

THE CORONATION OF NAPOLEON. In 1804, Napoleon restored monarchy to France when he crowned himself emperor. In the coronation scene painted by Jacques-Louis David, Napoleon is shown crowning the empress Josephine while the pope looks on. Shown seated in the box in the background is Napoleon's mother, even though she was in fact not present at the ceremony.

France did not have a single set of laws but rather a conglomeration of three hundred legal systems. During the Revolution, efforts were made to codify the laws for the entire nation, but it remained for Napoleon to bring the work to completion in seven codes of law, of which the most important was the Civil Code (or Code Napoléon). This preserved most of the revolutionary gains by recognizing the principle of the equality of all citizens before the law, the right of the individual to choose a profession, religious toleration, and the abolition of serfdom and feudalism. Property rights continued to be carefully protected, and the interests of employers were safeguarded by outlawing trade unions and strikes. The Civil Code clearly reflected the revolutionary aspirations for a uniform legal system, legal equality, and protection of property and individuals.

But the rights of some people were strictly curtailed by the Civil Code. During the radical phase of the French Revolution, new laws had made divorce an easy process for both husbands and wives, restricted the rights of fathers over their children (they could no longer have their children put in prison arbitrarily), and allowed all children (including daughters) to inherit property equally. Napoleon's Civil Code undid most of this legislation. The control of fathers over their families was restored. Divorce was still allowed but was made more difficult for women to obtain. A wife caught in adultery, for example, could be divorced by her husband and even imprisoned. A husband, however, could be accused of adultery only if he moved his mistress into his home. Women were now "less equal than men" in other ways as well. When they married, their property passed into the control of their husbands. In lawsuits, they were treated as minors, and their testimony was regarded as less reliable than that of men.

Napoleon also worked on rationalizing the bureaucratic structure of France by developing a powerful, centralized administrative machine. Administrative centralization required a bureaucracy of capable officials, and Napoleon worked hard to develop one. Early on, the regime showed its preference for experts and cared little whether that expertise had been acquired in royal or revolutionary bureaucracies. Promotion, whether in civil or military offices, was to be based not on rank or birth but only on demonstrated abilities. This was, of course, what many bourgeois had wanted before the Revolution. Napoleon, however, also created a new aristocracy based on merit in the state service. Napoleon created 3,263 nobles between 1808 and 1814; nearly 60 percent were military officers; the remainder came from the upper ranks of the civil service and other state and local officials. Socially, only 22 percent of Napoleon's aristocracy came from the nobility of the old regime; almost 60 percent were bourgeois in origin.

In his domestic policies, then, Napoleon both destroyed and preserved aspects of the Revolution. Although equality was preserved in the law code and the opening of careers to talent, the creation of a new aristocracy, the strong protection accorded to property rights, and the use of conscription for the military make it clear that much equality had been lost. Liberty had been replaced by an initially benevolent despotism that grew increasingly arbitrary. Napoleon shut down sixty of France's seventy-three newspapers and insisted that all manuscripts be subjected to government scrutiny before they were published. Even the mail was opened by government police. One prominent writer—Germaine de Staël—refused to accept Napoleon's growing despotism. Educated in Enlightenment ideas, Madame de Staël wrote novels and political works that denounced Napoleon's rule as tyrannical. Napoleon banned her books in France and exiled her to the German states, where she continued to write.

Napoleon's Empire and the European Response

When Napoleon became first consul in 1799, France was at war with a second European coalition of Russia, Great Britain, and Austria. Napoleon realized the need for a pause and achieved a peace treaty in 1802 that left France with new frontiers and a number of client territories from the North Sea to the Adriatic. But the peace did not last, and war was renewed in 1803 with Britain, which was soon joined by Austria, Russia, and Prussia in the Third Coalition. In a series of battles at Ulm, Austerlitz, Jena, and Eylau from 1805 to 1807, Napoleon's Grand Army defeated the Continental members of the Coalition, giving him the opportunity to create a new European order.

The Grand Empire was composed of three major parts: the French empire, dependent states, and allied states (see Map 19.3). The French empire, the inner core of the Grand Empire, consisted of an enlarged France extending to the Rhine in the east and including the western half of Italy north of Rome. Dependent states were kingdoms under the rule of Napoleon's relatives; these included Spain, Holland, the kingdom of Italy, the Swiss Republic, the Grand Duchy of Warsaw, and the Confederation of the

MAP 19.3 Napoleon's Grand Empire.

Rhine, the latter a union of all German states except Austria and Prussia. Allied states were those defeated by Napoleon and forced to join his struggle against Britain; they included Prussia, Austria, and Russia. Although the structure of the Grand Empire varied outside its inner core, Napoleon considered himself leader of the whole.

Within his empire, Napoleon sought acceptance everywhere of certain revolutionary principles, including legal equality, religious toleration, and economic freedom. As he explained to his brother Jerome after he had made him king of the new German state of Westphalia:

> What the peoples of Germany desire most impatiently is that talented commoners should have the same right to your esteem and to public employments as the nobles, that any trace of serfdom and of an intermediate hierarchy between the sovereign and the lowest class of the people should be completely abolished. The benefits of the Code Napoléon, the publicity of judicial procedure, the creation of juries must be so many distinguishing marks of your monarchy. . . . What nation would wish to return under the arbitrary Prussian government once it had tasted the benefits of a wise and liberal administration? The peoples of Germany, the peoples of France, of Italy, of Spain all desire equality and liberal ideas. I have guided the affairs of Europe for many years now, and I have had occasion to convince myself that the buzzing of the privileged classes is contrary to the general opinion. Be a constitutional king.[4]

In the inner core and dependent states of his Grand Empire, Napoleon tried to destroy the old order. Nobility and clergy everywhere in these states lost their special privileges. He decreed equality of opportunity with offices open to talent, equality before the law, and religious toleration. This spread of French revolutionary principles was an important factor in the development of liberal traditions in these countries.

Like Hitler 130 years later, Napoleon hoped that his Grand Empire would last for centuries; like Hitler's empire, it collapsed almost as rapidly as it had been formed. Two major reasons help explain this: the survival of Great Britain and the force of nationalism. Britain's survival was primarily due to its sea power. As long as Britain ruled the waves, it was almost invulnerable to military attack. Although Napoleon contemplated an invasion of Britain and even collected ships for it, he could not overcome the British navy's decisive defeat of a combined French-Spanish fleet at Trafalgar in 1805. Napoleon then turned to his Continental System to defeat Britain. Put into effect between 1806 and 1808, it attempted to prevent British goods from reaching the European continent in order to weaken Britain economically and destroy its capacity to wage war. But the Continental System failed. Allied states resented the ever-tightening French economic hegemony; some began to cheat and others to resist, thereby opening the door to British collaboration. New markets in the Levant (Middle East) and in Latin America also provided compensation for the British. Indeed, in 1809 and 1810, British overseas exports reached near-record highs.

The second important factor in the defeat of Napoleon was nationalism. This political creed had arisen during the French Revolution in the French people's emphasis on brotherhood (*fraternité*) and solidarity against other peoples. Nationalism involved the unique cultural identity of a people based on common language, religion, and national symbols. The spirit of French nationalism had made possible the mass armies of the revolutionary and Napoleonic eras. But Napoleon's spread of the principles of the French Revolution beyond France inadvertently brought a spread of nationalism as well. The French aroused nationalism in two ways: by making themselves hated oppressors and thus arousing the patriotism of others in opposition to French nationalism and by showing the people of Europe what nationalism was and what a nation in arms could do. The lesson was not lost on other peoples and rulers. A Spanish uprising against Napoleon's rule, aided by British support, kept a French force of 200,000 pinned down for years.

The beginning of Napoleon's downfall came in 1812 with the invasion of Russia. The latter's defection from the Continental System left Napoleon with little choice. Although aware of the risks of invading such a large country, he also knew that if the Russians were allowed to challenge the Continental System unopposed, others would soon follow suit. In June 1812, a Grand Army of more than 600,000 men entered Russia. Napoleon's hopes for victory depended on quickly meeting and defeating the Russian armies, but the Russian forces refused to give battle and retreated for hundreds of miles while torching their own villages and countryside to prevent Napoleon's army from finding food and forage. When the Russians did stop to fight at Borodino, Napoleon's forces won an indecisive and costly victory. When the remaining troops of the Grand Army arrived in Moscow, they found the city ablaze. Lacking food and supplies, Napoleon abandoned Moscow late in October and made the "Great Retreat" across Russia in terrible winter conditions. Only one-fifth of the original army managed to straggle back to Poland in January 1813. This military disaster then led to a war of liberation all over Europe, culminating in Napoleon's defeat in April 1814.

The defeated emperor of the French was allowed to play ruler on the island of Elba, off the coast of Tuscany, while the Bourbon monarchy was restored to France in the person of Louis XVIII, brother of the executed king. But the new king had little support, and Napoleon, bored on Elba, slipped back into France. The troops sent to capture him went over to his side, and Napoleon entered Paris in triumph on March 20, 1815. The powers who had defeated him pledged once more to fight this person they called the

CHRONOLOGY

The Napoleonic Era, 1799–1815

Napoleon as first consul	1799–1804
Concordat with Catholic church	1801
Emperor Napoleon I	1804–1815
Battles of Austerlitz; Trafalgar; Ulm	1805
Battle of Jena	1806
Continental System	1806
Battle of Eylau	1807
Invasion of Russia	1812
War of liberation	1813–1814
Exile to Elba	1814
Battle of Waterloo; exile to Saint Helena	1815

"enemy and disturber of the tranquillity of the world." Having decided to strike first at his enemies, Napoleon raised yet another army and moved to attack the nearest allied forces stationed in Belgium. At Waterloo on June 18, Napoleon met a combined English and Prussian army under the duke of Wellington and suffered a bloody defeat. This time the victorious Allies exiled him to St. Helena, a small and forsaken island in the South Atlantic. Only Napoleon's memory would continue to haunt French political life.

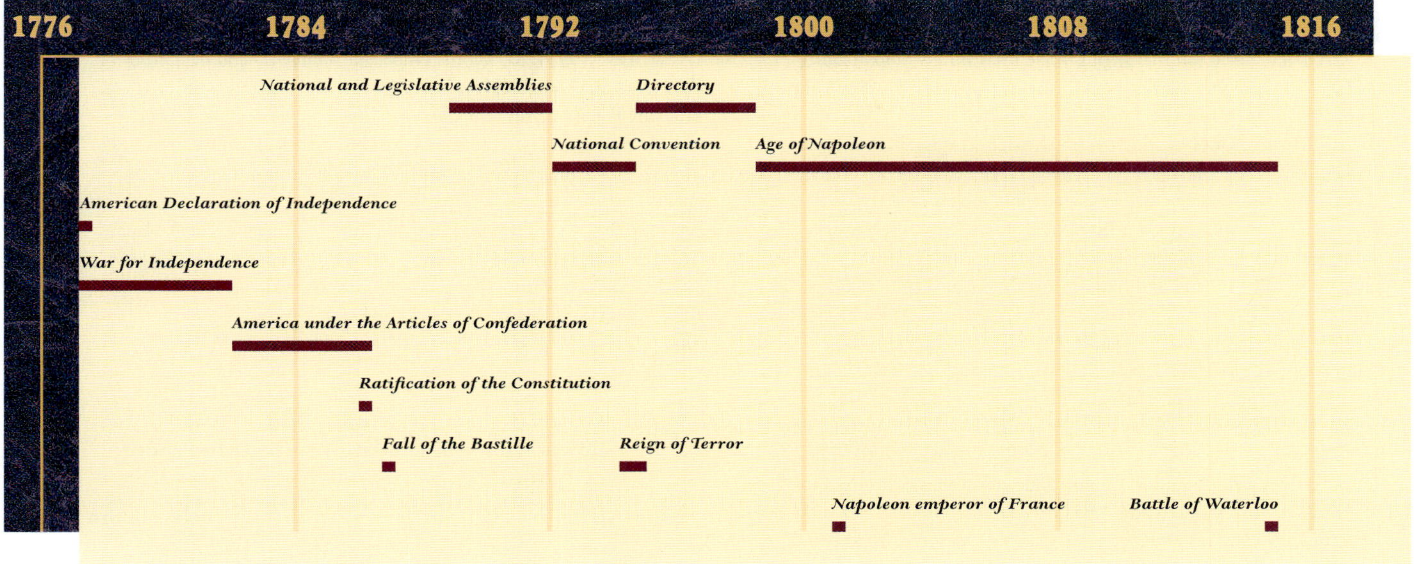

Conclusion

The revolutionary era of the late eighteenth century witnessed a dramatic political transformation. Revolutionary upheavals, beginning in North America and continuing in France, produced movements for political liberty and equality. The documents created by these revolutions, the Declaration of Independence and the Declaration of the Rights of Man and the Citizen, embodied the fundamental ideas of the Enlightenment and set forth a liberal political agenda based on a belief in popular sovereignty—the people as the source of political power—and the principles of liberty and equality. Liberty, frequently limited in practice, meant, in theory, freedom from arbitrary power as well as the freedom to think, write, and worship as one chose. Equality meant equality in rights and the equality of opportunity based on talent rather than birth. In practice, equality remained limited; those who owned property had greater opportunities for voting and officeholding, and there was no equality between men and women.

The French Revolution established a modern revolutionary concept. No one had foreseen or consciously planned the upheaval that began in 1789, but thereafter revolutionaries knew that the proper mobilization of the masses could succeed in overthrowing unwanted governments. For these people, the French Revolution became a symbol of hope; for those who feared such changes, it became a symbol of dread. The French Revolution became the classical political and social model for revolution. At the same time, the liberal and national political ideals fostered by the Revolution and spread through Europe by Napoleon dominated the political landscape of the nineteenth and early twentieth centuries. A new European era had begun.

Notes

1. Quoted in William Doyle, *The Oxford History of the French Revolution* (Oxford, 1989), p. 184.
2. Quoted in Leo Gershoy, *The Era of the French Revolution* (Princeton, N.J., 1957), p. 157.
3. Quoted in Doyle, *The Oxford History of the French Revolution*, p. 254.
4. Quoted in J. Christopher Herold, ed., *The Mind of Napoleon* (New York, 1955), pp. 74–75.

Suggestions for Further Reading

A well-written, up-to-date introduction to the French Revolution can be found in W. Doyle, *The Oxford History of the French Revolution* (Oxford, 1989). On the entire revolutionary and Napoleonic eras, see O. Connelly, *The French Revolution and Napoleonic Era*, 3d ed. (Fort Worth, Tex., 2000), and D. M. G. Sutherland, *France, 1789–1815: Revolution and Counter-Revolution* (New York, 1986). Two brief works are A. Forrest, *The French Revolution* (Oxford,

1995), and J. M. Roberts, *The French Revolution*, 2d ed. (New York, 1997). Three comprehensive reference works are S. F. Scott and B. Rothaus, eds., *Historical Dictionary of the French Revolution*, 2 vols. (Westport, Conn., 1985); F. Furet and M. Ozouf, *A Critical Dictionary of the French Revolution*, trans. A. Goldhammer (Cambridge, Mass., 1989); and O. Connelly et al., *Historical Dictionary of Napoleonic France, 1799–1815* (Westport, Conn., 1985).

The origins of the French Revolution are examined in W. Doyle, *Origins of the French Revolution* (Oxford, 1988). See also R. Chartier, *The Cultural Origins of the French Revolution* (Durham, N.C., 1991). On the early years of the Revolution, see N. Hampson, *Prelude to Terror* (Oxford, 1988); T. Tackett, *Becoming a Revolutionary* (Princeton, N.J., 1996), on the deputies to the National Assembly; and J. Markoff, *The Abolition of Feudalism: Peasants, Lords, and Legislators in the French Revolution* (University Park, Pa., 1996). Important works on the radical stage of the French Revolution include N. Hampson, *The Terror in the French Revolution* (London, 1981); R. R. Palmer, *Twelve Who Ruled* (New York, 1965); and R. Cobb, *The People's Armies* (London, 1987). For a biography of Robespierre, one of the leading figures of this period, see N. Hampson, *The Life and Opinions of Maximilien Robespierre* (London, 1974). The importance of the revolutionary wars in the radical stage of the Revolution is underscored in T. C. W. Blanning, *The French Revolutionary Wars, 1787–1802* (New York, 1996). The importance of the popular revolutionary crowds is examined in the classic work by G. Rudé, *The Crowd in the French Revolution* (Oxford, 1959), and D. Roche, *The People of Paris: An Essay in Popular Culture* (Berkeley, Calif., 1987). On the Directory, see M. Lyons, *France Under the Directory* (Cambridge, 1975).

On the Great Fear, there is the classic work by G. Lefebvre, *The Great Fear of 1789: Rural Panic in Revolutionary France* (London, 1973). On the role of women in revolutionary France, see O. Hufton, *Women and the Limits of Citizenship in the French Revolution* (Toronto, 1992); J. Landes, *Women and the Public Sphere in the Age of the French Revolution* (Ithaca, N.Y., 1988); and the essays in G. Fraisse and M. Perrot, eds., *A History of Women in the West*, vol. 4 (Cambridge, Mass., 1993). There is a good collection of essays in S. E. Melzer and L. Rabine, eds., *Rebel Daughters: Women and the French Revolution* (New York, 1992).

The best brief biography of Napoleon is F. Markham, *Napoleon* (New York, 1963). Also valuable are G. J. Ellis, *Napoleon* (New York, 1997); M. Lyons, *Napoleon Bonaparte and the Legacy of the French Revolution* (New York, 1994); and the massive biographies by F. J. McLynn, *Napoleon: A Biography* (London, 1997), and A. Schom, *Napoleon Bonaparte* (New York, 1997). On Napoleon's wars, see S. J. Woolf, *Napoleon's Integration of Europe* (New York, 1991).

A history of the revolutionary era in America can be found in R. Middlekauff, *The Glorious Cause: The American Revolution, 1763–1789* (New York, 1982), and C. Bonwick, *The American Revolution* (Charlottesville, Va., 1991).

For additional reading, go to InfoTrac College Edition, your online research library at http://web1.infotrac-college.com

Enter the search terms *French Revolution* using Key Terms.

Enter the search terms *American Revolution* using Key Terms.

Enter the search term *Napoleon* using Key Terms.

Enter the search terms *Napoleonic Wars* using Key Terms.

CHAPTER

20

The Industrial Revolution and Its Impact on European Society

CHAPTER OUTLINE

- The Industrial Revolution in Great Britain
- The Spread of Industrialization
- The Social Impact of the Industrial Revolution
- Conclusion

FOCUS QUESTIONS

- What conditions and developments coalesced in Great Britain to bring about the first Industrial Revolution?
- What were the basic features of the new industrial system created by the Industrial Revolution?
- How did the Industrial Revolution spread from Great Britain to the Continent and the United States, and how did industrialization in those areas differ from British industrialization?
- What effects did the Industrial Revolution have on urban life, social classes, and family life?
- What were working conditions like in the early decades of the Industrial Revolution, and what efforts were made to improve them?

THE FRENCH REVOLUTION dramatically altered the political structure of France; the Napoleonic conquests then spread many of the revolutionary principles to other parts of Europe. At the same time, during the late eighteenth and early nineteenth centuries, another revolution—an industrial one—was transforming the economic and social structure of Europe, although somewhat less radically and rapidly.

The Industrial Revolution initiated a quantum leap in industrial production. New sources of energy and power, especially coal and steam, replaced wind and water to create laborsaving machines that dramatically decreased the use of human and animal labor and at the same time increased the level of productivity. In turn, power machinery called for new ways of organizing human labor to maximize the benefits and profits

Discipline in the New Factories

Workers in the new factories of the Industrial Revolution had been accustomed to a lifestyle free of overseers. Unlike the cottages, where workers spun thread and wove cloth in their own rhythm and time, the factories demanded a new, rigorous discipline geared to the requirements of the machines. This selection is taken from a set of rules for a factory in Berlin in 1844. They were typical of company rules everywhere the factory system had been established.

The Foundry and Engineering Works of the Royal Overseas Trading Company, Factory Rules

In every large works, and in the co-ordination of any large number of workmen, good order and harmony must be looked upon as the fundamentals of success, and therefore the following rules shall be strictly observed.

1. The normal working day begins at all seasons at 6 A.M. precisely and ends, after the usual break of half an hour for breakfast, an hour for dinner and half an hour for tea, at 7 P.M., and it shall be strictly observed. . . .

   Workers arriving 2 minutes late shall lose half an hour's wages; whoever is more than 2 minutes late may not start work until after the next break; or at least shall lose his wages until then. Any disputes about the correct time shall be settled by the clock mounted above the gatekeeper's lodge. . . .

3. No workman, whether employed by time or piece, may leave before the end of the working day, without having first received permission from the overseer and having given his name to the gatekeeper. Omission of these two actions shall lead to a fine of ten silver groschen [pennies] payable to the sick fund.
4. Repeated irregular arrival at work shall lead to dismissal. This shall also apply to those who are found idling by an official or overseer, and refused to obey their order to resume work. . . .
6. No worker may leave his place of work otherwise than for reasons connected with his work.
7. All conversation with fellow-workers is prohibited; if any worker requires information about his work, he must turn to the overseer, or to the particular fellow-worker designated for the purpose.
8. Smoking in the workshops or in the yard is prohibited during working hours; anyone caught smoking shall be fined five silver groschen for the sick fund for every such offense. . . .
10. Natural functions must be performed at the appropriate places, and whoever is found soiling walls, fences, squares, etc., and similarly, whoever is found washing his face and hands in the workshop and not in the places assigned for the purpose, shall be fined five silver groschen for the sick fund. . . .
12. It goes without saying that all overseers and officials of the firm shall be obeyed without question, and shall be treated with due deference. Disobedience will be punished by dismissal.
13. Immediate dismissal shall also be the fate of anyone found drunk in any of the workshops. . . .
14. Every workman is obliged to report to his superiors any acts of dishonesty or embezzlement on the part of his fellow workmen. If he omits to do so, and it is shown after subsequent discovery of a misdemeanor that he knew about it at the time, he shall be liable to be taken to court as an accessory after the fact and the wage due to him shall be retained as punishment.

the costs of technical education, awarded grants to inventors and foreign entrepreneurs, exempted foreign industrial equipment from import duties, and in some places even financed factories. Of equal if not greater importance in the long run, governments actively bore much of the cost of building roads and canals, deepening and widening river channels, and constructing railroads. By 1850, a network of iron rails had spread across Europe, although only Germany and Belgium had largely completed their systems by that time.

The Industrial Revolution on the Continent occurred in three major centers between 1815 and

1850—Belgium, France, and the German states (see Map 20.2). Here, too, cotton played an important role, although it was not as significant as the iron and coal of heavy industry. As traditional methods persisted alongside the new methods in cotton manufacturing, the new steam engine came to be used primarily in mining and metallurgy on the Continent rather than in textile manufacturing.

The Industrial Revolution in the United States

In 1800, the United States was an agrarian society. There were no cities with populations of more than 100,000, and six out of every seven American workers were farmers. By 1860, however, the population had grown from 5 to 30 million people, larger than Great Britain. Almost half of them lived west of the Appalachian Mountains. The number of states had more than doubled, from sixteen to thirty-four, and nine American cities had populations of more than 100,000. Only 50 percent of American workers were farmers. In those sixty years, the United States was transformed from a farm-centered society of small communities to an industrializing, urbanizing nation.

The initial application of machinery to production was accomplished—as in Continental Europe—by borrowing from Great Britain. A British immigrant, Samuel Slater, established the first textile factory using water-powered spinning machines in Rhode Island in 1790. By 1813, factories with power looms copied from British versions were being established. Soon thereafter, however, Americans began to equal or surpass British technical inventions. The Harpers Ferry

MAP 20.2 The Industrialization of Europe by 1850.

arsenal, for example, built muskets with interchangeable parts. Because all the individual parts of a musket were identical (for example, all triggers were the same), the final product could be put together quickly and easily; this enabled Americans to avoid the more costly system in which skilled craftspeople fitted together individual parts made separately. The so-called American system reduced costs and revolutionized production by saving labor, important to a society that had few skilled artisans.

Unlike Britain, the United States was a large country. The lack of a good system of internal transportation seemed to limit American economic development by making the transport of goods prohibitively expensive. This was gradually remedied, however. Thousands of miles of roads and canals were built linking east and west. The steamboat facilitated transportation on the Great Lakes, Atlantic coastal waters, and rivers. It was especially important to the Mississippi River valley; by 1860, a thousand steamboats plied the Mississippi (see the box on p. 415). Most important of all in the development of an American transportation system was the railroad. Beginning with 100 miles in 1830, by 1860 there were more than 27,000 miles of railroad track covering the United States. This transportation revolution turned the United States into a single massive market for the manufactured goods of the Northeast, the early center of American industrialization.

Labor for the growing number of factories in this area came primarily from rural New England. The United States did not possess a large number of craftspeople, but it did have a rapidly expanding farm population; its size in the Northeast soon outstripped the available farmland. While some of this excess population, especially men, went west, others, mostly women, found work in the new textile and shoe factories of New England. Indeed, women made up more than 80 percent of the labor force in the large textile factories. In Massachusetts mill towns, company boarding houses provided rooms for large numbers of young women who worked for several years before marriage. Outside Massachusetts, factory owners sought entire families including children to work in their mills; one mill owner ran this advertisement in a newspaper in Utica, New York: "Wanted: A few sober and industrious families of at least five children each, over the age of eight years, are wanted at the Cotton Factory in Whitestown. Widows with large families would do well to attend this notice." When a decline in rural births threatened to dry up this labor pool in the 1830s and 1840s, European immigrants, especially poor and unskilled Irish, English, Scottish, and Welsh, appeared in large numbers to replace American women and children in the factories.

By 1860, the United States was well on its way to being an industrial nation. In the Northeast, the most industrialized section of the country, per capita income was 40 percent higher than the national average. Diets, it has been argued, were better and more varied; machine-made clothing was more abundant. Nevertheless, despite a growing belief in a myth of social mobility based on equality of economic opportunity, the reality was that the richest 10 percent of the population in the cities held 70 to 80 percent of the wealth, compared to 50 percent in 1800. Nevertheless, American historians generally argue that while the rich got richer, the poor, as a result of experiencing an increase in their purchasing power, did not get poorer.

◆ The Social Impact of the Industrial Revolution

The Industrial Revolution transfigured the social life of Europe and the world. Although much of Europe remained bound by its traditional ways, the social impact of the Industrial Revolution was already being felt in the first half of the nineteenth century, and future avenues of growth were becoming apparent. Vast changes in the number of people and where they lived were already dramatically evident.

Population Growth

Population increases had begun in the eighteenth century, but they became dramatic in the nineteenth century. In 1750, the total European population stood at an estimated 140 million; by 1800, it had increased to 187 million and by 1850 to 266 million, almost twice its 1750 level. The key to the expansion of population was the decline in death rates evident throughout Europe. Two major factors explain this decline: fewer deaths and better nutrition. The number of deaths from famines, epidemics, and war dropped substantially. Major epidemic diseases in particular, such as plague and smallpox, became less common, although small-scale epidemics did occur. The ordinary death rate also declined as a general increase in the food supply, already evident in the agricultural revolution of Britain in the late eighteenth century, spread to more areas. More food enabled a greater number of people to be better fed and therefore more resistant to disease. Famine largely dis-

"S-t-e-a-m-boat A-Comin'!"

Steamboats and railroads were crucial elements in a transportation revolution that enabled industrialists to expand markets by shipping goods cheaply and efficiently. At the same time, these marvels of technology aroused a sense of power and excitement that was an important aspect of the triumph of industrialization. The American writer Mark Twain captured this sense of excitement in this selection from Life on the Mississippi.

Mark Twain, Life on the Mississippi

After all these years I can picture that old time to myself now, just as it was then: the white town drowsing in the sunshine of a summer's morning; the streets empty, or pretty nearly so; one or two clerks sitting in front of the Water street stores, with their splint-bottomed chairs tilted back against the walls, chins on breasts, hats slouched over their faces, asleep; . . . two or three lonely little freight piles scattered about the "levee"; a pile of "skids" on the slope of the stone-paved wharf, and the fragrant town drunkard asleep in the shadow of them; . . . the great Mississippi, the majestic, the magnificent Mississippi, rolling its mile-wide along, shining in the sun; the dense forest away on the other side; the "point" above the town, and the "point" below, bounding the river glimpse and turning it into a sort of sea, and withal a very still and brilliant and lonely one. Presently a film of dark smoke appears above on those remote "points"; instantly a negro drayman, famous for his quick eye and prodigious voice, lifts up to cry, "S-t-e-a-m-boat a-comin'!" and the scene changes! The town drunkard stirs, the clerks wake up, a furious clatter of drays follows, every house and store pours out a human contribution, and all in a twinkling the dead town [Hannibal, Missouri] is alive and moving. Drays, carts, men, boys, all go hurrying from many quarters to a common center, the wharf. Assembled there, the people fasten their eyes upon the coming boat as upon a wonder they are seeing for the first time. And the boat is rather a handsome sight, too. She is long and sharp and trim and pretty; she has two tall, fancy-topped chimneys, with a gilded device of some kind swung between them; a fanciful pilot-house, all glass and "ginger bread," perched on top of the "texas" deck behind them; the paddle-boxes are gorgeous with a picture or with gilded rays above the boat's name; the boiler deck, the hurricane deck, and the texas deck are fenced and ornamented with clean white railings; there is a flag gallantly flying from the jack-staff; the furnace doors are open and the fires glaring bravely; the upper decks are black with passengers; the captain stands by the big bell, calm, imposing, the envy of all; great volumes of the blackest smoke are rolling and tumbling out of the chimneys—a husbanded grandeur created with a bit of pitch pine just before arriving at a town; the crew are grouped on the forecastle; the broad stage is run far out over the port bow, and an envied deck-hand stands picturesquely on the end of it with a coil of rope in his hand; the pent steam is screaming through the gauge-cocks; the captain lifts his hand, a bell rings, the wheels stop; then they turn back, churning the water to foam, and the steam is at rest. Then such a scramble as there is to get aboard, and to get ashore, and to take in freight and discharge freight, all at one and the same time; and such a yelling and cursing as the mates facilitate it all with! Ten minutes later the steamer is under way again, with no flag on the jack-staff and no black smoke issuing from the chimneys. After ten more minutes the town is dead again, and the town drunkard asleep by the skids once more.

appeared from western Europe, although there were dramatic exceptions in isolated areas where overpopulation magnified the problem of rural poverty. In Ireland, it produced the century's great catastrophe.

Ireland was one of the most oppressed areas in western Europe. The predominantly Catholic peasant population rented land from mostly absentee British Protestant landlords whose primary concern was collecting their rents. Irish peasants lived in mud hovels in desperate poverty. The cultivation of the potato, a nutritious and relatively easy crop to grow that produced three times as much food per acre as grain, gave Irish peasants a basic staple that enabled them to survive and even expand in numbers. Between 1781 and 1845, the Irish population doubled from four to eight million. Probably half of this population depended on

A NEW INDUSTRIAL TOWN. Cities and towns grew dramatically in Britain in the first half of the nineteenth century, largely as a result of industrialization. Pictured here is Saltaire, a model textile factory and town founded near Bradford by Titus Salt in 1851. To facilitate the transportation of goods, the town was built on the Leeds and Liverpool canals.

the potato for survival. In the summer of 1845, the potato crop in Ireland was struck by a fungus that turned the potato black. The resulting Great Famine decimated the Irish population between 1845 and 1851. More than one million inhabitants died of starvation and disease, and almost two million more emigrated to the United States and Britain. Of all the European nations, only Ireland had a declining population in the nineteenth century.

The flight of so many Irish to America reminds us that the traditional safety valve for overpopulation has always been emigration. Between 1821 and 1850, the number of emigrants from Europe averaged about 110,000 a year. Most of these emigrants came from places like Ireland and southern Germany, where peasant life had been reduced to a marginal existence. More often than emigration, however, the rural masses sought a solution to their poverty by moving to towns and cities within their own countries to find work. It should not astonish us then that the first half of the nineteenth century was a period of rapid urbanization.

The Growth of Cities

Cities and towns grew dramatically in the first half of the nineteenth century, a phenomenon related to industrialization. Cities had traditionally been centers for princely courts, government and military offices, churches, and commerce. By 1850, especially in Great Britain and Belgium, they were rapidly becoming places for manufacturing and industry. With the steam engine, entrepreneurs could locate their manufacturing plants in urban centers where they had ready access to transportation facilities and unemployed people from the country looking for work.

In 1800, Great Britain had one major city, London, with a population of one million and six cities that were home to 50,000 to 100,000 people. Fifty years later, London's population had swelled to 2,363,000, and there were nine cities with populations over 100,000 and eighteen cities with populations between 50,000 and 100,000. More than 50 percent of the British population now lived in towns and cities. Urban populations also grew on the Continent, but less dramatically.

URBAN LIVING CONDITIONS IN THE EARLY INDUSTRIAL REVOLUTION

The dramatic growth of cities in the first half of the nineteenth century produced miserable living conditions for many of the inhabitants. Of course, this had been true for centuries in European cities, but the rapid urbanization associated with the Industrial Revolution intensified the problems in the first half of the nineteenth century and made these wretched conditions all the more apparent. Wealthy, middle-class inhabitants, as usual, insulated themselves as best they could, often living in suburbs or the outer ring of the city where they could have individual houses and gardens. In the inner ring of the city stood the small row houses, some with gardens, of the artisans and lower middle class. Finally, located in the center of most industrial towns were the row houses of the industrial workers. This report on working-class housing in the British city of Birmingham in 1843 gives an idea of the general conditions they faced:

> The courts [of working class row houses] are extremely numerous; . . . a very large portion of the poorer classes of the inhabitants reside in them. . . . The courts vary in the

> number of the houses which they contain, from four to twenty, and most of these houses are three stories high, and built, as it is termed, back to back. There is a wash-house, an ash-pit, and a privy at the end, or on one side of the court, and not unfrequently one or more pigsties and heaps of manure. Generally speaking, the privies in the old courts are in a most filthy condition. Many which we have inspected were in a state which renders it impossible for us to conceive how they could be used; they were without doors and overflowing with filth.[1]

Rooms were not large and were frequently overcrowded, as this government report of 1838 revealed: "I entered several of the tenements. In one of them, on the ground floor, I found six persons occupying a very small room, two in bed, ill with fever. In the room above this were two more persons in one bed, ill with fever." Another report said: "There were 63 families where there were at least five persons to one bed; and there were some in which even six were packed in one bed, lying at the top and bottom—children and adults."[2]

Sanitary conditions in these towns were appalling. Due to the lack of municipal direction, city streets were often used as sewers and open drains: "In the centre of this street is a gutter, into which potato parings, the refuse of animal and vegetable matters of all kinds, the dirty water from the washing of clothes and of the houses, are all poured, and there they stagnate and putrefy."[3] Unable to deal with human excrement, cities in the new industrial era smelled horrible and were extraordinarily unhealthy. Towns and cities were fundamentally death traps. As deaths outnumbered births in most large cities in the first half of the nineteenth century, only a constant influx of people from the country kept them alive and growing.

To many of the well-to-do middle classes, this situation presented a clear danger to society. Were not these masses of workers, sunk in crime, filth, disease, and immorality, a potential threat to their own well-being? Might not the masses be organized and used by unscrupulous demagogues to overthrow the established order? Some observers, however, wondered if the workers could be held responsible for their fate. One of the best of a new breed of urban reformers was Edwin Chadwick (1800–1890). Chadwick became obsessed with eliminating the poverty and squalor of the metropolitan areas. As secretary of the Poor Law Commission, he initiated a passionate search for detailed facts about the living conditions of the working classes. After three years of investigation, Chadwick summarized the results in his *Report on the Condition of the Labouring Population of Great Britain*, published in 1842. In it he concluded that "the various forms of epidemic, endemic, and other disease" were directly caused by the "atmospheric impurities produced by decomposing animal and vegetable substances, by damp and filth, and close overcrowded dwellings [prevailing] amongst the population in every part of the kingdom." Such conditions, he argued, could be eliminated. As to the means: "The primary and most important measures, and at the same time the most practicable, and within the recognized province of public administration, are drainage, the removal of all refuse of habitations, streets, and roads, and the improvement of the supplies of water."[4] In other words, Chadwick was advocating a system of modern sanitary reforms consisting of efficient sewers and a supply of piped water. Six years after his report and largely due to his efforts, Britain's first Public Health Act created the National Board of Health, which was empowered to form local boards that would establish modern sanitary systems.

New Social Classes: The Industrial Middle Class

The rise of industrial capitalism added a new group to the middle class. The bourgeoisie or middle class was not new; it had existed since the emergence of cities in the Middle Ages. Originally, the bourgeois was a burgher or town dweller—a merchant, official, artisan, lawyer, or man of letters—who enjoyed a special set of rights from the charter of his town. As wealthy townspeople bought land, the term *bourgeois* came to include people involved in commerce, industry, and banking as well as professionals, such as lawyers, teachers, and physicians, and government officials at varying levels. At the lower end of the economic scale were master craftspeople and shopkeepers.

Lest we make the industrial middle class too much of an abstraction, we need to look at who the new industrial entrepreneurs actually were. These were the people who constructed the factories, purchased the machines, and figured out where the markets were. Their qualities included resourcefulness, single-mindedness, resolution, initiative, vision, ambition, and often greed. As Jedediah Strutt, a cotton manufacturer said, "Getting of money . . . is the main business of the life of men." But this was not an easy task. The early industrial entrepreneurs were called on to superintend an enormous array of functions that are handled today by teams of managers; they raised capital, determined markets, set company objectives, organized the factory and its labor, and trained supervisors who could act for them. The opportunities for making money were great, but the risks were also tremendous.

By 1850, in Britain at least, the kind of traditional entrepreneurship that had fueled the Industrial Revolution was declining and being replaced by a new business aristocracy. This new generation of entrepreneurs stemmed from the professional and industrial middle classes, especially as sons inherited successful businesses established by their fathers. Increasingly, the new industrial entrepreneurs—the bankers and owners of factories and mines—came to amass much wealth and play an important role alongside the traditional landed elites of their societies. The Industrial Revolution began at a time when the agrarian world was still largely dominated by landed elites. As members of the new bourgeoisie bought great estates and acquired social respectability, they also sought political power, and in the course of the nineteenth century, their wealthiest members would merge with those old elites.

New Social Classes: Workers in the Industrial Age

At the same time that the members of the industrial middle class were seeking to reduce the barriers between themselves and the landed elite, they were also trying to separate themselves from the laboring classes below them. The working class was actually a mixture of groups in the first half of the nineteenth century. Factory workers would eventually form an industrial proletariat, but they did not yet constitute a majority of the working class in any major city, even in Britain. According to the 1851 census in Britain, while there were 1.8 million agricultural laborers and 1 million domestic servants, there were only 811,000 workers in the cotton and woolen industries, and one-third of these were still working in small workshops or in their own homes.

WORKING CONDITIONS FOR THE INDUSTRIAL WORKING CLASS

Workers in the new industrial factories faced wretched working conditions. Unquestionably, in the early decades of the Industrial Revolution, "places of work," as early factories were called, were dreadful. Work hours ranged from twelve to sixteen hours a day, six days a week, with a half hour for lunch and dinner. There was no security of employment and no minimum wage. The worst conditions were endured by workers in the cotton mills, where temperatures were especially debilitating. One report noted that "in the cotton-spinning work, these creatures are kept, fourteen hours in each day, locked up, summer and winter, in a heat of from eighty to eighty-four degrees." Mills were also dirty, dusty, and unhealthy:

> Not only is there not a breath of sweet air in these truly infernal scenes, but . . . there is the abominable and pernicious stink of the gas to assist in the murderous effects of the heat. In addition to the noxious effluvia of the gas, mixed with the steam, there are the dust, and what is called cotton-flyings or fuz, which the unfortunate creatures have to inhale; and . . . the notorious fact is that well constitutioned men are rendered old and past labour at forty years of age, and that children are rendered decrepit and deformed, and thousands upon thousands of them slaughtered by consumptions [wasting away of body tissues, especially the lungs], before they arrive at the age of sixteen.[5]

Conditions in the coal mines were also harsh. The introduction of steam power in the coal mines meant only that steam-powered engines mechanically lifted coal to the top. Inside the mines, men still bore the burden of digging the coal out while horses, mules, women, and children hauled coal carts on rails to the lift. Dangers abounded in coal mines; cave-ins, explo-

WOMAN IN THE MINES. Women and children were often employed in the early factories and mines of the nineteenth century. As is evident in this illustration of a woman dragging a cart loaded with coal behind her, they often worked under very trying conditions.

Child Labor: Discipline in the Textile Mills

Child labor was not new, but in the early Industrial Revolution it was exploited more systematically. These selections are taken from the Report of Sadler's Committee, which was commissioned in 1832 to inquire into the condition of child factory workers.

How They Kept the Children Awake

It is a very frequent thing at Mr. Marshall's [at Shrewsbury] where the least children were employed (for there were plenty working at six years of age), for Mr. Horseman to start the mill earlier in the morning than he formerly did; and provided a child should be drowsy, the overlooker walks round the room with a stick in his hand, and he touches that child on the shoulder, and says, "Come here." In a corner of the room there is an iron cistern; it is filled with water; he takes this boy, and takes him up by the legs, and dips him over head in the cistern, and sends him to work for the remainder of the day. . . .

What means were taken to keep the children to their work?—Sometimes they would tap them over the head, or nip them over the nose, or give them a pinch of snuff, or throw water in their faces, or pull them off where they were, and job them about to keep them waking.

The Sadistic Overlooker

Samuel Downe, age 29, factory worker living near Leeds; at the age of about ten began work at Mr. Marshall's mills at Shrewsbury, where the customary hours when work was brisk were generally 5 A.M. to 8 P.M., sometimes from 5:30 A.M. to 8 or 9:

What means were taken to keep the children awake and vigilant, especially at the termination of such a day's labor as you have described?—There was generally a blow or a box, or a tap with a strap, or sometimes the hand.

Have you yourself been strapped?—Yes, most severely, till I could not bear to sit upon a chair without having pillows, and through that I left. I was strapped both on my own legs, and then I was put upon a man's back, and then strapped and buckled with two straps to an iron pillar, and flogged, and all by one overlooker; after that he took a piece of tow, and twisted it in the shape of a cord, and put it in my mouth, and tied it behind my head.

He gagged you?—Yes; and then he ordered me to run round a part of the machinery where he was overlooker, and he stood at one end, and every time I came there he struck me with a stick, which I believe was an ash plant, and which he generally carried in his hand, and sometimes he hit me, and sometimes he did not; and one of the men in the room came and begged me off, and that he let me go, and not beat me any more, and consequently he did.

You have been beaten with extraordinary severity?—Yes, I was beaten so that I had not power to cry at all, or hardly speak at one time. What age were you at that time?—Between 10 and 11.

sions, and gas fumes (called "bad air") were a way of life. The cramped conditions—tunnels often did not exceed 3 or 4 feet in height—and constant dampness in the mines resulted in deformed bodies and ruined lungs.

Both children and women were employed in large numbers in early factories and mines. Children had been an important part of the family economy in preindustrial times, working in the fields or carding and spinning wool at home with the growth of the cottage industry. In the Industrial Revolution, however, child labor was exploited more than ever and in a considerably more systematic fashion (see the box above). The owners of cotton factories appreciated certain features of child labor. Children had an especially delicate touch as spinners of cotton. Their smaller size made it easier for them to crawl under machines to gather loose cotton. Moreover, children were more easily accustomed to factory work. Above all, children represented a cheap supply of labor. In 1821, half the British population was under twenty years of age. Hence children made up a particularly abundant supply of labor, and they were paid only one-sixth to one-third of what a man was paid. In the cotton factories in 1838, children under eighteen made up 29 percent of the workforce; children as young as seven worked twelve to fifteen hours per day, six days a week, in the cotton mills.

By 1830, women and children made up two-thirds of the cotton industry's labor. However, as the number of children employed declined under the Factory Act of 1833, their places were taken by women, who came to dominate the labor forces of the early factories. Women made up 50 percent of the labor force in textile (cotton and woolen) factories before 1870. They were mostly unskilled labor and were paid half or less of what men received. Excessive working hours for women were outlawed in 1844, but only in textile factories and mines; not until 1867 were they outlawed in craft workshops.

The employment of children and women in large part represents a continuation of a preindustrial kinship pattern. The cottage industry had always involved the efforts of the entire family, and it seemed perfectly natural to continue this pattern. Men migrating from the countryside to industrial towns and cities took their wives and children with them into the factory or into the mines. Of 136 employees in Robert Peel's factory at Bury in 1801, 95 came from twenty-six families. The impetus for this family work often came from the family itself. The factory owner Jedediah Strutt was opposed to employing children under ten but was forced by parents to take children as young as seven.

The employment of large numbers of women in factories did not produce a significant transformation in female working patterns, as was once assumed. Studies of urban households in France and Britain, for example, have revealed that throughout the nineteenth century, traditional types of female labor still predominated in the women's work world. In 1851, fully 40 percent of the working women in Britain were employed as domestic servants. In France, the largest group of female workers, 40 percent, worked in agriculture. Only 20 percent of female workers labored in Britain's factories, and only 10 percent in France. Regional and local studies have also indicated that most of them were single women. Few married women worked outside the home.

The laws that limited the work hours of children and women also began to break up the traditional kinship pattern of work and led to a new pattern based on a separation of work and home. Men were expected to shoulder the primary work obligations while women assumed daily control of the family and performed low-paying jobs such as laundry work that could be done in the home. Domestic industry made it possible for women to continue their contributions to family survival.

Efforts at Change: The Workers

Before long, workers in Great Britain began to look to the formation of labor organizations to gain decent wages and working conditions. Despite government opposition, new associations known as trade unions were formed by skilled workers in a number of new industries, including the cotton spinners, ironworkers, coal miners, and shipwrights. These unions served two purposes. One was to preserve their own workers' positions by limiting entry into their trade; another was to

A TRADE UNION MEMBERSHIP CARD. Skilled workers in a number of new industries formed trade unions in an attempt to gain higher wages, better working conditions, and special benefits. The scenes at the bottom of this membership card for the Associated Shipwright's Society illustrate some of the medical and social benefits it provided for its members.

gain benefits from the employers. These early trade unions had limited goals. They favored a working-class struggle against employers, but only to win improvements for the members of their own trades. The largest and most successful was the Amalgamated Society of Engineers, formed in 1850. Its provision of generous unemployment benefits in return for a small weekly payment was precisely the kind of practical gains these trade unions sought.

Trade unionism was not the only type of collective action by workers in the early decades of the Industrial Revolution. The Luddites were skilled craftsmen in the Midlands and northern England who in 1812 physically attacked the machines that they believed threatened their livelihoods. Their actions failed to stop the industrial mechanization of Britain, but the inability of twelve thousand troops to track down the culprits provides stunning evidence of the local support they enjoyed.

A more meaningful expression of the attempts of British workers to improve their condition developed in the movement known as Chartism. Its aim was to achieve political democracy. The so-called People's Charter, drawn up in 1838, demanded universal male suffrage and payment for serving in Parliament. Two national petitions incorporating these points, bearing millions of signatures, were presented to Parliament in 1839 and 1842. Although both were rejected as "fatal to all the purposes for which government exists," Chartism had not been a total failure. Its true significance stemmed from its ability to arouse and organize millions of working-class men and women, to give them a sense of working-class consciousness that they had not really possessed before. The political education of working people was important to the ultimate acceptance of the goals expressed in the People's Charter.

Efforts at Change: Reformers and Government

Efforts to improve the worst conditions of the industrial factory system also came from outside the ranks of the working classes. Reform-minded individuals, be they factory owners who felt twinges of conscience or social reformers in Parliament, campaigned against the evils of the industrial factory, especially condemning the abuse of children. Their efforts eventually met with success, especially in the reform-minded decades of the 1830s and 1840s. The Factory Act of 1833 stipulated that children between nine and thirteen could work only eight hours a day; those between thirteen and eighteen, twelve hours. Another piece of legislation in 1833 required that children between nine and thirteen have at least two hours of elementary education during the working day. In 1847, the Ten Hours Act reduced the workday for children between thirteen and eighteen to ten hours. Women were also now included in the ten-hour limitation. In 1842, the Coal Mines Act eliminated the employment of boys under ten and all women in mines. Eventually, men too would benefit from the move to restrict factory hours.

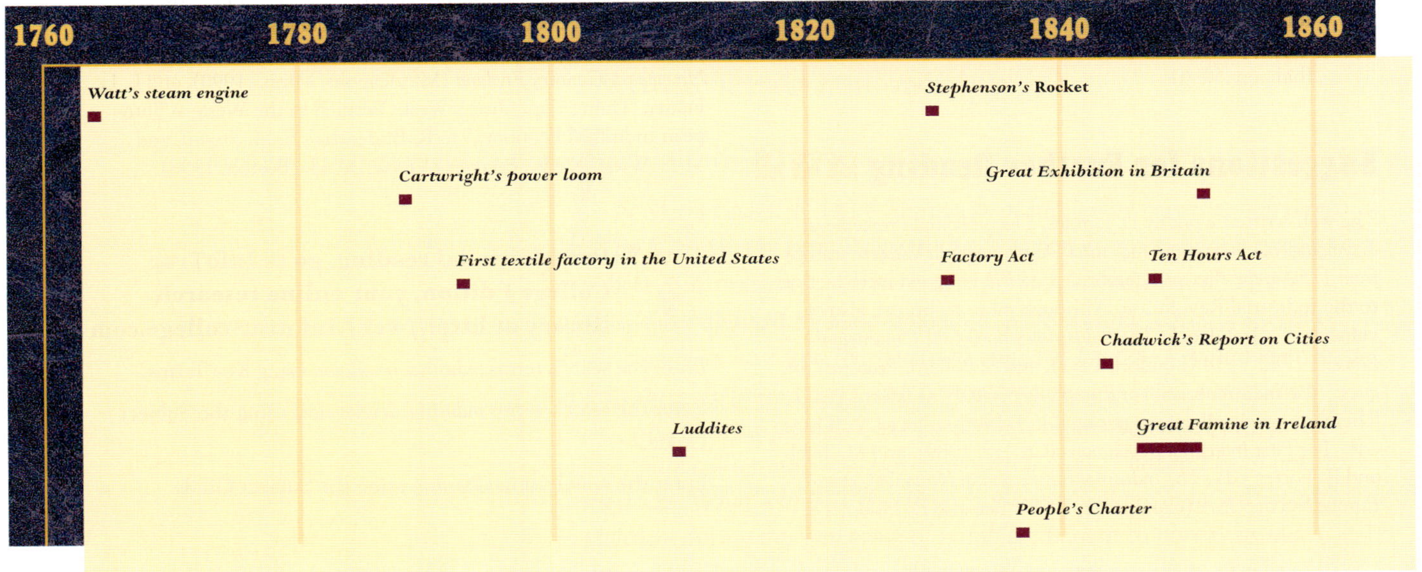

final peace settlement after almost a decade of war. On June 8, 1815, they finally completed their task.

The forces of upheaval unleashed during the French revolutionary and Napoleonic wars were temporarily quieted in 1815 as rulers sought to restore stability by reestablishing much of the old order to a Europe ravaged by war. Kings, landed aristocrats, and bureaucratic elites regained their control over domestic governments, while internationally the forces of conservatism tried to maintain the new status quo; some states even used military force to intervene in the internal affairs of other countries in their desire to crush revolutions.

But the Western world had been changed, and it would not readily go back to the old system. New ideologies, especially liberalism and nationalism, both products of the revolutionary upheaval initiated in France, had become too powerful to be contained. Not content with the status quo, the forces of change gave rise first to the revolts and revolutions that periodically shook Europe in the 1820s and 1830s and then to the widespread revolutions of 1848. Some of the revolutions and revolutionaries were successful; most were not. Although the old order usually appeared to have prevailed, by 1850 it was apparent that its days were numbered. This perception was reinforced by the changes wrought by the Industrial Revolution. Together the forces unleashed by the French Revolution and the Industrial Revolution made it impossible to turn back. Nevertheless, although these two revolutions initiated what historians like to call the modern European world, remnants of the old persisted in the midst of the new.

◆ The Conservative Order, 1815–1830

After the defeat of Napoleon, European rulers moved to restore the old order. This was the goal of the great powers—Great Britain, Austria, Prussia, and Russia—when they met at the Congress of Vienna in September 1814 to arrange a final peace settlement. The leader of the congress was the Austrian foreign minister, Prince Klemens von Metternich (1773–1859), who claimed that he was guided at Vienna by the principle of legitimacy. To keep peace and stability in Europe, he said it was necessary to restore the legitimate monarchs who would preserve traditional institutions. This had already been done in France by restoring the Bourbon monarchy.

METTERNICH. Prince Klemens von Metternich, the foreign minister of Austria, played a major role at the Congress of Vienna as the chief exponent of the principle of legitimacy. To maintain the new conservative order after 1815, Metternich espoused the principle of intervention, by which he meant that the great powers had the right to intervene militarily in other countries to crush revolutionary movements against legitimate rulers.

In fact, however, the principle of legitimacy was largely ignored elsewhere. At the Congress of Vienna, the great powers all grabbed land to add to their states. They believed that they were forming a new balance of power that would keep any one country from dominating Europe. For example, to balance Russian gains, Prussia and Austria had been strengthened (see Map 21.1). According to Metternich, this arrangement had clearly avoided a great danger: "Prussia and Austria are completing their systems of defence; united, the two monarchies form an unconquerable barrier against the enterprises of any conquering prince who might perhaps once again occupy the throne of France or that of Russia."[1]

The Conservative Domination: The Concert of Europe

The peace arrangements of 1815 were but the beginning of a conservative reaction determined to contain the liberal and nationalist forces unleashed by the French Revolution. Metternich and his kind were representatives of the ideology known as conservatism (see the box on p. 426). As a modern political philosophy, conservatism dates from 1790 when Edmund Burke wrote his *Reflections on the Revolution in France* in reaction to the French Revolution, especially its radical republican and democratic ideas. Burke maintained that society was a contract, but "the state ought not to be considered as nothing better than a partnership agreement in a trade of pepper and coffee, to be taken up for a temporary interest and to be dissolved by the fancy of the parties." The state was a partnership but one "not only between those who are living, but between those who are living, those who are dead and those who are to be born."[2] No one generation has the right to destroy this partnership; each generation has the duty to preserve and transmit it to the next. Burke advised against the violent overthrow of a government by revolution, but he did not reject the possibility of change. Sudden change was unacceptable, but that did not eliminate gradual or evolutionary improvements.

Most conservatives favored obedience to political authority, believed that organized religion was crucial to social order, hated revolutionary upheavals, and were unwilling to accept either the liberal demands for civil liberties and representative governments or the nationalistic aspirations generated by the French revolutionary era. The community took precedence over individual rights; society must be organized and ordered, and tradition remained the best guide for order. After 1815, the political philosophy of conservatism was supported by hereditary monarchs, government bureaucracies, landowning aristocracies, and revived churches, Protestant and Catholic alike. The conservative forces seemed dominant both internationally and domestically after 1815.

One method used by the great powers to maintain the new status quo they had constructed was the Concert of Europe, according to which Great Britain, Russia, Prussia, and Austria (and later France) agreed to meet periodically in conferences to discuss their common interests and examine measures that "will be judged most salutary for the repose and prosperity of peoples, and for the maintenance of peace in Europe."

Eventually, the five great powers formed the Quintuple Alliance and adopted a principle of intervention that was based on the right of the great powers to send armies into countries where there were revolutions to restore legitimate monarchs to their thrones. Britain refused to agree to the principle, arguing that it had never been the intention of the alliance to interfere in the internal affairs of other

MAP 21.1 Europe After the Congress of Vienna.

The Voice of Conservatism: Metternich of Austria

There was no greater symbol of conservatism in the first half of the nineteenth century than Prince Klemens von Metternich of Austria. Metternich played a crucial role at the Congress of Vienna and worked tirelessly for thirty years to repress the "revolutionary seed," as he called it, that had been spread to Europe by the "military despotism of Bonaparte."

Klemens von Metternich, Memoirs

We are convinced that society can no longer be saved without strong and vigorous resolutions on the part of the Governments still free in their opinions and actions.

We are also convinced that this may be, if the Governments face the truth, if they free themselves from all illusion, if they join their ranks and take their stand on a line of correct, unambiguous, and frankly announced principles.

By this course the monarchs will fulfill the duties imposed upon them by Him who, by entrusting them with power, has charged them to watch over the maintenance of justice, and the rights of all, to avoid the paths of error, and tread firmly in the way of truth. . . .

If the same elements of destruction which are now throwing society into convulsions have existed in all ages—for every age has seen immoral and ambitious men, hypocrites, men of heated imaginations, wrong motives, and wild projects—yet ours, by the single fact of the liberty of the press, possesses more than any preceding age the means of contact, seduction, and attraction whereby to act on these different classes of men.

We are certainly not alone in questioning if society can exist with the liberty of the press, a scourge unknown to the world before the latter half of the seventeenth century, and restrained until the end of the eighteenth, with scarcely any expectations but England—a part of Europe separated from the continent by the sea, as well as by her language and by her peculiar manners.

The first principle to be followed by the monarchs, united as they are by the coincidence of their desires and opinions, should be that of maintaining the stability of political institutions against the disorganized excitement which has taken possession of men's minds; the immutability of principles against the madness of their interpretation; and respect for laws actually in force against a desire for their destruction. . . .

The first and greatest concern for the immense majority of every nation is the stability of the laws, and their uninterrupted action—never their change. Therefore, let the Governments govern, let them maintain the groundwork of their institutions, both ancient and modern; for if it is at all times dangerous to touch them, it certainly would not now, in the general confusion, be wise to do so. . . .

Let them maintain religious principles in all their purity, and not allow the faith to be attacked and morality interpreted according to the social contract or the visions of foolish sectarians.

Let them suppress Secret Societies, that gangrene of society. . . .

To every great State determined to survive the storm there still remain many chances of salvation, and a strong union between the States on the principles we have announced will overcome the storm itself.

states. Ignoring the British response, Austria, Prussia, Russia, and France used military intervention to defeat revolutionary movements in Spain and Italy and to restore legitimate (and conservative) monarchs to their thrones. This success for the policy of intervention came at a price, however. The Concert of Europe had broken down when the British rejected Metternich's principle of intervention and ultimately prevented the Continental powers from intervening in the revolutions in Latin America.

THE REVOLT OF LATIN AMERICA

Whereas much of North America had been freed of European domination in the eighteenth century by the American Revolution, Latin America remained in the hands of the Spanish and Portuguese. However, when the Bourbon monarchy of Spain was toppled by Napoleon Bonaparte, Spanish authority in its colonial empire was weakened. By 1810, the disintegration of royal power in Argentina had led to that nation's independence. In Venezuela, a bitter struggle for independence was led by Simón Bolívar, hailed as "the Liberator." His forces freed Colombia in 1819 and Venezuela in 1821. A second liberator was José de San Martín, who freed Chile in 1817 and then in 1821 moved on to Lima, Peru, the center of Spanish authority. He was soon joined by Bolívar, who assumed the task of crushing the last significant Spanish army in 1824. Mexico and the Central American provinces also achieved their freedom, and by 1825, after Portugal had recognized the independence of Brazil, almost all of Latin America had been freed of colonial domination (see Map 21.2).

Although political independence brought economic independence, old patterns were quickly reestablished. Instead of Spain and Portugal, Great Britain now dominated the Latin American economy. British merchants moved in in large numbers, while British investors poured in funds, especially in the mining industry. Old trade patterns soon reemerged. Because Latin America served as a source of raw materials and foodstuffs for the industrializing nations of Europe and the United States, exports—especially wheat, tobacco, wool, sugar, coffee, and hides—to the North Atlantic countries increased noticeably. At the same time, finished consumer goods, especially textiles, were imported in increasing quantities, causing a decline in industrial production in Latin America. The emphasis on exporting raw materials and importing finished products ensured the ongoing domination of the Latin American economy by foreigners.

MAP 21.2 Latin America in the First Half of the Nineteenth Century.

THE GREEK REVOLT, 1821–1832

The principle of intervention proved to be a double-edged sword. Designed to prevent revolution, it could also be used to support revolution if the great powers found it in their interests to do so. In 1821, the Greeks revolted against their Turkish masters. Although subject to Muslim control for four hundred years, they had been allowed to maintain their language and their Greek Orthodox faith. A revival of Greek national sentiment at the beginning of the nineteenth century added to the growing desire for "the liberation of the fatherland from the terrible yoke of Turkish oppression." The Greek revolt was soon transformed into a noble cause by an outpouring of European sentiment for the Greeks' struggle. In 1827, a combined British and French fleet went to Greece and defeated a large Turkish armada. A year later, Russia declared war on the Ottoman Empire and invaded its European provinces of Moldavia and Wallachia. By the Treaty of Adrianople in 1829, which ended the Russian-Turkish war, the Russians received a protectorate over the two provinces. By the same treaty, the Turks agreed to allow Russia, France, and Britain to decide the fate of Greece. In 1830, the three powers declared Greece an independent kingdom, and two years later, a new royal dynasty was established. The revolution in Greece had been successful only because the great powers themselves supported it. Until 1830, the Greek revolt had been the only successful one in Europe; the conservative domination was still largely intact.

The Conservative Domination: The European States

Between 1815 and 1830, the conservative domination of Europe evident in the Concert of Europe was also apparent in domestic affairs as conservative governments throughout Europe worked to maintain the old order.

In 1815, Great Britain was governed by the aristocratic landowning classes that dominated both houses of Parliament. Within Parliament, there were two political factions, the Tories and the Whigs. Both were still dominated by members of the landed classes, although the Whigs were beginning to receive support from the new industrial middle class. Tory ministers largely dominated the government until 1830 and had little desire to change the existing political and electoral system. Calls for electoral reforms were met by repression and minor reforms that enabled the Tories to maintain their conservative domination.

In 1814, the Bourbon family was restored to the throne of France in the person of Louis XVIII (1814–1824). Louis understood the need to accept some of the changes brought to France by the revolutionary and Napoleonic eras. He accepted Napoleon's Civil Code, with its recognition of the principle of equality before the law. The property rights of those who had purchased confiscated lands during the Revolution were also preserved. In 1824, Louis died and was succeeded by his brother, who became Charles X (1824–1830). Charles' attempt to restore the old regime as far as possible led to public outrage. By 1830, France was on the brink of another revolution.

The Congress of Vienna had established nine states in Italy, including the kingdom of Sardinia in the north, ruled by the house of Savoy; the kingdom of the Two Sicilies (Naples and Sicily); the Papal States; a handful of small duchies ruled by relatives of the Austrian emperor; and the important northern provinces of Lombardy and Venetia, which were now part of the Austrian Empire. Italy was largely under Austrian domination, and all the states had extremely reactionary governments eager to smother any liberal or nationalist sentiment. Attempts at change were ruthlessly crushed.

After 1815, the forces of repression were particularly successful in central Europe. The Habsburg empire and its chief agent, Prince Klemens von Metternich, played an important role. Metternich boasted, "You see in me the chief Minister of Police in Europe. I keep an eye on everything. My contacts are such that nothing escapes me."[3] Metternich's spies were everywhere, searching for evidence of liberal or nationalist plots. Metternich worried too much in 1815. Although both liberalism and nationalism emerged in the German states and the Austrian Empire, they were initially weak as central Europe tended to remain under the domination of aristocratic landowning classes and autocratic, centralized monarchies.

The Vienna settlement in 1815 had recognized the existence of thirty-eight sovereign states (called the Germanic Confederation) in what had once been the Holy Roman Empire. Austria and Prussia were the two major powers; the other, smaller states varied considerably in size. The confederation had little real power. It had no real executive, and its only central organ was the federal diet, which needed the consent of all member states to take action. However, it also came to serve as Metternich's instrument to repress revolutionary movements within the German states and thus maintain the conservative status quo.

The Austrian Empire was a multinational state, a collection of different peoples under the Habsburg emperor, who provided a common bond. The empire contained people of eleven ethnicities, including Germans, Czechs, Slovaks, Magyars (Hungarians), Romanians, Slovenes, Poles, Serbs, and Italians. The Germans, accounting for only a quarter of the population, were economically the most advanced and played a leading role in governing Austria. Although these national groups, especially the Hungarians, began to favor the belief that each national group had the right to its own system of government, Metternich managed to repress the nationalist forces and hold the empire together.

At the beginning of the nineteenth century, Russia was overwhelmingly rural, agricultural, and autocratic. The Russian tsar was still regarded as a divine-right monarch. Alexander I (1801–1825) had been raised in the ideas of the Enlightenment and initially seemed willing to make reforms. He relaxed censorship, freed political prisoners, and reformed the educational system. But after the defeat of Napoleon, Alexander became a reactionary, and his government reverted to strict and arbitrary censorship. His brother Nicholas I (1825–1855), who succeeded him, was transformed from a conservative into a strict reactionary after a military revolt at the beginning of his reign. Nicholas strengthened both the bureaucracy and the secret police to maintain order. There would be no revolutions in Russia during the rest of his reign; if he could help it, there would be none in Europe either. Contemporaries called him the Policeman of Europe because of his willingness to use Russian troops to crush revolutions.

PORTRAIT OF NICHOLAS I. Tsar Nicholas I was a reactionary ruler who sought to prevent rebellion in Russia by strengthening the government bureaucracy, increasing censorship, and suppressing individual freedom by the use of political police. One of his enemies remarked about his facial characteristics: "The sharply retreating forehead and the lower jaw were expressive of iron will and feeble intelligence."

◆ The Ideologies of Change

Although the conservative forces were in the ascendancy from 1815 to 1830, powerful movements for change were also at work. These depended on ideas embodied in a series of political philosophies or ideologies that came into their own in the first half of the nineteenth century.

Liberalism

One of these ideologies was liberalism, which owed much to the Enlightenment of the eighteenth century and the American and French Revolutions at the end of that century. In addition, liberalism became even more significant as the Industrial Revolution progressed because the developing industrial middle class largely adopted the doctrine as its own. There were divergences of opinion among people classified as liberals, but all began with the belief that people should be as free from restraint as possible. This opinion is evident in both economic and political liberalism.

Also called classical economics, economic liberalism has as its primary tenet the concept of laissez-faire, the belief that the state should not interrupt the free play of natural economic forces, especially supply and demand. Government should not interfere with the economic liberty of the individual and should restrict itself to only three primary functions: defense of the country, police protection of individuals, and the construction and maintenance of public works too expensive for individuals to undertake. If individuals were allowed economic liberty, ultimately they would bring about the maximum good for the maximum number and benefit the general welfare of society.

Politically, liberals came to hold a common set of beliefs. Chief among them was the protection of civil liberties or the basic rights of all people, which included equality before the law; freedom of assembly, speech, and the press; and freedom from arbitrary arrest. All of these freedoms should be guaranteed by a written document, such as the American Bill of Rights or the French Declaration of the Rights of Man and the Citizen. In addition to religious toleration for all, most liberals advocated separation of church and state. The right of peaceful opposition to the government in and out of parliament and the making of laws by a representative assembly (legislature) elected by qualified voters constituted two other liberal demands. Many liberals believed, then, in a constitutional monarchy or constitutional state with limits on the powers of government in order to prevent despotism and in written constitutions that would also help guarantee these rights.

Many liberals also advocated ministerial responsibility, a system in which ministers of the king were responsible to the legislature rather than to the king, giving the legislative branch a check on the power of the executive. Liberals in the first half of the nineteenth century also believed in a limited suffrage. While all people were entitled to equal civil rights, they should not have equal political rights. The right to vote and hold office would be open only to men who met certain property qualifications. As a political philosophy, liberalism was tied to middle-class and especially industrial middle-class men who favored the extension of voting rights so that they could share power with the landowning classes. They had little desire to let the lower classes share that power. Liberals were not democrats.

One of the most prominent advocates of liberalism in the nineteenth century was the English philosopher John Stuart Mill (1806–1873). *On Liberty*, his most famous work, published in 1859, has long been regarded as a classic statement on the liberty of the individual (see the box on p. 431). Mill argued for an "absolute freedom of opinion and sentiment on all subjects" that needed to be protected from both government censorship and the tyranny of the majority.

Mill was also instrumental in expanding the meaning of liberalism by becoming an enthusiastic supporter of women's rights. When his attempt to include women in the voting reform bill of 1867 failed, Mill published an essay titled *On the Subjection of Women*, which he had written earlier with his wife, Harriet Taylor. He argued that "the legal subordination of one sex to the other" was wrong. Differences between women and men, he claimed, were not due to different natures but simply to social practices. With equal education, women could achieve as much as men. *On the Subjection of Women* would become an important work in the nineteenth-century movement for women's rights.

Nationalism

Nationalism was an even more powerful ideology for change in the nineteenth century. Nationalism arose out of an awareness of being part of a community that has common institutions, traditions, language, and customs. This community is called a "nation," and the primary political loyalty of individuals would be to the nation rather than to a dynasty or a city-state or other political unit. Nationalism did not become a popular force for change until the French Revolution. From then on, nationalists came to believe that each nationality should have its own government. Thus a divided people such as the Germans wanted national unity in a German nation-state with one central government. Subject peoples, such as the Hungarians, wanted national self-determination, or the right to establish their own autonomy, rather than be subject to a German minority in a multinational empire.

Nationalism threatened to upset the existing political order, both internationally and nationally (see Map 21.3). This meant that nationalism was fundamentally radical. A united Germany or united Italy would upset the balance of power established in 1815. By the same token, an independent Hungarian state would mean the breakup of the Austrian Empire. Because many European states were multinational, it is evident why conservatives tried so hard to repress the radical threat of nationalism.

At the same time, in the first half of the nineteenth century, nationalism and liberalism became strong allies. Most liberals believed that freedom could be realized only by peoples who ruled themselves. One British liberal said, "It is in general a necessary condition of free institutions that the boundaries of government should coincide in the main with those of nationalities." Many nationalists believed that once each people obtained its own state, all nations could be linked into a broader community of all humanity.

Early Socialism

In the first half of the nineteenth century, the pitiful conditions found in the slums, mines, and factories of the Industrial Revolution gave rise to another ideology for change known as socialism. The term even-

The Voice of Liberalism: John Stuart Mill on Liberty

John Stuart Mill was one of Britain's most famous philosophers of liberalism. Mill's On Liberty *is viewed as a classic statement of the liberal belief in the unfettered freedom of the individual. In this excerpt, Mill defends freedom of opinion from both government and the coercion of the majority.*

John Stuart Mill, On Liberty

The object of this Essay is to assert one very simple principle, as entitled to govern absolutely the dealings of society with the individual in the way of compulsion and control, whether the means used by physical force in the form of legal penalties, or the moral coercion of public opinion. That principle is, that the sole end for which mankind are warranted, individually or collectively, interfering with the liberty of action of any of their number, is self-protection. That the only purpose for which power can be rightfully exercised over any members of a civilized community, against his will, is to prevent harm to others. His own good, either physical or moral, is not a sufficient warrant. . . . These are good reasons for remonstrating with him, or reasoning with him, or persuading him, or entreating him, but not for compelling him, or visiting him with any evil in case he do otherwise. To justify that, the conduct from which it is desired to deter him, must be calculated to produce evil to some one else. The only part of the conduct of any one, for which he is amenable to society, is that which concerns others. In the part which merely concerns himself, his independence is, of right, absolute. Over himself, over his own body and mind, the individual is sovereign. . . .

Society can and does execute its own mandates: and if it issues wrong mandates instead of right, or any mandates at all in things with which it ought not to meddle, it practices a social tyranny more formidable than many kinds of political oppression, since, though not usually upheld by such extreme penalties, it leaves fewer means of escape, penetrating more deeply into the details of life, and enslaving the soul itself. Protection, therefore, against the tyranny of the magistrate is not enough: there needs protection also against the tyranny of prevailing opinion and feeling, against the tendency of society to impose, by other means than civil penalties, its own ideas and practices as rules of conduct on those who dissent from them. . . .

But there is a sphere of action in which society, as distinguished from the individual has, if any, only an indirect interest; comprehending all that portion of a person's life and conduct which affects only himself, or if it also affects others, only with their free, voluntary and undeceived consent and participation. . . . This then is the appropriate region of human liberty. It comprises, first, the inward domain of consciousness; demanding liberty of conscience in the most comprehensive sense; liberty of thought and feeling; absolute freedom of opinion and sentiment on all subjects, practical or speculative, scientific, moral, or theological. . . .

Let us suppose, therefore, that the government is entirely at one with the people, and never thinks of exerting any power of coercion unless in agreement with what it conceives to be their voice. But I deny the right of the people to exercise such coercion, either by themselves or by their government. The power itself is illegitimate. The best government has no more title to it than the worst. It is as noxious, or more noxious, when exerted in accordance with public opinion, than when in opposition to it. If all mankind minus one were of one opinion, and only one person were of the contrary opinion, mankind would be no more justified in silencing that one person, than he, if he had the power, would be justified in silencing mankind. . . . The peculiar evil of silencing the expression of an opinion is, that it is robbing the human race; posterity as well as the existing generation; those who dissent from the opinion, still more than those who hold it. If the opinion is right, they are deprived of the opportunity of exchanging error for truth: if wrong, they lose, what is almost as great a benefit, the clearer perception and livelier impression of truth, produced by its collision with error.

tually became associated with a Marxist analysis of human society (see Chapter 22), but early socialism was largely the product of political theorists or intellectuals who wanted to introduce equality into social conditions and believed that human cooperation was superior to the competition that characterized early industrial capitalism. To later Marxists, such ideas were impractical dreams, and they contemptuously labeled the theorists "utopian socialists." The term has endured to this day.

MAP 21.3 Nationalism in Europe in the Nineteenth Century.

The utopian socialists were against private property and the competitive spirit of early industrial capitalism. By eliminating these things and creating new systems of social organization, they thought, a better environment for humanity could be achieved. One prominent utopian socialist was Robert Owen (1771–1858), a British cotton manufacturer who believed that humans would reveal their true natural goodness if they lived in a cooperative environment. At New Lanark in Scotland, he was successful in transforming a squalid factory town into a flourishing, healthy community. But when he attempted to create a self-contained cooperative community at New Harmony, Indiana, in the United States in the 1820s, internal bickering within the community eventually destroyed his dream.

With their plans for the reconstruction of society, utopian socialists attracted a number of woman supporters who believed that only a reordering of society would help women. One of Owen's disciples, a wealthy woman named Frances Wright, bought slaves in order to set up a model community at Nashoba, Tennessee. The community failed, but Wright continued to work for women's rights.

◆ Revolution and Reform, 1830–1850

Beginning in 1830, the forces of change began to break through the conservative domination of Europe, more successfully in some places than in others. Finally, in 1848, a wave of revolutionary fervor moved through Europe, causing liberals and nationalists everywhere to think that they were on the verge of creating a new order.

The Revolutions of 1830

In France, the attempt of the ultraroyalists under the Bourbon monarch Charles X (1824–1830) to restore the old regime as far as possible led to a revolt by liberals in 1830 known as the July Revolution. Barricades went up in Paris as a provisional government led by a group of moderate, propertied liberals was hastily formed and appealed to Louis-Philippe, a cousin of Charles X, to become the constitutional king of France. Charles X fled to Britain; a new monarchy had been born.

Louis-Philippe (1830–1848) was soon called the bourgeois monarch because political support for his rule came from the upper middle class. Louis-Philippe even dressed like a member of the middle class, in business suits and hats. Constitutional changes that favored the interests of the upper bourgeoisie were instituted. Financial qualifications for voting were reduced yet remained sufficiently high that the number of voters only increased from 100,000 to barely 200,000 continuing to guarantee that only the wealthiest people would vote. To the upper middle class, the bourgeois monarchy represented the stopping place for political progress.

Supporters of liberalism played a primary role in the revolution in France, but nationalism was the crucial force in three other revolutionary outbursts in 1830. In an effort to create a stronger, larger state on France's northern border, the Congress of Vienna had added the area once known as the Austrian Netherlands (modern-day Belgium) to the Dutch Republic. But the Belgians rose up against the Dutch and succeeded in convincing the major European powers to accept an independent, neutral Belgium. The revolutionary scenarios in Poland and Italy were much less successful. Russian forces crushed the attempt of Poles to liberate themselves from foreign domination, and Metternich sent Austrian troops to crush revolts in three Italian states.

The successful July Revolution in France served to catalyze change in Britain. The Industrial Revolution had led to an expanding group of industrial leaders who objected to the corrupt British electoral system, which excluded them from political power. The Whigs, though also members of the landed classes, realized that concessions to reform were superior to revolution; the

THE JULY REVOLUTION IN PARIS. In 1830, the forces of change began to undo the conservative domination of Europe. In France, the reactionary Charles X was overthrown. In this painting, students, former soldiers of the empire, and middle-class citizens are seen joining the rebels who are marching on city hall to demand a republic. The forces of Charles X, seen firing from a building above, failed to halt the rebels.

demands of the wealthy industrial middle class could no longer be ignored. In 1832, Parliament passed a reform bill that increased the numbers of male voters, primarily benefiting the upper middle class; the lower middle class, artisans, and industrial workers still had no vote. Nevertheless, a significant step had been taken. The "monied, manufacturing, and educated elite" had been joined to the landed interest in ruling Britain. As a result of reforms, Britain would experience no revolutionary disturbances during 1848.

The Revolutions of 1848

Despite the successful revolutions in France, Belgium, and Greece, the conservative order remained in control of much of Europe. But liberalism and nationalism continued to grow. In 1848, these forces of change erupted once more. Yet again, revolution in France provided the spark for other countries, and soon most of central and southern Europe was ablaze with revolutionary fires. Tsar Nicholas I of Russia lamented to Queen Victoria in April 1848, "What remains standing in Europe? Great Britain and Russia."

ANOTHER FRENCH REVOLUTION

A severe industrial and agricultural depression beginning in 1846 brought great hardship in France to the lower middle class, workers, and peasants. Scandals, graft, and corruption were rife, and the government's persistent refusal to extend the suffrage angered the disenfranchised members of the middle class. As Louis-Philippe's government continued to refuse to make changes, opposition grew and finally overthrew the monarchy on February 24, 1848. A group of moderate and radical republicans established a provisional government and called for the election by universal manhood suffrage of a "constituent assembly" that would draw up a new constitution.

The provisional government also established national workshops, which were supposed to be cooperative factories run by the workers. In fact, the workshops came to provide jobs for unemployed workers, consisting primarly of leaf raking and ditch digging. The cost of the program became increasingly burdensome to the government.

The result was a growing split between the moderate republicans, who had the support of most of France, and the radical republicans, whose main support came from the Parisian working class. From March to June, the number of unemployed enrolled in the national workshops rose from 10,000 to almost 120,000, emptying the treasury and frightening the moderates, who responded by closing the workshops on June 23. The workers refused to accept this decision and poured into the streets. Four days of bitter and bloody fighting by government forces crushed the working-class revolt. Thousands were killed, and four thousand prisoners were deported to the French colony of Algeria in northern Africa.

The new constitution, ratified in November, established a republic (the Second Republic) with a one-house legislature with 750 members elected by universal male suffrage for three years and a president, also elected by universal male suffrage, for four years. In the elections for the presidency held in December 1848, Charles Louis Napoleon Bonaparte, the nephew of the famous French ruler, won a resounding victory. Within four years, President Napoleon would become Emperor Napoleon.

REVOLUTION IN CENTRAL EUROPE

News of the revolution in Paris in February 1848 led to upheavals in central Europe as well (see the box on p. 435). Revolutionary cries for change caused many German rulers to promise constitutions, a free press, jury trials, and other liberal reforms. Concessions to appease the revolutionaries were also made in Prussia. King Frederick William IV (1840–1861) agreed to abolish censorship, establish a new constitution, and work for a united Germany. This last promise had its counterpart throughout all the German states as governments allowed elections by universal male suffrage for deputies to an all-German parliament. Its purpose was to fulfill a liberal and nationalist dream—the preparation of a constitution for a new united Germany.

But the Frankfurt Assembly, as the all-German parliament was called, failed to achieve its goals. Although some members spoke of using force, they had no real means of compelling the German rulers to accept the constitution they had drawn up. The attempt of the German liberals at Frankfurt to create a German state had failed, and leadership for unification would now pass to the Prussian military monarchy.

The Austrian Empire also had its social, political, and nationalist grievances and needed only the news of the revolution in Paris to encourage it to erupt in flames in March 1848. The Hungarian liberals under Louis Kossuth agitated for "commonwealth" status; they were willing to keep the Habsburg monarch but wanted their own legislature. In March, demonstrations in Buda, Prague, and Vienna led to Metternich's dismissal, and the archsymbol of the conservative

Revolutionary Excitement: Carl Schurz and the Revolution of 1848 in Germany

The excitement with which German liberals and nationalists received the news of the February Revolution in France and their own expectations for Germany are well captured in this selection from the Reminiscences *of Carl Schurz (1829–1906). Schurz made his way to the United States after the failure of the German revolution and eventually became a United States senator.*

Carl Schurz, Reminiscences

One morning, toward the end of February, 1848, I sat quietly in my attic-chamber, working hard at my tragedy of "Ulrich von Hutten" [a sixteenth-century German knight], when suddenly a friend rushed breathlessly into the room, exclaiming: "What, you sitting here! Do you not know what has happened?"

"No, what?"

"The French have driven away Louis Philippe and proclaimed the republic."

I threw down my pen—and that was the end of "Ulrich von Hutten." I never touched the manuscript again. We tore down the stairs, into the street, to the market-square, the accustomed meeting-place for all the student societies after their midday dinner. Although it was still forenoon, the market was already crowded with young men talking excitedly. There was no shouting, no noise, only agitated conversation. What did we want there? This probably no one knew. But since the French had driven away Louis Philippe and proclaimed the republic, something of course must happen here, too. . . . We were dominated by a vague feeling as if a great outbreak of elemental forces had begun, as if an earthquake was impending of which we had felt the first shock, and we instinctively crowded together. . . .

The next morning there were the usual lectures to be attended. But how profitless! The voice of the professor sounded like a monotonous drone coming from far away. What he had to say did not seem to concern us. The pen that should have taken notes remained idle. At last we closed with a sigh the notebook and went away, impelled by a feeling that now we had something more important to do—to devote ourselves to the affairs of the fatherland. And this we did by seeking as quickly as possible again the company of our friends, in order to discuss what had happened and what was to come. In these conversations, excited as they were, certain ideas and catchwords worked themselves to the surface, which expressed more or less the feelings of the people. Now had arrived in Germany the day for the establishment of "German Unity," and the founding of a great, powerful national German Empire. In the first line the convocation of a national parliament. Then the demands for civil rights and liberties, free speech, free press, the right of free assembly, equality before the law, a freely elected representation of the people with legislative power, responsibility of ministers, self-government of the communes, the right of the people to carry arms, the formation of a civic guard with elective officers, and so on—in short, that which was called a "constitutional form of government on a broad democratic basis." Republican ideas were at first only sparingly expressed. But the word democracy was soon on all tongues, and many, too, thought it a matter of course that if the princes should try to withhold from the people the rights and liberties demanded, force would take the place of mere petition. Of course the regeneration of the fatherland must, if possible, be accomplished by peaceable means. . . . Like many of my friends, I was dominated by the feeling that at last the great opportunity had arrived for giving to the German people the liberty which was their birthright and to the German fatherland its unity and greatness, and that it was now the first duty of every German to do and to sacrifice everything for this sacred object.

order fled abroad. In Vienna, revolutionary forces, carefully guided by the educated and propertied classes, took control of the capital and insisted that a constituent assembly be summoned to draw up a liberal constitution. Hungary was granted its wish for its own legislature, a separate national army, and control over foreign policy and budget. In Bohemia, the Czechs began to demand their own government as well.

Although Emperor Ferdinand I (1835–1848) and Austrian officials had made concessions to appease the revolutionaries, they awaited an opportunity to reestablish their firm control. As in the German states, they were increasingly encouraged by the divisions between radical and moderate revolutionaries and played on the middle-class fear of a working-class social revolution. Their first success came in June 1848 when Austrian military forces under General Alfred Windischgrätz ruthlessly suppressed the Czech rebels in Prague. By the end of October, radical rebels had been crushed in Vienna. In December, the feebleminded Ferdinand agreed to abdicate in favor of his nephew, Francis Joseph I (1848–1916), who worked vigorously to restore the imperial government in Hungary. The Austrian armies, however, were unable to defeat Kossuth's forces, and it was only through the intervention of Nicholas I, who sent a Russian army of 140,000 men to aid the Austrians, that the Hungarian revolution was finally crushed in 1849. The revolutions in the Austrian Empire had also failed. Autocratic government was restored; emperor and propertied classes remained in control, and the numerous nationalities were still subject to the Austrian government.

REVOLTS IN THE ITALIAN STATES

The failure of revolutionary uprisings in Italy in 1830 and 1831 had encouraged the Italian movement for unification to take a new direction. The leadership of Italy's resurgence passed into the hands of Giuseppe Mazzini (1805–1872), a dedicated Italian nationalist who founded an organization known as Young Italy in 1831. This group set as its goal the creation of a united Italian republic. In *The Duties of Man*, Mazzini urged Italians to dedicate their lives to the Italian nation: "O my Brother! Love your country. Our Country is our home." A number of Italian women also took up Mazzini's call. Especially notable was Cristina Belgioioso (1808–1871), a wealthy aristocrat who worked to bring about Italian unification. Pursued by the Austrian authorities, she fled to Paris and started a newspaper to espouse the Italian cause.

The dreams of Mazzini and Belgioioso seemed on the verge of fulfillment when a number of Italian states rose in revolt in 1848. Beginning in Sicily, rebellions spread northward as ruler after ruler granted a constitution to his people. Citizens in Lombardy and Venetia also rebelled against their Austrian overlords. The Venetians declared a republic in Venice. The king of the northern Italian state of Piedmont, Charles Albert (1831–1849), took up the call and assumed the leadership for a war of liberation from Austrian domination. His invasion of Lombardy proved unsuccessful, however, and by 1849 the Austrians had reestablished complete control over Lombardy and Venetia. Counterrevolutionary forces also prevailed throughout Italy as Italian rulers managed to recover power on their own. Only Piedmont was able to keep its liberal constitution.

AUSTRIAN STUDENTS IN THE REVOLUTIONARY CIVIL GUARD. In 1848, revolutionary fervor swept through Europe and toppled governments in France, central Europe, and Italy. In the Austrian Empire, students joined the revolutionary civil guard in taking control of Vienna and forcing the Austrian emperor to call a constituent assembly to draft a liberal constitution.

CHRONOLOGY

Reaction, Reform, and Revolution: The European States, 1815–1850

Great Britain	
Reform Act	1832
France	
Louis XVIII	1814–1824
Charles X	1824–1830
July Revolution	1830
Louis-Philippe	1830–1848
Abdication of Louis-Philippe; formation of provisional government	1848 (February 22–24)
June Days: workers' revolt in Paris	1848 (June)
Establishment of Second Republic	1848 (November)
Election of Louis Napoleon as French president	1848 (December)
Low Countries	
Union of Netherlands and Belgium	1815
Belgian revolt and independence	1830
German States	
Germanic Confederation	1815
Frederick William IV of Prussia	1840–1861
Revolution in Germany	1848
Frankfurt Assembly	1848–1849
Austrian Empire	
Emperor Ferdinand I	1835–1848
Revolt in Austrian Empire; dismissal of Metternich	1848 (March)
Suppression of Czech rebels	1848 (June)
Suppression of Viennese rebels	1848 (October)
Francis Joseph I	1848–1916
Defeat of Hungarians with help of Russian troops	1849
Italian States	
King Charles Albert of Piedmont	1831–1849
Revolutions in Italy	1848
Attack on Austria	1848
Restoration of Austrian control in Lombardy and Venetia	1849
Russia	
Tsar Alexander I	1801–1825
Tsar Nicholas I	1825–1855
Suppression of Polish revolt	1831

Throughout Europe in 1848, popular revolts had initiated revolutionary upheavals that had prodded the formation of liberal constitutions and liberal governments. But the failure of the revolutionaries to stay united soon led to the reestablishment of the old regimes. In 1848, nationalities everywhere had also revolted in pursuit of self-government. But again frightfully little was achieved because divisions among nationalities proved utterly disastrous. Though the Hungarians demanded autonomy from the Austrians, at the same time they refused the same to their minorities—the Slovenes, Croats, and Serbs. Instead of joining together against the old empire, minorities fought each other.

The Growth of the United States

The American Constitution, ratified in 1789, committed the United States to two of the major forces of the first half of the nineteenth century, liberalism and nationalism. Initially, this constitutional commitment to national unity was challenged by divisions over the power of the federal government vis-à-vis the individual states. Bitter conflict erupted between the Federalists and the Republicans. Led by Alexander Hamilton (1757–1804), the Federalists favored a financial program that would establish a strong central government. The Republicans, guided by Thomas Jefferson (1743–1826) and James Madison (1751–1836), feared centralization and its consequences for popular liberties. These divisions were intensified by European rivalries because the Federalists were pro-British and the Republicans pro-French. The successful conclusion of the War of 1812 against the British brought an end to the Federalists, who had opposed the war, while the surge of national feeling generated by the war served to heal the nation's divisions.

Another strong force for national unity came from the Supreme Court while John Marshall

(1755–1835) was Chief Justice from 1801 to 1835. Marshall made the Supreme Court into an important national institution by asserting the right of the Court to overrule an act of Congress if the Court found it to be in violation of the Constitution. Under Marshall, the Supreme Court contributed further to establishing the supremacy of the national government by curbing the actions of state courts and legislatures.

The election of Andrew Jackson (1767–1845) as president in 1828 opened a new era in American politics. Jacksonian democracy introduced a mass democratic politics. The electorate was expanded by dropping traditional property qualifications; by the 1830s, suffrage had been extended to almost all adult white males. During the period from 1815 to 1850, the traditional liberal belief in the improvement of human beings was also given concrete expression. Americans developed detention schools for juvenile delinquents and new penal institutions, both motivated by the liberal belief that the right kind of environment would rehabilitate those in need of it.

Culture in an Age of Reaction and Revolution: The Mood of Romanticism

At the end of the eighteenth century, a new intellectual movement known as Romanticism emerged to challenge the Enlightenment's preoccupation with reason in discovering truth. The Romantics tried to balance the use of reason by stressing the importance of feeling, emotion, and imagination as sources of knowing. As one German Romantic put it, "It was my heart that counseled me to do it, and my heart cannot err."

The Characteristics of Romanticism

Romantic writers emphasized emotion, sentiment, and inner feelings in their works. An important model for Romantics was the tragic figure in *The Sorrows of the Young Werther*, a novel by the great German writer Johann Wolfgang von Goethe (1749–1832), who later rejected Romanticism in favor of classicism. Werther was a Romantic figure who sought freedom as the source of personal fulfillment. Misunderstood and rejected by society, he continued to believe in his own worth through his inner feelings, but his deep love for a girl who did not love him finally led him to commit suicide. After Goethe's *Sorrows of Young Werther*, numerous novels and plays appeared whose plots revolved around young maidens tragically carried off at an early age (twenty-three was most common) by disease (usually tuberculosis, at that time a protracted disease that was usually fatal) to the sorrow and sadness of their male lovers.

Another important characteristic of Romanticism was individualism, an interest in the unique traits of each person. The Romantics' desire to follow their inner drives led them to rebel against middle-class conventions. Long hair, beards, and outrageous clothes served to reinforce the individualism that young Romantics were trying to express.

Many Romantics possessed a passionate interest in the past. This historical focus was manifested in many ways. In Germany, the Grimm brothers collected and published local fairy tales, as Hans Christian Andersen did in Denmark. The revival of Gothic architecture left European countrysides adorned with pseudo-medieval castles and cities bedecked with grandiose neo-Gothic cathedrals, city halls, parliamentary buildings, and even railway stations. Literature, too, reflected this historical consciousness. The novels of Walter Scott (1771–1832) became European best-sellers in the first half of the nineteenth century. *Ivanhoe*, in which Scott tried to evoke the clash between Saxon and Norman knights in medieval England, became one of his most popular works.

To the historical mindedness of the Romantics could be added an attraction to the bizarre and unusual. In an exaggerated form, this preoccupation gave rise to so-called Gothic literature (see the box on p. 439), chillingly evident in short stories of horror by the American Edgar Allan Poe (1808–1849) and in *Frankenstein* by Mary Wollstonecraft Shelley (1797–1851). Shelley's novel was the story of a mad scientist who brings into being a humanlike monster who goes berserk. Some Romantics even sought the unusual in their own lives by pursuing extraordinary states of experience in dreams, nightmares, frenzies, and suicidal depression or by experimenting with cocaine, opium, and hashish to achieve altered states of consciousness.

Romantic Poets and the Love of Nature

To the Romantics, poetry ranked above all other literary forms because they believed it was the direct expression of one's soul. The Romantic poets were viewed as seers who could reveal the invisible world

Gothic Literature: Edgar Allan Poe

American writers and poets made significant contributions to the movement of Romanticism. Although Edgar Allan Poe was influenced by the German Romantic school of mystery and horror, many literary historians give him the credit for pioneering the modern short story. This selection from the conclusion of "The Fall of the House of Usher" gives a sense of the nature of so-called Gothic literature.

Edgar Allan Poe, "The Fall of the House of Usher"

No sooner had these syllables passed my lips, than—as if a shield of brass had indeed, at the moment, fallen heavily upon a floor of silver—I became aware of a distinct, hollow, metallic, and clangorous, yet apparently muffled, reverberation. Completely unnerved, I leaped to my feet; but the measured rocking movement of Usher was undisturbed. I rushed to the chair in which he sat. His eyes were bent fixedly before him, and throughout his whole countenance there reigned a stony rigidity. But, as I placed my hand upon his shoulder, there came a strong shudder over his whole person; a sickly smile quivered about his lips and I saw that he spoke in a low, hurried, and gibbering murmur, as if unconscious of my presence. Bending closely over him, I at length drank in the hideous import of his words.

"Not hear it?—yes, I hear it, and *have* heard it. Long-long-long-many minutes, many hours, many days, have I heard it—yet I dared not—oh, pity me, miserable wretch that I am!—I dared not—I *dared* not speak! *We have put her living in the tomb!* Said I not that my senses were acute? I *now* tell you that I heard her first feeble movements in the hollow coffin. I heard them—many, many days ago—yet I dared not—I *dared not speak!* And now—to-night— . . . the rending of her coffin, and the grating of the iron hinges of her prison, and her struggles within the coppered archway of the vault! Oh whither shall I fly? Will she not be here anon? Is she not hurrying to upbraid me for my haste? Have I not heard her footstep on the stair? Do I not distinguish that heavy and horrible beating of her heart? MADMAN!"—here he sprang furiously to his feet, and shrieked out his syllables, as if in the effort he were giving up his soul—"MADMAN! I TELL YOU THAT SHE NOW STANDS WITHOUT THE DOOR!"

As if in the superhuman energy of his utterance there had been found the potency of a spell, the huge antique panels to which the speaker pointed threw slowly back, upon the instant, their ponderous and ebony jaws. It was the work of the rushing gust—but then without those doors there DID stand the lofty and enshrouded figure of the lady Madeline of Usher. There was blood upon her white robes, and the evidence of some bitter struggle upon every portion of her emaciated frame. For a moment she remained trembling and reeling to and fro upon the threshold, then, with a low moaning cry, fell heavily inward upon the person of her brother, and in her violent and now final death-agonies, bore him to the floor a corpse, and a victim to the terrors he had anticipated.

to others. Their incredible sense of drama made some of them the most colorful figures of their era, living intense but short lives. Percy Bysshe Shelley (1792–1822), expelled from school for advocating atheism, set out to reform the world. His *Prometheus Unbound*, completed in 1820, is a portrait of the revolt of human beings against the laws and customs that oppress them. He drowned in a storm in the Mediterranean. Lord Byron (1788–1824) dramatized himself as the melancholy Romantic hero that he had described in his own work, *Childe Harold's Pilgrimage*. He participated in the movement for Greek independence and died in Greece fighting the Turks.

Romantic poetry gave full expression to one of the most important characteristics of Romanticism: love of nature, especially evident in William Wordsworth (1770–1850). His experience of nature was almost mystical as he claimed to receive "authentic tidings of invisible things":

> *One impulse from a vernal wood*
> *May teach you more of man,*
> *Of Moral Evil and of good,*
> *Than all the sages can.*[4]

To Wordsworth, nature contained a mysterious force that the poet could perceive and learn from. Nature served as a mirror into which humans could look to learn about themselves. Nature was, in fact, alive and sacred:

To every natural form, rock, fruit or flower,
Even the loose stones that cover the high-way,
I gave a moral life, I saw them feel,
Or link'd them to some feeling: the great mass
Lay bedded in a quickening soul, and all
That I beheld, respired with inward meaning.[5]

Other Romantics carried this worship of nature further into pantheism by identifying the great force in nature with God. As the German Romantic poet Friedrich Novalis said, "Anyone seeking God will find him anywhere."

Romanticism in Art and Music

Like the literary arts, the visual arts were also deeply affected by Romanticism. Although their works varied widely, Romantic artists shared at least two fundamental characteristics. All artistic expression to them was a reflection of the artist's inner feelings; a painting should mirror the artist's vision of the world and be the instrument of his own imagination. Moreover, Romantic artists deliberately rejected the principles of classicism. Beauty was not a timeless thing; its expression depended on one's culture and one's age. The Romantics abandoned classical restraint for warmth, emotion, and movement.

The early life experiences of Caspar David Friedrich (1774–1840) left him with a lifelong preoccupation with God and nature. Friedrich painted landscapes, but with an interest that transcended the mere presentation of natural details. His portrayal of mountains shrouded in mist, gnarled trees bathed in moonlight, and the stark ruins of monasteries surrounded by withered trees all conveyed a feeling of mystery and mysticism. For Friedrich, nature was a manifestation of divine life, as is evident in *Man and Woman Gazing at the Moon*. To Friedrich, the artistic process depended on the use of an unrestricted imagination that could only be achieved through inner vision. He advised artists: "Shut your physical eye and look first at your picture with your spiritual eye, then bring to the light of day what you have seen in the darkness."

Eugène Delacroix (1798–1863) was one of the most famous French exponents of the Romantic school of painting. Delacroix's paintings exhibited two primary characteristics, a fascination with the exotic and a passion for color. Both are visible in *Death of Sardanapalus*. Significant for its use of light and its patches of interrelated color, this portrayal of the world of the last Assyrian king was criticized at the time for its brilliant color. In Delacroix, theatricality and movement combined with a daring use of color. Many of his works reflect his own belief that "a painting should be a feast to the eye."

To many Romantics, music was the most Romantic of the arts because it enabled the composer to probe deeply into human emotions. Music historians have called the eighteenth century an age of classicism and the nineteenth the era of Romanticism. One of the greatest composers of all time, Ludwig van Beethoven, served as a bridge between the two.

Beethoven (1770–1827) was born in Bonn, Germany, but soon made his way to Vienna, then the musical capital of Europe, where he studied briefly

CASPAR DAVID FRIEDRICH, *MAN AND WOMAN GAZING AT THE MOON*. The German artist Caspar David Friedrich sought to express in painting his own mystical view of nature. "The divine is everywhere," he once wrote, "even in a grain of sand." In this painting, two solitary wanderers are shown from the back gazing at the moon. Overwhelmed by the all-pervasive presence of nature, the two figures express the human longing for infinity.

EUGÈNE DELACROIX, *DEATH OF SARDANAPALUS*. Delacroix's *Death of Sardanapalus* was based on Lord Byron's verse account of the decadent Assyrian king's dramatic last moments. Besieged by enemy troops and with little hope of survival, Sardanapalus orders that his harem women and prize horses go to their death with him. At the right, a guard stabs one of the women as the king looks on.

under Mozart and took up permanent residence. During his first major period of composing, from 1792 to 1802, his work was still largely within the classical framework of the eighteenth century, and the influences of Mozart and Haydn are paramount. But with the composition of the Third Symphony (1804), the *Eroica*, originally intended for Napoleon, Beethoven broke through to Romanticism in his use of uncontrolled rhythms to create dramatic struggle and uplifted resolutions. E. T. A. Hoffman, a contemporary composer and writer, said, "Beethoven's music opens the flood gates of fear, of terror, of horror, of pain, and arouses that longing for the eternal which is the essence of Romanticism. He is thus a pure Romantic composer."[6] Beethoven went on to write a vast quantity of works, but in the midst of this productivity and growing fame, he was more and more burdened by his growing deafness. One of the most moving pieces of music of all time, the chorale finale of his Ninth Symphony, was composed when Beethoven was totally deaf.

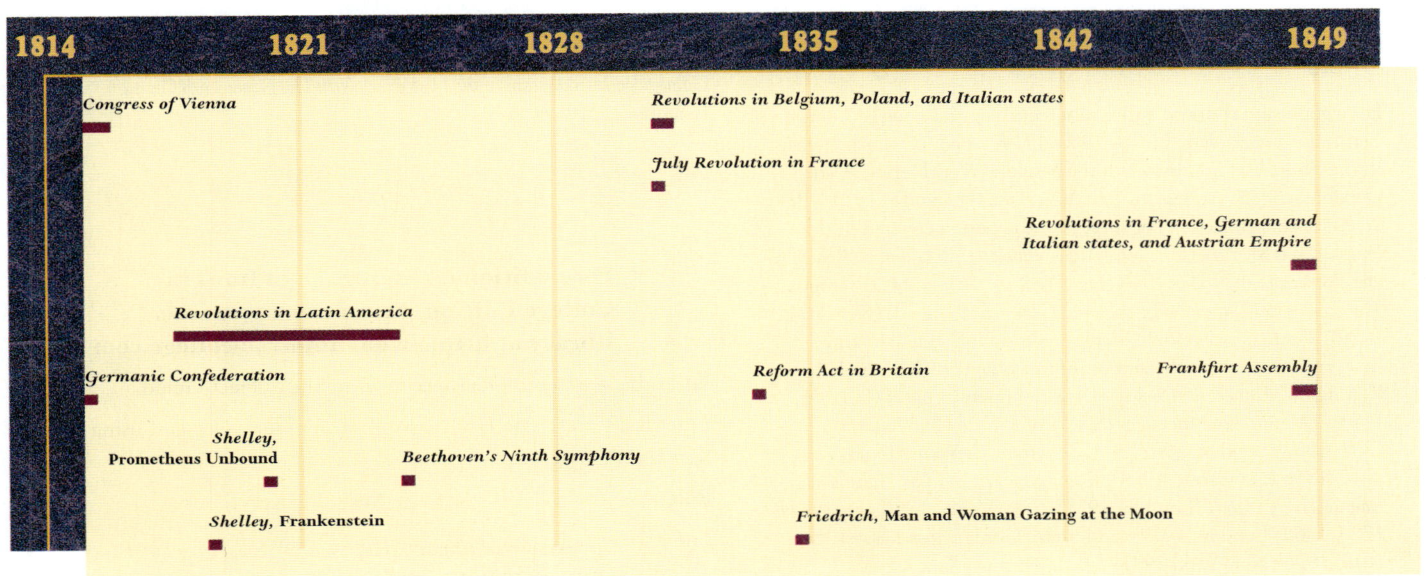

Conclusion

In 1815, a conservative order was reestablished throughout Europe, and the cooperation of the great powers, embodied in the Concert of Europe, tried to ensure its durability. But the revolutionary waves of the early 1820s and the early 1830s made it clear that the ideologies of liberalism and nationalism, unleashed by the French Revolution and now reinforced by the spread of the Industrial Revolution, were still alive and active. They faced enormous difficulties, however, as failed revolutions in Poland, Russia, Italy, and Germany all testify. At the same time, reform legislation in Britain and successful revolutions in Greece, France, and Belgium demonstrated the continuing strength of these forces of change. In 1848, they erupted once more all across Europe. And once more they failed. But all was not lost. Both liberalism and nationalism would succeed in the second half of the nineteenth century, but in ways not foreseen by the idealistic liberals and nationalists, who were utterly convinced that their time had come when they manned the barricades in 1848.

Notes

1. Quoted in M. S. Anderson, *The Ascendancy of Europe 1815–1914,* 2d ed. (London, 1985), p. 1.
2. Quoted in Peter Viereck, *Conservatism* (Princeton, N.J., 1956), p. 27.
3. Quoted in G. de Berthier de Sauvigny, *Metternich and His Times* (London, 1962), p. 105.
4. William Wordsworth, "The Tables Turned," *Poems of Wordsworth,* ed. Matthew Arnold (London, 1963), p. 138.
5. William Wordsworth, *The Prelude* (Harmondsworth, England, 1971), p. 109.
6. Quoted in Siegbert Prawer, ed., *The Romantic Period in Germany* (London, 1970), p. 285.

Suggestions for Further Reading 

For a good survey of the entire nineteenth century, see R. Gildea, *Barricades and Borders: Europe 1800–1914,* 2d ed. (Oxford, 1996), in the Short Oxford History of the Modern World series. Also valuable is M. S. Anderson, *The Ascendancy of Europe, 1815–1914,* 2d ed. (London, 1985). For surveys of the period covered in this chapter, see M. Broers, *Europe After Napoleon: Revolution, Reaction, and Romanticism, 1814–1848* (New York, 1996), and C. Breunig, *The Age of Revolution and Reaction, 1789–1850,* 2d ed. (New York, 1979). There are also some useful books on individual countries that cover more than the subject of this chapter. These include R. Magraw, *France, 1815–1914: The Bourgeois Century* (London, 1983); D. Saunders, *Russia in the Age of Reaction and Reform, 1801–1881* (London, 1992); J. J. Sheehan, *German History, 1770–1866* (New York, 1989); C. A. Macartney, *The Habsburg Empire, 1790–1918* (London, 1971); S. J. Woolf, *A History of Italy, 1700–1860* (London, 1979); and N. McCord, *British History, 1815–1906* (New York, 1991).

On the peace settlement of 1814–1815, see T. Chapman, *The Congress of Vienna* (London, 1998). A concise summary of the international events of the entire nineteenth century can be found in R. Bullen and F. R. Bridge, *The Great Powers and the European States System, 1815–1914* (London, 1980). See also N. Rich, *Great Power Diplomacy, 1814–1914* (New York, 1992). On the man whose conservative policies dominated this era, see the brief but good biography by A. Palmer, *Metternich* (New York, 1972). On the revolutions in Europe in 1830, see C. Church, *Europe in 1830: Revolution and Political Change* (Chapel Hill, N.C., 1983). On Great Britain's reform legislation, see M. Brock, *Great Reform Act* (London, 1973), and D. C. Moore, *The Politics of Deference: A Study of the Mid-Nineteenth-Century English Political System* (New York, 1976). The Greek revolt is examined in detail in D. Dakin, *The Greek Struggle for Independence, 1821–33* (Berkeley, Calif., 1973).

The best introduction to the revolutions of 1848 is J. Sperber, *The European Revolutions, 1848–1851* (New York, 1994). See also P. Stearns, *1848: The Revolutionary Tide in Europe* (New York, 1974). Good accounts of the revolutions in individual countries include G. Duveau, *1848: The Making of a Revolution* (New York, 1967); R. J. Rath, *The Viennese Revolution of 1848* (Austin, Tex., 1957); I. Déak, *The Lawful Revolution: Louis Kossuth and the Hungarians, 1848–49* (New York, 1979); R. Stadelmann, *Social and Political History of the German 1848 Revolution* (Athens, Ohio, 1975); and P. Ginsborg, *Daniele Manin and the Venetian Revolution of 1848–49* (New York, 1979). On Mazzini, see D. M. Smith, *Mazzini* (New Haven, Conn., 1994).

Good introductions to the major ideologies of the first half of the nineteenth century including both analysis and readings from the major figures can be found in H. Kohn, *Nationalism* (Princeton, N.J., 1955); J. S. Schapiro, *Liberalism: Its Meaning and History* (Princeton, N.J., 1958); and P. Viereck, *Conservatism* (Princeton, N.J., 1956). For a more detailed examination of liberalism, see J. Gray, *Liberalism* (Minneapolis, Minn., 1995).

On the ideas of the Romantics, see H. G. Schenk, *The Mind of the European Romantics* (Garden City, N.Y., 1969), and M. Cranston, *The Romantic Movement* (Oxford, 1994). An excellent collection of writings by Romantics is J. B. Halsted, ed., *Romanticism* (New York, 1969). On Wordsworth and English Romanticism, see J. Wordsworth, *William Wordsworth and the Age of English Romanticism* (New Brunswick, N.J., 1987). For an introduction to the arts, see W. Vaughan, *Romanticism and Art* (New York, 1994). A briefer survey (with illustrations) can be found in D. M. Reynolds, *Cambridge Introduction to the History of Art: The Nineteenth Century* (Cambridge, 1985).

For additional reading, go to InfoTrac College Edition, your online research library at http://webI.infotrac-college.com

Enter the search term *Romanticism* using the Subject Guide.

Enter the search term *Habsburg* and also the term *Hapsburg* using Key Terms.

Enter the search terms *John Stuart Mill* using Key Terms.

Enter the search term *Goethe* using Key Terms.

CHAPTER

22 An Age of Nationalism and Realism, 1850–1871

CHAPTER OUTLINE

- The France of Napoleon III
- National Unification: Italy and Germany
- Nation Building and Reform: The National State in Mid-Century
- Industrialization and the Marxist Response
- Science and Culture in an Age of Realism
- Conclusion

FOCUS QUESTIONS

- What were the characteristics of Napoleon III's government, and how did his foreign policy contribute to the unification of Italy and Germany?
- What actions did Cavour and Bismarck take to bring about unification in Italy and Germany, respectively, and what role did war play in their efforts?
- What efforts for reform occurred in the Austrian Empire and in Russia between 1850 and 1870, and how successful were they in alleviating each nation's problems?
- What were the main ideas of Karl Marx?
- How did the belief that the world should be viewed realistically manifest itself in science, art, and literature in the second half of the nineteenth century?

ACROSS THE CONTINENT, the revolutions of 1848 had failed. The forces of liberalism and nationalism appeared to have been decisively defeated as authoritarian governments reestablished their control almost everywhere in Europe by 1850. And yet within twenty-five years, many of the goals sought by the liberals and nationalists during the first half of the nineteenth century seemed to have been achieved. National unity became a reality in Italy and Germany, and many European states were governed by constitutional monarchies, even though the constitutional-parliamentary features were frequently facades.

All the same, these goals were not achieved by liberal and nationalist leaders but by a new generation of conservative leaders who were proud of being practitioners of Realpolitik, *the "politics of reality." One reaction to the failure of the revolutions of 1848 had been a new toughness of mind in which people prided themselves on being realistic in their handling of power. The new conservative leaders used armies and power politics to achieve their foreign policy goals. And they did not hesitate to manipulate liberal means to achieve conservative ends at home. Nationalism had failed as a revolutionary movement in 1848–1849, but between 1850 and 1871, these new leaders found a variety of ways to pursue nation building. One of the most successful was the Prussian Otto von Bismarck, who used both astute diplomacy and war to achieve the unification of Germany. On January 18, 1871, Bismarck and six hundred German princes, nobles, and generals filled the Hall of Mirrors in the palace of Versailles, 12 miles outside the city of Paris. The Prussian army had defeated the French, and the assembled notables were gathered for the proclamation of the Prussian king as the new emperor of a united German state. When the words "Long live His Imperial Majesty, the Emperor William!" rang out, the assembled guests took up the cry. One participant wrote, "A thundering cheer, repeated at least six times, thrilled through the room while the flags and standards waved over the head of the new emperor of Germany." European rulers who feared the power of the new German state were not so cheerful. "The balance of power has been entirely destroyed," declared the British prime minister.*

◆ The France of Napoleon III

After 1850, a new generation of conservative leaders came to power in Europe. Foremost among them was Napoleon III (1852–1870) of France, who taught his contemporaries how authoritarian governments could use liberal and nationalistic forces to bolster their own power. It was a lesson others quickly learned.

Louis Napoleon and the Second Napoleonic Empire

Even after his election as the president of the French Republic, many of his contemporaries dismissed Napoleon "the Small" as a nonentity whose success was due only to his name. But Louis Napoleon was a clever politician who was especially astute at understanding the popular forces of his day. After his election, he was at least clear about his desire to have personal power. He wrote, "I shall never submit to any attempt to influence me. . . . I follow only the promptings of my mind and heart. . . . Nothing, nothing shall trouble the clear vision of my judgment or the strength of my resolution."[1]

Louis Napoleon was a patient man. For three years, he persevered in winning the support of the French people, and when the National Assembly rejected his wish to be allowed to stand for reelection, Louis used troops to seize control of the government on December 1, 1851. After restoring universal male suffrage, Napoleon asked the French people to restore the empire. Ninety-seven percent responded affirmatively, and on December 2, 1852, Louis Napoleon assumed the title of Napoleon III (the first Napoleon had abdicated in favor of his son, Napoleon II, on April 6, 1814). The Second Empire had begun.

The government of Napoleon III was clearly authoritarian in a Bonapartist sense. As chief of state, Napoleon III controlled the armed forces, police, and civil service. Only he could introduce legislation and declare war. The Legislative Corps gave an appearance of representative government since its members were elected by universal male suffrage to six-year terms. But they could neither initiate legislation nor affect the budget.

The first five years of Napoleon III's reign were a spectacular success as he reaped the benefits of worldwide economic prosperity as well as some of his own economic policies. Napoleon believed in using the resources of government to stimulate the national economy and took many steps to expand industrial growth. Government subsidies were used to foster the rapid construction of railroads as well as harbors, roads, and canals. The major French railway lines were completed during Napoleon's reign, and industrial expansion was evident in the tripling of iron production. Napoleon III also undertook a vast reconstruction of the city of Paris. The medieval Paris of narrow streets and old city walls was destroyed and replaced by a modern Paris of broad boulevards, spacious buildings, public squares, an underground sewage system, a new public water supply, and gaslights. The new Paris served a military as well as an aesthetic purpose. Broad streets made it more difficult for would-be insurrectionists to throw up barricades and easier for troops to move rapidly through the city in the event of revolts.

In the 1860s, as opposition to some of his policies began to mount, Napoleon III liberalized his regime. He reached out to the working class by legalizing trade unions and granting them the right to strike. He also began to open up the political process. The Legislative Corps was permitted more say in affairs of state, including debate over the budget. Liberalization policies did serve initially to strengthen the hand of the government. In a plebiscite in May 1870 on whether to accept a new constitution that might have inaugurated a parliamentary regime, the French people gave Napoleon another resounding victory. This triumph was short-lived, however. Foreign policy failures led to growing criticism, and war with Prussia in 1870 turned out to be the death blow for Napoleon III's regime. Napoleon was ousted, and the Third Republic was proclaimed.

Foreign Policy: The Crimean War

As heir to the Napoleonic empire, Napoleon III was motivated by a desire to make France the chief arbiter of Europe. Although his foreign policy ultimately led to disaster and his own undoing, Napoleon had an initial success in the Crimean War (1854–1856).

The Crimean War was yet another chapter in the story of the "Eastern Question" as to who would be the chief beneficiaries of the disintegration of the Ottoman Empire. The Turks had long been in control of the Balkans, but by the beginning of the nineteenth century, their power had begun to decline. At the same time, European governments began to take an active interest in the empire's apparent demise. Russia's proximity to the Ottoman Empire naturally gave it special opportunities to enlarge its sphere of influence. In 1853, the Russians demanded the right to protect Christian shrines in Palestine, a privilege that had already been extended to the French. When the Turks refused, the Russians invaded Turkish Moldavia and Walachia. Failure to resolve the dispute by negotiations led the Turks to declare war on Russia on October 4, 1853. The following year, on March 28, Great Britain and France, fearful of Russian gains at the expense of the disintegrating Ottoman Empire, declared war on Russia.

EMPEROR NAPOLEON III. On December 2, 1852, Louis Napoleon took the title of Napoleon III and then proceeded to create an authoritarian monarchy. As opposition to his policies intensified in the 1860s, Napoleon III began to liberalize his government. However, a disastrous military defeat at the hands of Prussia in 1870–1871 brought the collapse of his regime.

The Crimean War was poorly planned and poorly fought. Britain and France decided to attack Russia's Crimean peninsula in the Black Sea. After a long siege and at a terrible cost in lives for both sides, the main Russian fortress of Sevastopol fell in September 1855, and the Russians soon sued for peace. By the Treaty of Paris, signed in March 1856, Russia was forced to give up Bessarabia and accept the neutrality of the Black Sea. In addition, Moldavia and Walachia were placed under the protection of all five great powers.

The Crimean War broke up long-standing European power relationships and effectively destroyed the Concert of Europe. Austria and Russia, the two chief powers maintaining the status quo in the first half of the nineteenth century, were now enemies because of Austria's unwillingness to support Russia in the war. Russia, defeated, humiliated, and weakened by the obvious failure of its armies, withdrew from European affairs for the next two decades to set its house in order. Great Britain, disillusioned by its role in the war, also pulled back from Continental affairs. Austria, paying the price for its neutrality, was now without friends among the great powers. Not until the 1870s were new combinations formed to replace those that had disappeared, and in the meantime the European international situation remained fluid. Leaders who were willing to pursue the "politics of reality" found themselves in a situation rife with opportunity. It was this new international situation that made possible the unification of Italy and Germany.

National Unification: Italy and Germany

The breakdown of the Concert of Europe opened the way for the Italians and the Germans to establish national states. Their successful unification transformed the power structure of the Continent. Well into the twentieth century, Europe and the world would still be dealing with the consequences.

The Unification of Italy

In 1850, Austria was still the dominant power on the Italian peninsula. After the failure of the revolution of 1848–1849, a growing number of advocates for Italian unification focused on the northern Italian state of Piedmont as their best hope to achieve their goal. The royal house of Savoy ruled the kingdom of Piedmont, which also included the island of Sardinia (see Map 22.1). The little state seemed unlikely to supply the needed leadership to unify Italy, however, until King Victor Emmanuel II (1849–1878) named Count Camillo di Cavour (1810–1861) as his prime minister in 1852.

Cavour was a consummate politician with the ability to persuade others of the rightness of his own convictions. After becoming prime minister in 1852, he pursued a policy of economic expansion that increased government revenues and enabled Cavour to pour money into equipping a large army. Cavour, however, had no illusions about Piedmont's military strength and was only too well aware that he could not challenge Austria directly. Consequently, he made an alliance in 1858 with the French emperor Louis Napoleon and then provoked the Austrians into invading Piedmont in 1859. In the initial stages of fighting, the Austrians were defeated in two major battles by mostly French armies. A peace settlement gave the French Nice and Savoy, which they had been promised for making the

MAP 22.1 The Unification of Italy.

CHRONOLOGY

The Unification of Italy

Victor Emmanuel II	1849–1878
Count Cavour prime minister of Piedmont	1852
Austrian War	1859
Plebiscites in the northern Italian states	1860
Garibaldi's invasion of the kingdom of the Two Sicilies	1860
Kingdom of Italy is proclaimed	1861
Italy's annexation of Venetia	1866
Italy's annexation of Rome	1870

alliance, and awarded Lombardy to Cavour and the Piedmontese. More important, however, Cavour's success caused nationalists in the northern Italian states of Parma, Modena, and Tuscany to overthrow their governments and join their states to Piedmont.

Meanwhile, in southern Italy, a new leader of Italian unification had come to the fore. Giuseppe Garibaldi (1807–1882), a dedicated Italian patriot, raised an army of a thousand Red Shirts, as his volunteers were called because of their distinctive dress, and landed in Sicily, where a revolt had broken out against the Bourbon king of the Two Sicilies. By the end of July 1860, most of Sicily had been pacified under Garibaldi's control. In August, Garibaldi and his forces crossed over to the mainland and began a victorious march up the Italian peninsula. Naples and the kingdom of the Two Sicilies fell in early September. Ever the patriot, Garibaldi chose to turn over his conquests to Cavour's Piedmontese forces. On March 17, 1861, a new kingdom of Italy was proclaimed under a centralized government subordinated to the control of Piedmont and King Victor Emmanuel II of the house of Savoy. Worn out by his efforts, Cavour died three months later.

Despite the proclamation of the new kingdom, unification was not yet complete because Venetia in the north was still held by Austria and Rome remained under papal control, supported by French troops. To attack either one meant war with a major European state, which the Italian army was not prepared to handle. It was the Prussian army that indirectly completed the task of Italian unification. In the Austro-Prussian War of 1866, the new Italian state became an ally of Prussia. Although the Italian army was defeated by the Austrians, Prussia's victory left the Italians with Venetia. In 1870, the Franco-Prussian War resulted in the withdrawal of French troops from Rome. The Italian army then annexed the city on September 20, 1870, and Rome became the new capital of the united Italian state.

The Unification of Germany

After the failure of the Frankfurt Assembly to achieve German unification in 1848–1849, German nationalists focused on Austria and Prussia as the only two states powerful enough to unify Germany. But Austria, a large multi-national empire, feared the creation of a strong German state in central Europe, and more and more Germans began to look to Prussia for leadership in the cause of German unification.

In the 1860s, King William I (1861–1888) attempted to enlarge and strengthen the Prussian army. When the Prussian legislature refused to levy new taxes for the proposed military changes in March 1862, William I appointed a new prime minister, Count Otto von Bismarck (1815–1898). Bismarck ignored the legislative opposition to the military reforms, arguing that "Germany does not look to Prussia's liberalism but to her power. . . . Not by speeches and majorities will the great questions of the day be decided—that was the mistake of 1848–1849—but by iron and blood."[2] Bismarck went ahead, collected the taxes, and reorganized the army anyway. From 1862 to 1866, Bismarck governed Prussia by simply ignoring parliament. Unwilling to revolt, parliament did nothing. In the meantime, opposition to his domestic policy determined Bismarck on an active foreign policy, which led to war and German unification.

Because Bismarck succeeded in guiding Prussia's unification of Germany, it is often assumed that he had determined on a course of action that led precisely to that goal. That is hardly the case. Bismarck was a consummate politician and opportunist. He was not a political gambler but rather a moderate who waged war only when all other diplomatic alternatives had been exhausted and when he was reasonably sure that all the military and diplomatic advantages were on his side. Bismarck has often been portrayed as the ultimate realist, the foremost nineteenth-century practitioner of *Realpolitik*. He was also quite open about his strong dislike of anyone who opposed him. He said one morning to his wife: "I could not sleep the whole night; I hated throughout the whole night."

Bismarck's first war was against Denmark and was fought over the duchies of Schleswig and Holstein. Bismarck persuaded the Austrians to join Prussia in declaring war on Denmark on February 1, 1864. The Danes were quickly defeated and surrendered Schleswig

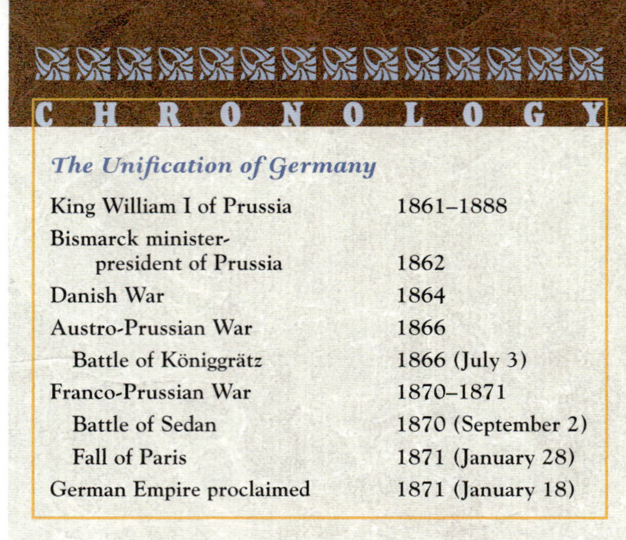

CHRONOLOGY

The Unification of Germany

King William I of Prussia	1861–1888
Bismarck minister-president of Prussia	1862
Danish War	1864
Austro-Prussian War	1866
Battle of Königgrätz	1866 (July 3)
Franco-Prussian War	1870–1871
Battle of Sedan	1870 (September 2)
Fall of Paris	1871 (January 28)
German Empire proclaimed	1871 (January 18)

and Holstein to the victors. Austria and Prussia then agreed to divide the administration of the two duchies; Prussia took Schleswig while Austria administered Holstein. But Bismarck used the joint administration of the two duchies to create friction with the Austrians and goad them into a war on June 14, 1866.

Many Europeans expected a quick Austrian victory, but they overlooked the effectiveness of the Prussian military reforms of the 1860s. The Prussian breech-loading needle gun had a much faster rate of fire than the Austrian muzzle-loader, and a superior network of railroads enabled the Prussians to mass troops quickly. At Königgrätz (or Sadowa) on July 3, the Austrian army was decisively defeated. Austria was now excluded from German affairs, and the German states north of the Main River were organized into a north German confederation controlled by Prussia. The south German states, largely Catholic, remained independent but were coerced into signing military agreements with Prussia.

THE FRANCO-PRUSSIAN WAR, 1870–1871

Bismarck and William I had achieved a major goal by 1866. Prussia now dominated all of northern Germany, and Austria had been excluded from any significant role in German affairs. Nevertheless, unsettled business led to new international complications and further change. Bismarck realized that France would never be content with a strong German state to its east because of the potential threat to French security. At the same time, after a series of setbacks, Napoleon III, the French ruler, needed a diplomatic triumph to offset his serious domestic problems. The French were not happy with the turn of events in Germany and looked for opportunities to humiliate the Prussians.

In 1870, Prussia and France became embroiled in a dispute over the candidacy of a relative of the Prussian king for the throne of Spain. Bismarck manipulated the misunderstandings between the French and Prussians to goad the French into declaring war on Prussia on July 15, 1870 (see the box on p. 449). The French proved no match for the better-led and better-organized Prussian forces. The south German states honored their military alliances with Prussia and joined the war effort against the French. The Prussian armies advanced into France, and at Sedan, on September 2, 1870, an entire French army and Napoleon III himself were captured. Paris finally capitulated on January 28, 1871, and an official peace treaty was signed in May. France had to pay an indemnity of 5 billion francs (about $1 billion) and give up the provinces of Alsace and Lorraine to the new German state, a loss that angered the French and left them burning for revenge.

Even before the war had ended, the south German states had agreed to enter the North German Confederation. On January 18, 1871, in the Hall of Mirrors in Louis XIV's palace at Versailles, William I was proclaimed kaiser or emperor of the Second German Empire (the first was the medieval

THE UNIFICATION OF GERMANY. Under Prussian leadership, a new German empire was proclaimed on January 18, 1871, in the Hall of Mirrors in the palace at Versailles. King William of Prussia became Emperor William I of the Second German Empire. In this painting by Anton von Werner, Otto von Bismarck, the man who had been so instrumental in creating the new German state, is shown, resplendently attired in his white uniform, standing at the foot of the throne.

Bismarck "Goads" France into War

After his meeting with the French ambassador at Ems, King William I of Prussia sent a telegraph to Bismarck with a report of their discussions. By editing the telegraph from King William I before releasing it to the press, Bismarck made it sound as if the Prussian king had treated the ambassador in a demeaning fashion. Six days later, France declared war on Prussia.

The Abeken [Privy Councillor] Text, Ems, July 13, 1870

To the Federal Chancellor, Count Bismarck. His Majesty the King writes to me:

"M. Benedetti intercepted me on the Promenade in order to demand of me most insistently that I should authorize him to telegraph immediately to Paris that I shall obligate myself for all future time never again to give my approval to the candidacy of the Hohenzollerns should it be renewed. I refused to agree to this, the last time somewhat severely, informing him that one dare not and cannot assume such obligations *à tout jamais* [forever]. Naturally, I informed him that I had received no news as yet, and since he had been informed earlier than I by way of Paris and Madrid, he could easily understand why my government was once again out of the matter."

Since then His Majesty has received a dispatch from the Prince [father of the Hohenzollern candidate for the Spanish throne]. As His Majesty has informed Count Benedetti that he was expecting news from the Prince, His Majesty himself, in view of the above-mentioned demand and in consonance with the advice of Count Eulenburg and myself, decided not to receive the French envoy again but to inform him through an adjutant that His Majesty had now received from the Prince confirmation of the news which Benedetti had already received from Paris, and that he had nothing further to say to the Ambassador. His Majesty leaves it to the judgment of Your Excellency whether or not to communicate at once the new demand by Benedetti and its rejection to our ambassadors and to the press.

Bismarck's Edited Version

After the reports of the renunciation by the hereditary Prince of Hohenzollern had been officially transmitted by the Royal Government of Spain to the Imperial Government of France, the French Ambassador presented to His Majesty the King at Ems the demand to authorize him to telegraph to Paris that His Majesty the King would obligate himself for all future time never again to give his approval to the candidacy of the Hohenzollerns should it be renewed.

His Majesty the King thereupon refused to receive the French envoy again and informed him through an adjutant that His Majesty had nothing further to say to the Ambassador.

Holy Roman Empire). German unity had been achieved by the Prussian monarchy and the Prussian army. In a real sense, Germany had been merged into Prussia, not Prussia into Germany (see Map 22.2). German liberals also rejoiced. They had dreamed of unity and freedom, but the achievement of unity now seemed much more important. One old liberal proclaimed:

> I cannot shake off the impression of this hour. I am no devotee of Mars; I feel more attached to the goddess of beauty and the mother of graces than to the powerful god of war, but the trophies of war exercise a magic charm even upon the child of peace. One's view is involuntarily chained and one's spirit goes along with the boundless row of men who acclaim the god of the moment—success.[3]

The Prussian leadership of German unification meant the triumph of authoritarian, militaristic values over liberal, constitutional sentiments in the development of the new German state. With its industrial resources and military might, the new state had become the strongest power on the Continent. A new European balance of power was at hand.

MAP 22.2 **The Unification of Germany.**

◆ Nation Building and Reform: The National State in Mid-Century

While European affairs were dominated by the unification of Italy and Germany, other states in the Western world were also undergoing transformations (see Map 22.3). War, civil war, and changing political alignments served as catalysts for domestic reforms.

The Austrian Empire: Toward a Dual Monarchy

After the Habsburgs had crushed the revolutions of 1848–1849, they restored centralized, autocratic government to the empire. But failure in war led to severe internal consequences for Austria. Austria's defeat at the hands of the Prussians in 1866 forced the Austrians to deal with the fiercely nationalistic Hungarians. The result was the negotiated *Ausgleich*, or Compromise, of 1867, which created the dual monarchy of Austria-Hungary. Each part of the empire now had its constitution, its own bicameral legislature, its own governmental machinery for domestic affairs, and its own capital (Vienna for Austria and Buda, which soon merged with the city of Pest to become Budapest, for Hungary). Holding the two states together were a single monarch (Francis Joseph was emperor of Austria and king of Hungary) and a common army, foreign policy, and system of finances. In domestic affairs, the Hungarians had become an independent nation. The *Ausgleich* did not, however, satisfy the other nationalities that made up the multinational Austro-Hungarian Empire (see Map 22.4). The dual monarchy

MAP 22.3 Europe in 1871.

simply enabled the German-speaking Austrians and Hungarian Magyars to dominate the minorities, especially the Slavs, in their respective states. As the Hungarian nationalist Louis Kossuth remarked, "Dualism is the alliance of the conservative, reactionary and any apparently liberal elements in Hungary with those of the Austrian Germans who despise liberty, for the oppression of the other nationalities and races."[4]

Imperial Russia

The defeat in the Crimean War in 1856 at the hands of the British and French revealed the blatant deficiencies behind the facade of absolute power and made it clear even to staunch conservatives that Russia was falling hopelessly behind the western European powers. Tsar Alexander II (1855–1881) turned his energies to a serious overhaul of the Russian system.

Serfdom was the most burdensome problem in tsarist Russia. The continuing subjugation of millions of peasants to the land and their landlords was an obviously corrupt and failing system. On March 3, 1861, Alexander issued his emancipation edict (see the box on p. 453). Peasants could now own property, marry as they chose, and bring suits in the law courts. Nevertheless, the benefits of emancipation were limited. The government provided land for the peasants

by purchasing it from the landlords, but the landowners often chose to keep the best lands. The Russian peasants soon found that they had inadequate amounts of good arable land to support themselves, a situation that worsened as the peasant population increased rapidly in the second half of the nineteenth century.

Nor were the peasants completely free. The state compensated the landowners for the land given to the peasants, but the peasants, in turn, were expected to repay the state in long-term installments. To ensure

EMANCIPATION OF THE SERFS. On March 3, 1861, Tsar Alexander II issued an edict emancipating the Russian serfs. This photograph shows a Russian noble on the steps of his country house reading the edict to a gathering of his serfs.

MAP 22.4 Ethnic Groups in the Dual Monarchy.

Germans
Poles
Croats
Czechs
Serbs
Italians
Little Russians
Magyars
Romanians
Slovaks
Slovenes
Boundary between Austria and Hungary

Emancipation: Serfs and Slaves

Although overall their histories have been quite different, Russia and the United States shared a common feature in the 1860s. They were the only states in the Western world that still had large enslaved populations (the Russian serfs were virtually slaves). The leaders of both countries issued emancipation proclamations within two years of each other. The first excerpt is taken from the Imperial Decree of March 3, 1861, which freed the Russian serfs. The second excerpt is from Abraham Lincoln's Emancipation Proclamation, issued on January 1, 1863.

The Imperial Decree, March 3, 1861

By the grace of God, we, Alexander II, Emperor and Autocrat of all the Russias, King of Poland, Grand Duke of Finland, etc., to all our faithful subjects, make known:

Called by Divine Providence and by the sacred right of inheritance to the throne of our ancestors, we took a vow in our innermost heart to respond to the mission which is intrusted to us as to surround with our affection and our Imperial solicitude all our faithful subjects of every rank and of every condition, from the warrior, who nobly bears arms for the defense of the country to the humble artisan devoted to the works of industry; from the official in the career of the high offices of the State to the laborer whose plow furrows the soil. . . .

We thus came to the conviction that the work of a serious improvement of the condition of the peasants was a sacred inheritance bequeathed to us by our ancestors, a mission which, in the course of events, Divine providence called upon us to fulfill. . . .

In virtue of the new dispositions above mentioned, the peasants attached to the soil will be invested within a term fixed by the law with all the rights of free cultivators. . . .

At the same time, they are granted the right of purchasing their close, and, with the consent of the proprietors, they may acquire in full property the arable lands and other appurtenances which are allotted to them as a permanent holding. By the acquisition in full property of the quantity of land fixed, the peasants are free from their obligations toward the proprietors for land thus purchased, and they enter definitely into the condition of free peasants—landholders.

The Emancipation Proclamation, January 1, 1863

Now therefore, I, Abraham Lincoln, President of the United States, by virtue of the power in me vested as Commander-in-Chief of the Army and Navy of the United States in time of actual armed rebellion against the authority and government of the United States, and as a fit and necessary war measure for suppressing such rebellion, do, on this 1st day of January, A.D. 1863, and in accordance with my purpose to do so, . . . order and designate as the States and parts of States wherein the people thereof, respectively, are this day in rebellion against the United States the following, to wit:

Arkansas, Texas, Louisiana, . . . Mississippi, Alabama, Florida, Georgia, South Carolina, North Carolina, and Virginia. . . .

And by virtue of the power for the purpose aforesaid, I do order and declare that all persons held as slaves within said designated States and parts of States are, and henceforward shall be free; and that the Executive Government of the United States, including the military and naval authorities thereof, will recognize and maintain the freedom of said persons.

that the payments were made, peasants were subjected to the authority of their *mir*, or village commune, which was collectively responsible for the land payments to the government. In a very real sense, then, the village commune, not the individual peasants, owned the land the peasants were purchasing. And since the village communes were responsible for the payments, they were reluctant to allow peasants to leave their land. Emancipation, then, led not to a free, landowning peasantry along the Western model but

Before 1870, capitalist factory owners remained largely free to hire labor on their own terms based on market forces. Although workers formed trade unions as organizations that would fight for improved working conditions and reasonable wages, they tended to represent only a small part of the industrial working class and proved largely ineffective. Real change for the industrial proletariat would come only with the development of socialist parties and socialist trade unions. These emerged after 1870, but the theory that made them possible had already been developed by mid-century in the work of Karl Marx.

Marx and Marxism

The beginnings of Marxism can be traced to the 1848 publication of a short treatise titled *The Communist Manifesto,* written by two Germans, Karl Marx (1818–1883) and Friedrich Engels (1820–1895). It became one of the most influential political treatises in modern European history.

Marx and Engels began their treatise with the statement that "the history of all hitherto existing society is the history of class struggles." Throughout history, oppressed and oppressor have "stood in constant opposition to one another." In an earlier struggle, the feudal classes of the Middle Ages were forced to accede to the emerging middle class or bourgeoisie. As the bourgeoisie took control in turn, its ideas became the dominant views of the era, and government became its instrument. Marx and Engels declared: "The executive of the modern State is but a committee for managing the common affairs of the whole bourgeoisie."[5] In other words, the government of the state reflected and defended the interests of the industrial middle class and its allies.

Although bourgeois society had emerged victorious out of the ruins of feudal society, Marx and Engels insisted that it had not triumphed completely. Now once again the bourgeois were antagonists in an emerging class struggle, but this time they faced the proletariat, or the industrial working class. The struggle would be fierce; in fact, Marx and Engels predicted that the workers would eventually overthrow their bourgeois masters. After their victory, the proletariat would form a dictatorship to reorganize the means of production. Then a classless society would emerge, and the state—itself an instrument of the bourgeoisie—would wither away, since it no longer represented the interests of a particular class. Class struggles would

KARL MARX. Karl Marx was a radical journalist who joined with Friedrich Engels to write *The Communist Manifesto,* which proclaimed the ideas of a revolutionary socialism. After the failure of the 1848 revolution in Germany, Marx fled to Britain, where he continued to write and became involved in the work of the first International Working Men's Association.

The Classless Society

In The Communist Manifesto, *Karl Marx and Friedrich Engels projected the creation of a classless society as the end product of the struggle between the bourgeoisie and the proletariat. In this selection, they discuss the steps by which that classless society would be reached.*

Karl Marx and Friedrich Engels, The Communist Manifesto

We have seen above, that the first step in the revolution by the working class, is to raise the proletariat to the position of ruling class. . . . The proletariat will use its political supremacy to wrest, by degrees, all capital from the bourgeoisie, to centralize all instruments of production in the hands of the State, i.e., of the proletariat organized as the ruling class; and to increase the total of productive forces as rapidly as possible.

Of course, in the beginning, this cannot be effected except by means of despotic inroads on the rights of property, and on the conditions of bourgeois production; by means of measures, therefore, which . . . necessitate further inroads upon the old social order, and are unavoidable as a means of entirely revolutionizing the mode of production.

These measures will of course be different in different countries.

Nevertheless, in the most advanced countries, the following will be pretty generally applicable:

1. Abolition of property in land and application of all rents of land to public purposes.
2. A heavy progressive or graduated income tax.
3. Abolition of all right of inheritance. . . .
5. Centralization of credit in the hands of the State, by means of a national bank with State capital and an exclusive monopoly.
6. Centralization of the means of communication and transport in the hands of the State.
7. Extension of factories and instruments of production owned by the State. . . .
8. Equal liability of all to labor. Establishment of industrial armies, especially for agriculture.
9. Combination of agriculture with manufacturing industries; gradual abolition of the distinction between town and country, by a more equable distribution of the population over the country.
10. Free education for all children in public schools. Abolition of children's factory labor in its present form. . . .

When, in the course of development, class distinctions have disappeared, and all production has been concentrated in the whole nation, the public power will lose its political character. Political power, properly so called, is merely the organized power of one class for oppressing another. If the proletariat during its contest with the bourgeoisie is compelled, by the force of circumstances, to organize itself as a class, if, by means of a revolution, it makes itself the ruling class, and, as such, sweeps away by force the old conditions of production, then it will, along with these conditions, have swept away the conditions for the existence of class antagonisms and of classes generally, and will thereby have abolished its own supremacy as a class.

In place of the old bourgeois society, with its classes and class antagonisms, we shall have an association, in which the free development of each is the condition for the free development of all.

be over (see the box above). Marx believed that the emergence of a classless society would lead to progress in science, technology, and industry and to greater wealth for all.

After the failure of the revolutions of 1848, Marx went to London, where he spent the rest of his life. Marx continued his writing on political economy, especially his famous work *Das Kapital* (*Capital*), but his own preoccupation with organizing the working-class movement kept Marx from ever finishing the book. In *The Communist Manifesto*, Marx had defined the communists as "the most advanced and resolute section of the working-class parties of every country." Their advantage was their ability to understand "the line of march, the conditions, and the ultimate general results of the proletarian movement."[6] Marx saw his role in this light and participated enthusiastically in the activities of the International Working Men's Association. Formed in 1864 by British and French trade unionists, this "First International" served as an umbrella organization for working-class interests. Marx was the dominant personality on the organization's General Council and devoted much time to its activities. Internal dissension, however, soon damaged the organization, and it failed in 1872. Although it would be revived in 1889, the fate of socialism by that time was in the hands of national socialist parties.

Science and Culture in an Age of Realism

Between 1850 and 1870, two major intellectual developments were evident: the growth of scientific knowledge, with its rapidly increasing impact on the Western worldview, and the shift from Romanticism, with its emphasis on the inner world of reality, to Realism, with its focus on the outer, material world.

A New Age of Science

By the mid-nineteenth century, science was having a greater and greater impact on European life. The Scientific Revolution of the sixteenth and seventeenth centuries had fundamentally transformed the Western worldview and fostered a modern, rational approach to the study of the natural world. Even in the eighteenth century, however, these intellectual developments had remained the preserve of an educated elite and resulted in few practical benefits. Moreover, the technical advances of the early Industrial Revolution had depended little on pure science and much more on the practical experiments of technologically oriented amateur inventors. Advances in industrial technology, however, fed an interest in basic scientific research, which in turn, in the 1830s and afterward, resulted in a rash of basic scientific discoveries that were soon transformed into technological improvements that affected all Europeans.

The development of the steam engine was important in encouraging scientists to work out its theoretical foundations, a preoccupation that led to the study of thermodynamics, the science of the relationship between heat and mechanical energy. The laws of thermodynamics were at the core of nineteenth-century physics. In biology, the Frenchman Louis Pasteur postulated the germ theory of disease, which had enormous practical applications in the development of modern, scientific medical practices. In chemistry, the Russian Dmitri Mendeleyev in the 1860s classified all the material elements then known on the basis of their atomic weights and provided the systematic foundation for the periodic law. The Briton Michael Faraday discovered the phenomenon of electromagnetic induction and put together a primitive generator that laid the groundwork for the use of electricity, although economically efficient generators were not built until the 1870s.

The steadily increasing and often dramatic material benefits generated by science and technology led Europeans to a growing faith in the benefits of science. The popularity of scientific and technological achievements produced a widespread acceptance of the scientific method, based on observation, experiment, and logical analysis, as the only path to objective truth and objective reality. This, in turn, undermined the faith of many people in religious revelation and truth. It is no accident that the nineteenth century was an age of increasing secularization, particularly evident in the growth of materialism or the belief that everything mental, spiritual, or ideal was simply an outgrowth of physical forces. Truth was to be found in the concrete material existence of human beings, not as Romanticists imagined in revelations gained by feeling or intuitive flashes. The importance of materialism was strikingly evident in the most important scientific event of the nineteenth century, the development of the theory of organic evolution according to natural selection. On the theories of Charles Darwin could be built a picture of humans as material beings that were simply part of the natural world.

Charles Darwin and the Theory of Organic Evolution

In 1859, Charles Darwin (1809–1882) published his celebrated book, *On the Origin of Species by Means of Natural Selection*. The basic idea of this book was that all plants and animals had evolved over a long period of time from earlier and simpler forms of life, a principle known as organic evolution. Darwin was important in explaining how this natural process worked. In every species, he argued, "many more individuals of each species are born than can possibly survive." This results in a "struggle for existence": "As more individuals are produced than can possibly survive, there must in every case be a struggle for existence, either one individual with another of the same species, or with the individuals of distinct species, or with the physical conditions of life." Those who succeeded in this struggle for existence had adapted better to their environment, a process made possible by the appearance of "variants." Chance variations that occurred in the process of inheritance enabled some organisms to be more adaptable to the environment than others, a process that Darwin called natural selection:

> Owing to this struggle [for existence], variations, however slight . . . , if they be in any degree profitable to the individuals of a species, in their infinitely complex relations to other organic beings and to their physical conditions of life, will tend to the preservation of such individuals, and will generally be inherited by the offspring.[7]

Those that were naturally selected for survival ("survival of the fit") survived. The unfit did not and became extinct. The fit who survived, in turn, propagated and passed on the variations that enabled them to survive until, from Darwin's point of view, a new separate species emerged.

In *On the Origin of Species*, Darwin discussed plant and animal species only. He was not concerned with humans themselves and only later applied his theory of natural selection to humans. In *The Descent of Man*, published in 1871, he argued for the animal origins of human beings: "Man is the co-descendant with other mammals of a common progenitor." Humans were not an exception to the rule governing other species.

Darwin's ideas were highly controversial at first. Some people fretted that Darwin's theory made human beings ordinary products of nature rather than unique beings. Others were disturbed by the implications of life as a struggle for survival, of "nature red in tooth and claw." Was there a place in the Darwinian world for moral values? For those who believed in a rational order in the world, Darwin's theory seemed to eliminate purpose and design from the universe. Gradually, however, Darwin's theory was accepted by scientists and other intellectuals. In the process of accepting Darwin's ideas, some people even tried to apply them to society, yet another example of science's increasing prestige.

Realism in Literature and Art

The belief that the world should be viewed realistically, frequently expressed after 1850, was closely related to the materialistic outlook. The word *Realism* was first employed in 1850 to describe a new style of painting and soon spread to literature.

THE REALISTIC NOVEL

The literary Realists of the mid-nineteenth century were distinguished by their deliberate rejection of Romanticism. The literary Realists wanted to deal with ordinary characters from actual life rather than Romantic heroes in unusual settings. They also sought to avoid flowery and sentimental language by using careful observation and accurate description, an approach that led them to eschew poetry in favor of prose and the novel. Realists often combined their interest in everyday life with a searching examination of social questions.

The leading novelist of the 1850s and 1860s, the Frenchman Gustave Flaubert (1821–1880), perfected the Realist novel. His *Madame Bovary* (1857) was a straightforward description of barren and sordid provincial life in France. Emma Bovary, a woman of some vitality, is trapped in a marriage to a drab provincial doctor. Impelled by the images of romantic love she has read about in novels, she seeks the same thing for herself in adulterous affairs. Unfulfilled, she is ultimately driven to suicide, unrepentant to the end for her lifestyle. Flaubert's contempt for bourgeois society was evident in his portrayal of middle-class hypocrisy and smugness.

William Thackeray (1811–1863) wrote the prototypical Realist novel in Britain: *Vanity Fair*, published in 1848. Subtitled *A Novel Without a Hero*, the book deliberately flaunted Romantic conventions. A novel,Thackeray said, should "convey as strongly as possible the sentiment of reality as opposed to a tragedy or poem, which may be heroical." Perhaps the greatest of the Victorian novelists was Charles Dickens (1812–1870), whose realistic novels focusing on the lower and middle classes in Britain's early industrial age became extraordinarily popular. His descriptions of the urban poor and the brutalization of human life were vividly realistic (see the box on p. 460).

REALISM IN ART

In art, too, Realism became dominant after 1850, although Romanticism was by no means dead. Among the most important characteristics of Realism are a desire to depict the everyday life of ordinary people,

Realism: Charles Dickens and an Image of Hell on Earth

Charles Dickens was one of Britain's greatest novelists. While he realistically portrayed the material, social, and psychological milieu of his time, an element of Romanticism still pervaded his novels. This is evident in this selection from The Old Curiosity Shop, *in which his description of the English mill town of Birmingham takes on the imagery of Dante's Hell.*

Charles Dickens, The Old Curiosity Shop

A long suburb of red brick houses,—some with patches of garden ground, where coal-dust and factory smoke darkened the shrinking leaves, and coarse rank flowers; and where the struggling vegetation sickened and sank under the hot breath of kiln and furnace, making them by its presence seem yet more blighting and unwholesome than in the town itself,—a long, flat, straggling suburb passed, they came by slow degrees upon a cheerless region, where not a blade of grass was seen to grow; where not a bud put forth its promise in the spring; where nothing green could live but on the surface of the stagnant pools, which here and there lay idly sweltering by the black roadside.

Advancing more and more into the shadow of this mournful place, its dark depressing influence stole upon their spirits, and filled them with a dismal gloom. On every side, and as far as the eye could see into the heavy distance, tall chimneys, crowding on each other, and presenting that endless repetition of the same dull, ugly form, which is the horror of oppressive dreams, poured out their plague of smoke, obscured the light, and made foul the melancholy air. On mounds of ashes by the wayside, sheltered only by a few rough boards, or rotten pent-house roofs, strange engines spun and writhed like tortured creatures; clanking their iron chains, shrieking in their rapid whirl from time to time as though in torment unendurable, and making the ground tremble with their agonies. Dismantled houses here and there appeared, tottering to the earth, propped up by fragments of others that had fallen down, unroofed, windowless, blackened, desolate, but yet inhabited. Men, women, children, wan in their looks and ragged in attire, tended the engines, fed their tributary fires, begged upon the road, or scowled half-naked from the doorless houses. Then came more of the wrathful monsters, whose like they almost seemed to be in their wildness and their untamed air, screeching and turning to the right and left, with the same interminable perspective of brick towers, never ceasing in their black vomit, blasting all things living or inanimate, shutting out the face of day, and closing in on all these horrors with a dense dark cloud.

But night-time in this dreadful spot!—night, when the smoke was changed to fire; when every chimney spurted up its flame; and places, that had been dark vaults all day, now shone red-hot, with figures moving to and fro within their blazing jaws, and calling to one another with hoarse cries—night, when the noise of every strange machine was aggravated by the darkness; when the people near them looked wilder and more savage; when bands of unemployed laborers paraded in the roads, or clustered by torchlight round their leaders, who told them in stern language of their wrongs, and urged them on by frightful cries and threats; when maddened men, armed with sword and firebrand, spurning the tears and prayers of women who would restrain them, rushed forth on errands of terror and destruction, to work no ruin half so surely as their own—night, when carts came rumbling by, filled with rude coffins (for contagious disease and death had been busy with the living crops); or when orphans cried, and distracted women shrieked and followed in their wake. . . .

whether peasants, workers, or prostitutes; an attempt at photographic realism; and an interest in the natural environment. The French became leaders in Realist painting.

Gustave Courbet (1819–1877) was the most famous artist of the Realist school. In fact, the word *Realism* was first coined in 1850 to describe one of his paintings. Courbet reveled in a realistic portrayal of everyday life. His subjects were factory workers, peasants, and the wives of saloon keepers. "I have never seen either angels or goddesses, so I am not interested in painting them," he exclaimed. One of his

GUSTAVE COURBET, *THE STONEBREAKERS.* **Realism, largely developed by French painters, aimed at a lifelike portrayal of the daily activities of ordinary people. Gustave Courbet was the most famous of the Realist artists. As is evident in *The Stonebreakers,* he sought to portray things as they really appear. He shows an old road builder and his young assistant in their tattered clothes, engrossed in their dreary work of breaking stones to construct a road.**

famous works, *The Stonebreakers*, painted in 1849, shows two workers engaged in the exhausting work of breaking stones to build a road. This representation of human misery was a scandal to those who objected to his "cult of ugliness." To Courbet, no subject was too ordinary, too harsh, or too ugly.

Jean-François Millet (1814–1875) was preoccupied with scenes from rural life, especially peasants laboring in the fields, although his Realism still contained an element of Romantic sentimentality. In *The Gleaners*, Millet's most famous work, three peasant women gather grain in a field, a centuries-old practice that for Millet showed the symbiotic relationship between humans and nature. Millet made landscapes and country life important subjects for French artists, but he too was criticized by his contemporaries for crude subject matter and unorthodox technique.

JEAN-FRANÇOIS MILLET, *THE GLEANERS.* **Jean-François Millet, another prominent French Realist painter, took a special interest in the daily activities of French peasants, although he tended to transform his peasants into heroic figures who dominated their environment. In *The Gleaners,* for example, the three peasant women who are engaged in the backbreaking work of gathering grain left after the harvest still appear as powerful figures, symbolizing the union of humans with the earth.**

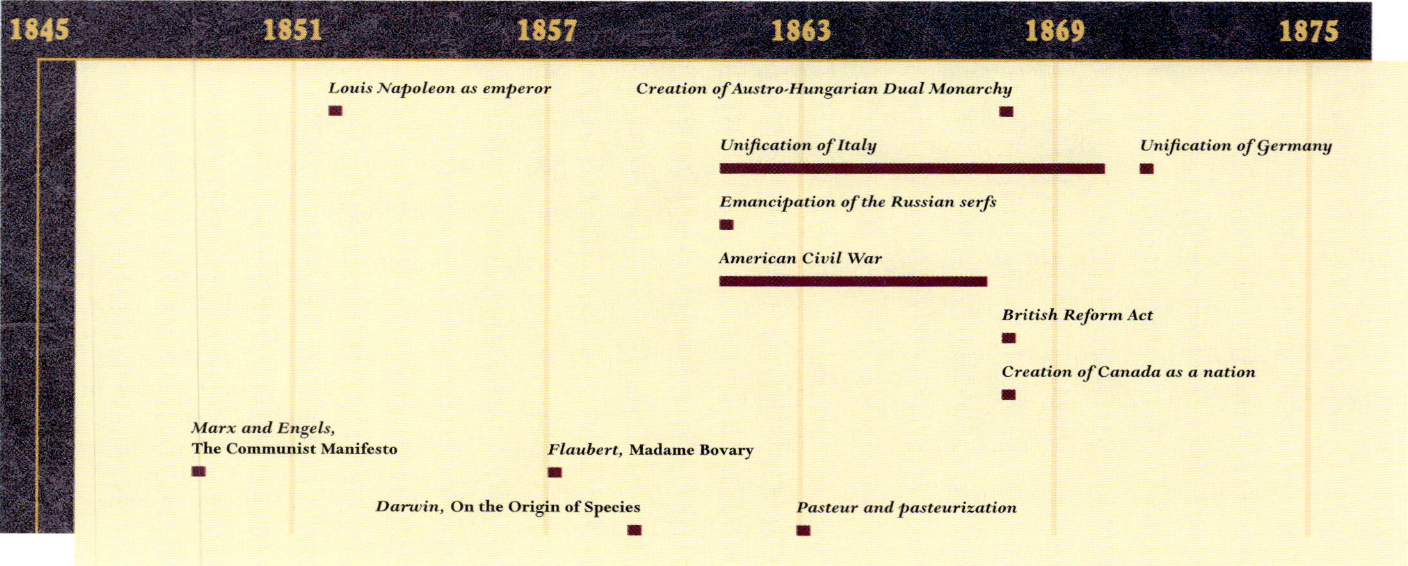

Conclusion

Between 1850 and 1871, the national state became the focus of people's loyalty. Wars, both foreign and civil, were fought to create unified nation-states. Political nationalism had emerged during the French revolutionary era and had become a powerful force of change during the first half of the nineteenth century, but its triumph came only after 1850. Tied initially to middle-class liberals, by the end of the nineteenth century it would have great appeal to the broad masses as well. In 1871, however, the political transformations stimulated by the force for nationalism were by no means complete. Large minorities, especially in the polyglot empires controlled by the Austrians, Ottoman Turks, and Russians, had not achieved the goal of their own national states. Moreover, the nationalism that had triumphed by 1871 was no longer the nationalism that had been closely identified with liberalism. Liberal nationalists had believed that unified nation-states would preserve individual rights and lead to a greater community of peoples. Rather than unifying people, however, the loud and chauvinistic nationalism of the late nineteenth century divided them as the new national states became embroiled in bitter competition after 1871.

Europeans, however, were hardly aware of nationalism's dangers in 1871. The spread of industrialization and the wealth of scientific and technological achievements were sources of optimism, not pessimism. After the revolutionary and military upheavals of the mid-century decades, many Europeans believed that they stood on the verge of a new age of progress.

Notes

1. Quoted in James F. McMillan, *Napoleon III* (New York, 1991), p. 37.
2. Quoted in Louis L. Snyder, ed., *Documents of German History* (New Brunswick, N.J., 1958), p. 202.
3. Quoted in Otto Pflanze, *Bismarck and the Development of Germany: The Period of Unification, 1815–1871* (Princeton, N.J., 1963), p. 327.
4. Quoted in György Szabad, *Hungarian Political Trends Between the Revolution and the Compromise, 1849–1867* (Budapest, 1977), p. 163.
5. Karl Marx and Friedrich Engels, *The Communist Manifesto* (Harmondsworth, England, 1967), pp. 79, 81, 82.
6. Ibid., p. 95.
7. Charles Darwin, *On the Origin of Species* (New York, 1872), vol. 1, pp. 77, 79.

Suggestions for Further Reading

Three general surveys of the mid-century decades are N. Rich, *The Age of Nationalism and Reform, 1850–1890*, 2d ed. (New York, 1979); E. Hobsbawm, *The Age of Capital, 1845–1875* (London, 1975); and J. A. S. Grenville, *Europe Reshaped, 1848–1878* (London, 1976). In addition to the books listed for individual countries in Chapter 21 that also cover the material of this chapter, see G. Craig, *Germany, 1866–1945* (Oxford, 1981); the two detailed volumes of T. Zeldin, *France, 1848–1945* (Oxford, 1973–1977); A. J. May, *The Habsburg Monarchy, 1867–1914* (Cambridge, Mass., 1951); and D. Read, *England, 1868–1914* (London, 1979).

For a good introduction to the French Second Empire, see A. Plessis, *The Rise and Fall of the Second Empire, 1852–1871*, trans. J. Mandelbaum (New York, 1985). Napoleon's role can be examined in J. F. McMillan, *Napoleon III* (New York, 1991). The

Crimean War and its impact are examined in P. W. Schroeder, *Austria, Great Britain, and the Crimean War: The Destruction of the European Concert* (Ithaca, N.Y., 1972), and N. Rich, *Why the Crimean War?* (Hanover, N.H., 1985).

The unification of Italy can best be examined in F. Coppa, *The Origins of the Italian Wars of Independence* (New York, 1992); the works of D. M. Smith, *Victor Emmanuel, Cavour and the Risorgimento* (London, 1971) and *Cavour* (London, 1985); and H. Hearder, *Cavour* (New York, 1994). The unification of Germany can be pursued first in W. Carr, *The Origins of the Wars of German Unification* (New York, 1991), and two good biographies of Bismarck, E. Crankshaw, *Bismarck* (New York, 1981), and G. O. Kent, *Bismarck and His Times* (Carbondale, Ill., 1978). See also the brief study by B. Waller, *Bismarck*, 2d ed. (Oxford, 1997). Also valuable is O. Pflanze, *Bismarck and the Development of Germany: The Period of Unification, 1815–1871* (Princeton, N.J., 1963). On the position of liberals in the unification of Germany, see J. J. Sheehan, *German Liberalism in the Nineteenth Century* (Chicago, 1978).

On the emancipation of the Russian serfs, see D. Field, *The End of Serfdom: Nobility and Bureaucracy in Russia, 1855–1861* (Cambridge, 1976). On Disraeli, see I. Machlin, *Disraeli* (London, 1995). A good one-volume survey of the American Civil War can be found in P. J. Parish, *The American Civil War* (New York, 1975).

In addition to the general works on economic development listed in Chapters 20 and 21, some specialized works on this period are worthwhile. These include W. O. Henderson. *The Rise of German Industrial Power, 1834–1914* (Berkeley, Calif., 1975), and F. Crouzet, *The Victorian Economy* (London, 1982). On Marx, the standard work by D. McLellan, *Karl Marx: His Life and Thought* (New York, 1975), can be supplemented by the interesting and comprehensive work by L. Kolakowki, *Main Currents of Marxism*, 3 vols. (Oxford, 1978).

For an introduction to the intellectual changes of the nineteenth century, see O. Chadwick, *The Secularization of the European Mind in the Nineteenth Century* (Cambridge, 1975). A detailed biography of Darwin can be found in J. Bowlby, *Charles Darwin: A Biography* (London, 1990). On the popularization of Darwinism, see A. Kelly, *The Descent of Darwin* (Chapel Hill, N.C., 1981). On Realism, J. Malpas, *Realism* (Cambridge, 1997), is a good introduction.

For additional reading, go to InfoTrac College Edition, your online research library at http://web1.infotrac-college.com

Enter the search terms *Crimean War* using Key Terms.

Enter the search term *Victorian* using Key Terms.

Enter the search terms *Karl Marx* using Key Terms.

Enter the search terms *Charles Darwin* using Key Terms.

CHAPTER

23

Mass Society in an "Age of Progress," 1871–1894

CHAPTER OUTLINE

FOCUS QUESTIONS

- What was the Second Industrial Revolution, and what effects did it have on European economic and social life?
- What roles did socialist parties and trade unions play in improving conditions for the working classes?
- What is meant by the term mass society, and what were its main characteristics?
- What role were women expected to play in society and family life in the latter half of the nineteenth century, and how closely did patterns of family life correspond to this ideal?
- What general political trends were evident in the nations of western Europe in the last decades of the nineteenth century, and how did these trends differ from the policies pursued in Germany, Austria-Hungary, and Russia?

IN THE LATE NINETEENTH CENTURY, Europe was enjoying a dynamic age of material prosperity. Bringing new industries, new sources of energy, and new goods, a second Industrial Revolution transformed the human environment, dazzled Europeans, and led them to believe that their material progress meant human progress. Scientific and technological achievements, many naively believed, would improve humanity's condition and solve all human problems. The doctrine of progress became an article of great faith.

The new urban and industrial world created by the rapid economic changes of the nineteenth century led to the emergence of a mass society by the late nineteenth century. A mass society meant improvements for the lower classes, who benefited from the extension of voting rights, a better standard of living, and mass education. It also brought mass leisure. New work patterns established the "weekend" as a distinct time of recreation and fun while new forms of mass transportation—railroads and streetcars—enabled even workers to make brief excursions to amusement parks. Coney Island was only 8 miles from central New York City; Blackpool in England was a short train ride from nearby industrial towns. With their Ferris wheels and other daring rides that threw young men and women together, amusement parks offered a whole new world of entertainment. Thanks to the railroad, seaside resorts, once the preserve of the wealthy, also became accessible to more people for weekend visits, much to the disgust of one upper-class regular who described the new "day-trippers": "They swarm upon the beach, wandering listlessly about with apparently no other aim than to get a mouthful of fresh air." Enterprising entrepreneurs in resorts like Blackpool, however, welcomed the masses of new visitors and built piers laden with food, drink, and entertainment to serve them.

The coming of mass society also created new roles for the governments of European nation-states, which now fostered national loyalty, formed mass armies by conscription, and took more responsibility for public health and housing measures in their cities. By 1871, the national state had become the focus of Europeans' lives. Within many of these nation-states, the growth of the middle class had led to the triumph of liberal practices: constitutional governments, parliaments, and principles of equality. The period after 1871 also witnessed the growth of political democracy as the right to vote was extended to all adult males; women, though, would still have to fight for the same political rights. With political democracy came a new mass politics and a new mass press. Both would become regular features of the twentieth century.

◆ The Growth of Industrial Prosperity

At the heart of Europeans' belief in progress after 1871 was the stunning material growth produced by what historians have called the Second Industrial Revolution. The first Industrial Revolution had given rise to textiles, railroads, iron, and coal. In the second revolution, steel, chemicals, electricity, and petroleum led the way to new industrial frontiers.

 *New Products and New Markets*

The first major change in industrial development after 1870 was the substitution of steel for iron. New methods of rolling and shaping steel made it useful in the construction of lighter, smaller, and faster machines and engines, as well as railways, ships, and armaments. In 1860, Great Britain, France, Germany, and Belgium produced 125,000 tons of steel; by 1913, the total was 32 million tons. By 1910, German steel production was double that of Great Britain, and both had been surpassed by the United States in 1890.

Electricity was a major new form of energy that proved to be of great value because it could be easily converted into other forms of energy, such as heat, light, and motion, and moved relatively effortlessly through wires. The first commercially practical generators of electrical current were developed in the 1870s. By 1910, hydroelectric power stations and coal-fired steam-generating plants enabled entire districts to be tied in to a single power distribution system that provided a common source of power for homes, shops, and industrial enterprises.

Electricity spawned spectacular new products. The invention of the lightbulb by the American Thomas Edison and the Briton Joseph Swan opened homes and cities to illumination by electric lights. A revolution in communications was fostered when Alexander Graham Bell invented the telephone in 1876 and Guglielmo Marconi sent the first radio waves across the Atlantic in 1901. Although most electricity was initially used for lighting, it was eventually put to use in transportation. By the 1880s, streetcars and subways had appeared in major European cities. Electricity also transformed the factory. Conveyor belts, cranes, machines, and machine tools could all be powered by electricity and located anywhere. Thanks to electricity, all countries could now enter the industrial age.

The development of the internal combustion engine had a similar effect. The processing of oil and gasoline made possible the widespread use of the internal combustion engine as a source of power in transportation. An oil-fired engine was made in 1897, and by 1902, the Hamburg-Amerika Line had switched from coal to oil on its new ocean liners. By the end of the nineteenth century, some naval fleets had been converted to oil burners as well.

The internal combustion engine gave rise to the automobile and airplane. In 1900, world production stood at 9,000 cars; by 1906, Americans had overtaken the initial lead of the French. It was an American, Henry Ford, who revolutionized the car industry with

AN AGE OF PROGRESS. **Between 1871 and 1914, the Second Industrial Revolution led many Europeans to believe that they were living in an age of progress when most human problems would be solved by scientific achievements. This illustration is taken from a special issue of *The Illustrated London News* celebrating the Diamond Jubilee of Queen Victoria in 1897. On the left are scenes from 1837, when Victoria came to the British throne; on the right are scenes from 1897. The vivid contrast underscored the magazine's conclusion: "The most striking . . . evidence of progress during the reign is the ever increasing speed which the discoveries of physical science have forced into everyday life. Steam and electricity have conquered time and space to a greater extent during the last sixty years than all the preceding six hundred years witnessed."**

the mass production of the Model T. By 1916, Ford's factories were producing 735,000 cars a year. In the meantime, air transportation began with the Zeppelin airship in 1900. In 1903, at Kitty Hawk, North Carolina, the Wright brothers, Orville and Wilbur, made the first flight in a fixed-wing plane powered by a gasoline engine. It took World War I to stimulate the aircraft industry, however, and the first regular passenger air service was not established until 1919.

The growth of industrial production depended on the development of markets for the sale of manufactured goods. After 1870, the best foreign markets were already heavily saturated, forcing Europeans to take a renewed look at their domestic markets. Between 1850 and 1900, real wages increased by two-thirds in Britain and by one-third in Germany. As the prices of both food and manufactured goods declined due to lower transportation costs, Europeans could spend more on consumer products. Businesses soon perceived the value of using new techniques of mass marketing to sell the consumer goods made possible by the development of the steel and electrical industries. By bringing together a vast array of new products in one place, they created the department store (see the box on p. 467). The desire to own sewing machines, clocks, bicycles, electric lights, and typewriters rapidly created a new consumer ethic that became a crucial part of the modern economy.

Meanwhile, increased competition for foreign markets and the growing importance of domestic demand led to a reaction against the free trade that had characterized much of the European economy between 1820 and 1870. To many industrial and political leaders, protective tariffs guaranteed domestic markets for the products of their own industries. By the 1870s, Europeans were returning to tariff protec-

The Department Store and the Beginnings of Mass Consumerism

Domestic markets were especially important for the sale of the goods being turned out by Europe's increasing number of industrial plants. New techniques of mass marketing arose to encourage people to purchase the new consumer goods. The Parisians pioneered in the development of the department store, and this selection is taken from a contemporary's account of the growth of these stores in the French capital city.

E. Lavasseur, On Parisian Department Stores, 1907

It was in the reign of Louis-Philippe that department stores for fashion goods and dresses, extending to material and other clothing, began to be distinguished. The type was already one of the notable developments of the Second Empire; it became one of the most important ones of the Third Republic. These stores have increased in number and several of them have become extremely large. Combining in their different departments all articles of clothing, toilet articles, furniture and many other ranges of goods, it is their special object so to combine all commodities as to attract and satisfy customers who will find conveniently together an assortment of a mass of articles corresponding to all their various needs. They attract customers by permanent display, by free entry into the shops, by periodic exhibitions, by special sales, by fixed prices, and by their ability to deliver the goods purchased to customers' homes, in Paris and to the provinces. Turning themselves into direct intermediaries between the producer and the consumer, even producing sometimes some of their articles in their own workshops, buying at lowest prices because of their large orders and because they are in a position to profit from bargains, working with large sums, and selling to most of their customers for cash only, they can transmit these benefits in lowered selling prices. They can even decide to sell at a loss, as an advertisement or to get rid of out-of-date fashions. Taking 5–6 percent on 100 million brings them in more than 20 percent would bring to a firm doing a turnover of 50,000 francs.

The success of these department stores is only possible thanks to the volume of their business and this volume needs considerable capital and a very large turnover. Now capital, having become abundant, is freely combined nowadays in large enterprises, although French capital has the reputation of being more wary of the risks of industry than of State or railway securities. On the other hand, the large urban agglomerations, the ease with which goods can be transported by the railways, the diffusion of some comforts to strata below the middle classes, have all favored these developments.

As example we may cite some figures relating to these stores, since they were brought to the notice of the public in the *Revue des Deux-Mondes*. . . .

Le Louvre, dating to the time of the extension of the rue de Rivoli under the Second Empire, did in 1893 a business of 120 million at a profit of 6.4 percent. *Le Bon-Marché,* which was a small shop when Mr. Boucicaut entered it in 1852, already did a business of 20 million at the end of the Empire. During the republic its new buildings were erected; Mme. Boucicaut turned it by her will into a kind of cooperative society, with shares and an ingenious organization; turnover reached 150 million in 1893, leaving a profit of 5 percent. . . .

According to the tax records of 1891, these stores in Paris, numbering 12, employed 1,708 persons and were rated on their site values at 2,159,000 francs; the largest had then 542 employees. These same stores had, in 1901, 9,784 employees; one of them over 2,000 and another over 1,600; their site value has doubled (4,089,000 francs).

tion. At the same time, cartels were being formed to decrease competition internally. In a cartel, independent enterprises worked together to control prices and fix production quotas, thereby restraining the kind of competition that led to reduced prices.

The formation of cartels was paralleled by a move toward ever-larger factories, especially in the iron and steel, machine, heavy electrical equipment, and chemical industries. This growth in the size of industrial plants led to pressure for greater efficiency in factory production at the same time that competition led to demands for greater economy. The result was a desire to streamline or rationalize production as much as possible. The development of precision tools enabled manufacturers to produce interchangeable parts, which in turn led to the creation of the assembly line for production. First used in the United States for small arms and clocks, the assembly line had moved to Europe by 1850. In the last half of the nineteenth century, it was primarily used in manufacturing nonmilitary goods, such as sewing machines, typewriters, bicycles, and finally the automobile.

New Patterns in an Industrial Economy

The Second Industrial Revolution played a role in the emergence of basic economic patterns that have characterized much of modern European economic life. Although we have described the period after 1871 as an age of material prosperity, recessions and crises were still very much a part of economic life. From 1873 to 1895, Europeans experienced a series of economic crises. Prices, especially those of agricultural products, fell dramatically. After 1895, however, until World War I, Europe overall experienced an economic boom and achieved a level of prosperity that encouraged people later to look back to that era as *la belle époque*—a golden age in European civilization.

After 1870, Germany replaced Great Britain as the industrial leader of Europe. Already in the 1890s, Germany's superiority was evident in new areas of manufacturing, such as organic chemicals and electrical equipment, and was increasingly apparent in its ever-greater share of worldwide trade. But the struggle for economic (and political) supremacy between Great Britain and Germany should not cause us to overlook the other great polarization of the age. By 1900, Europe was divided into two economic zones. Great Britain, Belgium, France, the Netherlands, Germany, the western part of the Austro-Hungarian Empire, and northern Italy constituted an advanced industrialized core that had a high standard of living, decent systems of transportation, and relatively healthy and educated populations (see Map 23.1). The backward and little industrialized areas to the south and east, consisting of southern Italy, most of Austria-Hungary, Spain, Portugal, the Balkan kingdoms, and Russia, were still largely agricultural and relegated by the industrial countries to the function of providing food and raw materials. The presence of Romanian oil, Greek olive oil, and Serbian pigs and prunes in western Europe served as reminders of an economic division of Europe that continued well into the twentieth century.

The economic developments of the late nineteenth century, combined with the transportation revolution that saw the growth of marine transport and railroads, also fostered a true world economy. By 1900, Europeans were importing beef and wool from Argentina and Australia, coffee from Brazil, nitrates from Chile, iron ore from Algeria, and sugar from Java. European capital was also invested abroad to develop railways, mines, electrical power plants, and banks. High rates of return, such as 11.3 percent on Latin American banking shares that were floated in London, provided plenty of incentive. Of course, foreign countries also provided markets for the surplus manufactured goods of Europe. With its capital, industries, and military might, Europe dominated the world economy by the end of the nineteenth century.

Women and Work: New Job Opportunities

The Second Industrial Revolution had an enormous impact on the position of women in the labor market. During the course of the nineteenth century, considerable controversy erupted over a woman's "right to work." Working-class organizations tended to reinforce the underlying ideal of domesticity: women should remain at home to bear and nurture children and should not be allowed in the industrial workforce. Working-class men argued that keeping women out of industrial work would ensure the moral and physical well-being of families. In reality, keeping women out of the industrial workforce simply made it easier to exploit them when they needed income to supplement their husbands' wages or to support their families when their husbands were unemployed. The desperate need to work at times forced women to do marginal work at home or piecework in sweatshops.

After 1870, however, new job opportunities for women became available. The development of larger industrial plants and the expansion of government services created a large number of service or white-collar jobs. The increased demand for white-collar workers at relatively low wages coupled with a shortage of male workers led employers to hire women. Big businesses and retail shops needed clerks, typists, secretaries, file clerks, and sales clerks. The expansion of government services created opportunities for women to be secretaries and telephone operators and to take jobs in health and social services. Compulsory education necessitated more teachers, and the development of modern hospital services opened the way for an increase in nurses.

Many of the new white-collar jobs were far from exciting. Their work was routine and, except for teaching and nursing, required few skills beyond basic literacy. Although there was little hope for advancement, these jobs had distinct advantages for the daughters of the middle classes and especially the upward-aspiring working classes. For some middle-class women, the new jobs offered freedom from the domestic patterns expected of them. Moreover, because middle-class women did not receive an education comparable to men's, they were limited in the careers they could pursue. Thus they found it easier to fill the jobs at the lower end of middle-class occupations, such as teaching and civil service jobs, especially in the postal service. Most of the new white-collar jobs, however, were filled by working-class females who saw their opportunity to escape from the physical labor of the lower-class world.

Organizing the Working Classes

The desire to improve their working and living conditions led many industrial workers to form political parties and labor unions. One of the most important of the working-class or socialist parties was formed in Germany in 1875. Under the direction of its two Marxist leaders, Wilhelm Liebknecht and August Bebel, the German Social Democratic Party (SPD) espoused revolutionary Marxist rhetoric while organizing itself as a mass political party competing in elections for the Reichstag (the German parliament). Once in the Reichstag, SPD delegates worked to enact legislation to improve the condition of the working class. As Bebel explained, "Pure negation would not be accepted by

MAP 23.1 The Industrial Regions of Europe at the Start of the Twentieth Century.

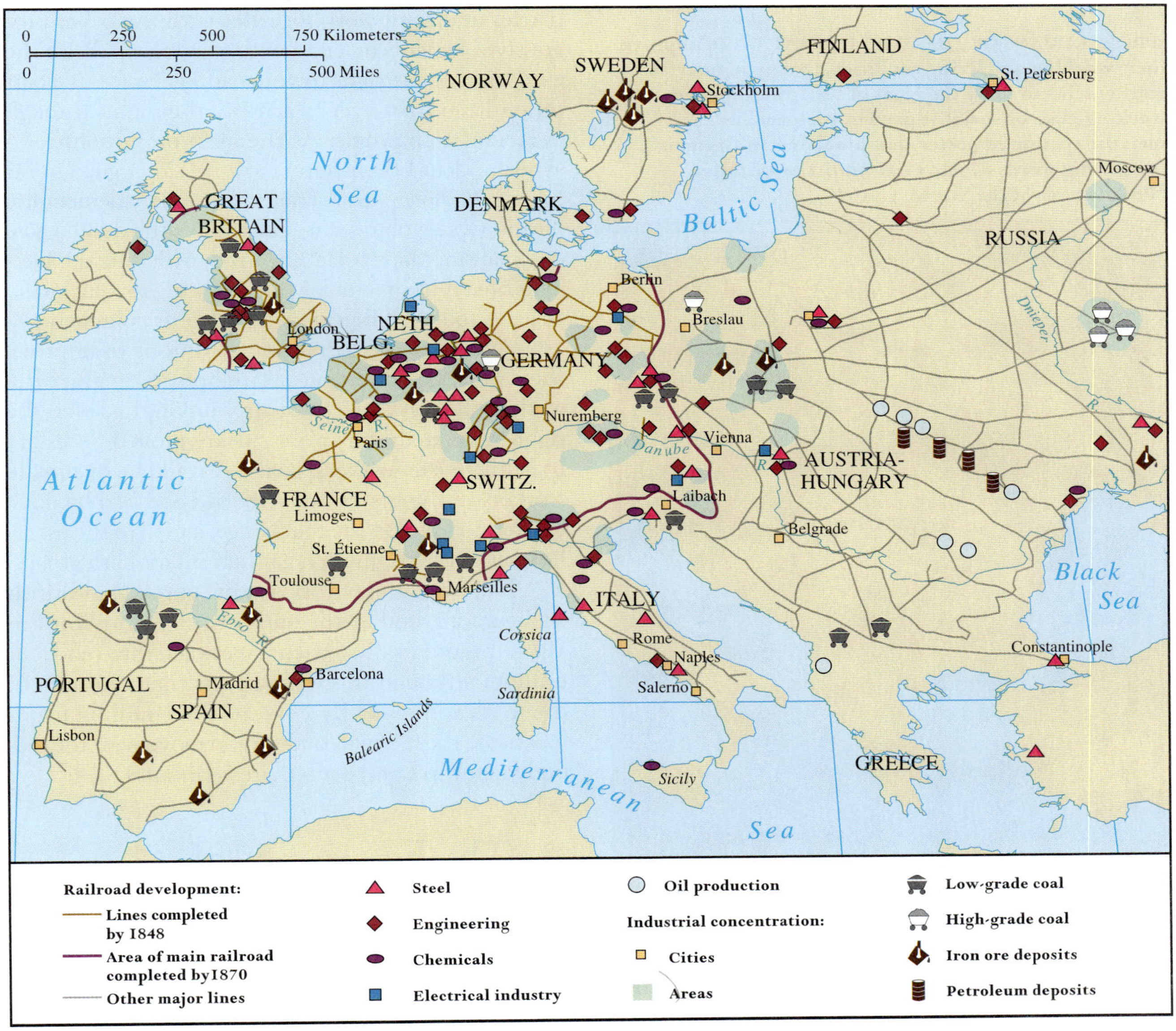

Railroad development:
Lines completed by 1848
Area of main railroad completed by 1870
Other major lines
Steel
Engineering
Chemicals
Electrical industry
Oil production
Industrial concentration:
Cities
Areas
Low-grade coal
High-grade coal
Iron ore deposits
Petroleum deposits

the voters. The masses demand that something should be done for today irrespective of what will happen on the morrow."[1] Despite government efforts to destroy it, the SPD continued to grow. In 1890, it received 1.5 million votes and thirty-five seats in the Reichstag. When it received 4 million votes in the 1912 elections, it became the largest single party in Germany.

Socialist parties also emerged in other European states, although none proved as successful as the German Social Democrats. As the socialist parties gained adherents, agitation for an international organization that would strengthen their position against international capitalism grew. In 1889, leaders of the various socialist parties formed the Second International, which was organized as a loose association of national groups. Though the Second International took some coordinated actions—for example, it proclaimed May Day (May 1) an international labor day to be marked by strikes and mass labor demonstrations—differences often wreaked havoc at the congresses of the organization. Two issues proved particularly divisive: nationalism and revisionism.

"PROLETARIANS OF THE WORLD, UNITE." To improve their working and living conditions, many industrial workers, inspired by the ideas of Karl Marx, joined working-class or socialist parties. Pictured here is a socialist-sponsored poster that proclaims in German the closing words of *The Communist Manifesto:* "Proletarians of the World, Unite!"

Despite the belief of Karl Marx and Friedrich Engels that "the working men have no country," in truth socialist parties varied from country to country and focused on national concerns and issues. Thus nationalism remained a much more powerful force than socialism.

Marxist parties also divided over the issue of revisionism. Some Marxists believed in a pure Marxism that accepted the imminent collapse of capitalism and the need for socialist ownership of the means of production. But others rejected the revolutionary approach and argued in a revisionist direction that the workers must continue to organize in mass political parties and even work together with the other progressive elements in a nation to gain reform. With the extension of the right to vote, workers were in a better position than ever to achieve their aims through democratic channels. As the most prominent revisionist, Eduard Bernstein (1850–1932), argued in his book *Evolutionary Socialism*, evolution by democratic means, not revolution, would achieve the desired goal of socialism. Many socialist parties, including the German Social Democrats, while spouting revolutionary slogans, followed Bernstein's gradualist approach.

Workers also formed trade unions to improve their working conditions. Attempts to organize the workers did not come until after unions had won the right to strike in the 1870s. Strikes proved necessary to achieve the workers' goals. A walkout by female workers in the match industry in 1888 and by dock workers in London the following year led to the establishment of trade union organizations for both groups. By 1900, two million workers were enrolled in British trade unions, and by the outbreak of World War I in 1914, this number had risen to between three and four million, although this was still less than one-fifth of the total workforce. By 1914, its three million members made the German trade union movement the second largest in Europe after Great Britain's.

◆ The Emergence of Mass Society

The new patterns of industrial production, mass consumption, and working-class organization that we identify with the Second Industrial Revolution were only one aspect of the new mass society that emerged in Europe after 1870. A larger and vastly improved urban environment, new patterns of social structure, gender issues, mass education, and mass leisure were also important features of Europe's mass society.

Population Growth

The European population increased dramatically between 1850 and 1910, rising from 270 million to more than 460 million by 1910 (see Table 23.1). After 1880, a noticeable decline in death rates largely explains the increase in population. Although the causes of this decline have been debated, two major factors—medical discoveries and environmental conditions—stand out. Some historians have stressed the importance of developments in medical science. Smallpox vaccinations, for example, were compulsory in many European countries by the mid-1850s. More important were improvements in the urban environment in the second half of the nineteenth century that greatly decreased fatalities from such infectious diseases as diarrhea, dysentery, typhoid fever, and cholera, which had been spread through contaminated water supplies and improper elimination of sewage. Improved nutrition also made a significant difference in the health of the population. The increase in agricultural productivity combined with improvements in transportation facilitated the shipment of food supplies from areas of surplus to regions with poor harvests.

Although growing agricultural and industrial prosperity supported an increase in European population, it could not do so indefinitely, especially in areas that had little industrialization and a severe problem of rural overpopulation. Some of the excess labor from underdeveloped areas migrated to the industrial regions of Europe (see Map 23.2). By 1913, more than 400,000 Poles were working in the heavily industrialized Ruhr region of western Germany. But a booming American economy and cheap shipping fares after 1898 led to mass emigration from southern and eastern Europe to America at the beginning of the twentieth century. In 1880, about 500,000 people left Europe each year on average; between 1906 and 1910, annual departures increased to 1,300,000, many of them from southern and eastern Europe.

Table 23.1 European Populations, 1851–1911

	1851	1881	1911
England and Wales	17,928,000	25,974,000	36,070,000
Scotland	2,889,000	3,736,000	4,761,000
Ireland	6,552,000	5,175,000	4,390,000
France	35,783,000	37,406,000	39,192,000
Germany	33,413,000	45,234,000	64,926,000
Belgium	4,530,000	5,520,000	7,424,000
Netherlands	3,309,000	4,013,000	5,858,000
Denmark	1,415,000	1,969,000	2,757,000
Norway	1,490,000	1,819,000	2,392,000
Sweden	3,471,000	4,169,000	5,522,000
Spain	15,455,000	16,622,000	19,927,000
Portugal	3,844,000	4,551,000	5,958,000
Italy	24,351,000	28,460,000	34,671,000
Switzerland	2,393,000	2,846,000	3,753,000
Austria	17,535,000	22,144,000	28,572,000
Hungary	18,192,000	15,739,000	20,886,000
Russia	68,500,000	97,700,000	160,700,000
Romania	—	4,600,000	7,000,000
Bulgaria	—	2,800,000	4,338,000
Greece	—	1,679,000	2,632,000
Serbia	—	1,700,000	2,912,000

SOURCE: B. R. Mitchell, *European Historical Statistics, 1750–1970* (1975).

Transformation of the Urban Environment

One of the most important consequences of industrialization and the population explosion of the nineteenth century was urbanization. In the course of the nineteenth century, urban dwellers came to make up an ever-increasing percentage of the European population. In 1800, they constituted 40 percent of the population in Britain, 25 percent in France and Germany, and only 10 percent in eastern Europe. By 1914, urban inhabitants had increased to 80 percent of the population in Britain, 45 percent in France, 60 percent in Germany, and 30 percent in eastern Europe. The size of cities also expanded dramatically, especially in industrialized countries. Between 1800 and 1900, London's population grew from 960,000 to 6,500,000 and Berlin's from 172,000 to 2,700,000.

Urban populations grew faster than the general population primarily because of the vast migration from rural areas to cities. People were driven from the countryside to the city by sheer economic necessity—unemployment, land hunger, and physical want. Urban centers offered something positive as well, usually mass employment in factories and later in service trades and professions. But cities also grew faster

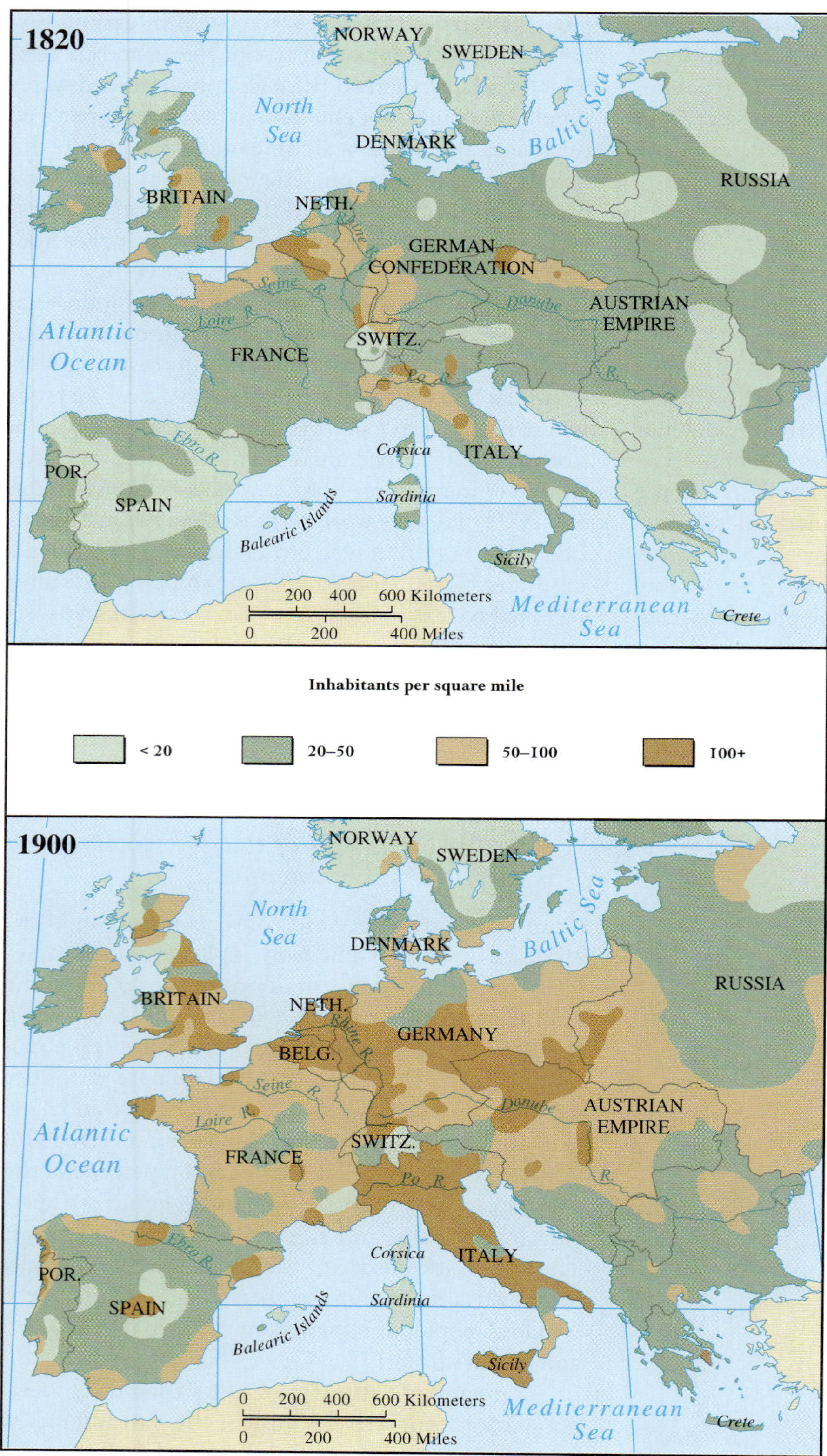

MAP 23.2 **Population Growth in Europe, 1820–1900.**

in the second half of the nineteenth century because health and living conditions in them were improving.

In the 1840s, a number of urban reformers, such as Edwin Chadwick in England and Rudolf Virchow and Solomon Neumann in Germany, had pointed to filthy living conditions as the primary cause of epidemic diseases and urged sanitary reforms to correct the problem. Soon legislative acts created boards of health that brought governmental action to bear on public health issues. Urban medical officers and building inspectors were authorized to inspect dwellings for public health hazards. New building regulations made it more difficult for private contractors to build shoddy housing. The Public Health Act of 1875 in Britain, for example, prohibited the construction of new buildings without running water and an internal drainage system. For the first time in Western history, the role of municipal governments had been expanded to include detailed regulations for the improvement of the living conditions of urban dwellers.

Essential to the public health of the modern European city was the ability to bring clean water into the city and to expel sewage from it. The problem of freshwater was solved by a system of dams and reservoirs that stored the water and aqueducts and tunnels that carried it from the countryside to the city and into individual dwellings. By the second half of the nineteenth century, regular private baths became accessible to many people as gas heaters in the 1860s and later electric heaters made hot baths possible. The treatment of sewage was also improved by building mammoth underground pipes that carried raw sewage far from the city for disposal. Unfortunately, in many places new underground sewers simply continued to discharge their raw sewage into what soon became highly polluted lakes and rivers. Nevertheless, the development of pure water and sewage systems dramatically improved the public health of European cities by 1914.

Middle-class reformers who denounced the unsanitary living conditions of the working class also

THE CITY AT NIGHT. Industrialization and the population explosion of the nineteenth century fostered the growth of cities. At the same time, technological innovations dramatically improved living conditions in European cities. Gas lighting and later electricity also transformed the nighttime environment of Europe's cities, as is evident in this painting of Liverpool.

focused on their housing needs. Overcrowded, disease-ridden slums were viewed as dangerous not only to physical health but also to the political and moral health of the entire nation. V. A. Huber, the foremost early German housing reformer, wrote in 1861: "Certainly it would not be too much to say that the home is the communal embodiment of family life. Thus the purity of the dwelling is almost as important for the family as is the cleanliness of the body for the individual."[2] To Huber, good housing was a prerequisite for stable family life, and without stable family life one of the "stabilising elements of society" would be dissolved, much to society's detriment.

Early efforts to attack the housing problem emphasized the middle-class, liberal belief in the efficacy of private enterprise. Reformers such as Huber believed that the construction of model dwellings renting at a reasonable price would force other private landlords to elevate their housing standards. A fine example of this approach was the work of Octavia Hill (see the box on p. 475). With the financial assistance of a friend, she rehabilitated some old dwellings and constructed new ones to create housing for 3,500 tenants.

As the number and size of cities continued to mushroom, governments by the 1880s came to the conclusion—although reluctantly—that private enterprise could not solve the housing crisis. In 1890, a British housing act empowered local town councils to construct cheap housing for the working classes. London and Liverpool were the first communities to take advantage of their new powers. Similar activity had been set in motion in Germany by 1900. Everywhere, however, these lukewarm measures failed to do much to meet the real housing needs of the working classes. In housing as in so many other areas of life in the late nineteenth and early twentieth centuries, the liberal principle that the government that governs least governs best had simply proved untrue. More and more, governments were stepping into areas of activity that they would have never touched earlier.

The Social Structure of Mass Society

At the top of European society stood a wealthy elite, constituting only 5 percent of the population but controlling 30 to 40 percent of its wealth. In the course of the nineteenth century, aristocrats coalesced with the most successful industrialists, bankers, and merchants (the wealthy upper middle class) to form this new elite. The growth of big business had produced this group of wealthy plutocrats, while aristocrats, whose income from landed estates declined, invested in railway shares, public utilities, government bonds, and even businesses.

Increasingly, aristocrats and plutocrats fused as the wealthy upper middle class purchased landed estates to join the aristocrats in the pleasures of country living while the aristocrats bought lavish town houses for part-time urban life. Common bonds were also forged when the sons of wealthy middle-class families were admitted to the elite schools dominated by the children of the aristocracy. This educated elite, whether aristocratic or middle class in background, assumed leadership roles in government bureaucracies and military hierarchies. Marriage also served to unite the two groups. Daughters of tycoons acquired titles while aristocratic heirs gained new sources of cash. Wealthy American heiresses were in special demand. When Consuelo Vanderbilt married the duke of Marlborough, the new duchess brought £2 million (approximately $10 million) to her husband.

The middle classes consisted of a variety of groups. Below the upper middle class was a level that included such traditional groups as professionals in law, medicine, and the civil service as well as moderately well-to-do industrialists and merchants. The industrial expansion of the nineteenth century also added new groups to this segment of the middle class. These included business managers and new professionals, such as the engineers, architects, accountants, and chemists who formed professional associations as the symbols of their newfound importance. A lower middle class of small shopkeepers, traders, manufacturers, and prosperous peasants provided goods and services for the classes above them.

Standing between the lower middle class and the lower classes were new groups of white-collar workers who were the product of the Second Industrial Revolution. They were the traveling salespeople, bookkeepers, bank tellers, telephone operators, department store clerks, and secretaries. Although largely propertyless and often paid only marginally more than skilled laborers, these white-collar workers were often committed to middle-class ideals and optimistic about improving their status.

The moderately prosperous and successful middle classes shared a common lifestyle, one whose values tended to dominate much of nineteenth-century society. The members of the middle class were especially active in preaching their worldview to their children and to the upper and lower classes of their society. This was especially evident in Victorian Britain, often considered a model of middle-class society. The European middle classes embraced and promulgated the importance of progress and science. They believed in hard work, which

The Housing Venture of Octavia Hill

Octavia Hill was a practical-minded British housing reformer who believed that workers and their families were entitled to happy homes. At the same time, she was convinced that the poor needed guidance and encouragement, not charity. In this selection, she describes her housing venture.

Octavia Hill, Homes of the London Poor

About four years ago I was put in possession of three houses in one of the worst courts of Marylebone. Six other houses were bought subsequently. All were crowded with inmates.

The first thing to be done was to put them in decent tenantable order. The set last purchased was a row of cottages facing a bit of desolate ground, occupied with wretched, dilapidated cow-sheds, manure heaps, old timber, and rubbish of every description. The houses were in a most deplorable condition—the plaster was dropping from the walls; on one staircase a pail was placed to catch the rain that fell through the roof. All the staircases were perfectly dark; the banisters were gone, having been burnt as firewood by tenants. The grates, with large holes in them, were falling forward into the rooms. The washhouse, full of lumber belonging to the landlord, was locked up; thus the inhabitants had to wash clothes, as well as to cook, eat and sleep in their small rooms. The dustbin, standing in the front part of the houses, was accessible to the whole neighbourhood, and boys often dragged from it quantities of unseemly objects and spread them over the court. The state of the drainage was in keeping with everything else. The pavement of the backyard was all broken up, and great puddles stood in it, so that the damp crept up the outer walls. . . .

As soon as I entered into possession, each family had an opportunity of doing better: those who would not pay, or who led clearly immoral lives, were ejected. The rooms they vacated were cleansed; the tenants who showed signs of improvement moved into them, and thus, in turn, an opportunity was obtained for having each room distempered and papered. The drains were put in order, a large slate cistern was fixed, the washhouse was cleared of its lumber, and thrown open on stated days to each tenant in turn. The roof, the plaster, the woodwork were repaired; the staircase walls were distempered; new grates were fixed; the layers of paper and rag (black with age) were torn from the windows, and glass put in; out of 192 panes only eight were found unbroken. The yard and footpath were paved.

The rooms, as a rule, were re-let at the same prices at which they had been let before; but tenants with large families were counselled to take two rooms, and for these much less was charged than if let singly: this plan I continue to pursue. In-coming tenants are not allowed to take a decidedly insufficient quantity of room, and no sub-letting is permitted. . . .

The pecuniary result has been very satisfactory. Five percent has been paid on all the capital invested. A fund for the repayment of capital is accumulating. A liberal allowance has been made for repairs. . . .

My tenants are mostly of a class far below that of mechanics. They are, indeed, of the very poor. And yet, although the gifts they have received have been next to nothing, none of the families who have passed under my care during the whole four years have continued in what is called "distress," except such as have been unwilling to exert themselves. Those who will not exert the necessary self-control cannot avail themselves of the means of livelihood held out to them. But, for those who are willing, some small assistance in the form of work has, from time to time, been provided—not much, but sufficient to keep them from want or despair.

they viewed as the primary human good, open to everyone and guaranteed to have positive results. They were also regular churchgoers who believed in the good conduct associated with traditional Christian morality. The middle class was concerned with propriety, the right way of doing things. This concern gave rise to an incessant number of books aimed at the middle-class market with such titles as *The Habits of Good Society* or *Don't: A Manual of Mistakes and Improprieties More or Less Prevalent in Conduct and Speech*.

Below the middle classes on the social scale were the working classes of European society, who made up almost 80 percent of the population. Many of the members of these classes were landholding peasants, farm laborers, and sharecroppers, especially in eastern Europe. The urban working class consisted of many different groups, including skilled artisans in such trades as cabinetmaking and printing and semiskilled laborers such as carpenters and many factory workers, who earned wages that were about two-thirds of those of highly skilled workers. At the bottom of the urban working class were the unskilled laborers. They were the largest group of workers and included day laborers and large numbers of domestic servants. One out of every seven employed persons in Great Britain in 1900 was a domestic servant. Most were women.

Urban workers did experience a real betterment in the material conditions of their lives after 1871. For one thing, urban improvements meant better living conditions. A rise in real wages, accompanied by a decline in many consumer costs, especially in the 1880s and 1890s, made it possible for workers to buy more than just food and housing. Workers' budgets now provided money for more clothes and even leisure at the same time that strikes and labor agitation were providing ten-hour days and Saturday afternoons off.

The "Woman Question": The Role of Women

The "woman question" was the term used to identify the debate over the role of women in society. In the nineteenth century, women remained legally inferior, economically dependent, and largely defined by family and household roles. Many women still aspired to the ideal of femininity popularized by writers and poets. Alfred Lord Tennyson's poem *The Princess* expressed it well:

> *Man for the field and woman for the hearth:*
> *Man for the sword and for the needle she:*
> *Man with the head and woman with the heart:*
> *Man to command and woman to obey;*
> *All else confusion.*

This traditional characterization of the sexes, based on gender-defined social roles, was elevated to the status of universal male and female attributes in the nineteenth century, due largely to the impact of the Industrial Revolution on the family. As the chief family wage earners, men worked outside the home while women were left with the care of the family, for which they were paid nothing. Of course, the ideal did not always match reality, especially for the lower classes, where the need for supplemental income drove women to do "sweated" work.

Throughout most of the nineteenth century, marriage was viewed as the only honorable and available career for most women. While the middle class glorified the ideal of domesticity (see the box on p. 478), for most women marriage was a matter of economic necessity. The lack of meaningful work and the lower wages paid to women made it difficult for single women to earn a living. Most women chose to marry, which was reflected in the increase in marriage rates and a decline in illegitimacy rates in the course of the nineteenth century.

Birthrates also dropped significantly at this time. A very important factor in the evolution of the modern family was the decline in the number of offspring born to the average woman. The change was not necessarily due to new technological products. Although the invention of vulcanized rubber in the 1840s made possible the production of condoms and diaphragms, they were not widely used as effective contraceptive devices until the era of World War I. Some historians maintain that the change in attitude that led parents to deliberately limit the number of offspring was more important than the method used. While some historians attribute increased birth control to more widespread use of coitus interruptus, or male withdrawal before ejaculation, others have emphasized the ability of women to restrict family size through abortion and even infanticide or abandonment. That a change in attitude occurred was apparent in the emergence of a movement to increase awareness of birth control methods. Europe's first birth control clinic, founded by Dr. Aletta Jacob, opened in Amsterdam in 1882.

THE MIDDLE-CLASS AND WORKING-CLASS FAMILY

The family was the central institution of middle-class life. Men provided the family income, while women focused on household and child care. The use of domestic servants in many middle-class homes, made possible by an abundant supply of cheap labor, reduced the amount of time middle-class women had to spend on household chores. At the same time, by reducing the number of children in the family, mothers could devote more time to child care and domestic leisure.

The middle-class family fostered an ideal of togetherness. The Victorians codified the family Christmas, with its yule log, Christmas tree, songs, and exchange of gifts. In the United States, Fourth of July celebrations changed from drunken revels to family picnics by the 1850s. The education of middle-class females in domestic crafts, singing, and piano play-

A MIDDLE-CLASS FAMILY. Nineteenth-century middle-class moralists considered the family the fundamental pillar of a healthy society, and family togetherness was an important ideal. This painting by William P. Frith, titled *Many Happy Returns of the Day,* shows a family birthday celebration for a little girl in which grandparents, parents, and children take part. The servant at the left holds presents for the little girl.

ing prepared them for their function of providing a proper environment for home recreation.

Women in working-class families were more accustomed to hard work. Daughters in working-class families were expected to work until they married; even after marriage, they often did piecework at home to support the family. For the children of the working classes, childhood was over by age of nine or ten when they became apprentices or were employed in odd jobs.

Between 1890 and 1914, however, family patterns among the working class began to change. High-paying jobs in heavy industry and improvements in the standard of living made it possible for working-class families to depend on the income of husbands and the wages of grown children. By the early twentieth century, some working-class mothers could afford to stay at home, following the pattern of middle-class women. At the same time, new consumer products, such as sewing machines, clocks, bicycles, and cast-iron stoves, created a new mass consumer society whose focus was on higher levels of consumption.

These working-class families also followed the middle classes in limiting the size of their families. Children began to be viewed as dependents rather than wage earners as child labor laws and compulsory education took children out of the workforce and into schools. Improvements in public health as well as advances in medicine and a better diet resulted in a decline in infant mortality rates for the lower classes and made it easier for working-class families to choose to have fewer children. At the same time, strikes and labor agitation led to laws that reduced work hours to ten per day by 1900 and eliminated work on Saturday afternoons, which enabled working-class parents to devote more attention to their children and develop deeper emotional ties with them.

Education and Leisure in the Mass Society

Mass education was a product of the mass society of the late nineteenth century. Being "educated" in the early nineteenth century meant attending a secondary school or possibly even a university. Secondary schools mostly emphasized a classical education based on the study of Greek and Latin. Secondary and university education were primarily for the elite, the sons of government officials, nobles, or the wealthier middle class. After 1850, secondary education was expanded as more middle-class families sought employment in public service and the professions or entry into elite scientific and technical schools.

In the decades after 1870, the functions of the state were extended to include the development of mass education in state-run systems. Between 1870 and 1914, most Western governments began to offer at least primary education to both boys and girls between the ages of six and twelve. States also assumed responsibility for the quality of teachers by establishing teacher-training schools. By 1900, many European states, especially in northern and western Europe, were providing state-financed primary schools, salaried and

Advice to Women: Be Dependent

Industrialization had a strong impact on middle-class women as gender-based social roles became the norm. Men worked outside the home to support the family while women provided for the needs of their children and husband at home. In this selection, one woman gives advice to middle-class women on their proper role and behavior.

Elizabeth Poole Sanford, Woman in Her Social and Domestic Character

The changes wrought by Time are many. It influences the opinions of men as familiarity does their feelings; it has a tendency to do away with superstition, and to reduce every thing to its real worth.

It is thus that the sentiment for woman has undergone a change. The romantic passion which once almost deified her is on the decline; and it is by intrinsic qualities that she must now inspire respect. She is no longer the queen of song and the star of chivalry. But if there is less of enthusiasm entertained for her, the sentiment is more rational, and, perhaps, equally sincere; for it is in relation to happiness that she is chiefly appreciated.

And in this respect it is, we must confess, that she is most useful and most important. Domestic life is the chief source of her influence; and the greatest debt society can owe to her is domestic comfort; for happiness is almost an element of virtue; and nothing conduces more to improve the character of men than domestic peace. A woman may make a man's home delightful, and may thus increase his motives for virtuous exertion. She may refine and tranquilize his mind,—may turn away his anger or allay his grief. Her smile may be the happy influence to gladden his heart, and to disperse the cloud that gathers on his brow. And in proportion to her endeavors to make those around her happy, she will be esteemed and loved. She will secure by her excellence that interest and that regard which she might formerly claim as the privilege of her sex, and will really merit the deference which was then conceded to her as a matter of course. . . .

Perhaps one of the first secrets of her influence is adaptation to the tastes, and sympathy in the feelings, of those around her. This holds true in lesser as well as in graver points. It is in the former, indeed, that the absence of interest in a companion is frequently most disappointing. Where want of congeniality impairs domestic comfort, the fault is generally chargeable on the female side. It is for woman, not for man, to make the sacrifice, especially in indifferent matters. She must, in a certain degree, be plastic herself if she would mould others. . . .

Nothing is so likely to conciliate the affections of the other sex as a feeling that woman looks to them for support and guidance. In proportion as men are themselves superior, they are accessible to this appeal. On the contrary, they never feel interested in one who seems disposed rather to offer than to ask assistance. There is, indeed, something unfeminine in independence. It is contrary to nature, and therefore it offends. We do not like to see a woman affecting tremors, but still less do we like to see her acting the amazon. A really sensible woman feels her dependence. She does what she can; but she is conscious of inferiority, and therefore grateful for support. She knows that she is the weaker vessel, and that as such she should receive honor. In this view, her weakness is an attraction, not a blemish.

In everything, therefore, that women attempt, they should show their consciousness of dependence. If they are learners, let them evince a teachable spirit; if they give an opinion, let them do it in an unassuming manner. There is something so unpleasant in female self-sufficiency that it not unfrequently deters instead of persuading, and prevents the adoption of advice which the judgment even approves.

trained teachers, and free, compulsory mass elementary education.

Why did European states make this commitment to mass education? Liberals believed that education was important to personal and social improvement and sought in Catholic countries to supplant Catholic education with moral and civic training based on secular values. Even conservatives were attracted to mass education as a means of improving the quality of military recruits and training people in social discipline. In 1875, a German military journal stated: "We in Germany consider education to be one of the principal ways of promoting the strength of the nation and above all military strength."[3]

Another incentive for mass education came from industrialization. In the early Industrial Revolution, unskilled labor was sufficient to meet factory needs, but the new firms of the Second Industrial Revolution demanded skilled labor. Both boys and girls with an elementary education had new possibilities of jobs beyond their villages or small towns, including white-collar jobs in railway and subway stations, post offices, banking and shipping firms, teaching, and nursing. To industrialists, then, mass education furnished the trained workers they needed.

Nevertheless, the chief motive for mass education was political. The expansion of voting rights necessitated a more educated electorate. Even more important, mass compulsory education instilled patriotism and nationalized the masses, providing an opportunity for even greater national integration. As people lost their ties to local regions and even to religion, nationalism supplied a new faith. The use of a single common language created greater national unity than loyalty to a ruler ever did.

A nation's motives for universal elementary education largely determined what was taught in the schools. Obviously, indoctrination in national values took on great importance. At the core of the academic curriculum were reading, writing, arithmetic, national history (especially geared to a patriotic view), geography, literature, and some singing and drawing. The education of boys and girls varied, however. Where possible, the sexes were separated. Girls did less math and no science but concentrated on such domestic skills as sewing, washing, ironing, and cooking, all prerequisites for providing a good home for husband and children. Boys were taught some practical skills, such as carpentry, and even some military drill. Most of the elementary schools also inculcated the middle-class virtues of hard work, thrift, sobriety, cleanliness, and respect for the family. For most students, elementary education led to apprenticeship and a job.

The development of compulsory elementary education created a demand for teachers, and most of them were female. In the United States, for example, females constituted two-thirds of all teachers by the 1880s. Many men viewed the teaching of children as an extension of women's "natural role" as nurturers of children. Moreover, females were paid lower salaries, in itself a considerable incentive for governments to encourage the establishment of teacher-training institutes for women. The first colleges for women were teacher-training schools; not until the beginning of the twentieth century were women permitted to enter

A WOMEN'S COLLEGE. Women were largely excluded from male-dominated universities before 1900. Consequently, the demand of women for higher education led to the establishment of women's colleges, most of which were primarily teacher-training schools. This photograph shows a group of women in an astronomy class at Vassar College in the United States in 1878. Maria Mitchell, a famous astronomer, was head of the department.

the male-dominated universities. In France, 3 percent of university students in 1902 were women; by 1914, their number had increased to 10 percent of the total.

The most immediate result of mass education was an increase in literacy. In Germany, Great Britain, France, and the Scandinavian countries, adult illiteracy was virtually eliminated by 1900. Where there was less schooling, the story is very different. Adult illiteracy rates were 79 percent in Serbia, 78 percent in Romania, and 79 percent in Russia. All of these countries had made only a minimal investment in mass education.

With the dramatic increase in literacy after 1871 came the rise of mass newspapers, such as the *Evening News* (1881) and *Daily Mail* (1896) in London, which sold millions of copies a day. These newspapers were written in an easily understood style and tended to be extremely sensational. Unlike eighteenth-century newspapers, which were full of serious editorials and lengthy political analysis, these tabloids provided lurid details of crimes, jingoistic diatribes, gossip, and sports news. There were other forms of cheap literature as well. Specialty magazines, such as the *Family Herald* for the entire family, and women's magazines began to appear in the 1860s. Pulp fiction for adults included the extremely popular westerns with their innumerable variations on conflicts between cowboys and Indians. Literature for the masses was but one feature of a new mass culture; another was the emergence of new forms of mass leisure.

MASS LEISURE

In the preindustrial centuries, play or leisure activities had been closely connected to work patterns based on the seasonal or daily cycles typical of the life of peasants and artisans. The process of industrialization in the nineteenth century had an enormous impact on that traditional pattern. The factory imposed new work patterns that were determined by the rhythms of machines and clocks and removed work time completely from the family environment of farms and workshops. Work and leisure became opposites as leisure came to be defined as what people did for fun after work. In fact, the new leisure hours created by the industrial system—evening hours after work, weekends, and later a week or two in the summer—largely determined the contours of the new mass leisure.

New technology also determined mass leisure pursuits. The new technology created novel experiences for leisure, such as the Ferris wheel at amusement parks, and the mechanized urban transportation systems of the 1880s meant that even the working classes were no longer dependent on neighborhood bars but could make their way to athletic games, amusement parks, and dance halls. Railroads could take people to the beaches on weekends.

The upper and middle classes had created the first market for tourism, but as wages increased and workers were given paid vacations, tourism became another form of mass leisure. Thomas Cook (1808–1892) was a British pioneer of mass tourism. Secretary to a British temperance group, Cook had been responsible for organizing a railroad trip to temperance gatherings in 1841. This experience led him to offer trips on a regular basis after he found that he could make substantial profits by renting special trains, lowering prices, and increasing the number of passengers.

By the late nineteenth century, team sports had also developed into yet another focus of mass leisure. Unlike the old rural games, however, they were no longer chaotic and spontaneous activities but became strictly organized with sets of rules and officials to enforce them. These rules were the products of organized athletic groups, such as the English Football Association (1863) and the American Bowling Congress (1895).

The new team sports rapidly became professionalized. In Britain, soccer had its Football Association in 1863 and rugby its Rugby Football Union in 1871. In the United States, the first national association to recognize professional baseball players was formed in 1863. By 1900, the National League and American League had a complete monopoly over professional baseball. The development of urban transportation systems made possible the construction of stadiums where thousands could attend, making mass spectator sports a big business.

Standardized forms of amusement drew mass audiences. Although some theorists argued that the new amusements were important for improving people, they served primarily to provide entertainment and distract people from the realities of their work lives. The new mass leisure also represented a significant change from earlier forms of popular culture. Festivals and fairs had been based on active and spontaneous community participation, whereas the new forms of mass leisure were businesses, standardized for largely passive mass audiences and organized to make profits.

◆ The National State

Within the major European states, considerable progress was made in achieving liberal practices (constitutions, parliaments, and individual liberties) and reforms that encouraged the expansion of political democracy through voting rights for men and mass political parties. At the same time, however, these developments were strongly resisted in parts of Europe where the old political forces remained strong.

Western Europe: The Growth of Political Democracy

Parliamentary government was most firmly rooted in the western European states. The growth of political democracy was one of the preoccupations of British politics after 1871, and its cause was pushed along by the expansion of suffrage. Much advanced by the Reform Act of 1867 (see Chapter 22), the right to vote was further extended during the second ministry of William Gladstone (1880–1885) with the passage of the Reform Act of 1884. It gave the vote to all men who paid regular rents or taxes, thus largely enfranchising the agricultural workers, a group previously excluded. The following year, the Redistribution Act eliminated historic boroughs and counties and established constituencies with approximately equal populations and one representative each. The payment of salaries to members of the House of Commons beginning in 1911 further democratized that institution by at least opening the door to people other than the wealthy. The British system of gradual reform through parliamentary institutions had become the way of British political life.

The defeat of France by the Prussian army in 1870 brought the downfall of Louis Napoleon's Second Empire. In new elections based on universal male suffrage, the French people rejected the republicans and overwhelmingly favored the monarchists, who won two-thirds of the seats in the new National Assembly. In response, on March 26, 1871, radical republicans formed an independent republican government in Paris known as the Commune.

But the National Assembly refused to give up its power and decided to crush the revolutionary Commune. Vicious fighting broke out in April. Many working-class men and women stepped forth to defend the Commune. At first, women's activities were the traditional ones: caring for the wounded soldiers and feeding the troops. Gradually, however, women expanded their activities to include taking care of weapons, working as scouts, and even setting up their own fighting brigades. Louise Michel (1830–1905), a schoolteacher, emerged as one of the leaders of the Paris Commune (see the box on p. 482). She proved tireless in forming committees for the defense of the revolutionary Commune.

All of these efforts were in vain, however. In the last week of May, government troops massacred thousands of the Commune's defenders. Estimates are that twenty thousand were shot; another ten thousand (including Louise Michel) were shipped to the French penal colony of New Caledonia. The brutal repression of the Commune bequeathed a legacy of hatred that continued to plague French politics for decades. The harsh punishment of women who participated in revolutionary activity also served to discourage any future action by working-class women to improve their conditions.

Although a majority of the members of the monarchist-dominated National Assembly wished to restore a monarchy in France, inability to agree on who should be king caused the monarchists to miss their opportunity and led in 1875 to an improvised constitution that established a republican form of government as the least divisive compromise. This constitution established a bicameral legislature with an upper house, the Senate, elected indirectly and a lower house, the Chamber of Deputies, chosen by universal male suffrage; a president, selected by the legislature for a term of seven years, served as executive of the government. The Constitution of 1875, intended only as a stopgap measure, solidified the republic—the Third Republic—which lasted sixty-five years. New elections in 1876 and 1877 strengthened the hands of the republicans who managed by 1879 to institute ministerial responsibility and establish the power of the Chamber of Deputies. The prime minister or premier and his ministers were now responsible not to the president but to the Chamber of Deputies.

By 1870, Italy had emerged as a geographically united state with pretensions to great power status. Its internal weaknesses, however, gave that claim a hollow ring. Sectional differences—a poverty-stricken south and an industrializing north—weakened any sense of community. Chronic turmoil between workers and industrialists undermined the social fabric. The Italian government was unable to deal effectively with these problems because of extensive corruption among government officials and the lack of stability created by ever-changing government coalitions. The granting of universal male suffrage in 1912 did little to correct the extensive corruption and weak government. Even Italy's pretensions to great power status came up empty when Italy became the first modern European power to be defeated in battle by an African state, Ethiopia.

A Leader of the Paris Commune

Louise Michel became active among revolutionary groups in Paris in 1870 and emerged the following year as a leader of the Paris Commune. Arrested and exiled to New Caledonia, she was allowed to return to France in 1880, where she became a heroic figure among radical groups. Later she spent three years in prison for anarchism and much of the time thereafter in England in self-imposed exile. In her memoirs, Louise Michel discussed what happened when the National Assembly sent troops on March 18, 1871, to seize cannon that had been moved earlier to the hills of Montmartre. She also reflected on her activities in the Commune.

Louise Michel, Memoirs

Learning that the Versailles soldiers [troops of the National Assembly] were trying to seize the cannon, men and women of Montmartre swarmed up the Butte in a surprise maneuver. Those people who were climbing believed they would die, but they were prepared to pay the price.

The Butte of Montmartre was bathed in the first light of day, through which things were glimpsed as if they were hidden behind a thin veil of water. Gradually the crowd increased. The other districts of Paris, hearing of the events taking place on the Butte of Montmartre, came to our assistance.

The women of Paris covered the cannon with their bodies. When their officers ordered the soldiers to fire, the men refused. The same army that would be used to crush Paris two months later decided now that it did not want to be an accomplice of the reaction. They gave up their attempt to seize the cannon from the National Guard. They understood that the people were defending the Republic by defending the arms that the royalists and imperialists would have turned on Paris in agreement with the Prussians. When we had won our victory, I looked around and noticed my poor mother, who had followed me to the Butte of Montmartre, believing that I was going to die.

On this day, the eighteenth of March, the people awakened. If they had not, it would have been the triumph of some king; instead it was a triumph of the people. The eighteenth of March could have belonged to the allies of kings, or to foreigners, or to the people. It was the people's. . . .

During the entire time of the Commune, I only spent one night at my poor mother's. I never really went to bed during that time. I just napped a little whenever there was nothing better to do, and many other people lived the same way. Everybody who wanted deliverance gave himself totally to the cause. . . . During the Commune I went unhurt except for a bullet that grazed my wrist, although my hat was literally riddled with bullet holes.

Central and Eastern Europe: Persistence of the Old Order

Germany, Austria-Hungary, and Russia pursued political policies that were quite different from those of the western European nations. Germany and Austria-Hungary had the trappings of parliamentary government, including legislative bodies and elections by universal male suffrage, but authoritarian forces, especially powerful monarchies and conservative social groups, remained strong. In eastern Europe, especially Russia, the old system of autocracy was barely touched by the winds of change.

The constitution of the new imperial Germany begun by Bismarck in 1871 provided for a federal system with a bicameral legislature. The lower house of the German parliament, known as the Reichstag, was elected on the basis of universal male suffrage, but it did not have ministerial responsibility. Ministers of government, the most important of which was the chancellor, were responsible not to the parliament but to the emperor. The emperor also commanded the armed forces and controlled foreign policy and internal administration. Although the creation of a parliament elected by universal male suffrage presented opportunities for the growth of a real political democracy, it failed to develop in Germany before World War I. The army and Bismarck were two major reasons why it did not.

The German (largely Prussian) army viewed itself as the defender of monarchy and aristocracy and sought to escape control by the Reichstag by operating under a general staff responsible only to the emperor. Prussian military tradition was strong, and

CHRONOLOGY

The National States, 1871–1894

Great Britain	
Second ministry of William Gladstone	1880–1885
Reform Act	1884
Redistribution Act	1885
France	
Paris Commune	1871 (March–May)
Republican constitution (Third Republic)	1875
Germany	
Bismarck as chancellor	1871–1890
Antisocialist law	1878
Social welfare legislation	1883–1889
Austria-Hungary	
Emperor Francis Joseph	1848–1916
Imperial Russia	
Tsar Alexander III	1881–1894

military officers took steps to ensure the loyalty of their subordinates to the emperor.

The policies of Bismarck, who served as chancellor of the new German state until 1890, often served to prevent the growth of more democratic institutions. At first, Bismarck worked with the liberals, especially in launching an attack on the Catholic church, the so-called *Kulturkampf* or "struggle for civilization." Like Bismarck, middle-class liberals distrusted Catholic loyalty to the new Germany. But Bismarck's tactics proved counterproductive, and Bismarck soon abandoned the attack on Catholicism by making an abrupt shift in policy.

In 1878, Bismarck abandoned the liberals and began to persecute the socialists. Bismarck became alarmed by the growth of the Social Democratic Party. He genuinely believed that the socialists' antinationalistic, anticapitalistic, and antimonarchical stance represented a danger to the empire. In 1878, Bismarck got the parliament to pass a law that limited socialist meetings and publications while still allowing socialist candidates to run for the Reichstag. Bismarck also attempted to woo workers away from socialism by enacting social welfare legislation. Between 1883 and 1889, the Reichstag passed laws that provided sickness, accident, and disability benefits as well as old-age pensions, financed by compulsory contributions from workers, employers, and the state. Bismarck's social security system was the most progressive the world had yet seen. Nevertheless, both the repressive and the social welfare measures failed to stop the growth of socialism. In his frustration, Bismarck planned still more antisocialist measures in 1890, but before he could carry them out, the new emperor, William II (1888–1918), eager to pursue his own policies, cashiered the aged chancellor.

After the creation of the dual monarchy of Austria-Hungary in 1867, the Austrian part received a constitution that established a parliamentary system with the principle of ministerial responsibility. But Emperor Francis Joseph (1848–1916) largely ignored ministerial responsibility and proceeded to personally appoint and dismiss his ministers and rule by decree when parliament was not in session.

The problem of the minorities continued to trouble the empire. The ethnic Germans, who made up only one-third of Austria's population, governed Austria but felt increasingly threatened by the Czechs, Poles, and other Slavic groups within the empire. The granting of universal male suffrage in 1907 served only to make the problem worse as nationalities that had played no role in the government now agitated in the

BISMARCK AND WILLIAM II. In 1890, Bismarck sought to undertake new repressive measures against the Social Democrats. Disagreeing with this policy, Emperor William II forced him to resign. This political cartoon shows William II reclining on a throne made of artillery and cannonballs and holding a doll labeled "socialism." Bismarck bids farewell while Germany, personified as a woman, looks on with grave concern.

parliament for autonomy. This led prime ministers after 1900 to ignore the parliament and rely increasingly on imperial emergency decrees to govern.

In Russia, the assassination of Alexander II in 1881 convinced his son and successor, Alexander III (1881–1894), that reform had been a mistake, and he quickly returned to the repressive measures of earlier tsars. Advocates of constitutional monarchy and social reform, along with revolutionary groups, were persecuted. Entire districts of Russia were placed under martial law if the government suspected the inhabitants of treason. The powers of the zemstvos, created by the reforms of Alexander II, were sharply curtailed. When Alexander III died, his weak son and successor, Nicholas II (1894–1917), began his rule with his father's conviction that the absolute power of the tsars should be preserved: "I shall maintain the principle of autocracy just as firmly and unflinchingly as did my unforgettable father."[4] But conditions were changing, especially with the growth of industrialization, and the tsar's approach was not realistic in view of the new circumstances he faced.

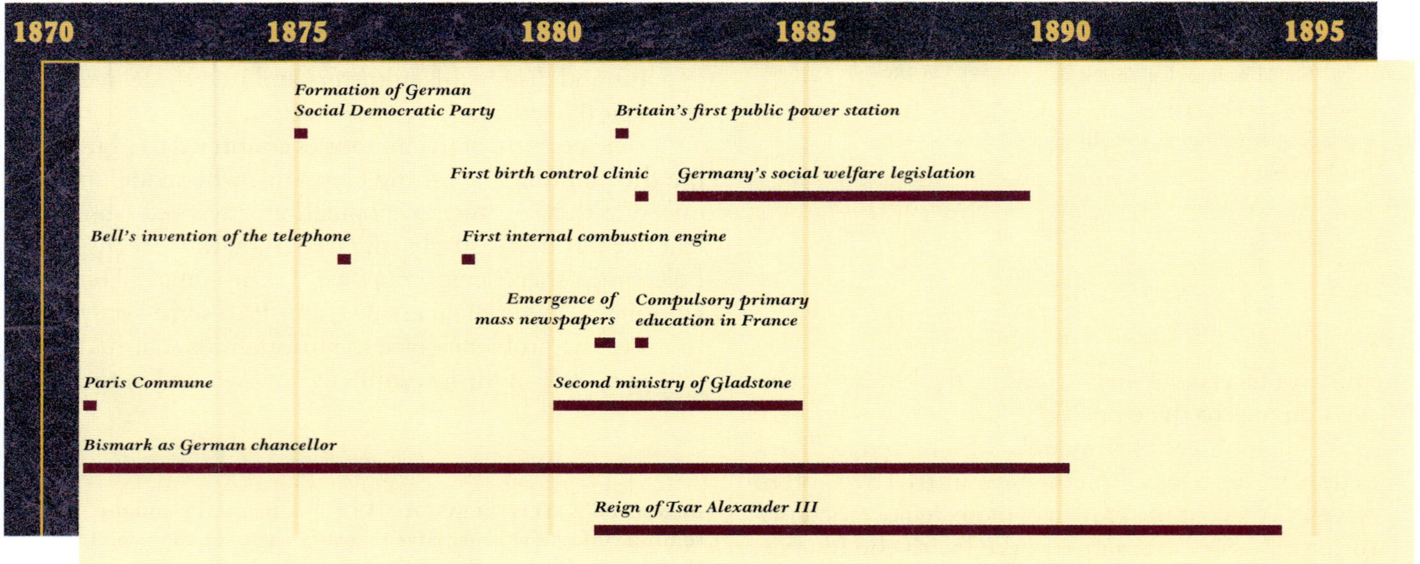

Conclusion

The Second Industrial Revolution helped create a new material prosperity that led Europeans to believe they had ushered in a new "age of progress." A major feature of this age was the emergence of a mass society. The lower classes in particular benefited from the right to vote, a higher standard of living, and new schools that provided them with an education. New forms of mass transportation, combined with new work patterns, enabled large numbers of people to enjoy weekend excursions to amusement parks and seaside resorts and to participate in new mass leisure activities.

By 1871, the national state had become the focus of people's lives. Liberal and democratic reforms brought new possibilities for greater participation in the political process, although women were still largely excluded from political rights. After 1871, the national state also began to expand its functions beyond all previous limits. Fearful of the growth of socialism and trade unions, governments attempted to appease the working masses by adopting such social insurance measures as protection against accidents, illness, and old age. These social welfare measures were narrow in scope and limited in benefits, but they signaled a new direction for state action to benefit the mass of its citizens. The enactment of public health and housing measures, designed to curb the worst ills of urban living, was yet another indication of how state power could be used to benefit the people.

This extension of state functions took place in an atmosphere of increased national loyalty. After 1871, nation-states increasingly sought to solidify the social order and win the active loyalty and support of their citizens by deliberately cultivating national feelings. Yet this policy contained potentially great dangers. As we shall see in the next chapter, nations had discovered once again that imperialistic adventures and military successes could arouse nationalistic passions and smother domestic political unrest. But they also found that nationalistic feelings could also lead to intense international rivalries that made war almost inevitable.

Notes

1. Quoted in W. L. Guttsman, *The German Social Democratic Party, 1875–1933* (London, 1981), p. 63.
2. Quoted in Nicholas Bullock and James Read, *The Movement for Housing Reform in Germany and France, 1840–1914* (Cambridge, 1985), p. 42.
3. Quoted in Robert Gildea, *Barricades and Borders: Europe, 1800–1914*, 2d ed. (Oxford, 1996), pp. 240–241.
4. Quoted in Shmuel Galai, *The Liberation Movement in Russia, 1900–1905* (Cambridge, 1973), p. 26.

Suggestions for Further Reading 

In addition to the general works on the nineteenth century and individual European countries cited in Chapters 21 and 22, two more specialized works on the subject matter of this chapter are available in N. Stone, *Europe Transformed, 1878–1919* (London, 1983), and F. Gilbert, *The End of the European Era, 1890 to the Present*, 4th ed. (New York, 1991).

The Second Industrial Revolution is well covered in D. Landes, *The Unbound Prometheus*, cited in Chapter 20. For a fundamental survey of European industrialization, see A. S. Milward and S. B. Saul, *The Development of the Economies of Continental Europe, 1850–1914* (Cambridge, Mass., 1977). For an introduction to the development of mass consumerism in Britain, see W. H. Fraser, *The Coming of the Mass Market, 1850–1914* (Hamden, Conn., 1981). The impact of the new technology on European thought is imaginatively discussed in S. Kern, *The Culture of Time and Space, 1880–1918* (Cambridge, Mass., 1983).

For an introduction to international socialism, see A. Lindemann, *A History of European Socialism* (New Haven, Conn., 1983), and L. Derfler, *Socialism Since Marx: A Century of the European Left* (New York, 1973). On the emergence of German social democracy, see W. L. Guttsman, *The German Social Democratic Party, 1875–1933* (London, 1981).

Demographic problems are examined in T. McKeown, *The Modern Rise of Population* (New York, 1976). On European emigration, see L. P. Moch, *Moving Europeans: Migration in Western Europe Since 1650* (Bloomington, Ind., 1993).

An interesting work on aristocratic life is D. Cannadine, *The Decline and Fall of the British Aristocracy* (New Haven, Conn., 1990). On the middle classes, see P. Pilbeam, *The Middle Classes in Europe, 1789–1914* (Basingstoke, England, 1990). On the working classes, see L. Berlanstein, *The Working People of Paris, 1871–1914* (Baltimore, 1984), and R. Magraw, *A History of the French Working Class* (Cambridge, Mass., 1992).

There are good overviews of women's experiences in the nineteenth century in B. Smith, *Changing Lives: Women in European History Since 1700* (Lexington, Mass., 1989), and M. J. Boxer and J. H. Quataert, eds., *Connecting Spheres: Women in the Western World, 1500 to the Present* (New York, 1987). The world of women's work is examined in L. A. Tilly and J. W. Scott, *Women, Work, and Family* (New York, 1978). Important studies of women include M. J. Peterson, *Family, Love, and Work in the Lives of Victorian Gentlewomen* (Bloomington, Ind., 1989); B. G. Smith, *Ladies of the Leisure Class: The Bourgeoises of Northern France in the Nineteenth Century* (Princeton, N.J., 1981); P. Robertson, *An Experience of Women: Pattern and Change in Nineteenth-Century Europe* (Philadelphia, 1982); and B. Franzoi, *At the Very Least She Pays the Rent: Women and German Industrialization, 1871–1914* (Westport, Conn., 1985).

On various aspects of education, see M. J. Maynes, *Schooling in Western Europe: A Social History* (Albany, N.Y., 1985), and J. S. Hurt, *Elementary Schooling and the Working Classes, 1860–1918* (London, 1979). A concise and well-presented survey of leisure patterns is G. Cross, *A Social History of Leisure Since 1600* (State College, Pa., 1990).

The domestic politics of the period can be examined in the general works on individual countries listed in the bibliographies for Chapters 21 and 22. There are also specialized works on aspects of each country's history. On Britain, see D. Read, *The Age of Urban Democracy: England, 1868–1914* (New York, 1994). For a detailed examination of French history from 1871 to 1914, see J. M. Mayeur and M. Reberioux, *The Third Republic from Its Origins to the Great War, 1871–1914* (Cambridge, 1984). On the Paris Commune, see R. Tombs, *The War Against Paris, 1871* (Cambridge, 1981). On Italy, see C. Seton-Watson, *Italy from Liberalism to Fascism* (London, 1967). On Germany, see W. J. Mommsen, *Imperial Germany, 1867–1918* (New York, 1995), and V. R. Berghahn, *Imperial Germany, 1871–1914* (Providence, R.I., 1995). On the nationalities problem in the Austro-Hungarian Empire, see R. Okey, *The Habsburg Monarchy* (New York, 2001). On aspects of Russian history, see H. Rogger, *Russia in the Age of Modernization and Revolution, 1881–1917* (London, 1983).

For additional reading, go to InfoTrac College Edition, your online research library at http://webI.infotrac-college.com

Enter the search term *Marxism* using Key Terms.

Enter the search terms *family nineteenth century* using Key Terms.

Enter the search terms *socialism history* using Key Terms.

thought to be composed of indivisible, solid material bodies called atoms.

These views were first seriously questioned at the end of the nineteenth century. The French scientist Marie Curie (1867–1934) and her husband Pierre (1859–1906) discovered that an element called radium gave off rays of radiation that apparently came from within the atom itself. Atoms were not simply hard, material bodies but small worlds containing such subatomic particles as electrons and protons that behaved in a seemingly random and inexplicable fashion. Inquiry into the disintegrative process within atoms became a central theme of the new physics.

MARIE CURIE. Marie Curie was born in Warsaw, Poland, but studied at the University of Paris, where she received degrees in both physics and mathematics. She was the first woman to win two Nobel Prizes, one in 1903 in physics and another in chemistry in 1911. She is shown here in her Paris laboratory in 1921.

Building on this work, in 1900 a Berlin physicist, Max Planck (1858–1947), rejected the belief that a heated body radiates energy in a steady stream but maintained instead that energy is radiated discontinuously, in irregular packets of energy that he called "quanta." The quantum theory raised fundamental questions about the subatomic realm of the atom. By 1900, the old view of atoms as the basic building blocks of the material world was being seriously questioned, and the world of Newtonian physics was in trouble.

Albert Einstein (1879–1955), a German-born patent officer working in Switzerland, pushed these new theories into new terrain. In 1905, Einstein published a paper titled "The Electro-Dynamics of Moving Bodies" that contained his special theory of relativity. According to relativity theory, space and time are not absolute but relative to the observer, and both are interwoven into what Einstein called a four-dimensional space-time continuum. Neither space nor time had an existence independent of human experience. As Einstein later explained simply to a journalist: "It was formerly believed that if all material things disappeared out of the universe, time and space would be left. According to the relativity theory, however, time and space disappear together with the things."[1] Moreover, matter and energy reflected the relativity of time and space. Einstein concluded that matter was nothing but another form of energy. His epochal formula $E = mc^2$—that each particle of matter is equivalent to its mass times the square of the velocity of light—was the key theory explaining the vast energies contained within the atom. It led to the atomic age.

Toward a New Understanding of the Irrational: Nietzsche

Intellectually, the decades before 1914 witnessed a combination of contradictory developments. Thanks to the influence of science, confidence in human reason and progress still remained a dominant thread. At the same time, however, a small group of intellectuals attacked the idea of optimistic progress, dethroned reason, and glorified the irrational.

Friedrich Nietzsche (1844–1900) was one of the intellectuals who glorified the irrational. According to Nietzsche, Western bourgeois society was decadent and incapable of any real cultural creativity, primarily because of its excessive emphasis on the rational faculty at the expense of emotions, passions, and instincts. Reason, claimed Nietzsche, actually played little role in human life because humans were at the mercy of irrational life forces.

Nietzsche believed that Christianity should shoulder much of the blame for Western civilization's enfeeblement. The "slave morality" of Christianity, he believed, had obliterated the human impulse for life and had crushed the human will:

> I call Christianity the one great curse, the one enormous and innermost perversion. . . . I call it the one immortal blemish of mankind. . . . Christianity has taken the side of everything weak, base, ill-constituted, it has made an ideal out of opposition to the preservative instincts of strong life.[2]

How, then, could Western society be renewed? First, said Nietzsche, one must recognize that "God is dead." Europeans had killed God, he said, and it was no longer possible to believe in some kind of cosmic order. Eliminating God and hence Christian morality had liberated human beings and made it possible to create a higher kind of being Nietzsche called the superman: "I teach you the Superman. Man is something that is to be surpassed."[3] Superior intellectuals must free themselves from the ordinary thinking of the masses, create their own values, and lead the masses. Nietzsche rejected and condemned political democracy, social reform, and universal suffrage.

Sigmund Freud and Psychoanalysis

At the end of the nineteenth and beginning of the twentieth centuries, the Viennese doctor Sigmund Freud (1856–1939) put forth a series of theories that undermined optimism about the rational nature of the human mind. Freud's thought, like the new physics, added to the uncertainties of the age. His major ideas were published in 1900 in *The Interpretation of Dreams*, which contained the basic foundation of what came to be known as psychoanalysis.

According to Freud, human behavior was strongly determined by the unconscious, by earlier experiences and inner forces of which people were largely oblivious. To explore the contents of the unconscious, Freud relied not only on hypnosis but also on dreams, but the latter were dressed in an elaborate code that had to be deciphered if the contents were to be properly understood.

But why did some experiences whose influence persisted in controlling an individual's life remain unconscious? According to Freud, the answer was repression (see the box on p. 490), a process by which unsettling experiences were blotted from conscious awareness but still continued to influence behavior because they had become part of the unconscious. To explain how repression worked, Freud elaborated an intricate theory of the inner life of human beings.

According to Freud, a human being's inner life was a battleground of three contending forces: the id, the ego, and the superego. The id was the center of unconscious drives and was ruled by what Freud termed the pleasure principle. As creatures of desire, human beings directed their energy toward pleasure and away from pain. The id contained all kinds of lustful drives and desires and crude appetites and impulses. The ego was the seat of reason and hence the coordinator of the inner life. It was governed by the reality principle. Although humans were dominated by the pleasure principle, a true pursuit of pleasure was not feasible. The reality principle meant that people rejected pleasure so that they might live together in society. The superego was the locus of conscience and represented the inhibitions and moral values that society in general and parents in particular imposed on people. The superego served to force the ego to curb the unsatisfactory drives of the id.

The human being was thus a battleground among id, ego, and superego. Ego and superego exerted restraining influences on the unconscious id and repressed or kept out of consciousness what they wanted to. Repression began in childhood, and psychoanalysis was accomplished through a dialogue between psychotherapist and patient in which the therapist probed deeply into memory in order to retrace the chain of repression all the way back to its childhood origins. By making the conscious mind aware of the unconscious and its repressed contents, the patient's psychic conflict was resolved.

The Impact of Darwin: Social Darwinism and Racism

In the second half of the nineteenth century, scientific theories were sometimes wrongly applied to achieve other ends. The application of Darwin's principle of organic evolution to the social order came to be known as Social Darwinism. Using Darwin's terminology, Social Darwinists argued that societies were organisms that evolved through time from a struggle with their environment. Progress came from the "struggle for survival," as the "fit"—the strong—advanced while the weak declined.

Freud and the Concept of Repression

Freud's psychoanalytical theories resulted from his attempt to understand the world of the unconscious. This excerpt is taken from a lecture given in 1909 in which Freud describes how he arrived at his theory of the role of repression. Although Freud valued science and reason, his theories of the unconscious produced a new image of the human being as governed less by reason than by irrational forces.

Sigmund Freud, Five Lectures on Psychoanalysis

I did not abandon it [his technique of encouraging patients to reveal forgotten experiences], however, before the observations I made during my use of it afforded me decisive evidence. I found confirmation of the fact that the forgotten memories were not lost. They were in the patient's possession and were ready to emerge in association to what was still known by him; but there was some force that prevented them from becoming conscious and compelled them to remain unconscious. The existence of this force could be assumed with certainty, since one became aware of an effort corresponding to it if, in opposition to it, one tried to introduce the unconscious memories into the patient's consciousness. The force which was maintaining the pathological condition became apparent in the form of resistance on the part of the patient.

It was on this idea of resistance, then, that I based my view of the course of physical events in hysteria. In order to effect a recovery, it had proved necessary to remove these resistances. Starting out from the mechanism of cure, it now became possible to construct quite definite ideas of the origin of the illness. The same forces which, in the form of resistance, were now offering opposition to the forgotten material's being made conscious, must formerly have brought about the forgetting and must have pushed the pathogenic experiences in question out of consciousness. I gave the name of "repression" to this hypothetical process, and I considered that it was proved by the undeniable existence of resistance.

The further question could then be raised as to what these forces were and what the determinants were of the repression in which we now recognized the pathogenic mechanism of hysteria. A comparative study of the pathogenic situations which we had come to know through the cathartic procedure made it possible to answer this question. All these experiences had involved the emergence of a wishful impulse which was in sharp contrast to the subject's other wishes and which proved incompatible with the ethical and aesthetic standards of his personality. There had been a short conflict, and the end of this internal struggle was that the idea which had appeared before consciousness as the vehicle of this irreconcilable wish fell a victim to repression, was pushed out of consciousness with all its attached memories, and was forgotten. Thus the incompatibility of the wish in question with the patient's ego was the motive for the repression; the subject's ethical and other standards were the repressing forces. An acceptance of the incompatible wishful impulse or a prolongation of the conflict would have produced a high degree of unpleasure; this unpleasure was avoided by means of repression, which was thus revealed as one of the devices serving to protect the mental personality.

Darwin's ideas were also applied to human society in an even more radical way by rabid nationalists and racists. In their pursuit of national greatness, extreme nationalists argued that nations, too, were engaged in a "struggle for existence" in which only the fittest survived. The German general Friedrich von Bernhardi argued in 1907 that

> war is a biological necessity of the first importance, a regulative element in the life of mankind which cannot be dispensed with, since without it an unhealthy development will follow, which excludes every advancement of the race, and therefore all real civilization. "War is the father of all things." The sages of antiquity long before Darwin recognized this.[4]

Numerous nationalist organizations preached the same doctrine as Bernhardi.

Racism, too, was dramatically revived and strengthened by new biological arguments. Perhaps nowhere was the combination of extreme nationalism and racism more evident and more dangerous than in Germany. The concept of the *Volk* (nation, people, or race) had been an underlying idea in German history since the beginning of the nineteenth century. One of the chief propagandists for German volkish ideology at the turn of the twentieth century was Houston Stewart Chamberlain (1855–1927), an Englishman who became a German citizen. His book, *The Foundations of the Nineteenth Century*, published in 1899, made a special impact on Germany. Modern-day Germans, according to Chamberlain, were the only pure successors of the Aryans, who were portrayed as the true and original creators of Western culture. The Aryan race, under German leadership, must be prepared to fight for Western civilization and save it from the destructive assaults of such "lower" races as Jews, Negroes, and Orientals. Increasingly, Jews were singled out by German volkish nationalists as the racial enemy in biological terms and as parasites who wanted to destroy the Aryan race (see "Jews in the European Nation-State" later in this chapter).

The Attack on Christianity and the Response of the Churches

Science became one of the chief threats to all the Christian churches and even to religion itself in the nineteenth century. Darwin's theory of evolution, accepted by ever-larger numbers of educated Europeans, seemed to contradict the doctrine of divine creation. By suppressing Darwin's books and forbidding the teaching of evolution, the churches often caused even more educated people to reject established religions.

Other churches sought compromise, an approach especially evident in the Catholic church during the pontificate of Leo XIII (1878–1903). Pope Leo permitted the teaching of evolution as a hypothesis in Catholic schools and also responded to the challenges of modernization in the economic and social spheres. In his encyclical *De Rerum Novarum*, issued in 1891, he upheld the individual's right to private property but at the same time criticized "naked" capitalism for the poverty and degradation in which it had left the working classes. Much in socialism, he declared, was Christian in principle, but he condemned Marxist socialism for its materialistic and antireligious foundations. The pope recommended that Catholics form socialist parties and labor unions of their own to help the workers.

The Culture of Modernity

The revolution in physics and psychology was paralleled by a revolution in literature and the arts. Before 1914, writers and artists were rebelling against the traditional literary and artistic styles that had dominated European cultural life since the Renaissance. The changes that they produced have since been called Modernism.

NATURALISM AND SYMBOLISM IN LITERATURE

Throughout much of the late nineteenth century, literature was dominated by Naturalism. Naturalists accepted the material world as real and felt that literature should be realistic. By addressing social problems, writers could contribute to an objective understanding of the world. Although Naturalism was a continuation of Realism, it lacked the underlying note of liberal optimism about people and society that had been prevalent in the 1850s. The Naturalists often portrayed characters caught in the grip of forces beyond their control.

The novels of the French writer Émile Zola (1840–1902) provide a good example of Naturalism. Against a backdrop of the urban slums and coalfields of northern France, Zola showed how alcoholism and different environments affected people's lives. He had read Darwin's *Origin of Species* and had been impressed by its emphasis on the struggle for survival and the importance of environment and heredity. These themes were central to his *Rougon-Macquart*, a twenty-volume series of novels on the "natural and social history of a family." Zola maintained that the artist must analyze and dissect life as a biologist would a living organism. He said, "I have simply done on living bodies the work of analysis which surgeons perform on corpses."

At the turn of the century, a new group of writers, known as the Symbolists, reacted against Realism. Primarily interested in writing poetry, the Symbolists believed that objective knowledge of the world was impossible. The external world was not real but only a collection of symbols that reflected the true reality of the individual human mind. Art, they believed, should function for its own sake instead of serving, criticizing, or seeking to understand society. In the works of two of the symbolist poets, William Butler Yeats and Rainer Maria Rilke, poetry ceased to be part of popular culture because only through a knowledge of the poet's personal language could one hope to understand what the poet was saying.

MODERNISM IN THE ARTS

Since the Renaissance, artists had tried to represent reality as accurately as possible. By the late nineteenth century, however, artists were seeking new forms of expression. The preamble to modern painting can be found in Impressionism, a movement that originated in France in the 1870s when a group of artists rejected the studios and museums and went out into the countryside to paint nature directly. Camille Pissarro (1830–1903), one of Impressionism's founders, expressed what they sought:

> Precise drawing is dry and hampers the impression of the whole, it destroys all sensations. Do not define too closely the outlines of things; it is the brush stroke of the right value and color which should produce the drawing. . . . Work at the same time upon sky, water, branches, ground, keeping everything going on an equal basis and unceasingly rework until you have got it. . . . Don't proceed according to rules and principles, but paint what you observe and feel. Paint generously and unhesitatingly, for it is best not to lose the first impression.[5]

Impressionists like Pissarro sought to put into painting their impressions of the changing effects of light on objects in nature.

An important Impressionist painter was Berthe Morisot (1841–1895), whose dedication to the new style of painting won her the disfavor of the traditional French academic artists. Morisot believed that women had a special vision, which was, as she said, "more delicate than that of men." Her special touch is evident in *Young Girl by the Window,* in which she makes use of lighter colors and flowing brushstrokes. Near the end of her life, she lamented the refusal of men to take her work seriously: "I don't think there has ever been a man who treated a woman as an equal, and that's all I would have asked, for I know I'm worth as much as they."[6]

BERTHE MORISOT, *YOUNG GIRL BY THE WINDOW.* Berthe Morisot came from a wealthy French family that settled in Paris when she was seven. The first female Impressionist painter, she developed her own unique style. Her gentle colors and strong use of pastels are especially evident in *Young Girl by the Window,* painted in 1878. Many of her paintings focus on women and domestic scenes.

By the 1880s, a new movement known as Post-Impressionism arose in France but soon spread to other European countries. Post-Impressionism retained the Impressionist emphasis on light and color but revolutionized it even further by paying more attention to structure and form. Post-Impressionists sought to use both color and line to express inner feelings and produce a personal statement of reality rather than an imitation of objects. Impressionist paintings had retained a sense of realism, but the Post-Impressionists shifted from objective reality to subjective reality and in so doing began to withdraw from the artist's traditional task of depicting the external world. The works of the Post-Impressionists were the real forerunners of modern art.

A famous Post-Impressionist was the tortured and tragic figure Vincent van Gogh (1853–1890). For van Gogh, art was a spiritual experience. He was especially interested in color and believed that it could act

VINCENT VAN GOGH, *THE STARRY NIGHT,* 1889. The Dutch painter Vincent van Gogh was a major figure among the Post-Impressionists. His originality and power of expression made a strong impact on his artistic successors. In *The Starry Night,* van Gogh's subjective vision was given full play as the dynamic swirling forms of the heavens above overwhelmed the village below. The heavens seem alive with a mysterious spiritual force.

as its own form of language. Van Gogh maintained that artists should paint what they feel. In *The Starry Night*, he painted a sky alive with whirling stars that overwhelmed the huddled buildings in the village below.

By the beginning of the twentieth century, the belief that the task of art was to represent "reality" had lost much of its meaning. By that time, the new psychology and the new physics had made it evident that many people were not sure what constituted reality anyway. Then, too, the development of photography gave artists another reason to reject visual realism. First invented in the 1830s, photography became popular and widespread after George Eastman created the first Kodak camera for the mass market in 1888. What was the point of an artist doing what the camera did better? Unlike the camera, which could only mirror reality, artists could *create* reality. As in literature, so also in modern art, individual consciousness became the source of meaning. Between 1905 and 1914, this search for individual expression produced a great variety of painting schools, all of which had their greatest impact after World War I.

By 1905, one of the most important figures in modern art was just beginning his career. Pablo Picasso (1881–1973) was from Spain but settled in Paris in 1904. Picasso was extremely flexible and painted in a remarkable variety of styles. He was instrumental in the development of a new style called Cubism that used geometric designs as visual stimuli to re-create reality in the viewer's mind. Picasso's 1907 work *Les Demoiselles d'Avignon* has been acknowledged as the first Cubist painting.

The modern artist's flight from "visual reality" reached a high point in 1910 with the beginning of abstract painting. Vasily Kandinsky (1866–1944), a Russian who worked in Germany, was one of the founders of Abstract Expressionism. As is evident in his *Painting with White Border,* Kandinsky sought to avoid representation altogether. He believed that art should speak directly to the soul. To do so, it must avoid any reference to visual reality and concentrate on color.

At the beginning of the twentieth century, developments in music paralleled those in painting. Expressionism in music was a Russian creation, the product of the composer Igor Stravinsky (1882–1971) and the Ballet Russe, the dancing company of Sergei Diaghilev (1872–1929). Together they revolutionized the world of music with Stravinsky's ballet *The Rite of Spring.* At the premiere on May 29, 1913, the pulsating rhythms, sharp dissonances, and unusual dancing overwhelmed the Paris audience and caused a riot at the theater.

PABLO PICASSO, *LES DEMOISELLES D'AVIGNON,* 1907. Pablo Picasso, a major pioneer and activist of modern art, experimented with a remarkable variety of modern styles. *Les Demoiselles d'Avignon* was the first great example of Cubism, which one art historian called the first style of the twentieth century to break radically with the past. Geometric shapes replace traditional forms, forcing the viewer to re-create reality in his or her own mind.

VASILY KANDINSKY, *COMPOSITION VIII, NO. 2 (PAINTING WITH WHITE BORDER).* One of the founders of Abstract Expressionism was the Russian Vasily Kandinsky, who sought to eliminate representation altogether by focusing on color and avoiding any resemblance to visual reality. In *Painting with White Border,* Kandinsky used color "to send light into the darkness of men's hearts." He believed that color, like music, could fulfill a spiritual goal of appealing directly to the human being.

◆ Politics: New Directions and New Uncertainties

The uncertainties in European intellectual and cultural life were paralleled by growing anxieties in European political life. The seemingly steady progress in the growth of liberal principles and political democracy after 1871 soon slowed or possibly even halted altogether after 1894. The new mass politics had opened the door to changes that many nineteenth-century liberals found unacceptable, and liberals themselves were forced to move in new directions. The appearance of a new right-wing politics based on racism added an ugly note to the already existing anxieties. With their newfound voting rights, workers elected socialists who demanded new reforms when they took their places in legislative bodies. Women, too, made new demands, insisting on the right to vote and using new tactics to gain it. In central and eastern Europe, tensions grew as authoritarian governments refused to meet the demands of reformers. And outside Europe, a new giant appeared in the Western world as the United States emerged as a great industrial power with immense potential.

The Movement for Women's Rights

In the 1830s, a number of women in the United States and Europe, who worked together in several reform movements, became frustrated by what they perceived as widespread prejudice against females. They sought improvements for women by focusing on specific goals. Family and marriage laws were especially singled out because it was difficult for women to secure divorces and because laws gave husbands almost complete control over the property of their wives. These early efforts, however, were not particularly successful. For example, women did not gain the right to their own property until 1870 in Britain, 1900 in Germany, and 1907 in France.

Custody and property rights were only a beginning for the women's movement, however. Some middle- and upper-middle-class women gained access to higher education while others sought entry into occupations dominated by men. The first to fall was teaching. Because medical training was largely closed to women, they sought alternatives in the development of nursing. One nursing pioneer was Amalie Sieveking (1794–1859), who founded the Female Association for the Care of the Poor and Sick in Hamburg, Germany. As she explained, "To me, at least as important were the benefits which [work with the poor] seemed to promise for those of my sisters who would join me in such a work of charity. The higher interests of my sex were close to my heart."[7] Sieveking's work was followed by the more famous British nurse Florence Nightingale (1820–1910), whose efforts during the Crimean War, combined with those of Clara Barton (1821–1912) in the American Civil War, transformed nursing into a profession of trained, middle-class "women in white."

By the 1840s and 1850s, the movement for women's rights had entered the political arena with the call for equal political rights. Many feminists believed that the right to vote was the key to all other reforms to improve the position of women. The British women's movement was the most vocal and active in Europe, but it divided over tactics. Moderates believed that women must demonstrate that they would use political power responsibly if they wanted Parliament to grant them the right to vote. Another group favored a more radical approach. Emmeline Pankhurst (1858–1928) and her daughters, Christabel and Sylvia, founded the Women's Social and Political Union, which enrolled mostly middle- and upper-class women, in 1903. Pankhurst's organization realized the value of the media and used unusual publicity stunts to call attention to its demands. Derisively labeled "suffragettes" by male politicians, they pelted government officials with eggs, chained themselves to lampposts, smashed the windows of department stores on fashionable shopping streets, burned railroad cars, and went on hunger strikes in jail.

Although demands for women's rights were heard throughout Europe and the United States before World War I, only in Finland, Norway, and a few American states did women actually receive the right to vote. It would take the dramatic upheaval of World War I before male-dominated governments capitulated on this basic issue.

Women reformers also took on issues besides suffrage. In many countries, women supported peace movements. Bertha von Suttner (1843–1914) became head of the Austrian Peace Society and protested against the growing arms race of the 1890s. Her novel, *Lay Down Your Arms*, became a best-seller and brought her the Nobel Peace Prize in 1905. Lower-class women also took up the cause of peace. A group of women workers marched in Vienna in 1911 and demanded, "We want an end to armaments, to the means of murder, and we want these millions to be spent on the needs of the people."[8]

THE NEW WOMAN

Bertha von Suttner was but one example of the "new women" who were becoming more prominent at the turn of the twentieth century. These women defied tradition in regard to traditional feminine roles (see the box on p. 497). Although some of them supported political ideologies, such as socialism, that flew in the face of the ruling classes, others simply sought new freedom outside the household and new roles other than those of wives and mothers.

Maria Montessori (1870–1952) was a good example of the "new woman." Breaking with tradition, she attended medical school at the University of Rome. Although often isolated by her fellow male students, she persisted and in 1896 became the first Italian woman to receive a medical degree. Three years later, she began a lecture tour in Italy on the subject of "The New Woman," whom she characterized as a woman who followed a rational, scientific perspective. In keeping with this ideal, Montessori put her medical background to work in a school for mentally retarded children. She devised new teaching materials that enabled these children to read and write and became convinced, as she later wrote, "that similar methods applied to normal students would develop or set free their personality in a marvelous and surprising way." Subsequently, she established a system of childhood education based on natural and spontaneous activities in which students learned at their own pace. By the 1930s, hundreds of Montessori schools had been established in Europe and the United States. As a professional woman and a woman who chose to have a child without being married, Montessori also embodied some of the freeedoms of the "new woman."

Jews in the European Nation-State

Near the end of the nineteenth century, a revival of racism combined with extreme nationalism to produce a new right-wing politics directed against the Jews. Anti-Semitism was not new to European civilization. Since the Middle Ages, Jews had been portrayed as the murderers of Jesus and subjected to mob violence; their rights had been restricted, and they had been physically separated from Christians in quarters known as ghettos.

In the nineteenth century, as a result of the ideals of the Enlightenment and the French Revolution, Jews were increasingly granted legal equality in many European countries. After the revolutions of 1848, emancipation became a fact of life for Jews throughout western and central Europe. Emancipation enabled many Jews to leave the ghetto and become assimilated, and hundreds of thousands of Jews entered the formerly closed worlds of parliaments and universities. Many Jews became successful as bankers, lawyers, scientists, scholars, journalists, and stage performers. In 1880, for example, Jews made up 10 percent of the population of the city of Vienna but 39 percent of its medical students and 23 percent of its law students.

These achievements represent only one side of the picture, however. In Germany and Austria during the 1880s and 1890s, conservatives founded right-wing anti-Semitic parties that used anti-Semitism to win the votes of traditional lower-middle-class groups who felt threatened by the new economic forces of the times. These German and Austrian anti-Semitic parties were based on race. To these anti-Semites, Jews were racially stained, a fact that could not be altered by conversion. One could not be both German and Jew.

The worst treatment of Jews in the last two decades of the nineteenth century and the first decade of the twentieth occurred in eastern Europe, where 72 percent of the entire world Jewish population lived. Russian Jews were admitted to secondary schools and universities only under a quota system and were forced to live in certain regions of the country. Persecutions and pogroms were widespread. Hundreds of thousands of Jews decided to emigrate to escape the persecution. Between 1881 and 1899, an average of 23,000 Jews left Russia each year. Many of them went to the United States, although some (probably about 25,000 in all) moved to Palestine, which soon became the focus for a Jewish nationalist movement called Zionism.

The emancipation of the nineteenth century had presented vast opportunities for some Jews but dilemmas for others. Did emancipation mean full assimilation, and did assimilation mean the disruption of traditional Jewish life? Many paid the price willingly, but others questioned its value and advocated a different answer, a return to Palestine. For many Jews, Palestine, the land of ancient Israel, had long been the land of their dreams. During the nineteenth century, as nationalist ideas spread and Italians, Poles, Irish, Greeks, and others sought national emancipation, so too did the idea of national independence capture the imagination of some Jews. A key figure in the growth of political Zionism was Theodor Herzl (1860–1904). In 1896, he published a book called *The Jewish State* in which he advocated that "the Jews who wish it will have their state." Financial support for the

Advice to Women: Be Independent

Although a majority of women probably followed the nineteenth-century middle-class ideal of women as keepers of the household and nurturers of husband and children, an increasing number of women fought for women's rights. This selection is taken from Act III of Henrik Ibsen's play A Doll's House *(1879), in which the character Nora Helmer declares her independence from her husband's control.*

❊ *Henrik Ibsen,* A Doll's House

NORA: *(Pause)* Does anything strike you as we sit here?

HELMER: What should strike me?

NORA: We've been married eight years; does it not strike you that this is the first time we two, you and I, man and wife, have talked together seriously?

HELMER: Seriously? What do you mean, *seriously?*

NORA: For eight whole years, and more—ever since the day we first met—we have never exchanged one serious word about serious things. . . .

HELMER: Why, my dearest Nora, what have you to do with serious things?

NORA: There we have it! You have never understood me. I've had great injustice done to me, Torvald; first by father, then by you.

HELMER: What! Your father *and* me? We, who have loved you more than all the world!

NORA: *(Shaking her head)* You have never loved me. You just found it amusing to think you were in love with me.

HELMER: Nora! What a thing to say!

NORA: Yes, it's true, Torvald. When I was living at home with father, he told me his opinions and mine were the same. If I had different opinions, I said nothing about them, because he would not have liked it. He used to call me his doll-child and played with me as I played with my dolls. Then I came to live in your house.

HELMER: What a way to speak of our marriage!

NORA: *(Undisturbed)* I mean that I passed from father's hands into yours. You arranged everything to your taste and I got the same tastes as you; or pretended to—I don't know which—both, perhaps; sometimes one, sometimes the other. . . . You and father have done me a great wrong. It is your fault that my life has come to naught.

HELMER: Why, Nora, how unreasonable and ungrateful! Haven't you been happy here?

NORA: No, never. I thought I was, but I never was.

HELMER: Not—not happy! . . .

NORA: I must stand quite alone if I am ever to know myself and my surroundings; so I cannot stay with you.

HELMER: Nora! Nora!

NORA: I am going at once. I daresay [my friend] Christina will take me in for tonight. . . .

HELMER: This is madness!

NORA: Tomorrow I shall go home—I mean to what was my home. It will be easier for me to find a job there.

HELMER: On, in your blind inexperience—

NORA: I must try to gain experience, Torvald.

HELMER: Forsake your home, your husband, your children! And you don't consider what the world will say.

NORA: I can't pay attention to that. I only know that I must do it.

HELMER: This is monstrous! Can you forsake your holiest duties?

NORA: What do you consider my holiest duties?

HELMER: Need I tell you that? Your duties to your husband and children.

NORA: I have other duties equally sacred.

HELMER: Impossible! What do you mean?

NORA: My duties toward myself.

HELMER: Before all else you are a wife and a mother.

NORA: That I no longer believe. Before all else I believe I am a human being just as much as you are—or at least that I should try to become one. I know that most people agree with you, Torvald, and that they say so in books. But I can no longer be satisfied with what most people say and what is in books. I must think things out for myself and try to get clear about them.

development of *yishuvs*, or settlements in Palestine, came from wealthy Jewish banking families who wanted a refuge in Palestine for persecuted Jews. Even settlements were difficult because Palestine was then part of the Ottoman Empire and Turkish authorities were opposed to Jewish immigration. Despite the problems, however, the First Zionist Congress, which met in Switzerland in 1897, proclaimed as its aim the creation of a "home in Palestine secured by public law" for the Jewish people. Although about a thousand Jews migrated to Palestine in 1900 and three thousand more each year after that, the Zionist dream remained a dream on the eve of World War I.

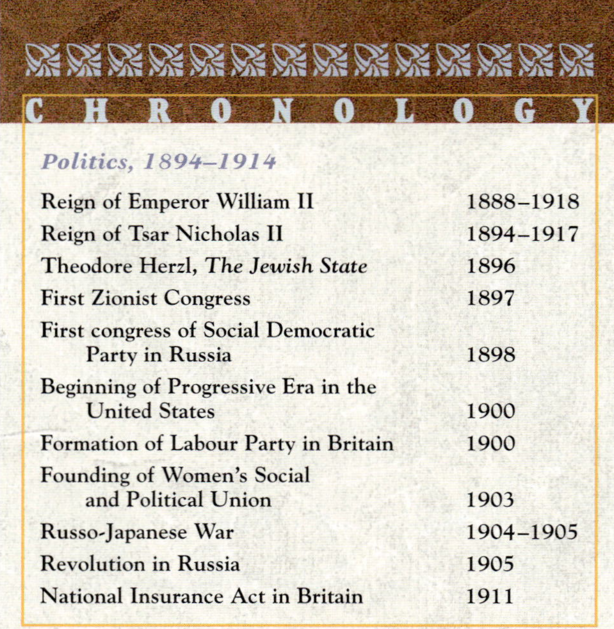

CHRONOLOGY

Politics, 1894–1914

Reign of Emperor William II	1888–1918
Reign of Tsar Nicholas II	1894–1917
Theodore Herzl, *The Jewish State*	1896
First Zionist Congress	1897
First congress of Social Democratic Party in Russia	1898
Beginning of Progressive Era in the United States	1900
Formation of Labour Party in Britain	1900
Founding of Women's Social and Political Union	1903
Russo-Japanese War	1904–1905
Revolution in Russia	1905
National Insurance Act in Britain	1911

The Transformation of Liberalism: Great Britain

In dealing with the problems created by the new mass politics, liberal governments often followed policies that undermined the basic tenets of liberalism. This was certainly true in Great Britain, where the demands of the working-class movement caused Liberals to move away from their ideals. Liberals were forced to adopt significant social reforms due to the pressure of two new working-class organizations: trade unions and the Labour Party.

Trade unions began to advocate more radical change of the economic system, calling for "collective ownership and control over production, distribution and exchange." At the same time, a movement for laborers emerged among a group of intellectuals known as the Fabian Socialists. Neither the Fabian Socialists nor the British trade unions were Marxist. They did not advocate class struggle and revolution but rather evolution toward a socialist state by democratic means. In 1900, representatives of the trade unions and Fabian Socialists coalesced to form the Labour Party. By 1906, they had managed to elect twenty-nine members to the House of Commons.

The Liberals, who held the government from 1906 to 1914, perceived that they would have to enact a program of social welfare or lose the support of the workers. Under the leadership of David Lloyd George (1863–1945), the Liberals abandoned the classical principles of laissez-faire and voted for a series of social reforms. The National Insurance Act of 1911 provided benefits for workers in case of sickness and unemployment, to be paid for by compulsory contributions from workers, employers, and the state. Additional legislation provided a small pension for retirees over seventy and compensation for workers injured in accidents on the job. Though the benefits of the program and tax increases were both modest, they were the first hesitant steps toward the future British welfare state.

Growing Tensions in Germany

The new imperial Germany begun by Bismarck continued as an "authoritarian, conservative, military-bureaucratic power state" during the reign of Emperor William II (1888–1918). By 1914, Germany had become the strongest military and industrial power on the Continent. More than 50 percent of German workers had jobs in industry, while only 30 percent of the workforce was still in agriculture. Urban centers had mushroomed in number and size. These rapid changes in William's Germany helped produce a society torn between modernization and traditionalism.

With the expansion of industry and cities came demands for more political participation and growing sentiment for reforms that would produce greater democratization. Conservative forces, especially the landowning nobility and representatives of heavy industry, two of the powerful ruling groups in Germany, tried to block it by supporting William II's activist foreign policy of finding Germany's "place in the sun." Expansionism, they believed, would divert people from further democratization.

The tensions in German society created by the conflict between modernization and traditionalism were also manifested in a new, radicalized, right-wing politics. A number of pressure groups arose to support nationalistic goals. Such groups as the Pan-German League stressed strong German nationalism and advocated imperialism as a tool to overcome social divisions and unite all classes. They were also anti-Semitic and denounced Jews as the destroyers of national community.

Industrialization and Revolution in Imperial Russia

Although industrialization came late to Russia, it progressed rapidly after 1890, especially with the assistance of foreign investment capital. By 1900, Russia had become the fourth-largest producer of steel, behind the United States, Germany, and Great Britain. With industrialization came factories, an industrial working class, and the development of socialist parties, although repression in Russia soon forced these parties to go underground and become revolutionary. The Marxist Social Democratic Party, for example, held its first congress in Minsk in 1898, but the arrest of its leaders caused the next one to be held in Brussels in 1903, attended by Russian émigrés. The Social Revolutionaries worked to overthrow the tsarist autocracy and establish peasant socialism. Having no other outlet for opposition to the regime, they advocated political terrorism, attempting to assassinate government officials and members of the ruling dynasty. The growing opposition to the tsarist regime finally exploded into revolution in 1905.

The defeat of the Russians by the Japanese in 1904–1905 encouraged antigovernment groups to rebel against the tsarist regime. After a general strike in October 1905, the government capitulated. Nicholas II granted civil liberties and agreed to create a legislative assembly, the Duma, elected directly by a broad franchise. But real constitutional monarchy proved short-lived. Already by 1907, the tsar had curtailed the power of the Duma, and he fell back on the army and bureaucracy to rule Russia.

The Rise of the United States

Between 1860 and World War I, the United States made the shift from an agrarian to a mighty industrial nation. American heavy industry stood unchallenged in 1900. In that year, the Carnegie Steel Company alone produced more steel than Great Britain's entire steel industry. Industrialization also led to urbanization. While established cities, such as New York, Philadelphia, and Boston, grew even larger, other moderate-size cities, such as Pittsburgh, grew by leaps and bounds because of industrialization. Whereas 20 percent of Americans lived in cities in 1860, more than 40 percent did in 1900.

NICHOLAS II. The last tsar of Russia hoped to preserve the traditional autocratic ways of his predecessors. In this photograph, Nicholas II and his wife, Alexandra, are shown returning from a church at Tsarskoe-Selo.

By 1900, the United States had become the world's richest nation and greatest industrial power. Yet serious questions remained about the quality of American life. In 1890, the richest 9 percent of Americans owned an incredible 71 percent of all the wealth. Labor unrest over unsafe working conditions, strict work discipline, and periodical cycles of devastating unemployment led workers to organize. By the turn of the century, one national organization, the American Federation of Labor, emerged as labor's dominant voice. Its lack of real power, however, is reflected in its membership figures. In 1900, it included only 8.4 percent of the American industrial labor force.

During the so-called Progressive Era after 1900, a wave of reform swept across the United States. State governments enacted economic and social legislation, such as laws that governed hours, wages, and working conditions, especially for women and children. But the realization that state laws were ineffective in dealing with nationwide problems led to a Progressive movement at the national level. The Meat Inspection Act and the Pure Food and Drug Act provided for a limited degree of federal regulation of corrupt industrial practices. The presidency of Woodrow Wilson (1913–1921) witnessed the imposition of a graduated federal income tax and the establishment of the Federal Reserve System, which permitted the federal government to play a role in important economic decisions formerly made by bankers. Like European states, the United States was moving slowly into policies that extended the functions of the state.

The Growth of Canada

Canada faced problems of national unity at the end of the nineteenth century. At the beginning of 1870, the Dominion of Canada had four provinces: Quebec, Ontario, Nova Scotia, and New Brunswick. With the addition of two more provinces in 1871—Manitoba and British Columbia—the Dominion of Canada extended from the Atlantic to the Pacific.

Real unity was difficult to achieve, however, because of the distrust between the English-speaking and French-speaking populations. Wilfred Laurier, who became the first French-Canadian prime minister in 1896, was able to reconcile Canada's two major groups. During his administration, industrialization boomed and immigrants from Europe helped populate Canada's vast territories.

The New Imperialism

Beginning in the 1880s, European states engaged in an intense scramble for overseas territory. This revival of imperialism, or the "new imperialism" as some have called it, led Europeans to carve up Asia and Africa. But why did Europeans begin their mad scramble for colonies after 1880?

The existence of competitive nation-states after 1870 was undoubtedly a major determinant in the growth of this new imperialism. As European affairs grew tense, heightened competition led European states to acquire colonies abroad that provided ports and coaling stations for their navies. Colonies were also a source of international prestige. Once the scramble for colonies began, failure to enter the race was perceived as a sign of weakness, totally unacceptable to an aspiring great power.

Then, too, imperialism was tied to Social Darwinism and racism. Social Darwinists believed that in the struggle between nations, the fit are victorious and survive. Superior races must dominate inferior races by military force to show how strong and virile they are. As one Englishman wrote: "To the development of the White Man, the Black Man and the Yellow must ever remain inferior, and as the former raised itself higher and yet higher, so did these latter seem to shrink out of humanity and appear nearer and nearer to the brutes."[9]

Some Europeans took a more religious-humanitarian approach to imperialism when they argued that Europeans had a moral responsibility to civilize "ignorant" peoples. This notion of the "white man's burden" (see the box on p. 501) helped at least the more idealistic individuals rationalize imperialism in their own minds. Nevertheless, the belief that the superiority of their civilization obligated them to impose modern industry, cities, and new medicines on supposedly primitive nonwhites, even if the primitives died in the process, was yet another manifestation of racism.

Some historians have emphasized an economic motivation for imperialism. There was a great demand for natural resources and products not found in Western countries, such as rubber, oil, and tin. Instead of just trading for these products, European investors advocated direct control of the raw material–producing areas.

SOAP AND THE WHITE MAN'S BURDEN. The concept of the "white man's burden" included the belief that the superiority of their civilization obligated Europeans to impose their practices on supposedly primitive nonwhites. This advertisement for Pears' Soap clearly communicates the Europeans' view of their responsibility toward other peoples.

The White Man's Burden

One of the justifications for European imperialism was the notion that superior white peoples had the moral responsibility to raise ignorant native peoples to a higher level of civilization. The British poet Rudyard Kipling (1865–1936) captured this notion in his poem, The White Man's Burden.

Rudyard Kipling, The White Man's Burden

Take up the White Man's burden—
Send forth the best ye breed—
Go bind your sons to exile
To serve your captives' needs;
To wait in heavy harness,
On fluttered folk and wild—
Your new-caught sullen peoples,
Half-devil and half-child.

Take up the White Man's burden—
In patience to abide,
To veil the threat of terror
And check the show of pride;
By open speech and simple,
An hundred times made plain
To seek another's profit,
And work another's gain.

Take up the White Man's burden—
The savage wars of peace—
Fill full the mouth of Famine
And bid the sickness cease;
And when your goal is nearest
The end for others sought,
Watch sloth and heathen Folly
Bring all your hopes to nought.

Take up the White Man's burden—
No tawdry rule of kings,
But toil of serf and sweeper—
The tale of common things.
The ports ye shall not enter,
The roads ye shall not tread,
Go mark them with your living,
And mark them with your dead.

Take up the White Man's burden—
And reap his old reward:
The blame of those ye better,
The hate of those ye guard—
The cry of hosts ye humour
(Ah, slowly) toward the light:—
"Why brought he us from bondage,
Our loved Egyptian night?"

Take up the White Man's burden—
Ye dare not stoop to less—
Nor call too loud on Freedom
To cloke your weariness;
By all ye cry or whisper,
By all you leave or do,
The silent, sullen peoples
Shall weigh your gods and you.

Take up the White Man's burden—
Have done with childish days—
The lightly proferred laurel,
The easy, ungrudged praise.
Comes now, to search your manhood
Through all the thankless years,
Cold, edged with dear-bought wisdom,
The judgment of your peers!

The large surpluses of capital that were being accumulated by bankers and industrialists often encouraged them to seek higher rates of profit in underdeveloped areas. All of these factors combined to form an economic imperialism whereby European finance dominated the economic activity of a large part of the world.

The Creation of Empires

Whatever the reasons for the new imperialism, it had a dramatic effect on Africa and Asia as European powers competed for control of the two continents.

THE SCRAMBLE FOR AFRICA

Europeans controlled relatively little of the African continent before 1880. During the Napoleonic wars, the British had established themselves in southern Africa by taking control of Cape Town, originally founded by the Dutch. After the wars, the British encouraged settlers to come to what they called the Cape Colony. British policies disgusted the Boers or Afrikaners, as the descendants of the Dutch colonists were called, and led them in 1835 to migrate north on the Great Trek to the region between the Orange and

CHRONOLOGY

The New Imperialism: Africa

Opening of the Suez Canal	1869
Leopold II of Belgium's settlements in the Congo	1876
French conquest of Algeria	1879
British expeditionary force in Egypt	1882
Defeat of Italians by Ethiopians	1896
Boer War	1899–1902
Union of South Africa	1910
Italian seizure of Tripoli	1911
French protectorate over Morocco	1912

Vaal Rivers (later known as the Orange Free State) and north of the Vaal River (the Transvaal). Hostilities between the British and the Boers continued.

In the 1880s, British policy in southern Africa was largely determined by Cecil Rhodes (1853–1902). Rhodes founded both diamond and gold companies that monopolized production of these precious commodities and enabled him to gain control of a territory north of Transvaal that he named Rhodesia after himself. His imperialist ambitions led to his downfall in 1896, however, when the British government forced him to resign as prime minister of Rhodesia after he conspired to overthrow the neighboring Boer government without British approval. Although the British government had hoped to avoid war with the Boers, it could not stop extremists on both sides from precipitating such action. The Boer War dragged on from 1899 to 1902, when the Boers were overwhelmed by the larger British army. British policy toward the defeated Boers was remarkably conciliatory. Transvaal and the Orange Free State had representative governments by 1907, and in 1910, the Union of South Africa was created. Like Canada, Australia, and New Zealand, it became a fully self-governing dominion within the British Empire.

Before 1880, the only other European settlements in Africa had been made by the French and Portuguese. The Portuguese had held on to their settlements in Angola on the west coast and Mozambique on the east coast. The French had started the conquest of Algeria in Muslim North Africa in 1830, although it was not until 1879 that French civilian rule was established there. The next year, 1880, the European scramble for possession of Africa began in earnest. By 1900, the French had added the huge area of French West Africa and Tunis to their African empire. In 1912, they created a protectorate over much of Morocco; the rest was left to Spain.

The British took an active interest in Egypt after the Suez Canal was opened by the French in 1869. Believing the canal their lifeline to India, the British sought to control the canal area. The British landed an expeditionary force in 1882 and soon established a protectorate over Egypt. From Egypt, the British moved south into the Sudan and seized it after narrowly averting a war with France. Not to be outdone, Italy joined in the imperialist scramble. Their humiliating defeat by the Ethiopians in 1896 only led the Italians to try again in 1911 by invading and seizing Ottoman Tripoli, which they renamed Libya.

Central Africa was also added to the list of European colonies. Popular interest in the forbiddingly dense tropical jungles of central Africa was first aroused in the 1860s and 1870s by explorers such as the Scottish missionary David Livingstone and the British-American journalist Henry M. Stanley. But the real driving force for the colonization of central Africa was King Leopold II (1865–1909) of Belgium, who had rushed enthusiastically into pursuit of empire in Africa: "To open to civilization," he said, "the only part of our globe where it has not yet penetrated, to pierce the darkness which envelops whole populations, is a crusade, if I may say so, a crusade worthy of this century of progess." Profit, however, was far more important to Leopold than progress. In 1876, Leopold engaged Stanley to establish Belgian settlements in the Congo. Alarmed by Leopold's actions, the French also moved into the territory north of the Congo River.

Between 1884 and 1900, most of the rest of Africa was carved up by the European powers. Germany also entered the ranks of the imperialist powers at this time. Initially, Bismarck had downplayed the significance of colonies, but as domestic political pressures for a German empire increased, Bismarck became a political convert to colonialism. As he expressed it, "All this colonial business is a sham, but we need it for the elections." The Germans established colonies in South West Africa, the Cameroons, Togoland, and East Africa.

By 1914, Britain, France, Germany, Belgium, Spain, and Portugal had divided Africa (see Map 24.1). Only Liberia, founded by emancipated American slaves, and Ethiopia remained free states. Despite the humanitarian rationalizations about the "white man's burden," Africa had been conquered by European states determined to create colonial empires. Any peoples who dared to resist (with the exception of the Ethiopians, who defeated the Italians) were simply devastated by the superior military force of the Europeans.

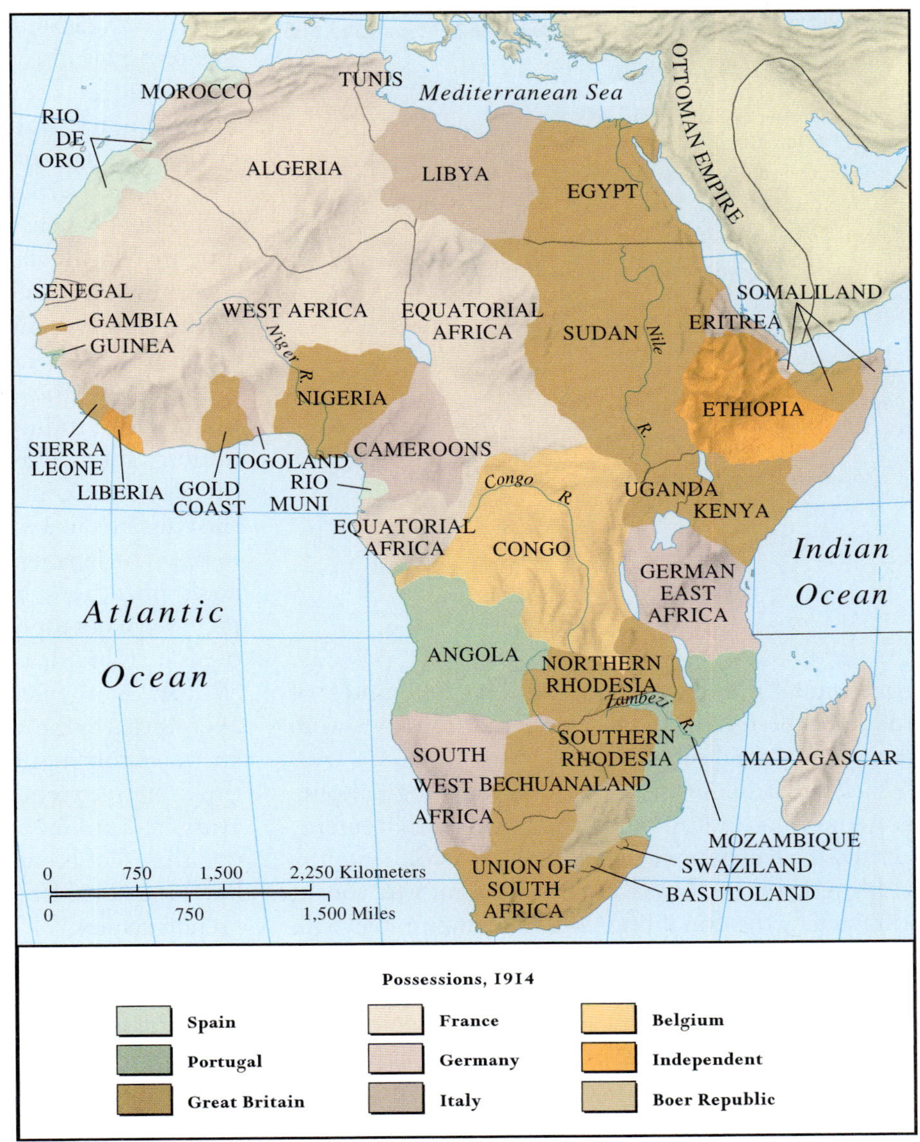

MAP 24.1 Africa in 1914.

IMPERIALISM IN ASIA

Although Asia had been open to Western influence since the sixteenth century, not much of its immense territory had fallen under direct European control. The Dutch were established in the East Indies and the Spanish in the Philippines, while the French and Portuguese had trading posts on the Indian coast. China, Japan, Korea, and Southeast Asia had largely managed to exclude Westerners.

It was not until the explorations of Australia by Captain James Cook between 1768 and 1771 that Britain took an active interest in the East. The availability of land for grazing sheep and the discovery of gold led to an influx of free settlers, who slaughtered many of the indigenous inhabitants. In 1850, the British government granted the various Australian colonies virtually complete self-government, and fifty years later, on January 1, 1901, all the colonies were unified into the Commonwealth of Australia. Nearby New Zealand, which the British had declared a colony in 1840, was also granted dominion status in 1907.

A private trading company known as the British East India Company had been responsible for subjugating much of India. In 1858, however, after a revolt of the sepoys, or Indian troops, of the East India Company's army had been crushed, the British Parliament transferred the company's powers directly to the

CHRONOLOGY

The New Imperialism: Asia

Hong Kong to Britain, along with trading rights in cities in China	1842
Commodore Perry's mission to Japan	1853–1854
Great Rebellion in India	1857–1858
Queen Victoria as Empress of India	1876
Russians in Central (trans-Caspian) Asia	1881
Spanish-American War; U.S. annexation of the Philippines	1898
Commonwealth of Australia	1901
Commonwealth of New Zealand	1907
Russian-British agreement over Afghanistan and Persia	1907
Japanese annexation of Korea	1910

government in London. In 1876, the title Empress of India was bestowed on Queen Victoria; Indians were now her colonial subjects.

Russian expansion in Asia was a logical outgrowth of its traditional territorial aggrandizement. Gradually, Russian settlers moved into cold and forbidding Siberia. The Russians also moved south, attracted by the crumbling Ottoman Empire. By 1830, the Russians had established control over the entire northern coast of the Black Sea and then pressed on into Central Asia, securing the trans-Caspian area by 1881 and Turkestan in 1885. These advances brought the Russians to the borders of Persia and Afghanistan, where the British also had interests because of their desire to protect their holdings in India. In 1907, the Russians and British agreed to make Afghanistan a buffer state between Russian Turkestan and British India and divide Persia into two spheres of influence. Halted by the British in their expansion to the south, the Russians moved east in Asia. The Russians' occupation of Manchuria and their attempt to move into Korea brought war with Japan. After losing the Russo-Japanese War in 1905, the Russians agreed to a Japanese protectorate in Korea; their Asian expansion was brought to a temporary halt (see Map 24.2).

The thrust of imperialism after 1880 led Westerners to move into new areas of Asia hitherto largely free of Western influence. By the nineteenth century, the ruling Manchu dynasty of the Chinese empire was showing signs of decline. In 1842, the British had obtained (through war) the island of Hong Kong and rights to trade in a number of Chinese cities. Other Western nations soon rushed in to gain similar trading privileges. Britain, France, Germany, Russia, the United States, and Japan established spheres of influence and long-term leases on Chinese territory.

Japan avoided Western intrusion until 1853–1854, when American naval forces under Commodore Matthew Perry forced the Japanese to grant the United States trading and diplomatic privileges. Japan, however, managed to avoid China's fate. By absorbing and adopting Western military and industrial methods, the Japanese developed a modern commercial and industrial system as well as a powerful military state. They established their own sphere of influence in China, and five years after they defeated the Russians in 1905, the Japanese formally annexed Korea. The Japanese had proved that an Eastern power could play the "white man's" imperialistic game and provided a potent example to peoples in other regions of Asia and Africa.

In Southeast Asia, Britain established control over Burma and the Malay States while France played an active role in subjugating Indochina. In the 1880s, the French extended "protection" over Cambodia, Annam, Tonkin, and Laos and organized them into the Union of French Indo-China. Only Siam (Thailand) remained free as a buffer state because of British-French rivalry.

The Pacific was also the scene of great power struggles and witnessed the entry of the United States onto the imperialist stage. Samoa became the first important American colony; the Hawaiian Islands were the next to fall. Soon after Americans had made Hawaii's Pearl Harbor into a naval station in 1887, American settlers gained control of the sugar industry on the islands. When Hawaiian natives tried to reassert their authority, the U.S. Marines were brought in to "protect" American lives. Hawaii was annexed by the United States in 1898 during the era of American nationalistic fervor generated by the Spanish-American War. The American defeat of Spain encouraged Americans to extend their empire by acquiring Cuba, Puerto Rico, Guam, and the Philippine Islands. Although the Filipinos hoped for independence, the Americans refused to grant it. As President McKinley said, the United States had the duty "to educate the Filipinos and uplift and Christianize them," a remarkable statement in view of the fact that most of them had been Roman Catholics for centuries. It took three years and sixty thousand troops to pacify the Philippines and establish American control.

MAP 24.2 Asia in 1914.

Asian Responses to Imperialism

When Europeans imposed their culture on peoples they considered inferior, how did the conquered peoples respond? Initial attempts to expel the foreigners only led to devastating defeats at the hands of Westerners, whose industrial technology gave them modern weapons of war with which to crush the indigenous peoples. Accustomed to rule by small elites, most people simply accepted their new governors, making Western rule relatively easy. The conquered peoples subsequently adjusted to foreign rule in different ways. Traditionalists sought to maintain their cultural traditions, but modernizers believed that adoption of Western ways would enable them to reform their societies and eventually challenge Western rule. Most people probably stood somewhere between these two extremes. By examining India, we can see how one Asian people responded to foreign rule.

INDIA

The British government had been in control of India since the mid-nineteeth century. After crushing a major revolt in 1858, the British ruled India directly. Under Parliament's supervision, a small group of British civil servants directed the affairs of India's almost 300 million people.

The British brought order to a society that had been divided by civil wars for some time and created a relatively honest and efficient government. They also brought Western technology—railroads, banks, mines, industry, medical knowledge, and hospitals. The British introduced Western-style secondary schools and colleges where the Indian upper and middle classes and professional classes were educated so that they could serve as trained subordinates in the government and the army.

But the Indian people paid a high price for the peace and stability brought by British rule. Due to population growth in the nineteenth century, extreme poverty was a way of life for most Indians; almost two-thirds of the population suffered from malnutrition in 1901. British industrialization brought little improvement for the masses. British manufactured goods destroyed local industries, and Indian wealth was used to pay British officials and the large army. The system of education served only elite, upper-class Indians, and it was conducted only in the rulers' English language, meaning that 90 percent of the population remained illiterate. Even for the Indians who benefited the most from their Western educations, British rule was degrading. The best jobs and the best housing were reserved for Britons. Despite their education, the Indians were never considered equals of the British, whose racial attitudes were made quite clear by Lord Kitchener, one of Britain's foremost military commanders in India, when he said: "It is this consciousness of the inherent superiority of the European which has won for us India. However well educated and clever a native may be, and however brave he may prove himself, I believe that no rank we can bestow on him would cause him to be considered an equal of the British officer."[10] Such smug racial attitudes made it difficult for British rule, no matter how beneficent, ever to be ultimately accepted and led to the rise of an Indian nationalist movement. By 1883, when the Indian National Congress was formed, moderate, educated Indians were beginning to seek self-government. By 1919, in response to British violence and British insensitivity, Indians were demanding complete independence.

International Rivalry and the Coming of War

Before 1914, Europeans had experienced almost fifty years of peace. There had been wars (including wars of conquest in the non-Western world), but none had involved the great powers. A series of crises occurred, however, that might easily have led to general war. One reason they did not is that until 1890, Bismarck of Germany exercised a restraining influence on the Europeans.

Bismarck knew that the emergence of a unified Germany in 1871 had upset the balance of power established at Vienna in 1815. Fearing a possible anti-German alliance between France, Russia, and possibly even Austria, Bismarck made a defensive alliance with Austria in 1879. In 1882, this German-Austrian alliance was enlarged with the entrance of Italy. The Triple Alliance of 1882 committed Germany, Austria-Hungary, and Italy to support the existing political order while providing a defense against France. At the same time, Bismarck maintained a separate treaty with Russia, hoping to prevent a French-Russian alliance that would threaten Germany with the possibility of a two-front war. The Bismarckian system of alliances, geared to preserving peace and the status quo, had worked, but in 1890, Emperor William II dismissed Bismarck and began to chart a new direction for Germany's foreign policy.

New Directions and New Crises

Emperor William II embarked on an activist foreign policy dedicated to enhancing German power by finding, as he put it, Germany's rightful "place in the sun." One of his changes in Bismarck's foreign policy was to drop the treaty with Russia, which he viewed as being at odds with Germany's alliance with Austria. The ending of the alliance achieved what Bismarck had feared: it brought France and Russia together. Republican France leapt at the chance to draw closer to tsarist Russia, and in 1894, the two powers concluded a military alliance.

During the next ten years, German policies abroad caused the British to draw closer to France (see the box on p. 507). By 1907, a loose confederation

The Emperor's "Big Mouth"

Emperor William II's world policy engendered considerable ill will and unrest among other European states, especially Britain. Moreover, the emperor had the unfortunate tendency to stir up trouble by his often tactless public remarks. In this 1908 interview, for example, William II intended to strengthen Germany's ties with Britain. His words had just the opposite effect and raised a storm of protest in both Britain and Germany.

Daily Telegraph *Interview, October 28, 1908*

As I have said, his Majesty honoured me with a long conversation, and spoke with impulsive and unusual frankness. "You English," he said, "are mad, mad, mad as March hares. What has come over you that you are so completely given over to suspicions quite unworthy of a great nation? What more can I do than I have done? I declared with all the emphasis at my command, in my speech at Guildhall, that my heart is set upon peace, and that it is one of my dearest wishes to live on the best of terms with England. Have I ever been false to my word? Falsehood and prevarication are alien to my nature. My actions ought to speak for themselves, but you listen not to them but to those who misinterpret and distort them. That is a personal insult which I feel and resent. To be forever misjudged, to have my repeated offers of friendship weighed and scrutinized with jealous, mistrustful eyes, taxes my patience severely. I have said time after time that I am a friend of England, and your Press—or, at least, a considerable section of it—bids the people of England to refuse my proffered hand, and insinuates that the other holds a dagger. How can I convince a nation against its will?

"I repeat," continued his Majesty, "that I am a friend of England, but you make things difficult for me. My task is not of the easiest. The prevailing sentiment among large sections of the middle and lower classes of my own people is not friendly to England. I am, therefore, so to speak, in a minority in my own land, but it is a minority of the best elements as it is in England with respect to Germany. That is another reason why I resent your refusal to accept my pledged word that I am the friend of England. I strive without ceasing to improve relations, and you retort that I am your arch-enemy. You make it hard for me. Why is it? . . .

"But, you will say, what of the German Navy? Surely, that is a menace to England! Against whom but England are my squadrons being prepared? If England is not in the minds of those Germans who are bent on creating a powerful fleet, why is Germany asked to consent to such new and heavy burdens of taxation? My answer is clear. Germany is a young and growing Empire. She has a world-wide commerce, which is rapidly expanding, and to which the legitimate ambition of patriotic Germans refuses to assign any bounds. Germany must have a powerful fleet to protect that commerce, and her manifold interests in even the most distant seas. She expects those interests to go on growing, and she must be able to champion them manfully in any quarter of the globe. Germany looks ahead. Her horizons stretch far away. She must be prepared for any eventualities in the Far East. Who can foresee what may take place in the Pacific in the days to come, days not so distant as some believe, but days, at any rate, for which all European Powers with Far Eastern interests ought steadily to prepare? Look at the accomplished rise of Japan; think of the possible national awakening of China; and then judge of the vast problems of the Pacific. Only those Powers which have great navies will be listened to with respect, when the future of the Pacific comes to be solved; and, if for that reason only, Germany must have a powerful fleet. It may even be that England herself will be glad that Germany has a fleet when they speak together on the same side in the great debates of the future."

of Great Britain, France, and Russia—known as the Triple Entente—stood opposed to the Triple Alliance of Germany, Austria-Hungary, and Italy. Europe became divided into two opposing camps that became more and more inflexible and unwilling to compromise. When the members of the two alliances became involved in a new series of crises between 1908 and 1913 over the struggle for the control of the remnants of the Ottoman Empire in the Balkans, the stage was set for World War I.

Crises in the Balkans, 1908–1913

The Bosnian Crisis of 1908–1909 initiated a chain of events that eventually spun out of control. Since 1878, Bosnia and Herzegovina had been under the protection of Austria, but in 1908, Austria took the drastic step of annexing these two Slavic-speaking territories. Serbia became outraged at this action because it dashed the Serbs' hopes of creating a large Serbian kingdom that would include most of the southern Slavs. But this possibility was why the Austrians had annexed Bosnia and Herzegovina. A large Serbia would be a threat to the unity of their empire with its large Slavic population. The Russians, as protectors of their fellow Slavs and with their own desire to increase their authority in the Balkans, supported the Serbs and opposed the Austrian action. Backed by the Russians, the Serbs prepared for war against Austria. At this point, William II intervened and demanded that the Russians accept Austria's annexation of Bosnia and Herzegovina or face war with Germany. Weakened from their defeat in the Russo-Japanese War in 1904–1905, the Russians backed down. Humiliated, they vowed revenge.

European attention returned to the Balkans in 1912 when Serbia, Bulgaria, Montenegro, and Greece organized the Balkan League and defeated the Ottomans in the First Balkan War. When the victorious allies were unable to agree on how to divide the conquered Ottoman territory, the Second Balkan War erupted in 1913. Greece, Serbia, Romania, and the Ottoman Empire attacked and defeated Bulgaria. As a result, Bulgaria obtained only a small part of Macedonia, and most of the rest was divided between Serbia and Greece (see Map 24.3). Yet Serbia's aspirations

MAP 24.3 The Balkans in 1913.

remained unfulfilled. The two Balkan wars left the inhabitants embittered and created more tensions among the great powers.

One of Serbia's major ambitions had been to acquire Albanian territory that would give it a port on the Adriatic. At the London Conference, arranged by Austria at the end of the two Balkan wars, the Austrians had blocked Serbia's wishes by creating an independent Albania. The Germans, as Austrian allies, had supported this move. In their frustration, Serbian nationalists increasingly portrayed the Austrians as monsters who were keeping the Serbs from becoming a great nation. As Serbia's chief supporters, the Russians were also upset by the turn of events in the Balkans. A feeling had grown among Russian leaders that they could not back down again in the event of a confrontation with Austria or Germany in the Balkans.

Austria-Hungary had achieved another of its aims, but it was still convinced that Serbia was a mortal threat to its empire and must at some point be crushed. Meanwhile, the French and Russian governments renewed their alliance and promised each other that they would not back down at the next crisis. Britain drew closer to France. By the beginning of 1914, two armed camps viewed each other with suspicion. The European "age of progress" was about to come to an inglorious and bloody end.

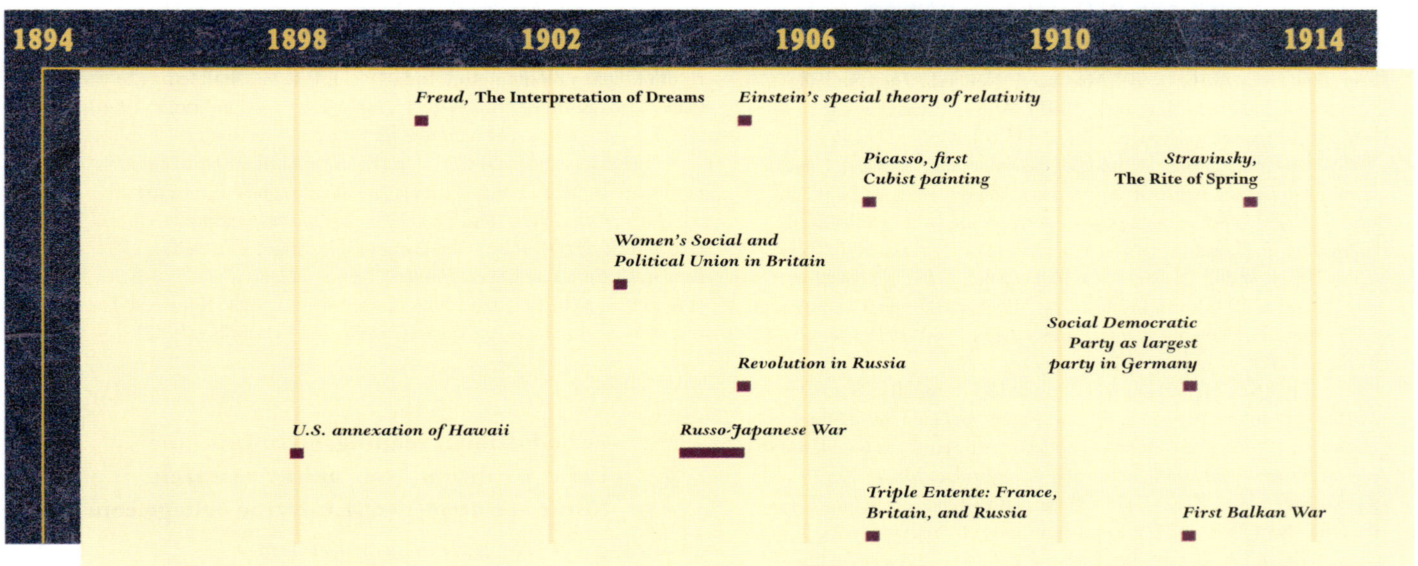

Conclusion

What many Europeans liked to call their "age of progress" in the decades before 1914 was also an era of anxiety. Frenzied imperialist expansion had created vast European empires and spheres of influence around the globe. This feverish competition for colonies, however, had markedly increased the existing antagonisms among the European states. At the same time, the Western treatment of non-Western peoples as racial inferiors impelled educated, non-Western elites in these colonies to found movements for national independence. Before these movements could succeed, however, the power that Europeans had achieved through their mass armies and technological superiority had to be weakened. The Europeans inadvertently accomplished this task for their colonial subjects by demolishing their own civilization on the battlegrounds of Europe in World War I and World War II.

The cultural revolutions before 1914 had also produced anxiety and a crisis of confidence in European civilization. A brilliant minority of intellectuals had created a modern consciousness that questioned most Europeans' optimistic faith in reason, the rational structure of nature, and the certainty of progress. The devastating experiences of World War I turned this culture of uncertainty into a way of life after 1918.

Notes

1. Quoted in Arthur E. E. McKenzie, *The Major Achievements of Science* (New York, 1960), vol. 1, p. 310.
2. Friedrich Nietzsche, *Twilight of the Idols and The Anti-Christ*, trans. R. J. Hollingdale (New York, 1972), pp. 117–118.
3. Friedrich Nietzsche, *Thus Spake Zarathustra*, in *The Philosophy of Nietzsche* (New York, 1954), p. 6.
4. Friedrich von Bernhardi, *Germany and the Next War*, trans. Allen H. Powles (New York, 1914), pp. 18–19.

5. Quoted in John Rewald, *History of Impressionism* (New York, 1961), pp. 456–458.
6. Quoted in Anne Higonnet, *Berthe Morisot's Images of Women* (Cambridge, Mass., 1992), p. 19.
7. Quoted in Catherine M. Prelinger, "Prelude to Consciousness: Amalie Sieveking and the Female Association for the Care of the Poor and the Sick," in John C. Fout, ed., *German Women in the Nineteenth Century: A Social History* (New York, 1984), p. 119.
8. Quoted in Bonnie Smith, *Changing Lives: Women in European History Since 1700* (Lexington, Mass., 1989), p. 379.
9. Quoted in John Ellis, *The Social History of the Machine Gun* (New York, 1975), p. 80.
10. Quoted in K. M. Panikkar, *Asia and Western Dominance* (London, 1959), p. 116.

Suggestions for Further Reading 

A well-regarded study of Sigmund Freud is P. Gay, *Freud: A Life for Our Time* (New York, 1988). Also, see J. Neu, ed., *The Cambridge Companion to Freud* (New York, 1991). A useful study on the impact of Darwinian thought on religion is J. Moore, *The Post-Darwinian Controversies: A Study of the Protestant Struggle to Come to Terms with Darwin in Great Britain and America, 1870–1900* (Cambridge, 1979). Very valuable on modern art are M. Powell-Jones, *Impressionism* (London, 1994); B. Denvir, *Post-Impressionism* (New York, 1992); and T. Parsons, *Post-Impressionism: The Rise of Modern Art* (London, 1992). On literature, see R. Pascal, *From Naturalism to Expressionism: German Literature and Society, 1880–1918* (New York, 1973).

The rise of feminism is examined in J. Rendall, *The Origins of Modern Feminism: Women in Britain, France and the United States* (London, 1985). The subject of modern anti-Semitism is covered in J. Katz, *From Prejudice to Destruction* (Cambridge, Mass., 1980), and A. S. Lindemann, *Esau's Tears: Modern Anti-Semitism and the Rise of the Jews* (New York, 1997). European racism is analyzed in G. L. Mosse, *Toward the Final Solution* (New York, 1980); German anti-Semitism as a political force is examined in P. J. Pulzer, *The Rise of Political Anti-Semitism in Germany and Austria* (New York, 1964). The problems of Jews in Russia are examined in J. Frankel, *Prophecy and Politics: Socialism, Nationalism and the Russian Jews, 1862–1917* (Cambridge, 1981). For a recent biography of Theodor Herzl, see J. Kornberg, *Theodor Herzl: From Assimilation to Zionism* (Bloomington, Ind., 1993). The beginnings of the Labour Party are examined in H. Pelling, *The Origins of the Labour Party*, 2d ed. (Oxford, 1965). There are good introductions to the political world of William II's Germany in T. A. Kohut, *Wilhelm II and the Germans: A Study in Leadership* (New York, 1991), and J. C. G. Röhl, *The Kaiser and His Court: Wilhelm II and the Government of Germany* (New York, 1994). On Russia, see T. H. von Laue, *Sergei Witte and the Industrialization of Russia* (New York, 1963), and A. Ascher, *The Revolution of 1905: Russia in Disarray*, 2 vols. (Stanford, Calif., 1988–1992).

For broad perspectives on imperialism, see T. Smith, *The Pattern of Imperialism* (Cambridge, 1981); M. W. Doyle, *Empires* (Ithaca, N.Y., 1986); and P. Darby, *Three Faces of Imperialism: British and American Approaches to Asia and Africa, 1870–1970* (New Haven, Conn., 1987). Different aspects of imperialism are covered in R. Robinson and J. Gallagher, *Africa and the Victorians*, 2d ed. (New York, 1981); A Burton, *Burdens of History: British Feminists, Indian Women, and Imperial Culture, 1865–1915* (Chapel Hill, N.C., 1994); M. Strobel, *European Women and the Second British Empire* (Bloomington, Ind., 1991); P. J. Marshall, ed., *The Cambridge Illustrated History of the British Empire* (Cambridge, 1996); and T. Pakhenham, *The Scramble for Africa* (New York, 1991).

Two fundamental works on the diplomatic history of the period are by W. L. Langer: *European Alliances and Alignments*, 2d ed. (New York, 1966), and *The Diplomacy of Imperialism*, 2d ed. (New York, 1965). Also valuable are G. Kennan, *The Decline of Bismarck's European Order: Franco-Prussian Relations, 1875–1890* (Princeton, N.J., 1979), and the masterful study by P. Kennedy, *The Rise of Anglo-German Antagonism, 1860–1914* (London, 1982).

For additional reading, go to InfoTrac College Edition, your online research library at http://web1.infotrac-college.com

Enter the search term *Nietzsche* using Key Terms.

Enter the search terms *Sigmund Freud* using Key Terms.

Enter the search terms *Social Darwinism* using Key Terms.

Enter the search term *imperialism* using the Subject Guide.

CHAPTER

25

The Beginning of the Twentieth-Century Crisis: War and Revolution

CHAPTER OUTLINE

- The Road to World War I
- The War
- War and Revolution
- The Peace Settlement
- Conclusion

FOCUS QUESTIONS

- What were the long-range and immediate causes of World War I?
- What did the belligerents expect at the beginning of World War I, and why did the course of the war turn out to be so different from their expectations?
- How did World War I affect the belligerents' governmental and political institutions, economic affairs, and social life?
- What were the causes of the Russian Revolution of 1917, and why did the Bolsheviks prevail in the civil war and gain control of Russia?
- What were the objectives of the chief participants at the Paris Peace Conference of 1919, and how closely did the final settlement reflect these objectives?

ON JULY 1, 1916, British and French infantry forces attacked German defensive lines along a 25-mile front near the Somme River in France. Each soldier carried almost 70 pounds of equipment, making it "impossible to move much quicker than a slow walk." German machine guns soon opened fire: "We were able to see our comrades move forward in an attempt to cross No-Man's Land, only to be mown down like meadow grass," recalled one British soldier. "I felt sick at the sight of this carnage and remember weeping." In one day more than 21,000 British soldiers died. After six months of fighting, the British had advanced 5 miles; one million British, French, and German soldiers had been killed or wounded.

World War I (1914–1918) was the defining event of the twentieth century. It devastated the prewar economic, social, and political order of

Europe, and its uncertain outcome prepared the way for an even more destructive war. Overwhelmed by the size of its battles, the extent of its casualties, and its effects on all facets of life, contemporaries referred to it simply as the "Great War."

The Great War was all the more disturbing to Europeans because it came after what many considered an age of progress. There had been international crises before 1914, but somehow Europeans had managed to avoid serious and prolonged military confrontations. When smaller European states had gone to war, as in the Balkans in 1912 and 1913, the great European powers had been able to keep the conflict localized. Material prosperity and a fervid belief in scientific and technological progress had convinced many people that the world was on the verge of creating the utopia that humans had dreamed of for centuries. The historian Arnold Toynbee expressed what the pre–World War I era had meant to his generation:

> *[We had expected] that life throughout the World would become more rational, more humane, and more democratic and that, slowly, but surely, political democracy would produce greater social justice. We had also expected that the progress of science and technology would make mankind richer, and that this increasing wealth would gradually spread from a minority to a majority. We had expected that all this would happen peacefully. In fact we thought that mankind's course was set for an earthly paradise.*[1]

After 1918, it was no longer possible to maintain naive illusions about the progress of Western civilization. As World War I was followed by the destructiveness of World War II and the mass murder machines of totalitarian regimes, it became all too apparent that instead of a utopia, European civilization had become a nightmare. The Great War resulted not only in great loss of life and property but also in the annihilation of one of the basic intellectual precepts on which Western civilization had been thought to have been founded—the belief in progress. World War I and the revolutions it spawned can properly be seen as the first stage in the crisis of the twentieth century.

◆ The Road to World War I

On June 28, 1914, the heir to the Austrian throne, Archduke Francis Ferdinand, was assassinated in the Bosnian city of Sarajevo. Although this event precipitated the confrontation between Austria and Serbia that led to World War I, there were also long-range, underlying forces that were propelling Europeans toward armed conflict.

Nationalism and Internal Dissent

In the first half of the nineteenth century, liberals had maintained that the organization of European states along national lines would lead to a peaceful Europe based on a sense of international fraternity. They were very wrong. The system of nation-states that had emerged in Europe in the second half of the nineteenth century led not to cooperation but to competition. Rivalries over colonial and commercial interests intensified during an era of frenzied imperialist expansion while the division of Europe's great powers into two loose alliances (Germany, Austria, and Italy versus France, Great Britain, and Russia; see Map 25.1) only added to the tensions. The series of crises that tested these alliances in the 1900s and early 1910s had left European states with the belief that their allies were important and that their security depended on supporting those allies, even when they took foolish risks.

The growth of nationalism in the nineteenth century had yet another serious consequence. Not all ethnic groups had achieved the goal of nationhood. Slavic minorities in the Balkans and the polyglot Habsburg empire, for example, still dreamed of creating their own national states. So did the Irish in the British Empire and the Poles in the Russian Empire.

National aspirations, however, were not the only source of internal strife at the beginning of the twentieth century. Socialist labor movements had grown more powerful and were increasingly inclined to use strikes, even violent ones, to achieve their goals. Some conservative leaders, alarmed at the increase in labor strife and class division, even feared that European nations were on the verge of revolution. Did these statesmen opt for war in 1914 because they believed that "prosecuting an active foreign policy," as one leader expressed it, would smother "internal troubles"? Some historians have argued that the desire to suppress internal disorder may have encouraged some leaders to take the plunge into war in 1914.

Militarism

The growth of large mass armies after 1900 not only heightened the existing tensions in Europe but made it inevitable that if war did come, it would be highly

MAP 25.1 Europe in 1914.

destructive. Conscription had been established as a regular practice in most Western countries before 1914 (the United States and Britain were major exceptions). European military machines had doubled in size between 1890 and 1914. With its 1.3 million men, the Russian army had grown to be the largest, while the French and Germans were not far behind with 900,000 each. The British, Italian, and Austrian armies numbered between 250,000 and 500,000 soldiers each.

Militarism, however, involved more than just large armies. As armies grew, so did the influence of military leaders, who drew up vast and complex plans for quickly mobilizing millions of men and enormous quantities of supplies in the event of war. Fearful that changes in these plans would cause chaos in the armed forces, military leaders insisted that their plans could not be altered. In the crises during the summer of 1914, the generals' lack of flexibility forced European political leaders to make decisions for military instead of political reasons.

The Outbreak of War: The Summer of 1914

Militarism, nationalism, and the desire to stifle internal dissent may all have played a role in the coming of World War I, but the decisions made by European leaders in the summer of 1914 directly precipitated the conflict. It was another crisis in the Balkans that forced this predicament on European statesmen.

As we have seen, states in southeastern Europe had struggled to free themselves of Ottoman rule in the course of the nineteenth and early twentieth centuries. But the rivalry between Austria-Hungary and Russia for domination of these new states created serious tensions in the region. By 1914, Serbia, supported by Russia, was determined to create a large, independent Slavic state in the Balkans, whereas Austria, which had its own Slavic minorities to contend with, was equally set on preventing that possibility. Many Europeans perceived the inherent dangers in this combination of Serbian ambition bolstered by Russian

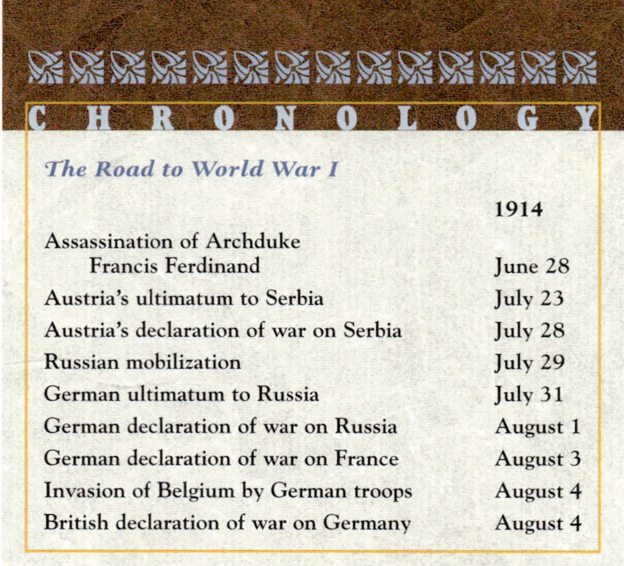

CHRONOLOGY

The Road to World War I

	1914
Assassination of Archduke Francis Ferdinand	June 28
Austria's ultimatum to Serbia	July 23
Austria's declaration of war on Serbia	July 28
Russian mobilization	July 29
German ultimatum to Russia	July 31
German declaration of war on Russia	August 1
German declaration of war on France	August 3
Invasion of Belgium by German troops	August 4
British declaration of war on Germany	August 4

hatred of Austria and Austrian conviction that Serbia's success would mean the end of its empire. The British ambassador to Vienna wrote in 1913:

> Serbia will some day set Europe by the ears, and bring about a universal war on the Continent. . . . I cannot tell you how exasperated people are getting here at the continual worry which that little country causes to Austria under encouragement from Russia. . . . It will be lucky if Europe succeeds in avoiding war as a result of the present crisis. The next time a Serbian crisis arises . . . , I feel sure that Austria-Hungary will refuse to admit of any Russian interference in the dispute and that she will proceed to settle her differences with her little neighbor by herself.[2]

It was against this backdrop of mutual distrust and hatred between Austria-Hungary and Russia, on the one hand, and Austria-Hungary and Serbia, on the other, that the events of the summer of 1914 were played out.

The assassination of the Austrian archduke Francis Ferdinand and his wife, Sophia, on June 28, 1914, was carried out by a Bosnian activist who worked for the Black Hand, a Serbian terrorist organization dedicated to the creation of a pan-Slavic kingdom. Although the Austrian government did not know whether the Serbian government had been directly involved in the archduke's assassination, it saw an opportunity to "render Serbia innocuous once and for all by a display of force," as the Austrian foreign minister put it. Fearful of Russian intervention on Serbia's behalf, Austrian leaders sought the backing of their German allies. Emperor William II and his chancellor gave their assurance that Austria-Hungary could rely on Germany's "full support," even if "matters went to the length of a war between Austria-Hungary and Russia."

Strengthened by German support, Austrian leaders issued an ultimatum to Serbia on July 23 in which they made such extreme demands that Serbia had little choice but to reject some of them in order to preserve its sovereignty. Austria then declared war on Serbia on July 28. Still smarting from its humiliation in the Bosnian crisis of 1908, Russia was determined to support Serbia's cause. On July 28, Tsar Nicholas II ordered partial mobilization of the Russian army against Austria. At this point, the Russian General Staff informed the tsar that its mobilization plans were based on a war against both Germany and Austria simultaneously. They could not execute partial mobilization without creating chaos in the army. Consequently, the Russian government ordered full mobilization of the Russian army on July 29, knowing that the Germans would consider this an act of war against them. Germany responded to Russian mobilization with its own ultimatum that the Russians must halt their mobilization within twelve hours. When the Russians ignored it, Germany declared war on Russia on August 1.

At this stage of the conflict, German war plans determined whether or not France would become involved in the war. Under the guidance of General Alfred von Schlieffen, chief of staff from 1891 to 1905, the German General Staff had devised a military plan based on the assumption of a two-front war with France and Russia, since the two powers had formed a military alliance in 1894. The Schlieffen plan called for a minimal troop deployment against Russia while most of the German army would rapidly invade western France by way of neutral Belgium. After the planned quick defeat of the French, the German army expected to redeploy to the east against Russia. Under the Schlieffen plan, Germany could not mobilize its troops solely against Russia and therefore declared war on France on August 3 after issuing an ultimatum to Belgium on August 2 demanding the right of German troops to pass through Belgian territory. On August 4, Great Britain declared war on Germany, officially over this violation of Belgian neutrality but in fact over the British desire to maintain world power. As one British diplomat argued, if Germany and Austria won the war, "what would be the position of a friendless England?" By August 4, all the great powers of Europe were at war.

◆ The War

Before 1914, many political leaders had become convinced that war involved so many political and economic risks that it was not worth fighting. Others had believed that "rational" diplomats could control any situation and prevent the outbreak of war. At the beginning of August 1914, both of these prewar illusions were shattered, but the new illusions that replaced them soon proved to be equally foolish.

1914–1915: Illusions and Stalemate

Europeans went to war in 1914 with remarkable enthusiasm. Government propaganda had been successful in stirring up national antagonisms before the war. Now in August 1914, the urgent pleas of governments for defense against aggressors fell on receptive ears in every belligerent nation. Most people seemed genuinely convinced that their nation's cause was just. A new set of illusions also fed the enthusiasm for war. Almost everyone in August 1914 believed that the war would be over in a few weeks. People were reminded that all European wars since 1815 had in fact ended in a matter of weeks, conveniently ignoring the American Civil War (1861–1865), which was the "real prototype" for World War I. Both the soldiers who exuberantly boarded the trains for the war front in August 1914 and the jubilant citizens who bombarded them with flowers when they departed believed that the warriors would be home by Christmas.

THE EXCITEMENT OF WAR. World War I was greeted with incredible enthusiasm. Each of the major belligerents was convinced of the rightness of its cause. Shown here are French soldiers in a jubilant mood departing for Gallipoli. Many of them did not return from that disastrous battle in 1915.

German hopes for a quick end to the war rested on a military gamble. The Schlieffen plan had called for the German army to make a vast encircling movement through Belgium into northern France that would sweep around Paris and encircle most of the French army. But the German advance was halted only 20 miles from Paris at the first Battle of the Marne (September 6–10; see Map 25.2). The war quickly turned into a stalemate—neither the Germans nor the French could dislodge each other from the trenches they had begun to dig for shelter. Two lines of trenches soon extended from the English Channel to the frontiers of Switzerland. The Western Front had become bogged down in trench warfare that kept both sides immobilized in virtually the same positions for four years.

In contrast to the west, the war in the east was marked by much more mobility, although the cost in lives was equally enormous. At the beginning of the war, the Russian army moved into eastern Germany but was decisively defeated at the Battles of Tannenberg on August 26–30 and the Masurian Lakes on September 15 (see Map 25.3). The Russians were no longer a threat to German territory.

The Austrians, Germany's allies, fared less well initially. They had been defeated by the Russians in Galicia and thrown out of Serbia as well. To make matters worse, the Italians betrayed the Germans and Austrians and entered the war on the Allied side by attacking Austria in May 1915. By this time, the Germans had come to the aid of the Austrians. A German-Austrian army defeated and routed the Russian army in Galicia and pushed the Russians back 300 miles into their own territory. Russian casualties stood at 2.5 million killed, captured, or wounded; the Russians had almost been knocked out of the war. Buoyed by their success, the Germans and Austrians,

MAP 25.2 The Western Front, 1914–1918.

joined by the Bulgarians in September 1915, attacked and eliminated Serbia from the war.

1916–1917: The Great Slaughter

The successes in the east enabled the Germans to move back to the offensive in the west. The early trenches dug in 1914 had by now become elaborate systems of defense. Both lines of trenches were protected by barbed wire entanglements 3 to 5 feet high and 30 yards wide, concrete machine-gun nests, and mortar batteries, supported farther back by heavy artillery. Troops lived in holes in the ground, separated from each other by a "no man's land."

The unexpected development of trench warfare baffled military leaders, who had been trained to fight wars of movement and maneuver. The only plan generals could devise was to attempt a breakthrough by throwing masses of men against enemy lines that had first been battered by artillery barrages. Once the decisive breakthrough had been achieved, they thought, they could then return to the war of movement that they knew best. Periodically, the high command on either side would order an offensive that would begin with an artillery barrage to flatten the enemy's barbed wire and leave the enemy in a state of shock. After "softening up" the enemy in this fashion, a mass of soldiers would climb out of their trenches with fixed bayonets and hope to work their way toward the enemy trenches. The attacks rarely worked, since the machine gun put hordes of men advancing unprotected across open fields at a severe disadvantage. In 1916 and 1917, millions of young men were sacrificed in the search for the elusive breakthrough. In the German offensive at Verdun in 1916, the British campaign on the Somme in 1916, and the French attack in the Champagne region in 1917, the senselessness of trench warfare became all too obvious. In ten months at Verdun, 700,000 men lost their lives over a few miles of terrain. At the Battle of the Somme, the British suffered 57,000 casualties, including 21,000 dead, on the first day of the battle, the heaviest one-day loss in World War I.

Warfare in the trenches of the Western Front produced unimaginable horrors (see the box on p. 519). Battlefields were hellish landscapes of barbed wire, shell holes, mud, and injured and dying men. The introduction of poison gas in 1915 produced new forms of injuries, as one British writer described:

> I wish those people who write so glibly about this being a holy war could see a case of mustard gas . . . could see the poor things burnt and blistered all over with great mustard-coloured suppurating blisters with blind eyes all sticky . . . and stuck together, and always fighting for breath, with voices a mere whisper, saying that their throats are closing and they know they will choke.[3]

Soldiers in the trenches also lived with the persistent presence of death. Because combat went on for months, soldiers had to carry on in the midst of countless bodies of dead men or the remains of men dismembered by artillery barrages. Many soldiers remembered the stench of decomposing bodies and the swarms of rats that grew fat in the trenches.

The Widening of the War

As another response to the stalemate on the Western Front, both sides sought to gain new allies who might provide a winning advantage. The Ottoman Empire had already come into the war on Germany's side in August 1914. Russia, Great Britain, and France declared war on the Ottoman Empire in November. Although the Allies attempted to open a Balkan front by landing forces at Gallipoli, southwest of Constantinople, in April 1915, the entry of Bulgaria into the war on the side of the Central Powers (as Germany, Austria-Hungary, and the Ottoman Empire were called) and a disastrous campaign at Gallipoli

IMPACT OF THE MACHINE GUN. Trench warfare on the Western Front stymied military leaders, who expected to fight a war based on movement and maneuver. Their efforts to advance by sending masses of men against enemy lines was the height of folly in view of the machine gun. Soldiers advancing across open land made magnificent targets.

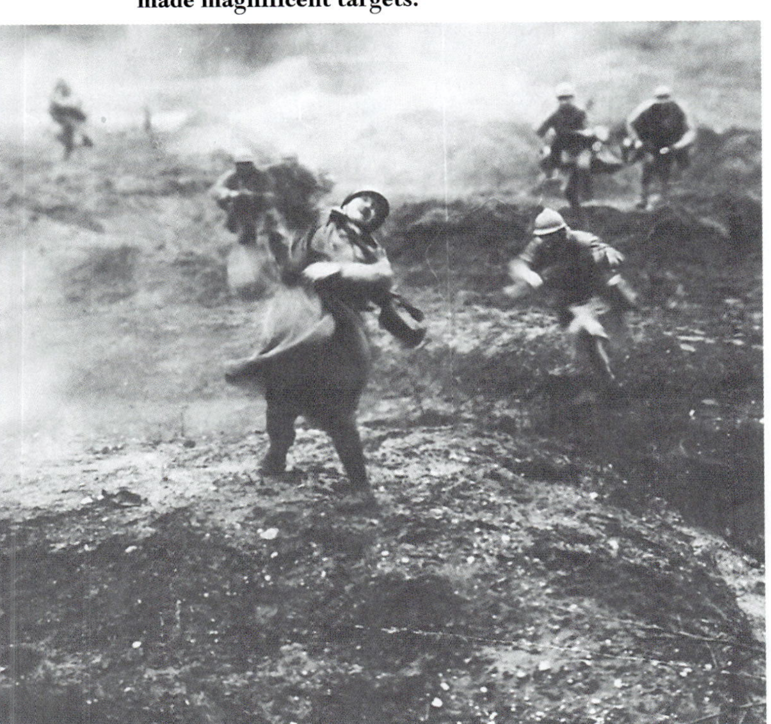

THE HORRORS OF WAR. The slaughter of millions of men in the trenches of World War I created unimaginable horrors for the participants. For the sake of survival, many soldiers learned to harden themselves against the stench of decomposing bodies and the sight of bodies horribly dismembered by artillery barrages.

MAP 25.3 **The Eastern Front, 1914–1918.**

caused them to withdraw. The Italians, as we have seen, also entered the war on the Allied side after France and Britain promised to further their acquisition of Austrian territory. In the long run, however, Italian military incompetence forced the Allies to come to the assistance of Italy.

By 1917, the war that had begun in Europe was having an increasing impact on other parts of the world. In the Middle East, a British officer who came to be known as Lawrence of Arabia incited Arab princes to revolt in 1917 against their Ottoman overlords. In 1918, British forces from Egypt destroyed the rest of the Ottoman Empire in the Middle East. For their Middle East campaigns, the British mobilized forces from India, Australia, and New Zealand. The Allies also took advantage of Germany's preoccupations in Europe and lack of naval strength to seize German colonies in the rest of the world.

Most important to the Allied cause was the entry of the United States into the war. At first, the United States tried to remain neutral in the Great War, but it found neutrality difficult to maintain as the war dragged on. The immediate cause of American involvement grew out of the naval conflict between Germany and Great Britain. Britain used its superior naval power to maximum effect by throwing up a naval blockade of Germany. Germany retaliated by imposing a counterblockade enforced by unrestricted submarine warfare. Strong American protests over the German sinking of passenger liners, especially the

The Reality of War: Trench Warfare

The romantic illusions about the excitement and adventure of war that filled the minds of so many young men who marched off to battle quickly disintegrated after a short time in the trenches on the Western Front. This description of trench warfare is taken from the most famous novel that emerged from World War I, Erich Maria Remarque's All Quiet on the Western Front, *written in 1929. Remarque had fought in the trenches in France.*

❊ *Erich Maria Remarque,* All Quiet on the Western Front

We wake up in the middle of the night. The earth booms. Heavy fire is falling on us. We crouch into corners. We distinguish shells of every calibre.

Each man lays hold of his things and looks again every minute to reassure himself that they are still there. The dug-out heaves, the night roars and flashes. We look at each other in the momentary flashes of light, and with pale faces and pressed lips shake our heads.

Every man is aware of the heavy shells tearing down the parapet, rooting up the embankment and demolishing the upper layers of concrete. . . . Already by morning a few of the recruits are green and vomiting. They are too inexperienced. . . .

The bombardment does not diminish. It is falling in the rear too. As far as one can see it spouts fountains of mud and iron. A wide belt is being raked.

The attack does not come, but the bombardment continues. Slowly we become mute. Hardly a man speaks. We cannot make ourselves understood.

Our trench is almost gone. At many places it is only eighteen inches high, it is broken by holes, and craters, and mountains of earth. A shell lands square in front of our post. At once it is dark. We are buried and must dig ourselves out. . . .

Towards morning, while it is still dark, there is some excitement. Through the entrance rushes in a swarm of fleeing rats that try to storm the walls. Torches light up the confusion. Everyone yells and curses and slaughters. The madness and despair of many hours unloads itself in this outburst. Faces are distorted, arms strike out, the beasts scream; we just stop in time to avoid attacking one another. . . .

Suddenly it howls and flashes terrifically, the dugout cracks in all its joints under a direct hit, fortunately only a light one that the concrete blocks are able to withstand. It rings metallically, the walls reel, rifles, helmets, earth, mud, and dust fly everywhere. Sulphur fumes pour in. . . . The recruit starts to rave again and two others follow suit. One jumps up and rushes out, we have trouble with the other two. I start after the one who escapes and wonder whether to shoot him in the leg—then it shrieks again, I fling myself down and when I stand up the wall of the trench is plastered with smoking splinters, lumps of flesh, and bits of uniform. I scramble back.

The first recruit seems actually to have gone insane. He butts his head against the wall like a goat. We must try tonight to take him to the rear. Meanwhile we bind him, but so that in case of attack he can be released.

Suddenly the nearer explosions cease. The shelling continues but it has lifted and falls behind us, our trench is free. We seize the hand-grenades, pitch them out in front of the dug-out and jump after them. The bombardment has stopped and a heavy barrage now falls behind us. The attack has come.

No one would believe that in this howling waste there could still be men; but steel helmets now appear on all sides out of the trench, and fifty yards from us a machine-gun is already in position and barking.

The wire-entanglements are torn to pieces. Yet they offer some obstacle. We see the storm-troops coming. Our artillery opens fire. Machine-guns rattle, rifles crack. The charge works its way across. Haie and Kropp begin with the hand-grenades. They throw as fast as they can, others pass them, the handles with the strings already pulled. Haie throws seventy-five yards, Kropp sixty, it has been measured, the distance is important. The enemy as they run cannot do much before they are within forty yards.

We recognize the distorted faces, the smooth helmets: they are French. They have already suffered heavily when they reach the remnants of the barbed-wire entanglements. A whole line has gone down before our machine-guns; then we have a lot of stoppages and they come nearer.

I see one of them, his face upturned, fall into a wire cradle. His body collapses, his hands remain suspended as though he were praying. Then his body drops clean away and only his hands with the stumps of his arms, shot off, now hang in the wire.

British ship *Lusitania* on May 7, 1915, when more than one hundred Americans lost their lives, forced the German government to suspend unrestricted submarine warfare in September 1915 to avoid further antagonizing the Americans.

In January 1917, however, eager to break the deadlock in the war, the Germans decided on another military gamble by returning to unrestricted submarine warfare. German naval officers convinced Emperor William II that the use of unrestricted submarine warfare could starve the British into submission within five months, certainly before the Americans could act. The return to unrestricted submarine warfare brought the United States into the war on April 6, 1917. Although American troops did not arrive in large numbers in Europe until 1918, the entry of the United States into the war in 1917 gave the Allied Powers a psychological boost when they needed it. The year 1917 was not a good year for them. Allied offensives on the Western Front were disastrously defeated. The Italian armies were smashed in October, and in November 1917 the Bolshevik revolution in Russia (see "The Russian Revolution" later in this chapter) led to Russia's withdrawal from the war. The cause of the Central Powers looked favorable, although war weariness in the Ottoman Empire, Bulgaria, Austria-Hungary, and Germany was beginning to take its toll. The home front was rapidly becoming a cause for as much concern as the war front.

The Home Front: The Impact of Total War

The prolongation of World War I made it a total war that affected the lives of all citizens, however remote they might be from the battlefields. The need to organize masses of men and matériel for years of combat (Germany alone had 5.5 million men in active units in 1916) led to increased centralization of government powers, economic regimentation, and manipulation of public opinion to keep the war effort going.

Because the war was expected to be short, little thought had been given to economic problems and long-term wartime needs. Governments had to respond quickly, however, when the war machines failed to achieve their knockout blows and made ever-greater demands for men and matériel. The extension of government power was a logical outgrowth of these needs. Most European countries had already devised some system of mass conscription or military draft. It was now carried to unprecedented heights as countries mobilized tens of millions of young men for that elusive breakthrough to victory. Even countries that continued to rely on volunteers (Great Britain had the largest volunteer army in modern history—one million men—in 1914 and 1915) were forced to resort to conscription, especially to ensure that skilled laborers did not enlist but remained in factories that were important to the production of munitions. In 1916, despite widespread resistance to this extension of government power, compulsory military service was introduced in Great Britain.

Throughout Europe, wartime governments expanded their powers over their economies. Free-market capitalistic systems were temporarily shelved as governments experimented with price, wage, and rent controls, the rationing of food supplies and materials, the regulation of imports and exports, the nation-

BRITISH RECRUITING POSTER. **As the conflict persisted month after month, governments resorted to active propaganda campaigns to generate enthusiasm for the war. In this British recruiting poster, the government tried to pressure men into volunteering for military service. By 1916, the British were forced to adopt compulsory military service.**

alization of transportation systems and industries, and compulsory labor employment. In effect, in order to mobilize the entire resources of their nations for the war effort, European nations had moved toward planned economies directed by government agencies. Under total war mobilization, the distinction between soldiers at war and civilians at home was narrowed. In the view of political leaders, all citizens constituted a national army dedicated to victory. As the American president Woodrow Wilson expressed it, the men and women "who remain to till the soil and man the factories are no less a part of the army than the men beneath the battle flags."

As the Great War dragged on and both casualties and privations worsened, internal dissatisfaction replaced the patriotic enthusiasm that had marked the early stages of World War I. By 1916, there were numerous signs that civilian morale was beginning to crack under the pressure of total war. War governments, however, fought back against the growing opposition to the war. Authoritarian regimes, such as those of Germany, Russia, and Austria-Hungary, had always relied on force to subdue their populations. Under the pressures of the war, however, even parliamentary regimes resorted to an expansion of police powers to stifle internal dissent. At the very beginning of the war, the British Parliament passed the Defence of the Realm Act (DORA), which allowed the public authorities to arrest dissenters as traitors. The act was later extended to authorize public officials to censor newspapers by deleting objectional material and even to suspend newspaper publication. In France, government authorities had initially been lenient about public opposition to the war. But by 1917, they began to fear that open opposition to the war might weaken the French will to fight. When Georges Clemenceau became premier near the end of 1917, the lenient French policies came to an end, and basic civil liberties were suppressed for the duration of the war. The editor of an antiwar newspaper was even executed on a charge of treason.

Wartime governments made active use of propaganda to arouse enthusiasm for the war. At the beginning, public officials needed to do little to achieve this goal. The British and French, for example, exaggerated German atrocities in Belgium and found that their citizens were only too willing to believe these accounts. But as the war progressed and morale sagged, governments were forced to devise new techniques for stimulating declining enthusiasm. In one British recruiting poster, for example, a small daughter asked her father, "Daddy, what did YOU do in the Great War?" while her younger brother played with toy soldiers and cannon.

THE SOCIAL IMPACT OF TOTAL WAR

Total war had a significant impact on European society, most visibly by bringing an end to unemployment. The withdrawal of millions of men from the labor market to fight, combined with the heightened demand for wartime products, led to jobs for everyone able to work.

World War I also created new roles for women. With so many men off fighting at the front, women were called on to take over jobs and responsibilities that had not been available to them before. Overall, 1,345,000 women in Britain obtained new jobs or replaced men during the war. Women were also now employed in jobs that had been considered beyond the "capacity of women." These included such occupations as chimney sweeps, truck drivers, farm laborers, and above all, factory workers in heavy industry (see the box on p. 522). Thirty-eight percent of the workers in the Krupp Armaments works in Germany in 1918 were women.

While male workers expressed concern that the employment of females at lower wages would depress their own wages, women began to demand equal pay. The French government passed a law in July 1915 that established a minimum wage for women homeworkers in textiles, an industry that had grown dramatically because of the need for military uniforms. Later in 1917, the government decreed that men and women should receive equal rates for piecework. Despite the noticeable increase in women's wages that resulted from government regulations, women's industrial wages still were not equal to men's wages by the end of the war.

Even worse, women had achieved little real security about their place in the workforce. Both men and women seemed to think that many of the new jobs for women were only temporary, an expectation quite evident in the British poem "War Girls," written in 1916:

There's the girl who clips your ticket for the train,
And the girl who speeds the lift from floor to floor,
There's the girl who does a milk-round in the rain,
And the girl who calls for orders at your door.
Strong, sensible, and fit,
They're out to show their grit,
And tackle jobs with energy and knack.
No longer caged and penned up,
They're going to keep their end up
Till the khaki soldier boys come marching back.[4]

THE BOLSHEVIK REVOLUTION

The Bolsheviks were a small faction of Marxist Social Democrats who had come under the leadership of Vladimir Ulianov, known to the world as V. I. Lenin (1870–1924). Arrested for his revolutionary activity, Lenin was shipped to Siberia. After his release, he chose to go into exile in Switzerland and eventually assumed the leadership of the Bolshevik wing of the Russian Social Democratic Party. Under Lenin's direction, the Bolsheviks became a party dedicated to a violent revolution that would destroy the capitalist system. He believed that a "vanguard" of activists must form a small party of well-disciplined professional revolutionaries to accomplish the task. Between 1900 and 1917, Lenin spent most of his time in Switzerland. When the Provisional Government was formed in March 1917, he believed that an opportunity for the Bolsheviks to seize power had come. In April 1917, with the connivance of the German High Command, who hoped to create disorder in Russia, Lenin was shipped to Russia in a "sealed train" by way of Finland.

Lenin's arrival in Russia on April 3 opened a new stage of the Russian Revolution. Lenin maintained that the soviets of soldiers, workers, and peasants were ready-made instruments of power. The Bolsheviks must work toward gaining control of these groups and then use them to overthrow the Provisional Government. At the same time, the Bolsheviks articulated the discontent and aspirations of the people, promising an end to the war, redistribution of all land to the peasants, the transfer of factories and industries from capitalists to committees of workers, and the relegation of government power from the Provisional Government to the soviets. Three simple slogans summed up the Bolshevik program: "Peace, Land, Bread," "Worker Control of Production," and "All Power to the Soviets."

By the end of October, the Bolsheviks had achieved a slight majority in the Petrograd and

CHRONOLOGY

The Russian Revolution

	1916
Murder of Rasputin	December
	1917
March of women in Petrograd	March 8
General strike in Petrograd	March 10
Establishment of Provisional Government	March 15
Abdication of the tsar	March 15
Formation of Petrograd soviet	March
Arrival of Lenin in Russia	April 3
Bolshevik majority in Petrograd soviet	October
Bolshevik overthrow of Provisional Government	November 6–7
	1918
Treaty of Brest-Litovsk	March 3
Civil war	1918–1921

LENIN ADDRESSING A CROWD. V. I. Lenin was the driving force behind the success of the Bolsheviks in seizing power in Russia and establishing the Union of Soviet Socialist Republics. Here Lenin is seen addressing a rally in Moscow in 1917.

Ten Days That Shook the World: Lenin and the Bolshevik Seizure of Power

John Reed was an American journalist who helped found the American Communist Labor Party. Accused of sedition, he fled the United States and went to Russia. In Ten Days That Shook the World, *Reed left an impassioned eyewitness account of the Russian Revolution. It is apparent from his comments that Reed considered Lenin the indispensable hero of the Bolshevik success.*

John Reed, Ten Days That Shook the World

It was just 8:40 when a thundering wave of cheers announced the entrance of the presidium, with Lenin—great Lenin—among them. A short, stocky figure, with a big head set down in his shoulders, bald and bulging. Little eyes, a snubbish nose, wide, generous mouth, and heavy chin; clean-shaven now, but already beginning to bristle with the well-known beard of his past and future. Dressed in shabby clothes, his trousers much too long for him. Unimpressive, to be the idol of a mob, loved and revered as perhaps few leaders in history have been. A strange popular leader—a leader purely by virtue of intellect; colorless, humorless, uncompromising and detached; without picturesque idiosyncrasies—but with the power of explaining profound ideas in simple terms, of analyzing a concrete situation. And combined with shrewdness, the greatest intellectual audacity. . . .

Now Lenin, gripping the edge of the reading stand, letting his little winking eyes travel over the crowd as he stood there waiting, apparently oblivious to the long-rolling ovation, which lasted several minutes. When it finished, he said simply, "We shall now proceed to construct the Socialist order!" Again that overwhelming human roar.

"The first thing is the adoption of practical measures to realize peace. . . . We shall offer peace to the peoples of all the belligerent countries upon the basis of the Soviet terms—no annexations, no indemnities, and the right of self-determination of peoples. At the same time, according to our promise, we shall publish and repudiate the secret treaties. . . . The question of War and Peace is so clear that I think that I may, without preamble, read the project of a Proclamation to the Peoples of All the Belligerent Countries. . . ."

His great mouth, seeming to smile, opened wide as he spoke; his voice was hoarse—not unpleasantly so, but as if it had hardened that way after years and years of speaking—and went on monotonously, with the effect of being able to go forever. . . . For emphasis he bent forward slightly. No gestures. And before him, a thousand simple faces looking up in intent adoration.

[Reed then reproduces the full text of the Proclamation.]

When the grave thunder of applause had died away, Lenin spoke again: "We propose to the Congress to ratify this declaration. . . . This proposal of peace will meet with resistance on the part of the imperialist governments—we don't fool ourselves on that score. But we hope that revolution will soon break out in all the belligerent countries; that is why we address ourselves especially to the workers of France, England, and Germany. . . ."

"The revolution of November 6th and 7th," he ended, "has opened the era of the Social Revolution. . . . The labor movement, in the name of peace and Socialism, shall win, and fulfill its destiny. . . ."

There was something quiet and powerful in all this, which stirred the souls of men. It was understandable why people believed when Lenin spoke.

Moscow soviets. The number of party members had also grown from 50,000 to 240,000. With Leon Trotsky (1877–1940), a fervid revolutionary, as chairman of the Petrograd soviet, the Bolsheviks were in a position to seize power in the name of the soviets. During the night of November 6, pro-soviet and pro-Bolshevik forces took control of Petrograd under the immensely popular slogan "All Power to the Soviets." The Provisional Government quickly collapsed with little bloodshed. The following night, the all-Russian Congress of Soviets, representing local soviets from all over the country, affirmed the transfer of power. At the second session, the night of November 8, Lenin announced the new Soviet government, the Council of People's Commissars, with himself as its head (see the box above).

But the Bolsheviks, soon renamed the Communists, still had a long way to go. Lenin had promised peace, and that, he realized, was not easy to deliver because of the humiliating losses of Russian territory that it would entail. There was no real choice, however. On March 3, 1918, Lenin signed the Treaty of Brest-Litovsk with Germany and gave up eastern Poland, the Ukraine, Finland, and the Baltic provinces. To his critics, Lenin argued that it made no difference since the spread of socialist revolution throughout Europe would make the treaty largely irrelevant. In any case, he had promised peace to the Russian people; but real peace did not come because the country soon sank into civil war.

CIVIL WAR

There was great opposition to the new Bolshevik or Communist regime, not only from groups loyal to the tsar but also from bourgeois and aristocratic liberals and anti-Leninist socialists. In addition, thousands of Allied troops were eventually sent to different parts of Russia in the hope of bringing Russia back into the war.

Between 1918 and 1921, the Bolshevik (or Red) Army was forced to fight on many fronts. The first serious threat to the Bolsheviks came from Siberia, where a White (anti-Bolshevik) force attacked westward and advanced almost to the Volga River before being stopped. Attacks also came from the Ukrainians in the southeast and from the Baltic regions. In mid-1919, White forces swept through the Ukraine and advanced almost to Moscow. At one point by late 1919, three separate White armies seemed to be closing in on the Bolsheviks but were eventually pushed back. By 1920, the major White forces had been defeated and the Ukraine had been retaken. The next year, the Communist regime regained control over the independent nationalist governments in the Caucasus: Georgia, Russian Armenia, and Azerbaijan.

How had Lenin and the Bolsheviks triumphed over what seemed at one time to be overwhelming forces? For one thing, the Red Army became a well-disciplined and formidable fighting force, largely due to the organizational genius of Leon Trotsky. As commissar of war, Trotsky reinstated the draft and insisted on rigid discipline; soldiers who deserted or refused to obey orders were summarily executed.

The disunity of the anti-Communist forces seriously weakened the efforts of the Whites. Political differences created distrust among the Whites and prevented them from cooperating effectively with each other. Some Whites insisted on restoring the tsarist regime, while others understood that only a more liberal and democratic program had any chance of success. It was difficult enough to achieve military cooperation; political differences made it virtually impossible. The lack of a common goal on the part of the Whites was paralleled by a clear sense of purpose on the part of the Communists. Inspired by their vision of a new socialist order, the Communists had the advantage of possessing that determination that comes from revolutionary fervor and revolutionary convictions.

The Communists also succeeded in translating their revolutionary faith into practical instruments of power. A policy of "war communism," for example, was used to ensure regular supplies for the Red Army. "War communism" included the nationalization of banks and most industries, the forcible requisition of grain from peasants, and the centralization of state administration under Bolshevik control. Another Bolshevik instrument was "revolutionary terror." Although the old tsarist secret police had been abolished, a new Red secret police—known as the Cheka—replaced it. The Red Terror instituted by the Cheka aimed at nothing less than the destruction of all who opposed the new regime. The Red Terror added an element of fear to the Bolshevik regime.

Finally, the intervention of foreign armies enabled the Communists to appeal to the powerful force of Russian patriotism. Although the Allied Powers had intervened initially in Russia to encourage the Russians to remain in the war, the end of the war on November 11, 1918, had made that purpose inconsequential. Nevertheless, Allied troops remained, and even more were sent because Allied countries did not hide their anti-Bolshevik feelings. At one point, more than 100,000 foreign troops, mostly Japanese, British, French, and American, were stationed on Russian soil. These forces rarely engaged in pitched battles, however, nor did they pursue a common strategy, although they did give material assistance to anti-Bolshevik forces. This intervention by the Allies enabled the Communist government to appeal to patriotic Russians to fight the attempts of foreigners to control their country. Allied interference was never substantial enough to win the civil war, but it did serve indirectly to help the Bolshevik cause.

By 1921, the Communists had succeeded in retaining control of Russia. In the course of the civil war, the Bolshevik regime had also transformed Russia into a bureaucratically centralized state dominated by a single party. It was also a state that was largely hostile to the Allied Powers that had sought to assist the Bolsheviks' enemies in the civil war.

CHRONOLOGY

World War I

	1914
Battle of Tannenberg	August 26–30
First Battle of the Marne	September 6–10
Battle of the Masurian Lakes	September 15
Russian, British, and French declaration of war on the Ottoman Empire	November
	1915
Start of Battle of Gallipoli	April 25
Italian declaration of war on Austria-Hungary	May 23
Entry of Bulgaria into the war	September
	1916
Battle of Verdun	February 21–December 18
	1917
German resumption of unrestricted submarine warfare	January
U.S. entry in the war	April 6
	1918
Last German offensive	March 21–July 18
Second Battle of the Marne	July 18
Allied counteroffensive	July 18–November 10
Armistice between Allies and Germany	November 11
	1919
Start of Paris Peace Conference	January 18
Peace of Versailles	June 28

The Last Year of the War

For Germany, the withdrawal of the Russians from the war in March 1918 offered renewed hope for a favorable end to the war. The victory over Russia persuaded Erich Ludendorff, who guided German military operations, and most German leaders to make one final military gamble—a grand offensive in the west to break the military stalemate. The German attack was launched in March and lasted into July, but an Allied counterattack, supported by the arrival of 140,000 fresh American troops, defeated the Germans at the Second Battle of the Marne on July 18. Ludendorff's gamble had failed. With the arrival of two million more American troops on the Continent, Allied forces began making a steady advance toward Germany.

On September 29, 1918, General Ludendorff informed German leaders that the war was lost and demanded that the government sue for peace at once. When German officials discovered that the Allies were unwilling to make peace with the autocratic imperial government, they instituted reforms to set up a liberal government. But these constitutional reforms came too late for the exhausted and angry German people. On November 3, naval units in Kiel mutinied, and within days, councils of workers and soldiers were forming throughout northern Germany and taking over the supervision of civilian and military administrations. William II capitulated to public pressure and abdicated on November 9, and the Socialists under Friedrich Ebert announced the establishment of a republic. Two days later, on November 11, 1918, the new German government agreed to an armistice. The war was over.

◆ The Peace Settlement

In January 1919, the delegations of twenty-seven victorious Allied nations gathered in Paris to conclude a final settlement of the Great War. Over the years, the reasons for fighting World War I had been transformed from selfish national interests to idealistic principles. No one expressed the latter better than Woodrow Wilson. Wilson's proposals for a truly just and lasting peace included "open covenants of peace, openly arrived at" instead of secret diplomacy; the reduction of national armaments to a "point consistent with domestic safety"; and the self-determination of people so that "all well-defined national aspirations shall be accorded the utmost satisfaction." Wilson characterized World War I as a people's war waged against "absolutism and militarism," two scourges of liberty that could be eliminated only by creating democratic governments and a "general association of nations" that would guarantee the "political independence and territorial integrity to great and small states alike" (see the box on p. 528). As the spokesman for a new world order based on democracy and international cooperation, Wilson was enthusiastically cheered by many Europeans when he arrived in Europe for the peace conference.

Wilson soon found, however, that other states at the Paris Peace Conference were guided by considerably more pragmatic motives. The secret treaties and agreements that had been made before the war could not be totally ignored, even if they did conflict with the principle of self-determination enunciated by

Two Voices of Peacemaking: Woodrow Wilson and Georges Clemenceau

When the Allied powers met at Paris in January 1919, it soon became apparent that the victors had different opinions on the kind of peace they expected. The first excerpt is from a speech of Woodrow Wilson in which the American president presented his idealistic goals for a peace based on justice and reconciliation. The French wanted revenge and security. In the second selection, from Georges Clemenceau's Grandeur and Misery of Victory, *the French premier revealed his fundamental dislike and distrust of Germany.*

Woodrow Wilson, May 26, 1917

We are fighting for the liberty, the self-government, and the undictated development of all peoples, and every feature of the settlement that concludes this war must be conceived and executed for that purpose. Wrongs must first be righted and then adequate safeguards must be created to prevent their being committed again. . . .

No people must be forced under sovereignty under which it does not wish to live. No territory must change hands except for the purpose of securing those who inhabit it a fair chance of life and liberty. No indemnities must be insisted on except those that constitute payment for manifest wrongs done. No readjustments of power must be made except such as will tend to secure the future peace of the world and the future welfare and happiness of its peoples.

And then the free peoples of the world must draw together in some common covenant, some genuine and practical cooperation that will in effect combine their force to secure peace and justice in the dealings of nations with one another.

Georges Clemenceau, Grandeur and Misery of Victory

War and peace, with their strong contrasts, alternate against a common background. For the catastrophe of 1914 the Germans are responsible. Only a professional liar would deny this. . . .

I have sometimes penetrated into the sacred cave of the Germanic cult, which is, as every one knows, the *Bierhaus* [beer hall]. A great aisle of massive humanity where there accumulate, amid the fumes of tobacco and beer, the popular rumblings of a nationalism upheld by the sonorous brasses blaring to the heavens the supreme voice of Germany, *Deutschland über alles! Germany above everything!* Men, women, and children, all petrified in reverence before the divine stoneware pot, brows furrowed with irrepressible power, eyes lost in a dream of infinity, mouths twisted by the intensity of willpower, drink in long draughts the celestial hope of vague expectations. These only remain to be realized presently when the chief marked out by Destiny shall have given the word. There you have the ultimate framework of an old but childish race.

Wilson. National interests also complicated the deliberations of the Paris Peace Conference. David Lloyd George, prime minister of Great Britain, had won a decisive electoral victory in December 1918 on a platform of making the Germans pay for this dreadful war.

France's approach to peace was determined primarily by considerations of national security. To Georges Clemenceau, the feisty premier of France who had led his country to victory, the French people had borne the brunt of German aggression. They deserved revenge and security against future German aggression. Clemenceau wanted a demilitarized Germany, vast German reparations to pay for the costs of the war, and a separate Rhineland as a buffer state between France and Germany, demands that Wilson viewed as vindictive and contrary to the principle of national self-determination.

Although twenty-seven nations were represented at the Paris Peace Conference, the most important decisions were made by Wilson, Clemenceau, and Lloyd George. Italy was considered one of the so-called Big Four powers but played a much less important role than the other three countries. Germany, of course, was not invited to attend, and Russia could not do so because of its civil war.

In view of the many conflicting demands at Versailles, it was inevitable that the Big Three would quarrel. Wilson was determined to create a "league of nations" to prevent future wars. Clemenceau and Lloyd George were equally determined to punish Ger-

THE BIG FOUR AT PARIS. Shown here are the Big Four at the Paris Peace Conference: David Lloyd George of Britain, Vittorio Orlando of Italy, Georges Clemenceau of France, and Woodrow Wilson of the United States. Although Italy was considered one of the Big Four powers, Britain, France, and the United States (the Big Three) made the major decisions at the peace conference.

many. In the end, only compromise made it possible to achieve a peace settlement. On January 25, 1919, the conference adopted the principle of a league of nations and Wilson agreed to make compromises on territorial arrangements. Clemenceau also compromised to obtain some guarantees for French security. He renounced France's desire for a separate Rhineland and instead accepted a defensive alliance with Great Britain and the United States. Both states pledged to help France if it were attacked by Germany.

The Treaty of Versailles

The final peace settlement of Paris consisted of five separate treaties with the defeated nations—Germany, Austria and Hungary (now separate nations), Bulgaria, and Turkey. The Treaty of Versailles with Germany, signed on June 28, 1919, was by far the most important one. The Germans considered it a harsh peace and were particularly unhappy with Article 231, the so-called War Guilt Clause, which declared Germany (and Austria) responsible for starting the war and ordered Germany to pay reparations for all the damage to which the Allied governments and their people were subjected as a result of the war "imposed upon them by the aggression of Germany and her allies."

The military and territorial provisions of the treaty also rankled Germans, although they were by no means as harsh as the Germans claimed. Germany had to reduce its army to 100,000 men, cut back its navy, and eliminate its air force. German territorial losses included the cession of Alsace and Lorraine to France and sections of Prussia to the new Polish state (see Map 25.4). German land west and as far as 30 miles east of the Rhine was established as a demilitarized zone and stripped of all armaments or fortifications to serve as a barrier to any future German military moves westward against France. Outraged by the "dictated peace," the new German government complained but accepted the treaty.

The Other Peace Treaties

The separate peace treaties made with the other Central Powers (Austria, Hungary, Bulgaria, and the Ottoman Empire) extensively redrew the map of eastern Europe. Many of these changes merely ratified what the war had already accomplished. Both the German and Russian empires lost considerable territory in eastern Europe, and the Austro-Hungarian Empire disappeared altogether. New nation-states emerged from the lands of these three empires: Finland, Latvia, Estonia, Lithuania, Poland, Czechoslovakia, Austria, and Hungary. Territorial rearrangements were also made in the Balkans. Romania acquired additional lands from Russia, Hungary, and Bulgaria. Serbia formed the nucleus

MAP 25.4 Europe in 1919.

of a new southern Slav state, the kingdom of the Serbs, Croats, and Slovenes (renamed Yugoslavia in 1929).

Although the Paris Peace Conference was supposedly guided by the principle of self-determination, the mixtures of peoples in eastern Europe made it impossible to draw boundaries along neat ethnic lines. As a result of compromises, virtually every eastern European state was left with a minorities problem that could lead to future conflicts. Germans in Poland; Hungarians, Poles, and Germans in Czechoslovakia; and the combination of Serbs, Croats, Slovenes, Macedonians, and Albanians in Yugoslavia all became sources of later conflict.

Yet another centuries-old empire—the Ottoman Empire—was dismembered by the peace settlement after the war. To gain Arab support against the Ottomans during the war, the Allies had promised to recognize the independence of Arab states in the Middle Eastern lands of the Ottoman Empire. But the imperialist habits of Europeans died hard. After the war, France took control of Lebanon and Syria while Britain received Iraq and Palestine. Officially, these acquisitions were called "mandates," meaning that the lands were to be officially administered on behalf of the newly formed League of Nations. The system of mandates could not hide the fact that the principle of national self-determination at the Paris Peace Conference was largely for Europeans.

The peace settlement negotiated at Paris soon came under attack, not only by the defeated Central Powers but also by others who felt that the peacemakers had been shortsighted. Some people, however, thought the peace settlement was the best that could be achieved under the circumstances. Self-determination, they believed, had served reasonably well as a central organizing principle, and the establishment of the League of Nations gave some hope that future conflicts could be resolved peacefully. And yet, within twenty years after the signing of the peace treaties, Europe was again engaged in deadly conflict. As some historians have suggested, perhaps lack of enforcement rather than the structure of the peace may have caused the failure of the peace of 1919.

Successful enforcement of the peace necessitated the active involvement of its principal architects, especially in helping the new German state set up a peaceful and democratic republic. The failure of the U.S. Senate to ratify the Treaty of Versailles, however, meant that the United States never joined the League of Nations. In addition, the Senate also rejected Wilson's defensive alliance with Great Britain and France. Already by the end of 1919, the United States was pursuing policies intended to limit its direct involvement in future European wars.

This retreat had dire consequences. American withdrawal from the defensive alliance with Britain and France led Britain to withdraw as well. By removing itself from European affairs, the United States forced France to stand alone facing its old enemy, leading the embittered nation to take strong actions against Germany that only intensified German resentment. By the end of 1919, it appeared that the peace of 1919 was already beginning to unravel.

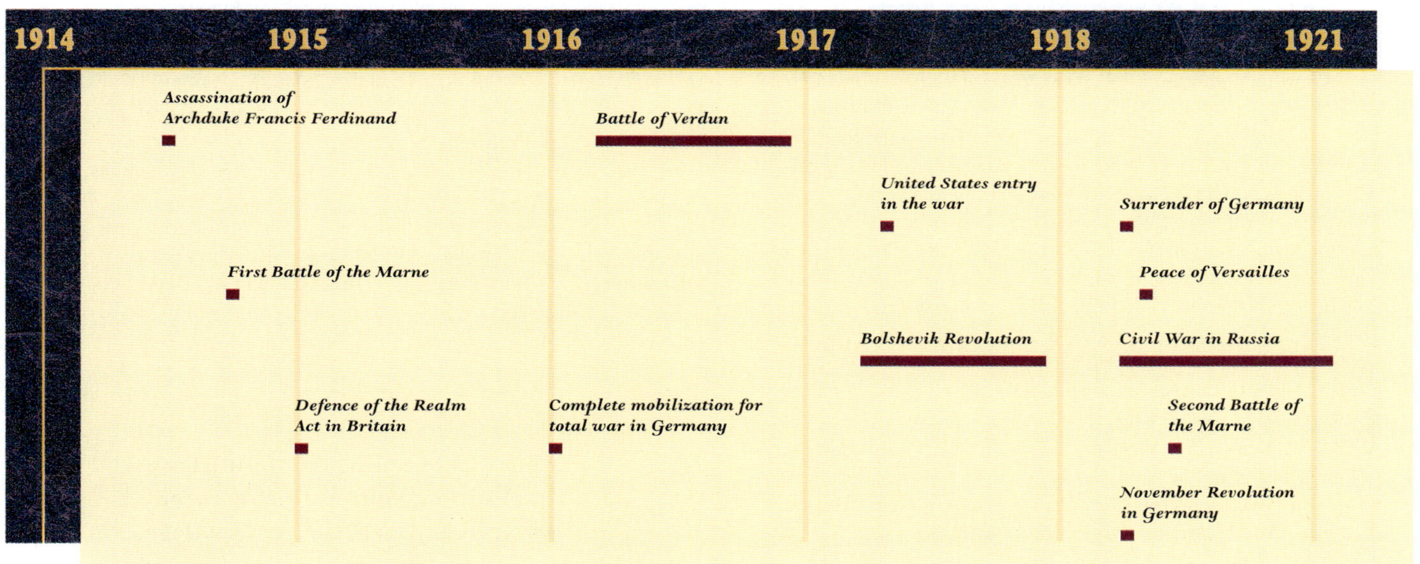

Conclusion

World War I shattered the liberal and rational assumptions of late-nineteenth- and early-twentieth-century Europe. The incredible destruction and the death of almost ten million people undermined the whole idea of progress. New propaganda techniques had manipulated entire populations into sustaining their involvement in a meaningless slaughter.

World War I was a total war and involved a mobilization of resources and populations and increased government centralization of power over the lives of its citizens. Civil liberties, such as freedom of the press, of speech, of assembly, and of movement, were circumscribed in the name of national security. Governments' need to plan the production and distribution of goods and to ration consumer goods restricted economic freedom. Although the late nineteenth and early twentieth centuries had witnessed the extension of government authority into such areas as mass education, social welfare legislation, and mass conscription, World War I made the practice of strong central authority a way of life.

Finally, World War I ended the age of European hegemony over world affairs. In 1917, the Russian Revolution laid the foundation for the creation of a new Soviet power, and the United States entered the war. The termination of the European age was not evident to all, however, for it was clouded by two developments—American isolationism and the withdrawal of the Soviets from world affairs while they nurtured their own socialist system. Although these developments were only temporary, they created a political vacuum in Europe that was filled all too soon by a resurgence of German power.

Notes

1. Arnold Toynbee, *Surviving the Future* (New York, 1971), pp. 106–107.
2. Quoted in Joachim Remak, "1914—The Third Balkan War: Origins Reconsidered," *Journal of Modern History*, 43 (1971): 364–365.
3. Quoted in J. M. Winter, *The Experience of World War I* (New York, 1989), p. 142.
4. Quoted in Catherine W. Reilly, ed., *Scars upon My Heart: Women's Poetry and Verse of the First World War* (London, 1981), p. 90.
5. Quoted in William M. Mandel, *Soviet Women* (Garden City, N.Y., 1975), p. 43.

Suggestions for Further Reading 

The historical literature on the causes of World War I is enormous. Good starting points are J. Joll, *The Origins of the First World War*, 2d ed. (London, 1992), and J. Remak, *The Origins of World War I, 1871–1914*, 2d ed. (Fort Worth, Tex., 1995). The belief that Germany was primarily responsible for the war was argued vigorously by the German scholar F. Fischer in *Germany's Aims in the First World War* (New York, 1967), *World Power or Decline: The Controversy over Germany's Aims in World War I* (New York, 1974), and *War of Illusions: German Policies from 1911 to 1914* (New York, 1975). The role of each great power has been reassessed in a series of books on the causes of World War I: V. R. Berghahn, *Germany and the Approach of War in 1914*, 2d ed. (London, 1993); Z. S. Steiner, *Britain and the Origins of the First World War* (New York, 1977); R. Bosworth, *Italy and the Approach of the First World War* (New York, 1983); J. F. Keiger, *France and the Origins of the First World War* (New York, 1984); and D. C. B. Lieven, *Russia and the Origins of the First World War* (New York, 1984). On the role of militarism, see D. Hermann, *The Arming of Europe and the Making of the First World War* (New York, 1997).

Two good recent accounts of World War I are M. Gilbert, *The First World War* (New York, 1994), and the lavishly illustrated book by J. M. Winter, *The Experience of World War I* (New York, 1989). See also the brief work by N. Heyman, *World War I* (Westport, Conn., 1997). H. Strachan, *The Oxford Illustrated History of the First World War* (New York, 1998), contains an excellent collection of articles. For an account of the military operations of the war, see the classic work by B. H. Liddell Hart, *History of the First World War* (Boston, 1970). The nature of trench warfare is examined in T. Ashworth, *Trench Warfare, 1914–1918: The Live-and-Let-Live System* (London, 1980). The use of poison gas is examined in L. F. Haber, *The Poisonous Cloud: Chemical Warfare in the First World War* (Oxford, 1985). The war at sea is examined in R. Hough, *The Great War at Sea, 1914–18* (Oxford, 1983). For an interesting perspective on World War I and the beginnings of the modern world, see M. Eksteins, *Rites of Spring: The Great War and the Birth of the Modern Age* (Boston, 1989).

On the role of women in World War I, see G. Braybon, *Women Workers in the First World War: The British Experience* (London, 1981); J. M. Winter and R. M. Wall, eds., *The Upheaval of War: Family, Work and Welfare in Europe, 1914–1918* (Cambridge, 1988); G. Braybon and P. Summerfield, *Women's Experiences in Two World Wars* (London, 1987); and M. R. Higonnet, J. Jensen, S. Michel, and M. C. Weitz, *Behind the Lines: Gender and the Two World Wars* (New Haven, Conn., 1987).

A good introduction to the Russian Revolution can be found in R. A. Wade, *The Russian Revolution, 1917* (Cambridge, 2000), and S. Fitzpatrick, *The Russian Revolution, 1917–1932*, 2d ed. (New York, 1994). See also R. Pipes, *The Russian Revolution* (New York, 1990). On Lenin, see R. W. Clark, *Lenin* (New York, 1988), and the valuable work by A. B. Ulam, *The Bolsheviks* (New York, 1965). A comprehensive study of the Russian civil war is W. B. Lincoln, *Red Victory: A History of the Russian Civil War* (New York, 1989).

The role of war aims in shaping the peace settlement is examined in V. H. Rothwell, *British War Aims and Peace Diplomacy, 1914–1918* (Oxford, 1971), and D. R. Stevenson, *French War Aims Against Germany, 1914–1919* (New York, 1982).

World War I and the Russian Revolution are also well covered in two good general surveys of European history in the twentieth century, R. Paxton, *Europe in the Twentieth Century*, 2d ed. (New York, 1985), and A. Rudhart, *Twentieth Century Europe* (Englewood Cliffs, N.J., 1986).

For additional reading, go to InfoTrac College Edition, your online research library at http://webI.infotrac-college.com

Enter the search terms *World War, 1914–1918* using the Subject Guide.

Enter the search terms *Russia Revolution* using Key Terms.

Enter the search term *Bolshevik* using Key Terms.

Enter the search terms *Versailles Treaty* using Key Terms.

C H A P T E R

26

The Futile Search for a New Stability: Europe Between the Wars, 1919–1939

CHAPTER OUTLINE

- An Uncertain Peace: The Search for Security
- The Democratic States
- Retreat from Democracy: The Authoritarian and Totalitarian States
- The Expansion of Mass Culture and Mass Leisure
- Cultural and Intellectual Trends in the Interwar Years
- Conclusion

FOCUS QUESTIONS

- How did France, Great Britain, and the United States respond to the various crises, including the Great Depression, that they faced in the interwar years?
- What conditions led to the emergence of Fascists in Italy and Nazis in Germany, and how did each group attain power?
- What are the characteristics of totalitarian states, and to what degree were these characteristics present in Fascist Italy, Nazi Germany, and Stalinist Russia?
- What new dimensions in mass culture and mass leisure emerged during the interwar years, and what role did these activities play in totalitarian states?
- What were the main cultural and intellectual trends in the interwar years?

ONLY TWENTY YEARS AFTER THE TREATY OF VERSAILLES, Europeans were again at war. And yet in the 1920s, many people assumed that Europe and the world were about to enter a new era of international peace, economic growth, and political democracy. In all of these areas, the optimistic hopes of the 1920s failed to be realized. After 1919, most people wanted peace but were unsure about how to maintain it. The League of Nations, conceived as a new instrument to provide for collective security, failed to work well. New treaties that renounced the use of war looked good on paper but had no means of enforcement. Then, too, virtually everyone favored disarmament, but few could agree on how to achieve it.

At home, Europe faced severe economic problems after World War I. The European economy did not begin to recover from the war until 1922, and even then it was beset by financial problems left over from the war and, most devastating of all, the severe depression that began at the end of 1929. The Great Depression brought untold misery to millions of people. Begging for food on the streets became widespread, especially when soup kitchens were unable to keep up with the demand. Larger and larger numbers of people were homeless and moved from place to place looking for work and shelter. In the United States, the homeless set up shantytowns they named "Hoovervilles" after the American president, Herbert Hoover. In their misery, some people saw but one solution, as one unemployed person expressed it: "Today, when I am experiencing this for the first time, I think that I should prefer to do away with myself, to take gas, to jump into the river, or leap from some high place. . . . Would I really come to such a decision? I do not know. Animals die, plants wither, but men always go on living." Social unrest spread rapidly, and some unemployed staged hunger marches to get attention. In democratic countries, more and more people began to listen to and vote for radical voices calling for extreme measures.

According to Woodrow Wilson, World War I had been fought to make the world safe for democracy, and for a while after 1919, political democracy seemed well established. But the hopes for democracy, too, soon faded as authoritarian regimes spread into Italy and Germany and across eastern Europe.

◆ An Uncertain Peace: The Search for Security

United States president Woodrow Wilson had recognized that the peace treaties ending World War I contained unwise provisions that could serve as new causes for conflicts, and he had placed his hopes for ensuring the future in the League of Nations. The League, however, was not particularly effective in maintaining the peace. The failure of the United States to join the League and the subsequent American retreat into isolationism undermined the League's effectiveness from the very start. Moreover, the League's sole weapon for halting aggression was economic sanctions.

The weakness of the League of Nations and the failure of both the United States and Great Britain to honor their promises to form defensive military alliances with France left France embittered and alone. France's search for security between 1919 and 1924 was founded primarily on a strict enforcement of the Treaty of Versailles. This tough policy toward Germany began with the issue of reparations, the payments that the Germans were to make to compensate for the "damage done to the civilian population of the Allied and Associated Powers and to their property," as the treaty asserted. In April 1921, the Allied Reparations Commission settled on a sum of 132 billion marks ($33 billion) for German reparations, payable in annual installments of 2.5 billion (gold) marks. The new German republic made its first payment in 1921, but by the following year, facing financial problems, it announced that it was unable to pay more. Outraged by what they considered Germany's violation of the peace settlement, the French government sent troops to occupy the Ruhr valley, Germany's chief industrial and mining center. Because the Germans would not pay reparations, the French would collect reparations in kind by operating and using the Ruhr mines and factories.

Both Germany and France suffered from the French occupation of the Ruhr. The German government adopted a policy of passive resistance that was largely financed by printing more paper money, but this only intensified the inflationary pressures that had already appeared in Germany by the end of the war. The German mark soon became worthless. In 1914, a dollar bought 4.2 marks; by the end of November 1923, a single dollar bought an incredible 4.2 trillion marks. Germany faced total economic collapse. The formation of new governments in both Great Britain and France opened the door to conciliatory approaches to Germany and the reparations problem. At the same time, a new German government led by Gustav Stresemann (1878–1929) ended the policy of passive resistance and committed Germany to carry out most of the provisions of the Versailles Treaty while seeking a new settlement of the reparations question.

In August 1924, an international commission produced a new plan for reparations. Named the Dawes plan after the American banker who chaired the commission, it reduced reparations and stabilized Germany's payments on the basis of its ability to pay. The Dawes plan also granted an initial $200 million loan for German recovery, which opened the door to heavy American investments in Europe that helped create a new era of European prosperity between 1924 and 1929.

With prosperity came a new era of European diplomacy. A spirit of international cooperation was fostered by Stresemann, the foreign minister of Germany, and his French counterpart, Aristide Briand (1862–1932), who concluded the Treaty of Locarno in 1925. This guaranteed Germany's new western borders with France and Belgium. Although Germany's new eastern borders with Poland were conspicuously absent from the agreement, the Locarno pact was viewed by many as the beginning of a new era of European peace. On the day after the pact was concluded, the headlines in the *New York Times* ran "France and Germany Ban War Forever," and the London *Times* declared, "Peace at Last."[1]

The spirit of Locarno was based on little real substance, however. Germany lacked the military power to alter its western borders even if it wanted to. And the issue of disarmament soon proved that even the spirit of Locarno could not bring nations to cut back on their weapons. The League of Nations covenant had suggested the "reduction of national armaments to the lowest point consistent with national safety." Germany, of course, had been disarmed with the expectation that other states would do likewise. Numerous disarmament conferences, however, failed to achieve anything substantial as states proved unwilling to trust their security to anyone but their own military forces. When a world disarmament conference finally met in Geneva in 1932, the issue was already dead.

 *The Great Depression*

Two factors played a major role in the coming of the Great Depression: a downturn in domestic economies and an international financial crisis created by the collapse of the American stock market in 1929. Already in the mid-1920s, prices for agricultural goods were beginning to decline rapidly due to overproduction of basic commodities, such as wheat. An increase in the use of oil and hydroelectricity led to a slump in the coal industry even before 1929.

In addition to these domestic economic troubles, much of the European prosperity between 1924 and 1929 had been built on American bank loans to Germany. Twenty-three billion marks had been invested in German municipal bonds and German industries since 1924. In 1928 and 1929, American investors began to pull money out of Germany in order to invest in the booming New York stock market. The crash of the American stock market in October 1929 led panicky American investors to withdraw even more of their funds from Germany and other European markets. The withdrawal of funds seriously weakened the banks of Germany and other central European states. The Credit-Anstalt, Vienna's most prestigious bank, collapsed on May 31, 1931. By that time, trade was slowing down, industrialists were cutting back production, and unemployment was increasing as the ripple effects of international bank failures had a devastating impact on domestic economies.

THE GREAT DEPRESSION: BREAD LINES IN PARIS. The Great Depression devastated the European economy and had serious political repercussions. Because of its more balanced economy, France did not feel the effects of the depression as quickly as other European countries. By 1931, however, even France was experiencing lines of unemployed people at free-food centers.

Economic depression was by no means a new phenomenon in European history. But the depth of the economic downturn after 1929 fully justifies calling it the Great Depression. During 1932, the worst year of the depression, 25 percent of the British and 40 percent of the German labor force was out of work. Between 1929 and 1932, industrial production plummeted almost 50 percent in the United States and more than 40 percent in Germany. The unemployed and homeless filled the streets of the cities throughout the industrialized countries (see the box on p. 537).

The economic crisis also had unexpected social repercussions. Women were often able to secure low-paying jobs as servants, housecleaners, or laundresses while many men remained unemployed, either begging on the streets or remaining at home to do household tasks. This reversal of traditional gender roles caused resentment on the part of many unemployed men, opening them to the shrill cries of demagogues with simple solutions to the economic crisis. High unemployment rates among young males often led them to join gangs that gathered in parks or other public places, spreading fear among local residents.

Governments seemed powerless to deal with the crisis. The classical liberal remedy for depression, a deflationary policy of balanced budgets, which involved cutting costs by lowering wages and raising tariffs to exclude other countries' goods from home markets, served only to worsen the economic crisis and create even greater mass discontent. This in turn led to serious political repercussions. Increased government activity in the economy was one reaction, even in countries like the United States that had a strong laissez-faire tradition. Another effect was a renewed interest in Marxist doctrines since Marx had predicted that capitalism would destroy itself through overproduction. Communism took on new popularity, especially among workers and intellectuals. Finally, the severity of the Great Depression increased the attractiveness of simplistic solutions, especially from a new authoritarian movement known as fascism. Everywhere, democracy seemed on the defensive in the 1930s.

◆ The Democratic States

Woodrow Wilson proclaimed that World War I had been fought to make the world safe for democracy, and in 1919, there seemed to be some justification for that claim. Four major European states and a host of minor ones had established functioning political democracies. In a number of nations, universal male suffrage had been replaced by universal suffrage as male politicians rewarded women for their contributions to World War I by granting them the right to vote (except in Italy, France, and Spain, where women had to wait until the end of World War II).

After World War I, Great Britain went through a period of painful readjustment and serious economic difficulties. During the war, Britain had lost many of the markets for its industrial products, especially to the United States and Japan. The postwar decline of such staple industries as coal, steel, and textiles led to a rise in unemployment, which reached the two million mark in 1921. But Britain soon rebounded and from 1925 to 1929 experienced an era of renewed prosperity.

By 1929, Britain faced the growing effects of the Great Depression. The Labour Party, now the largest party in Britain, failed to solve the nation's economic problems and fell from power in 1931. A national government (a coalition of Liberals, Conservatives, and Labour) claimed credit for bringing Britain out of the worst stages of the depression, primarily by using the traditional policies of balanced budgets and protective tariffs. British politicians largely ignored the new ideas of a Cambridge economist, John Maynard Keynes (1883–1946), who published his *General Theory of Employment, Interest, and Money* in 1936. He condemned the traditional view that in a free economy, depressions should be left to work themselves out. Instead, Keynes argued that unemployment stemmed not from overproduction but from a decline in demand and that demand could be increased by public works, financed, if necessary, through deficit spending to stimulate production.

After the defeat of Germany, France had become the strongest power on the European continent. Its greatest need was to rebuild the areas of northern and eastern France that had been devastated in World War I. But no French government seemed capable of solving France's financial problems between 1921 and 1926. Like other European countries, though, France did experience a period of relative prosperity between 1926 and 1929. By 1932, France began to feel the full effects of the Great Depression, and economic instability soon had political repercussions. During a nineteen-month period in 1932 and 1933, six different cabinets were formed as France faced political chaos. Finally, in 1936, fearful that rightists intended to seize power, a coalition of leftist parties—Communists, Socialists, and Radicals—formed a Popular Front government in June 1936.

The Popular Front succeeded in initiating a program for workers that established the right of collec-

The Great Depression: Unemployed and Homeless in Germany

In 1932, Germany had six million unemployed workers, many of them wandering aimlessly through the country, begging for food and seeking shelter in city lodgings for the homeless. The Great Depression was an important factor in the rise to power of Adolf Hitler and the Nazis. This selection presents a description of unemployed homeless in 1932.

Heinrich Hauser, "With Germany's Unemployed"

An almost unbroken chain of homeless men extends the whole length of the great Hamburg-Berlin highway. . . . All the highways in Germany over which I have traveled this year presented the same aspect. . . .

Most of the hikers paid no attention to me. They walked separately or in small groups, with their eyes on the ground. And they had the queer, stumbling gait of barefooted people, for their shoes were slung over their shoulders. . . . [most of them were] unskilled young people, for the most part, who had been unable to find a place for themselves in any city or town in Germany, and who had never had a job and never expected to have one. There was something else that had never been seen before—whole families that had piled all their goods into baby carriages and wheelbarrows that they were pushing along as they plodded forward in dumb despair. It was a whole nation on the march.

I saw them—and this was the strongest impression that the year 1932 left with me—I saw them, gathered into groups of fifty or a hundred men, attacking fields of potatoes. I saw them digging up the potatoes and throwing them into sacks while the farmer who owned the field watched them in despair and the local policeman looked on gloomily from the distance. I saw them staggering toward the lights of the city as night fell, with their sacks on their backs. What did it remind me of? Of the War, of the worst periods of starvation in 1917 and 1918, but even then people paid for the potatoes. . . .

I know what it is to be a tramp. I know what cold and hunger are. . . . But there are two things that I have only recently experienced—begging and spending the night in a municipal lodging house.

I entered the huge Berlin municipal lodging house in a northern quarter of the city. . . .

Distribution of spoons, distribution of enameledware bowls with the words "Property of the City of Berlin" written on their sides. Then the meal itself. A big kettle is carried. Men with yellow smocks have brought it in and men with yellow smocks ladle out the food. These men, too, are homeless and they have been expressly picked by the establishment and given free food and lodging and a little pocket money in exchange for their work about the house.

Where have I seen this kind of food distribution before? In a prison that I once helped to guard in the winter of 1919 during the German civil war. There was the same hunger then, the same trembling, anxious expectation of rations. Now the men are standing in a long row, dressed in their plain nightshirts that reach to the ground, and the noise of their shuffling feet is like the noise of big wild animals walking up and down the stone floor of their cages before feeding time. The men lean far over the kettle so that the warm steam from the food envelops them and they hold out their bowls as if begging and whisper to the attendant, "Give me a real helping. Give me a little more." A piece of bread is handed out with every bowl.

My next recollection is sitting at a table in another room on a crowded bench that is like a seat in a fourth-class railway carriage. Hundreds of hungry mouths make an enormous noise eating their food. The men sit bent over their food like animals who feel that someone is going to take it away from them. They hold their bowl with their left arm part way around it, so that nobody can take it away, and they also protect it with their other elbow and with their head and mouth, while they move the spoon as fast as they can between their mouth and the bowl.

tive bargaining, a forty-hour workweek, two-week paid vacations, and minimum wages. The Popular Front's policies failed to solve the problems of the depression, however. By 1938, the French were experiencing a serious decline of confidence in their political system that left them unprepared to deal with their aggressive enemy to the east, Nazi Germany.

With the exception of Germany, no Western nation was more affected by the Great Depression than the United States. By the end of 1932, industrial production had fallen to 50 percent of what it had been in 1929. Soon there were fifteen million unemployed. Under these circumstances, the Democrat Franklin Delano Roosevelt (1882–1945) won the 1932 presidential election by a landslide. He and his advisers pursued a policy of active government intervention in the economy that came to be known as the New Deal, which included a stepped-up program of public works, such as the Works Progress Administration (WPA), established in 1935. This government organization put between two and three million people to work building bridges, roads, post offices, and airports. The Roosevelt administration was also responsible for social legislation that launched the American welfare state. In 1935, the Social Security Act created a system of old-age pensions and unemployment insurance.

No doubt the New Deal provided some social reform measures that perhaps averted the possibility of social revolution in the United States. It did not, however, solve the unemployment problems of the Great Depression. In May 1937, during what was considered a period of full recovery, American unemployment still stood at seven million; by the following year, it had increased to eleven million. Only World War II and the subsequent growth of armament-related industries brought American workers back to full employment.

Retreat from Democracy: The Authoritarian and Totalitarian States

The apparent triumph of liberal democracy in 1919 proved extremely short-lived. By 1939, only two major states in Europe, France and Great Britain, remained democratic. Italy and Germany had succumbed to the political movement called fascism, while the Soviet Union, under Stalin, had moved toward a repressive totalitarian state. A host of other European nations, especially in eastern Europe, adopted authoritarian structures of various kinds.

The dictatorial regimes between the wars assumed both old and new forms. Dictatorship was not new, but the modern totalitarian state was. The totalitarian regimes, best exemplified by Stalinist Russia and Nazi Germany, extended the functions and powers of the central state far beyond what they had been in the past. The modern totalitarian state moved beyond the ideal of passive obedience expected in a traditional dictatorship or authoritarian monarchy. The new "total states" expected the active commitment of citizens to the regime's goals. They used modern mass propaganda techniques and high-speed communication media to conquer the minds and hearts of their subjects. The total state aimed to control not only the economic, political, and social aspects of life but the intellectual and cultural aspects as well. That control had a purpose: the involvement of the masses in the achievement of the regime's goals, whether they be war or a thousand-year Reich (empire).

The modern totalitarian state was to be led by a single leader and a single party. It ruthlessly rejected the liberal ideal of limited government power and constitutional guarantees of individual freedoms. Indeed, individual freedom was to be subordinated to the collective will of the masses, organized and determined for them by their leader. Modern technology also gave total states unprecedented police controls to enforce their wishes on their subjects. The fascist states—Italy and Germany—as well as Stalin's Soviet Union have all been labeled totalitarian, although their regimes exhibited significant differences and met with varying degrees of success.

Fascist Italy

In the early 1920s, in the wake of economic turmoil, political disorder, and the general insecurity and fear stemming from World War I, Benito Mussolini burst on the Italian scene with the first fascist movement in Europe. Mussolini (1883–1945) began his political career as a socialist but was expelled from the Socialist Party after supporting Italy's entry into World War I, a position contrary to the socialist position of ardent neutrality. In 1919, Mussolini established a new political group, the *Fascio di Combattimento,* or League of Combat. It received little attention in the elections of 1919, but political stalemate in Italy's parliamentary system and strong nationalist sentiment saved Mussolini and the Fascists.

The new parliament elected in November quickly proved incapable of governing Italy. The three major parties were unable to form an effective governmental coalition, and the Socialists, now the largest party, spoke theoretically of the need for revolution and alarmed conservatives, who quickly associated them with Bolsheviks or Communists. Thousands of industrial and agricultural strikes in 1919 and 1920 created a climate of class warfare and continual violence. In 1920 and 1921, bands of armed Fascists called *squadristi* were formed and turned loose in attacks on socialist offices and newspapers. Strikes by trade unionists and socialist workers and peasant leagues were broken up by force. Mussolini's Fascist movement began to gain support from middle-class industrialists fearful of working-class agitation and large landowners who objected to the agricultural strikes. Mussolini also perceived that Italians were angry over the failure of Italy to receive more territorial acquisitions after World War I. By 1922, the movement began to mushroom as Mussolini's nationalist rhetoric and the middle-class fear of socialism, Communist revolution, and disorder made the Fascists seem attractive. On October 29, 1922, after Mussolini and the Fascists threatened to march on Rome if they were not given power, King Victor Emmanuel III (1900–1946) capitulated and made Mussolini prime minister of Italy.

MUSSOLINI AND THE ITALIAN FASCIST STATE

By 1926, Mussolini had established his Fascist dictatorship. Press laws gave the government the right to suspend any publications that fostered disrespect for the Catholic church, the monarchy, or the state. The prime minister was made "head of government," with the power to legislate by decree. A police law empowered the police to arrest and confine anybody for political or nonpolitical crimes without due process of law. In 1926, all antifascist parties were outlawed, and a secret police force, known as the OVRA, was established. By the end of 1926, Mussolini ruled Italy as *Il Duce*, "the leader."

Mussolini conceived of the Fascist state as totalitarian: "Fascism is totalitarian, and the Fascist State, the synthesis and unity of all values, interprets, develops and gives strength to the whole life of the people."[2] Mussolini did try to create a totalitarian apparatus for police surveillance and for controlling mass communications, but this machinery was not particularly effective. Police activities in Italy were never as repressive, efficient, or savage as those of Nazi Germany. Likewise, the Italian Fascists' attempt to exercise control over all forms of mass media, including newspapers, radio, and cinema, in order to use propaganda as an instrument to integrate the masses into the state failed to achieve its major goals. Most commonly, Fascist propaganda was disseminated through simple slogans, such as "Mussolini is always right," plastered on walls all over Italy.

Mussolini and the Fascists also attempted to mold Italians into a single-minded community by developing Fascist organizations. Because the secondary schools maintained considerable freedom from Fascist control, the regime relied more and more on the activities of Fascist youth organizations, known as the Young Fascists, to indoctrinate the young people of the nation in Fascist ideals. By 1939, nearly seven

MUSSOLINI—THE IRON *DUCE*. **One of Mussolini's favorite images of himself was that of the iron *Duce*—the strong leader who is always right. Consequently, he was often seen in military-style uniforms and military poses. This photograph shows Mussolini in one of his numerous uniforms with his Black Shirt bodyguards giving the Fascist salute.**

million children and young adults of both sexes—two-thirds of the population between eight and eighteen—were enrolled in some kind of Fascist youth group. Activities for these groups included Saturday afternoon marching drills and calisthenics, seaside and mountain summer camps, and youth contests. Beginning in the 1930s, all male groups were given premilitary exercises to develop discipline and provide training for war. Results were mixed. Italian teenagers, who liked neither military training nor routine discipline of any kind, simply refused to attend Fascist youth group meetings on a regular basis.

The Fascist organizations hoped to create a new Italian, hardworking, physically fit, disciplined, intellectually sharp, and martially inclined. In practice, the Fascists largely reinforced traditional social attitudes in Italy, as is evident in their policies regarding women. The Fascists portrayed the family as the pillar of the state and women as the basic foundation of the family. "Woman into the home" became the Fascist slogan. Women were to be homemakers and baby producers, "their natural and fundamental mission in life," according to Mussolini, who viewed population growth as an indicator of national strength. Employment outside the home distracted women from conception. "It forms an independence and consequent physical and moral habits contrary to child bearing."[3] A practical consideration also underlay the Fascist attitude toward women: eliminating women from the job market reduced male unemployment figures in the depression economy of the 1930s.

Despite the instruments of repression, the use of propaganda, and the creation of numerous Fascist organizations, Mussolini never achieved the degree of totalitarian control accomplished in Hitler's Germany or Stalin's Soviet Union. Mussolini and the Fascist party never really destroyed the old power structure. Some institutions, including the armed forces and the monarchy, were never absorbed into the Fascist state and managed to maintain their independence. Mussolini had boasted that he would help workers and peasants, but instead he generally allied himself with the interests of industrialists and large landowners at the expense of the lower classes.

Even more indicative of Mussolini's compromise with the traditional institutions of Italy was his attempt to gain the support of the Catholic church. In the Lateran Accords of February 1929, Mussolini's regime recognized the sovereign independence of a small enclave of 109 acres in Rome, known as Vatican City, which had remained in the church's possession since unification in 1870; in return, the papacy recognized the Italian state. The Lateran Accords also guaranteed the church a large grant of money and recognized Catholicism as the "sole religion of the state." In return, the Catholic church urged Italians to support the Fascist regime.

CHRONOLOGY

Fascist Italy

Creation of *Fascio di Combattimento*	1919
Squadristi violence	1920–1921
Mussolini as prime minister	1922 (October 29)
Establishment of Fascist dictatorship	1925–1926
Lateran Accords with Catholic church	1929

In all areas of Italian life under Mussolini and the Fascists, there was a dichotomy between Fascist ideals and practice. The Italian Fascists promised much but actually delivered considerably less, and they were soon overshadowed by a much more powerful fascist movement to the north.

Hitler and Nazi Germany

In 1923, a small, south German rightist party known as the Nazis, led by an obscure Austrian rabble-rouser named Adolf Hitler, created a stir when it tried to seize power in southern Germany. Although the attempt failed, Hitler and the Nazis achieved sudden national prominence. Within ten years, Hitler and his party had taken over complete power.

WEIMAR GERMANY AND THE RISE OF THE NAZIS

After Germany's defeat in World War I, a German democratic state known as the Weimar Republic was established. From its beginnings, the Weimar Republic was plagued by a series of problems. The republic had no truly outstanding political leaders. In 1925, Paul von Hindenburg (1847–1934), a World War I military hero, was elected president. Hindenburg was a traditional military man, monarchist in sentiment, who at heart was not in favor of the republic. The young republic also suffered politically from attempted uprisings and attacks from both the left and right.

The Weimar Republic also faced serious economic difficulties. As Germany fell into the spiral of runaway inflation in 1922 and 1923, widows, orphans, the retired elderly, army officers, teachers, civil servants, and others who lived on fixed incomes all watched their monthly stipends become worthless or their lifetime savings disappear. Their economic losses increasingly pushed the middle class toward rightist parties that were hostile to the republic. To make matters worse, after a period of prosperity from 1924 to 1929, the Great Depression hit Germany hard. Unemployment increased to 4.38 million by December 1930. The depression fanned social discontent and fear and paved the way for extremist parties. The political, economic, and social problems of the Weimar Republic provided an environment in which Hitler and the Nazis were able to rise to power.

Born on April 20, 1889, Adolf Hitler was the son of an Austrian customs official. He was a total failure in secondary school and eventually made his way to Vienna to become an artist. In Vienna, Hitler established the basic ideas of an ideology from which he never deviated for the rest of his life. At the core of Hitler's ideas was racism, especially anti-Semitism. His hatred of the Jews lasted to the very end of his life. Hitler had also become an extreme German nationalist who had learned from the mass politics of Vienna how political parties could effectively use propaganda and terror. Finally, in his Viennese years, Hitler also came to a firm belief in the need for struggle, which he saw as the "granite foundation of the world."

At the end of World War I, after four years of service on the Western Front, Hitler went to Munich and decided to enter politics. He joined the obscure German Workers' Party, one of a number of right-wing extreme nationalist parties in Munich. By the summer of 1921, Hitler had assumed control of the party, which he renamed the National Socialist German Workers' Party (NSDAP), or Nazi for short. His idea was that the party's name would distinguish the Nazis from the socialist parties while gaining support from both working-class and nationalist circles. Hitler worked assiduously to develop the party into a mass political movement with flags, party badges, uniforms, its own newspaper, and its own police force or party militia known as the SA, the *Sturmabteilung*, or Storm Troops. The SA was used to defend the party in meeting halls and break up the meetings of other parties. Hitler's own oratorical skills were largely responsible for attracting an increasing number of followers. By 1923, the party had grown from its early hundreds into a membership of 55,000, with 15,000 SA members.

Overconfident, Hitler staged an armed uprising against the government in Munich in November 1923. The so-called Beer Hall Putsch was quickly crushed, and Hitler was sentenced to prison. During his brief stay in jail, Hitler wrote *Mein Kampf (My Struggle)*, an autobiographical account of his movement and its underlying ideology. Extreme German nationalism, virulent anti-Semitism, and vicious anticommunism are linked by a Social Darwinian theory of struggle that stresses the right of superior nations to *Lebensraum* (living space) through expansion and the right of superior individuals to secure authoritarian leadership over the masses.

During his imprisonment, Hitler also came to the realization that the Nazis would have to come to power by constitutional means, not by overthrowing the Weimar Republic. This implied the formation of a mass political party that would actively compete for votes with the other political parties. After his release from prison, Hitler worked to build such a party. He reorganized the Nazi party on a regional basis and expanded it to all parts of Germany. By 1929, the Nazi party had a national party organization. It also grew from 27,000 members in 1925 to 178,000 by the end of 1929. Especially noticeable was the youthfulness of the regional, district, and branch leaders of the Nazi organization. Many were under thirty and were fiercely committed to Hitler because he gave them the kind of active politics they sought. Rather than democratic debate, they wanted brawls in beer halls, enthusiastic speeches, and comradeship in the building of a new Germany. One new, young Nazi member expressed his excitement about the party:

> For me this was the start of a completely new life. There was only one thing in the world for me and that was service in the movement. All my thoughts were centred on the movement. I could talk only politics. I was no longer aware of anything else. At the time I was a promising athlete; I was very keen on sport, and it was going to be my career. But I had to give this up too. My only interest was agitation and propaganda.[4]

Such youthful enthusiasm gave the Nazi movement an aura of a "young man's movement" and a sense of dynamism that the other parties could not match.

By 1932, the Nazi party had 800,000 members and had become the largest party in the Reichstag. No doubt Germany's economic difficulties were a crucial factor in the Nazi rise to power. Unemployment rose dramatically, from 4.35 million in 1931 to 6 million by the winter of 1932. The economic and psychological impact of the Great Depression made extremist parties more attractive. The Nazis were especially effective in developing modern electioneering

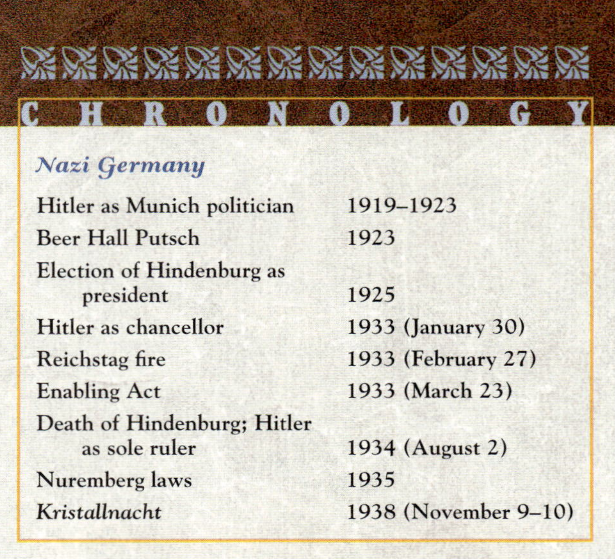
CHRONOLOGY

Nazi Germany

Hitler as Munich politician	1919–1923
Beer Hall Putsch	1923
Election of Hindenburg as president	1925
Hitler as chancellor	1933 (January 30)
Reichstag fire	1933 (February 27)
Enabling Act	1933 (March 23)
Death of Hindenburg; Hitler as sole ruler	1934 (August 2)
Nuremberg laws	1935
Kristallnacht	1938 (November 9–10)

techniques. In their election campaigns, party members pitched their themes to the needs and fears of different social groups. In working-class districts, for example, the Nazis attacked international high finance, but in middle-class neighborhoods, they exploited fears of a Communist revolution and its threat to private property. At the same time that the Nazis made blatant appeals to class interests, they were denouncing conflicts of interest and maintaining that they stood above classes and parties. Hitler, in particular, claimed to stand above all differences and promised to create a new Germany free of class differences and party infighting. His appeal to national pride, national honor, and traditional militarism struck chords of emotion in his listeners.

Increasingly, the right-wing elites of Germany—the industrial magnates, landed aristocrats, military establishment, and higher bureaucrats—began to see Hitler as the man who had the mass support to establish a right-wing, authoritarian regime that would save Germany and their privileged positions from a Communist takeover. Under pressure, President Hindenburg agreed to allow Hitler to become chancellor (on January 30, 1933) and form a new government.

Within two months, Hitler had laid the foundations for the Nazis' complete control over Germany. On the day after a fire broke out in the Reichstag building (February 27), supposedly caused by the Communists, Hitler convinced President Hindenburg to issue a decree that gave the government emergency powers. It suspended all basic rights of the citizens for the full duration of the emergency, thus enabling the Nazis to arrest and imprison anyone without redress. The crowning step of Hitler's "legal seizure" of power came on March 23 when a two-thirds vote of the Reichstag passed the Enabling Act, which empowered the government to dispense with constitutional forms for four years while it issued laws that would deal with the country's problems. The Enabling Act provided the legal basis for Hitler's subsequent actions. He no longer needed either the Reichstag or President Hindenburg. In effect, Hitler became a dictator appointed by the parliamentary body itself.

With their new source of power, the Nazis acted quickly to enforce *Gleichschaltung*, the coordination of all institutions under Nazi control. The civil service was purged of Jews and democratic elements, concentration camps were established for opponents of the new regime, the autonomy of the federal states was eliminated, trade unions were dissolved, and all political parties except the Nazis were abolished. By the end of the summer of 1933, within seven months of being appointed chancellor, Hitler and the Nazis had established the foundations for a totalitarian state. When Hindenburg died on August 2, 1934, the office of Reich president was abolished, and Hitler became sole ruler of Germany. Public officials and soldiers were all required to take a personal oath of loyalty to Hitler as the "Führer [leader] of the German Reich and people."

THE NAZI STATE, 1933–1939

Having demolished the parliamentary state, Hitler now felt that the real task was at hand: to develop the "total state." Hitler's aims had not been simply power for power's sake; he had larger ideological goals. The development of an Aryan racial state that would dominate Europe and possibly the world for generations to come required a movement in which the German people would be actively involved, not passively cowed by force. Hitler stated:

> We must develop organizations in which an individual's entire life can take place. Then every activity and every need of every individual will be regulated by the collectivity represented by the party. There is no longer any arbitrary will, there are no longer any free realms in which the individual belongs to himself. . . . The time of personal happiness is over.[5]

The Nazis pursued the creation of this totalitarian state in a variety of ways.

Mass demonstrations and spectacles were employed to integrate the German nation into a collective fellowship and to mobilize it as an instrument for Hitler's policies (see the box on p. 544). These mass demonstrations, especially the Nuremberg party rallies that were held every September, combined the symbolism of a religious service with the merriment of a popular amusement. They had great appeal and usually evoked mass enthusiasm and excitement.

Some features of the state apparatus of Hitler's total state seem contradictory. One usually thinks of Nazi Germany as having an all-powerful government that maintained absolute control and order. In truth, Nazi Germany was the scene of almost constant personal and institutional conflict, which resulted in administrative chaos. In matters such as foreign policy, education, and economics, parallel government and party bureaucracies competed over spheres of influence. Incessant struggle characterized relationships within the party, within the state, and between party and state. By fostering rivalry within the party and between party and state, Hitler became the ultimate decision maker.

In the economic sphere, Hitler and the Nazis also established control. Although the regime pursued the use of public works projects and "pump-priming" grants to private construction firms to foster employment and end the depression, there is little doubt that rearmament was a far more important contributor to solving the unemployment problem. Unemployment dropped to 2.6 million in 1934 and less than 500,000 in 1937. The regime claimed full credit for solving Germany's economic woes, an important factor that led many Germans to accept the new regime, despite its excesses.

For those who needed coercion, the Nazi total state had its instruments of terror and repression. Especially important was the SS. Originally created as Hitler's personal bodyguard, the SS, under the direction of Heinrich Himmler (1900–1945), came to control all of the regular and secret police forces. Himmler and the SS functioned on the basis of two principles: terror and ideology. Terror included the instruments of repression and murder: the secret police, criminal police, concentration camps, and later the execution squads and death camps for the extermination of the Jews. For Himmler, the primary goal of the SS was to further the Aryan master race. SS members, who constituted a carefully chosen elite, were thoroughly indoctrinated in racial ideology.

Other institutions, such as the Catholic and Protestant churches, primary and secondary schools, and universities, were also brought under the control of the Nazi total state. Nazi professional organizations and leagues were formed for civil servants, teachers, women, farmers, doctors, and lawyers. Because the early indoctrination of the youth would create the foundation for a strong totalitarian state for the future, youth organizations, the *Hitler Jugend* (Hitler Youth) and its female counterpart, the *Bund deutscher Mädel* (League of German Maidens), were given special attention. The oath required of Hitler Youth members demonstrates the degree of dedication expected of youth in the Nazi state: "In the presence of this blood banner, which represents our Führer, I swear to devote all my energies and my strength to the savior of our country, Adolf Hitler. I am willing and ready to give up my life for him, so help me God."

THE NAZI MASS SPECTACLE. Hitler and the Nazis made clever use of mass spectacles to rally the German people behind the Nazi regime. These mass demonstrations evoked intense enthusiasm, as is evident in this photograph of Hitler arriving at the Bückeberg near Hamelin for the Harvest Festival in 1937. Almost one million people were present for the celebration.

Propaganda and Mass Meetings in Nazi Germany

Propaganda and mass rallies were two of the chief instruments that Hitler used to prepare the German people for the tasks he set before them. In the first selection, taken from Mein Kampf, *Hitler explains the psychological importance of mass meetings in creating support for a political movement. In the second excerpt, taken from his speech to a crowd at Nuremberg, he describes the kind of mystical bond he hoped to create through his mass rallies.*

Adolf Hitler, Mein Kampf

The mass meeting is also necessary for the reason that in it the individual, who at first, while becoming a supporter of a young movement, feels lonely and easily succumbs to the fear of being alone, for the first time gets the picture of a larger community, which in most people has a strengthening, encouraging effect. . . . When from his little workshop or big factory, in which he feels very small, he steps for the first time into a mass meeting and has thousands and thousands of people of the same opinions around him, when, as a seeker, he is swept away by three or four thousand others into the mighty effect of suggestive intoxication and enthusiasm, when the visible success and agreement of thousands confirm to him the rightness of the new doctrine and for the first time arouse doubt in the truth of his previous conviction—then he himself has succumbed to the magic influence of what we designate as "mass suggestion." The will, the longing, and also the power of thousands are accumulated in every individual. The man who enters such a meeting doubting and wavering leaves it inwardly reinforced: he has become a link in the community.

Adolf Hitler, Speech at the Nuremberg Party Rally, 1936

Do we not feel once again in this hour the miracle that brought us together? Once you heard the voice of a man, and it struck deep into your hearts; it awakened you, and you followed this voice. Year after year you went after it, though him who had spoken you never even saw. You heard only a voice, and you followed it. When we meet each other here, the wonder of our coming together fills us all. Not everyone of you sees me, and I do not see everyone of you. But I feel you, and you feel me. It is the belief in our people that has made us small men great, that has made us poor men rich, that has made brave and courageous men out of us wavering, spiritless, timid folk; this belief made us see our road when we were astray; it joined us together into one whole! . . . You come, that . . . you may, once in a while, gain the feeling that now we are together; we are with him and he with us, and we are now Germany!

The creation of the Nazi total state also had an impact on women. The Nazi attitude toward women was largely determined by ideological considerations. Women played a crucial role in the Aryan racial state as bearers of the children who would bring about the triumph of the Aryan race. To the Nazis, the differences between men and women were quite natural. Men were warriors and political leaders, while women were destined to be wives and mothers. Motherhood was also exalted in an annual ceremony on August 12, Hitler's mother's birthday, when Hitler awarded the German Mother's Cross to a select group of German mothers. Those with four children received a bronze cross, those with six a silver cross, and those with eight or more a gold cross.

Nazi ideas determined employment opportunities for women. The Nazis hoped to drive women out of heavy industry or other jobs that might hinder women from bearing healthy children, as well as certain professions, including university teaching, law, and medicine, which were considered inappropriate for women, especially married women. The Nazis encouraged women to pursue professional occupations that had direct practical application, such as social work and nursing. In addition to restrictive legislation against females, the Nazi regime pushed its campaign against working women with such poster slogans as "Get hold of pots and pans and broom and sooner you will find a groom!"

The Nazi total state was intended to be an Aryan racial state. From its beginning, the Nazi party embraced the strong anti-Semitic beliefs of Adolf Hitler. Once in power, the Nazis translated anti-Semitic ideas into anti-Semitic policies. In September 1935, the Nazis announced new racial laws at the annual party rally in Nuremberg. These "Nuremberg laws" excluded German Jews from German citizenship, forbade marriages and extramarital relations between Jews and German citizens, and essentially separated Jews from the Germans politically, socially, and legally. They were the natural extension of Hitler's stress on the superiority of the pure Aryan race.

Another considerably more violent phase of anti-Jewish activity took place in 1938 and 1939; it was initiated on November 9–10, 1938, the infamous *Kristallnacht,* or Night of Shattered Glass. The assassination of a third secretary in the German embassy in Paris by a Polish Jew became the occasion for a Nazi-led destructive rampage against the Jews in which synagogues were burned, seven thousand Jewish businesses were destroyed, and at least one hundred Jews were killed. Moreover, thirty thousand Jewish males were rounded up and sent to concentration camps. *Kristallnacht* also led to further drastic steps. Jews were barred from all public buildings and prohibited from owning, managing, or working in any retail store. Finally, under the direction of the SS, Jews were encouraged to "emigrate from Germany." After the outbreak of World War II, the policy of emigration was replaced by a more gruesome one.

The Soviet Union

Yet another example of totalitarianism was to be found in the Soviet Union. The civil war in Russia had taken an enormous toll of life. Drought, which caused a great famine between 1920 and 1922, claimed as many as five million lives. Industrial collapse paralleled the agricultural disaster. By 1921, industrial output was only 20 percent of its 1913 level. Russia was exhausted. As Leon Trotsky said, "The collapse of the productive forces surpassed anything of the kind that history had ever seen. The country, and the government with it, were at the very edge of the abyss."[6]

In March 1921, Lenin pulled Russia back from the abyss by establishing his New Economic Policy (NEP). Lenin's New Economic Policy was a modified version of the old capitalist system. Peasants were now allowed to sell their produce openly, and retail stores and small industries that employed fewer than twenty employees could now operate under private ownership; heavy industry, banking, and mines remained in the hands of the government. In 1922, Lenin and the Communists formally created a new state called the Union of Soviet Socialist Republics, known by its initials as the U.S.S.R. and commonly called the Soviet Union. Already by that year, a revived market and a good harvest had brought the famine to an end; Soviet agriculture climbed to 75 percent of its prewar level. Industry, especially state-owned heavy industry, fared less well and continued to stagnate. Overall, the NEP had saved the Soviet Union from complete economic disaster even though Lenin and other leading Communists intended it to be only a temporary, tactical retreat from the goals of communism.

Lenin's death in 1924 provoked a struggle for power among the seven members of the Politburo, the institution that had become the leading organ of the party. The Politburo was severely divided over the future direction of the Soviet Union. The Left, led by Leon Trotsky, wanted to end the NEP and launch the U.S.S.R. on the path of rapid industrialization. This same group wanted to carry the revolution on, believing that the survival of the Russian Revolution ultimately depended on the spread of communism abroad. The Right rejected the cause of world revolution and wanted instead to concentrate on constructing a socialist state in the Soviet Union.

These ideological divisions were underscored by an intense personal rivalry between Leon Trotsky and Joseph Stalin. In 1924, Trotsky held the post of commissar of war and was the leading spokesman for the Left in the Politburo. Joseph Stalin (1879–1953) was content to hold the dull bureaucratic job of party general secretary. But Stalin was a good organizer, and the other members of the Politburo soon found that the position of party secretary was really the most important in the party hierarchy. Stalin used his post as party general secretary to gain control of the Communist Party. Trotsky was expelled from the party in 1927. By 1929, Stalin had succeeded in eliminating the Old Bolsheviks of the revolutionary era from the Politburo and establishing a dictatorship so powerful that the Russian tsars of old would have been envious.

THE STALIN ERA, 1929–1939

The Stalinist era marked the beginning of an economic, social, and political revolution that was more sweeping in its results than the revolutions of 1917. Stalin made a significant shift in economic policy in

CHRONOLOGY

The Soviet Union

New Economic Policy begins	1921
Death of Lenin	1924
Trotsky's expulsion from the Communist Party	1927
First five-year plan	1928–1932
Start of Stalin's dictatorship	1929
Stalin's purge	1936–1938

1928 when he launched his first five-year plan. Its real goal was nothing less than the transformation of the Soviet Union from an agricultural country into an industrial state virtually overnight. Instead of consumer goods, the first five-year plan emphasized maximum production of capital goods and armaments and succeeded in quadrupling the production of heavy machinery and doubling oil production. Between 1928 and 1937, during the first two five-year plans, steel production increased from 4 to 18 million tons per year and hard coal output went from 36 to 128 million tons.

The social and political costs of industrialization were enormous. While the industrial labor force increased by millions between 1932 and 1940, total investment in housing actually declined after 1929, with the result that millions of workers and their families lived in pitiful conditions. Real wages in industry also declined by 43 percent between 1928 and 1940, and strict laws limited workers' freedom of movement. To inspire and pacify the workers, government propaganda stressed the need for sacrifice to create the new socialist state.

Rapid industrialization was accompanied by an equally rapid collectivization of agriculture. Its goal was to eliminate private farms and push people into collective farms (see the box on p. 547). Strong resistance to his plans from peasants who hoarded crops and killed livestock only led him to step up the program. By 1930, 10 million peasant households had been collectivized; by 1934, the Soviet Union's 26 million family farms had been collectivized into 250,000 units. This was done at tremendous cost, since the hoarding of food and the slaughter of livestock produced widespread famine. Stalin himself is supposed to have told Winston Churchill during World War II that 10 million peasants died in the artificially created famines of 1932 and 1933. The only concession Stalin made to the peasants was to allow each collective farm worker to have one tiny, privately owned garden plot.

Stalin's program of rapid industrialization entailed additional costs as well. To achieve his goals, Stalin strengthened the party bureaucracy under his control. Those who resisted were sent into forced labor camps in Siberia. Stalin's desire for sole control of deci-

STALIN SIGNING A DEATH WARRANT. Terror played an important role in the authoritarian system established by Joseph Stalin. In this photograph, Stalin is shown signing what is supposedly a death warrant in 1933. As the terror increased in the late 1930s, Stalin signed such lists every day.

The Formation of Collective Farms

Accompanying the rapid industrialization of the Soviet Union was the collectivization of agriculture, a feat that involved nothing less than transforming Russia's 26 million family farms into 250,000 collective farms (kolkhozes). *This selection provides a firsthand account of how the process worked.*

Max Belov, The History of a Collective Farm

General collectivization in our village was brought about in the following manner: Two representatives of the [Communist] Party arrived in the village. All the inhabitants were summoned by the ringing of the church bell to a meeting at which the policy of general collectivization was announced. . . . The upshot was that although the meeting lasted two days, from the viewpoint of the Party representatives nothing was accomplished.

After this setback the Party representatives divided the village into two sections and worked each one separately. Two more officials were sent to reinforce the first two. A meeting of our section of the village was held in a stable which had previously belonged to a kulak. The meeting dragged on until dark. Suddenly someone threw a brick at the lamp, and in the dark the peasants began to beat the Party representatives who jumped out the window and escaped from the village barely alive. The following day seven people were arrested. The militia was called in and stayed in the village until the peasants, realizing their helplessness, calmed down. . . .

By the end of 1930 there were two kolkhozes in our village. Though at first these collectives embraced at most only 70 percent of the peasant households, in the months that followed they gradually absorbed more and more of them.

In these kolkhozes the great bulk of the land was held and worked communally, but each peasant household owned a house of some sort, a small plot of ground and perhaps some livestock. All the members of the kolkhoz were required to work on the kolkhoz a certain number of days each month; the rest of the time they were allowed to work on their own holdings. They derived their income partly from what they grew on their garden strips and partly from their work in the kolkhoz.

When the harvest was over, and after the farm had met its obligations to the state and to various special funds (for instance, seed, etc.) and had sold on the market whatever undesignated produce was left, the remaining produce and the farm's monetary income were divided among the kolkhoz members according to the number of "labor days" each one had contributed to the farm's work. . . . It was in 1930 that the kolkhoz members first received their portions out of the "communal kettle." After they had received their earnings, at the rate of 1 kilogram of grain and 55 kopecks per labor day, one of them remarked, "You will live, but you will be very, very thin."

In the spring of 1931 a tractor worked the fields of the kolkhoz for the first time. The tractor was "capable of plowing every kind of hard soil and virgin soil," as Party representatives told us at the meeting in celebration of its arrival. The peasants did not then know that these "steel horses" would carry away a good part of the harvest in return for their work. . . .

By late 1932 more than 80 percent of the peasant households . . . had been collectivized. . . . That year the peasants harvested a good crop and had hopes that the calculations would work out to their advantage and would help strengthen them economically. These hopes were in vain. The kolkhoz workers received only 200 grams of flour per labor day for the first half of the year; the remaining grain, including the seed fund, was taken by the government. The peasants were told that industrialization of the country, then in full swing, demanded grain and sacrifices from them.

sion making also led to purges of the Old Bolsheviks, army officers, diplomats, union officials, party members, intellectuals, and numerous ordinary citizens. Estimates are that between 1936 and 1938, eight million Soviets were arrested; millions were sent to Siberian forced labor camps, from which they never returned.

Disturbed by a rapidly declining birthrate, Stalin also reversed much of the permissive social legislation of the early 1920s. Advocating complete equality of rights for women, the Communists had made divorce and abortion easy to obtain while also encouraging women to work outside the home and liberate themselves sexually. After Stalin came to power, the family was praised as a miniature collective in which parents were responsible for inculcating values of duty, discipline, and hard work. Abortion was outlawed, and divorced fathers who did not support their children were fined heavily. The new divorce law of June 1936 imposed fines for repeated divorces, and homosexuality was declared a criminal activity. The regime now praised motherhood and urged women to have large families as a patriotic duty. But by this time, many Soviet women worked in factories and spent many additional hours in line waiting to purchase increasingly scarce consumer goods. There was no dramatic increase in the birthrate.

Authoritarian States

A number of other states in Europe were not totalitarian but did possess conservative authoritarian governments. These states adopted some of the trappings of totalitarian states, especially wide police powers, but their greatest concern was not the creation of a mass movement aimed at the establishment of a new kind of society but rather the defense of the existing social order. Consequently, the authoritarian states tended to limit the participation of the masses and were content with passive obedience rather than active involvement in the goals of the regime.

Nowhere had the map of Europe been more drastically altered by World War I than in eastern Europe. The new states of Austria, Poland, Czechoslovakia, and the kingdom of the Serbs, Croats, and Slovenes (Yugoslavia), adopted parliamentary systems while the preexisting kingdoms of Romania and Bulgaria gained new parliamentary constitutions in 1920. Greece became a republic in 1924. Hungary's government was parliamentary in form but was controlled by its landed aristocrats. At the beginning of the 1920s, political democracy seemed well established, but almost everywhere in eastern Europe, parliamentary governments soon gave way to authoritarian regimes.

Several problems helped create this situation. Eastern European states had little tradition of liberalism or parliamentary politics and no substantial middle class to support them. Then, too, these states were largely rural and agrarian in character. Much of the land was still dominated by large landowners who feared the growth of agrarian peasant parties with their schemes for land redistribution. Ethnic conflicts also threatened to tear these countries apart. Fearful of land reform, agrarian upheaval, and ethnic conflict, powerful landowners and the churches looked to authoritarian governments to maintain the old system. Only Czechoslovakia, with its substantial middle class, liberal tradition, and strong industrial base, maintained its political democracy.

In Spain, political democracy also failed to survive. Led by General Francisco Franco (1892–1975), Spanish military forces revolted against the democratic government in 1936 and launched a brutal and bloody civil war that lasted three years. Foreign intervention complicated the Spanish Civil War. Franco's forces were aided by arms, money, and men from the fascist regimes of Italy and Germany while the government was assisted by forty thousand foreign volunteers and trucks, planes, tanks, and military advisers from the Soviet Union. After Franco's forces captured Madrid on March 28, 1939, the Spanish Civil War finally came to an end. Franco soon established a dictatorship that favored large landowners, businessmen, and the Catholic clergy—yet another traditional, conservative, authoritarian regime.

The Expansion of Mass Culture and Mass Leisure

Technological innovations continued to have profound effects on European society. Nowhere is this more evident than in mass culture and mass leisure. The mass distribution of commercialized popular forms of entertainment had a major effect on European society.

Radio and Movies

A series of technological inventions in the late nineteenth century had prepared the way for a revolution in mass communications. Especially important was Marconi's discovery of "wireless" radio waves. But it was not until June 16, 1920, that a radio broadcast (of a concert by soprano Nellie Melba from London) for a mass audience was attempted. Permanent broadcasting facilities were then constructed in the United States, Europe, and Japan during 1921 and 1922, while mass production of radios (receiving sets) also began. In 1926, when the British Broadcasting Corporation (BBC) was made into a public corporation, there were 2.2 million radios in Great Britain. By the end of the 1930s, there were 9 million. The technical foundation for motion pictures had already been developed in the 1890s when short moving pictures were produced as novelties for music halls. Shortly before World War I, full-length features, such as the Italian film *Quo Vadis* and the American film *Birth of a Nation*, became available and made it apparent that cinema had created a new form of mass entertainment.

Mass forms of communication and entertainment were not new, but the increased size of mass audiences and the ability of radio and cinema, unlike the printed word, to provide an immediate experience did add new dimensions to mass culture. Favorite film actors and actresses became stars, whose lives then became subject to public adoration and scrutiny. Sensuous actresses such as Marlene Dietrich, whose appearance in the early sound film *The Blue Angel* catapulted her into fame, created new images of women's sexuality.

Of course, mass culture could also be used for political purposes. Film, for example, had propaganda potential, a possibility not lost on Joseph Goebbels (1897–1945), the propaganda minister of Nazi Germany. Believing that film constituted one of the "most modern and scientific means of influencing the masses," Goebbels created a special film section in his Propaganda Ministry and encouraged the production of both documentaries and popular feature films that carried the Nazi message. *The Triumph of the Will*, for example, was a documentary of the 1934 Nuremberg party rally that conveyed forcefully to viewers the power of Nazism.

Mass Leisure

Mass leisure activities had developed at the turn of the century, but new work patterns after World War I dramatically expanded the amount of free time available to take advantage of them. By 1920, the eight-hour day had become the norm for many office and factory workers in northern and western Europe.

Professional sporting events for mass audiences became an important aspect of mass leisure. Attendance at association football (soccer) games soared, and the inauguration of the World Cup contest in 1930 intensified the nationalistic rivalries that came to surround mass sporting events. Increased attendance also made the 1920s and 1930s a great era of stadium building. The Germans built a stadium in Berlin for the 1936 Olympics that seated 140,000 people.

Travel opportunities also added new dimensions to mass leisure activities. The military use of aircraft during World War I helped improve planes and make civilian air travel a reality. The first regular international mail service began in 1919, and regular passenger service soon followed. Although air travel remained the preserve of the wealthy or the adventurous, trains, buses, and private cars made excursions to beaches or holiday resorts more popular and possible for the less wealthy. Beaches were increasingly mobbed by crowds of people from all social classes.

Mass leisure provided totalitarian regimes with new ways to control their populations. The Nazi regime created a program known as *Kraft durch Freude* (Strength Through Joy) to coordinate the free time of the working class by offering a variety of activities, including concerts, operas, films, guided tours, and sporting events. Especially popular were the inexpensive vacations, essentially modern package tours. These could be cruises to Scandinavia or the Mediterranean or, more likely for workers, shorter trips to various sites in Germany. Essentially, *Kraft durch Freude* enabled the German government to supervise recreational activities. In doing so, the state imposed new rules and regulations on previously spontaneous activities, thus breaking down old group solidarities and allowing these groups to be guided by the goals of the state.

◆ Cultural and Intellectual Trends in the Interwar Years

The artistic and intellectual innovations of the pre–World War I period, which had shocked many Europeans, had been the preserve primarily of a small group of avant-garde artists and intellectuals. In the 1920s and 1930s, they became more widespread as intellectuals continued to work out the implications of the ideas developed before 1914. But what made the prewar avant-garde culture acceptable in the 1920s and the 1930s? Perhaps most important was the impact of World War I.

Four years of devastating war left many Europeans with a profound sense of despair and disillusionment. To many people, the experiences of World War I seemed to confirm the prewar avant-garde belief that human beings were really violent and irrational animals who were incapable of creating a sane and rational world. The Great Depression, as well as the growth of fascist movements based on violence and the degradation of individual rights, only added to the uncertainties generated by World War I. The crisis of confidence in Western civilization ran very deep.

Political and economic uncertainties were paralleled by social insecurities. World War I had served to break down many traditional middle-class attitudes, especially toward sexuality. In the 1920s, women's physical appearance changed dramatically. Short skirts, short hair, the use of cosmetics once thought suitable only for prostitutes, and the new practice of suntanning gave women a radically new image. This change in physical appearance, which exposed more of a woman's body than ever before, was also accompanied by frank discussions of sexual matters. In 1926, the Dutch physician Theodor van de Velde published *Ideal Marriage: Its Physiology and Technique*, which described female and male anatomy, discussed birth control techniques, and glorified sexual pleasure in marriage. Translated into a number of languages, it became an international best-seller. New ideas on sexuality and birth control were also spread to the working classes by family planning clinics, such as those of Margaret Sanger in the United States and Marie Stopes in Britain.

HANNAH HÖCH, *CUT WITH THE KITCHEN KNIFE DADA THROUGH THE LAST WEIMAR BEER BELLY CULTURAL EPOCH OF GERMANY.* **Hannah Höch, a prominent figure in the postwar Dada movement, used photomontage to create images that reflected on women's issues. In *Cut with the Kitchen Knife,* she combined pictures of German political leaders with sports stars, Dada artists, and scenes from urban life. One major theme emerged: the confrontation between the anti-Dada world of German political leaders and the Dada world of revolutionary ideals. Höch associated women with Dada and the new world.**

Nightmares and New Visions: Art and Music

Uncertainty also pervaded the cultural and intellectual achievements of the interwar years. Postwar artistic trends were largely a working out of the implications of prewar developments. Abstract Expressionism, for example, became ever more popular as many pioneering artists of the early twentieth century matured between the two world wars. In addition, prewar fascination with the absurd and the unconscious contents of the mind seemed even more appropriate after the nightmare landscapes of World War I battlefronts. This gave rise to both the Dada movement and Surrealism.

Dadaism attempted to enshrine the purposelessness of life. Tristan Tzara, a Romanian-French poet and one of the founders of Dadaism, expressed the Dadaist contempt for the Western tradition in a lecture on Dada in 1922: "The acts of life have no beginning or end. Everything happens in a completely idiotic way. . . . Like everything in life, Dada is useless."[7] Revolted by the insanity of life, the Dadaists tried to give it expression by creating anti-art. In the hands of Hannah Höch (1889–1978), however, Dada became an instrument to comment on women's roles in the new mass culture. In a number of works, she created positive images of the modern woman and expressed a keen interest in new freedoms for women.

Perhaps more important as an artistic movement was Surrealism, which sought a reality beyond the material, sensible world and found it in the world of the unconscious through the portrayal of fantasies, dreams, or nightmares. Employing logic to portray the illogical, the Surrealists created disturbing and evocative images. The Spaniard Salvador Dalí (1904–1989) became the high priest of Surrealism and in his mature phase became a master of representational Surrealism. In *The Persistence of Memory*, Dalí portrayed recognizable objects divorced from their normal context. By placing these objects into unrecognizable relationships, Dalí created a disturbing world in which the irrational had become tangible.

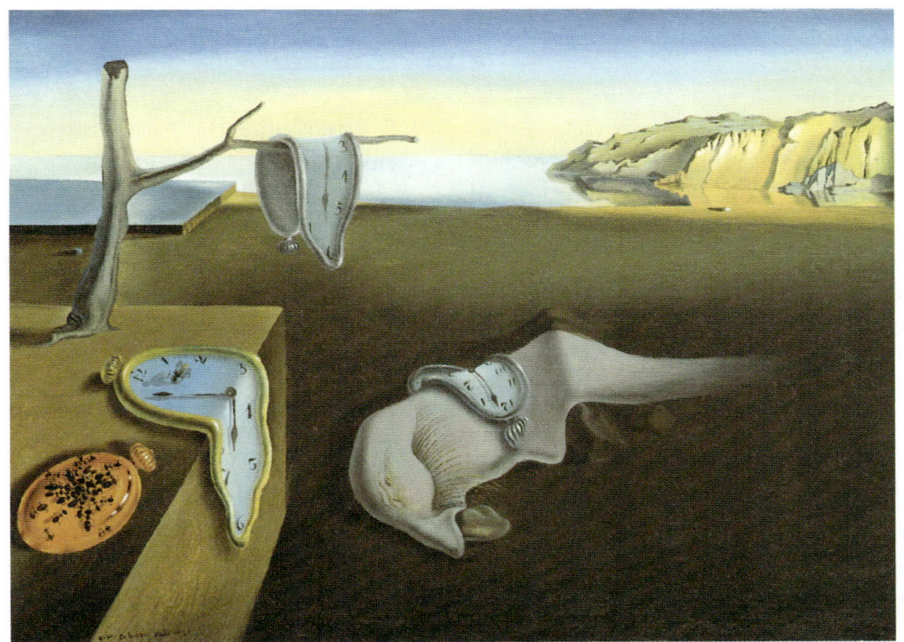

SALVADOR DALÍ, *THE PERSISTENCE OF MEMORY,* 1931. Surrealism was another important artistic movement between the wars. Influenced by the theories of Freudian psychology, Surrealists sought to reveal the world of the unconscious, or the "greater reality" that they believed existed beyond the world of physical appearances. As is evident in this painting, Salvador Dalí sought to portray the world of dreams by painting recognizable objects in unrecognizable relationships.

The move to functionalism in modern architecture also became more widespread in the 1920s and 1930s. First conceived near the end of the nineteenth century, functionalism meant that buildings should be "functional" or useful, fulfilling the purpose for which they were constructed. Art and engineering were to be unified, and all unnecessary ornamentation was to be stripped away. Especially important in the spread of functionalism was the Bauhaus school, founded in 1919 at Weimar, Germany, by the Berlin architect Walter Gropius. The Bauhaus teaching staff consisted of architects, artists, and designers who worked together to combine the study of fine arts (painting and sculpture) with the applied arts (printing, weaving, and furniture making).

The postwar acceptance of modern art forms was by no means universal. Many traditionalists denounced what they considered degeneracy and decadence in the arts. This was especially evident in the totalitarian state of Nazi Germany. In the 1920s, Weimar Germany was one of the chief European centers for modern arts and sciences. Hitler and the Nazis rejected modern art as "degenerate" or "Jewish" art. In 1937, Hitler said: "The people regarded this art as the outcome of an impudent and unashamed arrogance or of a simply shocking lack of skill; . . . these achievements which might have been produced by untalented children of from eight to ten years old could never be valued as an expression of our own times or of the German future."[8] Hitler and the Nazis believed that they had laid the foundation for a new and genuine German art, which would glorify the strong, the healthy, and the heroic—all of which were supposedly attributes of the Aryan race.

At the beginning of the twentieth century, a revolution in music parallel to the revolution in art had begun with the work of Igor Stravinsky. But Stravinksy still wrote music in a definite key. The Viennese composer Arnold Schönberg (1874–1951) began to experiment with a radically new style by creating musical pieces in which tonality is completely abandoned, a system that he called atonic music.

The Search for the Unconscious

The interest in the unconscious, evident in Surrealism, was also apparent in the development of new literary techniques that emerged in the 1920s. One of its most apparent manifestations was in a "stream of consciousness" technique in which the writer presented an interior monologue or a report of the innermost thoughts of each character. The most famous example of this genre was written by the Irish exile James Joyce (1882–1941). His *Ulysses*, published in 1922, told the story of one day in the life of ordinary people in Dublin by following the flow of their inner dialogue.

The German writer Hermann Hesse (1877–1962) dealt with the unconscious in a considerably different fashion. His novels reflected the influence of new psychological theories and Eastern religions and focused on, among other things, the spiritual loneliness of modern

Hesse and the Unconscious

The novels of Hermann Hesse made a strong impact on young people, first in Germany in the 1920s and then in the United States in the 1960s after they had been translated into English. Many of these young people shared Hesse's fascination with the unconscious and his dislike of modern industrial civilization. This excerpt from Demian *spoke directly to many of them.*

Hermann Hesse, Demian

The following spring I was to leave the preparatory school and enter a university. I was still undecided, however, as to where and what I was to study. I had grown a thin mustache, I was a full-grown man, and yet I was completely helpless and without a goal in life. Only one thing was certain: the voice within me, the dream image. I felt the duty to follow this voice blindly wherever it might lead me. But it was difficult and each day I rebelled against it anew. Perhaps I was mad, as I thought at moments; perhaps I was not like other men? But I was able to do the same things the others did; with a little effort and industry I could read Plato, was able to solve problems in trigonometry or follow a chemical analysis. There was only one thing I could not do: wrest the dark secret goal from myself and keep it before me as others did who knew exactly what they wanted to be—professors, lawyers, doctors, artists, however long this would take them and whatever difficulties and advantages this decision would bear in its wake. This I could not do. Perhaps I would become something similar, but how was I to know? Perhaps I would have to continue my search for years on end and would not become anything, and would not reach a goal. Perhaps I would reach this goal but it would turn out to be an evil, dangerous, horrible one?

I wanted only to try to live in accord with the promptings which came from my true self. Why was that so very difficult?

human beings in a mechanized urban society. *Demian* was a psychoanalytical study of incest, and *Steppenwolf* mirrored the psychological confusion of modern existence. Hesse's novels had a large impact on German youth in the 1920s (see the box above). He won the Nobel Prize for literature in 1946.

The growing concern with the unconscious also led to greater popular interest in psychology. The full impact of Sigmund Freud's thought was not felt until after World War I. The 1920s witnessed a worldwide acceptance of his ideas. Freudian terms, such as *unconscious, repression, id,* and *ego,* entered the popular vocabulary. Popularization of Freud's ideas led to the widespread misconception that an uninhibited sex life was necessary for a healthy mental life. Despite such misperceptions, psychoanalysis did develop into a major profession, especially in the United States. But Freud's ideas did not go unchallenged, even by his own pupils. One of the most prominent challenges came from Carl Jung.

A disciple of Freud, Carl Jung (1875–1961) came to believe that Freud's theories were too narrow and based on Freud's own personal biases. Jung's study of dreams—his own and others—led him to diverge sharply from Freud. Whereas for Freud the unconscious was the seat of repressed desires or appetites, for Jung it was an opening to deep spiritual needs and ever-greater vistas for humans.

Jung viewed the unconscious as twofold: a "personal unconscious" and a "collective unconscious," which existed at a deeper level of the unconscious. The collective unconscious was the repository of memories that all human beings share and consisted of archetypes, mental forms or images that appear in dreams. The archetypes are common to all people and have a special energy that creates myths, religions, and philosophies. To Jung, the archetypes proved that mind was only in part personal or individual because their origin was buried so far in the past that they seemed to have no human source. Their function was to bring the original mind of humans into a new, higher state of consciousness.

The "Heroic Age of Physics"

The prewar revolution in physics initiated by Max Planck and Albert Einstein continued in the interwar period. In fact, Ernest Rutherford (1871–1937), one of the physicists responsible for demonstrating that the atom could be split, dubbed the 1920s the "heroic age of physics."

The new picture of the universe that was unfolding continued to undermine the old scientific certainties of classical physics. Classical physics had rested on the fundamental belief that all phenomena could be predicted if they could be completely understood; thus the weather could be predicted if we knew everything about the wind, sun, and water. In 1927, the German physicist Werner Heisenberg (1901–1976) upset this belief when he posited the "uncertainty principle." In essence, Heisenberg posited that no one could determine the path of an electron because the very act of observing the electron with light affected the electron's location. The uncertainty principle was more than an explanation for the path of an electron, however; it was a new worldview. Heisenberg shattered confidence in predictability and dared to propose that uncertainty was at the root of all the physical laws.

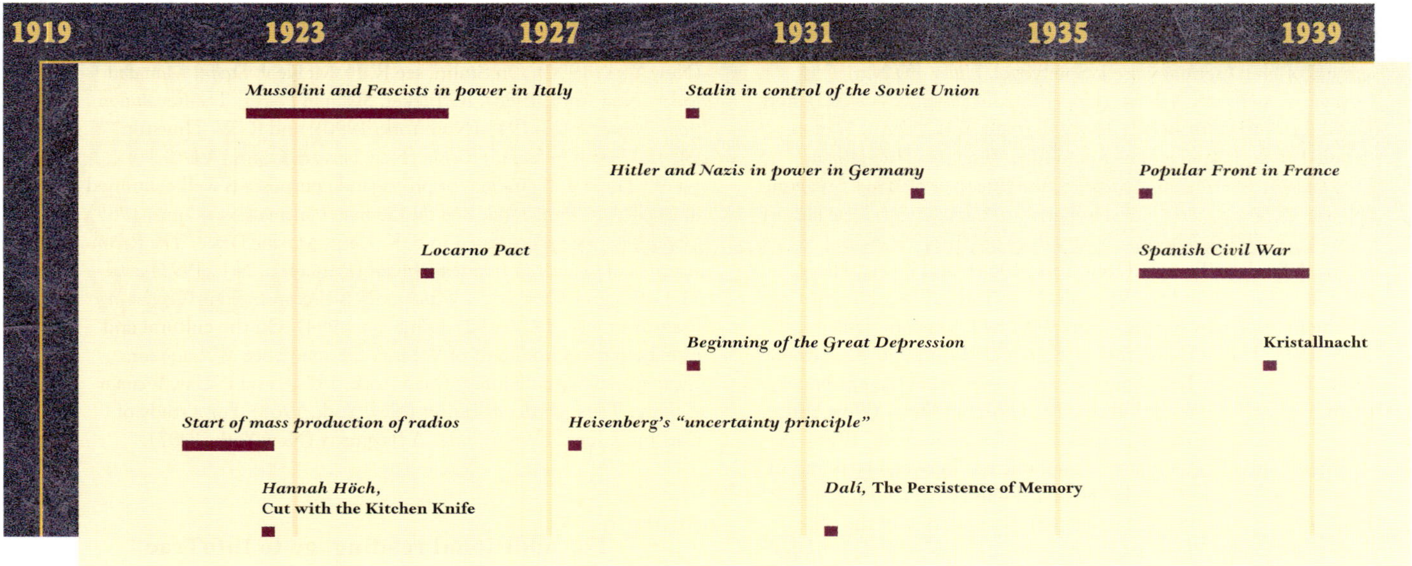

Conclusion

The devastation wrought by World War I destroyed the liberal optimism of the prewar era. Yet many people in the 1920s still hoped that the progress of Western civilization, so seemingly evident before 1914, could somehow be restored. These hopes proved largely unfounded as plans for economic reconstruction gave way to inflation and to an even more devastating Great Depression at the end of the 1920s. Likewise, confidence in political democracy was soon shattered by the rise of authoritarian governments that not only restricted individual freedoms but, in the cases of Italy, Germany, and the Soviet Union, sought even great control over the lives of their subjects in order to manipulate and guide them to achieve the goals of their totalitarian regimes. For many people, despite the loss of personal freedom, these mass movements at least offered some sense of security in a world that seemed fraught with uncertainties.

But the seeming security of these mass movements gave rise to even greater uncertainties as Europeans, after a brief twenty-year interlude of peace, once again plunged into war, this time on a scale even more horrendous than that of World War I. The twentieth-century crisis, begun in 1914, seemed only to be worsening in 1939.

Notes

1. Quoted in Robert Paxton, *Europe in the Twentieth Century*, 2d ed. (San Diego, Calif., 1985), p. 237.
2. Benito Mussolini, "The Doctrine of Fascism," in Adrian Lyttleton, ed., *Italian Fascisms from Pareto to Gentile* (London, 1973), p. 42.
3. Quoted in Alexander De Grand, "Women Under Italian Fascism," *Historical Journal*, 19 (1976): 958–959.
4. Quoted in Jeremy Noakes and Geoffrey Pridham, eds., *Nazism, 1919–1945* (Exeter, England, 1983), vol. 1, pp. 50–51.
5. Quoted in Joachim Fest, *Hitler*, trans. Richard and Clara Winston (New York, 1974), p. 418.
6. Irving Howe, ed., *The Basic Writings of Trotsky* (London, 1963), p. 162.
7. Tristan Tzara, "Lecture on Dada," in Robert Motherwell, ed., *The Dada Painters and Poets* (New York, 1951), p. 52.
8. Norman H. Baynes, ed., *The Speeches of Adolf Hitler, 1922–1939* (Oxford, 1942), vol. 1, p. 591.

Suggestions for Further Reading

For a general introduction to the interwar period, see R. J. Sontag, *A Broken World, 1919–39* (New York, 1971), and the general survey by R. Paxton, *Europe in the Twentieth Century*, 2d ed. (New York,

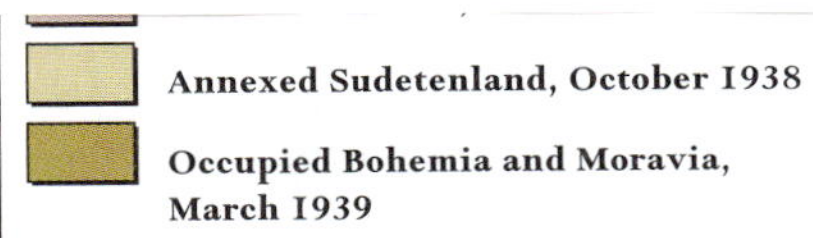

World War II was more than just Hitler's war, however. This chapter focuses on the European theater of war, but both European and American armies were involved in fighting around the world. World War II consisted of two conflicts, one provoked by the ambitions of Germany in

the Slavic population could be used as slave labor to build the Aryan racial state that would dominate Europe for a thousand years. Hitler's conclusion was apparent: Germany must prepare for its inevitable war with the Soviet Union. Hitler's ideas were by no means secret. He had spelled them out in *Mein Kampf*, a book

CHRONOLOGY

Prelude to War, 1933–1939

Hitler as chancellor	January 30, 1933
Hitler's announcement of a German air force	March 9, 1935
Hitler's announcement of military conscription	March 16, 1935
Mussolini's invasion of Ethiopia	October 1935
Hitler's occupation of the demilitarized Rhineland	March 7, 1936
Rome-Berlin Axis	October 1936
Anti-Comintern Pact (Japan and Germany)	November 1936
German annexation of Austria	March 13, 1938
Munich Conference: German occupation of Sudetenland	September 29, 1938
German occupation of the rest of Czechoslovakia	March 1939
German-Soviet Nonaggression Pact	August 23, 1939
German invasion of Poland	September 1, 1939
British and French declaration of war on Germany	September 3, 1939

might have seemed unrealistic since democratic Czechoslovakia was quite prepared to defend itself and was well supported by pacts with France and the Soviet Union. Nevertheless, Hitler believed that France and Britain would not use force to defend Czechoslovakia.

He was right again. When on September 15, 1938, Hitler demanded the cession to Germany of the Sudetenland, the mountainous northwestern border area of Czechoslovakia that was home to 3.5 million ethnic Germans, and expressed his willingness to risk "world war" to achieve his objective, the British, French, Germans, and Italians—at a hastily arranged conference at Munich—reached an agreement that essentially met all of Hitler's demands. German troops were allowed to occupy the Sudetenland as the Czechs, abandoned by their Western allies, stood by helplessly. The Munich Conference was the high point of Western appeasement of Hitler. When Neville Chamberlain, the British prime minister, returned to England from Munich, he boasted that the Munich agreement meant "peace in our times." Hitler had promised Chamberlain that he had made his last demand. Like many German politicians, Chamberlain had believed Hitler's assurances (see the box on p. 559).

In fact, Munich confirmed Hitler's perception that the Western democracies were weak and would not fight. Increasingly, Hitler was convinced of his own infallibility, and he had by no means been satisfied at Munich. In March 1939, Hitler occupied the Czech lands (Bohemia and Moravia) while the Slovaks, with Hitler's encouragement, declared their independence of the Czechs and became a puppet state (Slovakia) of Nazi Germany. On the evening of March 15, 1939,

HITLER ENTERING THE SUDETENLAND. The Sudetenland was an area of Czechoslovakia inhabited by 3.5 million ethnic Germans. The Munich Conference allowed the Germans to occupy the Sudetenland. This picture shows Hitler and his entourage arriving at Eger (now Cheb) in October 1938 to the cheers of an enthusiastic crowd.

The Munich Conference

At the Munich Conference, the leaders of France and Great Britain capitulated to Hitler's demands on Czechoslovakia. While the British prime minister, Neville Chamberlain, defended his actions at Munich as necessary for peace, another British statesman, Winston Churchill, characterized the settlement at Munich as "a disaster of the first magnitude."

Winston Churchill, Speech to the House of Commons, October 5, 1938

I will begin by saying what everybody would like to ignore or forget but which must nevertheless be stated, namely, that we have sustained a total and unmitigated defeat, and that France has suffered even more than we have. . . . The utmost my right honorable Friend the Prime Minister . . . has been able to gain for Czechoslovakia and in the matters which were in dispute has been that the German dictator, instead of snatching his victuals from the table, has been content to have them served to him course by course. . . . And I will say this, that I believe the Czechs, left to themselves and told they were going to get no help from the Western Powers, would have been able to make better terms than they have got. . . .

We are in the presence of a disaster of the first magnitude which has befallen Great Britain and France. Do not let us blind ourselves to that. . . .

And do not suppose that this is the end. This is only the beginning of the reckoning. This is only the first sip, the first foretaste of a bitter cup which will be proffered to us year by year unless by a supreme recovery of moral health and martial vigor, we arise again and take our stand for freedom as in the olden time.

Neville Chamberlain, Speech to the House of Commons, October 6, 1938

That is my answer to those who say that we should have told Germany weeks ago that, if her army crossed the border of Czechoslovakia, we should be at war with her. We had no treaty obligations and no legal obligations to Czechoslovakia. . . . When we were convinced, as we became convinced, that nothing any longer would keep the Sudetenland within the Czechoslovakian State, we urged the Czech Government as strongly as we could to agree to the cession of territory, and to agree promptly. . . . It was a hard decision for anyone who loved his country to take, but to accuse us of having by that advice betrayed the Czechoslovakian State is simply preposterous. What we did was to save her from annihilation and give her a chance of new life as a new State, which involves the loss of territory and fortifications, but may perhaps enable her to enjoy in the future and develop a national existence under a neutrality and security comparable to that which we see in Switzerland today. Therefore, I think the Government deserve the approval of this House for their conduct of affairs in this recent crisis which has saved Czechoslovakia from destruction and Europe from Armageddon.

Hitler triumphantly declared in Prague that he would be known as the greatest German of them all.

At last, the Western states reacted to Hitler's threat. Hitler's naked aggression made clear that his promises were utterly worthless. When Hitler began to demand the return to Germany of Danzig (which had been made a free city by the Treaty of Versailles to serve as a seaport for Poland), Britain recognized the danger and offered to protect Poland in the event of war. At the same time, both France and Britain realized that only the Soviet Union was powerful enough to help contain Nazi aggression and began political and military negotiations with Joseph Stalin and the Soviets. The West's distrust of Soviet communism, however, made an alliance unlikely.

Meanwhile, Hitler pressed on in the belief that the West would not really fight over Poland. To preclude an alliance between the West and the Soviet Union, which would create the danger of a two-front war, Hitler, ever the opportunist, negotiated his own nonaggression pact with Stalin and shocked the world with its announcement on August 23, 1939. The treaty with the Soviet Union gave Hitler the freedom to attack Poland. He told his generals: "Now Poland is in the position in which I wanted her. . . . I am only afraid that at the last moment some swine or other will yet submit to me a plan for mediation."[2] He need not have worried. On September 1, German forces invaded Poland; two days later, Britain and France declared war on Germany. Europe was again at war.

◆ The Course of World War II

Unleashing a *Blitzkrieg*, or "lightning war," Hitler stunned Europe with the speed and efficiency of the German attack. Armored columns or panzer divisions (a panzer division was a strike force of about three hundred tanks, with accompanying troops and supplies) supported by airplanes broke quickly through Polish lines and encircled the bewildered Polish troops. Regular infantry units then moved in to hold the newly conquered territory. Within four weeks, Poland had surrendered. On September 28, 1939, Germany and the Soviet Union officially divided Poland between them.

Victory and Stalemate

Although Hitler's hopes to avoid a war with the West were dashed when France and Britain declared war on September 3, he was confident that he could control the situation. After a winter of waiting (called the "phony war"), Hitler resumed the fight on April 9, 1940, with another *Blitzkrieg*, this time against Denmark and Norway. One month later, on May 10, the Germans launched their attack on the Netherlands, Belgium, and France. The main assault through Luxembourg and the Ardennes forest was completely unexpected by the French and British forces. German panzer divisions broke through the weak French defensive positions there and raced across northern France, splitting the Allied armies and trapping French troops and the entire British army on the beaches of Dunkirk. Only by heroic efforts did the British succeed in achieving an evacuation of 330,000 Allied (mostly British) troops. The French surrendered on June 22. German armies occupied about three-fifths of France while the French hero of World War I, Marshal Henri Pétain (1856–1951), established an authoritarian regime (known as Vichy France) over the remainder. Germany was now in control of western and central Europe, but Britain had still not been defeated.

As Hitler realized, an amphibious invasion of Britain would be possible only if Germany gained control of the air. At the beginning of August 1940, the *Luftwaffe* (the German air force) launched a major offensive against British air and naval bases, harbors, communication centers, and war industries. Led by the stubbornly determined Winston Churchill, now prime minister of Britain, the British fought back doggedly, supported by an effective radar system that gave them early warning of German attacks. Nevertheless, the British air force suffered critical losses by the end of the August and was probably saved by Hitler's change of strategy. In September, in retaliation for a British attack on Berlin, Hitler ordered a shift from military targets to massive bombing of British cities to break British morale. The British rebuilt their air strength quickly and were soon inflicting major losses on *Luftwaffe* bombers. By the end of September, Germany had lost the Battle of Britain, and the invasion of Britain had to be postponed.

At this point, Hitler pursued the possibility of a Mediterranean strategy, which would involve capturing Egypt and the Suez Canal and closing the Mediterranean to British ships, thereby shutting off Britain's supply of oil. Hitler's commitment to the Mediterranean was never wholehearted, however. His initial plan was to let the Italians defeat the British in North Africa, but this strategy failed when the British routed the Italian army. Although Hitler then sent German troops to the North African theater of war, his primary concern lay elsewhere; he had already reached the decision to fulfill his lifetime obsession with the acquisition of territory in the east.

Although he had no desire for a two-front war, Hitler became convinced that Britain was remaining in the war only because it expected Russian support. If Russia were smashed, Britain's last hope would be eliminated. Moreover, Hitler had convinced himself that the Soviet Union, with its Jewish-Bolshevik leadership and a pitiful army, could be defeated quickly and decisively. Although the invasion of the Soviet Union was scheduled for spring 1941, the attack was delayed because of problems in the Balkans. Hitler had already obtained the political cooperation of Hungary, Bulgaria, and Romania, but Mussolini's disastrous invasion of Greece in October 1940 exposed Hitler's southern flank to British air bases in Greece. To secure his Balkan flank, German troops seized both Yugoslavia and Greece in April. Now reassured, Hitler turned to the east and invaded the Soviet Union on June 22, 1941, in the belief that the Russians could still be decisively defeated before winter arrived.

The massive attack stretched out along an 1,800-mile front (see Map 27.2). German troops advanced rapidly, capturing two million Russian soldiers. By November, one German army group had swept through the Ukraine, while a second was besieging Leningrad; a third approached within 25 miles of Moscow, the Russian capital. An early winter and unexpected Russian resistance, however, brought a halt to the German advance. For the first time in the war, German armies had been stopped. A counterattack in December 1941 by the Soviet army, which Hitler assumed had been exhausted by Nazi victories, came as an ominous sign for the Germans. By then, another of Hitler's decisions—the declaration of war on the United States—had probably made Hitler's defeat inevitable and again turned a European conflict into a global war.

The War in Asia

On December 7, 1941, Japanese carrier-based aircraft attacked the United States naval base at Pearl Harbor in the Hawaiian Islands. The same day, other units launched additional assaults on the Philippines and began advancing toward the British colony of Malaya. Shortly after, Japanese forces invaded the Dutch East Indies and occupied a number of islands in the Pacific Ocean (see Map 27.3). In some cases, as on the Bataan peninsula and the island of Corregidor in the Philippines, resistance was fierce, but by the spring of 1942, almost all of Southeast Asia and much of the western Pacific had fallen into Japanese hands. Tokyo declared the creation of the Greater East-Asia Co-Prosperity Sphere, encompassing the entire region under Japanese tutelage, and announced its intention to liberate the colonial areas of Southeast Asia from Western colonial rule. For the moment, however, Japan needed the resources of the region for its war machine and placed the countries under its rule on a wartime basis.

Japanese leaders had hoped that their lightning strike at American bases would destroy the United States Pacific Fleet and persuade the Roosevelt administration to accept Japanese domination of the Pacific. The American people, in the eyes of Japanese leaders, had been made soft by material indulgence. But Tokyo had miscalculated. The attack on Pearl Harbor galvanized American opinion and won broad support for Roosevelt's war policy. The United States now joined with European nations and Nationalist China in a combined effort to defeat Japan and bring to an end its hegemony in the Pacific.

The Turning Point of the War, 1942–1943

The entry of the United States into the war created a coalition (the Grand Alliance) that ultimately defeated the Axis powers (Germany, Italy, Japan). Nevertheless, the three major Allies, Britain, the United States, and the Soviet Union, had to overcome mutual suspicions before they could operate as an effective alliance. Two factors aided that process. First, Hitler's declaration of war on the United States made

GERMAN PANZER TROOPS IN RUSSIA. At first, the German attack on Russia was enormously successful, leading one German general to remark in his diary, "It is probably no overstatement to say that the Russian campaign has been won in the space of two weeks." This picture shows German panzer troops jumping from their armored troop carriers to attack Red Army snipers who had taken refuge in a farmhouse.

MAP 27.2 World War II in Europe and North Africa.

it easier for the United States to accept the British and Russian contention that the defeat of Germany should be the first priority of the United States. For that reason, the United States increased the quantity of trucks, planes, and other arms that it sent to the British and Soviets. Also important to the alliance was the tacit agreement of the three chief Allies to stress military operations while ignoring political differences. At the beginning of 1943, the Allies agreed to fight until the Axis powers surrendered unconditionally. This principle of unconditional surrender had the effect of cementing the Grand Alliance by making it nearly impossible for Hitler to divide his foes.

Defeat was far from Hitler's mind at the beginning of 1942, however. As Japanese forces advanced into Southeast Asia and the Pacific, Hitler and his European allies continued the war in Europe against Britain and the Soviet Union. Until the fall of 1942, it appeared that the Germans might still prevail on the battlefield. Reinforcements in North Africa enabled the Afrika Korps under General Erwin Rommel to break through the British defenses in Egypt and advance toward Alexandria. In the spring of 1942, a renewed German offensive in Russia led to the capture of the entire Crimea, causing Hitler to boast in August 1942:

> As the next step, we are going to advance south of the Caucasus and then help the rebels in Iran and Iraq against the English. Another thrust will be directed along the Caspian Sea toward Afghanistan and India. Then the English will run out of oil. In two years we'll be on the borders of India. Twenty to thirty elite German divisions will do. Then the British Empire will collapse.[3]

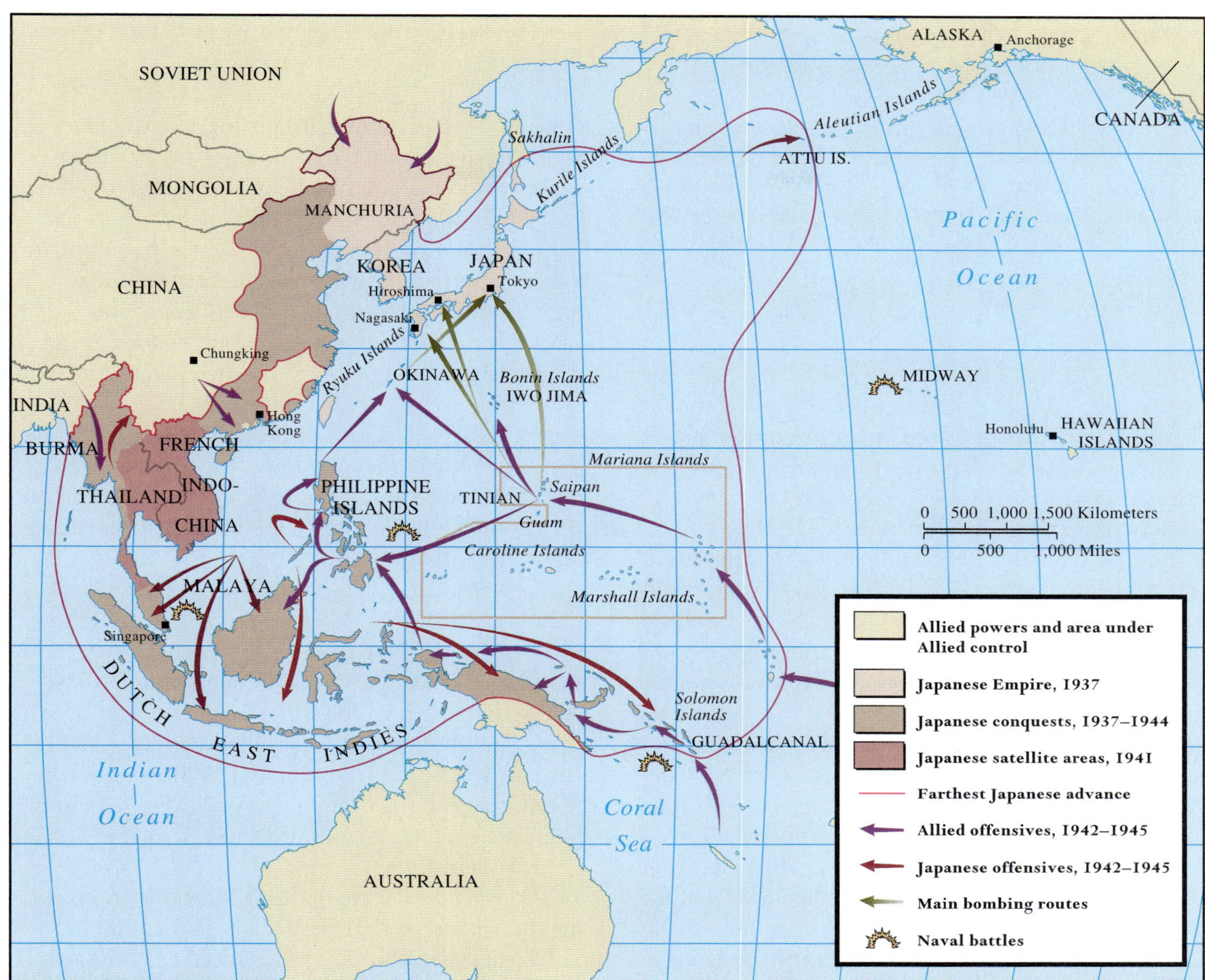

MAP 27.3 World War II in Asia and the Pacific.

But this would be Hitler's last optimistic outburst. By the fall of 1942, the war had turned against the Germans.

In North Africa, British forces had stopped Rommel's troops at El Alamein in the summer of 1942 and then forced them back across the desert. In November 1942, British and American forces invaded French North Africa and forced the German and Italian troops to surrender in May 1943. On the Eastern Front, the turning point of the war occurred at Stalingrad. After the capture of the Crimea, Hitler's generals wanted him to concentrate on the Caucasus and its oil fields, but Hitler decided that Stalingrad, a major industrial center on the Volga, should be taken first. Between November 1942 and February 1943, German troops were stopped, then encircled, and finally forced to surrender on February 2, 1943 (see the box on p. 564). The entire German Sixth Army of 300,000 men was lost. By February 1943, German forces in Russia were back to their positions of June 1942. By the spring of 1943, even Hitler knew that the Germans would not defeat the Soviet Union.

The tide of battle in the East also turned dramatically in 1942. In the Battle of the Coral Sea on May 7–8, 1942, American naval forces stopped the Japanese advance and temporarily relieved Australia of the threat of invasion. On June 4, at the Battle of Midway Island, American planes destroyed all four of the attacking Japanese aircraft carriers and established American naval superiority in the Pacific. After a series of bitter engagements in the waters of the Solomon Islands from August to November, Japanese fortunes began to fade.

A German Soldier at Stalingrad

The Russian victory at Stalingrad was a major turning point in World War II. This excerpt comes from the diary of a German soldier who fought and died in the Battle of Stalingrad. His dreams of victory and a return home with medals were soon dashed by the realities of Russian resistance.

Diary of a German Soldier

Today, after we'd had a bath, the company commander told us that if our future operations are as successful, we'll soon reach the Volga, take Stalingrad and then the war will inevitably soon be over. Perhaps we'll be home by Christmas.

July 29. The company commander says the Russian troops are completely broken, and cannot hold out any longer. To reach the Volga and take Stalingrad is not so difficult for us. The Führer knows where the Russians' weak point is. Victory is not far away. . . .

August 10. The Führer's orders were read out to us. He expects victory of us. We are all convinced that they can't stop us.

August 12. This morning outstanding soldiers were presented with decorations. . . . Will I really go back to Elsa without a decoration? I believe that for Stalingrad the Führer will decorate even me. . . .

September 4. We are being sent northward along the front toward Stalingrad. We marched all night and by dawn had reached Voroponovo Station. We can already see the smoking town. It's a happy thought that the end of the war is getting nearer. That's what everyone is saying. . . .

September 8. Two days of non-stop fighting. The Russians are defending themselves with insane stubbornness. Our regiment has lost many men. . . .

September 16. Our battalion, plus tanks, is attacking the [grain storage] elevator, from which smoke is pouring—the grain in it is burning, the Russians seem to have set light to it themselves. Barbarism. The battalion is suffering heavy losses. . . .

October 10. The Russians are so close to us that our planes cannot bomb them. We are preparing for a decisive attack. The Führer has ordered the whole of Stalingrad to be taken as rapidly as possible. . . .

October 22. Our regiment has failed to break into the factory. We have lost many men; every time you move you have to jump over bodies. . . .

November 10. A letter from Elsa today. Everyone expects us home for Christmas. In Germany everyone believes we already hold Stalingrad. How wrong they are. If they could only see what Stalingrad has done to our army. . . .

November 21. The Russians have gone over to the offensive along the whole front. Fierce fighting is going on. So, there it is—the Volga, victory and soon home to our families! We shall obviously be seeing them next in the other world.

November 29. We are encircled. It was announced this morning that the Führer has said: "The army can trust me to do everything necessary to ensure supplies and rapidly break the encirclement."

December 3. We are on hunger rations and waiting for the rescue that the Führer promised. . . .

December 14. Everybody is racked with hunger. Frozen potatoes are the best meal, but to get them out of the ice-covered ground under fire from Russian bullets is not so easy. . . .

December 26. The horses have already been eaten. I would eat a cat; they say its meat is also tasty. The soldiers look like corpses or lunatics, looking for something to put in their mouths. They no longer take cover from Russian shells; they haven't the strength to walk, run away and hide. A curse on this war!

The Last Years of the War

By the beginning of 1943, the tide of battle had turned against Germany, Italy, and Japan. After the Axis forces had surrendered in Tunisia on May 13, 1943, the Allies crossed the Mediterranean and carried the war to Italy. After taking Sicily, Allied troops began the invasion of mainland Italy in September. In the meantime, after the ouster and arrest of Benito Mussolini, a new Italian government offered to surrender to Allied forces. But Mussolini was liberated by the Germans in a daring raid and then set up as the head of a puppet German state in northern Italy while German troops moved in and occupied much of Italy. The new defensive lines established by the Germans in the hills south of Rome were so effective that the Allied advance up the Italian peninsula was a painstaking affair accompanied by heavy casualties. Rome did not fall to the Allies until June 4, 1944. By that time, the Italian war had assumed a secondary role anyway as the Allies opened their long-awaited "second front" in western Europe.

Since the autumn of 1943, the Allies had been planning a cross-channel invasion of France from Britain. Under the direction of the American general Dwight D. Eisenhower (1890–1969), the Allies landed five assault divisions on the Normandy beaches on June 6 in history's greatest naval invasion. An initially indecisive German response enabled the Allied forces to establish a beachhead. Within three months, they had landed two million men and a half-million vehicles that pushed inland and broke through German defensive lines.

After the breakout, Allied troops moved south and east and liberated Paris by the end of August. By March 1945, they had crossed the Rhine River and advanced farther into Germany. At the end of April, Allied forces in northern Germany moved toward the Elbe River, where they finally linked up with the Russians. The Russians had come a long way since the Battle of Stalingrad in 1943. In the summer of 1943, Hitler gambled on taking the offensive by making use of newly developed heavy tanks. German forces were soundly defeated by the Russians at the Battle of Kursk (July 5–12), the greatest tank battle of World War II. Soviet forces now began a relentless advance westward. The Soviets had reoccupied the Ukraine by the end of 1943 and lifted the siege of Leningrad and moved into the Baltic States by the beginning of 1944. Advancing along a northern front, Soviet troops occupied Warsaw in January 1945 and entered Berlin in April. Meanwhile, Soviet troops swept along a southern front through Hungary, Romania, and Bulgaria.

In January 1945, Adolf Hitler had moved into a bunker 55 feet under Berlin to direct the final stages of the war. In his final political testament, Hitler, consistent to the end in his rabid anti-Semitism, blamed the Jews for the war: "Above all I charge the leaders of the nation and those under them to scrupulous observance of the laws of race and to merciless opposition to the universal poisoner of all peoples, international Jewry."[4] Hitler committed suicide on April 30, two days after Mussolini had been shot by partisan Italian forces. On May 7, German commanders surrendered. The war in Europe was over.

The war in Asia continued. Beginning in 1943, American forces had gone on the offensive and advanced their way, slowly at times, across the Pacific. American forces took an increasing toll of enemy resources, especially at sea and in the air. When President Harry Truman (Roosevelt had died on April 12, 1945) and his advisers became convinced that American troops might suffer heavy casualties in an invasion

CROSSING THE RHINE. **After landing at Normandy, Allied forces liberated France and prepared to move into Germany. Makeshift bridges enabled the Allies to cross the Rhine in some areas and advance deeper into Germany. Units of the 7th United States Army of General Patch are shown here crossing the Rhine at Worms on a pontoon bridge constructed by battalions of engineers alongside the ruins of the old bridge.**

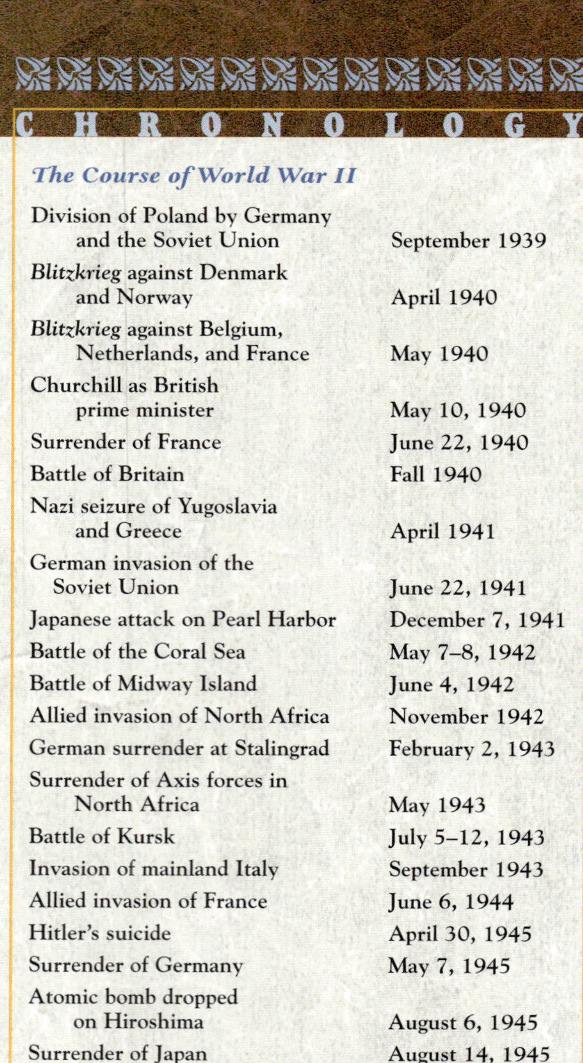
CHRONOLOGY

The Course of World War II

Division of Poland by Germany and the Soviet Union	September 1939
Blitzkrieg against Denmark and Norway	April 1940
Blitzkrieg against Belgium, Netherlands, and France	May 1940
Churchill as British prime minister	May 10, 1940
Surrender of France	June 22, 1940
Battle of Britain	Fall 1940
Nazi seizure of Yugoslavia and Greece	April 1941
German invasion of the Soviet Union	June 22, 1941
Japanese attack on Pearl Harbor	December 7, 1941
Battle of the Coral Sea	May 7–8, 1942
Battle of Midway Island	June 4, 1942
Allied invasion of North Africa	November 1942
German surrender at Stalingrad	February 2, 1943
Surrender of Axis forces in North Africa	May 1943
Battle of Kursk	July 5–12, 1943
Invasion of mainland Italy	September 1943
Allied invasion of France	June 6, 1944
Hitler's suicide	April 30, 1945
Surrender of Germany	May 7, 1945
Atomic bomb dropped on Hiroshima	August 6, 1945
Surrender of Japan	August 14, 1945

of the Japanese homeland, they made the decision to drop the newly developed atomic bomb on Hiroshima and Nagasaki. The Japanese surrendered unconditionally on August 14. World War II, in which seventeen million men died in battle and perhaps eighteen million civilians perished as well (some estimate total losses at fifty million), was finally over.

The Nazi New Order

After the German victories in Europe between 1939 and 1941, Nazi propagandists painted glowing images of a new European order based on "equal chances" for all nations and an integrated economic community. This was not Hitler's conception of a European New Order. He saw the Europe he had conquered simply as subject to German domination. Only the Germans, he once said, "can really organize Europe."

The Nazi Empire

The Nazi empire stretched across continental Europe from the English Channel in the west to the outskirts of Moscow in the east. In no way was this empire organized systematically or governed efficiently. Nazi-occupied Europe was organized in one of two ways. Some areas, such as western Poland, were annexed and made into German provinces. Most of occupied Europe was administered by German military or civilian officials, combined with different degrees of indirect control from collaborationist regimes.

Racial considerations played an important role in how conquered peoples were treated. German civil administrations were established in Norway, Denmark, and the Netherlands because the Nazis considered these populations Aryan, racially akin to the Germans and hence worthy of more lenient treatment. "Inferior" Latin peoples, such as the occupied French, were given military administrations. By 1943, however, as Nazi losses continued to mount, all the occupied territories of northern and western Europe were ruthlessly exploited for material goods and manpower for Germany's war needs.

Because the conquered lands in the east contained the living space for German expansion and were populated in Nazi eyes by racially inferior Slavic peoples, Nazi administration there was considerably more ruthless. Hitler's racial ideology and his plans for an Aryan racial empire were so important to him that he and the Nazis began to implement their racial program soon after the conquest of Poland. Heinrich Himmler, a strong believer in Nazi racial ideology and the leader of the SS, was put in charge of German resettlement plans in the east. Himmler's task was to evacuate the inferior Slavic peoples and replace them with Germans, a policy first applied to the new German provinces created from the lands of western Poland. One million Poles were uprooted and dumped in southern Poland. Hundreds of thousands of ethnic Germans (descendants of Germans who had migrated years earlier from Germany to different parts of southern and eastern Europe) were encouraged to colonize the designated areas in Poland. By 1942, two million ethnic Germans had been settled in Poland.

The invasion of the Soviet Union inflated Nazi visions of German colonization in the east. Hitler spoke to his intimate circle of a colossal project of social engineering after the war, in which Poles, Ukrainians, and Russians would become slave labor while German peasants settled on the abandoned lands and Germanized them. Nazis involved in this kind of planning were well aware of the human costs. Himmler told a gathering of SS officers that although the destruction of thirty million Slavs was a prerequisite for German plans in the east, "whether nations live in prosperity or starve to death interests me only insofar as we need them as slaves for our culture. Otherwise it is of no interest."[5]

Labor shortages in Germany led to a policy of ruthless mobilization of foreign labor for Germany. After the invasion of Russia, the four million Russian prisoners of war captured by the Germans became a major source of heavy labor, but it was wasted by allowing three million of them to die from neglect. In 1942, a special office was created to recruit labor for German farms and industries. By the summer of 1944, seven million foreign workers were laboring in Germany and constituted 20 percent of Germany's labor force. At the same time, another seven million workers were supplying forced labor in their own countries on farms, in industries, and even in military camps. Forced labor often proved counterproductive, however, because it created economic chaos in occupied countries and disrupted industrial production that could have helped Germany. Even worse for the Germans, the brutal character of Germany's recruitment policies often led more and more people to resist the Nazi occupation forces.

The Holocaust

There was no more terrifying aspect of the Nazi New Order than the deliberate attempt to exterminate the Jews of Europe. Racial struggle was a key element in Hitler's ideology and meant to him a clearly defined conflict of opposites: the Aryans, creators of human cultural development, against the Jews, parasites who were trying to destroy the Aryans. By the beginning of 1939, Nazi policy focused on promoting the "emigration" of German Jews from Germany. Once the war began in September 1939, however, the so-called "Jewish problem" took on new dimensions. For a while, there was discussion of the Madagascar plan, which aspired to the mass shipment of Jews to the African island of Madagascar. When war contingencies made this plan impractical, an even more drastic policy was conceived.

Heinrich Himmler and the SS organization closely shared Adolf Hitler's racial ideology. The SS was given responsibility for what the Nazis called their Final Solution to the Jewish problem, the annihilation of the Jews. Reinhard Heydrich (1904–1942), head of the SS's Security Service, was given administrative responsibility for the Final Solution. After the defeat of Poland, Heydrich ordered the special strike forces (*Einsatzgruppen*) that he had created to round up all Polish Jews and concentrate them in ghettos established in a number of Polish cities.

In June 1941, the *Einsatzgruppen* were given new responsibilities as mobile killing units. These SS death squads followed the regular army's advance into Russia. Their job was to round up Jews in their villages and execute and bury them in mass graves, often giant pits dug by the victims themselves before they were shot. Such regular killing produced morale problems among the SS executioners. During a visit to Minsk in the Soviet Union, SS leader Himmler tried to build morale by pointing out that "he would not like it if Germans did such a thing gladly. But their conscience was in no way impaired, for they were soldiers who had to carry out every order unconditionally. He alone had responsibility before God and Hitler for everything that was happening, . . . and he was acting from a deep understanding of the necessity for this operation."[6]

Although it has been estimated that as many as one million Jews were killed by the *Einsatzgruppen*, this approach to solving the Jewish problem was soon

THE HOLOCAUST: ACTIVITIES OF THE *EINSATZGRUPPEN*. The activities of the mobile killing units known as the *Einsatzgruppen* were the first stage in the mass killings of the Holocaust. This picture shows the execution of a Jew by a member of one of these SS killing squads. Onlookers include members of the German Army, the German Labor Service, and even Hitler Youth. When it became apparent that this method of killing was inefficient, it was replaced by the death camps.

MAP 27.4 The Holocaust.

perceived as inadequate. Instead, the Nazis opted for the systematic annihilation of the European Jewish population in specially built death camps. The plan was basically simple. Jews from countries occupied by Germany (or sympathetic to Germany) would be rounded up, packed like cattle into freight trains, and shipped to Poland, where six extermination centers were built for this purpose (see Map 27.4). The largest and most infamous was Auschwitz-Birkenau. Medical technicians chose Zyklon B (the commercial name for hydrogen cyanide) as the most effective gas for quickly killing large numbers of people in gas chambers designed to look like "shower rooms" to facilitate the cooperation of the victims. After gassing, the corpses would be burned in specially built crematoria.

By the spring of 1942, the death camps were in operation. Although initial priority was given to the elimination of the ghettos in Poland, by the summer of 1942, Jews were also being shipped from France, Belgium, and the Netherlands. Even as the Allies were making important advances in 1944, Jews were being shipped from Greece and Hungary. These shipments depended on the cooperation of Germany's Transport Ministry, and despite desperate military needs, the Final Solution had priority in using railroad cars for the transportation of Jews to death camps.

A harrowing experience awaited the Jews when they arrived at one of the six death camps. Rudolf Höss, commandant at Auschwitz-Birkenau, described it:

> We had two SS doctors on duty at Auschwitz to examine the incoming transports of prisoners. The prisoners would be marched by one of the doctors who would make spot decisions as they walked by. Those who were fit for work were sent into the camp. Others were sent immediately to

The Holocaust: The Camp Commandant and the Camp Victims

The systematic annihilation of millions of men, women, and children in extermination camps makes the Holocaust one of the most horrifying events in history. The first document is taken from an account by Rudolf Höss, commandant of the extermination camp at Auschwitz-Birkenau. In the second document, a French doctor explains what happened to the victims at one of the crematoria described by Höss.

Commandant Höss Describes the Equipment

The two large crematoria, Nos. I and II, were built during the winter of 1942–43. . . . They each . . . could cremate c. 2,000 corpses within twenty-four hours. . . . Crematoria I and II both had underground undressing and gassing rooms which could be completely ventilated. The corpses were brought up to the ovens on the floor above by lift. The gas chambers could hold c. 3,000 people.

The firm of Topf had calculated that the two smaller crematoria, III and IV, would each be able to cremate 1,500 corpses within twenty-four hours. However, owing to the wartime shortage of materials, the builders were obliged to economize and so the undressing rooms and gassing rooms were built above ground and the ovens were of a less solid construction. But it soon became apparent that the flimsy construction of these two four-retort ovens was not up to the demands made on it. No. III ceased operating altogether after a short time and later was no longer used. No. IV had to be repeatedly shut down since after a short period in operation of 4–6 weeks, the ovens and chimneys had burnt out. The victims of the gassing were mainly burnt in pits behind crematorium IV.

The largest number of people gassed and cremated within twenty-four hours was somewhat over 9,000.

A French Doctor Describes the Victims

It is mid-day, when a long line of women, children, and old people enter the yard. The senior official in charge . . . climbs on a bench to tell them that they are going to have a bath and that afterward they will get a drink of hot coffee. They all undress in the yard. . . . The doors are opened and an indescribable jostling begins. The first people to enter the gas chamber begin to draw back. They sense the death which awaits them. The SS men put an end to this pushing and shoving with blows from their rifle butts beating the heads of the horrified women who are desperately hugging their children. The massive oak double doors are shut. For two endless minutes one can hear banging on the walls and screams which are no longer human. And then—not a sound. Five minutes later the doors are opened. The corpses, squashed together and distorted, fall out like a waterfall. . . . The bodies which are still warm pass through the hands of the hairdresser who cuts their hair and the dentist who pulls out their gold teeth. . . . One more transport has just been processed through No. IV crematorium.

> the extermination plants. Children of tender years were invariably exterminated since by reason of their youth they were unable to work. . . . At Auschwitz we endeavored to fool the victims into thinking that they were to go through a delousing process. Of course, frequently they realized our true intentions and we sometimes had riots and difficulties due to that fact.[7]

About 30 percent of the arrivals at Auschwitz were sent to a labor camp; the remainder went to the gas chambers (see the box above). After they had been gassed, the bodies were burned in the crematoria. The victims' goods and even their bodies were used for economic gain. Women's hair was cut off, collected, and turned into mattresses or cloth. Some inmates were also subjected to cruel and painful "medical" experiments. The Germans killed between five and six million Jews, more than three million of them in the death camps. Virtually 90 percent of the Jewish populations of Poland, the Baltic countries, and Germany were exterminated. Overall, the Holocaust was responsible for the death of nearly two out of every three European Jews.

The Nazis were also responsible for the deliberate death by shooting, starvation, or overwork of at least another nine to ten million people. Because the Nazis also considered the Gypsies of Europe (like the Jews) a race containing alien blood, they were

The Bombing of Civilians

The home front became a battle front when civilian populations became the targets of mass bombing raids. Many people believed that mass bombing could effectively weaken the morale of the people and shorten the war. Rarely did it achieve its goal. In these selections, British, German, and Japanese civilians relate their experiences during bombing raids.

London, 1940

Early last evening, the noise was terrible. My husband and Mr. P. were trying to play chess in the kitchen. I was playing draughts with Kenneth in the cupboard. . . . Presently I heard a stifled voice "Mummy! I don't know what's become of my glasses." "I should think they are tied up in my wool." My knitting had disappeared and wool seemed to be everywhere! We heard a whistle, a bang which shook the house, and an explosion. . . . Well, we straightened out, decided draughts and chess were no use under the circumstances, and waited for a lull so we could have a pot of tea.

Hamburg, 1943

As the many fires broke through the roofs of the burning buildings, a column of heated air rose more than two and a half miles high and one and a half miles in diameter. . . . This column was turbulent, and it was fed from its base by in-rushing cooler ground-surface air. One and one half miles from the fires this draught increased the wind velocity from eleven to thirty-three miles per hour. At the edge of the area the velocities must have been appreciably greater, as trees three feet in diameter were uprooted. In a short time the temperature reached ignition point for all combustibles, and the entire area was ablaze. In such fires complete burn-out occurred; that is, no trace of combustible material remained, and only after two days were the areas cool enough to approach.

Hiroshima, August 6, 1945

I heard the airplane; I looked up at the sky, it was a sunny day, the sky was blue. . . . Then I saw something drop—and pow!—a big explosion knocked me down. Then I was unconscious—I don't know for how long. Then I was conscious but I couldn't see anything. . . . Then I see people moving away and I just follow them. It is not light like it was before, it is more like evening. I look around; houses are all flat! . . . I follow the people to the river. I couldn't hear anything, my ears are blocked up. I am thinking a bomb has dropped! . . . I didn't know my hands were burned, nor my face. . . . My eyes were swollen and felt closed up.

population by refusing to panic. But London morale was helped by the fact that German raids were widely scattered over a very large city. Smaller communities were more directly affected by the devastation. On November 14, 1940, for example, the *Luftwaffe* destroyed hundreds of shops and 100 acres of the city center of Coventry. Morale sank as wild rumors of heavy casualties spread in these communities but soon rebounded. War production in these areas seems to have been little affected by the raids.

The British failed to learn from their own experience, however, and soon proceeded with the bombing of Germany. Churchill and his advisers believed that destroying German communities would break civilian morale and bring victory. Major bombing raids began in 1942 under the direction of Arthur Harris, the wartime leader of the British air force's Bomber Command, which was rearmed with four-engine heavy bombers capable of taking the war into the center of occupied Europe. On May 31, 1942, Cologne became the first German city to be subjected to an attack by one thousand bombers.

With the entry of the Americans into the war, bombing strategy changed. American planes flew daytime missions aimed at the precision bombing of transportation facilities and wartime industries, while the British Bomber Command continued nighttime saturation bombing of all German cities with populations over 100,000. Bombing raids added an element of terror to circumstances already made difficult by growing shortages of food, clothing, and fuel. Germans especially feared incendiary bombs, which set off firestorms that swept destructive paths through the cities. Four raids on Hamburg in August 1943 produced temperatures of 1,800 degrees Fahrenheit, obliterated half the city's buildings, and killed fifty thousand civilians. The ferocious bombing of Dresden February 13–15, 1945, created a firestorm that may have killed as many as 100,000 inhabitants and refugees. Even some Allied leaders began to criticize what they saw as the unnecessary terror bombing of German cities.

Germany suffered enormously from the Allied bombing raids. Millions of buildings were destroyed, and possibly half a million civilians died in the raids. Nevertheless, it is highly unlikely that Allied bombing sapped the morale of the German people. Instead, Germans, whether pro-Nazi or anti-Nazi, fought on stubbornly, often driven simply by a desire to live. Nor did the bombing destroy Germany's industrial capacity. The Allied Strategic Bombing survey revealed that the production of war materials actually increased between 1942 and 1944. Even in 1944 and 1945, Allied raids cut German production of armaments by only 7 percent. Nevertheless, the widespread destruction of transportation systems and fuel supplies made it extremely difficult for the new materials to reach the German military.

The bombing of civilians eventually reached a new level with the dropping of the first atomic bomb. Japan was especially vulnerable to air raids because its air force had been virtually destroyed in the course of the war and its crowded cities were built of flimsy materials. Attacks on Japanese cities by the new American B-29 Superfortresses, the biggest bombers of the war, had begun on November 24, 1944. By the summer of 1945, many of Japan's factories had been destroyed along with one-fourth of its dwellings. After the Japanese government decreed the mobilization of all people between the ages of thirteen and sixty into the People's Volunteer Corps, President Truman and his advisers feared that Japanese fanaticism might mean a million American casualties. This concern led them to drop the atomic bomb on Hiroshima (August 6) and Nagasaki (August 9). The destruction was incredible. Of 76,000 buildings near the center of the explosion in Hiroshima, only 6,000 remained standing, and 140,000 of the city's 400,000 inhabitants had died by the end of 1945. Another 50,000 perished from the effects of radiation over the next five years.

Aftermath of the War: The Emergence of the Cold War

The total victory of the Allies in World War II was followed not by peace but by a new conflict known as the Cold War that dominated world politics until the end of the 1980s. The origins of the Cold War stemmed from the military, political, and ideological differences, especially between the Soviet Union and the United States, that became apparent at the Allied war conferences held in the last years of the war. Although Allied leaders were preoccupied primarily with how to end the war, they were also strongly motivated by differing and often conflicting visions of postwar Europe.

The Conferences at Tehran, Yalta, and Potsdam

Stalin, Roosevelt, and Churchill, the leaders of the Big Three of the Grand Alliance, met at Tehran (the capital of Iran) in November 1943 to decide the future course of the war. Their major tactical decision

THE VICTORIOUS ALLIED LEADERS AT YALTA. Even before World War II ended, the leaders of the Big Three of the Grand Alliance, Churchill, Roosevelt, and Stalin (shown from left to right), met in wartime conferences to plan the final assault on Germany and negotiate the outlines of the postwar settlement. At the Yalta meeting (February 5–11, 1945), the three leaders concentrated on postwar issues. The American president, who died two months later, was already a worn-out man at Yalta.

concerned the final assault on Germany. Stalin and Roosevelt argued successfully for an American-British invasion of the Continent through France, which they scheduled for the spring of 1944. The acceptance of this plan had important consequences. It meant that Soviet and British-American forces would meet in defeated Germany along a north-south dividing line and that, most likely, eastern Europe would be liberated by Soviet forces. The Allies also agreed to a partition of postwar Germany.

By the time of the conference at Yalta, in the Soviet republic of the Ukraine, in February 1945, the defeat of Germany was a foregone conclusion. The Western powers, which had earlier believed that the Soviets were in a weak position, now faced the reality of eleven million Red Army soldiers taking possession of eastern and much of central Europe. Stalin was still operating under the notion of spheres of influence. He was deeply suspicious of the Western powers and desired a buffer to protect the Soviet Union from possible future Western aggression. At the same time, however, Stalin was eager to obtain economically important resources and strategic military positions. Roosevelt by this time was moving away from the notion of spheres of influence to the ideal of self-determination. He called for "the end of the system of unilateral action, exclusive alliances, and spheres of influence." The Grand Alliance approved the "Declaration on Liberated Europe." This was a pledge to assist liberated European nations in the creation of "democratic institutions of their own choice." Liberated countries were to hold free elections to determine their political systems.

At Yalta, Roosevelt sought Soviet military help against Japan. The atomic bomb was not yet assured, and American military planners feared the possible loss of as many as one million men in amphibious assaults on the Japanese home islands. Roosevelt therefore agreed to Stalin's price for military assistance against Japan: possession of Sakhalin and the Kurile Islands, as well as two warm-water ports and railroad rights in Manchuria.

The creation of the United Nations was a major American concern at Yalta. Roosevelt hoped to ensure the participation of the Big Three powers in a postwar international organization before difficult issues divided them into hostile camps. After a number of compromises, both Churchill and Stalin accepted Roosevelt's plans for a United Nations organization and set the first meeting for San Francisco in April 1945.

The issues of Germany and eastern Europe were treated less decisively. The Big Three reaffirmed that Germany must surrender unconditionally and created four occupation zones. German reparations were set at $20 billion. A compromise was also worked out in regard to Poland. Stalin agreed to free elections in the future to determine a new government. But the issue of free elections in eastern Europe caused a serious rift between the Soviets and the Americans. The principle was that eastern European governments would be freely elected, but they were also supposed to be pro-Soviet. As Churchill expressed it: "The Poles will have their future in their own hands, with the single limitation that they must honestly follow in harmony with their allies, a policy friendly to Russia."[10] This attempt to reconcile two irreconcilable goals was doomed to failure, as soon became evident at the next conference of the Big Three powers.

Even before the conference at Potsdam, near Berlin, took place in July 1945, Western relations with the Soviets were deteriorating rapidly. The Grand Alliance had been one of necessity in which disagreements had been subordinated to the pragmatic concerns of the war. The Allied powers' only common aim was the defeat of Nazism. Once this aim had all but been accomplished, the many differences that troubled East-West relations came to the surface. Each side committed acts that the other viewed as unbecoming of "allies."

From the perspective of the Soviets, the United States' termination of lend-lease aid before the war was over and its failure to respond to a Soviet request for a $6 billion loan for reconstruction exposed the Western desire to keep the Soviet state weak. On the American side, the Soviet Union's failure to fulfill its Yalta pledge on the "Declaration on Liberated Europe" as applied to eastern Europe set a dangerous precedent. This was evident in Romania as early as February 1945, when the Soviets engineered a coup and installed a new government under the Communist Petra Groza, known as the "Little Stalin." One month later, the Soviets sabotaged the Polish settlement by arresting West-leaning Polish leaders and their sympathizers and placing Soviet-backed Poles in power. To the Americans, the Soviets seemed to be asserting control of eastern European countries under puppet Communist regimes.

The Potsdam conference of July 1945 consequently began under a cloud of mistrust. Roosevelt had died on April 12 and had been succeeded by Harry Truman. During the conference, Truman received word that the atomic bomb had been successfully tested. Some historians have argued that this knowledge resulted in Truman's stiffened resolve against the Soviets. Whatever the reasons, there was a new cold-

MAP 27.5 Territorial Changes After World War II.

ness in the relations between the Soviets and the Americans. At Potsdam, Truman demanded free elections throughout eastern Europe. Stalin responded: "A freely elected government in any of these East European countries would be anti-Soviet, and that we cannot allow."[11] After a bitterly fought and devastating war, Stalin sought absolute military security. To him, it could only be gained by the presence of Communist states in eastern Europe. Free elections might result in governments hostile to the Soviets. By the middle of 1945, only an invasion by Western forces could undo developments in eastern Europe, and after the world's most destructive conflict had ended, few people favored such a policy.

As the war slowly receded into the past, the reality of conflicting ideologies had reappeared. Many people in the West interpreted Soviet policy as part of a worldwide Communist conspiracy. The Soviets viewed Western, especially American, policy as global capitalist expansionism or, in Leninist terms, economic imperialism. Vyacheslav Molotov, the Russian foreign minister, referred to the Americans as "insatiable imperialists" and "war-mongering groups of adventurers."[12] In March 1946, in a speech to an American audience, former British prime minister Winston Churchill declared that "an iron curtain" had "descended across the continent," dividing Germany and Europe into two hostile camps (see Map 27.5). Stalin branded Churchill's speech a "call to war with the Soviet Union." Only months after the world's most devastating conflict had ended, the world seemed once again bitterly divided.

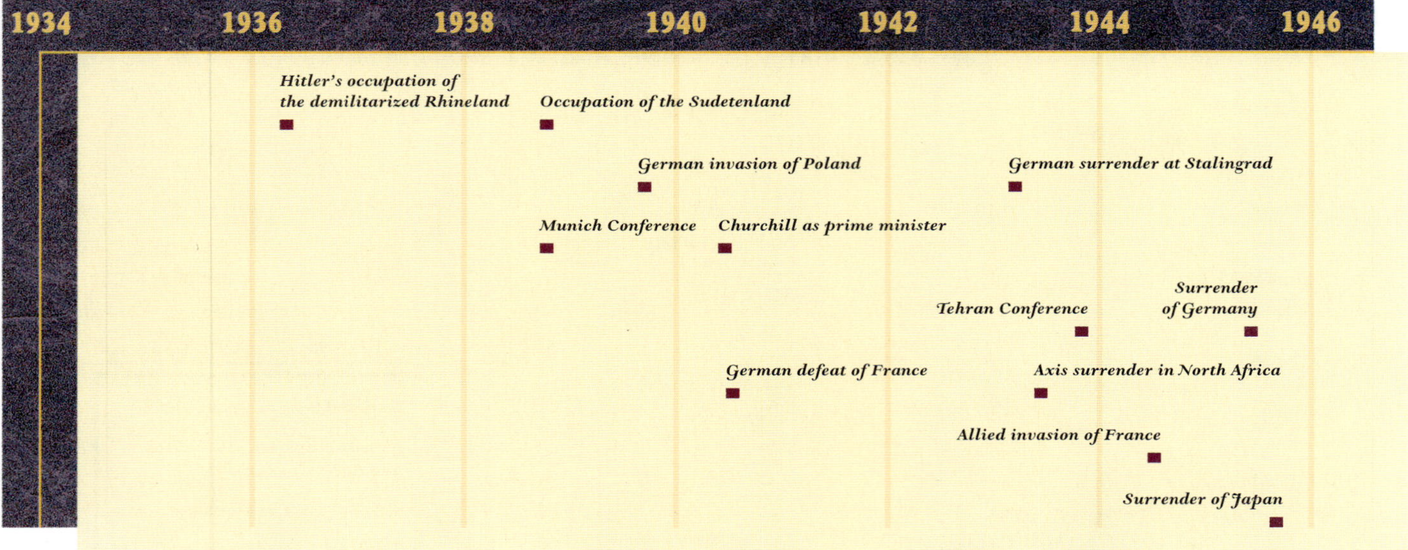

Conclusion

Between 1933 and 1939, Europeans watched as Adolf Hitler rebuilt Germany into a great military power. For Hitler, military power was an absolute prerequisite for the creation of a German racial empire that would dominate Europe and the world for generations to come. If Hitler had been successful, the Nazi New Order, built on authoritarianism, racial extermination, and the brutal oppression of peoples, would have meant a triumph of barbarism and the end of freedom and equality, which, however imperfectly realized, had become important ideals in Western civilization.

The Nazis lost, but only after tremendous sacrifices and costs. Much of European civilization lay in ruins, and the old Europe had disappeared forever. Europeans, who had been accustomed to dominating the world at the beginning of the twentieth century, now watched helplessly at mid-century as the two new superpowers created by the two world wars took control of their destinies. Even before the last battles had been fought, the United States and the Soviet Union had arrived at different visions of the postwar world. No sooner had the war ended than their differences sparked a new and potentially even more devastating conflict known as the Cold War. Yet even though Europeans seemed merely pawns in the struggle between the two superpowers, they managed to stage a remarkable recovery of their own civilization.

Notes

1. Adolf Hitler, *Mein Kampf*, trans. Ralph Manheim (Boston, 1971), p. 654.
2. *Documents on German Foreign Policy* (London, 1956), Series D, vol. 7, p. 204.
3. Quoted in Albert Speer, *Spandau*, trans. Richard Winston and Clara Winston (New York, 1976), p. 50.
4. *Nazi Conspiracy and Aggression* (Washington, D.C., 1946), vol. 6, p. 262.
5. International Military Tribunal, *Trial of the Major War Criminals* (Nuremberg, 1947–1949), vol. 22, p. 480.
6. Quoted in Raul Hilberg, *The Destruction of the European Jews*, rev. ed. (New York, 1985), vol. 1, pp. 332–333.
7. *Nazi Conspiracy and Aggression*, vol. 6, p. 789.
8. Quoted in John Campbell, *The Experience of World War II* (New York, 1989), p. 170.
9. Quoted in Claudia Koonz, "Mothers in the Fatherland: Women in Nazi Germany," in Renate Bridenthal and Claudia Koonz, eds., *Becoming Visible: Women in European History* (Boston, 1977), p. 466.
10. Quoted in Norman Graebner, *Cold War Diplomacy, 1945–1960* (Princeton, N.J., 1962), p. 117.
11. Ibid.
12. Quoted in Wilfried Loth, *The Division of the World, 1941–1955* (New York, 1988), p. 81.

Suggestions for Further Reading

The basic study of Germany's foreign policy from 1933 to 1939 can be found in G. Weinberg, *The Foreign Policy of Hitler's Germany: Diplomatic Revolution in Europe, 1933–36* (Chicago, 1970) and *The Foreign Policy of Hitler's Germany: Starting World War II, 1937–1939* (Chicago, 1980). For a detailed account of the immediate events leading to World War II, see D. C. Watt, *How War Came: The Immediate Origins of the Second World War, 1938–1939* (New York, 1989).

Hitler's war aims and the importance of ideology to those aims are examined in N. Rich, *Hitler's War Aims*, vol. 1, *Ideology, the Nazi State and the Course of Expansion* (New York, 1973), and vol. 2, *The Establishment of the New Order* (New York, 1974). On the origins of the war in the Pacific, see A. Iriye, *The Origins of the Second World War in Asia and the Pacific* (London, 1987). General works on World War II include the comprehensive work by

G. Weinberg, *A World at Arms: A Global History of World War II* (Cambridge, 1994); M. K. Dziewanowski, *War at Any Price: World War II in Europe, 1939–1945*, 2d ed. (Englewood Cliffs, N.J., 1991); J. Campbell, *The Experience of World War II* (New York, 1989); and G. Wright, *The Ordeal of Total War, 1939–1945* (New York, 1968). On Hitler as a military leader, see R. Lewin, *Hitler's Mistakes* (New York, 1986). The Eastern Front is covered in J. Erickson, *Stalin's War with Germany*, vol. 1, *The Road to Stalingrad* (London, 1973), and vol. 2, *The Road to Berlin* (London, 1985); and O. Bartov, *The Eastern Front, 1941–45: German Troops and the Barbarisation of Warfare* (London, 1986). The second front in Europe is examined in C. D'Este, *Decision in Normandy* (London, 1983).

A standard work on the German New Order in Russia is A. Dallin, *German Rule in Russia, 1941–1945*, rev. ed. (London, 1981). On Poland, see J. T. Gross, *Polish Society Under German Occupation* (Princeton, N.J., 1981). On foreign labor, see E. Homze, *Foreign Labor in Nazi Germany* (Princeton, N.J., 1967).

Among the best studies of the Holocaust are R. Hilberg, *The Destruction of the European Jews*, rev. ed., 3 vols. (New York, 1985); L. Dawidowicz, *The War Against the Jews* (New York, 1975); L. Yahil, *The Holocaust* (Oxford, 1990); and M. Gilbert, *The Holocaust: The History of the Jews of Europe During the Second World War* (New York, 1985). For brief studies, see J. Fischel, *The Holocaust* (Westport, Conn., 1998), and R. S. Botwinick, *A History of the Holocaust* (Upper Saddle River, N.J., 1996). A good overview of the scholarship on the Holocaust can be found in M. Marrus, *The Holocaust in History* (New York, 1987). On the extermination camps, see K. G. Feig, *Hitler's Death Camps: The Sanity of Madness* (New York, 1981). Other Nazi atrocities are examined in R. C. Lukas, *Forgotten Holocaust: The Poles Under German Occupation, 1939–44* (Lexington, Ky., 1986), and B. Wytwycky, *The Other Holocaust* (Washington, D.C., 1980).

General studies on the impact of total war include J. Costello, *Love, Sex and War: Changing Values, 1939–1945* (London, 1985); P. Summerfield, *Women Workers in the Second World War: Production and Patriarchy in Conflict* (London, 1984); and M. R. Marrus, *The Unwanted: European Refugees in the Twentieth Century* (New York, 1985). On the home front in Germany, see E. R. Beck, *Under the Bombs: The German Home Front, 1942–1945* (Lexington, Ky., 1986); M. Kitchen, *Nazi Germany at War* (New York, 1995); J. Stephenson, *The Nazi Organisation of Women* (London, 1981); and L. J. Rupp, *Mobilizing Women for War: German and American Propaganda, 1939–1945* (Princeton, N.J., 1978). The Soviet Union during the war is examined in M. Harrison, *Soviet Planning in Peace and War, 1938–1945* (Cambridge, 1985). On the American home front, see the collection of essays in K. P. O'Brien and L. H. Parsons, *The Home-Front War: World War II and American Society* (Westport, Conn., 1995).

On the destruction of Germany by bombing raids, see H. Rumpf, *The Bombing of Germany* (London, 1963). The German bombing of Britain is covered in T. Harrisson, *Living Through the Blitz* (London, 1985). On Hiroshima, see A. Chisholm, *Faces of Hiroshima* (London, 1985).

On the emergence of the Cold War, see W. Loth, *The Division of the World, 1941–1955* (New York, 1988), and the more extensive list of references at the end of Chapter 28. On the wartime summit conferences, see H. Feis, *Churchill, Roosevelt, Stalin: The War They Waged and the Peace They Sought*, 2d ed. (Princeton, N.J., 1967).

For additional reading, go to InfoTrac College Edition, your online research library at http://web1.infotrac-college.com

Enter the search terms *World War, 1939–1945* using the Subject Guide.

Enter the search terms *socialism history* using Key Terms.

Enter the search term *Holocaust* using the Subject Guide.

Enter the search term *Hitler* using Key Terms.

The Truman Doctrine

By 1947, the battle lines in the Cold War had been clearly drawn. This selection is taken from a speech by President Harry S Truman to the U.S. Congress in which he justified his request for aid to Greece and Turkey. Truman expressed the urgent need to contain the expansion of communism.

President Harry S Truman, Address to Congress, March 12, 1947

The peoples of a number of countries of the world have recently had totalitarian regimes forced upon them against their will. The Government of the United States has made frequent protests against coercion and intimidation, in violation of the Yalta agreement, in Poland, Romania, and Bulgaria. I must also state that in a number of other countries there have been similar developments.

At the present moment in world history nearly every nation must choose between alternative ways of life. The choice is too often not a free one.

One way of life is based upon the will of the majority, and is distinguished by free institutions, representative government, free elections, guarantees of individual liberty, freedom of speech and religion, and freedom from political oppression.

The second way of life is based upon the will of a minority forcibly imposed upon the majority. It relies upon terror and oppression, a controlled press and radio, fixed elections, and the suppression of personal freedoms.

I believe that it must be the policy of the United States to support free peoples who are resisting attempted subjugation by armed minorities or by outside pressures.

I believe that we must assist free people to work out their own destinies in their own way.

I believe that our help should be primarily through economic and financial aid which is essential to economic stability and orderly political processes. . . . I therefore ask the Congress for assistance to Greece and Turkey in the amount of $400,000,000.

requested $400 million in economic and military aid for Greece and Turkey from the U.S. Congress. The Truman Doctrine said in essence that the United States would provide money to countries that claimed they were threatened by Communist expansion. If the Soviets were not stopped in Greece, the Truman argument ran, the United States would have to face the spread of communism throughout the free world. As Dean Acheson, the American secretary of state, explained, "Like apples in a barrel infected by disease, the corruption of Greece would infect Iran and all the East . . . likewise Africa . . . Italy . . . France. . . . Not since Rome and Carthage had there been such a polarization of power on this earth."[1]

The proclamation of the Truman Doctrine was soon followed in June 1947 by the European Recovery Program, better known as the Marshall Plan. Intended to rebuild prosperity and stability, this program included $13 billion for the economic recovery of war-torn Europe. Underlying it was the belief that Communist aggression fed off economic turmoil. General George C. Marshall had noted in his commencement speech at Harvard: "Our policy is not directed against any country or doctrine but against hunger, poverty, desperation, and chaos."[2] From the Soviet perspective, the Marshall Plan aimed at "the construction of a bloc of states bound by obligations to the USA," and guaranteed "the American loans in return for the relinquishing by the European states of their economic and later also their political independence." The Marshall Plan was not intended to shut out either the Soviet Union or its Eastern European satellite states, but they refused to participate.

By 1947, the split in Europe between East and West had become a fact of life. At the end of World War II, the United States had favored a quick end to its commitments in Europe. But American fears of Soviet aims caused the United States to play an increasingly large role in Europe. In an important article in *Foreign Affairs* in July 1947, George Kennan, a well-known American diplomat with much knowledge of Soviet affairs, advocated a policy of containment against further aggression by the Soviets. Kennan favored the "adroit and vigilant application of counter-force at a series of constantly shifting geographical and political points, corresponding to the shifts and manoeuvres of Soviet policy." After the Soviets blockaded Berlin in 1948, containment of the Soviet Union became formal American policy.

The fate of Germany also became a source of heated contention between East and West. Besides the partitioning of Germany (and Berlin) into four occupied zones, the Allied powers had agreed on little else with regard to the conquered nation. The Soviets, hardest hit by the war, took reparations from Germany in the form of booty. The technology-starved Soviets dismantled and removed to Russia 380 factories from the western zones of Berlin before transferring their control to the Western powers. By the summer of 1946, two hundred chemical, paper, and textile factories in the Soviets' East German zone had likewise been shipped to the Soviet Union. At the same time, the German Communist Party was reestablished under the control of Walter Ulbricht (1893–1973) and was soon in charge of the political reconstruction of the Soviet zone in eastern Germany.

At the same time, the British, French, and Americans gradually began to merge their zones economically and by February 1948 were making plans for the unification of these three western sections of Germany and the formal creation of a West German federal government. The Soviets responded with a blockade of West Berlin that allowed neither trucks nor trains to enter the three western zones of Berlin.

The Western powers faced a dilemma. Direct military confrontation seemed dangerous, and no one wished to risk World War III. Therefore, an attempt to break through the blockade with tanks and trucks was ruled out. The solution was the Berlin air lift. At its peak, 13,000 tons of supplies were flown daily to Berlin. The Soviets, also not wanting war, did not interfere and finally lifted the blockade in May 1949. The blockade of Berlin had severely increased tensions between the United States and the Soviet Union and resulted in the separation of Germany into two states. The Federal Republic of Germany, known as West Germany, was formally created in September 1949, and a month later, the separate German Democratic Republic was established in East Germany. Berlin remained a divided city and the source of much contention between East and West.

In that same year, the Cold War spread from Europe to the rest of the world. The victory of the Chinese Communists in 1949 in the Chinese civil war brought a new Communist regime to power and intensified American fears about the spread of communism. The Soviet Union also detonated its first atomic bomb in 1949, and all too soon both powers were involved in an escalating arms race that resulted in the construction of ever more destructive nuclear weapons. Soon the search for security took the form of mutual deterrence, the belief that an arsenal of nuclear weapons prevented war by ensuring that if one nation launched its nuclear weapons in a preemptive first strike, the other nation would still be able to respond and devastate the attacker. It was assumed that neither side would risk using the massive arsenals that had been assembled.

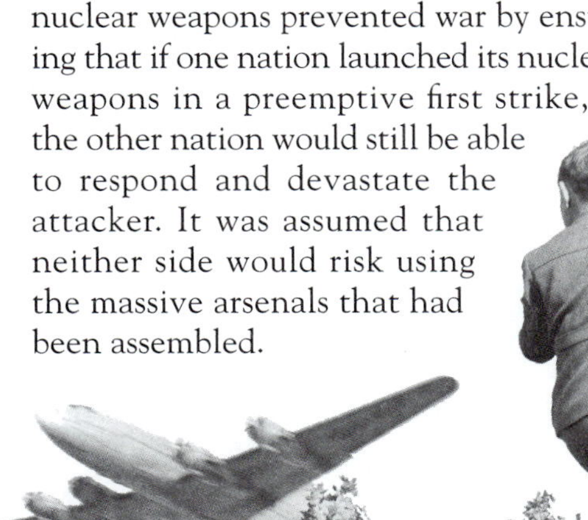

THE BERLIN AIR LIFT. The Berlin air lift enabled the United States to fly 13,000 tons of supplies daily to Berlin and thus break the Soviet land blockade of the city. In this photograph, children in West Berlin watch an American plane arrive with supplies for the city.

The search for security in the new world of the Cold War also led to the formation of military alliances. The North Atlantic Treaty Organization (NATO) was formed in April 1949 when Belgium, Luxembourg, the Netherlands, France, Britain, Italy, Denmark, Norway, Portugal, and Iceland signed a treaty with the United States and Canada. All the powers agreed to provide mutual assistance if any one of them was attacked. A few years later, West Germany, Greece, and Turkey joined NATO.

The Eastern European states soon followed suit. In 1949, they had already formed the Council for Mutual Economic Assistance (COMECON) for economic cooperation. Then in 1955, Albania, Bulgaria, Czechoslovakia, East Germany, Hungary, Poland, Romania, and the Soviet Union organized a formal military alliance in the Warsaw Pact. Once again, Europe was tragically divided into hostile alliance systems (see Map 28.1).

A system of military alliances spread to the rest of the world after the United States became involved in the Korean War in 1950. In 1950, probably with Stalin's approval, North Korean forces invaded South Korea. The Americans, seeing this as yet another example of Communist aggression and expansion, gained the support of the United Nations and intervened by sending American troops to turn back the invasion. When the American and South Korean

MAP 28.1 European Alliance Systems in the 1950s and 1960s.

forces pushed the North Koreans back toward the Chinese border, Chinese forces entered the fray and forced the American and South Korean troops to retreat back to South Korea. Believing that the Chinese were simply the puppets of Moscow, American policymakers created an image of communism as a monolithic force directed by the Soviet Union. After two more years of inconclusive fighting, an uneasy truce was reached in 1953, leaving Korea divided. To many Americans, the policy of containing communism had succeeded in Asia, just as it had earlier in Europe.

The Korean experience seemed to confirm American fears about Communist expansion and reinforced American determination to contain Soviet power. In the mid-1950s, the administration of President Dwight D. Eisenhower (1890–1969) adopted a policy of massive retaliation, which advocated the full use of American nuclear bombs to counteract even a Soviet ground attack in Europe. Moreover, American military alliances were extended around the world. The Central Treaty Organization (CENTO) of Turkey, Iraq, Iran, Pakistan, Britain, and the United States was intended to prevent the Soviet Union from expanding at the expense of its southern neighbors. To stem Soviet aggression in the East, the United States, Britain, France, Pakistan, Thailand, the Philippines, Australia, and New Zealand formed the Southeast Asia Treaty Organization (SEATO). By the mid-1950s, the United States found itself allied militarily with forty-two states around the world.

Despite the continued escalation of the Cold War, hopes for a new era of peaceful coexistence also appeared. The death of Stalin in 1953 caused some people in the West to think that the new Soviet leadership might be more flexible in its policies. But this optimism proved premature. A summit conference at Geneva in 1955 between President Eisenhower and Nikolai Bulganin, then leader of the Soviet government, produced no real benefits. A year later, all talk of rapprochement between East and West temporarily ceased when the Soviet Union used its armed forces in 1956 to crush Hungary's attempt to assert its independence from Soviet control.

A crisis over Berlin also added to the tension in the late 1950s. In August 1957, the Soviet Union had launched its first intercontinental ballistic missile (ICBM) and, shortly after, *Sputnik I,* the first space satellite. Fueled by partisan political debate, fears of a "missile gap" between the United States and the Soviet Union seized the American public. Nikita Khrushchev, the new leader of the Soviet Union, attempted to take advantage of the American frenzy over missiles to solve the problem of West Berlin. West Berlin had remained a "Western island" of prosperity in the midst of the relatively poverty-stricken East Germany. Many East Germans also managed to escape East Germany by fleeing through West Berlin.

In November 1958, Khrushchev announced that unless the West removed its forces from West Berlin within six months, he would turn over control of the access routes to Berlin to the East Germans. Unwilling to accept an ultimatum that would have abandoned West Berlin to the Communists, Eisenhower and the West stood firm, and Khrushchev eventually backed down. In 1961, the East German government built a wall separating West Berlin from East Berlin, and the Berlin issue faded.

It was revived when John F. Kennedy (1917–1963) became the U.S. president. During a summit meeting in Vienna in June 1961, Khrushchev threatened Kennedy with another six-month ultimatum over West Berlin. Kennedy left Vienna convinced of the need to deal firmly with the Soviet Union, and Khrushchev was forced once again to lift his six-month ultimatum. However, determined to achieve some foreign policy success, the Soviet leader soon embarked on an even more dangerous adventure in Cuba.

The Cuban Missile Crisis and the Move Toward Détente

The Cold War confrontation between the United States and the Soviet Union reached frightening levels during the Cuban Missile Crisis. In 1959, a left-wing revolutionary named Fidel Castro (b. 1927) had overthrown the Cuban dictator Fulgencio Batista and established a Soviet-supported totalitarian regime. In 1961, an American-supported attempt to invade via the Bay of Pigs and overthrow Castro's regime ended in utter failure. The next year, the Soviet Union decided to station nuclear missiles in Cuba. The United States was not prepared to allow nuclear weapons to be within such close striking distance of the American mainland, even though it had placed nuclear weapons in Turkey within easy range of the Soviet Union. Khrushchev was quick to point out that "your rockets are in Turkey. You are worried by Cuba . . . because it is 90 miles from the American coast. But Turkey is next to us."[3] When U.S. intelligence discovered that a Soviet fleet carrying missiles was heading to Cuba, President Kennedy decided to blockade Cuba and prevent the fleet from reaching its destination. This approach to the problem had the benefit of delaying confrontation and giving each side time to

The Cuban Missile Crisis: Khrushchev's Perspective

The Cuban Missile Crisis was one of the sobering experiences of the Cold War. It led the two superpowers to seek new ways to lessen the tensions between them. This version of the events is taken from the memoirs of Nikita Khrushchev.

Khrushchev Remembers

I will explain what the Caribbean crisis of October 1962, was all about. . . . At the time that Fidel Castro led his revolution to victory and entered Havana with his troops, we had no idea what political course his regime would follow. . . . All the while the Americans had been watching Castro closely. At first they thought that the capitalist underpinnings of the Cuban economy would remain intact. So by the time Castro announced that he was going to put Cuba on the road toward Socialism, the Americans had already missed their chance to do any thing about it by simply exerting their influence: there were no longer any forces left which could be organized to fight on America's behalf in Cuba. That left only one alternative—invasion! . . .

After Castro's crushing victory over the counterrevolutionaries we intensified our military aid to Cuba. . . . We were sure that the Americans would never reconcile themselves to the existence of Castro's Cuba. They feared, as much as we hoped, that a Socialist Cuba might become a magnet that would attract other Latin American countries to Socialism. . . . It was clear to me that we might very well lose Cuba if we didn't take some decisive steps in her defense. . . . We had to think up some way of confronting America with more than words. We had to establish a tangible and effective deterrent to American interference in the Caribbean. But what exactly? The logical answer was missiles. We knew that American missiles were aimed against us in Turkey and Italy, to say nothing of West Germany. . . . My thinking went like this: if we installed the missiles secretly and then if the United States discovered the missiles were there after they were already poised and ready to strike, the Americans would think twice before trying to liquidate our installations by military means. . . . I want to make one thing absolutely clear: when we put our ballistic missiles in Cuba we had no desire to start a war. On the contrary, our principal aim was only to deter America from starting a war. . . .

President Kennedy issued an ultimatum, demanding that we remove our missiles and bombers from Cuba. . . . We sent the Americans a note saying that we agreed to remove our missiles and bombers on the condition that the President give us his assurance that there would be no invasion of Cuba by the forces of the United States or anybody else. Finally Kennedy gave in and agreed to make a statement giving us such an assurance. . . . It had been, to say the least, an interesting and challenging situation. The two most powerful nations of the world had been squared off against each other, each with its finger on the button. You'd have thought that war was inevitable. But both sides showed that if the desire to avoid war is strong enough, even the most pressing dispute can be solved by compromise. And a compromise over Cuba was indeed found. The episode ended in a triumph of common sense. . . . It was a great victory for us, though, that we had been able to extract from Kennedy a promise that neither America nor any of her allies would invade Cuba. . . . The Caribbean crisis was a triumph of Soviet foreign policy and a personal triumph in my own career as a statesman and as a member of the collective leadership. We achieved, I would say, a spectacular success without having to fire a single shot!

find a peaceful solution (see the box above). Khrushchev agreed to turn back the fleet if Kennedy pledged not to invade Cuba.

The intense feeling that the world might have been annihilated in a few days had a profound influence on both sides. A hotline communication system between Moscow and Washington was installed in 1963 to expedite rapid communication between the two superpowers in time of crisis. In the same year, the two powers agreed to ban nuclear tests in the atmosphere, a step that served to lessen the tensions between the two nations.

By that time, the United States had also been drawn into a new confrontation that had an important impact on the Cold War—the Vietnam War. In 1964, under President Lyndon B. Johnson (1908–1973), increasing numbers of U.S. troops were sent to Vietnam to keep the Communist regime of the north from uniting the entire country under its control. Although nationalism played a powerful role in this conflict, the American policymakers saw it in terms of a "domino theory" concerning the spread of communism. If the Communists succeeded in Vietnam, the argument went, all the other countries in Asia freeing themselves from colonial domination would fall, like dominoes, to communism.

Despite their massive superiority in equipment and firepower, U.S. forces failed to prevail over the persistence of the North Vietnamese. The mounting destruction and increasing brutalization of the war, brought into American homes every evening on television, also turned American public opinion against U.S. participation in the war. In 1973, President Richard Nixon

THE VIETNAM WAR. Starting in 1964, U.S. troops fought against Vietcong guerrillas and North Vietnamese regular forces until they were withdrawn as a result of the Paris Agreement reached in January 1973. Shown here are U.S. troops after a Vietcong attack. The helicopter that is arriving would soon remove the American wounded from the battlefield.

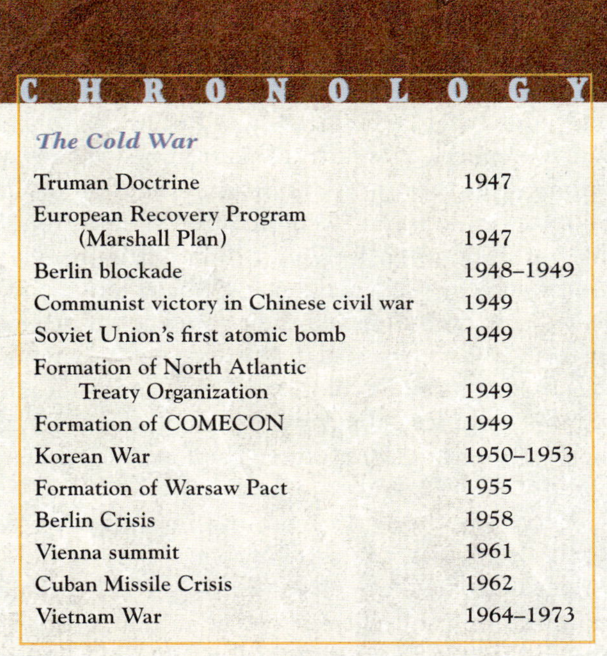

CHRONOLOGY

The Cold War

Truman Doctrine	1947
European Recovery Program (Marshall Plan)	1947
Berlin blockade	1948–1949
Communist victory in Chinese civil war	1949
Soviet Union's first atomic bomb	1949
Formation of North Atlantic Treaty Organization	1949
Formation of COMECON	1949
Korean War	1950–1953
Formation of Warsaw Pact	1955
Berlin Crisis	1958
Vienna summit	1961
Cuban Missile Crisis	1962
Vietnam War	1964–1973

(1913–1994) reached an agreement with North Vietnam that allowed the United States to withdraw its forces. Within two years, Vietnam had been forcibly reunited by Communist armies from the North.

Despite the success of the North Vietnamese Communists, the domino theory proved unfounded. A noisy rupture between Communist China and the Soviet Union put an end to the idea of a monolithic communism directed by Moscow. Under President Nixon, U.S. relations with China were resumed. New nations in Southeast Asia also managed to avoid Communist governments. Above all, Vietnam helped show the limitations of American power. By the end of the Vietnam War, a new era in American-Soviet relations, known as *détente*, had begun to emerge.

Recovery and Renewal in Europe

Within a few years after the defeat of Germany and Italy, economic revival brought renewed growth to European society, although major differences remained between Western and Eastern Europe. Moreover, many Europeans found that they could even adjust to decolonization.

The End of European Colonies

Not only did World War II leave Europe in ruins, but it also cost Europe its supremacy in world affairs. The power of the European states had been destroyed by the exhaustive struggles of World War II. The greatest colonial empire builder, Great Britain, no longer had the energy or wealth to maintain its colonial empire after the war and quickly sought to let its colonies go. A rush of decolonization swept through the world. Between 1947 and 1962, virtually every colony achieved independence. Some colonial powers willingly relinquished their control, but others, especially the French, had to be driven out by national wars of liberation. Decolonization was a difficult and even bitter process, but it reconfigured the world as the non-Western states halted the long-held ascendancy of the Western nations.

In Asia, the United States initiated the process of decolonization in 1946 when it granted independence to the Philippines (see Map 28.2). Britain soon followed suit with its oldest and largest nonwhite possession, India. Over the years, Mohandas "Mahatma" Gandhi (1869–1948) and his civil disobedience movement had greatly furthered the drive for India's independence. But unable to resolve the conflict between the Hindu and Muslim populations within India, the British created two states, a mostly Hindu India and a predominantly Muslim Pakistan in 1947. In 1948, Britain granted independence to Ceylon (modern Sri Lanka) and Burma (modern Myanmar). When the Dutch failed to reestablish control over the Dutch East Indies, Indonesia emerged as an independent nation in 1949. The French effort to remain in Indochina led to a bloody struggle with the Vietminh, Vietnamese nationalist guerrillas, led by Ho Chi Minh, the Communist and nationalist leader of the Vietnamese. After their defeat in 1954, the French granted independence to Laos and Cambodia, and Vietnam was temporarily divided in anticipation of elections in 1956 that would decide its fate. But the

MAP 28.2 Asia After World War II.

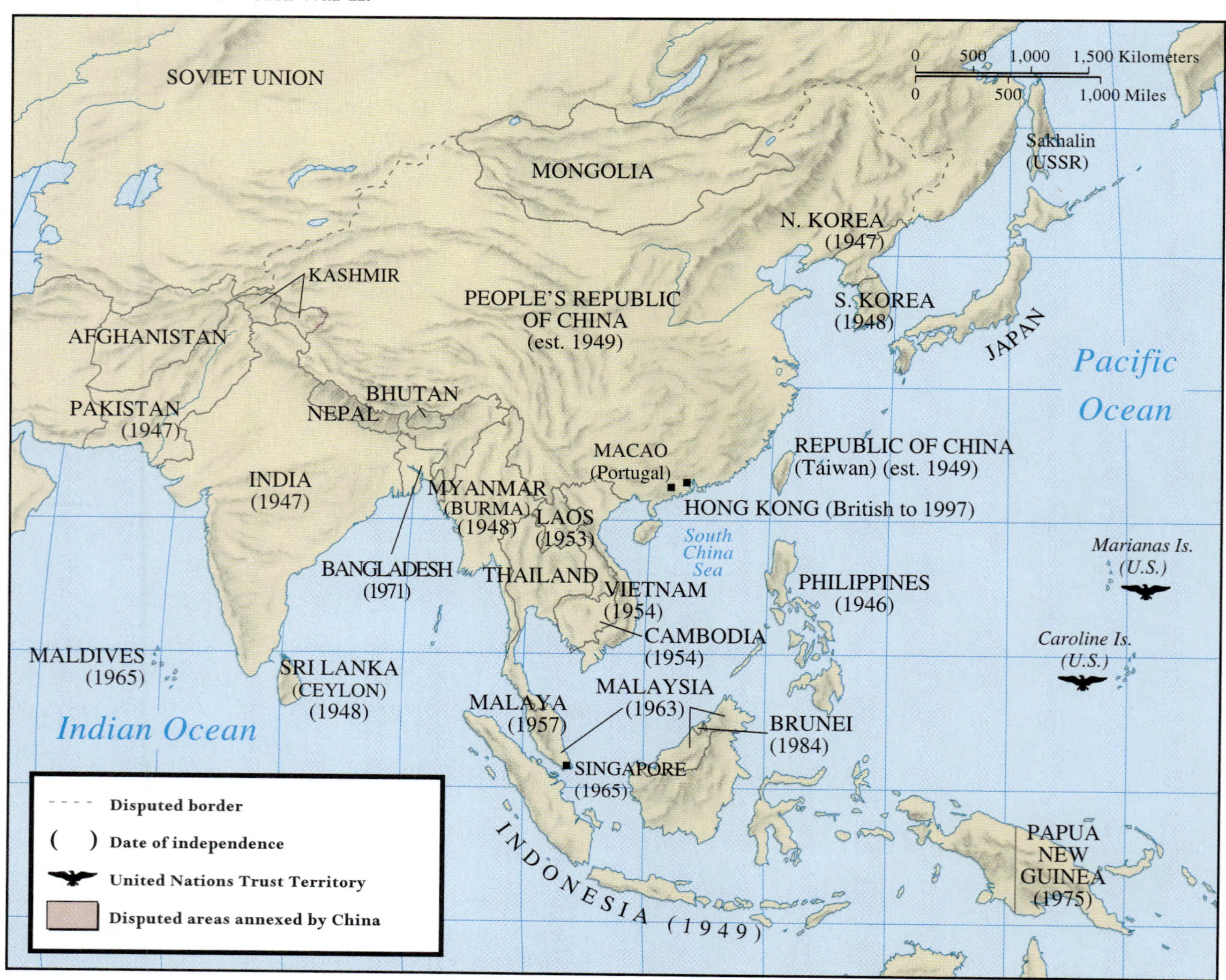

elections were never held, and the division of Vietnam by Communist and pro-Western regimes eventually led to the Vietnam War.

In the Middle East and North Africa, Arab nationalism was a powerful factor in ending colonial empires. Some Arab states had already become independent before the end of World War II. Now they were joined by other free Arab states, but not without considerable bloodshed and complications (see Map 28.3). When the British left Palestine in 1947, the United Nations voted to create both an Arab state and a Jewish state. When the Arabs attempted to destroy the new Jewish state of Israel, Israel's victories secured its existence. But the problem of the Palestinian refugees, who fled to the surrounding Arab states, perpetuated the Arab-Israeli conflict.

In North Africa, the French granted full independence to Morocco and Tunisia in 1956. Because Algeria was home to two million French settlers, however, France chose to retain its dominion there. But a group of Algerian nationalists organized the National Liberation Front (FLN) and in 1954 initiated a guerrilla war to liberate their homeland. The French leader, Charles de Gaulle, granted Algeria independence in 1962.

Decolonization in Africa south of the Sahara took place less turbulently. Ghana proclaimed its independence in 1957, and by 1960, almost all French and British possessions in Africa had gained their freedom (see Map 28.4). In 1960, the Belgians freed the Congo (the modern Democratic Republic of the Congo, formerly Zaire). The Portuguese held on stubbornly but were also driven out of Africa by 1975. Nevertheless, the continuing European economic presence in sub-Saharan Africa led radicals to accuse Europeans of "neocolonial" attitudes.

Although expectations ran high in the new states, they soon found themselves beset with problems of extreme poverty and antagonistic tribal groups that felt little loyalty to the new nations. These states came to be known collectively as the Third World (the First World consisted of the advanced industrial countries—Japan and the states of Western Europe and North America; the Second World comprised the Soviet Union and its satellites). Their status as "backward" nations led many Third World countries to modernize by pursuing Western technology and industrialization. In many instances, this meant that these peoples had to adjust to the continuing imposition of Western institutions and values on their societies.

The Soviet Union: From Stalin to Khrushchev

World War II devastated the Soviet Union. To create a new industrial base, Stalin returned to the method that he had used in the 1930s—the acquisition of development capital from Soviet labor. Working hard for

MAP 28.3 The Middle East After World War II.

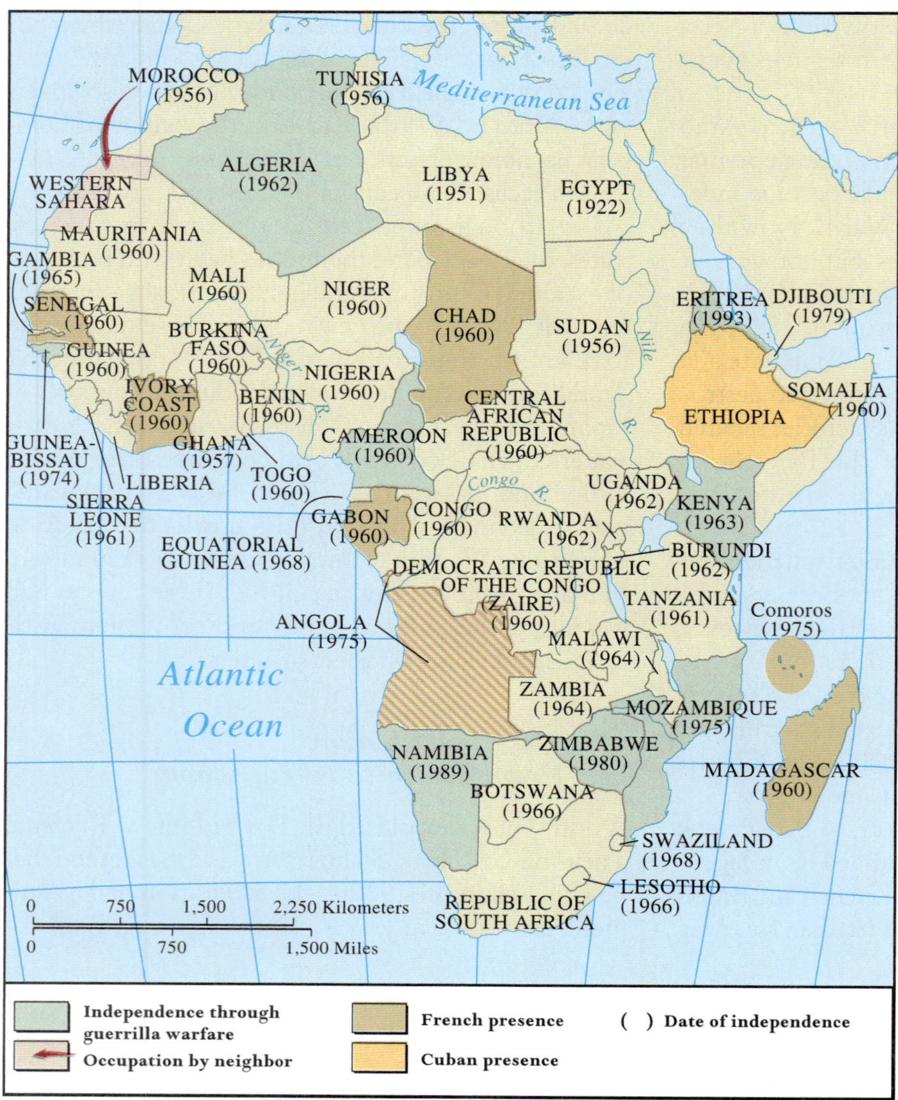

MAP 28.4 Africa After World War II.

little pay, poor housing, and precious few consumer goods, Soviet laborers were expected to produce goods for export with little in return for themselves. The incoming capital from abroad could then be used to purchase machinery and Western technology. The loss of millions of men in the war meant that much of this tremendous workload fell on Soviet women. Almost 40 percent of heavy manual labor was performed by women.

Economic recovery in the Soviet Union was nothing less than spectacular. By 1947, Russian industrial production had attained prewar levels; three years later, it had surpassed them by 40 percent. New power plants, canals, and giant factories were built, while new industrial plants and oil fields were established in Siberia and Soviet Central Asia. Stalin's five-year plan of 1946 reached its goals in less than five years.

Although Stalin's economic policy was successful in promoting growth in heavy industry, primarily for the benefit of the military, consumer goods were scarce. The development of thermonuclear weapons in 1953, MIG fighters from 1950 to 1953, and the first space satellite in 1957 may have elevated the Soviet state's reputation as a world power abroad, but domestically the Russian people were shortchanged. Heavy industry grew at a rate three times that of personal consumption. Moreover, the housing shortage was acute. A British military attaché in Moscow reported that "all houses, practically without exception, show lights from every window after dark. This seems to indicate that every room is both a living room by day and a bedroom by night. There is no place in overcrowded Moscow for the luxury of eating and sleeping in separate rooms."[4]

When World War II ended in 1945, Stalin had been in power for more than fifteen years. During that time, he had removed all opposition to his rule and remained the undisputed master of the Soviet Union. Other leading members of the Communist Party were completely obedient to his will. Increasingly distrustful of competitors, Stalin exercised sole authority and pitted his subordinates against one another.

Stalin's morbid suspicions fueled the constantly increasing repression that was a characteristic of his regime. In 1946, the government decreed that all literary and scientific works must conform to the political needs of the state. Along with this anti-intellectual campaign came political terror. A new series of purges seemed imminent in 1953, but Stalin's death on March 5, 1953, prevented more bloodletting.

A new collective leadership succeeded Stalin until Nikita Khrushchev (1894–1971) emerged as the chief Soviet policymaker. Khrushchev had been responsible for ending the system of forced-labor camps, a regular feature of Stalinist Russia. At the Twentieth Congress of the Communist Party in 1956, Khruschchev condemned Stalin for his "administrative violence, mass repression, and terror."

Once in power, Khrushchev took steps to undo some of the worst features of Stalin's repressive regime. A certain degree of intellectual freedom was now permitted; Khrushchev said that "readers should be given the chance to make their own judgments" regarding the acceptability of controversial literature and that "police measures shouldn't be used."[5] In 1962, he allowed the publication of Alexander Solzhenitsyn's novel *A Day in the Life of Ivan Denisovich*, a grim portrayal of the horrors of Russia's forced-labor camps. Most important, Khrushchev extended the process of destalinization by reducing the powers of the secret police and closing some of the Siberian prison camps. Nevertheless, Khrushchev's revelations about Stalin at the Twentieth Congress caused turmoil in Communist ranks everywhere and encouraged a spirit of rebellion in Soviet satellite countries in Eastern Europe. Soviet troops reacted by crushing an uprising in Hungary in 1956, and Khrushchev and the Soviet leaders, fearful of further undermining the basic foundations of the regime, downplayed their campaign of destalinization.

Economically, Khrushchev tried to place more emphasis on light industry and consumer goods. Khrushchev's attempts to increase agricultural output by cultivating vast lands east of the Ural Mountains proved less successful and damaged his reputation within the party. These failures, combined with increased military spending, hurt the Soviet economy. The industrial growth rate, which had soared in the early 1950s, now declined dramatically from 13 percent in 1953 to 7.5 percent in 1964.

Khrushchev's personality also did not endear him to the higher Soviet officials, who frowned at his tendency to crack jokes and play the clown. Nor were the higher members of the party bureaucracy pleased when Khruschchev tried to curb their privileges. Foreign policy failures caused additional damage to Khrushchev's reputation among his colleagues. His rash plan to place missiles in Cuba was the final straw. While he was on vacation in 1964, a special meeting of the Soviet Politburo voted him out of office (because of "deteriorating health") and forced him into retirement. Although a group of leaders succeeded him, real power came into the hands of Leonid Brezhnev (1906–1982), the "trusted" supporter of Khrushchev who had engineered his downfall.

Eastern Europe: Behind the Iron Curtain

At the end of World War II, Soviet military forces had occupied all of Eastern Europe and the Balkans (except for Greece, Albania, and Yugoslavia). All of the occupied states came to be part of the Soviet sphere of influence and, after 1945, experienced similar political developments. Between 1945 and 1947, one-party Communist governments became firmly entrenched in East Germany, Bulgaria, Romania, Poland, and Hungary. In Czechoslovakia, where there was a strong tradition of democratic institutions, the Communists did not achieve their goals until 1948 when all other parties were dissolved and Klement Gottwald, the leader of the Communists, became the new president of Czechoslovakia.

Albania and Yugoslavia were notable exceptions to this progression of Soviet dominance in Eastern Europe. Both had had strong Communist resistance movements during the war, and in both countries, the Communist Party simply assumed power when the war ended. In Albania, local Communists established a rigidly Stalinist regime that grew increasingly independent of the Soviet Union.

In Yugoslavia, Josip Broz, known as Tito (1892–1980), leader of the Communist resistance movement, seemed to be a loyal Stalinist. After the war, however, he moved toward the establishment of an independent Communist state in Yugoslavia. In 1958, the Yugoslav party congress asserted that Yugoslav

CHRONOLOGY

The Soviet Union and Satellite States in Eastern Europe

Death of Stalin	1953
Khrushchev's denunciation of Stalin	1956
Attempt at reforms in Poland	1956
Soviet suppression of Hungarian revolt	1956
Construction of Berlin Wall	1961
Brezhnev in power	1964
Soviet suppression of "Prague Spring" in Czechoslovakia	1968

Communists were not Stalinists but rather closer to the Marxist-Leninist ideal. This meant they would pursue a more decentralized economic and political system in which workers could manage themselves and local communes could exercise some political power.

Between 1948 and Stalin's death in 1953, the Eastern European satellite states followed a policy of Stalinization. They instituted Soviet-type five-year plans with an emphasis on heavy industry rather than consumer goods. They began to collectivize agriculture. They established the institutions of repression—secret police and military forces. But communism—a foreign product—had not developed deep roots among the peoples of Eastern Europe. Moreover, Soviet economic exploitation of Eastern Europe made living conditions harsh for most people. The Soviets demanded reparations from their defeated wartime enemies Bulgaria, Romania, and Hungary and forced all of the Eastern European states to trade with the Soviet Union to the latter's advantage.

After Stalin's death, many Eastern European states began to pursue a new, more nationalistically oriented course, while the new Soviet leaders, including Khrushchev, interfered less in the internal affairs of their satellites. But in the late 1950s and 1960s, the Soviet Union also made it clear, particularly in Poland, Hungary, and Czechoslovakia, that it would not allow its Eastern European satellites to become independent of Soviet control.

In 1956, worker protests erupted in Poland. In response, the Polish Communist Party adopted a series of reforms in October and elected Wladyslaw Gomulka (1905–1982) as first secretary. Gomulka declared that Poland had the right to follow its own socialist path. Fearful of Soviet armed response, however, the Poles compromised. Poland pledged to remain loyal to the Warsaw Pact, and the Soviets agreed to allow Poland to follow its own path to socialism.

The developments in Poland in 1956 inspired national Communists in Hungary to seek the same kinds of reforms and independence. Intense debates eventually resulted in the ouster of the ruling Stalinist and the selection of Imre Nagy (1896–1958) as the new Hungarian leader. Internal dissent, however, was not simply directed against the Soviets but against communism in general, which was viewed as a creation of the Soviets, not the Hungarians. The Stalinist secret police had also bred much terror and hatred. This dissatisfaction, combined with economic difficulties, created a situation ripe for revolt. To quell the rising rebellion, Nagy declared Hungary a free nation on November 1, 1956. He promised free elections, and the mood of the country made it clear that this could mean the end of Communist rule in Hungary. But Khrushchev was in no position at home to allow a member of the Communist flock to leave. Just three days after Nagy's declaration, the Red Army attacked Budapest (see the box on p. 591). The Soviets reestablished control over the country while János Kádár (1912–1989), a reform-minded cabinet minister, replaced Nagy. By collaborating with the Soviet invaders, Kádár saved many of Nagy's economic reforms.

The developments in Poland and Hungary in 1956 did not generate similar revolts in Czechoslovakia. The "Little Stalin," Antonin Novotny (1904–1975), placed in power in 1952 by Stalin himself, remained firmly in control. By the late 1960s, however, Novotny had alienated many members of his

SOVIET INVASION OF CZECHOSLOVAKIA, 1968. The attempt of Alexander Dubcek, the new first secretary of the Czech Communist Party, to liberalize Communist rule in Czechoslovakia failed when Soviet troops invaded and crushed the reform movement. This photograph shows a confrontation between Soviet tanks and Czechs in Prague. The tanks won.

Soviet Repression in Eastern Europe: Hungary, 1956

Developments in Poland in 1956 inspired the Communist leaders of Hungary to begin to remove their country from Soviet control. But there were limits to Khrushchev's tolerance, and he sent Soviet troops to crush Hungary's movement for independence. The first selection is a statement by the Soviet government justifying the use of Soviet troops; the second is a brief and tragic final statement from Imry Nagy, the Hungarian leader.

Statement of the Soviet Government, October 30, 1956

The Soviet Government regards it as indispensable to make a statement in connection with the events in Hungary.

The course of the events has shown that the working people of Hungary, who have achieved great progress on the basis of their people's democratic order, correctly raise the question of the necessity of eliminating serious shortcomings in the field of economic building, the further raising of the material well-being of the population, and the struggle against bureaucratic excesses in the state apparatus.

However, this just and progressive movement of the working people was soon joined by forces of black reaction and counterrevolution, which are trying to take advantage of the discontent of part of the working people to undermine the foundations of the people's democratic order in Hungary and to restore the old landlord and capitalist order.

The Soviet Government and all the Soviet people deeply regret that the development of events in Hungary has led to bloodshed. On the request of the Hungarian People's Government the Soviet Government consented to the entry into Budapest of the Soviet Army units to assist the Hungarian People's Army and the Hungarian authorities to establish order in the town.

The Last Message of Imry Nagy, November 4, 1956

This fight is the fight for freedom by the Hungarian people against the Russian intervention, and it is possible that I shall only be able to stay at my post for one or two hours. The whole world will see how the Russian armed forces, contrary to all treaties and conventions, are crushing the resistance of the Hungarian people. They will also see how they are kidnapping the Prime Minister of a country which is a Member of the United Nations, taking him from the capital, and therefore it cannot be doubted at all that this is the most brutal form of intervention. I should like in these last moments to ask the leaders of the revolution, if they can, to leave the country. I ask that all that I have said in my broadcast, and what we have agreed on with the revolutionary leaders during meetings in Parliament, should be put in a memorandum, and the leaders should turn to all the peoples of the world for help and explain that today it is Hungary and tomorrow, or the day after tomorrow, it will be the turn of other countries because the imperialism of Moscow does not know borders, and is only trying to play for time.

own party and was particularly resented by Czechoslovakia's writers, such as the playwright Vaclav Havel (b. 1936). A writers' rebellion late in 1967, in fact, led to Novotny's resignation. In January 1968, Alexander Dubcek (1921–1992) was elected first secretary of the Communist Party and soon introduced a number of reforms, including freedom of speech and of the press, freedom to travel abroad, and a relaxation of secret police activities. Dubcek hoped to create "communism with a human face." A period of euphoria erupted that came to be known as the "Prague Spring."

It proved short-lived. To forestall the spreading of this "spring fever," the Red Army invaded Czechoslovakia in August 1968 and crushed the reform movement. Gustav Husák (b. 1913), a committed nonreformist, replaced Dubcek, abolished his reforms, and reestablished the old order.

Western Europe: The Revival of Democracy and the Economy

Thanks to the economic aid of the Marshall Plan, the countries of Western Europe recovered relatively rapidly from the devastation of World War II. Between 1947 and 1950, European countries received $9.4 billion to be used for new equipment and raw materials.

By 1950, industrial output in Europe was 30 percent above prewar levels. And this economic recovery continued well into the 1950s and 1960s, both decades of dramatic economic growth and prosperity in Western Europe. Indeed, Western Europe experienced virtually full employment during these decades.

FRANCE: THE DOMINATION OF DE GAULLE

The history of France for nearly a quarter century after the war was dominated by one man—Charles de Gaulle (1890–1970)—who possessed an unshakable faith that he had a historical mission to reestablish the greatness of the French nation. During the war, de Gaulle had assumed leadership of some resistance groups and played an important role in ensuring the establishment of a French provisional government after the war. The declaration of the Fourth Republic, with a return to a parliamentary system based on parties that de Gaulle considered weak, led him to withdraw from politics. Eventually, he formed the French Popular Movement, a decidedly rightist organization. It blamed the parties for France's political mess and called for an even stronger presidency, a goal that de Gaulle finally achieved in 1958.

The fragile political stability of the Fourth Republic had been badly shaken by the Algerian crisis. The French army had suffered defeat in Indochina in 1954 and was determined to resist Algerian demands for independence. But a strong antiwar movement among French intellectuals and church leaders led to bitter divisions within France that opened the door to the possibility of civil war. The panic-stricken leaders of the Fourth Republic offered to let de Gaulle take over the government and revise the constitution.

In 1958, de Gaulle immediately drafted a new constitution for the Fifth Republic that greatly enhanced the power of the office of president, who now had the right to choose the prime minister, dissolve parliament, and supervise both defense and foreign policy. De Gaulle had always believed in strong leadership, and the new Fifth Republic was by no means a democratic system. As the new president, de Gaulle sought to return France to the position of a great power. He believed that playing a pivotal role in the Cold War might enhance France's stature. For that reason, he pulled France out of the NATO high command. He increased French prestige among the Third World countries by consenting to Algerian independence despite strenuous opposition from the army. With an eye toward achieving the status of a world power, de Gaulle invested heavily in the nuclear arms race. France exploded its first nuclear bomb in 1960. Despite his successes, de Gaulle did not really achieve his ambitious goals of world power. Although his successors maintained that France was the "third nuclear power" after the United States and the Soviet Union, in truth France was too small for such global ambitions.

Although the cost of the nuclear program increased the defense budget, de Gaulle did not neglect the French economy. Economic decision making was centralized. Between 1958 and 1968, the French gross national product experienced an annual increase of 5.5 percent, faster than that of the United States. By the end of de Gaulle's era, France was a major industrial producer and exporter, particularly in such areas as automobiles and armaments. Nevertheless, problems remained. The expansion of traditional industries, such as coal, steel, and railroads, which had all been nationalized (put under government ownership), led to large government deficits. The cost of living increased faster than in the rest of Europe.

Increased dissatisfaction with the inability of de Gaulle's government to deal with these problems soon led to more violent action. In May 1968, a series of student protests, followed by a general strike by the labor unions, shook the government. Although de Gaulle managed to restore order, the events of May 1968 had seriously undermined the French people's respect for their aloof and imperious president. Tired and discouraged, de Gaulle resigned from office in April 1969 and died within a year.

WEST GERMANY: A NEW NATION?

As a result of the pressures of the Cold War, the unification of the three western zones into the Federal Republic of Germany became a reality in 1949. Konrad Adenauer (1876–1967), the leader of the Christian Democratic Union (CDU) who served as chancellor from 1949 to 1963, became the "founding hero" of the Federal Republic. Adenauer sought respect for West Germany by cooperating with the United States and the other Western European nations. He was especially desirous of reconciliation with France—Germany's longtime enemy. The beginning of the Korean War in June 1950 had unexpected repercussions for West Germany. The fear that South Korea might fall to the Communist forces of the North led many Germans and Westerners to worry about the security of West Germany and led to calls for the rearmament of West Germany. Although many people, concerned about a revival of German militarism, condemned this proposal, Cold War tensions were decisive. West Germany rearmed in 1955 and became a member of NATO.

Adenauer's chancellorship is largely associated with the resurrection of the West German economy, often referred to as the "economic miracle." It was largely guided by the minister of finance, Ludwig Erhard. Although West Germany had only 75 percent of the population and 52 percent of the territory of prewar Germany, by 1955 the West German gross national product exceeded that of prewar Germany. Real wages doubled between 1950 and 1965 even though work hours were cut by 20 percent. Unemployment fell from 8 percent in 1950 to 0.4 percent in 1965. To maintain its economic expansion, West Germany even imported hundreds of thousands of "guest workers," primarily from Italy, Spain, Greece, Turkey, and Yugoslavia.

Throughout its postwar existence, West Germany was troubled by its Nazi past. The surviving major Nazi leaders had been tried and condemned as war criminals at the Nuremberg war crimes trials in 1945 and 1946. As part of the denazification of Germany, the victorious Allies continued war crimes trials of lesser officials, but these diminished as the Cold War produced a shift in attitudes. By 1950, German courts had begun to take over the war crimes trials, and the German legal machine persisted in prosecuting cases. Beginning in 1953, the West German government also began to make payments to Israel and to Holocaust survivors and their relatives in order to make some restitution for the crimes of the Nazi era.

Adenauer resigned in 1963, after fourteen years of firmly guiding West Germany through its postwar recovery. Adenauer had wanted no grand experimentation at home or abroad; he was content to give Germany time to regain its equilibrium. Ludwig Erhard succeeded Adenauer and largely continued his policies. But an economic downturn in the mid-1960s opened the door to the rise of the Social Democrats, and in 1969, they became the leading party.

GREAT BRITAIN: THE WELFARE STATE

The end of World War II left Britain with massive economic problems. In elections held immediately after the war, the Labour Party overwhelmingly defeated Churchill's Conservative Party. Labour had promised far-reaching reforms, particularly in the area of social welfare, and in a country with a tremendous shortage of consumer goods and housing, its platform was quite appealing. The new Labour government, with Clement Atlee (1883–1967) as prime minister, proceeded to enact the reforms that created a modern welfare state.

The establishment of the British welfare state began with the nationalization of the Bank of England, the coal and steel industries, public transportation, and public utilities, such as electricity and gas. In the area of social welfare, the new government enacted the National Insurance Act and the National Health Service Act in 1946. The insurance act established a comprehensive social security program and nationalized medical insurance, thereby enabling the state to subsidize the unemployed, the sick, and the aged. The health act created a system of socialized medicine that forced doctors and dentists to work with state hospitals, although private practices could be maintained. This measure was especially costly for the state, but within a few years, 90 percent of the medical profession were participating. The British welfare state

WELFARE STATE: FREE MILK AT SCHOOL. The creation of the welfare state was a prominent social development in postwar Europe. The desire to improve the health of children led to welfare programs that provided free food for young people. Pictured here are boys at Manchester Grammar School in England during a milk break.

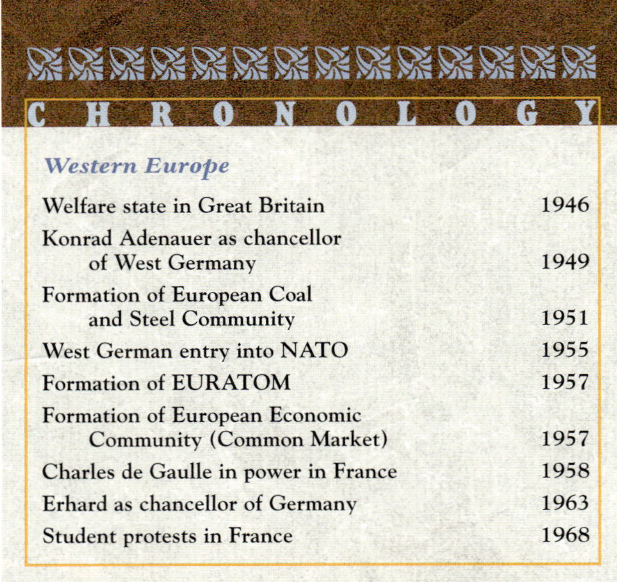

CHRONOLOGY

Western Europe

Welfare state in Great Britain	1946
Konrad Adenauer as chancellor of West Germany	1949
Formation of European Coal and Steel Community	1951
West German entry into NATO	1955
Formation of EURATOM	1957
Formation of European Economic Community (Common Market)	1957
Charles de Gaulle in power in France	1958
Erhard as chancellor of Germany	1963
Student protests in France	1968

became the model for most European states after the war.

The cost of building a welfare state at home forced the British to reduce expenses abroad. This meant the dismantling of the British Empire and the reduction of military aid to such countries as Greece and Turkey. Not a belief in the morality of self-determination but economic necessity brought an end to the British Empire.

Continuing economic problems brought the Conservatives back into power from 1951 to 1964. Although they favored private enterprise, the Conservatives accepted the welfare state and even extended it when they undertook an ambitious construction program to improve British housing. Although the British economy had recovered from the war, it had done so at a slower rate than other European countries. Moreover, the slow rate of recovery masked a long-term economic decline caused by a variety of factors. The demands of British trade unions for wages that rose faster than productivity were a problem in the 1950s and 1960s. The unwillingness of the British to invest in modern industrial machinery and to adopt new methods also did not help. Underlying the immediate problems, however, was a deeper issue. As a result of World War II, Britain had lost much of its prewar revenues from abroad but was left with a burden of debt from its many international commitments. At the same time, with the rise of the United States and the Soviet Union, Britain's ability to play the role of a world power declined substantially.

Western Europe: The Move Toward Unity

As we have seen, the divisions created by the Cold War led the nations of Western Europe to form the North Atlantic Treaty Organization in 1949. But military unity was not the only kind fostered in Europe after 1945. The destructiveness of two world wars caused many thoughtful Europeans to consider the need for some form of European pulling together. National feeling was still too powerful, however, for European nations to give up their political sovereignty. Consequently, the desire for a sense of solidarity was forced to focus primarily on the economic arena, not the political one.

In 1951, France, West Germany, the Benelux countries (Belgium, the Netherlands, and Luxembourg), and Italy formed the European Coal and Steel Community (ECSC). Its purpose was to create a common market for coal and steel products among the six nations by eliminating tariffs and other trade barriers. The success of the ECSC encouraged its members to proceed further, and in 1957 they created the European Atomic Energy Community (EURATOM) to further European research on the peaceful uses of nuclear energy.

In the same year, the same six nations signed the Rome treaty, which created the European Economic Community (EEC), also known as the Common Market. The EEC eliminated customs barriers for the six member nations and created a large free-trade area protected from the rest of the world by a common external tariff. By promoting free trade, the EEC also encouraged cooperation and standardization in many aspects of the six nations' economies. All the member nations benefited economically. With a total population of 165 million, the EEC became the world's largest exporter and purchaser of raw materials. Only the United States surpassed the EEC in steel production.

◆ The United States and Canada: A New Era

At the end of World War II, the United States emerged as one of the world's two superpowers. As the Cold War with the Soviet Union intensified, the United States worked hard to combat the spread of communism throughout the world. American domestic political life after 1945 was played out against a background of U.S. military power abroad.

American Politics and Society in the 1950s

Between 1945 and 1970, the ideals of Franklin Roosevelt's New Deal largely determined the patterns of American domestic politics. The New Deal had brought basic changes to American society. These included a dramatic increase in the role and power of the federal government, the rise of organized labor as a significant force in the economy and politics, the beginning of a welfare state, and a grudging realization of the need to deal fairly with the concerns of minorities.

The New Deal tradition in American politics was bolstered by the election of Democratic presidents—Harry Truman in 1948, John Kennedy in 1960, and Lyndon Johnson in 1964. Even the election of a Republican president, Dwight Eisenhower, in 1952 and 1956 did not change the basic direction of the New Deal. As Eisenhower stated, "Should any political party attempt to abolish Social Security and eliminate labor laws and farm programs, you would not hear of that party again in our political history."

The economic boom after World War II fueled confidence in the American way of life. A shortage of consumer goods during the war left Americans with both extra income and the desire to buy these goods after the war. Then, too, the growth of labor unions brought higher wages and gave more and more workers the ability to buy consumer goods. Between 1945 and 1973, real wages grew on an average of 3 percent a year, the most prolonged advance in American history.

Prosperity was not the only characteristic of the early 1950s. Cold War confrontations abroad had repercussions at home. The takeover of China by Mao Zedong's Communist forces in 1949 and Communist North Korea's invasion of South Korea in 1950 led to a fear that Communists had infiltrated America. President Truman's attorney general warned that Communists "are everywhere—in factories, offices, butcher stores, on street corners, in private businesses. And each carried in himself the germ of death for society." The demagogic senator from Wisconsin, Joseph R. McCarthy, helped intensify a massive "Red Scare" with his exposés of supposed Communists in high government positions. McCarthy went too far when he attacked alleged "Communist conspirators" in the United States Army and was censured by Congress in 1954. Very quickly, his anti-Communist crusade came to an end.

An Age of Upheaval: America in the 1960s

Between 1960 and 1970, the United States experienced a period of upheaval that brought to the fore problems that had been glossed over in the 1950s. The 1960s began on a youthful and optimistic note. At age forty-three, John F. Kennedy became the youngest elected president in the history of the United States. His own administration, cut short by an assassin's bullet on November 22, 1963, focused primarily on foreign affairs. Kennedy's successor, Lyndon B. Johnson, who won a new term as president in a landslide in 1964, used his stunning mandate to pursue what he called the Great Society, heir to the welfare state first begun in the New Deal. Johnson's programs included health care for the elderly, a War on Poverty to be fought with food stamps and a Job Corps, a new Department of Housing and Urban Development to deal with the problems of the cities, and federal assistance for education.

Johnson's other domestic passion was equal rights for African Americans. The civil rights movement had its beginnings in 1954 when the United States Supreme Court took the dramatic step of striking down the practice of racial segregation in public schools. The eloquent Martin Luther King Jr. (1929–1968) became the leader of a growing movement for racial equality, and by the early 1960s, a number of groups, including King's Southern Christian Leadership Conference (SCLC), were organizing sit-ins and demonstrations across the South to end racial segregation. In August 1963, King led the March on Washington for Jobs and Freedom to dramatize black Americans' desire for freedom. This march and King's impassioned plea for racial equality had an electrifying effect on the American people.

President Johnson took up the cause of civil rights. As a result of his initiative, Congress passed the Civil Rights Act of 1964, which created the machinery to end segregation and discrimination in the workplace and all public places. A voting rights act the following year made it easier for nonwhites to vote in southern states. But laws alone could not guarantee the Great Society, and Johnson soon faced bitter social unrest, both from African Americans and from the burgeoning movement opposing the Vietnam War.

In the North and West, African Americans had had voting rights for many years, but local patterns of segregation led to higher unemployment rates for blacks than for whites and left blacks segregated in urban ghettos. In these ghettos, the calls for action by radical black leaders, such as Malcolm X of the Black Muslims, attracted more attention than the nonviolent appeals of Martin Luther King. In the summer of 1965, race riots broke out in the Watts district of Los Angeles. Thirty-four people died and over one thousand buildings were destroyed. Cleveland, San Francisco, Chicago, Newark, and Detroit exploded in the summers of 1966 and 1967. The combination of riots and extremist comments by radical black leaders led to a "white backlash" and a severe division of America.

Antiwar protests also divided the American people after President Johnson sent American troops to Vietnam. As the war progressed and a military draft ensued, protests escalated. Teach-ins, sit-ins, and the occupation of buildings at universities alternated with more radical demonstrations that led to violence. The killing of four student protesters at Kent State University in 1970 by the Ohio National Guard caused a furor, and the antiwar movement began to decline. By that time, however, antiwar demonstrations had worn down the willingness of many Americans to continue the war. The combination of antiwar demonstrations and ghetto riots in the cities also heightened the appeal of a call for "law and order," used by Richard Nixon, the Republican presidential candidate in 1968. Nixon's election set in motion a shift to the right in American politics.

The Development of Canada

Canada experienced many of the same developments that the United States did in the postwar years. For twenty-five years after World War II, a prosperous Canada set out on a new path of industrial development. Canada had always had a strong export economy based on its abundant natural resources. Now it developed electronic, aircraft, nuclear, and chemical engineering industries as well on a large scale. Much of the Canadian growth, however, was financed by capital from the United States, which led to American ownership of Canadian businesses. Although many Canadians welcomed the economic growth, others feared American economic domination of Canada.

Canadians also worried about playing a secondary role politically and militarily to its neighboring superpower. Canadians agreed to join the North Atlantic Treaty Organization in 1949 and even sent military forces to fight in Korea the following year. But to avoid subordination to the United States, Canada actively supported the United Nations. Nevertheless, concerns about the United States did not keep Canada from maintaining a special relationship with its southern neighbor. The North American Air Defense Command (NORAD), formed in 1957, was based on close cooperation between the air forces of the two countries for the defense of North America against missile attack.

After 1945, the Liberal Party continued to dominate Canadian politics until 1957, when John Diefenbaker (1895–1979) achieved a Conservative Party victory. But major economic problems returned the Liberals to power, and under Lester Pearson (1897–1972), they created Canada's welfare state by enacting a national social security system (the Canada Pension Plan) and a national health insurance program.

The Emergence of a New Society

During the postwar era, Western society witnessed remarkably rapid change. Computers, television, jet planes, contraceptive devices, and new surgical techniques all dramatically and quickly altered the pace and nature of human life. The rapid changes in postwar society, fueled by scientific advances and rapid economic growth, led many people to view it as a new society. But waves of protest rocked this new society even as many aspects of life seemed to be getting better.

The Structure of European Society

The structure of European society was altered after 1945. Especially noticeable were the changes in the middle class. Such traditional middle-class groups as businesspeople and professionals in law, medicine, and the universities were joined by a new group of managers and technicians as large companies and government agencies employed increasing numbers of white-collar supervisory and administrative personnel. Whether in Eastern or Western Europe, the new managers and experts were very much alike. Everywhere their positions depended on specialized knowledge acquired from some form of higher education. Because their positions usually depended on their skills, they took steps to ensure that their own children would be educated.

Changes also occurred among the traditional lower classes. Especially noticeable was the dramatic shift of people from rural to urban areas. The number of people engaged in agriculture declined drastically; by the 1950s, the number of farmers throughout most of Europe had dropped by 50 percent. Nor did the size of the industrial working class expand. In West Germany, industrial workers made up 48 percent of the labor force throughout the 1950s and 1960s. Thereafter, the number of industrial workers began to dwindle as the number of white-collar service employees increased. At the same time, a substantial increase in their real wages enabled the working classes to aspire to the consumption patterns of the middle class, leading to what some observers have called the "consumer society." Buying on the installment plan, which was introduced in the 1930s, became widespread beginning in the 1950s and gave workers a chance to imitate the middle class by buying such products as televisions, washing machines, refrigerators, vacuum cleaners, and stereos. But the most visible symbol of mass consumerism was the automobile. Before World War II, cars were reserved mostly for the European upper classes. In 1948, there were 5 million cars in all of Europe, but by 1957, the number had tripled. By the 1960s, there were almost 45 million cars.

Rising incomes, combined with shorter working hours, created an even greater market for mass leisure activities. Between 1900 and 1960, the workweek was reduced from sixty hours to about forty hours, and the number of paid holidays increased. All aspects of popular culture—music, sports, media—became commercialized and offered opportunities for leisure activities including concerts, sporting events, and television viewing.

Another very visible symbol of mass leisure was the growth of mass tourism. Before World War II, mostly the upper and middle classes traveled for pleasure. After the war, the combination of more vacation time, increased prosperity, and the flexibility provided by package tours, with their lower rates and low-budget rooms, enabled millions to expand their travel possibilities. By the mid-1960s, some 100 million tourists were crossing European boundaries each year.

Patterns New and Old: Women in the Postwar Western World

Despite their enormous contributions to the war effort, women at the end of World War II were removed from the workforce to provide jobs for the soldiers returning home. After the horrors and separations of the war, people seemed willing for a while to return to traditional family life. Female participation in the workforce declined, and birthrates began to rise, creating a "baby boom." This increase in the birthrate, however, did not last, and thus the size of families began to decline by the end of the 1950s. Largely responsible for this decline was the widespread practice of birth control. Invented in the nineteenth century, the condom was already in wide use, but the development in the 1960s of oral contraceptives, known as birth control pills, provided a reliable means of birth control that quickly spread to all Western countries.

The trend toward smaller families contributed to the change in the nature of women's employment in both Europe and the United States as women spent considerably more years not involved in rearing children. The most important development was the increased number of married women in the workforce. At the beginning of the twentieth century, even working-class wives tended to stay at home if they could afford to do so. In the postwar period, this was no longer the case. In the United States, for example, in 1900, married women made up about 15 percent of the female labor force; by 1970, their number had increased to 62 percent. The percentage of married women in the female labor force in Sweden increased from 47 to 66 percent between 1963 and 1975.

But the increased number of women in the workforce did not change some old patterns. Working-class women in particular still earned salaries lower than those of men for equal work. In the 1960s, women earned only 60 percent of men's wages in Britain, 50 percent in France, and 63 percent in West Germany. In addition, women still tended to enter traditionally female jobs. Many European women also still faced the double burden of earning income on the one hand and raising a family and maintaining the household on the other. Such inequalities led increasing numbers of women to rebel.

THE FEMINIST MOVEMENT: THE SEARCH FOR LIBERATION

The participation of women in World Wars I and II helped them achieve one of the major aims of the nineteenth-century feminist movement—the right to vote. After World War I, many governments acknowledged the contributions of women to the war effort by granting them suffrage, although women in France and Italy did not obtain the vote until 1945. After World War II, European women tended to fall back into the traditional roles expected of them, but by the late 1960s, women began to assert their rights again. Along with the student upheavals of the late 1960s came renewed interest in feminism, or the women's liberation movement as it was now called. Increasingly, women protested that the acquisition of political and legal equality had not brought true equality with men:

> We are economically oppressed: in jobs we do full work for half pay, in the home we do unpaid work full time. We are commercially exploited by advertisement, television and the press; legally we often have only the status of children. We are brought up to feel inadequate, educated to narrower horizons than men. This is our specific oppression as women. It is as women that we are, therefore, organizing.[6]

These were the words of a British Woman's Liberation Workshop in 1969.

Of great importance to the emergence of the postwar women's liberation movement was the work of Simone de Beauvoir (1908–1986). Born into a Catholic middle-class family and educated at the Sorbonne in Paris, she supported herself as a teacher and later as a writer. She maintained a lifelong relationship (but not marriage) with the existentialist writer Jean-Paul Sartre and became actively involved in political causes. De Beauvoir believed that she lived a "liberated" life for a twentieth-century European woman, but for all her freedom, she still came to perceive that as a woman she faced limits that men did not. In 1949, she published her highly influential work, *The Second Sex,* in which she argued that as a result of male-dominated societies, women had been defined by their differences from men and consequently received second-class status. De Beauvoir took an active role in the French women's movement of the 1970s, and her book was a major influence on the feminist movement on both sides of the Atlantic.

The Permissive Society

The "permissive society" was yet another term applied to postwar Europe. World War I had seen the first significant crack in the rigid code of manners and morals of the nineteenth century. Subsequently, the 1920s had witnessed experimentation with drugs, the appearance of hard-core pornography, and a new sexual freedom (police in Berlin, for example, issued cards that permitted female and male homosexual prostitutes to practice their trade). But these indications of a new attitude appeared mostly in major cities and touched only small numbers of people. After World War II, changes in manners and morals were far more extensive and far more noticeable.

Sweden took the lead in the propagation of the so-called sexual revolution of the 1960s, but the rest of Europe and the United States soon followed. Sex education in the schools and the decriminalization of homosexuality were but two aspects of Sweden's liberal legislation. The

WOMEN'S LIBERATION MOVEMENT. In the late 1960s, as women began once again to assert their rights, a revived women's liberation movement emerged. Feminists in the movement maintained that women themselves must alter the conditions of their lives. During this women's liberation rally, some women climbed the statue of Admiral Farragut in Washington, D.C., to exhibit their signs.

introduction of the birth control pill, which became widely available by the mid-1960s, gave people more freedom in sexual behavior. Meanwhile, sexually explicit movies, plays, and books broke new ground in the treatment of once-hidden subjects.

The new standards were evident in the breakdown of the traditional family. Divorce rates increased dramatically, especially in the 1960s, and premarital and extramarital sexual experiences also rose substantially. A survey in the Netherlands in 1968 revealed that 78 percent of men and 86 percent of women had participated in extramarital sex. The appearance of *Playboy* magazine in the 1950s also added a new dimension to the sexual revolution for adult males. Along with photographs of nude women, *Playboy* offered well-written articles on various aspects of masculinity. *Playboy*'s message was clear: men were encouraged to seek sexual gratification outside of marriage.

The decade of the 1960s also saw the emergence of a drug culture. Marijuana was widely used among college and university students as a recreational drug. For young people more interested in mind expansion into higher levels of consciousness, Timothy Leary, who had done research at Harvard on the hallucinogenic effects of LSD (lysergic acid diethylamide), became the high priest of "psychedelic" experiences.

New attitudes toward sex and the use of drugs were only two manifestations of a growing youth movement in the 1960s that questioned authority and fostered rebellion against the older generation. Spurred on by the Vietnam War and a growing political consciousness, the youth rebellion became a youth protest movement by the second half of the 1960s (see the box on p. 600).

Education and Student Revolt

Before World War II, higher education had largely remained the preserve of Europe's wealthier classes. After the war, European states began to foster greater equality of opportunity in higher education by eliminating fees, and universities experienced an influx of students from the middle and lower classes. Enrollments grew dramatically: in France, 4.5 percent of young people went to a university in 1950. By 1965, the figure had increased to 14.5 percent.

But there were problems. Overcrowded classrooms, professors who paid little attention to students, administrators who acted in an authoritarian fashion, and an education that to many seemed irrelevant to the realities of the modern age led to an outburst of student revolts in the late 1960s. In part, these protests were an extension of the spontaneous disruptions in American universities in the mid-1960s, which were often sparked by student opposition to the Vietnam War. Perhaps the most famous student revolt occurred in France in 1968. It erupted at the University of Nanterre outside Paris but soon spread to the Sorbonne, the main campus of the University of Paris. French students demanded a greater voice in the administration of the university, took over buildings, and then expanded the scale of their protests by inviting workers to support them. Half of France's workforce went on strike in May 1968. After the Gaullist

THE "LOVE-IN." In the 1960s, a number of outdoor public festivals for young people combined music, drugs, and sex. Flamboyant dress, face painting, free-form dancing, and drugs were vital ingredients in creating an atmosphere dedicated to "love and peace." Shown here is a "love-in" that was held on the grounds of an English country estate in the Summer of Love, 1967.

"The Times They Are A-Changin'": The Music of Youthful Protest

In the 1960s, the lyrics of rock music reflected the rebellious mood of many young people. Bob Dylan (b. 1941), a popular recording artist, expressed the feelings of the younger generation. His song "The Times They Are A-Changin'," released in 1964, has been called an "anthem for the protest movement."

Bob Dylan, "The Times They Are A-Changin'"

Come gather round people
Wherever you roam
And admit that the waters
Around you have grown
And accept it that soon
You'll be drenched to the bone
If your time to you
Is worth savin'
Then you better start swimmin'
Or you'll sink like a stone
For the times they are a-changin'

Come writers and critics
Who prophesize with your pen
And keep your eyes wide
The chance won't come again
And don't speak too soon
For the wheel's still in spin
And there's no tellin' who
That it's namin'
For the loser now
Will be later to win
For the times they are a-changin'

Come senators, congressmen
please heed the call
Don't stand in the doorway
Don't block up the hall
For he that gets hurt
Will be he who has stalled
There's a battle outside
And it is ragin'
It'll soon shake your windows
And rattle your walls
For the times they are a-changin'

Come mothers and fathers
Throughout the land
And don't criticize
What you can't understand
Your sons and your daughters
Are beyond your command
Your old road
Is rapidly agin'
Please get out of the new one
If you can't lend your hand
For the times they are a-changin'

The line it is drawn
The curse it is cast
The slow one now
Will later be fast
As the present now
Will later be past
The order is
Rapidly fadin'
And the first one now
Will later be last
For the times they are a-changin'

government instituted a hefty wage hike, the workers returned to work and the police repressed the remaining student protesters.

The student protest movement reached its high point in 1968, although scattered incidents occurred into the early 1970s. There were several reasons for the student radicalism. Some students were genuinely motivated by the desire to reform the university. Others were protesting the Vietnam War, which they viewed as Western imperialism. They also attacked other aspects of Western society, such as its materialism, and expressed concern about becoming cogs in the large and impersonal bureaucratic jungles of the modern world. For many students, the calls for democratic decision making within the universities reflected their deeper concerns about the direction of Western society. Although student revolts fizzled out in the 1970s, the larger issues they raised revived in the 1990s.

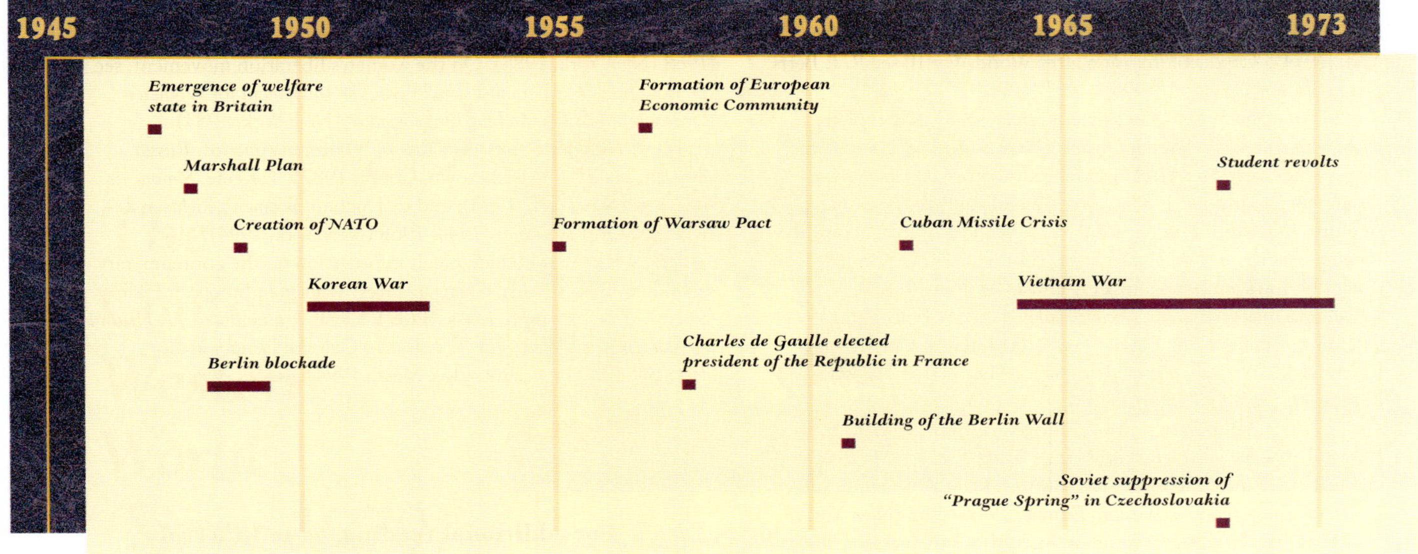

Conclusion

At the end of World War II, a new conflict erupted in the Western world as the two new superpowers, the United States and the Soviet Union, competed for political domination. Europeans, whether they wanted to or not, were forced to become supporters of one side or the other. But this ideological division also spread to the rest of the world as the United States fought in Korea and Vietnam to prevent the spread of communism, while the Soviet Union used its armies to prop up pro-Soviet regimes in Eastern Europe.

In addition to the Cold War conflict, the postwar era was characterized by decolonization. After World War II, the colonial empires of the European states were largely dissolved, and the liberated territories of Africa, Asia, and the Middle East emerged as sovereign states. By the late 1980s, the approximately 160 sovereign states of the world would become an emerging global community.

Western Europe also became a new community in the 1950s and 1960s. Although Western Europeans staged a remarkable economic recovery, the Cuban Missile Crisis made it clear that their future still depended on relations between the two superpowers. At the same time, the student protests of the late 1960s caused many to rethink some of their basic assumptions. And yet, looking back, the student upheavals were not a turning point in the history of postwar Europe, as some people thought at the time. Student rebels would become middle-class professionals, and the vision of a revolutionary politics would remain mostly a memory.

Notes

1. Quoted in Joseph M. Jones, *The Fifteen Weeks (February 21–June 5, 1947)*, 2d ed. (New York, 1964), pp. 140–141.
2. Quoted in Walter Laqueur, *Europe in Our Time* (New York, 1992), p. 111.
3. Quoted in Peter Lane, *Europe Since 1945: An Introduction* (Totowa, N.J., 1985), p. 248.
4. R. Hilton, *Military Attaché in Moscow* (London, 1949), p. 41.
5. Nikita S. Khrushchev, *Khrushchev Remembers*, trans. Strobe Talbott (Boston, 1970), p. 77.
6. Quoted in Marsha Rowe et al., *Spare Rib Reader* (Harmondsworth, England, 1982), p. 574.

Suggestions for Further Reading

Three introductory surveys on postwar Europe are P. Lane, *Europe Since 1945: An Introduction* (Totowa, N.J., 1985); J. R. Wegs, *Europe Since 1945: A Concise History*, 2d ed. (New York, 1984); and W. Laqueur, *Europe in Our Time* (New York, 1992). There is a detailed literature on the Cold War. A general account is J. W. Langdon, *A Hard and Bitter Peace: A Global History of the Cold War* (Englewood Cliffs, N.J., 1995). Two brief works on the entire Cold War are J. H. Mason, *The Cold War* (New York, 1996), and J. Smith, *The Cold War, 1945–1991* (Oxford, 1998). For an illustrated history, see J. Isaacs and T. Downing, *Cold War: An Illustrated History, 1945–1991* (Boston, 1998). There is a brief survey of the early Cold War in M. Dockrill, *The Cold War, 1945–1963* (Atlantic Highlands, N.J., 1988). For a study of Soviet foreign policy, see J. L. Nogee, *Soviet Foreign Policy Since World War I*, 4th ed. (New York, 1992). The effects of the Cold War on Germany are examined in J. H. Backer, *The Decision to Divide Germany: American Foreign Policy in Transition* (Durham, N.C., 1978). For a good introduction to the arms race, see E. M. Bottome, *The Balance of Terror:*

MAP 29.1 The New Europe.

◆ Toward a New Western Order

Between 1945 and 1970, economic recovery had brought renewed growth to Europe. Nevertheless, the political divisions between Western and Eastern Europe remained; so did the disparity in levels of prosperity. But in the late 1980s and early 1990s, the Soviet Union and its Eastern European satellite states underwent a revolutionary upheaval that dramatically altered the European scene and left many Europeans with both new hopes and new fears.

The Revolutionary Era in the Soviet Union

Between 1964 and 1982, significant change in the Soviet Union seemed highly unlikely. After the overthrow of Khrushchev in 1964, Leonid Brezhnev (1906–1982) had become head of both party and state. He was always optimistic yet reluctant to reform. The Brezhnev doctrine—the right of the Soviet Union to intervene if socialism was threatened in another "socialist state"—became an article of faith and led to the use of Soviet troops in Czechoslovakia in 1968.

Brezhnev benefited from the more relaxed atmosphere associated with détente. The Soviets had reached a rough parity with the United States in nuclear arms and enjoyed a sense of external security that seemed to allow for a relaxation of authoritarian rule. The regime permitted more access to Western styles of music, dress, and art, although dissenters were still punished. Andrei Sakharov, for example, who had played an important role in the development of the Soviet hydrogen bomb, was placed under house arrest for his defense of human rights.

In his economic policies, Brezhnev continued to emphasize heavy industry. Overall industrial growth declined, although the Soviet production of iron, steel, coal, and cement surpassed that of the United States. Two problems bedeviled the Soviet economy. The government's insistence on vigorous central planning led to a huge, complex bureaucracy that discouraged efficiency and reduced productivity. Moreover, the Soviet system, based on guaranteed employment and a lack of incentives, bred apathy, complacency, absenteeism, and drunkenness. Agricultural problems added to Soviet economic woes. Bad harvests in the mid-1970s, caused by a series of droughts, heavy rains, and early frosts, forced the Soviet government to buy grain from the West, particularly the United States. To their chagrin, the Soviets were increasingly dependent on capitalist countries.

By the 1970s, party and state leaders—as well as leaders of the army and secret police (KGB)—had come to expect numerous advantages and material privileges. Brezhnev was unwilling to tamper with the party leadership and state bureaucracy, regardless of the inefficiency and corruption that the system encouraged. By 1980, the Soviet Union was seriously ailing. A declining economy, a rise in infant mortality rates, a dramatic surge in alcoholism, and a deterioration in working conditions all gave impetus to a decline in morale and a growing perception that the system was floundering. Within the party, a small group of reformers emerged who understood the real condition of the Soviet Union, including a young reforming leader, Mikhail Gorbachev.

THE GORBACHEV ERA

Born into a peasant family in 1931, Mikhail Gorbachev combined farm work with school and received the Order of the Red Banner for his agricultural efforts. This award and his good school record enabled him to study law at the University of Moscow. After receiving his law degree in 1955, he returned to his native southern Russia, where he eventually became first secretary of the Communist Party in the city of Stavropol (he had joined the Communist Party in 1952). In 1978, Gorbachev was made a member of the party's Central Committee in Moscow. Two years later, he became a full member of the ruling Politburo and secretary of the Central Committee. In March 1985, party leaders elected him general secretary of the party, and he became the new leader of the Soviet Union.

Educated during the reform years of Khrushchev, Gorbachev seemed intent on taking earlier reforms to their logical conclusions. By the 1980s, Soviet economic problems were obvious. Rigid, centralized planning led to mismanagement and stifled innovation. Although the Soviets still excelled in space exploration, they fell behind the West in high technology, especially in the development and production of computers for private and public use. Most noticeable to the Soviet people was the actual decline in the standard of living. From the start, Gorbachev preached the need for radical reforms.

The cornerstone of Gorbachev's radical reforms was *perestroika*, or "restructuring" (see the box on p. 608). At first, this meant only a reordering of economic policy as Gorbachev called for the beginning of a market economy with limited free enterprise and some private property. However, Gorbachev soon perceived that in the Soviet system, the economic sphere was intimately tied to the social and political spheres. Attempting to reform the economy without political or social reform would be doomed to failure. One of the most important instruments of *perestroika* was *glasnost*, or "openness." Soviet citizens and officials were encouraged to discuss openly the strengths and weaknesses of the Soviet Union. *Pravda*, the official newspaper of the Communist Party, began to include reports of official corruption, sloppy factory work, and protests against government policy. The arts also benefited from the new policy. Previously banned works were now published, and music based on Western styles, such as jazz and rock, began to be performed openly.

Political reforms were equally revolutionary. At the Communist Party conference in 1988, Gorbachev called for the creation of a new Soviet parliament, the Congress of People's Deputies, whose members were to be chosen in competitive elections. It convened in 1989, the first such meeting in Russia since 1918. Early in 1990, Gorbachev legalized the formation of other political parties and struck out Article 6 of the Soviet constitution, which had guaranteed the "leading role" of the Communist Party. At the same time, Gorbachev attempted to consolidate his power by creating a new state presidency. Hitherto, the position of first secretary of the party was the most important post in the Soviet Union, but as the Communist Party became less closely associated with the state, the powers of this office diminished correspondingly. In March 1990, Gorbachev became the Soviet Union's first president.

One of Gorbachev's most serious problems stemmed from the character of the Soviet Union. The Union of Soviet Socialist Republics was a truly multiethnic country encompassing 92 nationalities and 112 recognized languages. Previously, the iron hand of the Communist Party, centered in Moscow, kept a

Gorbachev and Perestroika

After assuming the leadership of the Soviet Union in 1985, Mikhail Gorbachev worked to liberalize and restructure the country. His policies opened the door to rapid changes in Eastern Europe and in Soviet-American relations at the end of the 1980s. In his book Perestroika, *Gorbachev explained some of his "New Thinking."*

Mikhail Gorbachev, **Perestroika**

The fundamental principle of the new political outlook is very simple: *nuclear war cannot be a means of achieving political, economic, ideological or any other goals*. This conclusion is truly revolutionary, for it means discarding the traditional notions of war and peace. It is the political function of war that has always been a justification for war, a "rational" explanation. Nuclear war is senseless; it is irrational. There would be neither winners nor losers in a global nuclear conflict: world Civilization would inevitably perish. . . .

But military technology has developed to such an extent that even a non-nuclear war would now be comparable with a nuclear war in its destructive effect. That is why it is logical to include in our category of nuclear wars this "variant" of an armed clash between major powers as well.

Thereby, an altogether different situation has emerged. A way of thinking and a way of acting, based on the use of force in world politics, have formed over centuries, even millennia. It seems they have taken root as something unshakable. Today, they have lost all reasonable grounds. . . . For the first time in history, basing international politics on moral and ethical norms that are common to all humankind, as well as humanizing interstate relations, has become a vital requirement. . . .

There is a great thirst for mutual understanding and mutual communication in the world. It is felt among politicians, it is gaining momentum among the intelligentsia, representatives of culture, and the public at large. And if the Russian word "perestroika" has easily entered the international lexicon, this due to more than just interest in what is going on in the Soviet Union. Now the whole world needs restructuring, i.e., progressive development, a fundamental change.

People feel this and understand this. They have to find their bearings, to understand the problems besetting mankind, to realize how they should live in the future. The restructuring is a must for a world overflowing with nuclear weapons; for a world ridden with serious economic and ecological problems; for a world laden with poverty, backwardness and disease; for a human race now facing the urgent need of ensuring its own survival.

We are all students, and our teacher is life and time. I believe that more and more people will come to realize that through RESTRUCTURING in the broad sense of the word, the integrity of the world will be enhanced. Having earned good marks from our main teacher—life—we shall enter the twenty-first century well prepared and sure that there will be further progress.

lid on the centuries-old ethnic tensions that had periodically erupted in the history of this region. As Gorbachev released this iron grip, tensions resurfaced, a by-product of *glasnost* that Gorbachev had not anticipated. Ethnic groups took advantage of the new openness to protest what they perceived to be ethnically motivated slights. As violence erupted, the Soviet Army, in disrepair since the war in Afghanistan, had difficulty controlling the situation.

The period 1988 to 1990 also witnessed the appearance of nationalist movements in the republics of the Soviet Union. Many were motivated by ethnic concerns, with calls for sovereignty of the republics and independence from the Russian-based rule centered in Moscow. These movements first sprang up in Georgia in late 1988 and then in Latvia, Estonia, Moldavia, Uzbekistan, Azerbaijan, and most dramatically, Lithuania. On March 11, 1990, the Lithuanian Supreme Council proclaimed Lithuania an independent state.

THE END OF THE SOVIET UNION

During 1990 and 1991, Gorbachev struggled to deal with Lithuania and the other problems unleashed by his reforms. On one hand, he tried to appease conservative forces who complained about the growing disorder within the Soviet Union. On the other hand, he tried to accommodate the liberal forces, especially those in the Soviet republics, who increasingly favored a new kind of decentralized Soviet federation. In particular, Gorbachev labored to cooperate more closely with Boris Yeltsin, who had been elected president of the Russian Republic in June 1991.

By 1991, the conservative leaders of the traditional Soviet institutions—the army, government, KGB, and military industries—had grown increasingly worried about the impending dissolution of the Soviet Union and its impact on their own fortunes. On August 19, 1991, a group of these discontented rightists arrested Gorbachev and attempted to seize power. Gorbachev's unwillingness to work with the conspirators and the brave resistance in Moscow of Yeltsin and thousands of Russians who had grown accustomed to their new liberties caused the coup to disintegrate rapidly. The actions of these right-wing plotters, however, served to accelerate the very process they had hoped to stop—the disintegration of the Soviet Union.

Despite desperate pleas by Gorbachev, the Soviet republics soon moved for complete independence. Ukraine voted for independence on December 1, 1991, and, a week later, the leaders of Russia, Ukraine, and Belarus announced that the Soviet Union had "ceased to exist." Gorbachev resigned on December 25, 1991, and turned over his responsibilities as commander in chief to Boris Yeltsin, the president of Russia. By the end of 1991, one of the largest empires in world history had come to an end, and a new era had begun in its lands.

Within Russia, a new power struggle soon ensued. Yeltsin was committed to introducing a free market economy as quickly as possible, but the transition was not easy. Economic hardships and social disarray, made worse by a dramatic rise in the activities of organized crime mobs, led increasing numbers of Russians to support both former Communists and hard-line nationalists, who criticized Russia's loss of prestige in world affairs. Yeltsin's brutal use of force against the Chechens, who wanted to secede from Russia and create their own state, also undermined his support. Despite the odds against him, however, Yeltsin won reelection as Russian president in 1996, although his precarious health raised serious questions about his ability to govern. At the end of 1999, Yeltsin suddenly resigned and was replaced by Vladimir Putin, an ex-member of the KGB. Putin vowed to bring the breakaway state of Chechnya back under Russian authority while adopting a more assertive role in international affairs. Early in 2000, he was elected as Russia's president.

Eastern Europe: The Collapse of the Communist Order

Stalin's postwar order had imposed Communist regimes throughout Eastern Europe, and few people believed that the new order could be undone. But discontent with their Soviet-style regimes always simmered beneath the surface of these satellite states, and after Mikhail Gorbachev made it clear that his government would not intervene militarily, their Communist regimes fell quickly in the revolutions of 1989.

Poland had achieved a certain stability in the 1960s, but economic problems continued. Edward Gierek, who came to power in 1971, attempted to solve these problems by borrowing heavily from the West. But in 1980, when he announced huge increases in food prices in an effort to pay off part of the Western debt, workers' protests erupted and led directly to the rise of the independent labor movement called Solidarity. Led by Lech Walesa (b. 1943), Solidarity gained the support of the workers, many intellectuals, and the Catholic church and was able to win a series of concessions. In 1988, new demonstrations led the Polish regime to agree to free parliamentary elections—the first free elections in Eastern Europe in forty years. The newly elected Solidarity coalition formed a new government, ending forty-five years of Communist rule in Poland. In December 1990, Walesa was chosen as the new Polish president. But rapid free market reforms led to severe unemployment and popular discontent, and in November 1995, Alexander Kwasniewski, a former Communist, defeated Walesa and became the new Polish president. However, he has continued Poland's move toward an increasingly prosperous free market economy.

In Hungary, too, the process of liberation from Communist rule had begun before 1989. Remaining in power for more than thirty years, the government of János Kádár enacted the most far-reaching economic reforms in Eastern Europe. In the early 1980s, Kádár legalized small private enterprises, such as shops, restaurants, and artisan shops. Hungary moved slowly away from its strict adherence to Soviet dominance and even established fairly friendly relations with the West.

As the 1980s progressed, however, the economy sagged, and Kádár fell from power in 1988. By 1989, the Hungarian Communist government was aware of the growing dissatisfaction and began to undertake reforms. But they came too late as new political parties called for Hungary to become a democratic republic. In elections in March 1990, the Communists came in fourth, winning only 8.5 percent of the vote, a clear repudiation of communism. The Democratic Forum, a right-of-center, highly patriotic party, won the election and formed a new coalition government that committed Hungary to democratic government and the institution of a free market economy.

Communist regimes in Poland and Hungary had attempted to make some political and economic reforms in the 1970s and 1980s, but this was not the case in Czechoslovakia. After Soviet troops had crushed the reform movement in 1968, hard-line Czech Communists under Gustav Husák purged the party and instituted a policy of massive repression to maintain their power. Only writers and other intellectuals provided any real opposition to the government, but they did not meet with success until the late 1980s. Government attempts to suppress mass demonstrations in Prague and other Czechoslovakian cities in 1988 and 1989 only led to more and larger demonstrations. By November 1989, crowds as large as 500,000, which included many students, were forming in Prague. In December 1989, as demonstrations continued, the Communist government, lacking any real support, collapsed. President Husák resigned and at the end of December was replaced by Vaclav Havel, the dissident playwright who had played an important role in bringing the Communist government down. In January 1990, Havel declared amnesty for some thirty thousand political prisoners. He also set out on a goodwill visit to various Western countries in which he proved to be an eloquent spokesman for Czech democracy and a new order in Europe (see the box on p. 611).

Within Czechoslovakia, the shift to non-Communist rule was complicated by old problems, especially ethnic issues. Czechs and Slovaks disagreed over the makeup of the new state but were able to agree to a peaceful division of the country. On January 1, 1993, Czechoslovakia split into the Czech Republic and Slovakia. Vaclav Havel was elected the first president of the new Czech Republic.

Czechoslovakia's revolutionary path was considerably less violent than Romania's. In 1965, leadership of the Communist government in Romania passed into the hands of Nicolae Ceauşescu (1918–1989), who with his wife, Elena, established a rigid and dictatorial regime. Ceauşescu ruled Romania with an iron grip, using a secret police—the Securitate—as his personal weapon against any dissent. Nevertheless, opposition to his regime grew as Ceauşescu rejected the reforms in Eastern Europe promoted by Gorbachev. A small incident became the spark that ignited heretofore suppressed flames of discontent. The ruthless crushing of a demonstration in Timisoara in December 1989 led to other mass demonstrations. After the dictator was booed at a mass rally on December 21, the army refused to support any more repression. Ceauşescu and his wife were captured on December 22 and tried and executed on Christmas Day, 1989. Leadership now passed into the hands of a hastily formed National Salvation Front, which won elections in the spring of 1990. Questions remained, however, about the new government's commitment to democracy.

In Bulgaria, Todor Zhivkov (b. 1911) became leader of the Bulgarian Communist Party and hence leader of the nation in 1954. Not until the late 1980s did a number of small opposition groups begin to emerge. In October 1989, antigovernment demonstrations were held in the capital city of Sofia, and

CHRONOLOGY

The Soviet Bloc and Its Demise

Era of Brezhnev	1964–1982
Rule of Ceauşescu in Romania	1965–1989
Honecker as leader of East Germany	1971
Emergence of Solidarity in Poland	1980
Gorbachev in power in the Soviet Union	1985
	1989
Collapse of Communist government in Czechoslovakia	December
Collapse of East German government	December
Execution of Ceauşescu in Romania	December 25
	1990
East German elections—victory of Christian Democrats	March 18
Reunification of Germany	October 3
Walesa as president of Poland	December
	1991
Yeltsin as president of Russia	June
Slovenia and Croatia declarations of independence	June
Right-wing coup in the Soviet Union	August 19
Dissolution of the Soviet Union	December
	1993
Division of Czechoslovakia into Czech Republic and Slovakia	January 1
Havel as president of Czech Republic	February 2
	1995
Aleksander Kwasniewski as Polish president	November
Dayton accords—end of war in Bosnia	December
Russian presidential elections	1996
War in Kosovo	1999
Putin as president of Russia	2000

Vaclav Havel: The Call for a New Politics

In attempting to deal with the world's problems, some European leaders have pointed to the need for a new perspective, especially a moral one, if people are to live in a sane world. These two excerpts are taken from speeches by Vaclav Havel, who was elected the new president of Czechoslovakia at the end of 1989. The first is from his inaugural address as president of Czechoslovakia on January 1, 1990; the second is from a speech given to the United States Congress.

Vaclav Havel, Address to the People of Czechoslovakia, January 1, 1990

But all this is still not the main problem [the environmental devastation of the country by its Communist leaders]. The worst thing is that we live in a contaminated moral environment. We fell morally ill because we became used to saying something different from what we thought. We learned not to believe in anything, to ignore each other, to care only about ourselves. Concepts such as love, friendship, compassion, humility, or forgiveness lost their depth and dimensions, and for many of us they represented only psychological peculiarities, or they resembled gone astray greetings from ancients, a little ridiculous in the era of computers and spaceships. Only a few of us were able to cry out loud that the powers that be should not be all-powerful, and that special farms, which produce ecologically pure and top-quality food just for them should send their produce to schools, children's homes and hospitals if our agriculture was unable to offer them to all. The previous regime—armed with its arrogant and intolerant ideology—reduced man to a force of production and nature to a tool of production. In this it attacked both their very substance and their mutual relationship. It reduced gifted and autonomous people, skillfully working in their own country, to nuts and bolts of some monstrously huge, noisy, and stinking machine, whose real meaning is not clear to anyone.

Vaclav Havel, Speech to the U.S. Congress, February 21, 1990

For this reason, the salvation of this human world lies nowhere else than in the human heart, in the human power to reflect, in human meekness and in human responsibility.

Without a global revolution in the sphere of human consciousness, nothing will change for the better in the sphere of our being as humans, and the catastrophe toward which this world is headed—be it ecological, social, demographic or a general breakdown of civilization—will be unavoidable. . . .

We are still a long way from that "family of man." In fact, we seem to be receding from the ideal rather than growing closer to it. Interests of all kinds—personal, selfish, state, nation, group, and if you like, company interests—still considerably outweigh genuinely common and global interests. We are still under the sway of the destructive and vain belief that man is the pinnacle of creation and not just a part of it and that therefore everything is permitted. . . .

In other words, we still don't know how to put morality ahead of politics, science and economics. We are still incapable of understanding that the only genuine backbone of all our actions, if they are to be moral, is responsibility.

Responsibility to something higher than my family, my country, my company, my success—responsibility to the order of being where all our actions are indelibly recorded and where and only where they will be properly judged.

The interpreter or mediator between us and this higher authority is what is traditionally referred to as human conscience.

---

a month later, Zhivkov was unexpectedly relieved of his post as general secretary of the Communist Party, a position he had held for thirty-five years. Elections in November 1991 brought about a new government coalition, led by the United Democratic Front. Nevertheless, the Socialist Party (the former Communists) remained a potent force in Bulgarian politics.

The Reunification of Germany

Until 1989, the existence of West Germany and East Germany remained the most powerful symbol of divided postwar Europe. In the early 1950s, the ruling Communist government in East Germany, led by Walter Ulbricht, had consolidated its position and become a faithful Soviet satellite. Industry was nationalized and agriculture collectivized. After a workers' revolt in 1953 was crushed by Soviet tanks, a steady flight of East Germans to West Germany ensued, primarily through the city of Berlin. This exodus of mostly skilled laborers created economic problems and led the East German government in 1961 to build the infamous Berlin Wall separating West from East Berlin. After building the wall, East Germany succeeded in developing the strongest economy among the Soviet Union's Eastern European satellites. In 1971, Ulbricht was succeeded by Erich Honecker (b. 1912), a party hard-liner who made use of the *Stasi*, the secret police, to rule with an iron fist for the next eighteen years.

In 1988, however, popular unrest, fueled in part by the continual economic slump of the 1980s (which affected most of Eastern Europe) as well as the ongoing oppressiveness of Honecker's regime, caused another mass exodus of East German refugees. Violent repression and Honecker's refusal to institute reforms led to an even larger exodus and mass demonstrations against the regime in the summer and fall of 1989. Capituating to popular pressure on November 9, the Communist government opened the entire border with the West. Hundreds of thousands of Germans swarmed across the borders, mostly to visit and return. The Berlin Wall, long the symbol of the Cold War, became the site of massive celebrations as thousands of people used sledgehammers to demolish the wall. By December, new political parties had emerged, and on March 18, 1990, in East Germany's first free elections ever, the Christian Democrats won almost 50 percent of the vote. The Christian Democrats supported political unification with West Germany, which was achieved on October 3, 1990. What had seemed almost impossible at the beginning of 1989 had become a reality by the end of 1990—the countries of East and West Germany had reunited to form one Germany.

The Disintegration of Yugoslavia

From its beginning in 1919, Yugoslavia had been an artificial creation. After World War II, the dictatorial Marshal Tito had managed to hold the six republics and two autonomous provinces that constituted Yugoslavia together. After his death in 1980, no strong leader emerged, and his responsibilities passed to a collective state presidency and the League of Communists of Yugoslavia. At the end of the 1980s, Yugoslavia was caught up in the reform movements sweeping through Eastern Europe. The League of Communists collapsed, and new parties quickly emerged.

The development of separatist movements complicated the Yugoslav political scene. In 1990, the republics of Slovenia, Croatia, Bosnia-Herzegovina, and Macedonia began to lobby for a new federal structure of Yugoslavia that would fulfill their separatist desires. Slobodan Milosevic, who had become leader of the Serbian Communist Party in 1987 and had managed to stay in power by emphasizing his Serbian nationalism, rejected these efforts. He asserted that these republics could only be independent if new border arrangements were made to accommodate the Serb minorities in those republics who did not want to live outside the boundaries of a Greater Serbian state. Serbs constituted 11.6 percent of Croatia's population and 32 percent of Bosnia-Herzegovina's population in 1981.

AND THE WALL CAME TUMBLING DOWN. The Berlin Wall, long a symbol of Europe's Cold War divisions, became the site of massive celebrations after the East German government opened its border with the West. The activities included spontaneous acts of demolition as Germans used sledgehammers and crowbars to tear down parts of the wall.

After negotiations among the six republics failed, Slovenia and Croatia declared their independence in June 1991. Milosevic's government sent the Yugoslavian army, which it controlled, into Slovenia, without much success. In September 1991, it began a full assault against Croatia. Increasingly, the Yugoslavian army was becoming the Serbian army, while Serbian irregular forces played an important role in military operations. Before a cease-fire was arranged, the Serbian forces had captured one-third of Croatia's territory in brutal and destructive fighting. Early in 1992, the Serbs turned their guns on Bosnia-Herzegovina and by mid-1993 had acquired 70 percent of Bosnian territory. The Serbian policy of "ethnic cleansing"—killing or forcibly removing Bosnian Muslims from their lands—revived memories of Nazi atrocities in World War II. Nevertheless, despite worldwide outrage, European governments failed to take a decisive and forceful stand against these Serbian activities. By 1995, some 250,000 Bosnians had been killed and two million others left homeless.

In that same year, a sudden turn of events occurred. New offensives by mostly Muslim Bosnian government army forces and by the Croatian army regained considerable territory that had been lost to Serbian forces. Air strikes by NATO bombers, strongly advocated by U.S. President Bill Clinton, were launched in retaliation for Serb attacks on civilians and weakened the Serb military positions. A formal peace treaty was signed in Paris on December 14 that split Bosnia into a loose union of a Serb republic and a Muslim-Croat federation. NATO agreed to send a force of sixty thousand troops to monitor the frontier between the new political entities (see Map 29.2).

THE WAR IN KOSOVO

Peace in Bosnia, however, did not bring peace to the lands of the former Yugoslavia. A new war erupted in 1999 over Kosovo, which had been made an autonomous province within Yugoslavia by Tito in 1974. Kosovo's inhabitants were mainly ethnic Albanians. But the province was also home to a Serbian minority that considered it sacred territory where Serbian forces in the fourteenth century had been defeated by the Ottoman Turks.

In 1989, Slobodan Milosevic, the Yugoslav president, stripped Kosovo of its autonomous status and outlawed any official use of the Albanian language. In 1993, some groups of ethnic Albanians founded the Kosovo Liberation Army (KLA) and began a campaign against Serbian rule in Kosovo. When Serb forces began to massacre ethnic Albanians in an effort to crush the KLA, the United States and its NATO allies sought to arrange a settlement. After months of negotiations, the Kosovo Albanians agreed to a peace plan that would have given the ethnic Albanians in Kosovo broad autonomy for a three-year interim period. When Milosevic refused to sign the agreement, the United States and its NATO allies began a bombing campaign that forced the Yugoslavian government into compliance. In the fall elections of 2000, Milosevic himself was ousted from power.

Western Europe: The Winds of Change

After two decades of incredible economic growth, Europe experienced severe economic recessions in the mid-1970s and early 1980s. Both inflation and unemployment rose dramatically. A substantial increase in the price of oil in 1973 was a major cause of the first downturn. Moreover, a worldwide recession had led to a decline in demand for European goods. The economies of the Western European states recovered in the course of the 1980s, although problems remained.

Europeans also moved toward further integration of their economies after 1970. The European Economic Community expanded in 1973 when Great Britain, Ireland, and Denmark gained membership in what its members now called the European Community (EC). By 1986, three additional members—Spain, Portugal, and Greece—had been added. The European Community was primarily an economic union, not a political one. By 1992, the EC comprised 344 million people and constituted the world's largest single trading entity, transacting almost one-fourth of the world's commerce. In the 1980s and 1990s, the European Community moved toward even greater economic integration. The Treaty on European Union (also called the Maastricht Treaty after the city in the Netherlands where the agreement was reached) represented an attempt to create a true economic and monetary union of all EC members. On January 1, 1994, the European Community became the European Union (EU). One of its first goals was to introduce a common currency, called the *euro*, adopted by eleven EU nations.

GERMANY RESTORED

After the Adenauer era, German voters moved politically from the center-right politics of the Christian Democrats to center-left politics, and in 1969, the

MAP 29.2 **The Former Yugoslavia.**

Social Democrats became the leading party. The first Social Democratic chancellor was Willy Brandt (1913–1992). Brandt was especially successful with his "opening toward the east" (known as *Ostpolitik*), for which he received the Nobel Peace Prize in 1972. In that year, Brandt made a treaty with East Germany that called for "good neighborly" relations, which soon led to greater cultural, personal, and economic contacts between West and East Germany.

Brandt's successor, Helmut Schmidt (b. 1918), was more of a technocrat than a reform-minded socialist and concentrated primarily on the economic problems largely brought about by high oil prices between 1973 and 1975. Schmidt was successful in eliminating a deficit of 10 billion marks in three years. In 1982, when the coalition of Schmidt's Social Democrats with the Free Democrats fell apart over the reduction of social welfare expenditures, the Free Democrats joined with the Christian Democratic Union of Helmut Kohl (b. 1930) to form a new government.

Kohl was a clever politician who benefited greatly from the reunification of the two Germanies, which made the new Germany, with its 79 million people, the leading power in Europe. But the excitement over reunification soon dissipated as problems arose. The realization set in that the revitalization of eastern Germany would take far more money than was originally thought, and Kohl's government was soon forced to raise taxes. Moreover, the virtual collapse of the economy in eastern Germany led to extremely high levels of unemployment and severe discontent. One of the responses was a return to power for the Social Democrats as a result of elections in 1998.

GREAT BRITAIN: THATCHER AND THATCHERISM

Between 1964 and 1979, the Conservative and Labour Parties alternated in power. Neither could solve the problem of fighting between Catholics and Protestants in Northern Ireland. Violence increased as the Irish Republican Army (IRA) staged a series of dramatic terrorist acts in response to the suspension of Northern Ireland's parliament in 1972 and the establishment of direct rule by London. Nor was either party able to deal with Britain's ailing economy. Failure to modernize made British industry less and less competitive. Moreover, Britain was hampered by frequent labor strikes, many of them caused by conflicts between rival labor unions.

In 1979, the Conservatives returned to power under Margaret Thatcher (b. 1925), who became the first woman prime minister in British history (see the box on p. 616). Thatcher pledged to lower taxes, reduce government bureaucracy, limit social welfare, restrict union power, and end inflation. The "Iron Lady," as she was called, did break the power of the labor unions. Although she did not eliminate the basic components of the social welfare system, she did use austerity measures to control inflation. "Thatcherism," as her economic policy was termed, improved the British economic situation but at a price. The south of England, for example, prospered, but the old industrial areas of the Midlands and north declined and were beset by high unemployment and poverty.

In foreign policy, Thatcher, like Ronald Reagan in the United States, took a hard-line approach against communism. She oversaw a large military buildup aimed at replacing older technology and reestablishing Britain as a world policeman. In 1982, when Argentina attempted to take control of the Falkland Islands (one of Britain's few remaining colonial outposts) 300 miles off its coast, the British successfully rebuked the Argentines.

Thatcher dominated British politics in the 1980s. Only in 1990 did Labour's fortunes seem to revive when Thatcher's government attempted to replace local property taxes with a flat-rate tax payable by every adult to his or her local authority. Many argued that this was nothing more than a poll tax that would enable the rich to pay the same rate as the poor. In 1990, after antitax riots broke out, Thatcher's once remarkable popularity fell to all-time lows. At the end of November, a revolt within her own party caused

MARGARET THATCHER. Great Britain's first female prime minister, Margaret Thatcher was a strong leader who dominated British politics in the 1980s. This picture of Thatcher was taken at the Chelsea Flower Show in May 1990. Six months later, a revolt within her own party caused her to resign as prime minister.

Margaret Thatcher: Entering a Man's World

In this excerpt from her autobiography, Margaret Thatcher describes how she was interviewed by Conservative Party officials when they first considered her as a candidate for Parliament. Thatcher ran for Parliament for the first time in 1950; she lost, but increased the Conservative vote total in the district by 50 percent over the previous election.

Margaret Thatcher, The Path to Power

And, as always with me, there was politics. I immediately joined the Conservative Association and threw myself into the usual round of Party activities. In particular, I thoroughly enjoyed what was called the "'39–'45' discussion group, where Conservatives of the war generation met to exchange views and argue about the political topics of the day. . . . It was as a representative of the Oxford University Graduate Conservative Association (OUGCA) that I went to the Llandudno Conservative Party Conference in October 1948.

It had originally been intended that I should speak at the Conference. . . . It would have been my first Conference speech, but in the end the seconder chosen was a City man. . . .

My disappointment at this was, however, very quickly overcome and in a most unexpected way. After one of the debates, I found myself engaged in one of those speculative conversations which young people have about their future prospects. An Oxford friend, John Grant, said he supposed that one day I would like to be a Member of Parliament. "Well, yes," I replied, "but there's not much hope of that. The chances of my being selected are just nil at the moment." I might have added that with no private income of my own there was no way I could have afforded to be an MP on the salary then available. I had not even tried to get on the Party's list of approved candidates.

Later in the day, John Grant happened to be sitting next to the Chairman of the Dartford Conservative Association, John Miller. The Association was in search of a candidate. I learned afterwards that the conversation went something like this: "I understand that you're still looking for a candidate at Dartford?"

"That's right. Any suggestions?"

"Well, there's a young woman, Margaret Roberts, that you might look at. She's very good."

"Oh, but Dartford is a real industrial stronghold. I don't think a woman would do at all."

"Well, you know best of course. But why not just look at her?"

And they did. I was invited to have lunch with John Miller and his wife, Phee, and the Dartford Woman's Chairman, Mrs. Fletcher, on the Saturday on Llandudno Pier. Presumably, and in spite of any reservations about the suitability of a woman candidate for their seat, they liked what they saw. I certainly got on well with them. . . .

I did not hear from Dartford until December, when I was asked to attend an interview at Palace Chambers, Bridge Street. . . . I found myself short-listed, and was asked to go to Dartford itself for a further interview. . . . As one of five would-be candidates, I had to give a fifteen-minute speech and answer questions for a further ten minutes.

It was the questions which were more likely to cause me trouble. There was a good deal of suspicion of woman candidates, particularly in what was regarded as a tough industrial seat like Dartford. This was quite definitely a man's world into which not just angels feared to tread. . . .

The most reliable sign that a political occasion has gone well is that you have enjoyed it. I enjoyed that evening at Dartford, and the outcome justified my confidence. I was selected.

Thatcher to resign as prime minister and be replaced by John Major. His government, however, failed to capture the imagination of most Britons. In new elections on May 1, 1997, the Labour Party won a landslide victory. The new prime minister, Tony Blair (b. 1953), was a moderate whose youthful energy immediately instilled a new vigor on the political scene.

UNCERTAINTIES IN FRANCE

The worsening of France's economic situation in the 1970s brought a shift to the left politically. By 1981, the Socialists had become the dominant party in the National Assembly, and the Socialist leader, François Mitterrand (1916–1995), was elected president. His first

CHRONOLOGY

Western Europe

Willy Brandt as chancellor of West Germany	1969
Expansion of European Community	1973
Helmut Schmidt as chancellor of West Germany	1974
Margaret Thatcher as prime minister of Britain	1979
François Mitterrand as president of France	1981
Falklands War	1982
Helmut Kohl as chancellor of West Germany	1982
Reelection of Mitterrand	1988
Conservative victory in France	1993
Creation of European Union	1994
Jacques Chirac as president of France	1995
Victory of Labour Party in Britain	1997

concern was with France's economic difficulties. In 1982, Mitterrand froze prices and wages in the hope of reducing the huge budget deficit and high inflation. He also passed a number of liberal measures to aid workers: an increased minimum wage, expanded social benefits, a thirty-nine-hour workweek, higher taxes for the rich, and nationalization of major banks. Mitterrand's administrative reforms included both centralization (nationalization of banks and industry) and decentralization (granting local governments greater powers).

The Socialist policies largely failed to work, however, and within three years, a decline in support for the Socialists caused the Mitterrand government to turn portions of the economy back over to private enterprise. Economic improvements enabled Mitterrand to win a second seven-year term in the 1988 presidential election, but France's overall economic decline continued. In 1993, French unemployment stood at 10.6 percent, and in the elections in March of that year, the Socialists won only 28 percent of the vote while a coalition of conservative parties won 80 percent of the seats in the National Assembly. The move to the right was strengthened when the conservative mayor of Paris, Jacques Chirac, was elected president in May 1995.

The United States: The American Domestic Scene

With the election of Richard Nixon as president in 1968, American politics made a shift to the right. Nixon ended American involvement in Vietnam by gradually withdrawing American troops. Politically, he pursued a "southern strategy," carefully calculating that "law and order" issues and a slowdown in racial desegregation would appeal to southern whites. The South, which had once been a stronghold for the Democrats, began to form a new allegiance to the Republican party. The Republican strategy, however, also gained support among white Democrats in northern cities, where court-mandated busing to achieve racial integration had led to a white backlash.

As president, Nixon was paranoid about conspiracies and began to use illegal methods to gain political intelligence on his political opponents. Nixon's zeal led to the Watergate scandal—the attempted bugging of Democratic National Headquarters, located in the Watergate complex in Washington, D.C. Although Nixon repeatedly lied to the American public about his involvement in the affair, secret tapes of his own conversations in the White House revealed the truth. On August 9, 1974, Nixon resigned the presidency rather than face impeachment and then trial by the Senate.

After Watergate, American domestic politics focused on economic issues. Vice-President Gerald Ford (b. 1913) became president when Nixon resigned, only to lose in the 1976 election to the former governor of Georgia, Jimmy Carter (b. 1924). Both Ford and Carter faced severe economic problems. The period from 1973 to the mid-1980s was one of economic stagnation, which came to be known as stagflation—a combination of high inflation and high unemployment. In part, the economic downturn stemmed from a dramatic change in oil prices. An oil embargo and price increases by the Organization of Petroleum Exporting Countries (OPEC) in the aftermath of the Arab-Israel War in 1973 quadrupled oil prices. Additional price hikes led oil prices to increase twentyfold by the end of the 1970s, encouraging inflationary tendencies throughout the entire economy.

By 1980, the Carter administration faced two devastating problems. High inflation and a noticeable decline in average weekly earnings were causing a drop in American living standards. At the same time, a crisis abroad had erupted when fifty-three Americans were taken hostage by the Iranian government of Ayatollah Khomeini. Carter's inability to gain the release of the American hostages led to perceptions at home that he was a weak president. His overwhelming loss to Ronald Reagan (b. 1911) in the election of 1980 brought forward the chief exponent of right-wing Republican policies and a new political order.

The Reagan Revolution, as it has been called, consisted of a number of new directions. Reversing decades of changes, Reagan cut back on the welfare state by decreasing spending on food stamps, school lunch programs, and job programs. At the same time, his administration fostered the largest peacetime military buildup in American history. Total federal spending rose from $631 billion in 1981 to over $1 trillion by 1986. But instead of raising taxes to pay for the new expenditures, which far outweighed the budget cuts in social areas, Reagan convinced Congress to trust in "supply-side economics." Massive tax cuts would supposedly stimulate rapid economic growth and produce new revenues. Much of the tax cut went to the wealthy. Reagan's policies seemed to work in the short run as the United States experienced an economic upturn that lasted until the end of the 1980s. The spending policies of the Reagan administration, however, also produced record government deficits, which loomed as an obstacle to long-term growth. In the 1970s, the total deficit was $420 billion. Between 1981 and 1987, Reagan budget deficits were three times that amount.

The inability of George Bush (b. 1924), Reagan's successor, to deal with the deficit problem, accompanied by an economic downturn, enabled a Democrat, Bill Clinton (b. 1946), to become president in November 1992. The new president was a southern Democrat who claimed to be a new Democrat—one who favored a number of the Republican policies of the 1980s. This was a clear indication that the Democratic victory had by no means halted the rightward drift in American politics. In fact, Clinton's reelection in 1996 was due in part to his adoption of Republican ideas and policies. Much of Clinton's second term, however, was overshadowed by charges of presidential misconduct stemming from the president's sexual affair with Monica Lewinsky, a White House intern. After a bitter partisan struggle, the U.S. Senate acquitted the president on two articles of impeachment brought by the House of Representatives.

Contemporary Canada

In 1963, during a major economic recession, the Liberals had been returned to power in Canada. The most prominent Liberal government was that of Pierre Trudeau (1919–2000), who came to power in 1968. Although French in background, Trudeau was dedicated to Canada's federal union, and in 1968 his government passed the Official Languages Act, which allowed both English and French to be used in the federal civil service. Although Trudeau's government vigorously pushed an industrialization program, high inflation and Trudeau's efforts to impose the will of the federal government on the powerful provincial governments alienated voters and weakened his government. Economic recession in the early 1980s brought Brian Mulroney (b. 1939), leader of the Progressive Conservative party, to power in 1984. Mulroney's government sought greater privatization of Canada's state-run corporations and negotiated a free trade agreement with the United States. Bitterly resented by many Canadians, the agreement cost Mulroney's government much of its popularity. In 1993, the ruling Conservatives were drastically defeated, and the Liberal leader, Jean Chrétien (b. 1934), became prime minister.

Mulroney's government was also unable to settle the ongoing crisis over the French-speaking province of Quebec. In the late 1960s, the Parti Québécois, headed by René Lévesque, ran on a platform of Quebec's secession from the Canadian union. To pursue their dream of separation, some underground separatist groups even used terrorist bombings. In 1976, the Parti Québécois won Quebec's provincial elections and in 1980 called for a referendum that would enable the provincial government to negotiate Quebec's independence from the rest of Canada. Voters in Quebec narrowly rejected the plan in 1995, however, and debate over Quebec's status continues to divide Canada.

New Directions and New Problems in Western Society

Dramatic social developments have accompanied political and economic changes since the end of World War II. New opportunities for women emerged while new problems for Western society arose with the advent of terrorism and a growing awareness of environmental dangers.

Transformation in Women's Lives

It is estimated that women need to average 2.1 children in order to ensure a natural replacement of a country's population. In many European countries, the population stopped growing in the 1960s, and the trend has continued since then. By the 1990s, birthrates were down drastically; among the nations of the European Union, the average number of children per mother was 1.4. Italy's rate—1.2—was the lowest in the world in 1997.

At the same time, the number of women in the workforce has continued to rise. In Britain, for example, the number of women in the labor force went from 32 percent to 44 percent between 1970 and 1990. Moreover, women have entered new employment areas. Greater access to universities and professional schools enabled women to take jobs in law, medicine, government, business, and education. In the Soviet Union, for example, about 70 percent of doctors and teachers were women. Nevertheless, economic inequality still often prevailed; women received lower wages than men for comparable work and received fewer opportunities for advancement to management positions.

THE WOMEN'S MOVEMENT

Feminists in the women's liberation movement came to believe that women themselves must transform the fundamental conditions of their lives. They did so in a variety of ways after 1970. First, they formed numerous "consciousness-raising" groups to further awareness of women's issues. Women met to share their personal experiences and become aware of the many ways that male dominance affected their lives. This new consciousness helped many women become activists.

Women sought and gained a measure of control over their own bodies by seeking to overturn laws prohibiting contraception and abortion. Hundreds of thousands of European women worked to repeal those laws in the 1960s and 1970s, and began to meet with success. A French law in 1968 permitted the sale of contraceptive devices, and in the 1970s French feminists worked to legalize abortion. One group of 343 prominent French women even signed a manifesto declaring that they had had abortions. In 1979, a new French law legalized abortion. Even in Catholic countries, where the church remained strongly opposed to abortion, legislation allowing contraception and abortion was passed in the 1970s and 1980s.

As more women became activists, they also became involved in new issues. In the 1980s and 1990s, women faculty in universities concentrated on reforming cultural attitudes through the new academic field of women's studies. Courses in women's studies, which stressed the role and contributions of women in history, mushroomed in both American and European colleges and universities.

Other women began to try to affect the political environment by allying with the antinuclear movement. In 1981, a group of women protested American nuclear missiles in Britain by chaining themselves to the fence of an American military base. Thousands more joined

ANTINUCLEAR PROTEST. Women were active participants in the antinuclear movement of the 1980s. Shown here are some of the ten thousand antinuclear protesters who linked hands to form a human chain around the 9-mile perimeter of the U.S. Air Force base at Greenham Common, England, on December 13, 1982. They were protesting the planned siting of ninety-six U.S. cruise missiles at the base.

in creating a peace camp around the military compound. Enthusiasm ran high; one participant said: "I'll never forget that feeling; it'll live with me forever. . . . It was for women; it was for peace; it was for the world."[1]

Some women joined the ecological movement. As one German writer who was concerned with environmental issues said, it is women "who must give birth to children, willingly or unwillingly, in this polluted world of ours." Women became especially prominent members of the Green Party in Germany (see "The Environment and the Green Movements" later in this chapter), which supported environmental issues. One delegate was Petra Kelly (b. 1947), one of the founders of the German Green Party and a tireless campaigner for the preservation of the environment as well as human rights and equality.

Women in the West have also reached out to work with women from the rest of the world in international conferences to change the conditions of their lives. Between 1975 and 1995, the United Nations held conferences in Mexico City, Copenhagen, Nairobi, and Beijing. These meetings made clear the differences between women from Western and non-Western countries. Whereas women from Western countries spoke about political, economic, cultural, and sexual rights, women from developing countries in Latin America, Africa, and Asia focused their attention on bringing an end to the violence, hunger, and disease that haunted their lives. Despite these differences, these meetings made it clear that women in both developed and developing nations were organizing to make all people aware of women's issues.

The Growth of Terrorism

Acts of terror by opponents of governments became a frightening aspect of modern Western society. Bands of terrorists used assassination, indiscriminate bombing of civilians, the taking of hostages, and the hijacking of airplanes to draw attention to their demands or to destabilize governments in the hope of achieving their political goals. Terrorist acts garnered considerable media attention. When Palestinian terrorists kidnapped and killed eleven Israeli athletes at the Munich Olympic Games in 1972, hundreds of millions of people watched the drama unfold on television. Indeed, some observers believe that media exposure has been an important catalyst for some terrorist groups.

Motivations for terrorist acts varied considerably. Left-wing groups, such as the Baader-Meinhof gang (also known as the Red Army Faction) in Germany and the Red Brigades in Italy, consisted chiefly of affluent middle-class young people who denounced the injustices of capitalism and supported acts of "revolutionary terrorism" to bring down the system. Right-wing terrorist groups, such as the New Order in Italy and the Charles Martel Club in France, used bombings to foment disorder and bring about authoritarian regimes. These groups received little or no public support, and authorities were able to crush them fairly quickly.

But terrorist acts also stemmed from militant nationalists who wished to create separatist states. Because they received considerable support from local populations sympathetic to their cause, these terrorist groups could maintain their activities over a long period of time. Most prominent was the Irish Republican Army (IRA), which resorted to vicious attacks against the ruling government and innocent civilians in Northern Ireland. Over a period of twenty years, IRA terrorists were responsible for the deaths of two thousand people in Northern Ireland; three-fourths of them were civilians.

Governments fought back by creating special antiterrorist units that became extremely effective in responding to terrorist acts. In 1977, for example, the German special antiterrorist unit, known as GSG, rescued ninety-one hostages from a Lufthansa airplane that had been hijacked to Mogadishu in Somalia. Counterterrorism, or a calculated policy of direct retaliation against terrorists, also made states that sponsored terrorism more cautious. In 1986, the Reagan administration responded to the terrorist bombing of a West German disco club popular with American soldiers by an air attack on Libya, long suspected to be a major sponsor of terrorist organizations.

The Environment and the Green Movements

By the 1970s, serious ecological problems had become all too apparent. Air pollution, produced by nitrogen oxide and sulfur dioxide emissions from road vehicles, power plants, and industrial factories, was causing respiratory illnesses and having corrosive effects on buildings and monuments. Many rivers, lakes, and seas had become so polluted that they posed serious health risks. Dying forests and disappearing wildlife alarmed more and more people. The Soviet nuclear power disaster at Chernobyl in 1986 made Europeans even more aware of potential environmental hazards. The opening of Eastern Europe after the revolutions of 1989 brought to the world's attention the incredible environmental destruction of that region caused by unfettered industrial pollution. Environmental concerns forced the major political parties in Europe to advocate new regulations for the protection of the environment.

Growing ecological awareness also gave rise to Green movements and Green parties that emerged throughout Europe in the 1970s. Some of these parties came from the antinuclear movement; others came from such causes as women's liberation and concerns for foreign workers. Most visible was the Green Party in Germany, which was officially organized in 1979 and by 1987 had elected forty-two delegates to the West German parliament. Green parties also competed successfully in Sweden, Austria, and Switzerland.

Although the Green movements and parties have played an important role in making people aware of ecological problems, they have by no means replaced the traditional political parties, as some political analysts in the mid-1980s forecast. For one thing, the coalitions that made up the Greens found it difficult to agree on all issues and tended to splinter into cliques. Moreover, traditional political parties have co-opted the environmental issues of the Greens. By the 1990s, more and more European governments were beginning to sponsor projects to safeguard the environment and clean up the worst sources of pollution.

◆ The World of Western Culture

Intellectually and culturally, the Western world during the second half of the twentieth century was marked by diversity. Although many trends represented a continuation of prewar modern developments, new directions have led some observers to speak of a "postmodern" cultural world.

Trends in Art and Literature

For the most part, the United States has dominated the art world since the end of World War II. Often vibrantly colored and filled with activity, American art reflected the energy and exuberance of postwar America. After 1945, New York City became the artistic center of the Western world. The Guggenheim Museum, the Museum of Modern Art, and the Whitney Museum of American Art, along with New York's plethora of art galleries, promoted modern art and helped determine artistic tastes throughout much of the world.

Abstractionism, especially Abstract Expressionism, took over the artistic mainstream. Typical American exuberance is evident in the enormous Abstract Expressionist canvases of Jackson Pollock (1912–1956). In such works as *Lavender Mist* (1950), paint seems to explode, assaulting the viewer with emotion and movement. Pollock's swirling forms and seemingly chaotic patterns broke all conventions of form and structure. His drip paintings, which make no attempt at representationalism, were extremely influential with other artists, although the public was initially quite hostile to his work.

The early 1960s saw the emergence of Pop Art, which took images of popular culture and transformed them into works of fine art. Andy Warhol (1930–1987), who began as an advertising illustrator, was the most famous of the Pop artists. Warhol

JACKSON POLLOCK PAINTING. One of the best-known practitioners of Abstract Expressionism, which took over the artistic mainstream after World War II, was the American Jackson Pollock, who achieved his ideal of total abstraction in his drip paintings. He is shown here at work at his Long Island studio. Pollock found it easier to produce his large canvases, covered with exploding patterns of color, by laying them on the floor.

adapted images from commercial art, such as Campbell soup cans, and photographs of such celebrities as Marilyn Monroe.

In the 1980s, styles emerged that have sometimes been referred to as Postmodern. Though still ill defined, Postmodernism tends to move away from the futurism or "cutting edge" qualities of Modernism. Instead it favors tradition, whether that includes more styles of painting or elevating traditional craftsmanship to the level of fine art. Weavers, potters, glassmakers, and furniture makers gained respect as artists.

In postwar literature, the most significant new trend was called the "Theater of the Absurd." Its most famous proponent was the Irishman Samuel Beckett (1906–1990), who lived in France. In Beckett's *Waiting for Godot* (1952), two men wait incessantly for the appearance of someone, with whom they may or may not have an appointment. No background information on the two men is provided. During the course of the play, nothing seems to be happening. The audience is never told if the action in front of them is real or unreal. Unlike traditional theater, suspense is maintained not by having the audience wonder "What is going to happen next?" but simply "What is happening now?"

The sense of meaninglessness that inspired the Theater of the Absurd also underscored the philosophy of existentialism of Albert Camus (1913–1960) and Jean-Paul Sartre (1905–1980). The beginning point of the existentialism of Sartre and Camus was the absence of God in the universe. While the death of God was tragic, it meant that humans had no preordained destiny and were utterly alone in the universe, with no future and no hope. As Camus expressed it:

> A world that can be explained even with bad reasons is a familiar world. But, on the other hand, in a universe suddenly divested of illusions and lights, man feels an alien, a stranger. His exile is without remedy since he is deprived of the memory of a lost home or the hope of a promised land. This divorce between man and his life, the actor and his setting, is properly the feeling of absurdity.[2]

According to Camus, then, the world was absurd and without meaning; humans, too, are without meaning and purpose. Reduced to despair and depression, humans have but one ground of hope—themselves.

The Revival of Religion

Existentialism was one response to the despair generated by the apparent collapse of civilized values in the twentieth century. The revival of religion has been another. Ever since the Enlightenment of the eighteenth century, Christianity and religion had been on the defensive. But a number of religious thinkers and leaders attempted to bring new life to Christianity in the twentieth century.

One expression of this religious revival was the attempt by such theologians as the Protestant Karl Barth (1886–1968) and the Catholic Karl Rahner (1904–1984) to infuse traditional Christian teachings with new life. In his numerous writings, Barth attempted to reinterpret the religious insights of the Reformation era for the modern world. To Barth, the sinful and hence imperfect nature of human beings meant that humans could know religious truth not through reason but only through the grace of God. Rahner attempted to revitalize traditional Catholic theology by incorporating aspects of modern thought. He was careful, however, to emphasize the continuity between ancient and modern interpretations of Catholic doctrine.

In the Catholic church, attempts at religious renewal also came from two charismatic popes—John XXIII and John Paul II. Pope John XXIII (1881–1963) reigned as pope for only a short time (1958–1963) but sparked a dramatic revival of Catholicism when he summoned the twenty-first ecumenical council of the Catholic church. Known as Vatican II, the council liberalized a number of Catholic practices. The Mass was henceforth to be celebrated in the vernacular languages rather than Latin.

John Paul II (b. 1920), who had been the archbishop of Krakow in Poland before his elevation to the papacy in 1978, was the first non-Italian to be elected pope since the sixteenth century. Although he alienated a number of people by reasserting traditional Catholic teaching on such issues as birth control, women in the priesthood, and clerical celibacy, John Paul's numerous travels around the world helped strengthen the Catholic church throughout the non-Western world. A strong believer in social justice, the charismatic John Paul II has been a powerful figure in reminding Europeans of their spiritual heritage and the need to temper the pursuit of materialism with spiritual concerns.

The New World of Science and Technology

Many of the scientific and technological achievements since World War II have revolutionized people's lives. Before World War II, theoretical science and technology were largely separated. Pure science was the domain of university professors who were quite far removed from the practical technological matters of technicians and engineers. But during World War II, university scientists were recruited to work for their governments and develop new weapons and practical instruments of war. British physicists played a crucial role in the development of an improved radar system in 1940 that helped defeat the German air force in the Battle of Britain. German scientists created self-propelled rockets as well as jet airplanes to keep Hitler's hopes alive for a miraculous turnaround in the war. The computer, too, was a wartime creation. The British mathematician Alan Turing designed a primitive computer to assist British intelligence in breaking the secret codes of German ciphering machines. The most famous product of wartime scientific research was the atomic bomb, created by a team of American and European scientists under the guidance of the physicist J. Robert Oppenheimer. Obviously, most wartime devices were created for destructive purposes, but merely to mention computers and jet airplanes demonstrates that they could easily be adapted for peacetime uses.

The postwar alliance of science and technology led to an accelerated rate of change that became a fact of life in Western society. One product of this alliance—the computer—may yet prove to be the most revolutionary of all the technological inventions of the twentieth century. Early computers, which required thousands of vacuum tubes to function, were large and took up considerable space. The development of the transistor and then the silicon chip provided a revolutionary new approach to computers. In 1971, the invention of the microprocessor, a machine that combines the equivalent of thousands of transitors on a single, tiny silicon chip, opened the road for the development of the personal computer.

The computer is a new kind of machine whose chief function is to store and produce information, now considered a fundamental asset of our fast-paced civilization. By the 1990s, the personal computer had become a regular fixture in businesses, schools, and homes. Not only does it make a whole host of tasks much easier, but it has also become an important tool in virtually every area of modern life. Indeed, other tools and machines now depend for their functioning on computers. Many of the minute-by-minute decisions required to fly an airplane, for example, are done by a computer.

Despite the marvels that were produced by the alliance of science and technology, the underlying assumption of this alliance—that scientific knowledge gave human beings the ability to manipulate the environment for their benefit—was questioned by some in the 1960s and 1970s who believed that some technological advances had far-reaching side effects damaging to the environment. The chemical fertilizers, for example, that were touted for producing larger crops wreaked havoc with the ecological balance of streams, rivers, and woodlands. *Small Is Beautiful,* written by the British economist E. F. Schumacher (1911–1977), was a fundamental critique of the dangers of the new science and technology (see the box on p. 624). The threat of global warming and the dwindling of forests and lakes made environmentalism one of the important issues of the 1990s.

The Explosion of Popular Culture

Since World War II, popular culture has played an increasingly important role in helping Western people define themselves. The history of popular culture is also the history of the economic system that supports it, for it is this system that manufactures, distributes, and sells the images that people consume as popular culture. As popular culture and its economic support system became increasingly intertwined, industries of leisure emerged. As one historian of popular culture has argued, "Industrial societies turn the provision of leisure into a commercial activity, in which their citizens are sold entertainment, recreation, pleasure, and appearance as commodities that differ from the goods at the drugstore only in the way they are used."[3] Modern popular culture therefore is inextricably tied to the mass consumer society in which it has emerged.

POPULAR CULTURE AND THE AMERICANIZATION OF THE WORLD

The United States has been the most influential force in shaping popular culture in the West and, to a lesser degree, the rest of the world. Through movies, music, advertising, and television, the United States has spread its particular form of consumerism and the American dream to millions around the world. Already in 1923 the New York *Morning Post* noted that "the film is to America what the flag was once to Britain. By its means Uncle Sam may hope some day . . . to Americanize the world."[4] In movies,

Small Is Beautiful: The Limits of Modern Technology

Although science and technology have produced an amazing array of achievements in the postwar world, some voices have been raised in criticism of their sometimes destructive aspects. In 1975, in his book Small Is Beautiful, *the British economist E. F. Schumacher examined the effects modern industrial technology has had on the earth's resources.*

E. F. Schumacher, Small Is Beautiful

Is it not evident that our current methods of production are already eating into the very substance of industrial man? To many people this is not at all evident. Now that we have solved the problem of production, they say, have we ever had it so good? Are we not better fed, better clothed, and better housed than ever before—and better educated? Of course we are: most, but by no means all, of us: in the rich countries. But this is not what I mean by "substance." The substance of man cannot be measured by Gross National Product. Perhaps it cannot be measured at all, except for certain symptoms of loss. However, this is not the place to go into the statistics of these symptoms, such as crime, drug addiction, vandalism, mental breakdown, rebellion, and so forth. Statistics never prove anything.

I started by saying that one of the most fateful errors of our age is the belief that the problem of production has been solved. This illusion, I suggested, is mainly due to our inability to recognize that the modern industrial system, with all its intellectual sophistication, consumes the very basis on which it has been erected. To use the language of the economist, it lives on irreplaceable capital which it cheerfully treats as income. I specified three categories of such capital: fossil fuels, the tolerance margins of nature, and the human substance. Even if some readers should refuse to accept all three parts of my argument, I suggest that any one of them suffices to make my case.

And what is my case? Simply that our most important task is to get off our present collision course. And who is there to tackle such a task? I think every one of us. . . . To talk about the future is useful only if it leads to action *now.* And what can we do *now,* while we are still in the position of "never having had it so good"? To say the least . . . we must thoroughly understand the problem and begin to see the possibility of evolving a new life-style, with new methods of production and new patterns of consumption: a life-style designed for permanence. To give only three preliminary examples: in agriculture and horticulture, we can interest ourselves in the perfection of production methods which are biologically sound, build up soil fertility, and produce health, beauty and permanence. Productivity will then look after itself. In industry, we can interest ourselves in the evolution of small-scale technology, relatively nonviolent technology, "technology with a human face," so that people have a chance to enjoy themselves while they are working, instead of working solely for their pay packet and hoping, usually forlornly, for enjoyment solely during their leisure time.

television, and music, the impact of American popular culture on the Western world is apparent.

Motion pictures were the primary vehicle for the diffusion of American popular culture in the years immediately following the war, and they continued to dominate both European and American markets in the next decades. Although developed in the 1930s, television did not become readily available until the late 1940s. By 1954, there were 32 million sets in the United States as television became the centerpiece of middle-class life. In the 1960s, as television spread around the world, American networks unloaded their products on Europe and the Third World at extraordinarily low prices. The United States has also dominated popular music since the end of World War II. Jazz, blues, rhythm and blues, rap, and rock and roll have been by far the most popular music forms in the Western world—and much of the non-Western world—during this time. All of them originated in the United States, and all are rooted in African-American musical innovations. These forms later spread to the rest of the world, inspiring local artists who then transformed the music in their own way.

THE BEATLES IN CONCERT. Although rock and roll originated in the United States, it also inspired musical groups in Europe. This was certainly true of Britain's Beatles, who created a sensation among young people when they came to the United States in the 1960s. Here the Beatles are shown during a performance on *The Ed Sullivan Show*.

In the postwar years, sports have become a major product of both popular culture and the leisure industry. The development of satellite television and various electronic breakthroughs helped make sports a global phenomenon. Olympic Games could now be broadcast around the world from anywhere in the world. Sports became a cheap form of entertainment for the consumers, as fans did not have to leave their homes to enjoy athletic competitions.

◆ Toward a Global Civilization?

Increasingly, people are becoming aware of the political and economic interdependence of the world's nations and the global nature of our contemporary problems. At the beginning of the twenty-first century, human beings are coming to understand that destructive forces unleashed in any part of the world soon affect all of it. Nuclear proliferation makes nuclear war an ever-present possibility; such a war would mean radioactive fallout for the entire planet. Smokestack pollution in one nation can produce acid rain in another. Oil spills and dumping of wastes in the ocean have an impact on the shores of many nations. The consumption of drugs in the world's wealthy nations affects the stability of both wealthy and less developed nations. As crises involving food, water, energy, and natural resources proliferate, solutions implemented by one nation often affect other nations. The new globalism includes the recognition that the challenges that seem to threaten human existence at the beginning of the twenty-first century are global.

As the heirs of Western civilization have become aware that the problems humans face are global, not just national, they have responded to this challenge in different ways. One approach has been to develop grassroots social movements, including those devoted to the environment, women's and men's liberation, human potential, appropriate technologies, and nonviolence. "Think globally, act locally" is one slogan these groups use. Related to the emergence of these social movements is the growth of nongovernmental organizations (NGOs). According to one analyst, NGOs are an important instrument in the cultivation of global perspectives: "Since NGOs by definition are identified with interests that transcend national boundaries, we expect all NGOs to define problems in global terms, to take account of human interests and needs as they are found in all parts of the planet."[5] NGOs are often represented at the United Nations and include professional, business, and cooperative organizations; foundations; religious, peace, and disarmament groups; youth and women's organizations; environmental and human rights groups; and research institutes. The number of international NGOs increased from 176 in 1910 to 18,000 in 1990.

Yet hopes for global approaches to global problems have also been hindered by political, ethnic, and religious disputes. Pollution of the Rhine River by factories along its banks provokes angry disputes among European nations, while the United States and Canada have argued about the effects of acid rain on Canadian forests. The collapse of the Soviet Union and its satellite system between 1989 and 1991 seemed to provide an enormous boost to the potential for international cooperation on global issues. In fact, the collapse of the Soviet empire has had almost the opposite effect; its disintegration has led to the emergence of squabbling new nations and an atmosphere of conflict and tension throughout much of Eastern Europe. The bloody conflict in the former Yugoslavia clearly indicates the dangers in the rise of nationalist sentiment among various ethnic and religious groups in Eastern Europe.

Thus even as the world becomes more global in culture and interdependent in its mutual relations, centrifugal forces are still at work attempting to redefine the political, cultural, and ethnic ways in which the world is divided. Such efforts are often disruptive and can sometimes work against measures to enhance our human destiny.

Many lessons can be learned from the history of Western civilization, but one of them is especially clear. Lack of involvement in the affairs of one's society can lead to a sense of powerlessness. In an age that is often crisis-laden and chaotic, an understanding of our Western heritage and its lessons can be instrumental in helping us create new models for the future. For we are all creators of history, and the future of Western and indeed world civilization depends on us.

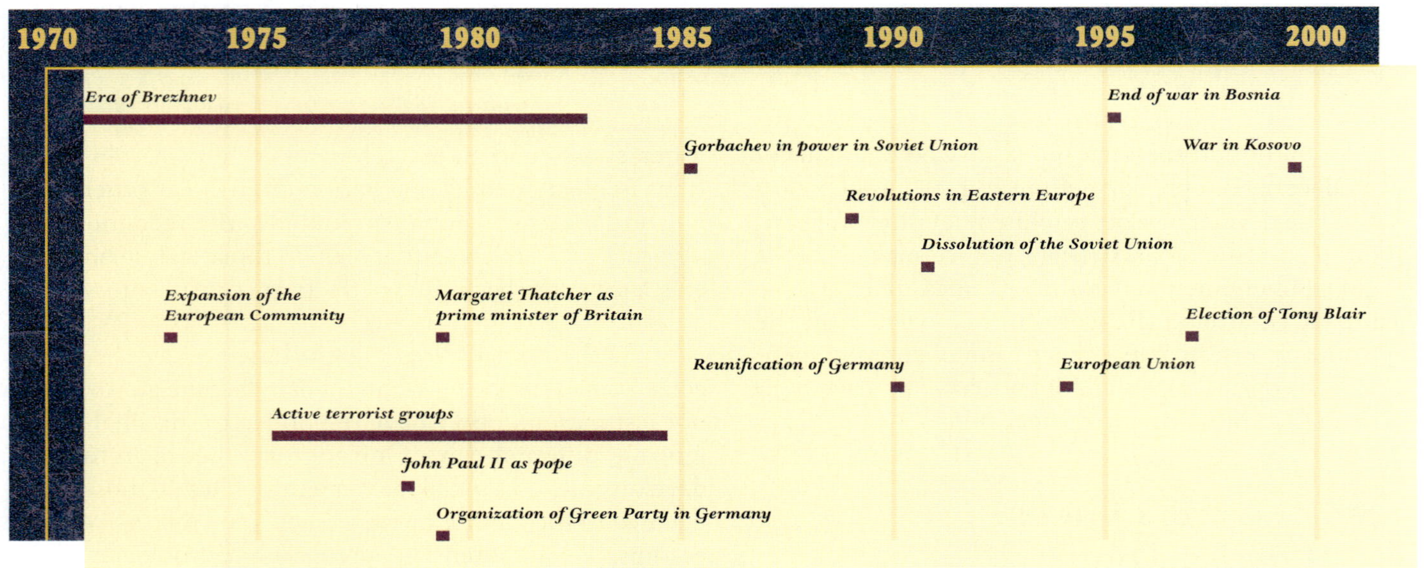

Notes

1. Quoted in Renate Bridenthal, "Women in the New Europe," in Renate Bridenthal, Susan Mosher Stuard, and Merry E. Wiesner, eds., *Becoming Visible: Women in European History,* 3d ed. (Boston, 1998), pp. 564–565.
2. Quoted in Henry Grosshans, *The Search for Modern Europe* (Boston, 1970), p. 421.
3. Richard Maltby, ed., *Passing Parade: A History of Popular Culture in the Twentieth Century* (New York, 1989), p. 8.
4. Quoted in ibid., p. 11.
5. Elise Boulding, *Women in the Twentieth Century World* (New York, 1977), p. 186.

Suggestions for Further Reading

For general surveys of contemporary European history, see the references in Chapter 28. General studies on the Cold War are also listed in Chapter 28. A detailed analysis of American-Soviet relations in the 1970s and 1980s is provided in R. Garthoff, *Détente and Confrontation: American-Soviet Relations from Nixon to Reagan* (Washington, D.C., 1985). On the end of the Cold War, see B. Denitch, *The End of the Cold War* (Minneapolis, Minn., 1990); W. G. Hyland, *The Cold War Is Over* (New York, 1990); and W. Laqueur, *Soviet Union, 2000: Reform or Revolution?* (New York, 1990).

Recent problems in the Soviet Union are analyzed in M. Lewin, *The Gorbachev Phenomenon* (Berkeley, Calif., 1988);

G. Hosking, *The Awakening of the Soviet Union* (London, 1990); and S. White, *Gorbachev and After* (Cambridge, 1991). For general studies of the Soviet satellites in Eastern Europe, see S. Fischer-Galati, *Eastern Europe in the 1980s* (London, 1981), and the references in Chapter 28. Additional studies on the recent history of these countries include T. G. Ash, *The Polish Revolution: Solidarity* (New York, 1984) and *The Magic Lantern: The Revolution of '89 Witnessed in Warsaw, Budapest, Berlin, and Prague* (New York, 1990); C. S. Maier, *Dissolution: The Crisis of Communism and the End of East Germany* (Princeton, N.J., 1997); and S. Ramet, *Nationalism and Federalism in Yugoslavia* (Bloomington, Ind., 1992).

For general works on Western Europe and individual countries, see the references in Chapter 28. On the recent history of these countries, see E. J. Evans, *Thatcher and Thatcherism* (New York, 1997); P. A. Hall, *Governing the Economy: The Politics of State Intervention in Britain and France* (New York, 1986); S. Baumann-Reynolds, *François Mitterrand* (Westport, Conn., 1995); and K. Jarausch, *The Rush to German Unity* (New York, 1994).

The changing role of women is examined in C. Duchen, *Feminism in France* (London, 1986). On terrorism, see W. Laqueur, *Terrorism*, 2d ed. (New York, 1988), and R. Rubenstein, *Alchemists of Revolution: Terrorism in the Modern World* (London, 1987). On the development of the Green parties, see M. O'Neill, *Green Parties and Political Change in Contemporary Europe* (Aldershot, England, 1997), and D. Richardson and C. Rootes, eds., *The Green Challenge: The Development of the Green Parties in Europe* (London, 1995).

For a general view of postwar thought, see R. N. Stromberg, *European Intellectual History Since 1789*, 5th ed. (Englewood Cliffs, N.J., 1990). On contemporary art, see R. Lambert, *Cambridge Introduction to the History of Art: The Twentieth Century* (Cambridge, 1981), and the general work by B. Cole and A. Gealt, *Art of the Western World* (New York, 1989). A physicist's view of science is contained in J. Ziman, *The Force of Knowledge: The Scientific Dimension of Society* (Cambridge, 1976). A physicist's view of a new conception of reality is D. Bohm, *Wholeness and the Implicate Order* (Boston, 1980). A classic work on existentialism is W. Barrett, *Irrational Man* (Garden City, N.Y., 1962). R. Maltby, ed., *Passing Parade: A History of Popular Culture in the Twentieth Century* (Oxford, 1989), is an excellent survey of twentieth-century popular culture. On film and the media, see L. May, *Screening Out the Past: The Birth of Mass Culture and the Motion Picture Industry* (New York, 1980), and F. Wheen, *Television* (London, 1985). On popular music, see P. Eberly, *Music in the Air* (New York, 1982). Sport is examined in A. Guttmann, *From Ritual to Record: The Nature of Modern Sports* (New York, 1978), and R. Mandell, *Sport: A Cultural History* (New York, 1984).

For additional reading, go to InfoTrac College Edition, your online research library at http://web1.infotrac-college.com

Enter the search terms *Single European Market* using the Subject Guide.

Enter the search terms *Europe Communism* using Key Terms.

Enter the search term *perestroika* using Key Terms.

Enter the search terms *Green Parties* using Key Terms.

Glossary

absolutism a form of government where the sovereign power or ultimate authority rested in the hands of a monarch who claimed to rule by divine right and was therefore responsible only to God.

Agricultural (Neolithic) Revolution the shift from hunting animals and gathering plants for sustenance to producing food by systematic agriculture that occurred gradually between 10,000 and 4000 B.C. (the Neolithic or "New Stone" Age).

agricultural revolution the application of new agricultural techniques that allowed for a large increase in productivity in the eighteenth century.

anarchism a political theory that holds that all governments and existing social institutions are unnecessary and advocates a society based on voluntary cooperation.

anti-Semitism hostility toward or discrimination against Jews.

appeasement the policy, followed by the European nations in the 1930s, of accepting Hitler's annexation of Austria and Czechoslovakia in the belief that meeting his demands would assure peace and stability.

Arianism a Christian heresy that taught that Jesus was inferior to God. Though condemned by the Council of Nicaea in 325, Arianism was adopted by many of the Germanic peoples who entered the Roman Empire over the next centuries.

aristocracy a class of hereditary nobility in medieval Europe; a warrior class who shared a distinctive lifestyle based on the institution of knighthood, although there were social divisions within the group based on extremes of wealth.

Ausgleich the "Compromise" of 1867 that created the dual monarchy of Austria-Hungary. Austria and Hungary each had its own capital, constitution, and legislative assembly, but were united under one monarch.

authoritarian state a state that has a dictatorial government and some other trappings of a totalitarian state, but does not demand that the masses be actively involved in the regime's goals as totalitarian states do.

auxiliaries troops enlisted from the subject peoples of the Roman Empire to supplement the regular legions composed of Roman citizens.

balance of power a distribution of power among several states such that no single nation can dominate or interfere with the interests of another.

benefice in the Christian church, a position, such as a bishopric, that consisted of both a sacred office and the right of the holder to the annual revenues from the position.

bicameral legislature a legislature with two houses.

Black Death the outbreak of plague (mostly bubonic) in the mid-fourteenth century that killed from 25 to 50 percent of Europe's population.

Blitzkrieg "lightning war." A war conducted with great speed and force, as in Germany's advance at the beginning of World War II.

Bolsheviks a small faction of the Russian Social Democratic Party who were led by Lenin and dedicated to violent revolution; seized power in Russia in 1917 and were subsequently renamed the Communists.

boyars the Russian nobility.

Brezhnev Doctrine the doctrine, enunciated by Leonid Brezhnev, that the Soviet Union had a right to intervene if socialism was threatened in another socialist state; used to justify the use of Soviet troops in Czechoslovakia in 1968.

caliph the secular leader of the Islamic community.

capital material wealth used or available for use in the production of more wealth.

cartel a combination of independent commercial enterprises that work together to control prices and limit competition.

Cartesian dualism Descartes' principle of the separation of mind and matter (and mind and body) that enabled scientists to view matter as something separate from themselves that could be investigated by reason.

chansons de geste a form of vernacular literature in the High Middle Ages that consisted of heroic epics focusing on the deeds of warriors.

chivalry the ideal of civilized behavior that emerged among the nobility in the eleventh and twelfth centuries under the influence of the church; a code of ethics knights were expected to uphold.

Christian (northern) humanism an intellectual movement in northern Europe in the late fifteenth and early sixteenth centuries that combined the interest in the classics of the Italian Renaissance with an interest in the sources of early Christianity, including the New Testament and the writings of the church fathers.

civic humanism an intellectual movement of the Italian Renaissance that saw Cicero, who was both an intellectual and a statesman, as the ideal and held that humanists should be involved in government and use their rhetorical training in the service of the state.

civil rights the basic rights of citizens including equality before the law, freedom of speech and press, and freedom from arbitrary arrest.

Cold War the ideological conflict between the Soviet Union and the United States after World War II.

collective farms large farms created in the Soviet Union by Stalin by combining many small holdings into one large farm worked by the peasants under government supervision.

collective security the use of an international army raised by an association of nations to deter aggression and keep the peace.

coloni free tenant farmers who worked as sharecroppers on the large estates of the Roman Empire (singular: *colonus*).

common law law common to the entire kingdom of England; imposed by the king's courts beginning in the twelfth century to replace the customary law used in county and feudal courts that varied from place to place.

commune in medieval Europe, an association of townspeople bound together by a sworn oath for the purpose of obtaining basic liberties from the lord of the territory in which the town was located; also, the self-governing town after receiving its liberties.

conciliarism a movement in fourteenth- and fifteenth-century Europe that held that final authority in spiritual matters resided with a general church council, not the pope; emerged in response to the Avignon papacy and the Great Schism and used to justify the summoning of the Council of Constance (1414–1418).

condottieri leaders of bands of mercenary soldiers in Renaissance Italy who sold their services to the highest bidder (singular: *condottiere*).

conquistadors "conquerors." Leaders in the Spanish conquests in the Americas, especially Mexico and Peru, in the sixteenth century.

conscription a military draft.

conservatism an ideology based on tradition and social stability that favored the maintenance of established institutions, organized religion, and obedience to authority and resisted change, especially abrupt change.

consuls the chief executive officers of the Roman Republic. Two were chosen annually to administer the government and lead the army in battle.

consumer society a term applied to Western society after World War II as the working classes adopted the consumption patterns of the middle class and installment plans, credit cards, and easy credit made consumer goods such as appliances and automobiles widely available.

Continental System Napoleon's effort to bar British goods from the Continent in the hope of weakening Britain's economy and destroying its capacity to wage war.

cosmopolitanism the quality of being sophisticated and having wide international experience.

cottage industry a system of textile manufacturing in which spinners and weavers worked at home in their cottages using raw materials supplied to them by capitalist entrepreneurs.

cultural relativism the belief that no culture is superior to another because culture is a matter of custom, not reason, and derives its meaning from the group holding it.

cuneiform "wedge-shaped." A system of writing developed by the Sumerians that consisted of wedge-shaped impressions made by a reed stylus on clay tablets.

decolonization the process of becoming free of colonial status and achieving statehood; occurred in most of the world's colonies between 1947 and 1962.

deism belief in God as the creator of the universe who, after setting it in motion, ceased to have any direct involvement in it and allowed it to run according to its own natural laws.

demesne the part of a manor retained under the direct control of the lord and worked by the serfs as part of their labor services.

depression a very severe, protracted economic downturn with high levels of unemployment.

destalinization the policy of denouncing and undoing the most repressive aspects of Stalin's regime; begun by Nikita Khrushchev in 1956.

détente the relaxation of tension between the Soviet Union and the United States that occurred in the 1970s.

dialectic logic, one of the seven liberal arts that made up the medieval curriculum. In Marxist thought, the process by which all change occurs through the clash of antagonistic elements.

Diaspora the scattering of Jews throughout the ancient world after the Babylonian captivity in the sixth century B.C.

dictator in the Roman Republic, an official granted unlimited power to run the state for a short period of time, usually six months, during an emergency.

diocese the area under the jurisdiction of a Christian bishop; based originally on Roman administrative districts.

direct representation a system of choosing delegates to a representative assembly in which citizens vote directly for the delegates who will represent them.

divination the practice of seeking to foretell future events by interpreting divine signs, which could appear in various forms, such as in entrails of animals, in patterns in smoke, or in dreams.

divine-right monarchy a monarchy based on the belief that monarchs receive their power directly from God and are responsible to no one except God.

domino theory the belief that if the Communists succeeded in Vietnam, other countries in Southeast and East Asia would also fall (like dominoes) to communism; a justification for the U.S. intervention in Vietnam.

dualism the belief that the universe is dominated by two opposing forces, one good and the other evil.

dynastic state a state where the maintenance and expansion of the interests of the ruling family is the primary consideration.

economic imperialism the process in which banks and corporations from developed nations invest in underdeveloped regions and establish a major presence there in the hope of making high profits; not necessarily the same as colonial expansion in that businesses invest where they can make a profit, which may not be in their own nation's colonies.

empiricism the practice of relying on observation and experiment.

enclosure movement in the eighteenth century, the fencing in of the old open fields, combining many small holdings into larger units that could be farmed more efficiently.

encyclical a letter from the pope to all the bishops of the Roman Catholic church.

enlightened absolutism an absolute monarchy where the ruler follows the principles of the Enlightenment by introducing reforms for the improvement of society, allowing freedom of speech and the press, permitting religious toleration, expanding education, and ruling in accordance with the laws.

Enlightenment an eighteenth-century intellectual movement, led by the philosophes, that stressed the application of reason and the scientific method to all aspects of life.

entrepreneur one who organizes, operates, and assumes the risk in a business venture in the expectation of making a profit.

Epicureanism a philosophy founded by Epicurus in the fourth century B.C. that taught that happiness (freedom from emotional turmoil) could be achieved through the pursuit of pleasure (intellectual rather than sensual pleasure).

equestrians a group of extremely wealthy men in the late Roman Republic who were effectively barred from high office, but sought political power commensurate with their wealth; called equestrians because many had gotten their start as cavalry officers (*equites*).

ethnic cleansing the policy of killing or forcibly removing people of another ethnic group; used by the Serbs against Bosnian Muslims in the 1990s.

eucharist a Christian sacrament in which consecrated bread and wine are consumed in celebration of Jesus' Last Supper; also called the Lord's Supper or communion.

evolutionary socialism a socialist doctrine espoused by Eduard Bernstein who argued that socialists should stress cooperation and evolution to attain power by democratic means rather than by conflict and revolution.

fascism an ideology or movement that exalts the nation above the individual and calls for a centralized government with a dictatorial leader, economic and social regimentation, and forcible suppression of opposition; in particular, the ideology of Mussolini's Fascist regime in Italy.

feminism the belief in the social, political, and economic equality of the sexes; also, organized activity to advance women's rights.

fief a landed estate granted to a vassal in exchange for military services.

Final Solution the physical extermination of the Jewish people by the Nazis during World War II.

folk culture the traditional arts and crafts, literature, music, and other customs of the people; something that people make, as opposed to modern popular culture, which is something people buy.

free trade the unrestricted international exchange of goods with low or no tariffs.

general strike a strike by all or most workers in an economy; espoused by Georges Sorel as the heroic action that could be used to inspire the workers to destroy capitalist society.

gentry well-to-do English landowners below the level of the nobility; played an important role in the English Civil War of the seventeenth century.

geocentric theory the idea that the earth is at the center of the universe and that the sun and other celestial objects revolve around the earth.

glasnost "openness." Mikhail Gorbachev's policy of encouraging Soviet citizens to openly discuss the strengths and weaknesses of the Soviet Union.

good emperors the five emperors who ruled from 96 to 180 (Nerva, Trajan, Hadrian, Antoninus Pius, and Marcus Aurelius), a period of peace and prosperity for the Roman Empire.

Great Schism the crisis in the late medieval church when there were first two and then three popes; ended by the Council of Constance (1414–1418).

guest workers foreign workers working temporarily in European countries.

guild an association of people with common interests and concerns, especially people working in the same craft. In medieval Europe, guilds came to control much of the production process and to restrict entry into various trades.

gymnasium in classical Greece, a place for athletics; in the Hellenistic Age, a secondary school with a curriculum centered on music, physical exercise, and literature.

heliocentric theory the idea that the sun (not the earth) is at the center of the universe.

Hellenistic literally, "to imitate the Greeks"; the era after the death of Alexander the Great when Greek culture spread into the Near East and blended with the culture of that region.

helots serfs in ancient Sparta, who were permanently bound to the land that they worked for their Spartan masters.

heresy the holding of religious doctrines different from the official teachings of the church.

Hermeticism an intellectual movement beginning in the fifteenth century that taught that divinity is embodied in all aspects of nature; included works on alchemy and magic as well as theology and philosophy. The tradition continued into the seventeenth century and influenced many of the leading figures of the Scientific Revolution.

hetairai highly sophisticated courtesans in ancient Athens who offered intellectual and musical entertainment as well as sex.

hieroglyphics a highly pictorial system of writing used in ancient Egypt.

high culture the literary and artistic culture of the educated and wealthy ruling classes.

Holocaust the mass slaughter of European Jews by the Nazis during World War II.

hoplites heavily armed infantry soldiers used in ancient Greece in a phalanx formation.

Huguenots French Calvinists.

humanism an intellectual movement in Renaissance Italy based upon the study of the Greek and Roman classics.

iconoclasm an eighth-century Byzantine movement against the use of icons (pictures of sacred figures), which was condemned as idolatry.

ideology a political philosophy such as conservatism or liberalism.

imperium "the right to command." In the Roman Republic, the chief executive officers (consuls and praetors) possessed the *imperium;* a military commander was an *imperator*. In the Roman Empire, the title *imperator,* or emperor, came to be used for the ruler.

indirect representation a system of choosing delegates to a representative assembly in which citizens do not choose the delegates directly but instead vote for electors who choose the delegates.

individualism emphasis on and interest in the unique traits of each person.

indulgence the remission of part or all of the temporal punishment in purgatory due to sin; granted for charitable contributions and other good deeds. Indulgences became a regular practice of the Christian church in the High Middle Ages, and their abuse was instrumental in sparking Luther's reform movement in the sixteenth century.

infanticide the practice of killing infants.

inflation a sustained rise in the price level.

intendants royal officials in seventeenth-century France who were sent into the provinces to execute the orders of the central government.

intervention, principle of the idea, after the Congress of Vienna, that the great powers of Europe had the right to send armies into countries experiencing revolution to restore legitimate monarchs to their thrones.

isolationism a foreign policy in which a nation refrains from making alliances or engaging actively in international affairs.

jihad "striving in the way of the Lord." In Islam, the practice of conducting raids against neighboring peoples, which was an expansion of the Arab tradition of tribal raids against their persecutors.

joint-stock company a company or association that raises capital by selling shares to individuals who receive dividends on their investment while a board of directors runs the company.

joint-stock investment bank a bank created by selling shares of stock to investors. Such banks potentially have access to much more capital than do private banks owned by one or a few individuals.

justification of faith the primary doctrine of the Protestant Reformation; taught that humans are saved not through good works, but by the grace of God, bestowed freely through the sacrifice of Jesus.

laissez-faire "to let alone." An economic doctrine that holds that an economy is best served when the government does not interfere but allows the economy to self-regulate according to the forces of supply and demand.

latifundia large landed estates in the Roman Empire (singular: *latifundium*).

lay investiture the practice in which a layperson invested a bishop with the symbols of both his temporal office and his spiritual office; led to the Investiture Controversy, which was ended by compromise in the Concordat of Worms in 1122.

Lebensraum "living space." The doctrine, adopted by Hitler, that a nation's power depends on the amount of land it occupies; thus, a nation must expand to be strong.

legitimacy, principle of the idea that after the Napoleonic wars peace could best be reestablished in Europe by restoring legitimate monarchs who would preserve traditional institutions; guided Metternich at the Congress of Vienna.

Leninism Lenin's revision of Marxism that held that Russia need not experience a bourgeois revolution before it could move toward socialism.

liberal arts the seven areas of study that formed the basis of education in medieval and early modern Europe. Following Boethius and other late Roman authors, they consisted of grammar, rhetoric, and dialectic or logic (the *trivium*) and arithmetic, geometry, astronomy, and music (the *quadrivium*).

liberalism an ideology based on the belief that people should be as free from restraint as possible. Economic liberalism is the idea that the government should not interfere in the workings of the economy. Political liberalism is the idea that there should be restraints on the exercise of power so that people can enjoy basic civil rights in a constitutional state with a representative assembly.

limited liability the principle that shareholders in a joint-stock corporation can be held responsible for the corporation's debts only up to the amount they have invested.

limited (constitutional) monarchy a system of government in which the monarch is limited by a representative assembly and by the duty to rule in accordance with the laws of the land.

mandates a system established after World War I whereby a nation officially administered a territory (mandate) on behalf of the League of Nations. Thus, France administered Lebanon and Syria as mandates, and Britain administered Iraq and Palestine.

manor an agricultural estate operated by a lord and worked by peasants who performed labor services and paid various rents and fees to the lord in exchange for protection and sustenance.

Marshall Plan the European Recovery Program, under which the United States provided financial aid to European countries to help them rebuild after World War II.

Marxism the political, economic, and social theories of Karl Marx, which included the idea that history is the story of class struggle and that ultimately the proletariat will overthrow the bourgeoisie and establish a dictatorship en route to a classless society.

mass education a state-run educational system, usually free and compulsory, that aims to ensure that all children in society have at least a basic education.

mass leisure forms of leisure that appeal to large numbers of people in a society including the working classes; emerged at the end of the nineteenth century to provide workers with amusements after work and on weekends; used during the twentieth century by totalitarian states to control their populations.

mass politics a political order characterized by mass political parties and universal male and (eventually) female suffrage.

mass society a society in which the concerns of the majority—the lower classes—play a prominent role; characterized by extension of voting rights, an improved standard of living for the lower classes, and mass education.

materialism the belief that everything mental, spiritual, or ideal is an outgrowth of physical forces and that truth is found in concrete material existence, not through feeling or intuition.

mercantilism an economic theory that held that a nation's prosperity depended on its supply of gold and silver and that the total volume of trade is unchangeable; therefore, advocated that the government play an active role in the economy by encouraging exports and discouraging imports, especially through the use of tariffs.

Mesolithic Age the period from 10,000 to 7000 B.C., characterized by a gradual transition from a food-gathering/hunting economy to a food-producing economy.

metics resident foreigners in ancient Athens; not permitted full rights of citizenship but did receive the protection of the laws.

militarism a policy of aggressive military preparedness; in particular, the large armies based on mass conscription and complex, inflexible plans for mobilization that most European nations had before World War I.

ministerial responsibility a tenet of nineteenth-century liberalism that held that ministers of the monarch should be responsible to the legislative assembly rather than to the monarch.

Modernism the new artistic and literary styles that emerged in the decades before 1914 as artists rebelled against traditional efforts to portray reality as accurately as possible (leading to Cubism and Abstract Expressionism) and writers explored new forms.

monotheistic/monotheism having only one god; the doctrine or belief that there is only one god.

mutual deterrence the belief that nuclear war could best be prevented if both the United States and the Soviet Union had sufficient nuclear weapons so that even if one nation launched a preemptive first strike, the other could respond and devastate the attacker.

mystery religions religions that involve initiation into secret rites that promise intense emotional involvement with spiritual forces and a greater chance of individual immortality.

nationalism a sense of national consciousness based on awareness of being part of a community—a "nation"—that has common institutions, traditions, language, and customs and that becomes the focus of the individual's primary political loyalty.

nationalities problem the dilemma faced by the Austro-Hungarian Empire in trying to unite a wide variety of ethnic groups including, among others, Austrians, Hungarians, Poles, Croats, Czechs, Serbs, Slovaks, and Slovenes in an era when nationalism and calls for self-determination were coming to the fore.

nationalization the process of converting a business or industry from private ownership to government control and ownership.

nation in arms the people's army raised by universal mobilization to repel the foreign enemies of the French Revolution.

nation-state a form of political organization in which a relatively homogeneous people inhabits a sovereign state, as opposed to a state containing people of several nationalities.

NATO the North Atlantic Treaty Organization; a military alliance formed in 1949 in which the signatories (Belgium, Canada, Denmark, France, Great Britain, Iceland, Italy, Luxembourg, the Netherlands, Norway, Portugal, and the United States) agreed to provide mutual assistance if any one of them was attacked; later expanded to include other nations.

natural laws a body of laws or specific principles held to be derived from nature and binding upon all human society even in the absence of positive laws.

natural rights certain inalienable rights to which all people are entitled; include the right to life, liberty, and property, freedom of speech and religion, and equality before the law.

natural selection Darwin's idea that organisms that are most adaptable to their environment survive and pass on the variations that enabled them to survive, while other, less adaptable organisms become extinct; "survival of the fittest."

Nazi New Order the Nazis' plan for their conquered territories; included the extermination of Jews and others considered inferior, ruthless exploitation of resources, German colonization in the east, and the use of Poles, Russians, and Ukrainians as slave labor.

Neoplatonism a revival of Platonic philosophy. In the third century A.D., a revival associated with Plotinus; in the Italian Renaissance, a revival associated with Marsilio Ficino who attempted to synthesize Christianity and Platonism.

New Economic Policy a modified version of the old capitalist system introduced in the Soviet Union by Lenin in 1921 to revive the economy after the ravages of the civil war and war communism.

new imperialism the revival of imperialism after 1880 in which European nations established colonies throughout much of Asia and Africa.

new monarchies the governments of France, England, and Spain at the end of the fifteenth century, where the rulers were successful in reestablishing or extending centralized royal authority, suppressing the nobility, controlling the church, and insisting upon the loyalty of all peoples living in their territories.

nobiles "nobles." The small group of families from both patrician and plebeian origins who produced most of the men who were elected to office in the late Roman Republic.

nominalism a school of thought in medieval Europe that, following Aristotle, held that only individual objects are real and that universals are only names created by humans.

nuclear family a family group consisting only of father, mother, and children.

old regime/old order the political and social system of France in the eighteenth century before the Revolution.

oligarchy rule by a few.

optimates "best men." Aristocratic leaders in the late Roman Republic who generally came from senatorial families and wished to retain their oligarchical privileges.

orders/estates the traditional tripartite division of European society based on heredity and quality rather than wealth or economic standing, first established in the Middle Ages and continuing into the eighteenth century; traditionally consisted of those who pray (the clergy), those who fight (the nobility), and those who work (all the rest).

organic evolution Darwin's principle that all plants and animals have evolved over a long period of time from earlier and simpler forms of life.

Paleolithic Age the period of human history when humans used simple stone tools (c. 2,500,000–10,000 B.C.).

pantheism a doctrine that equates God with the universe and all that is in it.

paterfamilias the dominant male in a Roman family whose powers over his wife and children were theoretically unlimited, though they were sometimes circumvented in practice.

patriarchal/patriarchy a society in which the father is supreme in the clan or family; more generally, a society dominated by men.

patriarchal family a family in which the husband/father dominates his wife and children.

patricians great landowners who became the ruling class in the Roman Republic.

patronage the practice of awarding titles and making appointments to government and other positions to gain political support.

Pax Romana "Roman peace." A term used to refer to the stability and prosperity that Roman rule brought to the Mediterranean world and much of western Europe during the first and second centuries A.D.

Pentateuch the first five books of the Hebrew Bible (Genesis, Exodus, Leviticus, Numbers, and Deuteronomy).

perestroika "restructuring." A term applied to Mikhail Gorbachev's economic, political, and social reforms in the Soviet Union.

permissive society a term applied to Western society after World War II to reflect the new sexual freedom and the emergence of a drug culture.

Petrine supremacy the doctrine that the bishop of Rome—the pope—as the successor of Saint Peter (traditionally considered the first bishop of Rome) should hold a preeminent position in the church.

phalanx a rectangular formation of tightly massed infantry soldiers.

philosophes intellectuals of the eighteenth-century Enlightenment who believed in applying a spirit of rational criticism to all things, including religion and politics, and who focused on improving and enjoying this world, rather than on the afterlife.

plebeians the class of Roman citizens who included nonpatrician landowners, craftspeople, merchants, and small farmers in the Roman Republic. Their struggle for equal rights with the patricians dominated much of the Republic's history.

pluralism the practice in which one person holds several church offices simultaneously; a problem of the late medieval church.

pogroms organized massacres of Jews.

polis an ancient Greek city-state encompassing both an urban area and its surrounding countryside; a small but autonomous political unit where all major political and social activities were carried out in a central location.

political democracy a form of government characterized by universal suffrage and mass political parties.

politiques a group who emerged during the French Wars of Religion in the sixteenth century; placed politics above religion and believed that no religious truth was worth the ravages of civil war.

polytheistic/polytheism having many gods; belief in or the worship of more than one god.

popular culture as opposed to high culture, the unofficial, written and unwritten culture of the masses, much of which was passed down orally; centers on public and group activities such as festivals. In the twentieth century, refers to the entertainment, recreation, and pleasures that people purchase as part of mass consumer society.

populares "favoring the people." Aristocratic leaders in the late Roman Republic who tended to use the people's assemblies in an effort to break the stranglehold of the *nobiles* on political offices.

popular sovereignty the doctrine that government is created by and subject to the will of the people, who are the source of all political power.

praetorian guard the military unit that served as the personal bodyguard of the Roman emperors.

predestination the belief, associated with Calvinism, that God, as a consequence of his foreknowledge of all events, has predetermined those who will be saved (the elect) and those who will be damned.

price revolution the dramatic rise in prices (inflation) that occurred throughout Europe in the sixteenth and early seventeenth centuries.

primogeniture an inheritance practice in which the eldest son receives all or the largest share of the parents' estate.

principate the form of government established by Augustus for the Roman Empire; continued the constitutional forms of the Republic and consisted of the *princeps* ("first citizen") and the senate, although the *princeps* was clearly the dominant partner.

proletariat the industrial working class. In Marxism, the class who will ultimately overthrow the bourgeoisie.

Puritans English Protestants inspired by Calvinist theology who wished to remove all traces of Catholicism from the Church of England.

querelles des femmes "arguments about women." A centuries-old debate about the nature of women that continued during the Scientific Revolution as those who argued for the inferiority of women found additional support in the new anatomy and medicine.

rationalism a system of thought based on the belief that human reason and experience are the chief sources of knowledge.

realism in medieval Europe, the school of thought that, following Plato, held that the individual objects we perceive are not real but merely manifestations of universal ideas existing in the mind of God. In the nineteenth century, a school of painting that emphasized the everyday life of ordinary people, depicted with photographic realism.

Realpolitik "politics of reality." Politics based on practical concerns rather than theory or ethics.

real wages/income/prices wages/income/prices that have been adjusted for inflation.

reason of state the principle that a nation should act on the basis of its long-term interests and not merely to further the dynastic interests of its ruling family.

relativity theory Einstein's theory that holds, among other things, that (1) space and time are not absolute but are relative to the observer and interwoven into a four-dimensional space-time continuum and (2) matter is a form of energy ($E = mc^2$).

relics the bones of Christian saints or objects intimately associated with saints that were considered worthy of veneration.

Renaissance the "rebirth" of classical culture that occurred in Italy between c. 1350 and c. 1550; also, the earlier revivals of classical culture that occurred under Charlemagne and in the twelfth century.

rentier a person who lives on income from property and is not personally involved in its operation.

reparations payments made by a defeated nation after a war to compensate another nation for damage sustained as a result of the war; required from Germany after World War I.

revisionism a socialist doctrine that rejected Marx's emphasis on class struggle and revolution and argued instead that workers should work through political parties to bring about gradual change.

revolution a fundamental change in the political and social organization of a state.

revolutionary socialism the socialist doctrine espoused by Georges Sorel who held that violent action was the only way to achieve the goals of socialism.

rhetoric the art of persuasive speaking; in the Middle Ages, one of the seven liberal arts.

sacraments rites considered imperative for a Christian's salvation. By the thirteenth century consisted of the eucharist or Lord's Supper, baptism, marriage, penance, extreme unction, holy orders, and confirmation of children; Protestant reformers of the sixteenth century generally recognized only two—baptism and communion (the Lord's Supper).

salons gatherings of philosophes and other notables to discuss the ideas of the Enlightenment; so-called from the elegant drawing rooms (salons) where they met.

sans-culottes the common people who did not wear the fine clothes of the upper classes (sans-culottes means "without breeches") and played an important role in the radical phase of the French Revolution.

satrap/satrapy a governor with both civil and military duties in the ancient Persian Empire, which was divided into satrapies, or provinces, each administered by a satrap.

scholasticism the philosophical and theological system of the medieval schools, which emphasized rigorous analysis of contradictory authorities; often used to try to reconcile faith and reason.

scientific method a method of seeking knowledge through inductive principles; uses experiments and observations to develop generalizations.

Scientific Revolution the transition from the medieval worldview to a largely secular, rational, and materialistic perspective; began in the seventeenth century and was popularized in the eighteenth.

secularization the process of becoming more concerned with material, worldly, temporal things and less with spiritual and religious things.

self-determination the doctrine that the people of a given territory or a particular nationality should have the right to determine their own government and political future.

senate/senators the leading council of the Roman Republic; composed of about 300 men (senators) who served for life and dominated much of the political life of the Republic.

serf a peasant who is bound to the land and obliged to provide labor services and pay various rents and fees to the lord; considered unfree but not a slave because serfs could not be bought and sold.

skepticism a doubtful or questioning attitude, especially about religion.

Social Darwinism the application of Darwin's principle of organic evolution to the social order; led to the belief that progress comes from the struggle for survival as the fittest advance and the weak decline.

socialism an ideology that calls for collective or government ownership of the means of production and the distribution of goods.

social security/social insurance government programs that provide social welfare measures such as old age pensions and sickness, accident, and disability insurance.

Socratic method a form of teaching that uses a question-and-answer format to enable students to reach conclusions by using their own reasoning.

Sophists wandering scholars and professional teachers in ancient Greece who stressed the importance of rhetoric and tended toward skepticism and relativism.

soviets councils of workers' and soldiers' deputies formed throughout Russia in 1917; played an important role in the Bolshevik Revolution.

sphere of influence a territory or region over which an outside nation exercises political or economic influence.

Stoicism a philosophy founded by Zeno in the fourth century B.C. that taught that happiness could be obtained by accepting one's lot and living in harmony with the will of God, thereby achieving inner peace.

subinfeudation the practice in which a lord's greatest vassals subdivided their fiefs and had vassals of their own, and those vassals, in turn, subdivided their fiefs and so on down to simple knights whose fiefs were too small to subdivide.

suffrage the right to vote.

suffragists those who advocate the extension of the right to vote (suffrage), especially to women.

surplus value in Marxism, the difference between a product's real value and the wages of the worker who produced the product.

syncretism the combining of different forms of belief or practice, as, for example, when two gods are regarded as different forms of the same underlying divine force and are fused together.

tariffs duties (taxes) imposed on imported goods; usually imposed both to raise revenue and to discourage imports and protect domestic industries.

tetrarchy rule by four; the system of government established by Diocletian (284–305) in which the Roman Empire was divided into two parts, each ruled by an "Augustus" assisted by a "Caesar."

theocracy a government ruled by a divine authority.

three-field system in medieval agriculture, the practice of dividing the arable land into three fields so that one could lie fallow while the others were planted in winter grains and spring crops.

tithe a tenth of one's harvest or income; paid by medieval peasants to the village church.

Torah the body of law in Hebrew Scripture, contained in the Pentateuch (the first five books of the Hebrew Bible).

totalitarian state a state characterized by government control over all aspects of economic, social, political, cultural, and intellectual life, the subordination of the individual to the state, and insistence that the masses be actively involved in the regime's goals.

total war warfare in which all of a nation's resources, including civilians at home as well as soldiers in the field, are mobilized for the war effort.

trade union an association of workers in the same trade, formed to help members secure better wages, benefits, and working conditions.

transubstantiation a doctrine of the Roman Catholic church that teaches that during the eucharist the substance of the bread and wine is miraculously transformed into the body and blood of Jesus.

trench warfare warfare in which the opposing forces attack and counterattack from a relatively permanent system of trenches protected by barbed wire; characteristic of World War I.

trivium* and *quadrivium together formed the seven liberal arts that were the basis of medieval and early modern education. Grammar, rhetoric, and dialectic or logic made up the *trivium;* arithmetic, geometry, astronomy, and music made up the *quadrivium.*

Truman Doctrine the doctrine, enunciated by Harry Truman in 1947, that the United States would provide economic aid to countries that said they were threatened by Communist expansion.

tyrant/tyranny in an ancient Greek *polis* (or an Italian city-state during the Renaissance), a ruler who came to power in an unconstitutional way and ruled without being subject to the law.

uncertainty principle a principle in quantum mechanics, posited by Heisenberg, that holds that one cannot determine the path of an electron because the very act of observing the electron would affect its location.

unconditional surrender complete, unqualified surrender of a belligerent nation.

utopian socialists intellectuals and theorists in the early nineteenth century who favored equality in social and economic conditions and wished to replace private property and competition with collective ownership and cooperation; deemed impractical and "utopian" by later socialists.

vassal a person granted a fief, or landed estate, in exchange for providing military services to the lord and fulfilling certain other obligations such as appearing at the lord's court when summoned and making a payment on the knighting of the lord's eldest son.

vernacular the everyday language of a region, as distinguished from a language used for special purposes. For example, in medieval Paris, French was the vernacular, but Latin was used for academic writing and for classes at the University of Paris.

volkish thought the belief that German culture is superior and that the German people have a universal mission to save Western civilization from inferior races.

war communism Lenin's policy of nationalizing industrial and other facilities and requisitioning the peasants' produce during the civil war in Russia.

War Guilt Clause the clause in the Treaty of Versailles that declared that Germany (and Austria) were responsible for starting World War I and ordered Germany to pay reparations for the damage the Allies had suffered as a result of the war.

Warsaw Pact a military alliance, formed in 1955, in which Albania, Bulgaria, Czechoslovakia, East Germany, Hungary, Poland, Romania, and the Soviet Union agreed to provide mutual assistance.

welfare state a social/political system in which the government assumes the primary responsibility for the social welfare of its citizens by providing such things as social security, unemployment benefits, and health care.

wergeld "money for a man." In early Germanic law, a person's value in monetary terms, which was paid by a wrongdoer to the family of the person who had been injured or killed.

world-machine Newton's conception of the universe as one huge, regulated, and uniform machine that operated according to natural laws in absolute time, space, and motion.

ziggurat a massive stepped tower upon which a temple dedicated to the chief god or goddess of a Sumerian city was built.

Zionism an international movement that called for the establishment of a Jewish state or a refuge for Jews in Palestine.

Zoroastrianism a religion founded by the Persian Zoroaster in the seventh century B.C.; characterized by worship of a supreme god Ahuramazda who represents the good against the evil spirit, identified as Ahriman.

Pronunciation Guide

al-Abbas, Abu al-AH-bus, AH-boo
Abbasid AB-uh-sid *or* a-BA-sid
Adenauer, Konrad AD-n'our-er
aediles EE-diles
Aeolians ee-OH-lee-uns
Aeschylus ESS-kuh-lus
Afrikaners a-fri-KAH-ners
Agincourt AJ-in-kor
Ahuramazda ah-HOOR-ah-MAHZ-duh
Akhenaton ah-kuh-NAH-tun
Akkadians a-KAY-dee-uns
Albigensians al-bi-GEN-see-uns
d'Albret, Jeanne dahl-BRAy, ZHAHN
Albuquerque, Afonso de AL-buh-kur-kee, ah-FON-soh d'
Alcibiades al-suh-BY-uh-deez
Alcuin AL-kwin
Aliz, Ramiz AL-ee-uh, ra-MEEZ
Allah AH-luh *or* AL-uh
Amenhotep ah-mun-HOE-tep
Andreotti, Giulio ahn-dray-AH-tee, JOOL-yoh
Andropov, Yuri an-DROP-ov, YOOR-ee
Anjou AN-joo
Antigonid an-TIG-oh-nid
Antigonus Gonatus an-TIG-oh-nus goh-NAH-tus
Antiochus an-TIE-uh-kus
Antonescu, Ion An-tuh-NES-koo, YON
Antoninus Pius an-toh-NIGH-nus PIE-us
apella a-PELL-uh
Apollonius ap-uh-LOH-nee-us
Aquinas, Thomas uh-KWIGH-nus
aratrum a-RA-trum
Archimedes are-kuh-MEE-deez
Argonautica ARE-guh-NOT-i-kuh
Aristarchus ar-is-TAR-kus
Aristotle ar-i-STAH-tul
Arsinoë ar-SIN-oh-ee
artium baccalarius are-TEE-um back-uh-LAR-ee-us
artium magister are-TEE-um ma-GIS-ter
Ashkenazic ash-kuh-NAH-zic
Ashurnasirpal ah-shoor-NAH-suh-pul
asiento a-SEE-en-toh
assignat as-seen-YAH *or* AS-sig-nat
Assyrians uh-SEER-ee-uns
Atahualpa ah-tuh-WALL-puh
Attalid AT-a-lid
audiencias ah-DEE-en-CEE-ahs
Augustine AW-gus-STEEN
Avicenna av-i-SEN-uh
Avignon ah-veen-YONE
Auschwitz-Birkenau OUSH-vitz-BUR-kuh-now
Ausgleich OUS-glike
Babeuf, Gracchus bah-BUHF, GRAK-us
Bach, Johann Sebastian BAHK, yoh-HAHN suh-BASS-chen
Bakunin, Michael ba-KOO-nin
Balboa, Vasco Nuñez de bal-BOH-uh, VASH-koh NOON-yez duh
Ballin, Albert BAHLL-een
Barbarossa bar-buh-ROH-suh
Bastille ba-STEEL
Bayle, Pierre BAYL, PYER
Beauvoir, Simone de boh-VWAH, see-MOAN duh
Bebel, August BAY-bul
Beccaria, Cesare bek-KAH-ree-uh, CHAY-zahr-ay
Beguines bi-GEENS
Belisarius bell-i-SAR-ee-us
benefice BEN-uh-fiss
Bergson, Henri BERG-son, AWN-ree
Bernini, Gian Lorenzo bur-NEE-nee, JAHN loh-RENT-soh
Bernstein, Eduard BURN-stine, AY-doo-art
Blitzkrieg BLITZ-kreeg
Blum, Léon BLOOM, LAY-OHN
Boccaccio, Giovanni boh-KAH-chee-oh, joe-VAHN-nee
Bodichon, Barbara BOH-duh-chon
Boer BOHR
Boethius boh-EETH-ee-us
Boleyn, Anne BUH-lin
Bólívar, Simón BOH-luh-VAR, see-MOAN
Bologna buh-LOHN-yuh
Bossuet, Jacques baw-SWAY, ZHAHK
Bottai, Giuseppe BOT-tah, joo-ZEP-pay
Botticelli, Sandro BOT-i-CHELL-ee, SAHN-droh
Boulanger, Georges boo-lahn-ZHAY, ZHORZH
Bracciolini, Poggio braht-choh-LEE-nee, POD-joh

Brahe, Tycho BRAH, TIE-koh
Bramante, Donato brah-MAHN-tee, doe-NAY-toe
Brandt, Willy BRAHNT, VIL-ee
Brétigny bray-tee-NYEE
Brezhnev, Leonid BREZH-nef, lyi-on-YEET
Briand, Aristide bree-AHN, a-ree-STEED
Brunelleschi, Filippo BROO-nuh-LES-kee, fee-LEEP-poe
Brüning, Heinrich BROO-ning, HINE-rik
Bulganin, Nilolai bul-GAN-in, nyik-uh-LYE
Bund deutscher Mädel BUNT DOICHer MAIR-del
Burschenschaften BOOR-shen-shaft-un
Calais ka-LAY
Caligula ka-LIG-yuh-luh
caliph/caliphate KAY-lif/KAY-li-FATE
Calonne, Charles de kah-LAWN, SHARL duh
Cambyses kam-BY-seez
Camus, Albert kuh-MOO, al-BEAR
Canaanites KAY-nuh-nites
Capet/Capetian ka-PAY or KAY-put/kuh-PEE-shun
Caraffa, Gian Pietro kah-RAH-fuh, JAHN PYEE-troh
carbonari kar-buh-NAH-ree
Carolingian kar-oh-LIN-jun
carruca ca-ruh-kuh
Carthage/Carthaginian KAR-thij/KAR-thuh-JIN-ee-un
Cassiodorus kass-ee-oh-DOR-us
Castlereagh, Viscount KAS-ul-RAY
Catharism KA-tha-ri-zem
Catullus ka-TULL-us
Cavendish, Margaret KAV-un-dish
Cavour, Camillo di ka-VOOR, kah-MIL-oh
Ceausescu, Nicolai chow-SHES-koo, nee-koh-LYE
cenobitic sen-oh-BIT-ik
Cèzanne, Paul say-ZAN
Chaeronea ker-oh-NEE-uh
Chaldean kal-DEE-un
chanson de geste shahn-SAWN duh ZHEST
Charlemagne SHAR-luh-mane
Chateaubriand, François-René de shah-TOH-bree-AHN, FRAN-swah-ruh-NAY duh
Chernenko, Konstantin cher-NYEN-koh, kon-stunTEEN
Chiang Kai-Shek CHANG KIGH-shek
Chrétien de Troyes KRAY-tee-ahn duh TRWAH
Cicero SIS-uh-roh
ciompi CHOM-pee
Cistercians si-STIR-shuns
Claudius KLAW-dee-us
Cleisthenes KLISE-thuh-neez
Clemenceau, Georges klem-un-SOH, ZHORZH
Clovis KLOH-vis
Codreanu, Corneliu kaw-dree-AH-noo, kor-NELL-yoo
colonus kuh-LOH-nus
Columbanus kol-um-BAHN-us
comitia centuriata kuh-MISH-ee-uh sen-TYOO-ree-ah-tuh
Commodus KOM-uh-dus
Comnenus kom-NEE-nus
Comte, Auguste KOHNT
concilium plebis con-CIL-ee-um PLE-bis
Concordat of Worms kon-KOR-dat of WURMZ *or* VAWRMZ
Condorcet, Marie-Jean de kawn-dar-SAY, mur-REE-ZHAHN duh
condottieri kon-dah-TEE-AIR-ee
consul KON-sul
Contarini, Gasparo kahn-tuh-REE-nee, Gahs-pah-roh
conversos kon-VAIR-sohs
Copernicus, Nicolaus koh-PURR-nuh-kus, nee-koh-LAH-us
Corinth KOR-inth
corregidores kor-REG-uh-DOR-ays
Cortés, Hernán kor-TEZ, er-NAHN
Corvinus, Matthias kor-VIE-nus, muh-THIGH-us
Courbet, Gustave koor-BAY, guh-STAWV
Crassus KRASS-us
Crécy kray-SEE
Crédit Mobilier kred-EE mohb-eel-YAY
Croesus KREE-sus
Danton, Georges dahn-TAWN, Zhorzh
Darius duh-RYE-us
dauphin DAW-fin
David, Jacques-Louis dah-VEED, ZHAHK-LWEE
Debussy, Claude de-BYOO-see, KLODE
Decameron di-KAM-uh-run
Deffand, marquise du di-FAHN, mar-KEEZ doo
de Gaulle, Charles duh GOLL, SHARL
Delacroix, Eugène del-uh-KWAW, yoo-ZHAHN
Demosthenes di-MOSS-thuh-neez
Denikin, Anton dyi-NYEE-kin, an-TAWN
Descartes, René day-KART, ruh-NAY
Diaghilev, Sergei dee-AHG-uh-lef, syir-GYAY
Dias, Bartholomeu DEE-us, bar-too-loo-MAY
Diaspora die-AS-pur-uh
Diderot, Denis DEE-duh-roh, duh-NEE
Diocletian die-uh-KLEE-shun
Disraeli, Benjamin diz-RAY-lee
Dollfuss, Engelbert DOLL-foos
Domesday Book DOOMZ-day
Domitian doh-MISH-un
Donatus/Donatist doh-NAY-tus/DOH-nuh-tist
Dorians DOR-ee-uns
Dostoevsky, Fyodor DOS-tuh-YEF-skee, FYOD-ur
Douhet, Giulio doo-EE, JOOL-yoh
Dreyfus, Alfred DRY-fus

Dubcek, Alexander DOOB-chek
Duma DOO-muh
Dürer, Albrecht DOO-er, AWL-brekt
ecclesia eh-KLEE-zee-uh
Eckhart, Meister EK-hart, MY-ster
encomienda en-koh-mee-EN-dah
Engels, Friedrich ENG-ulz, FREE-drik
Entente Cordiale ahn-TAHNT kor-DYALL
Epaminondas i-PAM-uh-NAHN-dus
ephor EF-or
Epicurus/Epicureanism EP-i-KYOOR-us/EP-i-kyoo-REE-uh-ni-zem
equestrians i-KWES-tree-uns
equites EK-wuh-tays
Erasistratus er-uh-SIS-truh-tus
Erasmus, Desiderius i-RAZZ-mus, des-i-DIR-ee-us
Eratosthenes er-uh-TOSS-thuh-neez
eremitical air-uh-MITT-i-cul
d'Este, Isabella ES-tay
Erhard, Ludwig AIR-hart
Etruscans i-TRUSS-kuhns
Euclid YOO-klid
Euripides yoo-RIP-i-deez
exchequer EX-chek-ur
fasces FASS-eez
Fascio di Combattimento FASH-ee-oh di com-BATT-ee-men-toh
Fatimid FAT-i-mid
Fedele, Cassandra FAY-del-ee
Feltre, Vittorino da FELL-tree, vee-tor-EE-noh dah
Ficino, Marsilio fee-CHEE-noh, mar-SIL-ee-oh
Flaubert, Gustave floh-BEAR, guh-STAWV
Fleury, Cardinal floe-REE
Fontainebleau FAWN-tin-BLOW
Fontenelle, Bernard de fawnt-NELL, Ber-nar duh
Fouquet, Nicolas foo-KAY, nee-KOH-lah
Frequens FREE-kwens
Friedan, Betty fri-DAN
Frimaire free-MARE
Fronde FROND
Führerprinzip FYOOR-ur-PRIN-tseep
gabelle gah-BELL
Gama, Vasco da GAM-uh, VASH-koh duh
Gamond, Zoé Gatti de gah-MAHN, zaw-ay GAHT-tee duh
Garibaldi, Giuseppe gar-uh-BAWL-dee, joo-ZEP-pay
Gasperi, Alcide de GAHS-pe-ree, awl-CHEE-day de
Gaugamela gaw-guh-MEE-luh
Gentileschi, Artemisia jen-tul-ESS-kee, are-tee-MISS-ee-uh
gerousia juh-ROO-see-uh
Gierek, Edward GYER-ek
Gilgamesh GILL-guh-mesh
Giolitti, Giovanni joh-LEET-tee, joe-VAHN-nee
Giotto JAW-toh
Girondins juh-RAHN-dins
glasnost GLAZ-nohst
Gleichschaltung GLIKE-shalt-ung
Goebbels, Joseph GUHR-bulz
Gomulka, Wladyslaw goh-MOOL-kuh, vla-DIS-lawf
gonfaloniere gon-fa-loh-NEE-ree
Gorbachev, Mikhail GOR-buh-chof, meek-HALE
Gracchus, Tiberius and Gaius GRAK-us, tie-BIR-ee-us and GAY-us *or* GUY-us
grandi GRAHN-dee
Grieg, Edvard GREEG, ED-vart
Groote, Gerard GROH-tuh
Gropius, Walter GROH-pee-us, VAHL-ter
Grossdeutsch gross-DOICH
Guicciardini, Francesco gwee-char-DEE-nee, frahn-CHASE-koh
Guizot, François gee-ZOH, FRAN-swah
Gustavus Adolphus gus-STAY-vus a-DOLF-us
Guzman, Gaspar de goos-MAHN, gahs-PAR day
Habsburg HAPS-burg
Hadrian HAY-dree-un
Hagia Sophia HAG-ee-uh soh-FEE-uh
hajj HAJ
Hammurabi ham-uh-RAH-bee
Handel, George Friedrich HAN-dul
Hannibal HAN-uh-bul
Hanukkah HAH-nuh-kuh
Hardenberg, Karl von HAR-d'n-burg
Harun al-Rashid huh-ROON al-ra-SHEED
Hatshepsut hat-SHEP-soot
Haussmann, Baron HOUS-mun
Havel, Vaclav HAH-vuhl, VAHT-slaf
Haydn, Franz Joseph HIDE-n, FRAHNTS
hegemon HEJ-uh-mon
Heisenberg, Werner HIGH-zun-burg, VUR-nur
Hellenistic hell-uh-NIS-tik
helots HELL-uts
hermandades er-mahn-DAHDH-ays
Herodotus hi-ROD-oh-tus
Herophilus hi-ROF-uh-lus
Herzen, Alexander HER-tsun
Herzl, Theodor HERT-sul, TAY-oh-dor
Hesiod HEE-see-ud
Heydrich, Reinhard HIGH-drik, RINE-hart
hieroglyph HIGH-ur-oh-glif
Hildegard of Bingen HILL-duh-gard of BING-en
Hitler Jugend JOO-gunt
Ho Chi Minh HOE CHEE MIN
Höch, Hannah HOKH
Hohenstaufen HOE-un-SHTAU-fun

Hohenzollern HOE-un-ZAHL-lurn
d'Holbach, Paul awl-BAHK
Honecker, Erich HOE-nuh-ker
hoplites HOP-lites
Horace HOR-us
Horthy, Miklós HOR-tee, MIK-lohsh
Hoxha, Enver HAW-jah
Huguenots HYOO-guh-nots
Husák, Gustav HOO-sahk, guh-STAHV
Ibn Sina ib-en SEE-nuh
Ignatius of Loyola ig-NAY-shus of loi-OH-luh
Il Duce eel DOO-chay
imperator im-puh-RAH-tor
imperium im-PIER-ee-um
intendant in-TEN-duhnt
Isis EYE-sis
Issus ISS-us
ius gentium YOOS GEN-tee-um
Jacobin JAK-uh-bin
Jacquerie zhah-KREE
Jagiello yah-GYELL-oh
Jahn, Friedrich Ludwig YAHN, FREE-drik
Jaruzelski, Wojciech yahr-uh-ZEL-skee, VOI-chek
Jaurés, Jean zhaw-RESS, ZHAHN
jihad ji-HAHD
Judaea joo-DEE-uh
Judas Maccabaeus JOO-dus mak-uh-BEE-us
Jung, Carl YOONG
Junkers YOONG-kers
Jupiter Optimus Maximus JOO-pi-ter OPP-tuh-mus MAK-suh-mus
Justinian juh-STIN-ee-un
Juvenal JOO-vuh-nul
Kádár, János KAY-dahr, YAHN-us
Kadinsky, Vasily kan-DIN-skee, vus-YEEL-yee
Karlowitz KARL-oh-vitz
Kaunitz, Wenzel von KOU-nits, VENT-sul
Kerensky, Alexander kuh-REN-skee
Keynes, John Maynard KAYNZ
Khrushchev, Nikita KROOSH-chef, nuh-KEE-tuh
Kleindeutsch kline-DOICH
Kohl, Helmut KOLE, HELL-mut
koiné koi-NAY
Kolchak, Alexander KAWL-chok
Kollantai, Alexandra kawl-un-TIE
Kosciuszko, Thaddeus kos-ee-US-koh, tah-DE-us
Kossuth, Louis KOSS-ooth
kouros KOO-raws
Kraft durch Freude CRAFT durch FROI-duh
Kristallnacht KRIS-tal-NAHCHT
Krupp, Alfred KROOP
Kuchuk-Kainarji koo-CHOOK-kigh-NAR-jee
kulaks koo-LAKS
kulturkampf kool-TOOR-kahmf
Kun, Béla KOON, Bay-luh
Lafayette, marquis de lah-fee-ETTE, mar-KEE duh
laissez-faire les-ay-FAIR
Lamarck, Jean-Baptiste luh-MAHRK, ZHAHN-buh-TEEST
Lancaster LAN-kas-ter
latifundia lat-uh-FUN-dee-uh
Latium LAY-shee-um
Laurier, Wilfred LAWR-ee-ay
Lebensraum LAY-benz-roum
Lespinasse, Julie de les-peen-AHS
Le Tellier, François Michel luh tel-YAY, FRAN-swah-mee-SHELL
Lévesque, René luh-VEK, ruh-NAY
Leyster, Judith LE-ster
Liebenfels, Lanz von LEE-bun-felz, LAHNZ
Liebknecht, Karl LEEP-knekt
Liebknecht, Wilhelm LEEP-knekt, VIL-helm
Lionne, Hugues de LYAWN, UGH
List, Friedrich LIST, FREE-drik
Liszt, Franz LIST, FRAHNZ
Livy LIV-ee
Lucretius loo-KREE-shus
Luddites LUD-ites
Ludendorff, Erich LOOD-un-dorf
Lueger, Karl LOO-ger
Luftwaffe LUFT-vaf-uh
Luxemburg, Rosa LUK-sum-burg
Machiavelli, Niccolò mak-ee-uh-VELL-ee, nee-koh-LOH
Magna Graecia MAG-nuh GREE-shuh
Magyars MAG-yars
Maistre, Joseph de MES-truh
Malleus Maleficarum mall-EE-us mal-uh-FIK-ar-um
al-Ma'mun al-MAH-moon
Manetho MAN-uh-THOH
Mao Zedong mau zee-DONG
Marcus Aurelius MAR-kus au-REE-lee-us
Marcuse, Herbert mar-KOO-zuh
Marie Antoinette muh-REE an-twuh-NET
Marius MAR-ee-us
Marsiglio of Padua mar-SIL-ee-oh of PA-juh-wuh
Masaryk, Thomas MAS-uh-rik
Matteotti, Giacomo mat-ee-OH-tee, Jahk-oh-moh
Mazarin maz-uh-RAN
Mazzini, Giuseppe maht-SEE-nee, joo-ZEP-pay
Meiji MAY-jee
Mein Kampf mine KAHMF
Melanchthon, Philip muh-LANGK-thun
Menander me-NAN-der
Mendeleyev, Dmitri men-duh-LAY-ef, di-MEE-tri

Merian, Maria Sibylla MARE-ee-un
Mesopotamia mess-oh-poh-TAME-ee-uh
Messiaen, Olivier me-SYAHN, O-LEEV-yay
Metaxas, John me-TAK-sus
Metternich, Klemens von MET-er-nik, KLAY-mens
Michel, Louise mee-SHELL
Michelangelo my-kell-AN-juh-loh
Mieszko MYESH-koh
Millet, Jean-François mi-LAY, ZHAHN-FRAN-swah
Milošević, Slobodan mi-LOH-suh-vik, SLOW-buh-dan
Miltiades mil-TIE-uh-deez
Mirandola, Pico della muh-RAN-duh-luh, PEE-koh DELL-uh
missi dominici MISS-ee doe-MIN-ee-chee
Moctezuma mahk-tuh-ZOO-muh
Mohács MOH-hach
Moldavia mahl-DAY-vee-uh
Molière, Jean-Baptiste mole-YAIR, ZHAHN-buh-TEEST
Moltke, Helmuth von MOLT-kuh, HELL-mut fahn
Monet, Claude moh-NAY, KLODE
Montaigne, Michel de mahn-TANE, mee-SHELL duh
Montefeltro, Federigo da mahn-tuh-FELL-troh, fay-day-REE-goh dah
Montesquieu MONT-ess-skyoo
Montessori, Maria mon-ti-SOR-ee
Morisot, Berthe mor-ee-ZOH, BERT
Muawiyah moo-AH-wee-yah
Mühlberg mool-BERK
Muhammad moe-HA-mud
Müntzer, Thomas MOON-tsur
Muslim MUZ-lum
Mutsuhito moo-tsoo-HEE-toe
Mycenaean my-suh-NEE-un
Nabonidas na-bun-EYE-dus
Nagy, Imry NAHJD, IM-re
Navarre nuh-VARR
Nebuchadnezzar neb-uh-kad-NWZZ-ar
Nero NEE-roh
Nerva NUR-vuh
Neumann, Balthasar NOI-mahn, BAHL-tah-zar
Neumann, Solomon NOI-mahn
Nevsky, Alexander NEW-skee
Newcomen, Thomas new-KUH-mun
Ngo Dinh Diem NGOH din dee-EM
Nietzsche, Friedrich NEE-chuh, FREE-drik
Nimwegen NIM-vay-gun
Ninhursaga nin-HUR-sah-guh
Nogaret, William de noh-guh-RAY
Nogarola, Isotta NOH-guh-roll-uh, eye-SOT-tuh
Novalis, Friedrich noh-VAH-lis, FREE-drik
Novotny, Antonin noh-VOT-nee, AN-ton-yeen
Nystadt nee-STAHD
Octavian ok-TAY-vee-un
Odoacer oh-doh-AY-ser
optimates opp-tuh-MAH-tays
Osiris oh-SIGH-ris
Ovid OV-id
Paleologus pay-lee-OHL-uh-gus
papal curia PAY-pul KOOR-ee-uh
Papen, Franz von PAH-pun, FRAHNTZ fahn
Paracelsus par-uh-SELL-sus
Parlement par-luh-MAHN
Pascal, Blaise pass-KAL, BLEZ
paterfamilias pay-ter-fuh-MILL-ee-us
Pentateuch PEN-tuh-tuke
Pepin PEP-in
perestroika pair-ess-TROY-kuh
Pergamum PURR-guh-mum
Pericles PER-i-kleez
perioeci per-ee-EE-sie
Pétain, Henri pay-TAN, AHN-ree
Petrarch PE-trark
Petronius pi-TROH-nee-us
philosophe fee-luh-ZAWF
Phoenicians fi-NISH-uns
Photius FOH-shus
Picasso, Pablo pi-KAW-soh
Pilsudski, Joseph peel-SOOT-skee
Pisistratus pi-SIS-truh-tus
Pissaro, Camille pi-SARR-oh, kah-MEEYL
Pizarro, Francesco pi-ZARR-oh, frahn-CHASE-koh
Planck, Max PLAHNK
Plantagenet plan-TA-juh-net
Plato PLAY-toe
Plautus PLAW-tus
Poincaré, Raymond pwan-kah-RAY, re-MOAN
polis POE-lis
politiques puh-lee-TEEKS
Polybius poe-LIB-ee-us
Pombal, marquis de pom-BAHL, mar-KEE duh
Pompadour, madame de POM-puh-door, muh-DAM duh
Pompey POM-pee
pontifex maximus PON-ti-feks MAK-suh-mus
populares POP-yoo-lar-ays
populo grasso POP-uh-loh GRAH-soh
Poussin, Nicholas poo-SAN, NEE-kaw-lah
Praecepter Germaniae PREE-sep-ter ger-MAN-ee-eye
praetor PREE-ter
princeps PRIN-seps
Procopius proh-KOH-pee-us
procurator PROK-yuh-ray-ter
Ptolemy/Ptolemaic TOL-uh-mee/TOL-uh-MAY-ik

Pugachev, Emelyan POO-guh-choff, yim-yil-YAHN
Punic PYOO-nik
Pyrrhus/Pyrrhic PIR-us/PIR-ik
quaestors KWES-ters
Quetzelcoatl ket-SAHL-koh-ATE-ul
Quran kuh-RAN
Racine, Jean-Baptiste ra-SEEN, ZHAHN-buh-TEEST
al-Rahman, Abd al-RAH-mun, abd
Ramesses RAM-i-seez
Raphael RAFF-ee-ul
Rasputin rass-PYOO-tin
Realpolitik ray-AHL-poe-li-teek
Reichsrat RIKES-raht
Rembrandt van Rijn REM-brant vahn RINE
Renan, Ernst re-NAHN
Ricci, Matteo REECH-ee, mah-TAY-oh
Richelieu RISH-uh-loo
Rilke, Rainer Maria RILL-kuh, RYE-ner
risorgimento ree-SOR-jee-men-toe
Robespierre, Maximilien ROHBZ-pee-air, mak-SEE-meel-yahn
Rococo ro-KOH-koh
Röhm, Ernst RURM
Roon, Albrecht von ROHN AHL-brekt
Rousseau, Jean-Jacques roo-SOH ZHAHN-ZHAHK
Rurik ROOR-ik
Ryswick RIZ-wik
Sacrosancta sak-roh-SANK-tuh
Saint-Just san-ZHOOST
Saint-Simon, Henri de san-see-MOAN, AHN-ree duh
Sakharov, Andrei SAH-kuh-rof, ahn-DRAY
Saladin SAL-uh-din
Sallust SALL-ust
Samnites SAM-nites
San Martín, José de san mar-TEEN, hoe-Say day
Sartre, Jean-Paul SAR-truh, ZHAHN-PAUL
satrap/satrapy SAY-trap/SAY-truh-pee
Satyricon SAY-tir-ee-kon
Schaumburg-Lippe SHAHM-berkh-LI-puh
Schleswig-Holstein SCHLES-vig-HOLE-stine
Schlieffen, Alfred von SHLEE-fun
Schmidt, Helmut SHMIT, HELL-mut
Schönberg, Arnold SHURN-burg, ARR-nawlt
Schönerer, George von SHURN-er-er, ZHORSH
Schuschnigg, Karl von SHOOSH-nik
Schutzmannschaft SHOOTS-mun-shaft
Scipio Africanus SI-pee-oh af-ri-KAY-nus
Scipio Aemilianus SI-pee-oh i-mill-ee-AY-nus
scriptoria skrip-TOR-ee-uh
Sejm SAME
Seleucus/Seleucid si-LOO-kus/si-LOO-sid
Seljuk Turks SELL-juke
Seneca SEN-i-kuh
Sephardic suh-FAR-dik
Septimius Severus sep-TIM-ee-us se-VIR-us
Sforza, Ludovico SFORT-zuh, loo-doe-VEE-koh
Sieveking, Amalie SEEVE-king
Sieyès, Abbé sye-YES, a-BAY
signoria seen-YOOR-ee-uh
Socrates SOK-ruh-teez
Solon SOH-lun
Solzhenitsyn, Alexander SOLE-zhuh-NEET-sin
Sophocles SOF-uh-kleez
Sorel, Georges sah-RELL, ZHORZH
Spartacus SPAR-tuh-kus
Speer, Albert SHPIER
Speransky, Michael spyuh-RAHN-skee
Spinoza, Benedict de spi-NOH-zuh
squadristi sqah-DREES-tee
Staël, Germaine de STAWL, ZHER-men duh
Stein, Heinrich von STINE, HINE-rik
Stoicism STOH-i-siz-um
Stolypin, Peter stuh-LEE-pyin
Stravinsky, Igor struh-VIN-skee, EE-gor
Stresemann, Gustav SHTRAY-zuh-mahn, GUS-tahf
Struensee, John Frederick SHTROO-un-zay
Sulla SULL-uh
Sumerians soo-MER-ee-uns
Suppiluliumas suh-pil-oo-LEE-uh-mus
Suttner, Bertha von ZOOT-ner
Taafe, Edward von TAH-fuh
Tacitus TASS-i-tus
taille TAH-yuh or TIE
Talleyrand, Prince TAL-ee-ran
Tauler, Johannes TOU-ler, yoh-HAHN-us
Tenochtitlán tay-NAWCH-teet-LAWN
Tertullian tur-TULL-yun
Theocritus thee-OCK-ri-tus
Theodora thee-uh-DOR-uh
Theognis thee-OGG-nus
Thermidor ter-mee-DOR
Thermopylae thur-MOP-uh-lee
Thiers, Adolphe tee-ER, a-DOLF
Thucydides thoo-SID-uh-deez
Thutmosis thoot-MOH-sus
Tiberius tie-BIR-ee-us
Tiepolo, Giovanni Battista tee-AY-puh-loh, joe-VAHN-ee baht-TEES-tah
Tiglath-pileser TIG-lath-puh-LEE-zur
Tirpitz, Admiral von TUR-puts
Tito TEE-toh
Tlaxcala tlah-SKAHL-uh
Torah TOR-uh
Tordesillas tor-duh-SEE-yus

Trajan TRAY-jun
Trevithick, Richard TREV-uh-thik
Tristan, Flora TRIS-tun
Tyche TIE-kee
Ulbricht, Walter UL-brikt, VAHL-ter
Umayyads oo-MY-ads
Unam Sanctam OON-ahm SANK-tahm
universitas yoo-ni-VER-si-tahs
Valois VAL-wah
van Eyck, Jan van IKE
van Gogh, Vincent van GOE
Vasa, Gustavus VAH-suh, gus-STAY-vus
Vega, Lope de VAY-guh, LOH-pay day
Vendée vahn-DAY
Venetia vuh-NEE-shee-uh
Vesalius, Andreas vi-SAY-lee-us, ahn-DRAY-us
Vespasian ves-PAY-zhun
Vespucci, Amerigo ves-POO-chee, ahm-ay-REE-goe
Vichy VISH-ee
Vierzenheiligen feer-tsun-HILE-i-gun
Virchow, Rudolf FEER-koh, roo-DOLF
Virgil VUR-jul
Volkschulen FOLK-shool-un
Voltaire vole-TAIR
von Bora, Katherina BOR-uh
Wagner, Richard VAHG-ner, RIK-art
Walesa, Lech va-WENZ-uh, LEK
Wallachia wah-lay-KEE-uh
Wallenstein, Albrecht von WOLL-un-stine, AWL-brekt
Watteau, Antoine wah-TOE, AHN-twahn
Wannsee VAHN-say
Weizsäcker, Richard von VITS-zek-er, RIK-art
wergeld wur-GELD
Windischgrätz, Alfred vin-dish-GRETS
Winkelmann, Maria VING-kul-mun
Witte, Sergei VIT-uh, syir-GYAY
Worms, Edict of WURMZ *or* VAWRMZ
Wyclif, John WIK-lif
Xavier, Francis ZAY-vee-ur
Xerxes ZURK-seez
Xhosa KOH-suh
Ximenes hee-MAY-nus
Yahweh YAH-wah
Yeats, William Butler YATES
Yeltsin, Boris YELT-sun
yishuv Yish-uv
Zemsky Sobor ZEM-skee SOH-bur
zemstvos ZEMPST-voh
Zeno ZEE-noh
Zeus ZOOS
Zhivkov, Todor ZHEV-kof, toh-DOR
ziggurat ZIG-guh-rat
Zimmermann, Domenikus TSIM-ur-mahn, doe-MEE-nee-kus
Zinzendorf, Nikolaus von ZIN-zun-dorf, nee-koh-LAH-us
Zola, Emile ZOH-luh, ay-MEEL
zollverein TSOL-fuh-rine
Zoroaster ZOR-oh-as-ter

Photo Credits

CHAPTER 14

280 Courtesy of J. K. Wingfield Digby, Sherborne Castle; **284** North Wind Picture Archives; **285** *The Massacre of Indian at Cholula on the orders of Cortes, 1519* William Clements Library, University of Michigan, USA/Bridgeman Art Library, London/New York; **291** Private Collection; **297** *Laocöon*, El Greco, National Gallery of Art, Washington: Samuel H. Kress Collection; **298** Reunion des Musees Nationaux/Art Resource, NY; **299** Giraudon/Art Resource, NY

CHAPTER 15

303 Jacob van der Ulft, *The Square of the Dam at Amsterdam*, 1659, Musee Conde, Chantilly, Photo Giraudon/Art Resource, NY; **305** Reunion des Musees Nationaux/Art Resource, NY; **307** Giraudon/Art Resource, NY; **312** Russian School, Czar Peter the Great, Rijksmuseum, Amsterdam; **317** Robert Walker, *Oliver Cromwell*, 1649, By Courtesy of the National Portrait Gallery; **322 (top)** Leyster, Judith (Dutch, 1609– 1660) *Self-Portrait* c. 1630, oil on canvas, (29 3/8″ x 25 5/8″); National Gallery of Art, Washington, Gift of Mr. and Mrs. Robert Woods Bliss; **322 (bottom)** Rembrandt Van Rijn, *Syndics of the Cloth Guild*, Rijksmuseum, Amsterdam

CHAPTER 16

325 Reunion des Musees Nationaux/Art Resource, NY; **328** Courtesy of the Lilly Library, Indiana University, Bloomington, Indiana; **329** Courtesy of the Lilly Library, Indiana University, Bloomington, Indiana; **332** National Portrait Gallery, London; **334** CORBIS; **336** Reunion des Musees Nationaux/Art Resource, NY; **340** Giraudon/Art Resource, NY

CHAPTER 17

343 Photo © Michael Holford; **345** By permission of the Houghton Library, Harvard University; **347** Mary Evans Picture Library; **353** Giraudon/Art Resource, NY; **354 (top)** Reunion des Musees Nationaux/Art Resource, NY; **354 (bottom)** Courtesy of James R. Spencer; **356** Photo © Michael Holford

CHAPTER 18

362 Erich Lessing/Art Resource, NY; **365** National Portrait Gallery, London; **367** Giraudon/Art Resource, NY; **369** Scala/Art Resource, NY; **373** Benjamin West, *The Death of General Wolfe*, Transfer from the Canadian War Memorial, 1921, Gift of the second Duke of Westminster, Eaton Hall, Cheshire, 1918, National Gallery of Canada, Ottawa; **376** Bibliotheque des Arts Decoratifs, Photo © J. L. Charmet; **379 (left)** Erich Lessing/Art Resource, NY; **379 (right)** Wilton House, *East View Showing the Old Entrance* by Richard Wilson (1714–82) Collection of the Earl of Pembroke, Wilton House, Wilts., UK/Bridgeman Art Library, London/New York

CHAPTER 19

383 Reunion des Musees Nationaux/Art Resource, NY; **388** Giraudon/Art Resource, NY; **389** Reunion des Musees Nationaux/Art Resource, NY; **393** ET Archive, London; **395** Giraudon/Art Resource, NY; **396** Giraudon/Art Resource, NY; **399** Reunion des Musees Nationaux/Art Resource, NY

CHAPTER 20

405 Photo Bulloz; **408** Reproduced by Permission of the Trustees of the Science Museum (neg. 607.56); **409** Mansell/Time, Inc; **411** *Great Exhibition, 1851: South side of Crystal Palace from near Prince's Gate*, engraved by P. Brannon and T. Picken (colour litho) Guildhall Library, Corporation of London, UK/Bridgeman Art Library; **416** © Ann Ronan/Image Select; **418** CORBIS; **420** Trade Emblems of the Associated Shipwrights Society Trades Union Congress, London, UK/Bridgeman Art Library

CHAPTER 21

423 Giraudon/Art Resource, NY; **424** Austrian Information Service; **429** © British Museum; **433** Giraudon, Art Resource, NY; **436** Historisches Museum der Stadt Wien; **440** Caspar David Friedrich, *Man and Woman Gazing at the Moon*, Nationalgalerie SMPK Berlin, Photo Jorg P. Anders, © Bildarchiv Preussischer Kulturbesitz, Berlin; **441** Erich Lessing/Art Resource, NY

CHAPTER 22

443 *Proclamation of the German Empire at Versailles*, 1871, Anton von Werner, Photo © Bildarchiv Preussischer Kulturbesitz, Berlin; **445** Reunion des Musees Nationaux/Art Resource, NY; **448** *Proclamation of the German Empire at Versailles*, 1871, Anton von Werner, Photo © Bildarchiv Preussischer Kulturbesitz, Berlin; **452** Novosti Agency; **456** The Granger Collection, New York; **461 (top)** Gustave Courbet, *The Stonebreakers*, Gemaldegalerie Neue Meister, Staatliche Kunstsammlungen Dresden, Photo by Reinhold, Leipzig-Molkau; **461 (bottom)** Erich Lessing/Art Resource, NY

CHAPTER 23

464 William Powell Firth, *Many Happy Returns of the Day*, Harrogate Museums and Art Gallery/Bridgeman Art Library, London; **466** The Fotomas Index; **470** Verein fur Geschichte der Arbeiterbewegung, Vienna; **473** Tate Gallery/Art Resource, NY; **477** William Powell Firth, *Many Happy Returns of the Day*, Harrogate Museums and Art Gallery/Bridgeman Art Library, London; **479** Courtesy, Vassar College Library; **483** CORBIS

CHAPTER 24

486 Hulton Getty/Liaison Agency, Inc.; **488** Wide World Photos; **492** Erich Lessing/Art Resource, NY; **493** Vincent van Gogh, *The Starry Night*, (1889) Oil on canvas 29 x 36 1/4″ (73.7x92.1 cm), Collection, The Museum of Modern Art, New York, Acquired through the Lillie P. Bliss Bequest. Photograph © 1998 The Museum of Modern Art, New York; **494 (top)** Pablo Picasso, *Les Demoiselles d"Avignon*, Paris (Begun May reworked July 1907), Oil on canvas, 8′ x 7′8″ (243.9x233.7cm), Collection, The Museum of Modern Art, New York, Acquired through the Lillie P. Bliss Bequest, Photograph © 1998 the Museum of Modern Art, New York © 2000 Estate of Pablo Picasso/Artist Right's Society (ARS), New York; **494 (bottom)** Vasily Kandinsky, *Painting with White Border*, May 1913, The Solomon R. Guggenheim Museum, New York; **499** David King Collection, London; **500** North Wind Picture Archives

CHAPTER 25

511 Hulton-Deutsch Collection/CORBIS; **515** Hulton-Deutsch Collection/CORBIS; **517 (left)** Bilderdienst Suddeutscher Verlag, Munich; **517 (right)** Roger-Viollet/Liaison Agency, Inc.; **520** E.T. Archive, London; **524** Brown Brothers; **529** Hulton Getty/Liaison Agency, Inc.

CHAPTER 26

533 Hugo Jaeger, Life Magazine, © Time Warner, Inc.; **535** Roger-Viollet/Liaison Agency, Inc.; **539** Wide World Photos; **543** Hugo Jaeger, Life Magazine, © Time Warner, Inc.; **546** David King Collection, London; **550** Erich Lessing/Art Resource, NY Hoech, Hannah. *The Kitchen knife cuts through Germany's first Weimar beer-belly culture*. Photomontage. 1919. © 2000 Copyright Artist's Rights Society, (ARS), NY, VG Bild-Kunst, Bonn; **551** Salvador Dali, *The Persistence of Memory*, 1931, Oil on canvas, 9 1/2 x 13″, Collection the Museum of Modern Art, New York, Given Anonymously, © 2000 Artist Right's Society, (ARS), New York

CHAPTER 27

555 Hugo Jaeger, Life Magazine, © Time Warner, Inc.; **558** Hugo Jaeger, Life Magazine, © Time Warner, Inc.; **561** Hulton Getty/Liaison Agency, Inc.; **565** National Archives, (#111-C-273); **566** Library of Congress (2391, folder 401); **571** The Herald and Evening Times Picture Library, © Caledonian Newspapers, LTD.; **573** E.T. Archive, London

CHAPTER 28

578 © Prache-Lewin/Sygma; **581** CORBIS; **585** CORBIS; **590** © Prache-Lewin/Sygma; **593** Hulton Getty/Liaison Agency, Inc.; **598** Wide World Photos; **599** Popperfoto/Archive Photos

CHAPTER 29

603 Wide World Photos; **605** Wide World Photos; **612** Alexandra Avakian/Woodfin Camp & Associates; **615** Mark Stewart/Camera Press, London; **619** Wide World Photos; **621** Hans Namuth/Photo Researchers, Inc.; **625** Wide World Photos

Documents

We are grateful to the authors and publishers acknowledged here for their permission to reprint copyrighted material. We have made every reasonable effort to identify copyright owners of materials in the boxed documents. If any information is found to be incomplete, we will gladly make whatever additional acknowledgments might be necessary.

Stone, ed., *Women War Workers* (London: George Harrap & Co., 1917), pp. 25, 35–38.

Hans Rumpf, *The Bombing of Germany* (New York: Holt, Rinehart and Winston, 1963), p. 94. From John Campbell, ed., *The Experience of World War II* (New York: Oxford University Press, 1989), p. 180.

CHAPTER 18

Frederick the Great and His Father 368
From James Harvey Robinson, *Readings in European History* (Lexington, Mass.: Ginn & Co.), 1934. Reprinted by permission of Silver, Burdett, & Ginn, Inc.

British Victory in India 372
From James Harvey Robinson, *Readings in European History* (Lexington, Mass.: Ginn & Co.), 1934. Reprinted by permission of Silver, Burdett, & Ginn, Inc.

The Atlantic Slave Trade 377

"S-t-e-a-m-boat A-Comin'!" 415
From Mark Twain, *Life on the Mississippi*. Copyright © 1911 by Harper & Brothers. Reprinted by permission of Harper & Row, Publishers, Inc.

Child Labor: Discipline in the Textile Mills 419
From E. Royston Pike, *Human Documents of the Industrial Revolution*. Copyright © 1966. Reprinted by permission of Unwin Hyman, Ltd.

CHAPTER 21

S

T

Y

Z